Conceivability and Po̲_____

Conceivability and Possibility

EDITED BY

Tamar Szabó Gendler

John Hawthorne

CLARENDON PRESS · OXFORD

OXFORD
UNIVERSITY PRESS

Great Clarendon Street, Oxford OX2 6DP

Oxford University Press is a department of the University of Oxford.
It furthers the University's objective of excellence in research, scholarship,
and education by publishing worldwide in

Oxford New York

Auckland Bangkok Buenos Aires Cape Town Chennai
Dar es Salaam Delhi Hong Kong Istanbul Karachi Kolkata
Kuala Lumpur Madrid Melbourne Mexico City Mumbai Nairobi
São Paulo Shanghai Taipei Tokyo Toronto

Oxford is a registered trade mark of Oxford University Press
in the UK and in certain other countries

Published in the United States
by Oxford University Press Inc., New York

British Library Cataloguing in Publication Data

Data available

Library of Congress Cataloging in Publication Data

Conceivability and possibility / edited by Tamar Szabó Gendler and John Hawthorne.
p. cm.
Includes bibliographical references and index.
1. Possibility. 2. Concepts. I. Gendler, Tamar. II. O'Leary-Hawthorne, John.
BC199.P7 .C66 2002   110–dc21   2002019755

ISBN 0–19–825089–4
ISBN 0–19–825090–8 (Pbk.)

3 5 7 9 10 8 6 4 2

Typeset in Bembo
by Newgen Imaging Systems (P) Ltd., Chennai, India
Printed in Great Britain
on acid-free paper by
T.J. International Ltd.,
Padstow, Cornwall

ACKNOWLEDGEMENTS

All of the papers in this volume appear for the first time in this collection, and most were written especially for it. Knowing this, the reader may be puzzled by the fact that many of the papers include author-generated cross-references to other essays within the volume. This fruitful exchange of ideas is the consequence of the authors' willingness to share draft copies of their papers with the other contributors. We had feared that such a process, though philosophically rewarding, might delay publication of the volume unreasonably; that it did not is due to the extraordinary good will of the contributors, whose universal co-operation in responding to comments and meeting deadlines enabled timely publication of the volume without sacrifice in quality.

We are grateful to Syracuse University for financial support in the preparation of this volume, and to Philosophy Department Chair Tom McKay, Dean of Arts and Sciences Cathy Newton, and Vice Chancellor Debbie Freund for their extraordinary commitment to its philosophy department. David Chalmers, Brendan Murday, Ted Sider, Zoltán Gendler Szabó, Brian Weatherson, and Dean Zimmerman offered sage advice throughout the process. Thanks also to Peter Momtchiloff of Oxford University Press for seeing the publication through from beginning to end, and to the other staff at OUP with whom we had the pleasure of working, particularly Charlotte Jenkins and Rebecca Bryant.

Finally, our thanks are due to Brendan Murday, graduate assistant *extraordinaire*, for his spectacular work preparing the volume's index and his outstanding work in readying the manuscripts for publication. A better graduate assistant is inconceivable—indeed, perhaps, impossible.

CONTENTS

CONTRIBUTORS

GEORGE BEALER Professor of Philosophy, University of Colorado at Boulder

JOHN CAMPBELL Wilde Professor of Mental Philosophy in the University of Oxford; Fellow of Corpus Christi College

DAVID J. CHALMERS Professor of Philosophy, University of Arizona; Associate Director, Center for Consciousness Studies

GREGORY CURRIE Professor of Philosophy, University of Nottingham

MICHAEL DELLA ROCCA Professor of Philosophy, Yale University

KIT FINE Professor of Philosophy, New York University

TAMAR SZABÓ GENDLER Associate Professor of Philosophy, Syracuse University

JOHN HAWTHORNE Professor of Philosophy, Rutgers University

GIDEON ROSEN Associate Professor of Philosophy, Princeton University

ALAN SIDELLE Professor of Philosophy, University of Wisconsin at Madison

ROY SORENSEN Professor of Philosophy, Dartmouth College

ERNEST SOSA Romeo Elton Professor of Natural Theology and Professor of Philosophy, Brown University; Distinguished Visiting Professor, Rutgers University

ROBERT STALNAKER Professor of Philosophy, Massachusetts Institute of Technology

CRISPIN WRIGHT Professor of Logic and Metaphysics, Wardlaw University Professor and Leverhulme Research Professor, University of St. Andrews

STEPHEN YABLO Professor of Philosophy, Massachusetts Institute of Technology

Introduction: Conceivability and Possibility

TAMAR SZABÓ GENDLER AND
JOHN HAWTHORNE

Overview

We have, it seems, a capacity that enables us to represent scenarios to ourselves using words or concepts or sensory images, scenarios that purport to involve actual or non-actual things in actual or non-actual configurations. There is a natural way of using the term 'conceive' that refers to this activity in its broadest sense.[1]

When we engage in such conceivings, the things we depict to ourselves frequently present themselves *as possible*, and we have an associated tendency to judge that they *are possible*. Indeed, when invited to consider whether something is possible, we often engage in a deliberate effort to conceive of it; upon

For comments and conversation concerning this introduction, we are grateful to George Bealer, David Chalmers, Brendan Murday, Ted Sider, Zoltán Gendler Szabó, and Steve Yablo.

[1] The term 'conceive' shares a root with the term 'concept'—the former is traceable to the Latin verb *concipere*, the latter to its past participle *conceptus*. But while the verb *concipere* is used frequently throughout antiquity, employment of the nominal form term *conceptus* does not seem to emerge until the third or fourth century CE; instead, the term *notio* (roughly 'notion') was employed. (Thanks to Charles Brittain for research into this question.) In this light, it seems reasonable to follow modern usage in allowing a broad sense for the term 'conceive' that permits as instances certain uses of (see *Roget's Thesaurus*, 3rd edn.) 'envisage, envision, fancy, fantasize, image, imagine, picture, see, think, vision, visualize'—that is, a use of the term that is non-committal on the relation between conceiving and concept-deployment. Imagining and conceiving in the narrow sense are special cases of conceiving in this broad sense.

finding ourselves able to do so, we conclude that it is. We may even decide that something is impossible on the basis of our apparent inability to conceive of it.

The technique just described is a pervasive feature of our mental life—both in day-to-day decision making and in philosophical reasoning. We might conceive of a scenario in which the couch fits through the door or the Democrats take control of the Senate, and conclude that such events could occur; if we cannot conceive of any such scenario involving the piano or the House of Representatives, we may conclude that such events could not. We might conceive of a scenario in which there is a golden mountain or a red square, and conclude that such entities could exist; if we cannot conceive of any scenario involving a mountain without a valley or a round square, we may conclude that such entities could not. We might conceive of a scenario in which there are exact physical duplicates of actual human beings who lack consciousness, and conclude that such beings are possible; if we cannot conceive of any such scenario, we may conclude that such beings are not.

Although there are numerous differences among the cases just described—in the sorts of conceiving in which they ask us to engage, the extent to which they involve sensory imagination, the sorts of possibility they apparently invoke, the generality of the conclusions they purport to establish,—there are also important similarities. In particular, each employs what is sometimes called a *conceivability–possibility* (or *inconceivability–impossibility*) move: from the fact that we are (or are not) able to depict to ourselves a scenario in which thus-and-such obtains, we take ourselves to have learned something about whether thus-and-such *could* (or could not) obtain. The very existence of such a practice raises a number of perplexing philosophical questions. Of these, four stand out as particularly central to traditional and contemporary discussions of the topic:[2]

(a) What sorts of possibility are there, such that the conceivability of a scenario might be thought to be an indicator of that scenario's being possible?

(b) What is it to conceive of something?

(c) When is conceivability a reliable guide to possibility?

(d) How, if at all, might conceivability–possibility reasoning be employed in particular cases to establish claims about the actual world?

In the remainder of this introduction, we discuss these questions from various perspectives. In section 1, we provide a broad overview of some of the general philosophical issues raised by consideration of them. Sections 2–4 are devoted to surveying in somewhat more detail some of the highlights of

---

[2] Note that in asking these questions, we are using 'conceive' in the broad sense described in the opening paragraph. There is an important tradition of trying to clarify the relevant notion of conceiving in terms of the notion of a priori (or rational) intuition; see Bealer, Ch. 1 below; see also Yablo (1993) and various of the papers in DePaul and Ramsey (1998).

traditional and recent discussions of these and related issues: section 2 describes accounts due to Descartes and Hume; section 3 describes an account due to Saul Kripke; and section 4 presents an overview of a family of accounts commonly referred to as *two-dimensionalist*. Finally, in section 5, we present brief summaries of each of the chapters in this volume.

1 General Issues

1.1 *Possibility*

Our faculty of perception reveals to us what is actual. And there is a widely accepted explanation of why this is so: our perceptual mechanisms are sensitive to features of the actual world, which impinge on them causally to produce systematic patterns of stimulus and response. Likewise, it seems, our faculty of conception reveals to us what is possible. But here there is no widely accepted explanation of why and to what extent this is so.

There are two reasons for this. The first is that the term 'possible' is used in a number of different ways, resulting in a certain ambiguity in what is being claimed. But even when this is sorted out, a deeper problem in the epistemology of modality remains. We address these issues in turn.

If I claim that thus-and-such is possible, there are a number of things I might mean. One thing I might mean is that, for all I know, thus-and-such obtains. In so doing, I invoke one of the family of notions of *epistemic possibility*: notions of possibility that are defined relative to some subject (or set of subjects) in terms of some body of knowledge or evidence available to (or otherwise associated with) the subject(s) in question.[3] So, for example, one might offer a *permissive* account of epistemic possibility, according to which P is epistemically possible for S just in case S does not know that not-P, or a *strict* account, according to which P is epistemically possible for S just in case P is consistent (metaphysically compossible) with all that S knows.[4] There are important differences

---

[3] For a systematic discussion of various established epistemic uses of 'possible' in English (and for a challenge to certain further alleged such uses), see Bealer, Ch. 1, sect. 1.3, below. See also Yablo (1993: 22–5).

[4] In addition to these permissive and strict notions, intermediate characterizations might also be offered: for instance, P is epistemically possible for S just in case S's evidence does not warrant S's believing not-P; or P is epistemically possible for S just in case S could not reasonably be expected to ascertain not-P on the basis of what S knows. Spelling out precisely what these amount to requires fully characterizing what is meant by 'warrant' and 'reasonable expectation'. Occasionally, the term is used in an even broader—and impersonal—sense: P is epistemically possible just in case it is not a priori that not-P (see, e.g., Chalmers, Ch. 3 below). Spelling out precisely what this amounts to requires fully characterizing what is meant by 'a priori'.

between these characterizations: on the strict account, epistemic possibility entails metaphysical possibility; on the permissive account, it does not. But, regardless of the details of the characterization, conceivability is clearly *not* a general guide to epistemic possibility, in either of these senses. If I know that the cat is on the mat, then it is not epistemically possible for me that the cat is not on the mat, even in the permissive sense.[5] Still, I can easily conceive a situation in which the cat is not on the mat—so I can easily conceive something epistemically impossible. Those who claim conceivability as a guide to possibility, then, presumably do not mean that it is a guide to *epistemic* possibility.[6]

So what they mean is that it is a guide to *non*-epistemic possibility. But in what sense? Consider three candidate notions of non-epistemic possibility with which philosophers have traditionally been concerned: (narrow) logical possibility, metaphysical possibility, and nomological (for example, physical or biological) possibility.[7] On a standard sort of characterization, P is *logically possible* just in case no contradiction can be proved from P using the standard rules of deductive inference (in conjunction, perhaps, with certain definitions). On a similarly standard characterization, P is *nomologically possible* for a relevant body of *nomos* just in case P is consistent with the body of truths expressed by those laws. (For example, P is physically possible iff P is compossible with the laws of physics, biologically possible iff it is compossible with the laws of biology, and so on.) The notion of *metaphysical possibility*, meanwhile, is standardly taken to be primitive.[8] It is taken as the most basic conception of 'how things

---

[5] Note that it *is* epistemically possible in the broad impersonal sense employed by Chalmers (since presumably my knowledge that the cat is on the mat is not a priori); for an argument that conceivability (of the requisite sort) is indeed a guide to epistemic possibility (in this sense), see Chalmers, Ch. 3 below.

[6] One might object that the permissive notion of epistemic possibility is not a notion of *possibility* at all, since (as we noted in the text) P can be epistemically possible in this sense without being metaphysically possible.

[7] We are not taking a stand on whether these notions are, on final analysis, distinct—only observing that they have been, at various times by various philosophers, treated as such. (A complicating terminological factor is the following: as George Bealer (Ch. 1) reminds us, before Kripke introduced the expression 'metaphysical possibility', many philosophers (including Kripke) used 'logical possibility' for what is now called 'metaphysical possibility'. Where this consideration may lead to confusion, we flag divergent uses.) For discussion of the question of how many primitive forms of possibility there are, see Fine, Ch. 6 below; for additional discussion of the relation between nomological and metaphysical possibility, see Shoemaker (1998), Sidelle (Ch. 8 below and references therein); for additional general discussion of varieties of possibility, see also the chapters in this volume by Bealer, Chalmers, Della Rocca, Wright, and Yablo. For discussion of what is sometimes called *conceptual possibility*, see sections 3 and 4 below.

[8] In contemporary discussions, at any rate.

might have been'—gestured at by talk of how 'God might have made things' or 'ways it is possible for things to be'.[9] Using the terminology of possible worlds, actuality and possibility in this sense can be characterized in parallel fashion: it is *actual* that P just in case P in the actual world, and (metaphysically) *possible* that P just in case P in some possible world.[10] On the characterizations we have offered, then, it would appear that metaphysical possibility is more expansive than nomological possibility, less expansive than narrow logical possibility:[11] it is possible in none of the senses that something is both red and not red, logically but not metaphysically possible that something is both red and non-extended, metaphysically but not physically possible that something travel faster than the speed of light, and possible in all three senses that something travel faster than the space shuttle.

As a guide to logical possibility in the sense we have characterized it, conceivability seems somewhat superfluous; whether or not a contradiction can be derived from P seems better determined by proof procedures than by scenario depiction. If it is this notion of possibility that is at issue, the activity of conceiving seems largely irrelevant (or at least inessential) to the determination of possibility.[12] As a guide to nomological possibility, conceivability seems to confront many of the problems confronted in the epistemic case—namely, that it seems all too easy for us to conceive of situations that are not possible in the relevant sense. So if it is this notion of possibility that is at issue, the activity of conceiving seems largely ineffective to the task at hand.[13] Rather, it is as a guide to metaphysical possibility that conceivability is typically taken as having a central role to play. On the standard view, our ability to conceive of a scenario

[9] The distinction between essential and inessential properties is standardly glossed in terms of metaphysical possibility: a property is essential to a thing just in case it is not metaphysically possible that the thing lacks it.

[10] Correspondingly, it is *necessary* that P just in case P in all possible worlds, *impossible* that P just in case P in no possible world, and *contingent* whether P just in case it is possible that P and not necessary that P.

[11] While the majority of the authors in this volume follow roughly this terminological practice, a few employ certain of the terms somewhat differently (e.g., Chalmers's uses of ('epistemic')); in all cases where authors' use differs significantly from that which we have introduced here, explicit characterizations of the terms in question are provided in the author's main text. Note also that while several of the authors are directly interested in contrasting the various sorts of possibility introduced thus far (e.g., Fine, Sidelle), a number of others are primarily interested in the contrast (to be discussed in sections 3 and 4 below) between metaphysical and conceptual possibility (e.g., Chalmers, Della Rocca, Stalnaker, Wright, and Yablo), while still others are interested in additional uses of possibility: for instance, those relating to normative notions (e.g., Currie, Fine, and Yablo).   [12] For arguments that it is irrelevant in general, see Bealer, Ch. 1 below.

[13] See, however, next paragraph and n. 15.

where P obtains is reckoned as constituting at least prima-facie reason for supposing that P is metaphysically possible. This issue is addressed, directly or indirectly, by nearly all the authors in the volume.

If conceivability is a good guide to metaphysical possibility, it is easy enough to see how—given the requisite additional nomological (or epistemic) information—it could in a derivative way be a good guide to various species of nomological and epistemic possibility. If what it means for P to be nomologic-ally possible relative to some body of laws L (or epistemically possible relative to some body of knowledge K) is for P and L (or P and K) to be metaphysic-ally compossible,[14] then the question of whether P is L-nomologically (or K-epistemically) possible can be tested by attempting to conceive of a scenario where L and P hold (or where K and P hold).[15] Of course, if we are misinformed about L (or K), we will go astray. But since conceivability can only work in this way as a guide to epistemic and nomological possibility on the assumption that it is a good guide to metaphysical possibility, it is the latter assumption that has been the primary object of philosophical attention.

While these clarifications dispel a certain amount of confusion, they do lit-tle to resolve an obvious puzzle: on the face of it, the idea that conceivability is a guide to metaphysical possibility is extremely problematic. According to current orthodoxy, metaphysical possibility can neither be reduced to, nor eliminated in favour of, linguistic rules and conventions; it constitutes a funda-mental, mind-independent subject-matter for thought and talk. Given this picture, it is rather baffling what sort of explanation there could be for conceiving's ability to reveal its character. It seems clear that the causal explana-tion for the reliability of perception is unsuitable here—and it is profoundly difficult to see what to put in its place. A number of authors in the volume take up just this issue.[16]

---

[14] Note while most of the notions of possibility described above can be characterized in this way, not all can; in particular, neither (narrow) logical possibility nor the permissive notion of epistemic possibility can be spelled out in such relative terms.

[15] Matters may be more complex than this simple sketch allows. Perhaps, for instance, we have an evolutionarily instilled capacity for physical intuition that is psychologically distinct from what philosophers call 'conceiving' on the basis of which we are able to draw reliable conclusions about what is physically possible. At the same time, we sometimes set out to learn about the actual world by deliberately conceiving of idealized situations where certain laws of nature—say, laws govern-ing friction—fail to hold. (These topics fall largely outside the scope of this volume. For an overview of such issues, see papers collected in Horowitz and Massey (1991), DePaul and Ramsey (1998), and additional works cited in the 'Bibliography on Experiment and Thought Experiment' in Gendler (2000: 229–50).)

[16] See in particular the chapters by Bealer, Chalmers, Rosen, and Sosa.

1.2 *Conceiving and Imagining*

While the notion of possibility has received fairly thorough philosophical
consideration, much less attention has been devoted to the second element in the
supposed equation: conceiving.[17] In the opening paragraph, we characterized
the activity extremely broadly—broadly enough to include any sort of mental
depiction of a scenario, whether in words or concepts or pictures.[18] But, pressing a bit harder, one might wonder what sort of underlying psychological kind
(or cluster of kinds) the notion is meant to capture. Consider the following
rather diverse list of mental activities, each arguably related to the requisite
notion of conceiving:

> Rationally intuiting that it is possible that P
> Realizing that not-P is not necessary
> Imagining (that) P
> Conjecturing that P
> Accepting that P for the sake of argument
> Describing to oneself a scenario where P obtains
> Telling oneself a coherent story in which P obtains
> Pretending that P
> Make-believing that P
> Supposing (that) P

[17] Indeed, it is far from clear how its nature should even be investigated. One might, it seems,
fruitfully explore it in light of recent work in (i) empirical psychology, (ii) general philosophy of
mind, (iii) phenomenology, or (iv) general work on the nature of pretence, make-belief, and fiction—though it remains an open question how, if at all, such results could illuminate the relation
between this capacity and our knowledge of modality. Regarding (i), one might consider the
empirical psychological literature on (a) mental imagery (for an overview of these issues, see
papers collected in Block (1981), Shepard and Cooper (1982); for developmental perspectives, see
Piaget and Inhelder (1971)); (b) imagination and pretence (for a general overview of the psychological literature on imagination, particularly in children, see Harris (2000); for developmental
perspectives, see papers collected in Lewis and Mitchell (1994), esp. part III, as well as numerous
recent papers in the *British Journal of Developmental Psychology, Child Development, Cognition,* and
Cognitive Development); (c) conceptions of possibility and necessity in developmental perspective
(for classic discussion, see Piaget (1987*a*, 1987*b*); for more recent essays, see papers collected in
Overton (1990)). Regarding (ii), one might consider in particular discussions of mental simulation and other sorts of non-belief-like attitudes (for a general philosophical overview of the issues
relating to mental simulation, see papers collected in Davies and Stone (1995*a*, 1995*b*), as well as
numerous recent papers in *Mind and Language*). Regarding (iii), one might begin with Casey
(1976/2000), Sartre (1939/1962 and 1940/1963), or, for more general discussions of imagination,
Brann (1991) and Warnock (1976). Regarding (iv), one might consider Walton (1990) and
Currie and Ravenscroft (2002).   [18] Cf. n. 1.

Understanding the proposition that P
Entertaining (that) P
Mentally simulating P's obtaining
Engaging in off-line processing concerning P

If conceiving is a natural psychological kind, then it presumably corresponds to something like one of these items (or to some natural cluster of them). But the wide variability among their features suggests that the notion in question may be highly elusive.[19] Some, for example, are propositional attitudes; some are attitudes towards scenarios or states of affairs; and still others are activities. Some seem explicitly sensory; others explicitly non-sensory; still others are neutral on this question. Some are highly conceptual; others are strongly language-based; still others are, perhaps, non-conceptual. Some seem to take place primarily spontaneously, others only under our deliberate control; others in both ways. All seem capable of being directed both towards propositions (or states of affairs) involving particular individuals, as well as towards propositions (or states of affairs) that are general. And both within and among them there seem to be variations in the degree of privileged access associated with the attitude/activity and its content/object.[20] In light of these differences, one might reasonably wonder which, if any, of the features alluded to is required by conceivability in the sense we seek.

---

[19] Cf. P. F. Strawson who writes, concerning the notion of imagination: 'the uses, and applications, of the terms "image", "imagine", "imagination" and so forth, make up a very diverse and scattered family. Even this image of a family seems too definite. It would be a matter of more than difficulty to identify and list the family's members, let alone their relations of parenthood and cousinhood' (Strawson 1970: 31). Or again, Brian O'Shaughnessy: 'What is the *imagination*? What is it to *imagine*? These perfectly natural questions already assume too much: the first question assumes there exists something that is the Imagination, presumably a distinctive faculty; the second that there is some one thing that is the phenomenon of Imagining, doubtless instantiated in diverse phenomenal forms. These assumptions may be valid, but they need not be. We ought not to prejudge these questions' (2000: 339–40). (After detailed discussion, O'Shaughnessy provisionally concludes that 'the doctrine of an essential common imagination agency is unacceptable, along with the theory of a common intrinsic imagining essence' (2000: 361), though he leaves room for looser uses of the term.) To the extent that we are taking 'conceiving' to be even broader than 'imagining', such problems are only magnified.

[20] Cf. Wittgenstein: 'Someone says, he imagines King's College is on fire. We ask him: How do you know that it's *King's College* you imagine on fire? Couldn't it be a different building very much like it. In fact, is your imagination so absolutely exact that there might not be a dozen buildings whose representation your image could be?—And still you say: "There's no doubt I imagine King's College and no other Building"' (Wittgenstein 1958/1965, 39). The question 'how do you know that it is really X that you imagine' may be absurd in the case of imagining King's College; but its analogue for certain other attitude-content pairs seems perfectly reasonable.

There is a traditional distinction made between (sensory) imagining on the one hand, and (non-sensory) non-imagistic conceiving on the other.[21] But it is far from settled whether the distinction has a proper role to play in circumscribing the appropriate subject-matter for an investigation of conceivability as a guide to possibility.[22] Certainly, it seems, there are things that we can (non-sensorily) conceive that we cannot (sensorily) imagine: but is the modal status of one or the other of these categories more or less apt to be illuminated by the associated mental act?[23] Perhaps there is an alternative distinction to be made between imagining and mere conceiving—wherein imagining is somehow perspectival or self-involving, whereas mere conceiving is not. If so, there may again be a difference between their relative capacities to illuminate certain sorts of modal and non-modal subject-matter.[24] More generally, one might wonder about the relation between imagination/conception, on the one hand, and perception/intellection, on the other: is the former parasitic on the latter, merely *re*-presenting perhaps in slightly modified form, what the latter presents, or is it somehow productive, enabling us to gain access to genuinely novel experiences or ideas?[25]

While the general notion of conceiving and its connections to the notion of imagining have not been well investigated, a few attempts have been made to systematize what is meant by these terms,[26] and a number of the authors in this volume offer significant refinements on the traditional 'placeholder' use.[27]

1.3 *Reliability Conditions*

Even if we lack a fully satisfying explanation for the link, conceivability does seem to provide at least a prima-facie guide to possibility; that something is conceivable is at least a good indicator that it is possible. At the same time, it is uncontroversial that there are cases where we are misled. Some Greeks found it conceivable (in some decent sense of 'conceivable') that stars are holes in the

---

[21] This distinction is explored in more detail in our discussion of Descartes and Hume in section 2 below.

[22] For an argument suggesting that failure to make such a distinction may lead to mistaken philosophical conclusions, see Hill (1997).

[23] For an exploration of the question of whether impossibilities that can be represented in non-sensory modalities can be depicted visually, see Sorensen, Ch. 9 below.

[24] For an exploration of this question with regard to morality, see Currie, Ch. 4 below.

[25] For a discussion of the contrastive roles of experience and mere representation, see Campbell, Ch. 2 below.

[26] For an influential attempt to provide such a taxonomy, see Yablo (1993). Some attention is also given to this question in van Cleve (1983) and Tidman (1994).

[27] In this regard, see especially the chapters by Bealer, Chalmers, and Yablo.

sky. George Berkeley found it conceivable that chairs are mere agglomerations of sensory experiences. Various mathematicians have found it conceivable that Goldbach's conjecture is wrong. Some philosophers have found it conceivable that seven hairs marks the borderline between being bald and not being bald, others that nominalism is true, that immanent universals exist,[28] or that there are exact physical duplicates of human beings who lack consciousness. Some find it conceivable that Hesperus is not Phosphorus, or that water is not H_2O. In each of these cases, the content that is conceived may well be metaphysically impossible. But if so, conceivability has failed as a guide to the relevant sort of possibility.

Can these cases be cordoned off in a principled way, so that one can explain the failure of conceivability in particular cases while maintaining the general reliability of the practice described? Or can nothing systematic be said in this regard?

In responding to this challenge, three families of strategies suggest themselves. The first cordons off on the basis of subject-matter. Perhaps certain classes of propositions—abstract metaphysical ones, ones concerning necessary beings, ones that turn on actual empirical matters of fact, and so on—are illegitimate targets for conceivability–possibility arguments. Perhaps our conceiving faculty (whatever that turns out to be) is simply ill-suited to the task of providing reliable guidance concerning such realms. At the same time, it might be suggested, other topics are such that conceiving can deliver reliable modal verdicts concerning them. As long as we circumscribe subject-matter properly, conceivability will be a reliable guide to possibility.

A second strategy cordons off by way of procedure. Perhaps certain sorts of conceivings—clear and distinct conceivings, or conceivings accompanied by rational insight, or conceivings that involve a detailed intellectual vision of a possible scenario—are able to deliver reliable modal verdicts. And perhaps there is a straightforwardly detectable difference between these sorts of conceivings and their unreliable counterparts. As long as we restrict ourselves to the relevant sorts of conceiving, conceivability will be a reliable guide to possibility.

Finally, one might combine the two strategies, either by relativizing types of conceiving to types of subject-matter or by restricting both domains on independent grounds. Perhaps for each sort of subject-matter, there is an associated form of conceiving that is possibility-revealing in the requisite sense. Or perhaps only certain sorts of subject-matter are tractable in this way, and only on the basis of certain sorts of conceiving.

---

[28] That is, that qualities exist that are actually located in space and time and are fully capable of bi-location.

In each case, the challenge is to come up with characterizations that are both sufficient to the task at hand and non-circular. For, of course, one might define 'conceivable' in such a way that P is not *really* conceivable unless P is possible. While this will solve the problem of reliability, unless there is an independent way of determining that we are conceiving in the relevant sense (and not merely seeming to conceive), the practical significance of the link will be negligible. And one might safely claim that one class of propositions for which conceivability implies possibility is the class of propositions that are possible— but here again, the practical significance of the observation is negligible.

How one goes about providing useful characterizations of the relevant notion of conceivability and the relevant class of propositions will depend on the sorts of answers one offers to the questions raised in the two previous sections—that is, on the views one has about the nature of possibility, the nature of conceiving, and the resultant reasons (if any) for expecting the latter to be a reliable guide to the former. Issues of this sort are addressed, directly and indirectly, by nearly all of the volume's authors.

1.4 *Applications*

Assuming that one can successfully establish a link between (certain sorts of) conceivability and possibility (within certain realms), one might wonder what philosophical work the connection can do. Of course, it is of independent philosophical interest to know what is and is not metaphysically possible. But it is the strategy of employing conceivability arguments to establish claims of identity and distinctness that has been the primary target of such reasoning.

The idea behind such arguments is the following. If it is possible that a exist without b, it seems to follow that, as a matter of fact, a and b are distinct: after all, nothing can exist without itself, so if a *is* b, then presumably a cannot exist *without* b.[29] But if this line of reasoning is correct, and conceivability is a guide to possibility, then the mere conceivability of a's existing without b will be sufficient to establish the possibility of a's existing without b, which in turn will be sufficient to establish the actual distinctness of a and b.

This means that conceivability–possibility arguments are potentially quite powerful: if the conceivability of a's existing without b is capable of revealing the metaphysical possibility of a's existing without b, then conceivability would be able to reveal something about the actual lay of the land: namely, a's distinctness from b. Faced with such a connection between actuality and possibility,

---

[29] For a challenge to this view, see Della Rocca, Ch. 5 below.

two attitudes towards the epistemic role of conceiving suggest themselves. The optimist will insist that since conceiving is a guide to possibility, it can reveal the actual distinctness of things; the pessimist will insist that since conceiving can never reveal actual facts of identity and distinctness, it is ill-suited to judging possibility in such cases.[30]

The most famous of such arguments, of course, is that which attempts to establish some sort of mind–body dualism on conceivability grounds alone.[31] If it is conceivable that mind exist without body, and conceivability implies possibility, then it is possible that mind exist without body, and thus actual that mind and body are distinct. The argument in question can be traced to Descartes, and it is for this reason that, as noted above, we devote the next section (2) of the introduction to a detailed presentation of Descartes's version of it, in the context of a more general presentation of his (and Hume's) views on conceivability and possibility. Contemporary interest in the question, however, is due largely to the work of Saul Kripke, and in the subsequent section (3), we introduce the Kripkean framework, connecting Kripke's discussion to more general issues of conceivability and possibility. Even more recently, there has been a groundswell of interest in the relation between the viability of such arguments and so-called two-dimensionalist modal logics; in section 4, we present a framework for thinking about this most recent round of the debate between optimists and pessimists. With this background in place, we hope that even the previously uninitiated reader will be in a position to appreciate the volume's papers, the contents of which are summarized in section 5.

---

[30] Note that on some metaphysical views, the connection between possibility and actuality runs so deep as to (apparently) render pessimism mandatory. Consider, for example, the causal theory of properties, according to which the causal role of a property is essential to that property. On such a conception, the shortcomings of conceivability as a guide to nomological possibility would seem to carry over to metaphysical possibility: since the (metaphysical) essence of a property is tied to the actual laws that govern it, our ability to mix and match qualities in thought and imagination will cause us to neglect certain necessary connections. Commitment to an optimistic perspective, meanwhile, would seem on the face of it to license dismissal of any such metaphysical picture. (But see Fine and Sidelle, Chapters 6 and 8 below.)

[31] Such arguments are explicitly addressed in a number of chapters in this volume: see those by Bealer, Chalmers, Della Rocca, Sidelle, Stalnaker, Wright, and Yablo. Among the numerous discussions of the topic in the last decade or so, we direct readers who are particularly interested in conceivability–possibility issues to the following: (optimists) Bealer (1987, 1992), Chalmers (1996, 1999), Chalmers and Jackson (2002), Hart (1988), Jackson (1993, 1998); (pessimists, generally speaking) Balog (1999), Block and Stalnaker (1999), Levine (1998, 2000), Loar (1999), McLaughlin and Hill (1999), Yablo (2000). (Extensive lists of additional references can be found in the pieces mentioned.)

2 Descartes and Hume

As we have just noted, contemporary discussions of conceivability and possibility trace their ancestry to the early modern period—particularly to the writings of Descartes and, to some extent, Hume. In situating the volume's papers in their historical context, then, it may be helpful for the reader to have some sense of how Descartes—and, where relevant, Hume—respond to the four questions posed in the introductory section.

Throughout, we will provide the reader with extensive quotations from the relevant texts. In this way, she may judge for herself to what extent these representative early modern discussions do and do not correspond to their contemporary analogues.[32]

2.1 *Possibility and Necessity*

Like most philosophers before him, Descartes is concerned with a notion of possibility where what it is to be possible is to be non self-contradictory.[33] As he observes in the *Second Set of Replies*:

All self-contradictoriness or impossibility resides solely in our thought, when we make the mistake of joining together mutually inconsistent ideas; it cannot occur in anything outside the intellect. For the very fact that something exists outside the intellect manifestly shows that it is not self-contradictory, but possible. (CSM II, 108; AT VII, 152)[34]

---

[32] In the pages that follow references to the work of Descartes are to the three-volume edition *The Philosophical Writings of Descartes*, ed. John Cottingham, Robert Stoothof, Dugald Murdoch, and (in the case of vol. III) Anthony Kenny. References to vols. I and II respectively are of the form 'CSM I' or 'CSM II' followed by the relevant page number; references to volume III are in the form 'CSMK' followed by the relevant page number. The CSM(K) references are followed by references to the corresponding page in the standard twelve-volume edition of Descartes produced by Adam and Tannery; references to these pages are of the form 'AT' followed by the relevant page number. References David Hume's *Treatise of Human Nature* are made in the form [book, part, section] indicated respectively by [(large roman numeral), (small roman numeral), (arabic numeral)]. So, e.g., '*Treatise*, I. iii. 14' refers to book I, part iii, section 14 of the *Treatise*. These references are followed by the corresponding page and paragraph in the Oxford Philosophical Texts (2000) edition of Hume's *Treatise*, ed. David Fate Norton and Mary J. Norton. These are of the form 'NN', followed by [(page): (paragraph number)]. So, e.g., 'NN 112: 23' refers to the paragraph numbered 23 on p. 112 of the Oxford edition of the *Treatise*.

[33] For discussion of the historical background to Descartes's conception of modality, see Alanen and Knuuttila (1988) and detailed bibliographic references provided therein.

[34] Descartes does not mean that impossibilities are explicitly contradictory. At CSM II, 108; AT VII, 151, he speaks of the relevant test as being whether or not a concept *implies* a contradiction (our emphasis). We will not pursue this topic further.

Descartes is also explicit about the subject-matter for such thoughts of possibility and necessity: such thoughts (unlike thoughts that encode impossible combinations of properties) concern a realm of essences that are external to our minds (though dependent on God's will[35]). For Descartes, that is, eternal truths do not 'depend on the human intellect or on other existing things'; rather, they have reality whether or not anything actual possesses them. So writes Descartes in the *Fifth Meditation*:

When, for example, I imagine a triangle, even if perhaps no such figure exists, or has ever existed, anywhere outside my thought, there is still a determinate nature, or essence, or form of the triangle which is immutable and eternal, and not invented by me or dependent on my mind. (CSM II, 44–5; AT VII, 64)

On what grounds does he think this? Descartes's reasoning seems to be something like the following: (a) the properties of imagined entities outstrip those that we explicitly recognize in forming the image; (b) only those properties that we explicitly recognize in forming an image could be the products of our invention; therefore (c) at least some of the properties of imagined entities are not the products of our invention. Descartes presents this reasoning in the continuation of the passage just cited. The next sentence reads:

This is clear from the fact that various properties can be demonstrated of the triangle, for example . . . that its greatest side subtends its greatest angle . . . and since these properties are ones which I now clearly recognize whether I want to or not, even if I never thought of them at all when I previously imagined the triangle, it follows that they cannot have been invented by me. (CSM II, 45; AT VII, 64)

The move from this negative conclusion ('they cannot have been invented by me') to the positive claim ('there is . . . a determinate nature, or essence, or form . . . which is immutable and eternal') is left somewhat enthymematic. Still, it is clear that Descartes is committed to this stronger result. Later in the same *Meditation*, applying the principle just presented to the Ontological Argument for God's existence, Descartes writes:

from the fact that I cannot think of God except as existing, it follows that existence is inseparable from God. It is not that my thought makes it so, or imposes any necessity on the thing; on the contrary, it is the necessity of the thing itself, namely the existence of God, which determines my thinking in this respect. (CSM II, 46; AT VII, 67)

---

[35] For expressions of Descartes's notorious commitment to God's role in the creation of eternal truths, see, e.g., CSM II, 291, 294; AT VII, 432, 436. For the purposes of our discussion, we will set this complicated issue to one side.

For Descartes, that is, the direction of explanation runs from the necessities contained in the natures of things to the perceptions of the intellect, and not the other way around.

By contrast, an important theme in Hume's work is the mind-dependence of necessity:

> Thus as the necessity, which makes two times two equal to four, or three angles of a triangle equal to two right ones lies only in the act of the understanding, by which we consider and compare these idea; in like manner the necessity or power, which unites causes and effects, lies in the determination of the mind to pass from the one to the other. (*Treatise*, I. iii. 14; NN 112: 23)[36]

The modern reader will wonder why Hume does not say the same about possibility. If even logical necessity has its source 'in the act of understanding'— and, Hume insists, 'there is but one kind of *necessity*' (*Treatise*, I. iii. 14; NN 115: 33, italics in original) why not think the same is true of possibility? After all, for P to be possible is just for it not to be necessary that not-P. Though Hume never confronts the issue directly, one might extend his views on necessity as follows: the possibility of a given proposition is constituted by the capacity of the fancy to imagine its holding. As we noted in the prefatory section, this sort of projectivism about modality is currently out of favour—though (as we will discuss in section 3.2 below) it, like the full-blooded Cartesian picture, offers a sort of grounding for the conceivability–possibility link that is unavailable to those who hold certain sorts of post-Kripkean views.

2.2 *Conceiving and Other Faculties*

Descartes distinguishes sharply between intellection and understanding, on the one hand, and imagination and sensation, on the other. Whereas the former are general cognitive faculties that belong to us essentially *qua* thinking things, the latter are limited cognitive faculties that belong to us contingently *qua* embodied beings (cf. CSM II, 51; AT VII, 73). The faculties differ not only in their range of subject-matter—imagination being 'nothing but an application of the cognitive faculty to a body which is intimately present to it' (CSM II, 50; AT VII, 72)—but also in their phenomenology. As Descartes writes in the *Sixth Meditation*: 'When I imagine a triangle, for example, I do not merely understand that it is a figure bounded by three lines, but at the same time I also see the three

---

[36] Hume's ideas on this subject are, of course, most fully developed in his discussion of causality, where the appearance of necessity in the natural order is attributed to the mind's 'great propensity to spread itself on external objects'. See *Treatise*, I. iii. 14; NN 112: 25.

lines with my mind's eye as if they were present before me' (CSM II, 50; AT VII, 72). And again, in a July 1641 letter to Mersenne: 'whatever we conceive without an image is an idea of the pure mind, and whatever we conceive with an image is an idea of the imagination' (CSMK, 186; AT III, 395).

The primary task of metaphysical inquiry, according to Descartes, is the understanding of the immutable natures of things. And it is the intellect—not the imagination—that Descartes repeatedly credits with being suited to the task of revealing things as they actually are. Nonetheless, the faculty of imagination may serve as a useful supplement to the intellect in certain special cases. This ability to 'see [a shape] with my mind's eye as if [it] were present before me' (CSM II, 50; AT VII, 72) facilitates our grasping of certain simple truths about geometry and motion. As Descartes writes in a letter to Elizabeth on 28 June 1643:

body (i.e. extension, shapes and motions) can . . . be known by the intellect alone, but much better by the intellect aided by the imagination . . . and the study of mathematics, which exercises mainly the imagination in the consideration of shapes and motions, accustoms us to form very distinct notions of body. (CSMK, 227; AT III, 691–2)

Even in the case of geometrical figures, however, the imagination faces certain limitations: our finite representational capacities are restricted to the portrayal of fairly simple shapes. In his discussion of the chiliagon at the beginning of the *Sixth Meditation*, Descartes insists that while we can well understand what a chiliagon is, we cannot represent it in imagination:

if I want to think of a chiliagon, although I understand that it is a figure consisting of a thousand sides just as well as I understand the triangle to be a three-sided figure, I do not in the same way imagine the thousand sides or see them as if they were present before me. . . . I may construct in my mind a confused representation of some figure; but it is clear that this is not a chiliagon. For it differs in no way from the representation I should form if I were thinking of a myriagon, or any figure with very many sides (CSM II, 50; AT VII, 72)

And he is insistent that the faculty of imagination is an outright impediment to understanding when the subject-matter in question is metaphysical. In a letter to Mersenne dated 13 November 1639, he writes: 'The imagination, which is the part of the mind that most helps mathematics, is more of a hindrance than a help in metaphysical speculation' (CSMK, 141; AT II, 622).

In the case of body, the hindrance is due to the imagination's inability to grasp the relevant complexity in sufficient detail. In the *Second Meditation*, Descartes writes:

I can grasp that the wax is capable of countless changes of this kind, yet I am unable to run through this immeasurable number of changes in my imagination, from which it follows that it is not the faculty of imagination that gives me my grasp of the wax as flexible and changeable. . . . I would not be making a correct judgment about the nature of wax unless I believed it capable of being extended in many more different ways than I will ever encompass in my imagination. I must therefore admit that the nature of this piece of wax is in no way revealed by my imagination, but is perceived by the mind alone. (CSM II, 20–1; AT VII, 31)

In the case of the soul, the hindrance is even more direct: since the soul cannot be depicted by imagery, the imagination is completely unsuited to reveal its nature. Earlier in the *Second Meditation*, Descartes writes:

it would . . . be a case of fictitious invention if I used my imagination to establish that I was something or other; for imagining is simply contemplating the shape or image of a corporeal thing . . . thus . . . none of the things that imagination enables me to grasp is at all relevant to this knowledge of myself which I possess. (CSM II, 19; AT VII, 28)

Thus, for Descartes, the proper vehicles for metaphysical inquiry are understanding and intellection, which are sharply distinguished from imagination. Hume, by contrast, blurs the distinction between imagining and conceiving. He writes:

'Tis an established maxim in metaphysics, *That whatever the mind clearly conceives includes the idea of possible existence*, or in other words, *that nothing we imagine is absolutely impossible*. (*Treatise*, I. ii. 2; NN 26: 8; italics in original)

His use of the expression 'in other words' to link the two italicized phrases suggests that he takes them to be equivalent. But the purportedly equivalent precepts differ in at least two crucial ways: the first concerns conceiving, the second imagining; and the first is concerned with the relation between bearing a certain attitude towards P and P's *seeming* possible, whereas the second is concerned with the relation between bearing a certain attitude towards P and P's as a matter of fact *being* possible.[37]

The source of his indifference to the first is fairly straightforward: it is a consequence of his philosophical psychology (permitting only sensory experiences ('impressions') and their copies ('ideas') to serve as the building-blocks of the mind) coupled with an outright rejection of the rationalist distinction between imagination and understanding. (The source of his apparent indifference to the second is more controversial and would take us too far afield.)

While some attention has been paid in contemporary discussions to the question of how imagination and conception differ in their modality-revealing

---

[37] We assume here an equivalence between 'nothing we imagine is (absolutely) impossible' and 'anything we imagine is (strictly) possible'.

character (see section 1.2 above), the question has not been explored fully. A number of the authors in this volume offer reasons for re-examining the issue.[38]

2.3   *Reliability Conditions*

Descartes is explicit in endorsing the second of the strategies introduced in section 1.3 above: it is only certain sorts of conceiving that provide us with guidance concerning what is and is not possible. In particular, it is clear and distinct[39] understanding that provides us with the knowledge we seek. In the *Sixth Meditation*, he writes: 'I know that everything which I clearly and distinctly understand is capable of being created by God so as to correspond exactly with my understanding of it' (CSM II, 54; AT VII, 78). Or again, in *Comments on a Certain Broadsheet*:

the rule 'whatever we can conceive of can exist' is my own, [but] it is true only so long as we are dealing with a conception which is clear and distinct, a conception which embraces the possibility of the thing in question, since God can bring about whatever we clearly perceive to be possible. (CSM I, 299; AT VIIIB, 352)[40]

---

[38]   For extended discussions of imagination, see chapters in this volume by Campbell, Currie, and Sorensen.

[39]   Strictly speaking, the expression is redundant, as clarity is a special case of distinctness. In the *Principles of Philosophy*, Descartes explains: 'I call a perception "clear" when it is present and accessible to the attentive mind . . . I call a perception "distinct" if, as well as being clear, it is so sharply separated from all other perceptions that it contains within itself only what is clear' (CSM I, 207–8; AT VIII A, 22). Despite the redundancy, we follow Descartes in using the phrase 'clear and distinct' throughout.

[40]   What is the relation between this and the truth rule of the *Third Meditation*: viz., that 'whatever I perceive very clearly and distinctly is true'? Prima facie, they differ markedly: the one is a rule connecting understanding with possibility, the other a rule connecting perception with truth. On a certain reading, however, the one can be seen as a special case of the other: if understanding involves a perception of possibility, then the conceivability–possibility rule is just the truth rule, applied to some particular subject-matter. Some of Descartes's writings support such an account. For instance, the *Sixth Meditation* claim that 'everything which I clearly and distinctly understand is capable of being created by God so as to correspond exactly with my understanding' (CSM II, 54; AT VII, 78) is elsewhere presented in terms of perception of the possible: 'I boldly assert that God can do everything which I perceive to be possible' (CSMK, 363; AT V, 272, writing to More on 5 February 1649). Note that the notion of 'clear understanding' required is a strong one. In one sense we have an understanding of 'something is both round and square' clear enough to recognize it as necessarily false. But the sort of clear understanding required here is one allied to the intellectual perception of possibility.

In order for the clearness and distinctness condition to be a useful one, it must have two characteristics. First of all, clearness and distinctness of understanding must be *reliable*, in the sense that it serves as a fail-safe (or at least reasonably fail-safe) guide to the potentialities accruing to the immutable natures willed by God, and thereby to possibility. At the same time, clearness and distinctness of understanding must be *introspectively identifiable*, in the sense that we are able, as Descartes writes in the *Fifth Set of Replies* (to Gassendi), 'to distinguish between the things that we really perceive clearly and those that we merely think we perceive clearly' (CSM II, 260; AT VII, 379). As we noted above, one could introduce a notion of 'clearness' according to which, as a matter of stipulation, its being clear that p is a state that couldn't obtain without p being true[41]—but unless we have some way of *telling* that we are in such a state, the notion will be of little epistemic value.

Two challenges might here be raised. First, why think that clearness and distinctness would be introspectively identifiable, let alone introspectively identifiable in the infallible way that Descartes seems to require? And second, even if we set aside the question of (infallible) introspective identifiability, why think that any such capacity would be a reliable guide to that which it is intended to illuminate?

The first challenge is a serious one—many of the objectors raise it in one form or another. Mersenne, for instance, asks (in the *Second Set of Objections*): 'how can you establish with certainty that you are not deceived, or capable of being deceived, in matters which you think you know clearly and distinctly?' (CSM II, 90; AT VII, 126). And Gassendi complains (in the *Fifth Set of Objections*) that 'the difficulty does not seem to be about whether we must clearly and distinctly understand something if we are to avoid error, but about what possible skill or method will permit us to discover that our understanding is so clear and distinct as to be true and to make it impossible that we are mistaken' (CSM II, 221; AT VII, 318).

Descartes is rather impatient with this line of attack—not only with Gassendi, but with the others as well—insinuating that it arises from a stubborn and deliberate unwillingness to engage in introspection. Such introspection, he suggests, would reveal to the objector his own obvious capacity to identify instances in which his understanding or perception is 'transparently clear' (*Fifth Meditation*, CSM II, 48; AT VII, 70)—indeed, cases where 'perceptions are so transparently clear and at the same time so simple that we cannot even think of

---

[41] Indeed, it is arguable that the English construction 'it is clear that p' is factive in this sense. If p turned out to be false, one would need to retreat to the claim that it merely *seemed* clear that p.

them without believing them to be true' (*Second Set of Replies*, CSM II, 104; AT VII, 145). Whether this answer is satisfactory is not a question we will attempt to adjudicate.

The second challenge is met as follows. As we noted at the outset, the sort of possibility to which clear and distinct understanding is supposed to be a guide is non-self-contradictoriness. But, as Descartes writes in the *Second Set of Replies*, 'Self-contradictoriness in our concepts arises merely from their obscurity and confusion' (CSM II, 108; AT VII, 152). And if self-contradictoriness arises only from obscurity and confusion, then if a concept is not obscure and confused, it will not be self-contradictory. But a concept that is not obscure and confused is a concept that is clear and distinct. And a concept that is not self-contradictory is a concept of something that is possible. So a concept that is clear and distinct is a concept of something that is possible.

Not only does clear and distinct understanding of a concept guarantee that the concept is of something possible; clear and distinct understanding is understanding *as* possible. As Descartes writes in the *First Set of Replies*, 'Possible existence is contained in the concept or idea of everything that we clearly and distinctly understand' (CSM II, 83; AT VII, 116). For Descartes, then, there is a straightforwardly circumscribed class of cases for which a certain sort of mental act provides us with reliable knowledge of possibility: things that are clearly and distinctly understood both *seem* possible and *are* possible.

Still, one might wonder what grounds the link between obscurity and confusion, on the one hand, and self-contradictoriness, on the other: why mightn't self-contradictoriness arise in the case of thoughts that are clear and distinct? (Of course, one could stipulate that thoughts that entailed a contradiction were thereby not clear. But, to rehearse a point made already, this would serve to problematize the claim of introspective identifiability.) At the very least, Descartes has a theological answer available. While acknowledging that 'In the case of our clearest and most careful judgments . . . if such judgments were false they could not be corrected by any clearer judgments or by means of any other natural faculty' (CSM II, 102–3; AT VII, 143–4). Descartes nonetheless maintains that we have reason to be sanguine. For, Descartes contends, it is incoherent to suppose that God would allow us to be deceived under such circumstances, since it would be contradictory to suppose 'anything should be created by him which positively tends towards falsehood' (CSM II, 103; AT VII, 144). As we noted at the end of section 1.1 above, for those of us unwilling to appeal to divine benevolence, the problem is not so easily escaped.

2.4 *Applications*

2.4.1 *General Issues: Cut and Paste*

While there are a number of conspicuous differences between Descartes and Hume at the level of substance[42] and at the level of practice,[43] there are also important points of agreement. Of these, the one most central to contemporary discussions derives from Hume's use of the Cartesian thesis that when a pair of things are distinct,[44] each can exist without the other. Such arguments make direct use of conceivability–possibility reasoning: when we conceive (or imagine) one of two non-overlapping things without the other, we establish the thing's possible distinct existence, thereby establishing their actual distinctness. In the context of Hume's philosophical psychology, our ability to separate distinguishable objects in thought is a corollary of one of the most basic traits of the faculty in question, namely, '*the liberty of imagination to transpose and change its ideas*' (*Treatise*, I. i. 3; NN 12:4; italics in original), which has as a straightforward corollary that: 'Where-ever the imagination perceives a difference among ideas, it can easily produce a separation' (*Treatise*, I. i. 3; NN 12: 4).

From (a) the liberty of imagination and (b) the imagination–possibility link, we can extract from Hume something like a 'cut and paste' story about possibility. The liberty of imagination underwrites the following two principles:

Cut$_I$: If we can imagine a region that is (intrinsically) F adjacent to a (non-overlapping) region that is (intrinsically) G, then we can imagine a region that is F and withhold imagining a region that is G (where the regions can be either spatial or temporal).

---

[42] Most striking, perhaps, are the sharply different conclusions they draw when it comes to questions of space and finitude. Descartes uses the principles that whatever is clearly and distinctly understood is possible to argue that the idea of an extended indivisible atom is incoherent (cf. CSMK, 202–3; AT III, 477–8; cf. also CSM I, 231–2; AT VIIIA, 51) and that a finitely bounded space is unimaginable (cf. CSM I, 232; AT VIII A, 51); whereas Hume argues from facts about imaginability to the possibility that space is composed of a finite number of extended atoms—and thus to the conclusion that it could be only finitely divisible and of finite extent (cf. *Treatise*, I. ii. 2; NN 25: 2).

[43] In general, Hume is quite ready to conclude that a thing is possible on the basis of his capacity to imagine it sensorily. See, e.g., his arguments '*that an object may exist, and yet be no where*' (*Treatise*, I. iv. 5; NN 154: 10, italics in original); 'that any object may be . . . annihilated in a moment' (I. iv. 5; NN 164: 35); that any material particle can exist in the absence of any other, distinct quantity (I. ii. 5; NN 40: 3); or that it is possible for any given thing to exist without any cause at all (I. iii. 3; NN 56–8: 1–9). To the extent that Descartes would reject such reasoning, he would presumably do so on the grounds that the supposedly imagined content was not clearly and distinctly understood.

[44] Where this means non-overlapping.

Paste$_1$: If we can imagine a region that is (intrinsically) F, and we can imagine another region that is (intrinsically) G, then we can imagine adjacent F and G regions (where the regions can be either spatial or temporal).

If we accept these principles, along with the inference from imaginability to possibility, we now get:

Cut$_p$: If we can imagine a region that is (intrinsically) F adjacent to a (non-overlapping) region that is (intrinsically) G, then it is possible that there is a region that is F in a world where no non-overlapping region is G.

Paste$_p$: If we can imagine a region that is (intrinsically) F, and we can imagine another region that is (intrinsically) G, then it is possible that there is a region that contains two adjacent sub-regions, one F, another G.

Coupled with facts about identity, Cut$_p$ and Paste$_p$—and their conceivability-based analogues—can serve as extremely powerful tools.[45] For example, it is on the basis of Cut$_p$, that Hume derives the conclusion that any material particle can exist in the absence of any other, distinct quantity. And one can readily reconstruct much of his reasoning about causation on the basis of Cut$_p$ and Paste$_p$—for instance, his commitment to the thesis that any 'cause' may be followed by any 'effect' or that it is possible for any given thing to exist without any cause at all.

2.4.2 *Mind–Body Dualism*

By far the most famous application of conceivability–possibility reasoning is Descartes's effort to establish the 'real distinction' between mind and body. The crucial thought here is that since we can clearly and distinctly understand the mind being apart from the body, it is possible that the mind be apart from the body; hence mind and body are possibly distinct; hence mind and body are actually distinct.

In somewhat more detail, the argument runs as follows. Using the principle—call it the *conceivability–possibility principle*—put forth in the *Sixth Meditation* and cited above, namely that 'everything which I clearly and distinctly understand is capable of being created by God so as to correspond exactly with my understanding of it' (CSM II, 54; AT VII, 78). Descartes applies it to a particular case: 'the fact that I can clearly and distinctly understand one thing apart from another is enough to make me certain that the two things

---

[45] For a modern descendant, see David Lewis: 'I suggest we look to the Humean denial of necessary connections between distinct existences. To express the plenitude of possible worlds, I require a principle of recombination according to which patching together parts of different possible worlds yields another possible world' (1986: 87–8).

are distinct, since they are capable of being separated, at least by God' (CSM II, 54; AT VII, 78). The argument for this principle—call it the *distinctness principle*—relies on the conceivability–possibility principle coupled with the thesis that for any x and y, if x and y can exist apart from each other, x and y are in reality distinct. Descartes goes on to apply the distinctness principle to a particular case of clear and distinct understanding of one thing apart from another: namely, the case of mind and body. The *Sixth Meditation* text continues:

I have a clear and distinct sense of myself, in so far as I am simply a thinking, non-extended thing; and on the other hand I have a distinct idea of body, in so far as this is simply an extended, non-thinking thing. And, accordingly, it is certain that I am really distinct from my body, and can exist without it. (CSM II, 54; AT VII, 78)

Here, as elsewhere, Descartes places great weight on the clarity and distinctness restriction. As he notes in an August 1641 letter to 'Hyperaspites', our ability confusedly and obscurely to understand one thing apart from another would enable us to draw no such conclusion:

Of course someone whose eyes are unsteady may take one thing for two, as people often do when drunk; and philosophers may do the like . . . when in the same body they make a distinction between the matter, the form and the various accidents as if there were so many different things. In such cases . . . if they paid more careful attention they would notice that they do not have completely distinct ideas of the things they thus suppose to be distinct. (CSMK, 197; AT III, 435)

2.4.3 *Arnauld's Objection*

But how is Descartes so sure that his argument for the real distinction between mind and body is not trading off a similarly inadequate conception? Arnauld raises such a worry in the *Fourth Set of Objections*:

Suppose someone knows for certain that the angle in a semi-circle is a right angle, and hence that the triangle formed by this angle and the diameter of the circle is right-angled. In spite of this, he may doubt, or not yet have grasped for certain, that the square on the hypotenuse is equal to the squares on the other two sides. . . . [He] clearly and distinctly understand[s] that this triangle is right-angled, without understanding that the square on the hypotenuse is equal to the squares on the other sides. It follows on this reasoning that God, at least, could create a right-angled triangle with the square on its hypotenuse not equal to the square on the other sides. (CSM II, 141–2; AT VII, 201–2)

Moreover, Arnauld continues:

although the man in the example clearly and distinctly knows that the triangle is right-angled, he is wrong in thinking that the aforesaid relationship between the squares on the sides does not belong to the nature of the triangle. Similarly, although I clearly and distinctly know my nature to be something that thinks, may I, too, not perhaps be wrong in thinking that nothing else belongs to my nature apart from the fact that I am a thinking thing? Perhaps the fact that I am an extended thing may also belong to my nature. (CSM II, 142–3; AT VII, 202–3)

Arnauld anticipates the obvious retort—that 'the person in this example does not clearly and distinctly perceive that the triangle is right-angled' (CSM II, 142; AT VII, 202). But, he responds, 'how is my perception of the nature of my mind any clearer than his perception of the nature of the triangle? He is just as certain that the triangle in the semi-circle has one right angle (which is the criterion of a right-angled triangle) as I am certain that I exist because I am thinking' (CSM II, 142; AT VII, 202). And he goes on to underscore the fact that we do not have a 'complete and adequate conception' of mind: 'I conceive of it only inadequately, and by a certain intellectual abstraction' (CSM II, 143; AT VII, 203).

But when a substance is thought about in abstracted terms, there may well be unnoticed elements of the nature of the substance to which the abstracted conception applies. Arnauld again offers an analogy from geometry:

Geometers conceive of a line as a length without breadth, and they conceive of a surface as length and breadth without depth, despite the fact that no length exists without breadth and no breadth without depth. In the same way, someone may perhaps suspect that every thinking thing is also an extended thing . . . although simply in terms of this power [thought], it can by an intellectual abstraction be app-rehended as a thinking thing, in reality bodily attributes may belong to this think-ing thing. (CSM II, 143; AT VII, 203–4)

So Arnauld's concern is the following: Even if I have a clear and distinct sense of myself as simply a thinking, thing, I have no way of ruling out that my conception of thinking substance is the result of intellectual abstraction; if this is so, I have no way of ruling out that the natures(s) of which I have a concep-tion include(s) a good deal more than thought, and hence no grounds for applying the distinctness principle to the case of mind and body.

2.4.4 *Descartes's Reply*

Arnauld's worry is widely echoed in contemporary discussions, and in this light, it is instructive to consider Descartes's various replies.[46] Importantly, he does not try to defend the view that our conception of substance is 'adequate'

---

[46] Because they are somewhat orthogonal to the central issue, we do not present in detail Descartes's discussion of the disanalogies between the geometrical cases that Arnauld presents, and the particular case they are intended to illuminate; see CSM II, 157–9; AT VII, 224–6.

in the sense of containing 'absolutely all the properties that are in the thing which is the object of knowledge', since a 'created intellect . . . can never know it has such knowledge unless God grants it a special revelation of the fact' (CSM II, 155; AT VII, 220). Rather, he insists, what is required is that I 'understand the thing well enough to know that my understanding is *complete*'—that is, that I understand the thing in question to be a 'complete thing . . . a substance endowed with the forms or attributes which enable me to recognize that it is a substance' (CSM II, 156; AT VII, 221–2), where 'the notion of a *substance* is just this—that it can exist by itself, that is without the aid of any other substance' (CSM II, 159; AT VII, 226; italics in original).

But, one might object, even if I know that everything that has the attribute of being a thinking thing is a substance, my conception of the nature of that substance may be deficient in exactly the ways at issue. For the sceptical hypothesis is not that mental substance needs the aid of another substance to exist; rather, the worry is that mental substance, while independent of all other substance, is such that a fully adequate conception of it reveals corporeality to be part of its nature.

Descartes's discussion elsewhere is more helpful in advancing the dialectic. In the letter to Gibieuf dated 19 January 1642, he offers the following gloss on 'completeness':

the idea of a substance with extension and shape is a complete idea, because I can conceive it entirely on its own, and deny of it everything else of which I have an idea. Now it seems to me very clear that the idea which I have of a thinking substance is complete in this sense. (CSMK, 202; AT III, 475)

The idea seems to be that we have an insight that it is possible that there be a self-standing thing enjoying some determinate version of extension and shape and no other intrinsic properties[47] (or at least nothing else in our repertoire of determinables). By contrast, perhaps, we realize that no self-standing thing could have merely colour and nothing else, or motion and nothing else, or smell and nothing else. For a conception of a substance to be complete, then, is for it to specify some determinable(s) such that a thing could exist with just some version of those determinables.[48] And, insists Descartes, our conception of thinking substance is complete in just this way.

The point can be put even more straightforwardly, employing terminology from the *Principles of Philosophy*. To each substance, Descartes explains, there belongs one principal attribute 'which constitutes its nature and essence, and to

---

[47] That it may have various relations to other things is beside the point.
[48] Among those determinables of which we have some notion.

which all its other properties are referred' (CSM I, 210;AT VIIIA, 25). In the case of mind, this is thought; in the case of body, extension: 'Everything else which can be attributed to a body . . . is merely a mode of an extended thing; and . . . whatever we find in the mind is simply one of the various modes of thinking (CSM I, 210;ATVIIIA, 25). Thus, concludes Descartes, 'we can easily have two clear and distinct notions or ideas, one of created thinking substance, and the other of corporeal substance, provided we are careful to distinguish all the attributes of thought from the attributes of extension' (CSM I, 211;AT VIIIA, 25).

Readers may well wonder why Descartes is entitled to move from the possibility that there be a thinking thing that exists without corporeality to the general conclusion that *all* thinking things can exist without corporeality: after all, perhaps some thinking things are essentially embodied, others not. Descartes's thought here seems to be that, since the attribute of thought is sufficient for yielding a self-standing substance, then once one has a thing that *inter alia* thinks, one can strip away all other attributes and still be left with the same self-standing substance. After all, if the addition of corporeality to a thinking thing would not destroy it, why should subtraction of corporeality have a different effect?

While there is much more to be said on these matters, further exploration of the Cartesian argument lies beyond our current purview.[49] Instead, we turn to its distinguished contemporary revival (and refinement) in the writings of Saul Kripke.[50]

3 Kripke

Even authors who disagree with Kripke's fundamental picture tend to present their arguments against an implicitly or explicitly Kripkean backdrop— including most of the authors in this volume.

3.1 *Key Distinctions*

Most readers will be aware of three key distinctions that drive Kripke's discussion: the distinction between rigid and non-rigid designators, the distinction

---

[49] For discussion of Descartes's argument with particular attention to conceivability–possibility questions, see van Cleve (1983) and Yablo (1990).

[50] While there are numerous important moments in the discussion of conceivability–possibility arguments from Hume to the present—to mention but three, consider Kant's Copernican turn, positivism's conventionalist approach to modality, and Quine's scepticism about the coherence of modal discourse—it is Kripke's *Naming and Necessity* that sets the stage for most contemporary discussions of our topic.

between reference-fixers and definitions, and the distinction between apriority and necessity (and, correspondingly, between aposteriority and contingency). But, given the centrality of these distinctions to Kripke's diagnosis of how and when conceivability–possibility arguments can be successfully deployed, it is worth reviewing them before continuing.

3.1.1 *Rigid versus Non-Rigid Designators*

A *rigid designator* is a term that picks out the same thing 'across possible worlds'.[51] Names ('Pierre', 'London'), demonstratives ('that', 'I'), and natural kind terms ('water', 'light') are rigid designators—they designate the same individual or kind in all possible worlds (where that individual or kind exists). A term that designates *non-rigidly*, by contrast, may pick out different objects in different worlds. Definite descriptions are generally treated as non-rigid[52] ('the most interesting person in the room', 'the oldest line in the book')—these terms designate different individuals or categories in different possible worlds.

Often, we pick out the same individual in the actual world by employing diverse descriptions and names: 'Cicero', 'Tully', 'the prosecutor of Cataline', and 'the man who was consul in 63BC' are all ways of referring to the same individual. In many contexts (so-called transparent contexts), which of the terms we choose will make no difference to the truth-value of the sentence in which it appears. The following sentences, for example, stand or fall together:

(1) Cicero was wise.
(2) Tully was wise.
(3) The prosecutor of Cataline was wise.
(4) The man who was consul in 63BC was wise.

By contrast, suppose we wish to consider how what is expressed by (5) and (6) respectively might not have been true:

(5) Cicero is wise.
(6) The man who was consul in 63BC is wise.

Because 'Cicero' is rigid, it picks out the same individual in all possible worlds. So to entertain a possible world where what is said by (5) is false, we need to think of a possible situation in which a certain actual individual—Cicero—is not wise. By contrast, because 'The man who was consul in 63BC' is non-rigid,

---

[51] More precisely, in all possible worlds where it picks out anything at all. For the sake of simplicity, we will generally omit this caveat in our discussion below. And we will set to one side the issues raised by reference failure and its cousins.

[52] There are exceptions—for instance, 'the smallest prime number'.

it picks out different individuals in different possible worlds. So to entertain a possible world where what is said by (6) is false, we need, for example, only to think of a possible situation in which someone or other—never mind whether he is Cicero—is, in that situation, both non-wise and consul in 63BC.

With these considerations in mind, we can see that the second of the following sentences expresses a proposition that might have been true, whereas the first does not:

(7) Cicero is not Tully.
(8) Cicero is not the prosecutor of Cataline.

Because 'Cicero' and 'Tully' are rigid designators, each picks out the same individual in all possible worlds. So, since Cicero is Tully in the actual world, Cicero is Tully in all possible worlds, hence (7) does not express a proposition that might have been true.[53] Identity claims flanked by a pair of rigid designators are, if true, necessarily true, and if false, necessarily false.[54] But the same does not hold in the case of (8). 'The prosecutor of Cataline' may pick out different individuals in different possible worlds. So, even though Cicero is the prosecutor of Cataline in the actual world, he is not the prosecutor of Cataline in all possible worlds; hence (8) expresses a proposition that might have been true.

3.1.2 *Reference-Fixers versus Definitions*

To the extent that names are treated as rigid designators and descriptions as non-rigid designators, a description cannot be used to *define* a name. That is, we cannot give a rule for determining the name's meaning across possible worlds that coincides with the rule for determining the meaning of the description, for the (rigid) name picks out the same individual across possible worlds, whereas the (non-rigid) description picks out different ones. There is a second way, however, that a name and a description might be associated: the description might be used to 'fix the reference' of the name. In this sense, we can give a rule for determining that name's meaning across possible worlds that *makes use of* the rule for determining the meaning of the description; in particular, we can let the name pick out across possible worlds whatever the description picks out in the actual world. Here again the (rigid) name will pick out the same individual across possible worlds, whereas the (non-rigid) description will

---

[53] This follows from the nature of rigid designation, coupled with the highly intuitive theses of the necessity of identity and diversity (implicit in Descartes's musings about separability): $\Box [(x) (y) (x = y) \supset \Box (x = y); \Box [(x) (y) (x \neq y) \supset \Box (x \neq y)]$

[54] For a challenge to this thesis, see Della Rocca, Ch. 5 below.

pick out different ones. But what the name picks out across possible worlds will, in some important intuitive sense, *depend on* what the description picks out in the actual world. Kripke writes:

suppose we say, 'Aristotle is the greatest man who studied with Plato'. If we used that as a *definition*, the name 'Aristotle' is to mean 'the greatest man who studied with Plato'. Then of course in some other possible world that man might not have studied with Plato and some other man would have been Aristotle. If, on the other hand, we merely use the description to *fix the referent* then that man will be the referent of 'Aristotle' in all possible worlds. The only use of the description will have been to pick out to which man we mean to refer. But then, when we say counterfactually 'suppose Aristotle had never gone into philosophy at all', we need not mean 'suppose a man who studied with Plato, and taught Alexander the Great, and wrote this and that, and so on, had never gone into philosophy at all', which might seem like a contradiction. We need only mean, 'suppose that *that man* had never gone into philosophy at all'. (1980: 57, italics in original)

What goes for proper names goes for other rigid terms, such as natural kind terms. Here again, we might introduce a term that is intended to be rigid by use of a description that is not: 'let *jooce* name the liquid that is in that test-tube', 'let *woozle* name the species of animal that raided the hen-house', and so on. Because we are generally ignorant of the 'real definition' or 'real essence' of the kinds that comprise the joints in nature, our access to the referents of natural kind terms frequently proceeds in this way: we (rightly or wrongly) reckon some (set of) manifest qualities as indicating the presence of a natural kind, and we use those qualities to fix the reference of what we take to be a rigid term.[55] Thus it is plausible that the reference of 'light' was fixed by the visual appearance it produces, 'heat' by the sensation it engenders, and so on. Idealizing somewhat for heuristic purposes, we might even suppose that the term 'heat' was explicitly introduced via the dictum: 'Let "heat" denote whatever kind it is in the actual world that produces such-and-such sensations.'

Recognizing that manifest qualities can serve as mere reference-fixers allows us to explain our apparent capacity coherently to conceive of situations where the relevant kind is present but produces different manifest qualities (light produces sensations of darkness, heat sensations of chill) and situations where the relevant kind is absent but where some other kind(s) produce(s) the qualities that serve to fix the reference of the kind term in the actual world (something other than light produces sensations of brightness, something other than heat produces sensations of warmth).

[55] For discussion of complications related to this strategy, see Wright, Ch. 12 below.

3.1.3 *A Priority versus Necessity*

On one traditional conception of their relation, apriority and necessity coincide, as do their counterparts, aposteriority and contingency.[56] On this traditional conception, all truths knowable a priori are necessary truths, and all necessary truths are (at least in principle) knowable a priori. Correlatively, all truths knowable only a posteriori are contingent truths, and all contingent truths are knowable only a posteriori. One of the central accomplishments of *Naming and Necessity* was explicitly to challenge this purported equivalence.

Whether a proposition is a priori or a posteriori, observes Kripke, is an epistemic question: it turns, roughly, on whether we can know the proposition to be true independently of any experience. Whether a proposition is necessary or contingent is a metaphysical question: it turns on whether its truth is independent of what the world is like. The two concepts deal 'with two different domains, two different areas, the epistemological and the metaphysical' (Kripke 1980: 36). Kripke continues:

> More important than any particular example of something which is alleged to be necessary and not *a priori* or *a priori* and not necessary, is to see that the notions are different, that it's not trivial to argue on the basis of something's being something which maybe we can know only *a posteriori*, that it's not a necessary truth. It's not trivial, just because something is known in some sense *a priori*, that what is known is a necessary truth. (1980: 38–9)

Not only do the concepts differ in intension; they also differ in extension: there are necessary a priori and contingent a posteriori truths, but there are also contingent a priori and necessary a posteriori truths.

Why might one have thought otherwise? 'I guess it's thought that . . . if something is known *a priori* it must be necessary, because it was known without looking at the world. If it depended on some contingent feature of the actual world, how could you know it without looking?' (Kripke 1980: 38). The answer to this latter question exploits the reference-fixer/definition distinction. Suppose I introduce 'Bob' by the reference-fixer 'the number of the planets'. Then the sentence

(9) Bob is the number of the planets

will be a priori knowable—but it will not be necessary. It will be a priori knowable because I can know without looking at the world that the numbers

---

[56] For example, on the positivist picture, both 'a priori' and 'necessary' were to be explicated in terms of analyticity (which in turn, for the positivists, was to be explained in terms of convention). On the Kantian picture, necessity is to be explained in terms of apriority (though apriority outstrips analyticity). Both are species of this 'traditional conception'.

designated by 'Bob' and 'the number of the planets' are the same,[57] and hence that (9) is true; but it will not be necessary because 'Bob' is a rigid term, whereas 'the number of the planets' is not, so there will be worlds where 'Bob' picks out one number (namely, the number of planets in the actual world), whereas 'the number of the planets' picks out another (namely, the number of planets in that world).[58] By similar reasoning, if 'heat' has its reference fixed by 'the phenomenon that produces sensations of warmth', then the statement

(10) If heat exists, it produces sensations of warmth

will likewise be contingent a priori.

The same goes for the other direction of the supposed necessity–apriority equivalence. Initially, it may appear that all necessary truths are knowable (at least in principle) a priori. The thought behind this, suggests Kripke, is something like the following: 'if something not only happens to be true in the actual world but is also true in all possible worlds, then, of course, just by running through all the possible worlds in our head, we ought to be able with enough effort to see, if a statement is necessary, that it is necessary, and thus know it *a priori*' (1980: 38). Kripke mentions in passing possible counter-examples from mathematics: it is far from trivial that every mathematical truth is a priori knowable, while it is fairly clear that every mathematical truth is necessary. But the best-known class of counter-examples proceeds via the observation that there are necessary truths that, while unknowable a priori, are knowable a posteriori. The most straightforward examples are provided by identities expressed by statements in which the copula is flanked by rigid designators, but where empirical investigation is required to determine whether the terms co-refer. For example,

(11) Hesperus is Phosphorus
(12) Water is H_2O

are necessary but a posteriori. They are necessary because the rigid designators on each side of the copula co-refer in the actual world, and hence in all possible worlds; but they are knowable only a posteriori because the co-reference of the terms is itself contingent. Other examples can be generated by appeal to the real essence of any given thing or kind, in cases where reference to the thing

---

[57] Of course, for all I know a priori, that number may be zero.

[58] While Kripke's examples of contingent a priori identities involve one rigid and one non-rigid designator, there are examples of contingent a priori identities that do not. Suppose Saul is a book in a row of books, and suppose I introduce 'David' by the reference-fixer 'Let "David" be the book two to the right of Saul'. Then the statement 'If Saul and David exist, then the book to the right of Saul is the book to the left of David' expresses a contingent a priori truth.

or kind does not require epistemic access to that essence.[59] Thus the following sentences are necessary a posteriori:

(13) Water has hydrogen as a constituent.[60]

(14) Prince Charles is the son of Queen Elizabeth.[61]

3.2 *Conceivability and Possibility*

3.2.1 *The Problem*

On the traditional picture adverted to above, there is a straightforward, if idealized, way to explain the connection between conceivability and possibility. Recall that P is possible iff it is not necessary that not-P. Let us introduce, as a term of art, that P is *Conceivable* iff it is not a priori that not-P. If all and only a priori truths are necessary truths, then all and only Conceivable truths are possible truths. For the Conceivable truths are just those whose negations are not a priori, and the possible truths are just those whose negations are not necessary. And since the latter two classes coincide, so do the former two.

As we noted above, some version of this form of reasoning is implicit both in Descartes and in Hume, though the two accounts differ in their order of explanation. Put crudely, in Descartes, the direction of explanation runs from the metaphysical to the epistemic: something is knowable by reflection because it is necessary; in Hume, the direction of explanation runs from the epistemic to the metaphysical: something is necessary because the mind treats it as such.[62] Yet in each case the metaphysical and epistemic categories coincide.

---

[59] So whether an identity is a priori or a posteriori knowable will depend on how the references of its terms are fixed. If we can know that humans are essentially humans—let's not worry about Jesus—then if a's reference is fixed by the attribute 'human', one can know a priori that if a exists, a is essentially human. But if a name b refers to a human without having its reference fixed by the attribute of humanity, then the corresponding conditional may be knowable only a posteriori.

[60] Whether we can know a priori the necessary statement that H_2O has hydrogen as a constituent is a trickier question; on this issue, Kripke offers little explicit guidance.

[61] Assuming that our parental origins are necessary.

[62] This oversimplifies the views of the actual historical figures. For example, Descartes is explicitly sensitive to the possibility of truths that transcend our cognitive powers altogether, so unless a priori means something like 'a priori knowable by God', then what we described as the traditional equation will not apply straightforwardly to him. But it remains plausible that Descartes believes that *for any proposition we can grasp*, it is necessary iff it is a priori knowable, and thus possible iff it is conceivable. Note, though, that the fact that there may be ungraspable propositions suggests that Conceivability (as defined above) and conceivability (in the intuitive sense) may come apart fairly radically. These issues are discussed at some length in Chalmers's contribution to this volume (Ch. 3).

On the post-Kripkean picture, however, no such explanation is available. For if there are a posteriori necessities and a priori contingencies, no such grounds can be appealed to in establishing a conceivability–possibility link. On the post-Kripkean picture, even if it is not necessary that not-P, it may still be a priori that not-P (contingent a priori); and even if it is not a priori that not-P, it may still be necessary that not-P (necessary a posteriori). But then, by substitution, it may be possible that P but not Conceivable that P, or Conceivable that P but not possible that P. Thus the contingent a priori seems to guarantee that there will be cases of possibility without Conceivability; the necessary a posteriori seems to guarantee that there will be cases of Conceivability without possibility.

In the face of such discrepancies, some have been inclined to give up on the link between conceivability and possibility. As Hilary Putnam writes in 'The Meaning of "Meaning" ':

> we can perfectly well imagine having experiences that would convince us (and that would make it rational to believe that) water isn't H_2O. In that sense, it is conceivable that water isn't H_2O. It is conceivable but it isn't logically possible! Conceivability is no proof of logical possibility . . . Human intuition has no privileged access to metaphysical necessity. (1975*b*: 233)[63]

3.2.2 *The Diagnosis*

Kripke, however, is more sanguine. While it is not his ambition to offer some general epistemology of modality—in favour of his positive modal claims, he is content to appeal to the fact that they are highly intuitive—he does offer a strategy for re-establishing a link between intuitions of possibility and what is in fact possible. There will, he acknowledges, be cases where it seems (at least to some of us) to be possible that not-P, but where, in fact, P is necessary: a posteriori necessities provide us with a class of such cases.[64] In such cases, we will be faced with an *illusion of possibility*—not-P will *seem* possible, though in fact it is not. At the same time, there will also be cases where it seems (at least

---

[63] In earlier writings, for instance, in his (1962) 'It ain't necessarily so', Putnam is similarly dubious of the possibility- and necessity-revealing powers of conceivability and apriority respectively. But there his motivation is essentially Quinean: 'the traditional philosophical distinction between statements necessary in some eternal sense and statements contingent in some eternal sense is not workable' (1975*a*: 248).

[64] Does Kripke think that it seems to ordinary people to be metaphysically possible that Hesperus is not Phosphorus and metaphysically necessary that the metre stick is a metre long, or is this an illusion that has occurred only to philosophers in the grip of a picture? We shall not take a stand on this finer point of exegesis. For more on this topic, see Bealer, Ch.1 below, and Della Rocca, Ch. 5 below.

to some of us) to be necessary that P, but where, in fact, not-P is possible: a priori contingencies provide us with a class of such cases. In such cases, there will be an *illusion of necessity*—P will seem necessary, though in fact it is not. But Kripke also offers a general strategy for dealing with such cases. We can explain these illusions by adverting to certain conflations that systematically give rise to them, notably:

(i)   between reference-fixing descriptions and the rigid terms they introduce
(ii) between the possibility of a community in an epistemically analogous situation saying something true by a sentence and the possibility of what a sentence says being true.

3.2.3 *Reference-fixing Surrogates*

Recall the following examples:

(9)   Bob is the number of the planets.
(11) Hesperus is Phosphorus.

The contingent a priori (9) has seemed to some to express a necessary truth, the necessary a posteriori (11) a contingent one. But, of course, these appearances are misleading: the negation of (11) expresses a necessary falsehood, whereas the negation of (9) expresses a possible truth. (There is no possible world in which Hesperus is not Phosphorus, but there is a possible world in which Bob is not the number of the planets.) In both cases, the explanation for the modal status of the proposition relies on the distinction between rigid and non-rigid designation. 'Hesperus' and 'Phosphorus' are rigid designators that pick out the same object in the actual world, and hence in all possible worlds. But whereas 'Bob' is rigid, 'the number of planets' is not, so there are worlds where 'Bob' picks out one object and 'the number of planets' another.

Why, then, does the negation of (11) seem to express a possible truth, whereas the negation of (9) does not? In this case, the explanation relies on the fact that our modal intuitions will go astray in so far as we conflate a reference-fixer with the term it introduces.

Suppose that 'Hesperus' and 'Phosphorus' were introduced by the reference-fixers 'the heavenly body that appears at thus-and-such location in the morning sky' and 'the heavenly body that appears at thus-and-such location in the evening sky', respectively. There are certainly worlds where these descriptions pick out distinct objects. If we are careless in distinguishing the terms in question from the descriptions by which their reference is fixed, we may confusedly think that the question whether it is possible that Hesperus is not Phosphorus is the same as the question whether it is possible that the heavenly body that appears at thus-and-such location in the morning sky is not the heavenly body that appears at thus-and-such location in the evening sky.[65] A parallel explanation can be offered for the apparent necessity of (9), where 'Bob' has its reference fixed by the description 'the number of planets'. Here again, if we are careless in distinguishing terms from reference-fixers, we may find ourselves thinking that the question whether it is possible that Bob is not the number of planets is the same as the question whether it is possible that the number of planets is not the number of planets.

Let us generalize the point. Call a statement s2 the *reference-fixing surrogate* of s1 when each term in s1 that was introduced by a reference-fixing description is replaced in s2 by the reference-fixing description itself. The reference-fixing surrogate of an a posteriori necessary truth will be contingent, and the reference-fixing surrogate of an a priori contingent truth will be necessary. It is no wonder that in so far as statements are conflated with their reference-fixing surrogates, modal illusions arise.[66]

3.2.4 *Epistemic Duplicates*

There is a second, though related, strategy deployed by Kripke for explaining modal illusion. He does not, after all, think that all rigid designators are introduced by reference-fixing descriptions: sometimes such terms are introduced by a baptismal act whereby an individual or kind is ostended.[67] And even when a term is originally introduced by a reference-fixing description, a competent user of the term need not be familiar with the description that introduced it (and so may lack grounds for conflating the term with its associated reference-fixing description). Return to the case of 'Hesperus' and 'Phosphorus': What is certainly possible (whether or not the terms were originally introduced by reference-fixing description or ostension) is that there be a community meeting two conditions: (a) their epistemic situation is identical to that of our

---

[65] Cf. Kripke: 'Of course, it is only a contingent truth . . . that the star seen over there in the evening is the star seen over there in the morning . . . But that contingent truth shouldn't be identified with the statement that Hesperus is Phosphorus' (1980: 105).

[66] Kripke writes: 'Let "R_1," and "R_2," be the two rigid designators which flank the identity sign . . . The references of "R_1," and "R_2,", respectively, may well be fixed by nonrigid designators "D_1," and "D_2," . . . Then although "$R_1 = R_2$," is necessary, "$D_1 = D_2$," may well be contingent, and this is often what leads to the erroneous view that "$R_1 = R_2$," might have turned out otherwise' (1980: 143–4).

[67] 'Usually a baptizer is acquainted with some sense with the object he names and is able to name it ostensively' (1980: 96 n. 42).

term-introducing community's, and (b) they express something false by the sentence 'Hesperus is Phosphorus':

> There certainly is a possible world in which a man should have seen a certain star at a certain position in the evening and called it 'Hesperus' and a certain star in the morning and called it 'Phosphorus'; and should have concluded—should have found out by empirical investigation—that he names two different . . . heavenly bodies. . . . And so it's true that given the evidence someone has antecedent to his empirical investigation, he can be placed in a sense in exactly the same situation, that is a qualitatively identical epistemic situation, and call two heavenly bodies 'Hesperus' and 'Phosphorus', without their being identical. (1980: 103–4)

Generalizing, let us call a community C_1 an *epistemic duplicate* of a community C_2 just in case for every proposition known by someone in C_1, someone in C_2 knows that proposition (or an analogous proposition), and vice versa.[68] Even when an utterance expresses a necessary truth in our mouths, there may nevertheless be some possible epistemic duplicate community for whom it or its analogue would express a (necessary) falsehood. Insofar as we conflate the latter possibility with the possible falsity of the original statement, modal illusion will arise. Meanwhile, even when an utterance expresses a contingent truth in our mouths, there may nevertheless be no possible epistemic duplicate community for whom it or its analogue would express a falsehood. Insofar as we conflate the latter impossibility with the necessary truth of the original statement, modal illusion will similarly arise.[69]

3.2.5 *General Morals*

The modal illusions that we have been trying to make sense of arise from some sort of genuine modal insight, distorted by some sort of conflation. Once the conflation is ironed out, the modal insight can be expressed in a trouble-free way. Thus:

> The loose and inaccurate statement that gold might have turned out to be a compound should be replaced (roughly) by the statement that it is logically possible that

[68] Of course, if the members of C_1 and C_2 are wholly distinct, no one in C_1 will know quite what a member of C_2 knows when that member utters 'I exist'. But that member's 'counterpart' will, in some intuitive sense, know a counterpart singular proposition—hence the 'analogous proposition' clause. The task of making the notion of 'analogous' proposition precise in this sense is a daunting one—which we leave to others. For discussion of these issues, see the contributions to this volume by Bealer, Chalmers, and Yablo.

[69] Note that in the case of a term introduced by a reference-fixing description, epistemic duplicate confusion will induce reference-fixing surrogate confusion.

there should have been a compound with all the properties originally known to hold of gold. (1980: 142–3)[70]

Similarly, the loose and inaccurate statement that water might not have been H_2O is a faulty attempt to convey the perfectly acceptable thought that there might have been a community that was an epistemic duplicate of our predecessors that rigidly denoted some stuff other than H_2O by 'water'.[71] Those who conflate this possibility with the possibility that water is not H_2O may be duped into thinking that any possible stuff with those manifest qualities originally known to hold of water counts as water. They may also be induced to suppose that in possible worlds where H_2O does not generate those manifest qualities originally known to hold of water, it will not count as water. (After all, in a world where XYZ has those properties and H_2O does not, the epistemic duplicate will not refer to H_2O by 'water'.) The latter style of mistake is particularly tempting, Kripke notes, in the case of heat. While the sensation of heat fixes the reference of 'heat', it does not define it. Heat, after all, is identical to molecular motion:

Suppose we imagine God creating the world; what does He need to do to make the identity of heat and molecular motion obtain? Here it would seem that all He needs

[70] And again: '*it could have turned out that P* entails that P could have been the case. What, then, does the intuition that the table might have turned out to have been made of ice or of anything else . . . amount to? I think that it means simply that there might have been *a table* looking and feeling just like this one and placed in this very position in the room, which was in fact made of ice. In other words, I (or some conscious being) could have been *qualitatively in the same epistemic situation* that in fact obtains, I could have the same sensory evidence that I in fact have, about *a table* which was made of ice. . . . Something like counterpart theory is thus applicable to the situation, but it applies only because we are *not* interested in what might have been true of *this particular* table, but in what might or might not be true of *a table* given certain evidence' (1980: 141–2, italics in original).

[71] Note that the strategy just described will not work for certain sorts of statements: for instance, those concerning mathematics. (Wright (Ch. 12 below) discusses potential implications of this fact.) If Goldbach's conjecture is true, then the statement that it might have turned out to be false should presumably *not* be replaced, even roughly, by the statement that one might, in an epistemically identical situation, encounter an analogous mathematical conjecture that is false. Rather, the statement that Goldbach's conjecture might have turned out to have been false is to be replaced, roughly, by an acknowledgement of our uncertainty about the conjecture's truth or falsity. Kripke writes: 'there's one sense in which things might turn out either way, in which it's clear that that doesn't imply that the way it finally turns out isn't necessary. For example, the four color theorem might turn out to be true and might turn out to be false. It might turn out either way. . . . Obviously, the "might" here is purely "epistemic"—it merely expresses our present state of ignorance, or uncertainty' (1980: 103). Note that certain constructions are better suited than others to express the 'might' of ignorance: it is relatively difficult to think of the sentence 'It might not have been the case that water is H_2O' being used in this way (unless the utterer wishes to express the thought that perhaps in the past water had a different chemical constitution). For a general strategy for distinguishing uses of the 'epistemic might', see Bealer, Ch. 1 below.

to do is to create the heat, that is, the molecular motion itself. . . . How then does it appear to us that the identity of molecular motion with heat is a substantive scientific fact, that the mere creation of molecular motion still leaves God with the additional task of making molecular motion into heat? This feeling is indeed illusory, but what *is* a substantive task for the Deity is the task of making molecular motion felt as heat. (1980: 153, italics in original)

Once our thinking has been purged of such conflations, Kripke holds, we can happily rely on the modal intuitions that remain intact.

3.3   *Dualism*

One such case, Kripke argues, is the case of our modal intuitions concerning the distinctness of mental and physical phenomena. Here, he maintains, the conceivability of their distinctness *is* a guide to possibility—and hence to actuality.

Consider some candidate materialist claim of property identity:

(15) Pain is C-fibre stimulation.

As with heat, it seems that the mere creation of C-fibre stimulation leaves God with an additional task: namely, that of bringing pain into the world. Moreover, it seems that God could have brought pain into the world without creating C-fibres. But 'pain' and 'C-fibre stimulation' both seem to be rigid designators, so it would seem that the identity theorist cannot coherently maintain that 'pain is C-fibre stimulation' is a mere contingent truth (1980: 148–9). A natural strategy would be to defend it as a necessary truth—and explain away the appearance of contingency using one of the strategies just presented. So, for instance, the defender of materialism might say: 'What you call an intuition to the effect that C-fibre stimulation could exist without pain and vice versa is just a loose and misleading way of saying that C-fibre stimulation could fail to satisfy the description that is used to fix the reference of "pain" .' Or he might say: 'What you call an intuition to the effect that C-fibre stimulation could exist without pain and vice versa is just a loose and misleading way of saying that there is some possible epistemic duplicate community (of ourselves or our predecessors) such that "pain" in their mouths does not apply to C-fibre stimulation.'

But, Kripke maintains, these strategies for explaining the appearance of contingency will not work for 'pain'.[72] 'In the case of molecular motion and heat there is something, namely, the sensation of heat, which is an intermediary between the external phenomenon and the observer. In the mental-physical

---

[72] Kripke (1980: 151–3); Bealer (Ch. 1 below) argues that Kripke is too quick here.

case no such intermediary is possible' (1980: 151). So, while there is a distinction between the manifest qualities that can be used to fix the reference of a natural kind term like 'heat' and the reference of the natural kind term itself, there seems to be no such distinction available between the quality that is used to fix the referent of 'pain' and pain itself (cf. 1980: 152–3). Likewise in the case of the second speech:

> Someone can be in the same epistemic situation as he would be if there were heat, even in the absence of heat, simply by feeling the sensation of heat; and even in the presence of heat, he can have the same evidence as he would have in the absence of heat simply by lacking the sensation *S*. No such possibility exists in the case of pain and other mental phenomena. To be in the same epistemic situation that would obtain if one had a pain *is* to have a pain; to be in the same epistemic situation that would obtain in the absence of a pain *is* not to have a pain. (1980: 152, italics in original)[73]

So, maintains Kripke, neither of the strategies available for explaining modal illusion can be applied in this case: the appearance of possibility is a reflection of genuine possibility. (15) is not merely a posteriori, but contingent.

4 Two-Dimensionalism

Crucial to Kripke's diagnosis of our tendency to modal illusions, is the contrast between the modal status of the proposition expressed by a sentence and modal facts about what that sentence would have expressed in the mouths of other possible communities. This makes for two different perspectives upon any given assertoric utterance. On the one hand, we might wish to consider which possible worlds are in accord with how the sentence *does* represent things to be. On the other hand, we might wish to consider how that sentence would have represented things as being had it been uttered in a different setting (and to consider which possible worlds are in accord with how the sentence *would have* represented things to be). 'Two-dimensional' approaches to modal discourse attempt to accommodate both perspectives, using the machinery of two-dimensional modal logic.[74]

---

[73] Though Kripke does not emphasize the point, the heat/molecular motion strategy has more promise for explaining the appearance that I can exist without my body. Assuming that I am identical to a certain organism, there may be a possible being for which Cartesian dualism is true, whose evidential situation is analogous to mine, and for which an analogous claim of separability is correct.

[74] For conversations and advice concerning this section, we are grateful to David Chalmers, Ted Sider, and Brian Weatherson. In thinking about these issues, we have been much influenced by Stalnaker (2001).

4.1 *Standard 'One-Dimensional' Modal Logic*

There are many ways that the world could have been. If the world had been some of those ways—ways such that snow is white—then what is said by the assertoric utterance 'Snow is white' would have been true. If the world had been others of those ways—ways such that snow is not white—then what is said by the utterance would have been false.

Facts such as these are represented within standard modal logic using a familiar formal framework.[75] Speaking at a maximal level of abstraction, a modal propositional language consists of the symbols of propositional logic plus two monadic sentential operators $\Box$ and $\Diamond$. The usual semantics for this language consists of a set of indices or 'points', a valuation function that assigns to each atomic sentence of the language one of the values 1,0 at each point, and an accessibility relation that specifies which points are accessible from any given point. Complex formulas are then assigned values at points in ways that depend on the values of atomic sentences at various points. The value of a Boolean combination of formulas depends only on the values of those formulas *at that point*, in the usual way. (For example, the formula that results from prefixing a formula ϕ with ~ gets the value 1 at a point if ϕ has the value 0 at that point, 0 if ϕ has the value 1.) But the value of modal formulas $\Box \phi$ and $\Diamond \phi$ at a point depends on the value of ϕ *at other points*. $\Diamond \phi$ has the value 1 at a point i iff ϕ has the value 1 at some point j accessible from i. $\Box \phi$ has the value 1 at i iff ϕ has the value 1 at all points j accessible from i.

For the purposes of shedding light on discourse about possibility and necessity, there is a natural interpretation of this formal framework. We think of $\Box$ and $\Diamond$ as representing necessity and possibility, respectively. We think of the points in the intended interpretation as being an array of possible worlds (with one of the worlds earmarked as the actual world). We think of '1' and '0' as standing for the truth-values true and false, respectively. And we think of the formulas as representing assertoric sentences of some natural language. The valuation function will thus be in the business of assigning truth-values to assertoric sentences of natural language relative to possible worlds.

Suppose that one such model is correct for the set of assertoric utterances of English.[76] To simplify, let us suppose that the model is one according to which

[75] How one understands general issues of modality will turn to some extent on fundamental philosophical questions of priority—between worlds and propositions, between sentential truth and propositional truth, between sentential operators and propositional operators. Our discussion here does not explore these foundational issues. For critique of some widely accepted views on these matters, see Bealer, Ch. 1 below.

[76] Of course, if we are simply interested in determining which modal formulas are valid (given, say, certain constraints on accessibility), we will be concerned with which formulas are true at

every world is accessible from every other (so that from the perspective of any world, every world is a possible world).[77] Each assertoric utterance will now have, associated with it, a function from possible worlds to truth-values. Associated with the English sentence 'Snow is white' is one such function: a function that delivers the value 'true' for all worlds where snow is white, and 'false' for all other worlds. This function specifies a condition that a world must satisfy in order for this English sentence to be true relative to it: the world must be such that snow is white in that world. Call this function the utterance's *content*. The content of an utterance will associate two sets of worlds with it: a set of worlds that are the way the utterance represents the world as being, and a set of worlds that are not. Necessary truth and possible truth will be explicable in terms of the □ and ◊ operators described earlier. Given the simplifying assumptions about accessibility, an utterance is necessarily true if the second set is empty (that is, if every world is the way the utterance represents the world as being), necessarily false if the first set is empty (that is, if no world is the way the utterance represents the world as being), possibly true if the first set is non-empty (that is, if some world is the way the utterance represents the world as being), and true if the first set contains the actual world (that is, if the actual world is the way the utterance represents the world as being).

In so far as an assertoric utterance is neither necessarily true nor necessarily false, the utterance effects a cut in possibility space. It is natural to suppose that the truth-conditions of the utterance are given by this cut. And it is standard to suppose that the meaning of an utterance is intimately linked to its truth-conditions. Suppose, for example, you ask me what my utterance of 'pachyderms are macrotous' means, and I answer by conveying to you that the utterance is true in all and only those worlds where elephants, rhinoceroses, hippopotami, and the like have big ears. It seems reasonable to say that I have done a tolerably good job in answering your question. What we have called the 'content' of an assertion is thus closely associated with what in ordinary English would be called its *meaning*. And it has seemed to many philosophers that this might serve as a promising centre-piece for an analysis of the ordinary notion of what is said.[78]

---

every point in every model (that obeys those accessibility constraints), and not with which formulas come out true on some particular intended interpretation.

[77] This is the framework of S5 modal logic.

[78] The most obvious stumbling-block for content-based analyses of meaning is, of course, the account they offer of necessary truths and falsehoods. Intuitively, I have fallen far short of conveying the meaning of a complex mathematical expression if I simply convey to you that the utterance is true/false in all possible worlds. Related problems of coarse-grainedness arise in

4.2 *The Two-Dimensional Framework*

Let's return to our old friend Bob, who, you will recall, was introduced by the reference-fixer 'the number of the planets'. Now suppose that I utter the following sentence:

  (16) Bob is odd.

An utterance of (16) is true just in case the number designated by 'Bob' is odd. Since 'Bob' is rigid, the utterance will express a necessary truth if it expresses a truth at all (assuming that any truth of mathematics is necessary).[79] Reflecting on how the name 'Bob' is introduced, however, it is readily apparent that there are possible worlds where the name 'Bob' is introduced in just the way We actually introduced it, but where the content of the sentence 'Bob is odd' is different. Although the sentence actually expresses a necessary truth, there will be possible tokens of 'Bob is odd' that express necessary falsehoods—for in some worlds, 'Bob' picks out a different (even) number that in that world numbers the planets. So the content associated with 'Bob is odd' depends on contingent facts about the world at which it is uttered. Our competence with various sorts of indicative conditionals—such as 'If, to our great surprise, it turns out that there are in actual fact only four planets, then in actual fact Bob is identical to four, and so Bob is not odd'—seems to turn on an appreciation of something like this dependency.[80]

This discussion makes obvious two kinds of interest that we might have in an utterance. On the one hand, we might be interested in its content. On the other hand, we might be interested in what content that utterance might have had if it had been made in different circumstances. Two-dimensional approaches attempt to accommodate facts corresponding to both kinds of interest within the formal framework of two-dimensional modal logic.

Speaking at a maximal level of abstraction, while one-dimensional modal semantics deploys a valuation function that evaluates formulas relative to a single index, a two-dimensional modal semantics deploys a valuation function that evaluates formulas relative to an ordered pair of indices. Thus the valuation

other cases of extensional equivalence. Addressing such issues would take us beyond the scope of this introduction. Bealer (Ch. 1 below) argues that two-dimensional semantics cannot deal with a number of outstanding problems of 'fine-grained content' relevant to modal epistemology (Frege's puzzle, Mates's puzzle, Kripke's puzzle, etc.), and he outlines an algebraic semantical account designed to handle such phenomena.

[79] Whether it expresses a truth, of course, will depend on the ultimate classificatory fate of poor Pluto.

[80] A satisfying account of what such appreciation comes to will require, *inter alia*, some decision as to which of the versions of two-dimensionalism that we describe in sect. 4.3 is best suited to the job.

function will assign one of the values 1,0 to each atomic formula relative to each ordered pair $<i,j>$. How a formula gets evaluated now depends upon two dimensions of variation, not one. The truth-value of a Boolean combination at a pair depends on the truth-values of its parts at that same pair, in the usual way. (For example, the formula $\sim \phi$ has the value 1 at a pair $<i,j>$ if and only if ϕ has the value 0 at $<i,j>$.) The truth-values of the modal formulas $\Box$ ϕ and $\Diamond \phi$ at a pair $<i,j>$ depend on the truth-values of ϕ at pairs $<i,k>$: the modal operators $\Box$ and $\Diamond$ are in this way 'tied to' the second index. For example, $\Diamond \phi$ gets the value 1 at $<i,j>$ iff ϕ gets the value 1 at some pair $<i,k>$ where k is accessible from j. But the language of propositional modal logic may be enriched by other operators as well, operators that are tied to the first index, or even operators that are tied to each index. For example, one might introduce the operator 'Act' with a corresponding valuation condition: Act ϕ gets the value 1 at pair $<i,j>$ iff ϕ has the value 1 at $<i,i>$.

For the purposes of shedding light on discourse about possibility and necessity, there is a natural interpretation of this formal framework. We think of $\Box$ and $\Diamond$ as representing necessity and possibility, respectively. We think of the points in the intended interpretation as being an array of possible worlds (with one of the worlds earmarked as the actual world). We treat '1' and '0' as standing for the truth-values true and false. And we think of the formulas as representing assertoric sentences of some natural language. The valuation function will thus be in the business of assigning truth-values to assertoric sentences of natural language relative to possible worlds.

For the purpose of representing the facts that we are interested in, there is, once again, a natural interpretation of this formal framework. As before, we think of formulas as sentences of a natural language, and the values 1 and 0 as truth-values. A formula ϕ will have a truth-value relative to an ordered pair of indices $<i,j>$. We can think of i as representing a possible occasion of use[81] of ϕ. To this end we might usefully think of i as what many philosophers, following Quine, call a 'centred world'[82]—roughly, an ordered pair of a possible world and a location in that world. Then ϕ's content on that possible occasion of use delivers a truth-value relative to j. We thus think of j as a possible world. $\Box$ and $\Diamond$, as before, may be thought of as representing the standard notions of necessity and possibility; and 'Act' can be thought of as representing the English operator 'It is actually the case that'.[83] To think of ϕ as being true relative to

---

[81] This oversimplifies things a little: not everyone who uses the two-dimensional framework in this area deploys centred worlds for representing possible occasions of utterance. (For more, see sect. 4.3.) [82] Quine 1969.

[83] This definition secures that if P is true, then it is necessarily actually the case that P. The best-known discussion of the 'Actuality' operator and its relation to the contingent a priori and

<i,j>, then, is to think of the content that it would have at i delivering the value true at world j.[84]

Suppose that one such model is correct for the assertoric sentences of English. Return now to our 'Bob is odd' example. Suppose an index i is a centred world where 'Bob is odd' is uttered and the number of planets in the world associated with i is five. Suppose further that the same reference-fixing mechanism is employed for 'Bob' as in the actual world. Then, for every pair <i,j>, the valuation function will assign the value 1 to 'Bob is odd'. Suppose, meanwhile, an index k is a centred world where 'Bob is odd' is uttered and where the number of planets is six. And suppose, as before, that the same reference-fixing mechanism is employed for 'Bob' as in the actual world. Then, for every pair <k,j>, the valuation function will assign the value 0 to 'Bob is odd'.

For each assertoric sentence, our model will determine what might be called a *two-dimensional* or *2D* function. The arguments of that function will be centred worlds. The values of the function will be contents (which are themselves functions from worlds to truth-values). The variation in contents that the 2D function assigns to a sentence relative to different centred worlds as arguments will represent the way that the content of a sentence can vary in different contexts of use—how its content is determined by contingent facts about the world. Meanwhile, the value of the function given some centred world based on[85] the actual world—corresponding to some particular deployment of that sentence—will describe the content of some actual assertion. If one is interested in whether that actual assertion is true, or possibly true, or necessarily true (in the sense of 'possibly' and 'necessarily' that has traditionally interested those concerned with modality), it is the content assigned by the 2D function relative to the centred world corresponding to that speech act that will be of interest. If one is interested in how the truth-value of that sentence might have

necessary a posteriori is Davies and Humberstone (1980). While noting the adequacy of two-dimensional modal logic to explain the behaviour of 'Actually', they deploy a slightly different formal framework that relies on considering sets of models that differ only in which world is tagged as actual. Clearly, the notation of two-dimensionalism is not the only way to encode the sorts of philosophical ideas that it is standardly used to express.

[84] The contrast between considering a world as occupying the first index and considering it as occupying the second corresponds to what Jackson and Chalmers call the difference between considering a world 'as actual' and considering it 'as counterfactual'.

[85] Each centred world can be mapped on to a world that is the world for which it provides a centre. Assuming a centred world is an ordered pair of world and location, let us say that a centred world is 'based on' a world w iff w is the first member of the ordered pair that is that centred world.

been different had the circumstances of utterance been different, then further aspects of the 2D function will be what is of interest.

In some contexts of inquiry, what Stalnaker calls the 'diagonal proposition' will be of special interest. This can be thought of as a function from centred worlds to truth-values, where the value true is assigned to a centred world just in case the sentence expresses a truth at that world (that is, at the world upon which the centred world is based).[86] In effect, the diagonal proposition tells us, for a given sentence, which possible and actual speakers succeed in saying something true by means of it. (The term 'diagonal' is used because the function is determined by the values along the diagonal of a two-dimensional matrix representing the sentence's two-dimensional function.[87]) Return to our 'Bob is odd' example. Suppose 'Bob is odd' picks out a necessary truth. Still, there is an evident epistemic risk to an utterance of 'Bob is odd', one that is highlighted by the diagonal proposition: there will be many possible contexts in which 'Bob is odd' expresses a falsehood, and thus many centred worlds for which its diagonal proposition gives the value false. Meanwhile, there are sentences with contingent contents that appear to enjoy a special epistemic security—such as Kripke's examples of contingent a priori truths. Return to our earlier example, 'Bob is the number of the planets'. At any world where 'Bob' is introduced by the same reference-fixing device as we have specified, and 'is the number of the planets' expresses the property that it does at the actual world, the diagonal proposition will deliver the value true.[88]

4.3 *Sub-semantic, Semantic, and Epistemic Two-Dimensionalism*

The discussion so far has deliberately masked a number of issues that divide those who deploy the two-dimensionalist framework. It is time to bring those to the surface, and to explain their significance.[89]

---

[86] The diagonal proposition will be determined by how values are assigned to a particular class of ordered pairs: those where the very same world occurs in both places (or as the first member of the pair, supposing that centred worlds are themselves ordered pairs of worlds and locations).

[87] See Stalnaker (1978). Stalnaker's discussion there streamlines matters by using worlds rather than centred worlds for the purposes of both indices.

[88] Can we say that a claim is a priori when its associated diagonal proposition is necessary, and a posteriori when its diagonal proposition is contingent? Such questions cannot be settled prior to deciding which version of two-dimensionalism one is deploying. For example, on the sub-semantic version of two-dimensionalism, such equations are hopeless.

[89] We are indebted to David Chalmers for a number of the ideas in this section, both taxonomic and substantive. In addition, our discussion in this section has been very much influenced by Stalnaker (2001).

Of special note is the fact that the abstract 2D framework can be combined with a number of different ways of defining the 2D evaluation of statements at worlds. Correlatively, 2D approaches can be conducted with or without a specialized notion of meaning, and with or without an idealized notion of apriority. These variations are of great significance in the current context: for, as we shall see, the extent to which the 2D framework has any prospect of illuminating the connections between apriority and necessity, and between conceivability and possibility, depends very much on the kinds of two-dimensional evaluation that are available.

To begin, the reader may have noticed that the 2D function, as just described, was characterized with regard to some sentence: arguments for which the 2D function delivers values correspond to possible occasions of use of that sentence. But what counts as a use of *that* sentence rather than some other sentence? What criterion of sameness of sentence type is to govern the philosophical interpretation of the framework?

Return to 'Bob is odd'. On one approach, any possible occurrence of a contentful string of sounds that is suitably similar by phonetic (or graphemic) standards (or some other relatively superficial linguistic criterion) will serve as a suitable argument for the two-dimensional function. Some possible use of the sounds 'Bob is odd' express the content that Plato was tall. The two-dimensional function will take such a value as argument and yield as content the function that assigns truth to all worlds in which Plato was tall. (Presumably, the 2D function will be a partial function: given a centred world as argument that does not correspond to a possible use of that string of noises, the 2D function will deliver no value. From the current perspective, its job will be to codify what content that string would have on possible occasions of use. The 2D function for 'Bob is odd' will have nothing to say regarding occasions of use of a different string.) From this perspective, no diagonal proposition will be such as to always deliver the value true for any centred world (where it delivers a value at all), since any phonemically or graphemically individuated sentence type could have been used to express a falsehood. Call this the *sub-semantic 2D function* associated with an utterance.[90]

There, are, however, other ways of thinking about the 2D approach. Intuitively, there is a notion of meaning that is orthogonal to the notion of content adumbrated earlier. Begin with David Kaplan's notion of the *character* of an indexical.[91] There is an obvious sense in which you and I mean the same thing when each of us says 'I am hungry'—even though the contents of our utterances are different. We both grasp a rule associated with the lexical

---

[90] For exploration of one such approach, see Stalnaker (2001).   [91] See Kaplan (1989).

expression 'I', a rule that generates different contents in different contexts of use. This commonality of rule grounds our sense that the English pronoun 'I' in some sense means the same thing on different occasions of use.

It seems plausible to think that this notion of meaning can be generalized beyond standard indexicals. Consider 'Bob is odd'. Suppose someone in another possible world—call him my 'counterpart'—introduces a name with the same reference-fixing description (which may or may not bear a superficial resemblance to 'Bob'), but rigidly designates a different number thereby. There is an obvious sense in which there is a common rule to my use of 'Bob' and his use of the term he introduces, so that it is not implausible to say that in some sense, my counterpart and I mean the same by our respective terms. Moreover, it is prima-facie natural to think that it is meaning in this sense that is more closely tied to the intuitive notion of understanding. Understanding the expression 'Bob' appears to have little to do with possessing a substantive conception of which thing it is that 'Bob' refers to. Indeed, if—due to astronomical ignorance—I mistakenly believe that Bob is identical to the number 6, that is quite consistent with my understanding the term 'Bob' perfectly well. On the face of it, my understanding of the expression is determined by my knowledge of the reference-fixing description that serves as the rule by which a referent is determined and my knowledge that the term so introduced functions rigidly. But this seems to be knowledge that I share with my counterpart.[92]

While reserving the term 'content' for the notion previously explained (see section 4.1), let us henceforth use the term 'meaning' for the phenomenon just identified. If one finds something like this conception of meaning compelling, one might well find it useful to build some two-dimensional apparatus around it. In particular, the notion of meaning will provide us with a way to type utterances that serve as arguments for the 2D function. Return to 'Bob is odd'. While we have little interest in uses of 'Bob is odd' that are phonetically similar but different in meaning, we may very well be interested in uses that share its meaning but differ in content.

A 2D function will nicely represent how content varies according to the interaction between contingent facts and fixed meanings. In this connection,

---

[92] We might allow that the rule is sometimes deferential: In my mouth, the referent of 'quark' might be given by the rule 'Whatever the experts refer to by "quark" ', and in that sense, a possible duplicate of me embedded in a community that used 'quark' to pick out a different kind of fundamental particle would mean the same by 'quark' as me in the relevant 'character-theoretic' sense (cf. Chalmers's discussion of Neptune, Ch. 3 below). More generally, the notion of meaning that will maximally illuminate epistemic matters may differ from ordinary notions of linguistic meaning in being far less public.

the function's arguments will be possible utterances with the same meaning, rather than, for instance, possible utterances typed by superficial similarity. Call this the *semantic two-dimensional function.*[93]

(Perhaps we can generalize even further: for every possible space-time location, we associate a content with the meaning of 'Bob is odd', regardless of whether there is at that location a speaker who makes an utterance with that meaning.[94] The content will be a function from worlds to truth-values that delivers True at all worlds iff the number of planets at the time associated with the location is odd, and delivers False at all worlds otherwise. Note that it is now no longer clear that the 2D function need be a partial function.[95])

Not everyone will think that the notion of meaning that is required for the semantic 2D function is coherent. One might in particular worry whether there are disciplined standards for sameness and difference of meaning—as opposed to content—of natural language expressions.[96] The formal machinery of two-dimensionalism cannot serve to explicate any notion of meaning, since it is presupposed by the very idea of a function from meanings to contents: the concept of meaning is thus used to introduce the notion of a semantic 2D function, not the other way around.[97] But if there is such a coherent notion of meaning, one might reasonably hope that semantic two-dimensionalism would shed some useful light on our main topics.

In this connection, note that while the diagonal proposition of a sub-semantic 2D function is always contingent, it is natural to suppose that the diagonal proposition of a semantic 2D function is sometimes necessary. Consider 'Bob is the number of the planets' (where 'Bob', as before, is introduced by the reference-fixer 'the number of the planets'). The content is contingent. But

---

[93] Note that our use of 'semantic' here differs from Stalnaker's.

[94] After all, if someone had actually introduced 'Bob' into English in this way, it wouldn't really have been crucial for anyone to actually utter 'Bob is odd' in order that that sentence get a truth-value relative to the actual world. And in a world where we never even introduce 'Bob' into English (or any other name like it), it seems that we can nevertheless think of that enrichment of English (English + 'Bob') as being available at that world.

[95] This is the version of semantic two-dimensionalism that comes closest to Chalmers's epistemic version of two-dimensionalism. Note that on this version of semantic two-dimensionalism what is crucial is how meanings (suitably conceived) deliver different contents relative to various hypotheses about which world is actual, not what contents are enjoyed by particular utterances relative to various hypotheses about which world is actual (holding fixed the meaning).

[96] Cf. in this regard Yablo's discussion (Ch. 13 below) of the connection of these issues to the issue of narrow content.

[97] It would similarly be absurd to suppose that the machinery of sub-semantic two-dimensionalism is a useful way of explicating what it is for two possible utterances to be phonetic or graphemic duplicates.

any possible utterance that means the same as 'Bob is the number of the planets' will, it seems, express a truth on that occasion of use.[98] Thus the diagonal proposition of the semantic 2D function for 'Bob is the number of the planets' will be necessary. While the necessity of the content does not appear sufficient or necessary for apriority, there appears to be a tighter connection between a statement's apriority and the diagonal proposition of its semantic 2D function.[99] After all, if its diagonal proposition is contingent, then there will be possible worlds where someone who means the same thing will express something false.[100] Relatedly, where 'S' has a contingent diagonal proposition, there would seem to be true indicative conditions of the form 'If such-and-such a situation is actual, S is false', where we have no way of telling a priori whether the situation described in the antecedent is actual. So it is hard to see how a statement with a contingent semantic diagonal proposition could be a priori.[101] Correlatively, while conceivability may be an insecure guide to whether the content of a statement is possibly true,[102] it may be a much better guide to whether or not the semantic diagonal proposition is contingent. Note in this connection that 'Hesperus is not Phosphorus' does enjoy a possibly true diagonal proposition—that is, there is some circumstance where 'Hesperus is not Phosphorus' has the same meaning (though not the same content) as it

---

[98] We assume for now that the concept of meaning is well enough understood to permit such judgements. Not everyone will agree. Here is one potential source of obscurity: Does sameness of meaning of the term introduced require merely that the reference-fixing descriptions used to introduce the term have the same meaning? Or must these descriptions also have the same content?

[99] One might even think that the ordinary 'necessity' is ambiguous between what we have been calling metaphysical necessity and necessity of diagonal proposition.

[100] There are complications here. We noted above that a semantic 2D function might evaluate formulas at locations where they are not uttered. If we make use of this conception, we may well allow the sentence 'I exist' to count as a contingent semantic 2D diagonal proposition. But no possible utterance of 'I exist' with the same meaning as its meaning in English will express a falsehood. Call a sentence 'weakly contingent' if semantic diagonal proposition assigns it falsity only at centred worlds that are not associated with possible utterances with the same meaning. One now has to classify weak contingency in relation to apriority and conceivability—a task we leave to others.

[101] Quite obviously, the contingency of the diagonal proposition associated with a sub-semantic 2D function will not tell against apriority. If the sub-semantic two-dimensionalist is to explain apriority and conceivability, it will have to be by supplemental theory.

[102] Of course, one might stipulate that 'conceive' is a success term, so that one can only conceive of the possibility of some content if that content is possible: thus one cannot conceive that Hesperus is not Phosphorus, but only seem to conceive it. But, as before, such a stipulation will restore a tight connection between conceivability and possibility (and may even have some plausibility as a matter of capturing the ordinary language use of 'conceive'), at the expense of making one's success at conceiving inscrutable to oneself.

does for us, yet expresses a truth. So someone wishing to defend the view that conceivability is a guide to semantic diagonal possibility[103] need not be embarrassed to concede that we can conceive that Hesperus is not Phosphorus.[104]

In addition to the two just canvassed, a third version of two-dimensionalism has recently been advanced.[105] Begin by noting that the evaluation of such indicative conditionals as

> (17) If the star seen in the morning is not in actual fact the star seen in the evening, then Hesperus is not Phosphorus[106]

cannot proceed simply via the contents of the antecedent and consequent. But there does seem to be an epistemic connection between the antecedent and the consequent, and it seems that it is this connection that grounds our confidence in the conditional. Why not, then, build a framework directly around this notion of epistemic connection?[107] *Epistemic two-dimensionalism*[108] does just this. Here—in extremely sketchy form—is the basic picture. Associated with each world w is a world description d. Our two-dimensional modal logic now evaluates claims relative to pairs of world descriptions. We proceed as follows. Take an ordered pair of world descriptions $<d_1, d_2>$ and a statement s. Assume that d_1 describes the actual world. Now determine, on a priori grounds alone, whether on this assumption s is true at the world described by d_2. For example, assume d_1 is a description that says, *inter alia*, that the lakes and rivers are filled with a transparent, flavourless liquid that is XYZ. Suppose d_2 is a description that says, *inter alia*, that Dave has XYZ in his pool.

---

[103] Once again, though, we need to get clearer about what 'conceivability' is supposed to be. It is intuitively possible that Bob is not the number of the planets. Yet 'Bob is the number of the planets' is diagonally necessary. In so far as conceiving is a guide to diagonal possibility, we need a notion of conceiving according to which our finding it intuitively possible that Bob is not the number of the planets doesn't count as a case of conceiving. (See Chalmers (Ch. 3 below) for a detailed treatment of such issues, noting especially his distinction between primary and secondary conceivability.)

[104] A number of philosophers have suggested that the necessary a posteriori can be demystified via the 2D framework, although the underlying idea can be expressed without the formalism that the framework provides. The basic idea is that a necessary a posteriori truth of the form □P can be factorized into an empirical premiss about the underlying structure of the actual world, together with an a priori conditional whose antecedent is that empirical premiss and whose consequent is □P. See, e.g., Sidelle, Ch. 8 below.

[105] Cf. Chalmers, Ch. 3 below, and other papers at http://www.u.arizona.edu/~chalmers/.

[106] Yablo (Ch. 13 below) argues that it is in fact conditionals of the form 'If it had turned out that P . . .' that best capture the explanandum here. For critique see Chalmers, Ch. 3 below.

[107] One could in principle develop versions of epistemic two-dimensionalism that exploit a notion other than that of a priori connection: relevant here is Yablo, Ch. 13 below.

[108] Thanks to David Chalmers for suggesting this label.

And suppose s is the sentence 'Dave has water in his pool'. Now determine, on a priori grounds alone, whether Dave has water in his pool at the world described by d_2 on the assumption that d_1 describes the actual world. (Intuitively, our verdict will be 'yes': if the lakes and rivers are filled with XYZ in the actual world, then water is XYZ at every world, so at the world described by d_2, Dave has water in his pool.)

Of special interest will be the epistemic diagonal proposition for a given statement, s.[109] This proposition will be determined, for each value of d, by whether the material conditional 'd $\supset$ s' is a priori true or a priori false. The a priori evaluation of such conditionals will fix the value of s at all pairs $<d_1, d_2>$ where $d_1 = d_2$. (To inquire a priori whether or not s is true is at a world described by d_1 on the assumption that d_1 is the actual world is just to inquire a priori whether or not $d_1 \supset$ s.) The epistemic diagonal will assign to s at a pair $<d_1, d_1>$ the value true or false depending on whether $d_1 \supset$ s is a priori true or a priori false (and will be indeterminate to the extent that there is no a priori decision either way[110]).[111]

Obviously the details of such a picture will depend a good deal upon what the 'world descriptions' look like. A few points to bear in mind:[112] (1) To

---

[109] Chalmers calls the content of a statement its 'secondary intension' and the diagonal proposition associated with epistemic two-dimensionalism its 'primary intension'. Note that what is common among the three sorts of diagonal is purely formal: in each case the diagonal proposition is determined by how the valuation function operates on those ordered pairs of indices $<i\,j>$ where $i = j$.

[110] If the descriptions are framed so that there will always be an a priori decision with regard to any statement evaluated with respect to them, they will be what Chalmers calls 'epistemically complete'.

[111] There is no analogously simple procedure for assigning values to the values of the epistemic 2D function for a pair of indices associated with different worlds. One promising way to think about the general case is as follows: The evaluation of some claim s at some index d_2 given that d_1 is actual turns on the a priori evaluation of the more complex conditional:

$d_1 \supset$ s (if d_2 were true, s would be true).

Where $d_1 = d_2$, this reduces to the a priori evaluation of

$d_1 \supset$ s.

Given the extra cognitive demands imposed by pairs of indices based upon different worlds, it should not be assumed that our facility with the primary intension associated with an epistemic 2D proposition is cognitively derivative from a facility with the 2D function itself. (Chalmers himself is emphatic that, on his view, primary intension is not to be thought of as the by-product of an epistemic 2D function, and for that reason holds that a primary intension is not fundamentally the diagonal of a 2D function.)

[112] Our discussion in this paragraph owes much to conversations with David Chalmers.

the extent that d is descriptively thin, the epistemic diagonal proposition for certain claims may yield highly indeterminate results. For example, if the continuum hypothesis is true as a matter of metaphysical necessity, but a priori undecidable, then in so far as the 'world description' for each world is silent concerning the truth of the continuum hypothesis, the epistemic diagonal for 'The continuum hypothesis is true' will be correspondingly indeterminate. (Note that, intuitively, the semantic diagonal will yield the value True at every world in this case.) (2) To the extent that d is descriptively thick, epistemic diagonal possibility will not correspond to anything like conceivability. For example, if the world description for each H_2O world contains the sentence 'Water is H_2O', then 'Water is not H_2O' will not be an epistemic diagonal possibility.[113] (3) The view requires as an epistemic primitive a highly idealized notion of apriority.[114]

It is an open question which, if any, versions of a 'conceivability entails epistemic diagonal possibility' thesis are true. Take the following toy example: Suppose space, if it exists at all, is necessarily non-Euclidean. Then, relative to any world description d, it will presumably be a priori false that 'If d, then a Euclidean space exists'. But it may none the less be conceivable that space is Euclidean. One who wishes to maintain that conceivability entails epistemic diagonal possibility will presumably wish to maintain that this kind of a posteriori necessity cannot arise.[115]

Sub-semantic two-dimensionalism is, quite obviously, very different from epistemic two-dimensionalism. There appears to be a far greater affinity between semantic and epistemic two-dimensionalism, though we leave an exploration of their relationship to others. We also leave it to readers to explore other possible applications of the formal framework of two-dimensionalism. After all, the versions presented above hardly exhaust the conceptual space. We have in effect indicated a variety of axes along which applications of the

---

[113] On Chalmers's view, the water/H_2O problem is avoided by requiring canonical descriptions to be couched in an appropriately neutral vocabulary. The continuum hypothesis problem will not arise if Chalmers's substantive claims about conceivability and possibility are correct; but if such cases can arise, they are handled by requiring that canonical descriptions are epistemically complete.

[114] For example, (i) it applies to infinitary descriptions; (ii) it applies to descriptions involving vocabulary expressing concepts alien to the human mind; (iii) the inference from a given world description to a given statement will often require a good deal more than narrow logical competence, since the vocabulary of the statement may not appear in the world description (as should be clear from the example just given).

[115] Chalmers calls purported necessities like these 'strong necessities', and argues against their existence (Ch. 3 below).

framework might differ: whether they deploy worlds, centred worlds, or some style or other of world description; whether the evaluation is by truth-value or a priori recognizable truth-value; whether the two-dimensional function can yield values relative to centred worlds where no speech act or thought token occurs; whether the selection of the functions (perhaps partial) from pairs of indices to truth-values is governed by considerations of superficial properties of utterances, or considerations about meaning, or interest in some kind of epistemic connections, and so on. We leave it to readers to consider how these parameters might be juggled, and how yet further interests or parameters might be brought into play.[116]

4.4 *Two-Dimensionalism and the Mind–Body Problem*

Both the semantic and epistemic versions of two-dimensionalism have prima-facie application to the mind–body problem. By way of example, we offer in what follows a reconstruction of Kripke's anti-materialism argument through the lens of semantic two-dimensionalism.

We begin by noting that, arguably, there are cases where content cannot vary while meaning is preserved. In such cases, meaning determines content. For example, one might think that any possible person who means what I mean by '2 is odd' will express the same content. Where meaning and content march in step in this way, the content of an utterance will be necessary iff the diagonal proposition is necessary as well. Content and meaning seem to collapse in precisely this way for predicates describing phenomenal experience: Any possible person that means what I do by 'there is pain' will (it would seem) express the same content by it. It is this that Kripke's argument trades on. In the terminology of our semantic two-dimensionalist, while there are possible uses

---

[116] For example, a more austerely Kripkean implementation of the 2D formal framework might associate a partial 2D function with some claim c such that pairs of indices for which the function gives a value will have a first index that is either (a) a centred world where someone issues an utterance (or thought token) which expresses the proposition actually expressed by c or (b) a world centred upon someone who is an epistemic duplicate—here we have in mind Kripke's notion of an epistemic counterpart—of someone at the centre of one of the worlds captured by (a). The value delivered by the function will depend upon whether the proposition expressed by the utterance associated with the first index is true at the world that serves as the second index. This version of the framework does not appear to require that we bifurcate notions of meaning. Arguably, something like it can implement a Kripkean account of the sense in which it is conceivable that 'Hesperus is not Phosphorus': there is possible being who is (i) an epistemic duplicate of someone who thinks (falsely) that Hesperus is not Phosphorus, and (ii) thinks something true.

of 'There is heat' that have the same meaning (via the same reference-fixing mechanisms) but different contents, no such separation of meaning and content can be effected for descriptions of experience.

Let us now re-articulate Kripke's line of thought within the semantic 2D framework.[117] We appear to be able to conceive of the possibility that there is C-fibre stimulation but no pain—a state of affairs incompatible with the identity of C-fibre stimulation and pain. We can concede that, in general, the ability to conceive of 'a is not b', where 'a' and 'b' are rigid, is evidence only for the diagonal possibility of the statement. But in the case of 'Pain is not C-fibre stimulation', it would seem, the statement is diagonally possible if and only if it is possibly true (there being no gap between meaning and content).[118] If one concedes the diagonal possibility of 'Pain is not C-fibre stimulation', it seems, one is forced to relinquish materialism.

The argument is successful only if our conceiving P succeeds in establishing P's diagonal possibility. How secure is that assumption? An ambitious project in this area is to find some suitable sense of 'conceiving' according to which conceiving that P is sufficient for the possible truth of the diagonal proposition of the semantic 2D function—that is, diagonal possibility—for each utterance.[119] Even if we grant that the notion of meaning required for semantic two-dimensionalism is coherent, this project faces considerable difficulties. If one is to maintain the thesis that conceiving is an infallible (or near-infallible) guide to diagonal possibility, one needs to deploy a highly idealized notion of conceiving. For example, there is an obvious sense in which we can conceive of the possible truth of necessary falsehoods of mathematics of whose truth-values we are ignorant—but such claims are not, it would seem, diagonally

---

[117] Note that what follows is a semantic two-dimensionalist reconstruction of Kripke, not of more recent extant dualist arguments.

[118] Though, as Bealer urges (1994 and Ch. 1 below) there is a worry here that we are forgetting the gap between meaning and content associated with the expression 'C-fibre stimulation'. One response is to point out that even if there is a gap between meaning and content for 'Pain is C-fibre stimulation', there is no such gap for 'Pain is had by an unextended individual', and that the diagonal possibility of the latter is enough to make trouble for at least some versions of materialism. (Reconstructing modal arguments this way is an instance of a general strategy—defended by Bealer (1994, 1996, and Ch. 1 below)—according to which 'semantically unstable' terms—'C-fiber', 'water', 'heat', etc.—are replaced with associated 'semantically stable' terms—'pain', 'individual', 'nested functional part', etc. Bealer argues that, since the resulting sentences are semantically stable, their epistemic possibility entails their metaphysical possibility, therefore yielding the desired outcome in a significant range of cases, but without commitment to any particular controversial semantic scheme.) Further explorations of these issues are offered below by Chalmers, Stalnaker, Yablo, and Wright.

[119] An even more ambitious project is to find some sense of 'conceivable' according to which being conceivable is necessary for diagonal possibility.

possible: any possible mathematical utterance with that meaning is false.[120] For the thesis to be maintained, then, there must be a demanding conception of conceiving—which, to be interesting, must not be tied to diagonal possibility by mere stipulation—according to which what we do in these mathematical cases will not count as conceiving.[121] Call this stronger notion of conceiving— conceiving that entails diagonal possibility—*superconceiving*. If superconceiving were (a) internally scrutable, and (as defined) (b) such as to guarantee diagonal possibility, then one could, potentially, justify anti-materialism in the philosophy of mind using the following style of argument:

(1) A statement is superconceivable iff it is diagonally possible.
(2) 'Pain is not C-fibre stimulation' is superconceivable.
(3) 'Pain is not C-fibre stimulation' is diagonally possible iff it is possible
(4) Therefore 'Pain is not C-fibre stimulation' is possibly true.
(5) Where a claim of distinctness flanked by two rigid designators is possibly true, it is necessarily true.
(6) Therefore 'Pain is not C-fibre stimulation' is actually true.

Can two-dimensional reflection ultimately serve to deliver on the Cartesian dream of refuting materialism in the philosophy of mind through a priori reflection? On this matter, an introduction like this should remain silent.

5 Summaries of Papers

In this section, we provide brief summaries of each of the papers in the volume, so as to permit the reader to identify those most likely to be of interest to her.

5.1 *George Bealer*

In 'Modal Epistemology and the Rationalist Renaissance', George Bealer defends a view he calls *moderate rationalism*: that for a certain distinguished class of propositions—those that are *semantically stable*[122]—necessity and a priori knowability coincide. Because many recent discussions of modal epistemology have misidentified or mischaracterized their subject-matter, he suggests, the existence of such an equivalence (with proper scope) has often been challenged or supported for philosophically unsound reasons. By way of corrective, Bealer

---

[120] But see Rosen, Ch. 7 below.

[121] Chalmers (Ch. 3 below) is helpful here; see also the chapters by Bealer, Wright, and Yablo.

[122] A proposition is semantically stable if it is invariant across communities whose epistemic situations are qualitatively identical.

offers positive characterizations of apriority/aposteriority, possibility/necessity, the nature of propositions, and the nature of understanding that together serve to ground an alternative picture.

Many discussions of the epistemology of modality, he suggests, founder at the outset through their failure to recognize that the source of all (non-stipulative) a priori knowledge is the *sui generis* propositional attitude of *rational intuition* (and not, as many people suppose, conceivability). Recognizing this makes possible a positive characterization of a priori knowledge: knowledge that is directly intuitive, or stipulative, or based wholly upon intuition and/or stipulation.

Apriority in this sense is, Bealer claims, a guide to metaphysical possibility and necessity. In contrast to the latter notions, epistemic possibility and necessity concern a different phenomenon: namely, the quality and character of our evidential relation to p. Proper attention to the details of these distinctions, Bealer suggests, permits proper appreciation of Kripke's contribution to modal epistemology, and points towards ways in which two-dimensionalist accounts are doomed to inadequacy.

Such accounts misfire, Bealer suggests, in failing to recognize that notions of possibility should be accommodated not by distinguishing different kinds of meaning (primary, secondary, etc.), but by distinguishing different kinds of modal operators that can be applied to a fixed domain of propositions. Because they do not, he argues, two-dimensionalist approaches to epistemic possibility, meaning, and understanding such as those proposed by Frank Jackson and David Chalmers fall short in a number of ways: they run a foul of Frege's puzzle, posit ambiguities where there are none, wrongly reckon only sentences (never propositions) to enjoy the property of being necessary a posteriori, and overestimate the centrality of reference-fixing descriptions to linguistic understanding.

As a corrective, Bealer develops a modal epistemology that takes propositions as more basic than possible worlds and that attempts to ground the reliability of intuition by locating it within an account of what it is to understand a concept or proposition. With a sketch of this theory in place, Bealer presents a taxonomy of sources of modal error, and applies his analysis to recent versions of anti-materialist arguments in the philosophy of mind.

5.2 *John Campbell*

In 'Berkeley's Puzzle', John Campbell offers an interpretation of Berkeley's famous argument that it is impossible to conceive of existence unperceived, suggesting that the argument is best understood as making appeal to a principle that Campbell calls *the explanatory role of experience*: that concepts of physical objects, and of their observable characteristics, are made available by our experience of the world. The puzzle that confronts Berkeley, Campbell suggests, is that it is difficult to see how experience could provide us with such concepts if the objects it concerns are mind-independent. Hence, concludes Berkeley, we do not have concepts of mind-independent objects.

Campbell accepts that the puzzle raises a challenge, but rejects Berkeley's solution. Instead, Campbell contends, we need to take what he calls a *relational view* of experience, according to which experience is a primitive cognitive relation that explains, rather than depends upon, the possibility of thoughts about objects. The view is *disjunctivist* in holding that there is no experiential factor in common between a case where one sees an object and a case where one has a hallucination as of such an object. On such a view, experience of objects *can* provide us with concepts of mind-independent objects in ways that mere imagination cannot, for experience has mind-independent objects as its constituent ingredients.

5.3 *David Chalmers*

In 'Does Conceivability Entail Possibility?', David Chalmers presents a detailed taxonomy for exploring the relationship between conceivability and possibility, examines and defends the most promising versions of the thesis that conceivability entails possibility, and applies these results to the question of mind–body dualism.

Chalmers's taxonomy of types of conceivability employs three (independent) distinctions: between (a) finding oneself prima facie able to conceive of P and (b) being able to conceive of P on ideal rational reflection (*prima-facie* versus *ideal* conceivability); between (c) being unable to rule out P and (d) being able to form a detailed positive conception of a situation in which P (*negative* versus *positive* conceivability); and between (e) its being conceivable that P is actually the case and (f) its being conceivable that P might have been the case (*primary/epistemic* versus *secondary/subjunctive* conceivability). This final distinction is paired with an associated distinction between two corresponding notions of possibility: P is primarily possible iff there is a world w such that if w is actual, P is the case; P is secondarily possible iff there is a world w such that if w had been actual, P would have been the case. (So, for example, it is primarily, though not secondarily, possible that Hesperus is not Phosphorus.)

Of these, it is primary conceivability that is of greatest interest to modal rationalism, primary possibility to which primary conceivability offers the most promising guide, and ideal conceivability that provides a credible

candidate for reliable guidance. The conceivability–possibility theses of principal interest, then, are (1) that ideal primary positive conceivability entails primary possibility, and (2) that ideal primary negative conceivability entails primary
possibility. If (1) and (2) are true (as Chalmers believes they are), then instances
of modal error will be traceable to cases where (non-possibility entailing)
prima-facie conceivability is (mistakenly) taken as a guide to possibility, and
cases where (non-secondary possibility entailing) primary conceivability is
(mistakenly) taken as a guide to secondary possibility.

Chalmers points out that for (1) to be true but (2) to be false, there would need
to be statements that fall in what he calls the *twilight zone*: statements that are negatively but not positively conceivable. Such statements, he suggests, would need
to be either *inscrutable*, in the sense that they are not epistemically accessible on the
basis of a complete qualitative description of the world, or *openly inconceivable*, in
the sense that they cannot be ruled out a priori, but are verified by no positively
conceivable situation. Chalmers suggests that both of these classes are empty, so
that if (1) is true, (2) is true as well. But for (1) to be false, there would have to be
instances of *strong necessities*—statements true in all possible worlds that are falsified by some positively conceivable situation considered as actual. But, Chalmers
argues, there are no such instances, so (1) (and hence (2)) is true.

Chalmers then applies this result to the mind–body problem, offering an
argument against materialism that moves from the premiss that zombies are
ideally primarily positively (or negatively) conceivable to the conclusion that
they are primarily possible, and thence to the conclusion that materialism (of
the standard sort) is false.

5.4 *Gregory Currie*

In 'Desire in Imagination', Gregory Currie contends that we need to distinguish between two sorts of imagining, belief-like imagining, on the one hand,
and desire-like imagining, on the other. In imagining of the first sort, one
imaginatively projects into the situation of one who believes P; in imagining of
the second sort, one imaginatively projects into the situation of one who
desires Q. Recognizing these two categories, contends Currie, allows one to
account for a phenomenon—first identified by Hume—that has come to be
known as the puzzle of *imaginative resistance*: whereas we have no systematic difficulty imagining non-moral facts to be otherwise than they are—even to the
point of imagining straightforward impossibilities—we tend to find ourselves
unwilling or unable to imagine alien moral facts.

The explanation for this, on Currie's account, is that imaginative resistance
arises primarily in cases of desire-like imagining, and only derivatively in cases

of belief-like imagining. For, whereas belief-like imagining is carried out in a largely 'off-line' fashion, largely unconstrained by the beliefs that one holds about the actual world, desire-like imagining, according to Currie, engages the imaginer's moral character; as a result, desire-like imagining is constrained by factors that belief-like imagining is not, and hence is more restricted in its range.

5.5 *Michael Della Rocca*

In 'Essentialism versus Essentialism', Michael Della Rocca challenges an assumption generally taken as common ground in contemporary debates about the relation between conceivability and possibility: namely, the assumption that if a and b differ in their possible features, then a and b are non-identical. As Della Rocca observes, Cartesian-style conceivability–possibility arguments for the dualism of phenomenal and physical properties (versions of which are advanced by Kripke and Chalmers) proceed in two steps: (i) from the conceivability of a's having some feature F and the inconceivability of b's having that feature F, it is concluded that a and b differ modally (that they have different possible features); (ii) from the fact that a and b differ modally, it is concluded that a and b are non-identical. In challenging the second step of such arguments, Della Rocca aims to call into question the metaphysical significance of the conceivability–possibility debate; for if modal difference does not imply distinctness, then even granting the conceivability–possibility move will not allow proponents of Cartesian-style arguments to establish non-identity claims on conceivability grounds.

Della Rocca suggests that the move from modal difference to non-identity presupposes essentialism, which he glosses as the two-part thesis that (i) objects have their modal properties independently of how they are described, and (ii) have certain properties essentially. Working with largely Kripkean materials, he attempts to raise doubts concerning the first of these theses.

It is characteristic of essentialists, he contends, to suppose that the modal properties of an individual are not to be explained in terms of facts of similarity between that individual and various possibilia. By contrast, anti-essentialists— and especially 'counterpart theorists'—frequently make use of facts of similarity to account for the truth and falsity of modal property ascriptions (and for the description dependence of such ascriptions). Della Rocca is struck by the fact that there are certain contexts in which Kripke himself is more than willing to deploy facts of similarity in order to make sense of modal intuitions. For example, in explaining away intuitions of contingency accruing to 'Hesperus is Phosphorus', Kripke invokes epistemically similar scenarios where there are two objects in the sky. If facts of similarity are to be invoked there, why should they not be invoked more generally to account for modal property ascriptions (as many anti-essentialists would recommend)? Della Rocca suggests that the essentialist has no good answer to this query.

5.6 *Kit Fine*

In 'The Varieties of Necessity', Kit Fine argues that there are three main forms of necessity—the metaphysical, the natural, and the normative—none reducible to either of the others, or to any other form of necessity. Metaphysical necessity is logical necessity 'in the broad sense'—necessity that obtains in virtue of the identity of things, broadly conceived. So, for instance, the truths of logic are metaphysically necessary (it is metaphysically necessary that anything red is red), as are mathematical truths (there are prime numbers less than 10), conceptual truths (nothing red is green), and truths of identity broadly understood (2 is a number). Natural necessity is the form of necessity standardly associated with laws of nature. So, for instance, certain propositions describing the motions of objects or kinds of objects express natural necessities (it is naturally necessary that billiard-ball B moves in thus-and-such manner when impacted by billiard-ball A; it is naturally necessary that bodies attract one another according to an inverse square law). Normative necessity is the form of necessity that pertains to moral claims—and perhaps to normative claims more generally. So, for instance, certain propositions expressing judgements of rightness and wrongness express normative necessities (it may be normatively necessary that war or murder or lying is wrong, or that if I make a promise I am obliged to keep it).

After providing reasons for thinking that metaphysical necessity (as opposed to some more restricted notion such as mathematical necessity or logical necessity 'in the narrow sense') is properly taken to be a primitive notion of necessity, Fine devotes the bulk of his discussion to showing that neither natural nor normative necessity can be assimilated—either by subsumption or by definition—to metaphysical necessity. Natural necessity cannot be subsumed under metaphysical necessity, for the laws that govern the natural world cannot be fully explained by essentialist truths arising from the identity of things. As a result, attempts to subsume the natural under metaphysical will mislocate the source of the necessity. Nor can natural necessity be defined in terms of metaphysical necessity by characterizing it as a form of metaphysical necessity *relative to* some set of assumptions about the natural world. For such a strategy renders the necessity of the propositions with respect to which the necessity is relative a trivial matter, whereas we are aiming for an account of their necessity that does not trivialize it. Parallel arguments are offered for the case of normative necessity: it cannot be subsumed under metaphysical (or conceptual) necessity on pain of mislocating the source of its normative force, and it cannot be defined in terms of metaphysical necessity on pain of trivializing its content.

Fine closes by considering whether all three forms of necessity might be defined as restrictions of some more comprehensive form of necessity, but rejects this on the grounds that such a characterization would fail to capture the sense in which these three forms of necessity seem, at base, to describe three fundamentally different sorts of constraints upon the world.

5.7 *Gideon Rosen*

In 'A Study in Modal Deviance', Gideon Rosen describes an imaginary tribe—the Q—who hold that the existential truths of number theory—and with them, the related truths of arithmetic—are contingent: according to the Q, there might have been no numbers, in which case it would be false, for instance, that $7 + 5 = 12$, or that there are 10 prime numbers less than 30.

Rosen provides the Q with three arguments in favour of their position: an argument from 'vivid conceivability', a 'Humean argument', and an argument from 'strong coherence'. According to the first, we can vividly conceive a world in which there are no numbers, and hence, barring some special reason for thinking the conception misleading, we are entitled to conclude that such a world is possible. The recipe for such conception goes as follows: start by conceiving a world in which standard arithmetic is true—a world containing both concreta and an infinite number of abstracta. Now eliminate the abstracta, and you have conceived a world in which there are no numbers. The second argument employs the ingredients of the first, without direct appeal to conceiving. Assuming with Hume that there are no necessary connections between distinct existences, it follows that there is a world of concreta without associated abstracta—and hence a world in which arithmetic is false. The third argument makes appeal to the principle that any hypothesis that is 'strongly coherent' is possibly true, where a strongly coherent hypothesis is any hypothesis whose truth in some possible world is consistent with all non-modal facts about the actual world. The hypothesis that there are no numbers seems strongly coherent in this sense, and hence, according to the principle in question, possibly true.

Rosen goes on to describe another imaginary tribe—the Z—who defend the necessary truth of sentences couched in their arithmetical vocabulary on the basis of a 'modal structuralist' construal of such claims. Because of the ontological innocence of arithmetical claims in their mouths, the Z are untroubled by the arguments of the Q. Whether we can follow suit in this regard depends crucially, Rosen suggests, on subtle issues concerning the meaning of 'exists'.

5.8 *Alan Sidelle*

In 'On the Metaphysical Contingency of Laws of Nature', Alan Sidelle aims to defend the traditional role of imagining and conceiving as a means to modal knowledge: while there are, he concedes, necessary a posteriori truths, their existence should not undermine our general reliance on imagination and conception as guides to possibility.

Sidelle makes his case by focusing on the particular example of laws of nature, which some philosophers have recently maintained to be—'in the strongest sense'—necessary. Against this, Sidelle tries to show that the laws of nature are contingent—or, if necessary, necessary in metaphysically uninteresting ways.

Sidelle begins by enumerating a number of prima-facie reasons for thinking the laws of nature to be contingent: namely, that it seems fully imaginable that they might have been otherwise. Kripke- and Putnam-style arguments cannot, Sidelle contends, provide a metaphysically interesting challenge to such imaginative exercises, for necessary a posteriori truths are the result of filling 'gaps' in analytic principles of individuation with particular empirical findings. For example, water is the substance that has the same deep explanatory feature as the stuff we call 'water', and that deep explanatory feature is: being H_2O. As a result, to say that such facts are necessary—that water is necessarily H_2O, or that the laws of nature are necessarily thus-and-such—turns out not to describe an interesting constraint on ways it is possible for the world to have been, but rather to describe an uninteresting constraint on ways it is possible for us to *describe* the world as having been.

Sidelle considers in detail two main arguments in favour of the necessity of laws of nature. According to the first, it is only by taking laws of nature to be metaphysically necessary that we can explain their modal force and their capacity to support counterfactuals; according to the second, it is only by taking laws of nature to be metaphysically necessary that we can understand them as governing the properties that they do. Neither succeeds in motivating metaphysically robust claims of necessity for laws of nature, he argues. Generalizing these results, Sidelle concludes that we have categorical grounds for rejecting challenges to the overall reliability of conceiving and imagining as guides to possibility.

5.9 *Roy Sorensen*

In 'The Art of the Impossible', Roy Sorensen explores the question of what would be required for the visual depiction of a logical impossibility. (If such impossibilities are visually representable, then presumably they are imaginable; if they are not visually representable, then their imaginability may be more difficult to maintain.)

Biological, physical, and conceptual impossibilities, Sorensen contends, can be straightforwardly depicted visually: mermaids, floating rocks, and Escher staircases provide examples of each in turn. In exploring the question of whether one might similarly depict a logical impossibility, Sorensen articulates a set of standards for what such a depiction would require. In particular, the depiction must be (a) open to inspection, in the sense that it places no limit on potential detail concerning the item represented; (b) equivocation-free, in the sense that contradiction depicted does not exploit an ambiguity in language or representational convention; (c) perceptual, in the sense that the impossibility is not a consequence of how the depiction is labelled or described; (d) not merely adverbially inconsistent, in the sense that the impossibility is not the result of treating inaccuracies as inconsistencies; (e) not merely inconsistent at the level of infrastructure, in the sense that the impossibility is not merely the result of the interplay between two distinct perceptual capacities; and (f) not merely ambiguous, in the sense that the impossibility is not a consequence of treating the depiction as simultaneously characterized by two of its ambiguous readings.

Though Sorensen does not present an example of a visual depiction of a logical impossibility—indeed, he offers a reward of $100 to the first reader who provides him with one—he is optimistic about the prospects of there being such. After all, he insists, logical impossibilities can be depicted narratively. So, unless there is an in principle consistency constraint governing perceptual representation that does not govern its linguistic and conceptual cousins, then, presumably, logical inconsistencies can be depicted visually as well.

5.10 *Ernest Sosa*

In 'Reliability and the A Priori', Ernest Sosa considers various responses to what he terms *the Platonist's dilemma*—the problem of explaining our reliable knowledge of mathematical truths, assuming that these truths concern a realm of abstracta that lies beyond space-time. The dilemma is this: according to the Platonist, (i) mathematical objects are acausal and mind-independent. But, it seems that (ii) causal explanations of our mathematical reliability are incompatible with the acausality of mathematical objects, and that (iii) non-causal explanations of our mathematical reliability are incompatible with their mind-independence. So, given Platonist commitments, it seems that (iv) there is no explanation of our mathematical reliability.

Sosa considers two families of response to this dilemma. The first sort of response involves rejecting (iii) (and in its extreme form, the second clause of (i)) on the grounds that mathematical truths are *judgement-dependent*, in the sense that the truths about mathematical objects are determined by our best judgements about them. Sosa presents various refinements of this view, but ultimately rejects them because he thinks they cannot account for the purported necessity of mathematical truths. The second sort of response rejects (iii) by exploiting an analogy between thoughts about mathematics and *cogito*-like thoughts. Sosa suggests that where the content-determining conditions of a thought imply that to have such a thought is to have a thought that is true, we may have a non-causal explanation of the reliability of that thought without abandoning our commitment to the mind-independence of its content. Mathematical facts may be of this sort: in the case of mathematical truths, understanding and knowledge go hand in hand. While conceding that such responses leave certain sorts of questions unanswered, Sosa is sanguine about the general strategy. We can, it seems, offer a fairly satisfactory explanation of our knowledge of certain necessary truths.

5.11 *Robert Stalnaker*

In 'What is it Like to be a Zombie?', Robert Stalnaker seeks to throw light on general questions about the nature of modal claims and the relations among metaphysical, semantic, and empirical questions by examining the debate between those who think zombies are (metaphysically) possible and those who think they are not. (Zombies are creatures that physically duplicate ordinary people, but lack phenomenal consciousness.) Stalnaker frames the debate as a conversation among three imaginary philosophers with real-world counterparts (Dave, Patricia, and Sydney) and a fourth (Anne) who steps in at the end for clarification. Dave (whose real-world counterpart is David Chalmers) holds that zombies are possible but non-actual; Patricia (whose real-world counterpart is Patricia Churchland) holds that zombies are possible and, indeed, actual; and Sydney (whose real-world counterpart is Sydney Shoemaker) holds that zombies are neither actual nor possible. Anne (who lacks a particular real-world counterpart) holds that *if* materialism is false (as Dave holds), then zombies are possible though non-actual, but if materialism is true (as Sydney holds), then they are neither actual nor possible.

Patricia, Sydney, and Anne agree on the empirical question of whether materialism is true; Dave demurs. Sydney, Anne, and Dave agree on the empirical question of whether there is (actually) phenomenal consciousness; Patricia demurs. Sydney holds that phenomenal consciousness is a functional property that would be (and is) present in what Stalnaker calls a *z-world*: a world exactly like the actual world in all physical respects, containing nothing that does not supervene on the physical. Moreover, he believes it is built into the meanings of experiential vocabulary that its terms denote functional properties. Dave, by contrast, holds that phenomenal consciousness is an irreducible non-physical property that would be absent in a z-world; the world *we* live in, he maintains, is what Stalnaker calls an *a-world*: a world physically just like a z-world that has, in addition, certain properties not instantiated in the z-world—in particular, properties of conscious beings that are the properties we refer to when we talk about phenomenal consciousness. So, while Dave and Sydney agree that z-worlds are both conceivable and metaphysically possible, Dave holds that z-worlds are zombie worlds, whereas Sydney holds that they are not.

Anne regards experiential concepts as less theoretically loaded than either Dave or Sydney. According to Anne, if the actual world is a z-world, then phenomenal consciousness is a functional property of the kind Sydney takes it to be; if the actual world is an a-world, then phenomenal consciousness is an irreducible non-physical property of the kind Dave takes it to be. But this means that such concepts cannot carry with them either an a priori requirement that they refer to irreducible non-physical properties (as Dave requires) or an a priori requirement that they refer to functional properties (as Sydney requires). For Anne, the prima-facie conceivability of zombies establishes their metaphysical possibility only if we know on independent grounds that our world is not, in fact, a z-world.

5.12 *Crispin Wright*

In 'The Conceivability of Naturalism', Crispin Wright explores Kripke's well-known argument concerning materialism, generalizes it, and then raises questions concerning its adequacy. He begins by pointing out that Kripke's argument depends on what Wright calls the *Counter-Conceivability Principle*, that if we can clearly and distinctly conceive of a scenario in which not-P, then it is not necessary that P. An apparently lucid conception of a scenario in which a and b are distinct is thus sufficient to establish the non-identity of a and b—except where the conception can be discounted as misleading. Wright notes that Kripke's method for identifying such deficiencies relies on a particular insight: an apparently lucid conception of a situation where some kind (or individual) is F may latch on to nothing more than a possible situation where a symptomatic counterpart of that kind (or individual) is F. Central to Wright's presentation of Kripke's argument, then, is the observation that there is no distinction between a symptomatic counterpart of pain and pain itself. Thus the general strategy for blocking deployment of the Counter-Conceivability Principle cannot be invoked in this case.

Wright defends Kripke's argument against objections by Boyd (to the effect that Kripke's argument neglects the relevance of the distinction between C-fibre stimulation and a symptomatic counterpart of it) and McGinn (to the effect that a token-identity version of physicalism remains intact). He then generalizes the argument, suggesting that analogous anti-materialist arguments can be run for any concept that is what he calls *Euthyphronic*—such that it is a priori that (when certain specified conditions hold) if it seems to a thinker that the concept is instantiated, then it is.

None the less, Wright maintains, the generalized Kripke argument is unsuccessful. For, while Kripke offers one recipe for blocking conceivability–possibility arguments, he is insensitive to other ways to defuse such reasoning. In particular, Wright contends, there are cases where an apparently lucid conception that purports to be of a *possible* scenario in which not-P is in fact a conception of what it would be like if—*per impossibile*—P were (found to be) false. In such cases, he argues, the Counter-Conceivability Principle cannot be employed to establish claims of non-identity.

5.13   *Stephen Yablo*

In 'Coulda, Woulda, Shoulda', Stephen Yablo offers a critique of modal rationalism through careful examination of a notion he calls *conceptual possibility*, which can be characterized in contrast to its more familiar metaphysical counterpart: it is metaphysically, but not conceptually, possible that the metre stick exist without being a metre long, conceptually, but not metaphysically, possible that Hesperus exist without Phosphorus. In general, suggests Yablo, we can express the difference between the two notions as follows: S is metaphysically possible iff it could have been that S (iff some world w is such that it would have been that S, had w obtained), and conceptually possible iff it could have turned out that S (iff some world w is such that it would have turned out that S, had w turned out to be actual). To consider a world as metaphysically possible is to consider it as *counterfactual*; to consider a world as conceptually possible, he suggests, is to consider it as *counteractual*.

Using this terminology, modal rationalism can be characterized as the thesis that (although metaphysical necessity and apriority may come apart in certain cases) conceptual necessity and apriority coincide: P is knowable a priori iff P holds in all counteractual worlds. But, contends Yablo, the thesis fails in both directions: there are a priori knowable statements that are false at some counteractual worlds, and statements true at all counteractual worlds that are knowable only a posteriori. This can be seen, for example, by considering how we come to know the truth or falsity of conditionals of the form: 'If w had turned out to be actual, it would have turned out that Q', where w is some detailed world description, and Q is some candidate conceptual possibility. For modal rationalism to be correct, we would need in all such cases to be able to deduce (or recognize that one cannot deduce) Q from w by a priori methods. But, argues Yablo, in a wide range of cases, we cannot. In particular, we cannot do so for Qs that involve predicates that are *recognitional* (like 'painful'), otherwise *observational* (like 'jagged'), *evaluative* (like 'wrong'), or *theoretical* (like 'energy'). In these cases, he argues, we can determine whether Q given w only by means of engaging in a sort of 'off-line' simulation that allows us to exercise our (perceptual or non-perceptual) sensibilities—and judgements formed on such a basis do not provide us with knowledge that is a priori.

For a statement S to be known a priori by me, Yablo suggests, is for me to possess some information G such that (a) I grasp the meaning of 'S' in part by knowing that 'S' is G, and (b) that 'S' is G conceptually necessitates that 'S' is true. Since there may be statements that are conceptually necessary for which there is no such G possessable by me, there will be conceptually necessary truths that I cannot know a priori. And since the information G that conceptually necessitates that 'S' is true may itself not be conceptually necessary, there will be a priori truths that are conceptually contingent.

REFERENCES

Alanen, Lilli, and Knuuttila, Simo (1988), 'The Foundations of Modality and Conceivability in Descartes and his Predecessors', in Simo Knuuttila (ed.), *Modern Modalities* (Dordrecht: Kluwer), 1–69.

Balog, Katalin (1999), 'Conceivability, Possibility and the Mind–Body Problem', *Philosophical Review*, 108(4): 497–528.

Bealer, George (1987), 'Philosophical Limits of Scientific Essentialism', *Philosophical Perspectives*, 1: 289–365.

—— (1992), 'The Incoherence of Empiricism', *Aristotelian Society*, Supp. Vol. 66: 99–138.

—— (1994), 'Mental Properties', *Journal of Philosophy*, 91: 185–208.

—— (1996), '*A Priori* Knowledge and the Scope of Philosophy', *Philosophical Studies*, 81(2–3): 121–42.

Block, Ned, (1981) (ed.), *Imagery* (Cambridge, Mass.: MIT Press).

Block, Ned and Stalnaker, Robert (1999), 'Conceptual Analysis, Dualism, and the Explanatory Gap', *Philosophical Review*, 108(1): 1–46.

Brann, Eva (1991), *The World of the Imagination: Sum and Substance* (Lanham, Md.: Rowman and Littlefield).

Casey, Edward S. (1976/2000), *Imagining: A Phenomenological Study*, 2nd edn. (Bloomington, Ind.: Indiana University Press).

Chalmers, David (1996), *The Conscious Mind* (New York: Oxford University Press).

—— (1999), 'Materialism and the Metaphysics of Modality', *Philosophy and Phenomenological Research*, 59(2): 473–96.

—— and Jackson, Frank (2001), 'Conceptual Analysis and Reductive Explanation', *Philosophical Review*, 110: 315–61.

Currie, Gregory, and Ravenscroft, Ian (2002), *Recreative Minds: Image and Imagination in Philosophy and Psychology* (Oxford: Oxford University Press).

Davies, Martin, and Humberstone, Lloyd (1980), 'Two Notions of Necessity', *Philosophical Studies*, 38: 1–30.

—— and Stone, Tony (1995a) (eds.), *Folk Psychology: The Theory of Mind Debate* (Oxford: Blackwell).

—— —— (1995b) (eds.), *Mental Simulation: Evaluations and Applications* (Oxford: Blackwell).

DePaul, Michael, and Ramsey, William (1998) (eds.), *Rethinking Intuition* (Lanham, Md.: Rowman and Littlefield).

Descartes, René ([1619–64] 1990), *The Philosophical Writings of Descartes*, vol. I, trans. John Cottingham, Robert Stoothoff, and Dugald Murdoch (Cambridge: Cambridge University Press).

—— ([1641–2, 1701] 1989), *The Philosophical Writings of Descartes*, vol. II, trans. John Cottingham, Robert Stoothoff, and Dugald Murdoch (Cambridge: Cambridge University Press).

—— ([1619–50] 1991), *The Philosophical Writings of Descartes*, vol. III, trans. John Cottingham, Robert Stoothoff, Dugald Murdoch, and Anthony Kenny (Cambridge: Cambridge University Press).

Gendler, Tamar Szabó (2000), *Thought Experiment: On the Powers and Limits of Imaginary Cases* (New York: Garland Routledge).

Harris, Paul (2000), *The Work of the Imagination* (Oxford: Blackwell).

Hart, W. D. (1988), *Engines of the Soul* (Cambridge: Cambridge University Press).

Hill, Christopher (1997), 'Imaginability, Conceivability, Possibility and the Mind–Body Problem', *Philosophical Studies*, 87(1): 61–85.

Horowitz, Tamara, and Massey, Gerald (1991) (eds.), *Thought Experiments in Science and Philosophy* (Savage, Md.: Rowman and Littlefield).

Hume, David ([1739–40] 2000), *A Treatise of Human Nature*, ed. David Fate Norton and Mary Norton (Oxford: Oxford University Press).

Jackson, Frank (1993), 'Armchair Metaphysics', in Michaelis Michael and John O'Leary-Hawthorne (eds.), *Philosophy in Mind* (Dordrecht: Kluwer), 23–42.

—— (1998), *From Metaphysics to Ethics: A Defense of Conceptual Analysis* (New York: Oxford University Press).

Kaplan, David (1989), 'Demonstratives', in Joseph Almog, John Perry, and Howard Wettstein (eds.), *Themes from Kaplan* (New York: Oxford University Press), 481–564.

Kripke, Saul (1980), *Naming and Necessity* (Cambridge, Mass.: Harvard University Press).

Levine, Joseph (1998), 'Conceivability and the Metaphysics of Mind', *Nous*, 32(4): 449–80.

—— (2001), *Purple Haze: The Puzzle of Consciousness* (New York: Oxford University Press.)

Lewis, Charles, and Mitchell, Peter (1994) (eds.), *Children's Early Understanding of Mind* (Hillsdale, NJ: Laurence Erlbaum).

Lewis, David (1986), *On the Plurality of Worlds* (Oxford: Blackwell).

Loar, Brian (1999), 'David Chalmers's "The Conscious Mind"', *Philosophy and Phenomenological Research*, 59(2): 465–72.

McLaughlin, Brian, and Hill, Christopher (1999), 'There Are Fewer Things in Reality Than Are Dreamt of in Chalmers's Philosophy', *Philosophy and Phenomenological Research*, 59(2): 445–54.

O'Shaughnessy, Brian (2000), *Consciousness and the World* (Oxford: Clarendon Press).

Overton, W. F. (1990) (ed.), *Reasoning, Necessity and Logic: Developmental Perspectives* (Hillsdale, NJ: Laurence Erlbaum).

Piaget, Jean (1987a), *Possibility and Necessity: The Role of Necessity in Cognitive Development*, trans. Helga Feider (Minneapolis: University of Minnesota Press).

—— (1987b), *Possibility and Necessity: The Role of Possibility in Cognitive Development*, trans. Helga Feider (Minneapolis: University of Minnesota Press).

—— and Inhelder, Bärbel (1971), *Mental Imagery in the Child: A Study of the Development of Imaginal Representation*, trans. P. A. Chilton (New York: Basic Books).

Putnam, Hilary (1975a), *Mathematics, Matter and Method, Philosophical Papers*, i (Cambridge: Cambridge University Press).

—— (1975b), *Mind, Language and Reality, Philosophical Papers*, ii (Cambridge: Cambridge University Press).

Quine, Willard van Orman (1969), *Ontological Relativity and Other Essays* (London: Columbia University Press).

Sartre, Jean-Paul (1939/1962), *Imagination: A Psychological Critique*, trans. Forrest Williams (Ann Arbor: University of Michigan Press).

—— (1940/1963), *The Psychology of Imagination*, trans. Forrest Williams (New York: Citadel Press).

Shepard, Roger, and Cooper, Lynn (1982), *Mental Images and their Transformations* (Cambridge, Mass.: MIT Press).

Shoemaker, Sydney (1998), 'Causal and Metaphysical Necessity', *Pacific Philosophical Quarterly*, 79: 59–77.

Stalnaker, Robert (1978), 'Assertion', in Peter Cole (ed.), *Syntax and Semantics*, ix: *Pragmatics* (New York: Academic Press), 315–32.

—— (2001), 'On Considering a Possible World as Actual', *Proceedings of the Aristotelian Society*, supp. vol. 65: 141–56.

Strawson, P. F. (1970), 'Imagination and Perception', in L. Foster and J. W. Swanson (eds.), *Experience and Theory* (Amherst, Mass.: University of Massachusetts Press), 31–54.

Tidman, Paul (1994), 'Conceivability as a Test for Possibility', *American Philosophical Quarterly*, 31(4): 297–309.

van Cleve, James (1983), 'Conceivability and the Cartesian Argument for Dualism', *Pacific Philosophical Quarterly*, 64: 35–45.

Walton, Kendall (1990), *Mimesis as Make-Believe: On the Foundations of the Representational Arts* (Cambridge, Mass.: Harvard University Press).

Warnock, Mary (1976), *Imagination* (Berkeley and Los Angeles: University of California Press).

Wittgenstein, Ludwig ([1958] 1965), *The Blue and Brown Books* (New York: Harper Torchbacks).

Yablo, Stephen (1990), 'The Real Distinction Between Mind and Body', *Canadian Journal of Philosophy*, supp. vol. 16: 149–201.

—— (1993), 'Is Conceivability a Guide to Possibility?', *Philosophy and Phenomenological Research*, 53(1): 1–42.

—— (2000), 'Textbook Kripkeanism and the Open Texture of Concepts', *Pacific Philosophical Quarterly*, 81(1): 98–122.

I

Modal Epistemology and the Rationalist Renaissance

GEORGE BEALER

The term 'modal epistemology' may be understood in three ways. First, as the theory of *modal* knowledge—knowledge of what is necessary and possible. Second, as the theory of *possible* knowledge—what sorts of knowledge are *possible*. Third, as the intersection of the first two: the theory of *possible modal knowledge*—that is, of what modal knowledge is possible.

The primary question of modal epistemology in this third sense is this. What is the relationship between the a priori and the modal? Most traditional rationalists held that, for all p, p is necessary iff p is knowable a priori. But Saul Kripke (1980) taught us that this traditional equivalence fails in both directions. His meter-stick case is a counter-example to the right-to-left direction. And he argued, along with Putnam (1975), that natural kind identities (e.g., water = H_2O) are counter-examples to the left-to-right direction. In addition, every 'actualization' of any true contingent proposition (e.g., the proposition that *in the actual world* Aristotle taught Alexander) is another sort of counter-example to the left-to-right direction. In fact, because of actualizations, the

I wish to thank Iain Martel for insightful discussions and advice during the preparation of the chapter, Mark Moffett, Michael Peirce, and Stephen Biggs for discerning critical suggestions on the completed manuscript, and Tamar Gendler and John Hawthorne for judicious editorial guidance and general philosophical acumen.

left-to-right direction wrongly implies that every true proposition is knowable a priori. Finally, independently of such broadly Kripkean considerations, the left-to-right direction also fails if there are necessary propositions that in principle cannot be thought. There are such unthinkable propositions if, for example, there could be individual entities that cannot coexist in any one possible world (or properties F and G that cannot both have instances in any common world), and whose unique descriptions are beyond any one person's descriptive powers. At least relative to minds like ours, it seems that there could be such things.

These considerations lead naturally to the further question: for which *types* of proposition p does the traditional equivalence hold? (Or, for which types do the separate halves of the equivalence hold?) The safest interesting generalization is this: the equivalence holds for all (or at least most) *semantically stable* propositions p—roughly, propositions that are invariant across communities whose epistemic situations are qualitatively identical.[1] What this means is that p is the sort of proposition immune to scientific essentialism and externalism generally, as well as to the other counter-examples to traditional rationalism. Semantically stable propositions include virtually all central propositions of the traditional a priori disciplines—logic, mathematics, and philosophy. Accordingly, these disciplines can, at least in principle, be independent of the empirical sciences, as traditional rationalists believed. Since this autonomy thesis is at the same time consistent with the truth of scientific essentialism and other phenomena that brought down traditional rationalism, this view may rightly be called *moderate rationalism*.

I have defended a qualified form of moderate rationalism in a series of papers (1987, 1992, 1994, 1996, 1999). A large number of other contemporary philosophers have also become convinced of one form of moderate rationalism or another. While agreeing with their general conclusion, I believe that in many cases their path to it is flawed—often in the conceptual and logical preliminaries. Additional problems arise from terminology itself: sometimes traditional debates are distorted, even trivialized, by nonstandard uses of well-established (and acceptably clear) ordinary-language expressions and traditional philosophical vocabulary. As Frank Jackson puts it (1998: 31), such terminological distortions can turn 'interesting philosophical debates into easy exercises in deductions from stipulative definitions'.

---

[1] More precisely, (for thinkable p) p is semantically stable iff, necessarily, if p plays some cognitive role in the mental life of a community c, then it is necessary that for any other community c in qualitatively the same epistemic situation as c, no proposition can play that role other than p itself. See Bealer (1987, 1994). I should note that Eli Hirsch (1986) advocates a similar, independently arrived at, position in his elegant paper.

My aim here is to correct a number of these problems, laying the groundwork for a more acceptable modal epistemology and its correct application. In section 1, I clarify a number of (often nontrivial) conceptual and terminological preliminaries concerning intuition (and, in particular, modal intuition), modal error, conceivability, metaphysical possibility, and epistemic possibility. Section 2 is concerned with the appropriate logical (and semantical) framework for modal epistemology, the main conclusion being that two-dimensionalism is unfit for this role and that a certain nonreductionist approach to the theory of concepts and propositions is required instead. In section 3 I turn to the positive story—a moderate rationalist modal epistemology which includes an account of what it is to understand one's concepts and, as a corollary, an account of an important family of modal errors (namely, those that arise from misunderstanding one's categorial concepts). In section 4, I examine moderate rationalism's impact on modal arguments in the philosophy of mind—for example, Yablo's disembodiment argument and Chalmers's two-dimensional modal arguments. I close by defending a less vulnerable style of modal argument, which nevertheless wins the same anti-materialist conclusions sought by these other arguments.

1 Intuition, Conceivability, Possibility

1.1 *Intuition and the A Priori*

Intuition is the source of all a priori knowledge—except, of course, for that which is merely stipulative. The use of intuitions as evidence (reasons) is ubiquitous in our standard justificatory practices in the a priori disciplines—Gettier intuitions, twin-earth intuitions, transitivity intuitions, etc. By intuitions here, we mean *seemings*: for you to have an intuition that A is just for it to *seem* to you that A. Of course, this kind of seeming is *intellectual*, not experiential—sensory, introspective, imaginative. Typically, the contents of intellectual and experiential seeming cannot overlap. You can intuit that there could be infinitely many marbles, but such a thing cannot seem experientially (say, imaginatively) to be so. Intuition and imagination are in this way distinct. Descartes was right, I believe, to distinguish sharply between imagination and understanding, especially intuitive understanding.[2]

Intuition is different from belief: you can believe things that you do not intuit (e.g., that Rome is the capital of Italy), and you can intuit things that you do not believe (e.g., the axioms of naïve set theory). The experiential parallel is that

---

[2] [See Introduction, sect. 2.2—eds.]

you can believe things that do not appear (seem sensorily) to be so, and vice versa. Intuition is in similar ways different from other propositional attitudes (judging, guessing, etc.) and from common sense. After surveying the alternatives, I can see no choice but that intuition is a *sui generis* propositional attitude.

The set-theoretic paradoxes establish an important moral: namely, that intuition can be fallible, and that a priori belief is not unrevisable. Infallibilism and unrevisability have often been red herrings in modal epistemology. An alternative tradition—from Plato to Gödel—recognizes that a priori justification is fallible and holistic, relying respectively on dialectic and theory construction.

The sort of intuitions relevant to the a priori disciplines are *rational* intuitions, not *physical* intuitions; only the former present themselves as necessary. According to traditional usage, 'thought experiments' appeal, not to rational intuition, but to physical intuitions (and the like). Here one constructs a hypothetical case about which one tries to elicit, say, a physical intuition deriving from one's implicit mastery of relevant physical laws (as, for example, in Newton's bucket thought experiment). The contrast with Gettier cases, de Morgan's laws, and so forth is plain.

A tendency of late has been to stretch the traditional term 'a priori knowledge' by artificially restricting what is meant by 'experience'—for example, by omitting wholesale Locke's second category of experience, knowledge by reflection (or introspection). Accordingly, one's knowledge of one's self-intimating conscious states is wrongly classified as a priori. An easy way to avoid such confusions is to give a *positive* characterization of a priori knowledge—as opposed to the customary negative characterization as knowledge not based on experience. Perhaps one could do so along the following lines: x knows p a priori iff x knows p and this is direct intuitive knowledge or stipulative knowledge or is based wholly upon such knowledge and/or intuitional evidence.[3]

It is our standard epistemic practice to use intuitions as evidence (or reasons): by virtue of having an intuition that p, one has a prima-facie reason or prima-facie evidence for p. Much as we take our ostensible sense perceptions to be prima-facie evidence if we lack special reason not to do so, it would be unreasonable not to do the same for intuitions. I have argued (1992), however, that we have no special reason not to take intuitions this way and, moreover, that if we deny that intuitions are prima-facie evidence, we are put in an epistemically self-defeating situation. For these reasons, I conclude, we are justified in continuing with our standard practice. In what follows I will assume that this is correct.

---

[3] Is a priori knowledge exhausted by conceptual analysis? No, not unless the latter includes various necessities that traditionally were thought to be synthetic, not analytic.

There is no relevant phenomenological difference between modal and nonmodal intuitions. For example, there is no relevant phenomenological difference between your intuition that any arbitrary object that has a shape has a size and your intuition that it is possible for something to have a shape and a size, or your intuition that it is not possible for there to be something having a shape but no size. Nor are there good grounds for thinking that modal intuition is not prima-facie evidence whereas nonmodal intuition is. In particular, modal intuition's tie to the truth has a satisfactory explanation and is no more prone to uncorrectable error (see section 3). For these reasons, it would be unreasonable to deny the evidential force of modal intuition and, in turn, unreasonable to deny that just as your nonmodal intuitions are a (fallible) guide to nonmodal truth, so your modal intuitions are a (fallible) guide to modal truth. As a special case, therefore, it would be unreasonable to deny that your possibility intuitions are a guide to possibility. In what follows I will assume that this too is correct.

1.2 *Conceivability and Imaginability*

There is a venerable tradition of taking conceivability and inconceivability to be the evidential basis for, and guide to, a priori knowledge of possibility and impossibility. I think this is a mistake. Intuition is, as we have seen, comparatively easy to characterize—at least provisionally. Not so conceivability and inconceivability (at least if the scholarly literature is any indication). Or maybe I am wrong about this; maybe these, too, are easy to characterize. Perhaps when I say 'It is conceivable that p', all I am saying (at least conversationally) is that I have an intuition that p is possible; and when I say 'It is inconceivable that p', all I am saying is that I have an intuition that it is impossible that p. If so, a great amount of unnecessary confusion would be avoided if we were simply to stop using 'conceivable' and 'inconceivable' and to confine ourselves to talking directly about possibility and impossibility intuitions. The same goes for 'imaginable' and 'unimaginable'.

Suppose, however, that this easy idiomatic gloss on 'conceivable' and 'inconceivable' is not correct, and that these terms are instead taken at face value as literal expressions of certain modal facts: it is conceivable that p iff it is possible for someone to conceive that p; it is inconceivable that p iff it is not possible for someone to conceive that p. Then we have a pair of problems. First, unlike intuitions of possibility and impossibility, conceivability and inconceivability would not be suited to play their reputed evidential role in modal epistemology. That it is possible, or impossible, to conceive that p is itself a mere modal fact. But in order for someone to acquire evidence (reasons), something must *actually happen*: a datable psychological episode must occur (the occurrence of a sensation, an introspective or imaginative experience, a seeming memory, an intuition). Modal facts do not occur. Nothing *happens* when something is conceivable or inconceivable. So something's merely being conceivable or inconceivable cannot provide anyone with evidence (reasons) for anything.

Not only that, our beliefs about what is conceivable and inconceivable can be highly inferential and are often theoretical. True, one way you can come to believe that it is possible for someone to conceive that p is for *you actually* to conceive that p. But why should your conceiving that p provide you with evidence that p is possible? I can see no reason why it should, unless conceiving that p involves intuiting that p is possible.[4] But this takes us back to relying evidentially on modal intuition.[5] In any case, many of our beliefs about conceivability arise, not by way of actual conceivings, but indirectly via our (implicit) modal epistemology—our general beliefs about what classes of propositions can and cannot be conceived. And in the case of inconceivability, something like this *must* be the case. The mere fact that I tried, but happened to fail, to conceive that p is not a good guide to what is in principle possible in this regard for any being whatsoever; maybe I am just not sharp enough. Of course, there is another way we could come to have beliefs about what is and what is not possible to conceive: we can just have modal intuitions to that effect. But then, once again, we are back to relying on modal intuitions as our source of evidence, except that these intuitions are one step removed, for they do not directly concern the possibility or impossibility of p, but only an associated psychological possibility or impossibility of conceiving that p. The moral is simple: in the matter of evidence for possibility and impossibility, talk of conceivability and inconceivability is an idle complication that only breeds confusion. Again, these points hold for 'imaginable' and 'unimaginable'.

As observed at the outset, most traditional rationalists held that, for all p, p is necessary iff p is knowable a priori. Many traditionalists also accepted an associated equivalence between conceivability and possibility: it is possible that

---

[4] Suppose instead that x conceives that p iff x conceives *of* a possible situation in which p. But what is it to conceive of a situation in which p? In one sense of 'conceive', conceiving of a situation is merely thinking of it. But this sort of conceiving would provide no evidence that p is possible: after all, one can think of impossible situations (e.g., that the square root of 2 is rational); moreover, if one succeeds in thinking of a situation that happens to be possible, that could be a matter of pure chance (e.g., a result of reading the works of the monkeys at the typewriters). Conceiving of a possible situation can be evidential only if, in the very conceiving of the situation, the situation *seems* possible—that is, only if the conceiving involves the intuition that it is possible. As Stephen Yablo tells us: 'In slogan form: *conceiving involves the appearance of possibility*' (1993: 5). But then we are right back to relying on modal intuitions.

[5] As we saw above, intuiting that p is possible *does* provide evidence that p is possible, for this is just a special case of the fact that intuiting that q provides evidence that q.

p iff it is conceivable that p. On the literal, face-value interpretation, this equivalence is: p is possible iff it is possible for someone to conceive that p. On the supposition that x conceives that p iff x intuits that p is possible, the traditional equivalence is then: p is possible iff it is possible for someone to intuit that p is possible. This equivalence fails in both directions. (1) We know that the right-to-left direction fails, because intuitions are fallible (e.g., in view of the paradoxes). (2) The left-to-right direction fails in the event that there are unthinkable propositions p of the sort discussed at the outset.[6]

Returning to the general matter of terminology, my overall judgment is that it is safest simply to avoid the minefield of 'conceivability' and 'inconceivability' and to stick to the unproblematic idiom of intuitions of possibility and impossibility.[7]

1.3 *Metaphysical Possibility and Epistemic Possibility*

The modal expressions 'could', 'can', 'might', 'possible' are used in diverse ways that fall into two broad classes: (i) epistemic and (ii) nonepistemic. (An analogous division holds for 'must' and 'necessary'.) The first thing to note about these two classes of uses is that they do not mark out two associated *genuses*—epistemic possibility and nonepistemic possibility—of some common still more general modal category *Possibility*. The analogous point holds for the specific properties expressed by the various epistemic and nonepistemic uses of 'could': for any pair of properties, one of which is associated with the former class and the second with the latter, these properties are not *kinds* or *species* of some common, still more general modal category *Possibility*. Take, for example, the properties expressed, respectively, by the 'could'-of-less-than-complete-certainty and the 'could'-of-metaphysical-possibility. There simply is no common general modal category *Possibility* of which these two properties are kinds or species. (This of course is not to say that such properties are entirely unrelated, but if they are related, this would result from a much deeper connection—perhaps revealed in the genesis of our concepts.)

---

[6] It has been suggested (e.g., Chalmers 1996: 68) that we understand 'conceivable' to be equivalent to 'conceivable by a being with maximal cognitive powers', but this is not the standard use of the term in the history of philosophy. It is likewise nonstandard to use 'p is conceivable' to mean 'the possibility of p would be affirmed at the close of a priori deliberation by a being with maximal cognitive powers' (or something of the sort). But, for what it is worth, on these nonstandard readings, the resulting equivalences are threatened by much the same problems as those that undermined traditional rationalism.

[7] In support of the centrality of modal intuition, Stephen Yablo tells us that 'modal intuition *must* be accounted reliable if we are to credit ourselves with modal knowledge' (1990: 179).

In logic and metaphysics the primary focus is, in Kripke's words, necessity *tout court*. The dual of this use of 'necessary' is the weakest of the nonepistemic uses of 'possible'—weakest in the sense that its extension always includes the extensions of all other nonepistemic uses of 'possible'.

Because 'possible' and 'necessary' have diverse uses in ordinary language (both epistemic and nonepistemic), confusion easily creeps in. In logic and metaphysics there is an easy antidote. Most of us are inclined to hear the terms 'contingent' and 'noncontingent' univocally. So we can almost always head off misunderstanding in logic and metaphysics simply by 'translating' modal remarks into this univocal idiom. p is necessary iff p is true but not contingent. p is impossible iff p is false but not contingent. p is possible iff p is necessary or contingent. (That is, p is possible iff either p is true but noncontingent or p is contingent.) For example, when I say, 'Despite the recent proof, there is still a possibility that Fermat's Last Theorem is false', I am certainly not asserting that Fermat's Last Theorem is either necessarily false or contingently false! Likewise, when I say, 'It could have turned out that Hesperus was not Phosphorus', I am assuredly not asserting that it is either necessarily false or contingently false that Hesperus is Phosphorus. Using this 'translation' test will dispel virtually all such confusions.

Various species of possibility (in the identified sense) may be isolated as follows: p is nomologically possible iff p and the laws of nature are compossible (i.e., it is possible for p and the laws of nature to be true together); p is physically possible iff p and the laws of physics are compossible.[8] What about logical possibility? Well, mimicking this pattern of definition, we would have: p is logically possible iff p and the laws of logic are compossible. But *every* possibility p is compossible with the laws of logic, so logic rules out nothing that is not *already* ruled out. Therefore, according to this definition, logical possibility and possibility coincide. That is, logical possibility is not a *species* of possibility; rather, it is just possibility itself. And this is precisely how 'logical possibility' has historically been used by a great many philosophers—for example, by Kripke himself at the advent of *Naming and Necessity*. What about 'metaphysical possibility'? This is a technical term which Kripke stipulatively introduced, solely for heuristic purposes, as a synonym of his term 'logically possible'—that is, of 'possible'. Thus, according to this standard philosophical usage, p is possible iff p is logically possible iff p is metaphysically possible iff p is necessary or contingent iff either p is true but noncontingent or p is contingent.

Despite this fully documented history, some people insist on distinguishing logical possibility and metaphysical possibility and so are led to the following: p is logically possible iff p is merely *consistent* with the laws of logic (i.e., not

---

[8]   For challenges to this suggestion, cf. Fine, Ch. 6 below.

ruled out by logic alone). This usage, however, invites confusion.[9] There are many logically consistent sentences that express obvious impossibilities (e.g., 'Bachelors are necessarily women', 'Triangles are necessarily circles', 'Water contains no hydrogen'). If you buy into calling mere logical consistency a kind of possibility, why not keep going? For example: p is 'sententially possible' iff p is consistent with the laws of sentential logic. Then, since 'Everything is both F and not F' is not ruled out by sentential logic (quantifier logic is what rules it out), would it be possible in some sense (i.e., sententially possible) that everything is both F and not F?![10] Certainly not to my ear! At this juncture it seems to me that the best policy is simply to eschew the problematical term 'logically possible' and to confine ourselves to the well-demarcated terms 'logically consistent' and 'metaphysically possible'.

Let us return to standard epistemic uses of 'could'.[11] To illustrate some of them, consider any thinkable necessary truth p. The first use is the 'could'-of-ignorance: absent what we deem to be adequate evidence (or adequate justification) one way or the other about p, we can truly say, 'It could be that p, and it could be that not p. We just do not know yet.' (For example, this can be truly said of Goldbach's conjecture.) But once we have adequate evidence (justification) one way or the other, what was meant in speaking *that way* can no longer be truly said. Second, there is the 'could'-of-less-than-complete-certainty: if we have less than complete certainty about p (even if we have adequate evidence, or justification, for p), we can still truly say, 'We still could be mistaken; we know we can be wrong about almost anything.' (For example, even though we now have a proof of Fermat's Last Theorem, this can still be truly said of it.) Third, there is the 'could'-of-qualitative-evidential-neutrality: for a posteriori necessities, we can often truly say, 'It could have turned out that p, and it could have turned out that not p.' And this is so, even though, meant this way, it cannot be said of any traditional a priori necessities. For example, meant this way, 'Whether Hesperus was Phosphorus could have turned out

---

[9] This is certainly not to say that the (very well-studied) notion of logical consistency is unimportant.

[10] Some people also hypothesize a use of 'possible' for what they call 'conceptual possibility': p is possible (in the hypothesized sense) iff it is impossible for anyone to know a priori that p is false. Two points: first, even if there were such a use of 'possible' in ordinary English, it would (just as in earlier cases) not expresses a *kind* of possibility; second, there is in fact no such use of 'possible' in ordinary English. Here is one among many counts on which this is so: if p is an unthinkable proposition, then the proposition that p is false is likewise unthinkable. Thus, it is impossible for anyone to know—and hence, think—that p is false. So, on the hypothesized use, it would be possible (i.e., 'conceptually possible') that p. And this would be so even if p were *logically inconsistent*!

[11] These uses of 'could' need not correspond to distinct *literal meanings*; it is enough that they are standard uses of the term in the sort of ordinary contexts relevant to modal epistemology.

either way' would be true, even though, when meant the same way, 'Fermat's Last Theorem could have turned out either way' would be false.

A few semi-formal remarks about these epistemic uses of 'could' might be helpful. Suppose someone intends the 'could'-of-ignorance when uttering the sentence 'It could be that p' in some relevant conversational context.[12] Then, the asserted proposition would be the proposition that results when an associated propositional operation $\Diamond_{ignorance}$ is applied to the proposition P. (In symbols: $\Diamond_{ignorance}$ p.) The truth-conditions are: the proposition that $\Diamond_{ignorance}$ p is true iff it is unknown, one way or the other, whether p. Likewise, the 'could'-of-less-than-complete-certainty may be represented with the operator '$\Diamond_{uncertainty}$'. The truth-conditions are: the proposition that $\Diamond_{uncertainty}$ p is true iff it is not completely certain that p. Finally, the 'could'-of-qualitative-evidential-neutrality may be represented with '$\Diamond_{qual\text{-}evid\text{-}neut}$'. The truth-conditions are: the proposition that $\Diamond_{qual\text{-}evid\text{-}neut}$ p is true iff it is possible for there to be a population c with attitudes toward p and it is possible for there to be a population c' whose epistemic situation is qualitatively identical to that of c such that the proposition which in c' is the epistemic counterpart of p in c is true.[13]

Note that in each of these three biconditionals the whole proposition mentioned on the left-hand side need not be *identical* to that expressed by the associated right-hand side, and intuitively, they are indeed different. This feature allows the above account to avoid various difficulties that undermine other accounts of epistemic uses of 'could'. A case in point is Kripke's account of the 'could'-of-qualitative-evidential-neutrality. As we shall see in section 1.4, the above account avoids problems confronting Kripke's account, while at the same time preserving a thesis latent in Kripke's discussion—namely, that it could have turned out epistemically that p iff p has a qualitative epistemic counterpart (in the above sense) that is metaphysically possible. In other words, this sort of epistemic possibility entails the existence of the associated sort of metaphysical possibility.

Kripke's modal argument against materialism is based on the premise that, for a certain proposition p (i.e., that there could turn out to be pain without firing C-fibers, and firing C-fibers without pain), p's epistemic possibility entails its metaphysical possibility. His argument fails, however. Since p is semantically *unstable*, its epistemic possibility entails merely that some qualitative epistemic counterpart be metaphysically possible; it does not entail that p itself is metaphysically possible. But the latter sort of metaphysical possibility is what

---

[12] Here and certain other places I use single quotes where, strictly, corner quotes are required.

[13] In symbols: $\Diamond(\exists c)\ \Diamond(\exists c')(\exists p')[\text{QualitativelyIdentical}(c', c)\ \&\ \text{Counterparts}(<p', c'>, <p, c>)\ \&\ \text{True}(p')]$.

Kripke's argument requires. In section 4.3 we shall see that Chalmers's zombie argument—and other two-dimensional modal arguments—resemble Kripke's argument in this respect, and that they fail for the same reason. If, however, p is semantically *stable*, p's epistemic possibility *does* entail p's metaphysical possibility. This follows from the definition of semantic stability: a semantically stable proposition is, by definition, one that is *identical* to all of its epistemic counterparts (see n. 1). It turns out that, for certain semantically stable propositions p, p's epistemic possibility—and hence p's metaphysical possibility—entails the falsity of associated instances of the Identity Theory. For example, if p is the proposition that some being feels pain but does not have 74,985,263 or more functionally related nonconscious parts (or whatever is the minimum number needed for having firing C-fibers), p's epistemic possibility entails its metaphysical possibility. In turn, this entails that having firing C-fibers is not a necessary condition for being in pain and, therefore, that these two properties are not identical. This epistemic possibility suffices as the first step in the anti-materialist argument described in section 4.4.[14]

1.4 *Modal Error I: Epistemic Possibility and Rephrasals*

An important task for modal epistemology is to identify the sources of—and defenses against—erroneous or misleading modal intuitions. In this section, I will consider one such source: namely, confusion between metaphysical possibility and epistemic possibility. The threat of such confusion plays a significant role in Kripke's discussion of scientific essentialism (hereafter SE). In section 3.3, I will return to the topic of modal error, and the account of it offered by Stephen Yablo.

Kripke holds that, taken literally, there is a conflict between his thesis that, say, it is necessary that Hesperus = Phosphorus and our ordinary intuition that it could have turned out that Hesperus was not Phosphorus (1980: 103–5, 140–4).

---

[14] The foregoing dialectic is spelled out in Bealer (1994). Note that, besides the indicated epistemic intuition, most of us have a direct metaphysical intuition that there could be a being that feels pain but lacks 74,985,263 or more functionally related nonconscious parts. (Our little 'translation' test can be used to establish that this is indeed the 'could' of metaphysical possibility.) Like the epistemic intuition, this intuition also contradicts the thesis that firing C-fibers is a necessary condition for being in pain. And, because this intuition is semantically stable, it too avoids the sort of scientific essentialist worries that confront the traditional modal arguments (i.e., traditional multiple-realizability, zombie, and disembodiment arguments, including Yablo's disembodiment argument; cf. sect. 4.2). We thus have *two* arguments against the Identity Theory that are immune to scientific essentialist worries.

Kripke takes there to be a conflict because he believes that '*it could have turned out that p* entails that p could have been the case' (1980: 141–2). And he believes that, if conflicts like this cannot be resolved, his argument for SE would be foiled.

His resolution is to hold that the apparent conflict among our intuitions is an illusion. All, or most, of our intuitions are correct, but many are *misreported*. For example, our intuitions supporting the necessary identity of Hesperus and Phosphorus are correctly reported, but when we report our apparently contrary intuitions, we confuse ordinary possibility with the possibility of a certain kind of epistemic situation:

And so it's true that given the evidence that someone has antecedent to his empirical investigation, he can be placed in a sense in exactly the same situation, that is a qualitatively identical epistemic situation [to ours], and call two heavenly bodies 'Hesperus' and 'Phosphorus', without their being identical. So in that sense we can say that it might have turned out either way. (1980: 103–4)

Generalizing from Kripke's remarks, one arrives at the following rephrasal schema: The inaccurate statement 'It could have turned out that A' is to be rephrased with the accurate statement 'It is possible that a population of speakers in an epistemic situation qualitatively identical to ours would make a true statement by uttering "A" with normal literal intent'.

But this sort of metalinguistic rephrasal is untenable because of familiar problems concerning fine-grained intensional content. For example, it runs afoul of the Langford–Church translation test.[15] It also runs afoul of the sort of arguments Tyler Burge (1979) and Stephen Schiffer (1987) give against metalinguistic rephrasals of attitude reports.

There is, however, an extremely simple resolution of the problem: namely, to deny that there is conflict in the first place. When people say that it could have turned out that Hesperus was not Phosphorus, they are simply not contradicting the SE thesis that it is necessary that Hesperus = Phosphorus. Why? Because they are just employing a straightforward epistemic use of 'could': namely, the 'could'-of-qualitative-evidential-neutrality. As we saw in the previous section, this use of 'could' does not collide with the metaphysical use. End of story. Kripke took there to be a conflict because '*it could have turned out that p* entails that p could have been the case'. True enough—when the two uses of 'could' are the same. But our little 'translation' test from section 1.3 easily shows

---

[15] Church (1950: 98) describes this test thus: '[W]e may bring out more sharply the inadequacy of [an analysis] by translating into another language . . . and observing that the two translated statements would obviously convey different meanings to [a speaker of the other language] (whom we may suppose to have no knowledge of English).'

that in the context of Kripke's discussion his first and second uses of 'could' are not the same. (When Kripke granted, 'It could have turned out that Hesperus was not Phosphorus', he was assuredly not committing himself to the claim that it is either necessary that Hesperus ≠ Phosphorus or contingent that Hesperus ≠ Phosphorus. But when he told us, 'Hesperus could not be different from Phosphorus', he was committing himself to the claim that it is neither necessary that Hesperus ≠ Phosphorus nor contingent that Hesperus ≠ Phosphorus.) As soon as we see this, the appearance of conflict vanishes. Moreover, by identifying the first occurrence of 'could' with the 'could'-of-qualitative-evidential-neutrality and by analyzing it in the way proposed in section 1.3, we are able to preserve Kripke's underlying insight, but without the problematic features of his official metalinguistic approach.

Besides Kripke's approach (just discussed), there have been many others. For example, Kripke offers a second style of rephrasal based on the idea that the intuition that the Hesperus–Phosphorus identity 'could have turned out otherwise' is misreported, and that it is correctly reported with definite descriptions ('the so and so heavenly body', 'the such and such heavenly body') rather than names ('Hesperus', 'Phosphorus'). This, too, is seriously flawed (see Bealer, 1994). Another general approach also holds that the intuitions are indeed in conflict, but that the conflict results from an understandable conceptual illusion: specifically, a subtle slipping back and forth between very similar but conflicting intuitions—for example, an intuition about the thing, whatever it is, and an intuition involving the thing's contingent macroscopic properties. A third general approach (see section 4.1 for criticism of this idea) is to hold that, although the conflict is genuine, one of the conflicting intuitions is of a generally unreliable sort and so on that ground should be dismissed. In any case, the simple logico-linguistic account given in the previous section vitiates these three approaches, for each is based on the false assumption that there *is* a conflict in the intuitions at issue.

1.5 *Epistemic Possibility in Two-Dimensionalism*

A final approach to the problem just discussed, which is espoused by David Chalmers, is a variant of the account I have given. On Chalmers's approach (as I understand it) the intuitions at issue are correctly reported from the start, but the intuition-reports are *ambiguous*. There simply is no conflict between the reported intuitions as long as the reports are understood correctly. If (i) 'Hesperus could not have been different from Phosphorus' is understood metaphysically and (ii) 'It could have turned out that Hesperus ≠ Phosphorus' is understood epistemically, there is no conflict. In other words: (iii) although it is not metaphysically possible, it is nevertheless epistemically possible that Hesperus ≠ Phosphorus. Up to this point, this is just what I have said.

The difference emerges in the way (iii) is dealt with. I represent (iii) in the following straightforward way (where p is that Hesperus ≠ Phosphorus): $\neg \lozenge p$ & $\lozenge_e p$. Here I am using '$\lozenge$' for metaphysical possibility and '$\lozenge_e$' for the relevant epistemic use of 'possible', whatever it is. By contrast, to deal with (iii), Chalmers posits a very different sort of ambiguity: namely, an ambiguity in the *sentence* 'Hesperus ≠ Phosphorus' itself. As we will see (section 2.2), Chalmers holds that there are two distinct sorts of meaning: 'primary' and 'secondary'. He holds in particular that a sentence is semantically correlated to what he calls a 'primary proposition' and a 'secondary proposition'. (For Chalmers (1996: 63–4) , a proposition, whether primary or secondary, is a function from possible worlds to truth-values; accordingly, he holds that a proposition is possible iff it is true in some possible world iff it has the value True for some possible world.) Let p_1 be the primary proposition of 'Hesperus ≠ Phosphorus', and p_2 its secondary proposition. Then, according to Chalmers (if I understand him), 'It is epistemically possible that Hesperus ≠ Phosphorus' is equivalent to 'p_1 is possible [i.e., true in some possible world]'. And 'It is not metaphysically possible that Hesperus ≠ Phosphorus' is equivalent to 'p_2 is not possible [i.e., true in no possible world]'. Accordingly, (iii) would be represented thus: $\neg \lozenge p_2$ & $\lozenge p_1$. So, despite all the talk of epistemic possibility, the epistemic use of 'could' disappears; the only use of 'could' is the one for metaphysical possibility. (This fact comes to the foreground in Chalmers's zombie argument; see section 4.3.)

This picture has very implausible consequences. Intuitively, statement (iii) entails the following: (iv) there is something which, although not metaphysically possible, is nevertheless epistemically possible, namely, *that Hesperus ≠ Phosphorus*.[16] But, on the present theory, (iv) cannot be true. Why? Because on the theory, the only ambiguity in sentences like (iii)—and hence, the only ambiguity in sentences like (iv)—is between the primary and secondary intensions associated with 'Hesperus ≠ Phosphorus', and there is only one modality relevant to such sentences: namely, truth in some possible world. Therefore, on the theory, '$\lozenge_e p$' just collapses into '$\lozenge p$'. Consequently, on the theory, (iv) implies that there is something p that both is and is not possible (true in some possible world): namely, that Hesperus ≠ Phosphorus.[17] A contradiction. And this is so whether p is a 'primary proposition', a 'secondary proposition', or any other sort of proposition. Furthermore, this problem generalizes, yielding

---

[16] That is, there is something p such that p is not metaphysically possible and p is epistemically possible and p is that Hesperus ≠ Phosphorus. In symbols: $(\exists p)(\neg \lozenge p$ & $\lozenge_e p$ & $p = [H \neq P])$.

[17] In symbols, $(\exists p)((\neg \lozenge p$ & $\lozenge p)$ & $p = [H \neq P])$.

the conclusion that, on this theory, there is *not one* proposition that, although not metaphysically possible, is nevertheless epistemically possible.

In the face of this contradiction, Chalmers has no choice but to retreat to a metalinguistic analysis of sentences like (iv), according to which only a *sentence*—never a proposition—can be said to be both epistemically possible and metaphysically impossible.[18] But such metalinguistic analyses run afoul of a host of well-known problems (including, e.g., the very sort of problem that confronted Kripke's metalinguistic rephrasals in section 1.3). For this reason, a satisfactory logico-linguistic treatment of epistemic possibility turns out to be out of the reach of Chalmers's two-dimensionalism.

The fact that Chalmers has no choice but to accept the thesis that sentences (never propositions) are the only sort of thing that can be at once epistemically possible and metaphysically impossible should be no surprise, for it is entailed by the Jackson–Chalmers thesis that sentences, never propositions, are the only sort of thing that can be at once necessary and a posteriori. Like the former thesis, the latter thesis is subject to a wealth of well-known arguments against metalinguistic treatments of 'that'-clauses and their interaction with 'could' and 'possible' and other key expressions ('knows', 'believes', etc.).[19] Such 'mixed' constructions, however, form the very heart of intensional logic— which is, of course, the logical framework of modal epistemology. In section 2, I will discuss a number of other reasons why the Jackson–Chalmers two-dimensional framework is incapable of fulfilling this role.

2 Logical Framework for Modal Epistemology

As I mentioned in the introduction, many defenses of moderate rationalism fail right in the conceptual and logical preliminaries. If we are to have an adequate

---

[18] There are a few minor variants. Chalmers could hold that there are certain other *sentence-like* entities (asserted sentences, Mentalese representations, etc.) which, by virtue of having both primary and secondary intensions, can be both epistemically possible and metaphysically impossible. But this proposals falls prey to analogues of the problems that undermine the metalinguistic analysis in the text. Chalmers also speaks as though 'concepts' (1996: 56ff.) and 'thoughts' (1996: 65) have primary and secondary intensions, but he offers no theory of what 'concepts' and 'thoughts' are, or of what this relation of *having* a primary and secondary intension is. Maybe Chalmers's 'thoughts' are sentence-like entities (as above). Or maybe they are ordered pairs consisting of a primary intension and a secondary intension. But such proposals fall prey to a host of difficulties. For example, they amount to category errors: thoughts are not *really* English sentences, asserted sentences, Mentalese sentences, or ordered pairs! Moreover, these proposals fall prey to a multitude of insurmountable Benacerraf-style problems; see sect. 2.2. (The present note is also intended to apply to the remarks in the next paragraph in the text.)

[19] Section 2.3 provides a new style of argument. See also Bealer (1993*b*).

modal epistemology, it is essential that we first have an adequate logical framework. In this section, after showing in some detail why the two-dimensionalist approach cannot provide one, I will then briefly outline a more satisfactory framework, the nonreductive algebraic framework.

2.1   *Propositions*

There is very strong logical and linguistic evidence for the following tenets. (1) 'Say', 'mean', 'believe', 'is possible', and so forth often function as predicates, and 'that'-clauses function as singular terms in companion sentences (e.g., 'I believe that A', 'It is possible that A'). I propose to use 'proposition' as a technical term for the sorts of entity—*whatever they turn out to be*—denoted by 'that'-clauses occurring in the indicated family of sentences. (2) Propositions (in this neutral sense) are not sentences, uttered sentences, utterances of sentences, or any other such linguistic entities. For example, speakers of diverse languages can believe various common propositions; animals and infants have beliefs but no language; metalinguistic treatments of 'that'-clause sentences do not pass the Langford–Church translation test, and so forth. (3) Propositions can be very fine-grained. For example, it is a truth of logic that triangles are triangles, but a truth of geometry, not logic, that trilaterals are triangles. (Of course, our proposed use of 'proposition' is consistent with the idea that there are also families of propositions that are not so fine-grained, and, indeed, that there could be a spectrum of 'granularities'.)

Frege's puzzle (how can sentences of the form 'A = A' and 'A = B' be true but be different in meaning) also calls for very fine-grained propositions: 'A = A' means that A = A, and 'A = B' means that A = B; therefore, since the two sentences are different in meaning, the associated 'that'-clauses must denote different propositions (in our neutral sense). How can these propositions be different? Frege's solution no longer seems feasible, for Marcus, Kripke, Kaplan, Putnam, and others have convincingly argued that names do not have descriptive content. The problem is compounded by the fact that, if 'A' and 'B' are names such as 'Hesperus' and 'Phosphorus', the proposition that A = B is both necessarily true and knowable only a posteriori, as Kripke and Putnam have shown.

A great irony in contemporary philosophy of language is that most people originally moved by the Kripke–Putnam arguments advocate theories according to which there exist *no* such necessary a posteriori propositions. I have in mind hidden-indexical theories and most other direct-reference theories and the Jackson–Chalmers two-dimensional theory. This creates a special problem in our context, for there can be no satisfactory modal epistemology without such propositions. Reserving critical discussion of hidden-indexicalism for another setting, I will here examine two-dimensionalism and follow that discussion with a proposal of what I believe is a more satisfactory framework.

2.2 *Two-Dimensionalism, Possibilia, and Understanding Language*

Frank Jackson (1993, 1998) and David Chalmers (1995, 1996) have each proposed a new 'two-dimensional' logical framework, adapted from prior work of David Kaplan, Robert Stalnaker, Martin Davies and Lloyd Humberstone, David Lewis, and Pavel Tichy (see Jackson 1998: 47 n.). The resulting theory is at once a formal semantics, a foundation for intensional logic, a theory of understanding of words and language, and a modal epistemology. I believe that this framework and the theory that flows from it are inadequate.

2.2.1 *The Possible-Worlds Background*

A preliminary concern is that two-dimensionalism is developed within a meta-physics that assumes both possible worlds and possible individuals (nonactual as well as actual) and that constructs all the intensional entities required by philo-sophical semantics from such possibilia. This applies to propositions, concepts, senses, meanings, mental contents—and so, presumably, also to properties and relations.

There are, I believe, overwhelming reasons for holding that this analytical order is backwards. The notions of concepts and/or properties and relations are fundamental. They, together with modal notions and certain other logical notions, are the basic notions in terms of which the notions of proposition, state of affairs, maximal state of affairs, and so forth are to be characterized and pos-sibilist language is to be analyzed.

Here is one of many arguments for this assessment.[20] Intuitively, it is neces-sary *that some proposition is necessary*. On the possible-worlds reduction, the property (concept) of being a necessary proposition is a function (set of ordered pairs) from possible worlds to the set of necessary propositions. But this set includes the proposition that some proposition is necessary (because, as just indicated, this proposition is itself necessary). Thus, this proposition belongs to a set belonging to an ordered pair belonging to the property of being necessary.

---

[20] Two other problems: (1) identifying properties (red) and propositions (that I am thinking) with functions is, other things being equal, simply a category mistake—these things are not func-tions, not *really*; (2) this reduction is subject to a wealth of Benacerraf-style problems. See Bealer (1993*a*: 20, 22) and Jubien (2001). These two problems, and that in the text, are avoided by the approach in sect. 2.5.

But, to avoid the problem of logical omniscience, our reductionists are forced to treat this proposition as a *structured proposition*, one of whose constituents is the property (concept) of being necessary. Hence, this property belongs to an ordered set that belongs to a set that belongs to an ordered pair that belongs to the property of being necessary. That is, being necessary ∈ . . . ∈ being necessary. Hence, the property of being necessary cannot be a set-theoretical construct built up entirely from possible *particulars* (possible people, possible stones, and the like). Thus, the possible-worlds construction fails for the property of being necessary—in general, for most every iteratable property. Hence, these properties are irreducible *sui generis* entities. But, then, uniformity supports the thesis that all other properties (concepts) are *sui generis* as well.

Chalmers responds to concerns of this sort by holding that the possible-worlds framework and its reductions of propositions (concepts, senses, meanings, thoughts) to possible-worlds constructs is only a tool, which may be taken for granted 'in much the way one takes mathematics for granted' (1996:66). And Jackson tells us that refusing the possible-worlds approach would be 'not that different from refusing to count one's change at the supermarket because of the ontological mysteries raised by numbers' (1998: 11). But the implied analogy is unsound: the questions at hand concern the ultimate *foundations* of philosophy; at this point one can no longer simply defer the issue. Is two-dimensionalism a satisfactory framework for understanding the fundamental concepts of modal epistemology: necessity, possibility, meaning, property, concept, proposition, mental content, a posteriori necessity, epistemic possibility, and so forth? Considerations like the one given above strongly suggest that it is not.[21]

2.2.2 *The Key Idea of Two-Dimensionalism*

Jackson puts it thus:

We can think of the [things] to which a term *applies* in two different ways, depending on whether we are considering what the term applies to under various hypotheses about which world is the actual world, or whether we are considering what the term applies to under various counterfactual hypotheses. (1998: 48, emphasis added)

In the former case, the term has an 'A-intension' (A for actual), a 'primary intension' in Chalmers's terminology; in the latter case, a 'C-intension' (C for counterfactual), a 'secondary intension' in Chalmers's terminology. In conventional

---

[21] A related point concerns the actualism/possibilism debate. Other things being equal, economy makes actualism preferable to possibilism. It is often claimed, however, that possibilist language has a useful expressive power not available to actualist language. The fact of the matter is that an actualist semantics can be given for possibilist language, and this settles the matter in favor of actualism. See Bealer (1998: 25 f.).

possible-worlds terminology, the intension of a term is the C-intension (secondary intension). The A-intension (primary intension) is very different and is characterized by Jackson as follows:

What then does the word 'water' *denote* in a world where the kind common to the relevant watery exemplars in that world is kind K under the hypothesis that that world is the actual world? Kind K, of course, be that kind H_2O, XYZ, or whatever. (1998: 49, emphasis added)

Chalmers states the idea thus:

When the XYZ world is considered as actual, my term 'water' *picks out* XYZ in the world. (1996: 60, emphasis added)

But these claims are simply mistaken. The English word 'water' denotes H_2O, as we all know. Kripke and Putnam taught us that, for *every possible situation*, the English word 'water' denotes H_2O in that situation. This just reflects the standard use of the English expressions 'water' and 'denote'. It is simply false that, for some possible situation, the English word 'water' denotes XYZ in that situation! This is so no matter how we might be 'considering' these situations or what 'hypotheses' we might be entertaining about them. For the same reason, it is false that, for some possible situation, the English word 'water' *applies* to picks out, refers to, designates) XYZ in that situation. All such uses of these key English semantical expressions are blatant violations of Jackson's own terminological dictum (cited at the outset)![22]

In Chalmers the problem is even more graphic, for he holds that *concepts* (as well as words) have primary intensions:

Take the concept 'water'. [T]he primary intension of 'water' maps the XYZ world to XYZ and the H_2O world to H_2O. . . . [I]t picks out the *watery stuff* in a world. (1996: 57; see also 65)

---

[22]   The following alternative definition (cf. Chalmers 1996: 364 n. 21; 365 n. 25) is no better: the A-intension (primary intension) of the English word 'water' is a function from worlds w to the object in w denoted by the sound-alike word 'water' in the counterpart language of the beings in w whose epistemic situation is qualitatively the same as ours. Analogously for sentences. But, as before, such A-intenstions (primary intensions) do not correspond to any standard notion from the semantics for English. For example, the English word 'water' does not *express*, or have as its *meaning*, a function that identifies what *other* speakers of *other* languages would denote with *their* word 'water'! In the case of sentences, there is another way to make the point. Propositions of the following form fix the meaning relation (and, in turn, reference) for English: the English sentence 'S' means *that S*. For example, the English sentence 'Hesperus=Phosphorus' means *that Hesperus=Phosphorus*. But this proposition cannot be the primary intension because, unlike the primary intension, it is necessary; nor can it be the secondary intension because, unlike the secondary intension, it cannot be know a priori (sect. 2.3 elaborates this argument).

From Putnam we know that, for every possible situation, XYZ is not water in that situation. It is simply a misuse of the English expressions 'concept of being water' and 'pick out' (or 'applies to') to say that, for some possible situation, the concept of being water picks out (applies to) XYZ in that situation. Again, this is so regardless of how we might happen to be considering these situations or what hypotheses we might be entertaining about them. To hold otherwise is to hold that, for some possible situations, the concept of *being water* picks out (applies to) things that are *not water* in those situations! And, by parity, this would lead one to hold that, for certain reptilian worlds, the concept of being a human being applies to beings that are not even human beings in those worlds: namely, to human-looking reptiles! *Reductio ad absurdum.*[23]

These and related considerations show that A-intensions (primary intensions) and their kin do not match any of the standard semantical notions from the theory of reference and meaning for natural language. Likewise, the incongruity between C-intensions (secondary intensions) and the fine-grained distinctions exemplified in Frege's puzzle shows that they too do not match any of the standard semantical notions. The problem here is not merely 'terminological'; rather, it occupies the core of philosophy of language. What is linguistic meaning? What do words and sentences really mean (given that their meanings are not primary or secondary intensions)? What is it to understand a language? How are we to solve Frege's Puzzle? How can a sentence express something that is both necessary and a posteriori? How can language be both public and anti-individualistic in nature? On the Jackson–Chalmers theory, these questions prove unanswerable.

2.2.3 *Understanding Language*

As indicated, Jackson and Chalmers also intend their theory to provide an account of what it is to understand a word, a sentence, and, more generally, a language. Put briefly, their view is that to understand an English sentence is just to know its A-intension (i.e., primary intension). As Jackson tells us: '[U]nderstanding the sentence only requires knowing the A-proposition' (1998: 77); '[U]nderstanding "Water covers most of the Earth" does not require knowing the conditions under which it is true, that is, the proposition it expresses [i.e., its C-intension]. Rather it requires knowing how the proposition expressed depends on the context of utterance—in this case, how it depends on which stuff in the world of utterance is the watery stuff of our acquaintance in it [i.e., its

---

[23] In Chalmers there is also a use/mention problem: standard quotation names (e.g., 'water') are, throughout, used ambiguously as names of both words and concepts; and, contrary to standard usage, concepts are said to have 'meanings' and 'references'.

A-intension]' (1998: 73–4).[24] But this account is surely mistaken. Consider the two-planet version of the twin-earth example: in that world, earth exists with all its inhabitants, languages, etc., and, in addition, so does a twin earth that is a macroscopic duplicate of earth except that XYZ fills the lakes and rivers, etc. Given that on the Jackson–Chalmers theory A-intensions (primary intensions) are defined on 'centered worlds', the words and sentences of Twin English would have the same A-intensions as they do in English. Moreover, Twin English would be syntactically and phonetically the same as English. It would then follow that in this envisaged world you already would understand, and know how to speak, Twin English.[25] I find this wholly counter-intuitive. In radio 'conversations' with your twin earth counterpart, each of you would seriously misunderstand the other's sentences. Suppose each of you simultaneously asserts 'Water contains hydrogen.' Then, each one would misunderstand the sentence he receives. After all, you know that in your language 'Water contains hydrogen' means *that water contains hydrogen*, but you wrongly believe that in your counterpart's language 'Water contains hydrogen' means *that water contains hydrogen*. (Analogously for your counterpart.) In fact, *no* sentence in your counterpart's language can even express this proposition! (And the other way round.) Still worse, not only does the present theory wrongly imply that your counterpart *does* understand your sentence, it also implies that even your most intimate friends *cannot* understand it! (Likewise for you counterpart's most intimate friends and his sentence.)

2.3   *Two-Dimensionalism, the Necessary A Posteriori, and Frege's Puzzle*

The primary tenet of the Jackson–Chalmers theory of the necessary a posteriori is that only sentences, never propositions, have this key property. But this is not so.

[24] Accordingly, Jackson tells us that his theory of understanding language 'can be put in Stalnaker's terminology by saying that understanding requires knowing the propositional concept associated with a sentence, though not necessarily the proposition expressed, and in Kaplan's by saying that understanding requires knowing character but not necessarily content' (1998: 72 n. 26). But, as Chalmers emphasizes, 'Kaplan uses his account to deal with indexical and demonstrative terms like "I" and "that", but does not extend it to deal with natural-kind terms such as "water", as he takes "water" to pick out H_2O in all contexts (the sound-alike word on Twin Earth is simply a different word)', (1996: 365–6 n. 25). (Kaplan seems clearly right.)

On the Jackson-Chalmers theory of linguistic understanding, not even your most intimate friend understands what you do by 'Water contains hydrogen'; only your twin-earth counterpart does!

[25] This is avoided if your words' primary intensions were *partial funcitons* defined for a centered world only if in that world you truly occupy the relevant location. Still, all the problems in sects. 2.3 and 2.4 (and the privacy problem just below) survive.

As I indicated earlier, to avoid the problem of logical omniscience (i.e., knowing every truth of logic if you know any), Jackson and Chalmers must incorporate structured propositions (ordered sets, labeled trees, or whatever). Jackson ought to accept this solution, for he himself endorses an analogous solution to a very similar problem (1998: 34). The idea is that, if a 'that'-clause denotes one of these structured propositions, the latter's 'constituents' would be either logical particles or intensions, associated in the obvious way with corresponding primitive expressions occurring in the embedded sentence. For example, 'that everything is even or odd' might denote the structured proposition: <universal generalization, <being even, disjunction, being odd>>. Universal generalization is the logical particle associated with 'everything'; being even, the primary intension (and also the secondary intension) of 'is even'; disjunction, the logical particle associated with 'or'; being odd, the primary (and also secondary) intension of 'is odd'.

Consider the following intuitive schemas: (i) If a sincere English speaker x utters an English sentence 'A' with literal, assertoric intent, then x thereby sincerely asserts that A; (ii) If x sincerely states that A, then x believes that A. Now, famously, Saul Kripke sincerely uttered 'It is necessarily true that Hesperus = Phosphorus' with literal, assertoric intent. So, by (i), Kripke thereby sincerely asserted that it is necessarily true that Hesperus = Phosphorus. Hence, by (ii), Kripke believed that it is necessarily true that Hesperus = Phosphorus. As history showed, this proposition which Kripke believed proved to be highly nontrivial. Like so many of us, Kripke once believed the negation of this proposition, and only with argument did he come to believe the unnegated proposition. What proposition is this? Within Jackson–Chalmers semantics there are two candidates: (a) the secondary intension of the embedded sentence 'It is necessarily true that Hesperus = Phosphorus' and (b) the primary intension of this sentence.[26] But neither option works.

(a) The secondary intension is the following structured proposition (where h is the constant function from worlds to Hesperus—i.e., to Phosphorus): <necessity, <h, identity, h>>. But this structured proposition is a triviality, so cannot be the one Kripke believed. (I think this would be Jackson's and Chalmers's assessment, for they take primary, not secondary, intensions to be the objects of the attitudes.)

(b) The primary intension of 'It is necessarily true that Hesperus = Phosphorus' is the following structured proposition (where h and p and are the

---

[26] I am supposing that hidden-indexicalism is not available (see Bealer (forthcoming)). Nor is treating 'water' as synonymous to the description 'the *actual* watery stuff of our acquaintance', because of various well-known difficulties.

primary intensions of 'Hesperus' and 'Phosphorus', respectively): <necessity, <h, identity, p >>. Unlike the secondary intension, this structured proposition is not a triviality. But this proposition is true iff the structured proposition <h, identity, p > is necessary. The latter structured proposition, however, is the primary intension of 'Hesperus = Phosphorus', and this primary intension is contingent, according to Jackson and Chalmers. It follows, therefore, that the former structured proposition must be false. Thus, given option (b), the proposition Kripke believed when he uttered 'It is necessarily true that Hesperus = Phosphorus' was false.

Now it is a truism that the sentence 'Hesperus = Phosphorus' is necessary iff the sentence 'It is necessarily true that Hesperus = Phosphorus' is true. Since all participants in the present debate (two-dimensionalists and their opponents alike) accept the left-hand side, they must accept the right-hand side as well: namely, that the sentence 'It is necessarily true that Hesperus = Phosphorus' is true. This, of course, is the reason Kripke chose to utter this sentence: he believed that it is true. Now when he uttered this sentence, what he said—namely, that it is necessarily true that Hesperus = Phosphorus—was true. And, since he was sincere, he believed this proposition. Therefore, the proposition he believed when he uttered 'It is necessarily true that Hesperus = Phosphorus' was true. But this contradicts the conclusion we reached in the preceding paragraph. So option (b) cannot be right, either.

Since neither option (a) nor (b) works, Jackson–Chalmers semantics is evidently unable to represent our sample sentence—and a great many other such sentences mixing modalities and attitudes—and, for this reason, it is evidently unable to deal successfully with one of the central phenomena of modal epistemology: the necessary a posteriori.[27]

---

[27] Someone might propose a more complicated two-dimensional semantics designed to avoid the above problem. It seems, however, that problems of the same general type will continue to recur. But even if this is not so, how far from commonsense semantics should one be willing to go? Incidentally, there is a quicker, but less rigorous, way to formulate the above problem. Kripke, and almost everyone else, accepts the following sentence: 'It is a posteriori that it is necessary that Hesperus = Phosphorus'. But if the second 'that'-clause denotes the secondary intension of 'Hesperus = Phosphorus', then the whole sentence is false because the proposition that this proposition is necessary is a priori (vs. a posteriori). Conversely, if the indicated 'that'-clause denotes the primary intension, then the whole sentence is again false because the primary intension is a contingent (vs. necessary) proposition. Put another way, when you utter 'Hesperus = Phosphorus' with sincere assertoric intent, what are you asserting and consciously and explicitly thinking? The necessary a priori secondary intension? The contingent a posteriori primary intension? Both?! The ordered-pair of the two?! None of these answers is acceptable. By the way, many of my criticisms in this section can be applied *mutatis mutandis* to the theory that intentional states have two kinds of content—'narrow' and 'wide'.

The underlying problem is, of course, that two-dimensionalism has no solution to Frege's puzzle. As we saw in section 2.1, a solution requires an explanation of how, for example, the propositions that Hesperus = Hesperus and that Hesperus = Phosphorus can be different. So (by generalization), a solution also requires an explanation of how the proposition that it is necessarily true that Hesperus = Hesperus and the proposition that it is necessarily true that Hesperus = Phosphorus can be different. Since, as we have just seen, two-dimensionalism cannot explain this difference, it has no general solution to Frege's puzzle. That is to say, two-dimensionalism cannot solve the first problem in philosophy of language. What is missing, of course, is a satisfactory theory of fine-grained propositions. If one is feasible (see sect. 2.5), however, the complicated apparatus of two-dimensional semantics is rendered superfluous.

2.4   *Two-Dimensionalism, Public Language, and Anti-Individualism*

In this section we will see that two-dimensional semantics runs into two other fundamental challenges in philosophy of language: namely, how to deal with the public and anti-individualistic character of language. A convenient way to bring this out is to examine Jackson and Chalmers's commitment to implicit descriptivism.[28] By implicit descriptivism, I mean the thesis that, if a Jackson–Chalmers primary intension (e.g., being-the-watery-stuff-of-our-acquaintance) were analyzed completely, the result would be a descriptive analysis. (It is understood that the envisaged analysis may be infinitary.) This implicit descriptivism is consistent with the thesis that, phenomenologically, primary intensions present themselves as nondescriptive simples. Since Jackson's commitment to implicit descriptivism is more straightforward (e.g., 1998: 40 n.), I will formulate the discussion in Jackson's idiom. (For Chalmers's commitment, see n. 29 below.)

---

[28] This implicit descriptivism plays the role in the Jackson-Chalmers account of the alleged 'a priori link' between the microphysical and macrophysical and between the physical and the mental, so if their implicit descriptivism is problematic, so is this account. (For another problem, see Bealer 1997, 2000.) Further, since Chalmers's implicit descriptivism also plays an essential role in his zombie argument, that argument will likewise be deficient, as we shall see in sect. 4.3. A note on terminology. In my remarks on the two-planet version of the twin-earth story in section 2.2.3, I noted that two-dimensionalism's account of linguistic understanding is rendered untenable by the fact that (as defined) the primary intensions of corresponding words in English and Twin English are identical. In n. 23 I indicated how this consequence could be avoided if the notion of primary intension were redefined in a certain way. In the present section, 'primary intension' may be understood in either the first or second way; the criticisms in this section apply either way.

2.4.1 *Platitudinous Conceptions*

According to Jackson, the primary intension of 'water' (i.e., being-the-watery-stuff-of-our-acquaintance) is encoded in our 'conception' of water. Hence, if this conception were converted into a Ramsified definition (i.e., an implicit-turned-direct second-order definition), the result would be a correct analysis of the original primary intension. Since this qualifies as a descriptive analysis, Jackson's view qualifies as an implicit descriptivism in the above sense.

What, for Jackson, is a 'conception'? It is a certain kind of theory: namely, one that is revealed by one's intuitions about possible cases. For example, in connection with his 'conception' of free action, Jackson tell us, '[M]y intuitions about possible cases reveal my theory of free action' (1998: 32). On one natural way of taking this, a conception is an aggregation of widely accepted platitudes (general truths)—for example, that water is the stuff of our acquaintance that is 'a clear potable liquid and all that; for short, being watery' (1998: 38). Though this is not Jackson's official way of taking 'conception', for the time being let us adopt it, for it is important to see that the resulting view (which many two-dimensionalists seem to accept) suffers from two serious problems. (a) Either it wrongly implies that natural language is not *public* in the way we know it is, or it leads to a mistaken account of what it is to *understand* a language. (b) It wrongly implies that platitudinous conceptions are *a priori* and, since in many cases they are not, that ordinary English speakers do not understand many everyday English words.

(a) The Public-Language Dilemma.[29] Suppose that there are two English-speaking communities c_1 and c_n who are 'joined' to one another by a chain of English-speaking communities $c_2, \ldots, c_{n-1}$, each of which has regular contact with its flanking communities, and with whom it has significant overlap in water platitudes (i.e., the theory-like general principles). But suppose that at the extremes c_1 and c_n (e.g. the English speakers on "Waterworld" and "Dune") have little or no overlap in their water platitudes. In this case, we would still want to say that they share the term 'water'. Indeed, if the two

---

[29] In effect, the argument of sect. 2.3.3 already demonstrates the public language dilemma. On the one hand, we saw that when primary intensions are defined in the original way, the resulting theory of linguistic understanding is mistaken, for it wrongly implies that every English speaker would already understand Twin English, and conversely. On the other hand, we saw that this unwanted consequence could be avoided by redefining primary intensions in accordance with the corrective given in n. 23. But given this definition, it trivially follows that primary intensions of every English speaker's words are private (not public), for these primary intensions are defined only in those centered worlds in which that speaker is the person at the center. The argument I am about to give (as well as the public-language argument in sect. 2.4.2) is independent of this earlier argument for the public-language dilemma.

groups got together, we can easily imagine how the conversations about water would go. In such conversations, the participants would mean and understand the same thing by their 'water' sentences (namely, what those sentences mean *in English*), and they would be communicating as well. But this would not be so on the present construal of 'conceptions', for their conceptions of water differ so radically.

There is, however, a natural fall-back position, namely, to base the implicit-turned-direct definition of water on the water platitudes *common to* the various communities of English speakers. The problem with this is that (at least in some worlds) hardly any water platitudes would be shared by all these communities, and, therefore, the resulting platitudes would not support an implicit-turned-direct definition that picks out water uniquely. Well, I take that back. The shared platitudes could support such a definition, but only if they included highly *deferential* platitudes (including platitudes concerning causal information chains). But this would only trigger the other horn of the dilemma. If the primary things you understand by 'water' are, for example, that it refers to the thing that English speakers refer to with 'water' (and/or other such deferential facts), then even though you are able to use the word passably in various conversations, you would not really *understand* it. Moreover, even though this fall-back position has many variations, as far as I can see they all either let in too much or exclude too much, making this an unsolvable problem for the Jackson–Chalmers picture (even when understood as in section 2.4.2).

(b) A Priori Conceptions and Linguistic Understanding. On Jackson's account of linguistic understanding (1998: 73 f.), an ordinary English speaker understands the English word 'water' only if he or she is in a position to know a priori the propositions making up our ordinary conception of water. So, if (as we are supposing temporarily) our ordinary conception consisted of widely accepted platitudes, we should be in a position to have a priori knowledge of those platitudes (or, at least, that a majority of them hold). But this knowledge is in fact a posteriori, not a priori. Why? Because *intuition* constitutes the evidential basis of a priori knowledge;[30] and, even if we initially have intuitions supporting the platitudes, we are readily disabused of them as soon as we come upon our intuitions that it could have turned out (i.e., it is epistemically possible) that, as a result of systematic illusions, water is not really clear or potable or . . . (for the majority of the platitudinous properties of water). Given this, it

---

[30] Except for stipulative knowledge, which is not relevant here, since we may assume that our English speaker (and, for that matter, *every* English speaker; see sect. 3.2 below) did not stipulatively introduce the word 'water' to English.

follows on the present theory that, since the requisite knowledge is not a priori, ordinary English speakers do not understand the English word 'water'.

2.4.2 *The Jackson–Chalmers Picture*

It is now time to see what happens when we take 'conception' in the way Jackson really intends—that is, as *the whatever it is* that our intuitions about relevant possible cases reveal. Understood this way, Jackson's picture and Chalmer's picture pretty much coincide.[31] When 'conceptions' are taken this way, however, there are two unacceptable consequences: (a) once again, language cannot be public in the way we know it is; (b) language cannot be anti-individualistic in the way we know it is.

(a) Public Language.   Rather than establishing this point in detail, I will give an example indicative of the problem. It should be clear how to extend the argument to other examples. Consider Kripke's original meter-man. Suppose that he perished immediately after he stipulatively introduced his word 'meter'. Suppose that meter-man's stipulation was witnessed by someone, and that a causal naming chain flowed out from this person and eventually came to include utterances to which you have been party (but with only a deferential understanding). In this connection, suppose that the primary intension of your word 'meter' was fixed at the time solely by virtue of your being party to these utterances. When this primary intension is analyzed, the result is a description of a causal information chain descending from your exposure to these utterances through other people and terminating in a naming ceremony in which a name denoting one meter was stipulatively introduced. By contrast, when the primary intension of meter-man's word 'meter' is analyzed, the result is a description of a naming ceremony in which he himself is stipulatively introducing his word for one meter by reference to the length of a stick he is looking at. Since there are plainly centered worlds in which the denotations of

---

[31] How so? Well, Chalmers tell us that 'what makes an actual-world X *qualify* as the referent of "X" ' is provided by an 'analysis of the primary intension [which is] an a priori enterprise' (1996: 59). Primary intensions just encode *all* the correct, determinate answers to 'questions about what our concept [*sic*] *would* refer to if the actual world turned out in various ways' (1996: 60). 'The true intension can be determined only from detailed consideration of specific scenarios: What would we say if the world turned out this way? What would we say if it turned out that way?' (1996: 57 f.) Thus, on Chalmers's picture (and Jackson's too), if no finitary descriptive analysis is available, then there always exists a default descriptive analysis consisting of a definite description 'the x such that . . .' formed from an infinitary (cf. Chalmers 1996: 84 n. 45) conjunction of conditionals in which (i) the antecedent characterizes some relevant possible case (scenario) from the perspective of the individual at the center of a corresponding centered world, and (ii) the consequent correctly identifies the indicated entity x with one of the entities described by that antecedent.

these two descriptions come apart, it follows that the primary intensions of meter-man's word 'meter' and your word 'meter' are different.[32] Similar considerations (i.e., a different description for each personalized mode of access) show that this conclusion generalizes to all speakers who have a word 'meter' in their vocabularies: the primary intension of each such speaker's word differs from that of meter-man's word (and, indeed, from everyone else's). Thus, meter-man's word is private not public.

(b) Anti-Individualism and Linguistic Misunderstanding.   On the Jackson–Chalmers picture, the primary intension of, say, *your* word 'know' is uniquely determined by your 'conception of knowledge', where the latter is uniquely revealed by your intuitions about relevant possible cases (e.g., your intuition that it is, or is not, possible for a certain Gettier scenario to occur and the person in the case to have the relevant bit of knowledge; and so forth). On this picture, therefore, you could not fail to understand your word 'know'. To illustrate, suppose there are various people (perhaps you?) who resolutely insist that the Gettier examples are examples of knowledge. Then, as Jackson tells us, 'In these cases, it is . . . misguided to accuse them of error' (1998: 32); '[They are] right about what counts as knowledge in *their* sense' (1998: 36). Naturally, this generalizes from your word 'know' to your other words.

This picture, however, is mistaken, for it overlooks the phenomenon of anti-individualism, which is convincingly illustrated by Tyler Burge's (1979) arthritis example. When the patient in Burge's example sincerely utters 'I have arthritis in my thigh', he asserts and believes that he has arthritis in his thigh, which of course is impossible. (If the patient did not believe this, he would not be relieved if the doctor were to tell him that arthritis in the thigh is impossible because arthritis is a joint disease. But he plainly would be relieved!) Now suppose that right after his original assertion the patient had gone on to consider the question whether having arthritis in the thigh is possible, he would have had the intuition that it is—or, at least, he would have lacked the (correct) intuition that it is impossible. The Burgean explanation would be that the patient does not understand his concept, for if he did, he would instead have had the intuition that arthritis in the thigh is impossible. If this is right, as it surely is, it is clear the patient does not understand what he himself means when he utters

---

[32] Indeed, these two primary intensions do not even have the same *extension* in the centered *actual* world where meter-man is flagged as the person at the center and the time of the dubbing is flagged as the time at the center. Nor do these primary intensions have the same extension in the centered *actual* world where you are flagged as the person at the center and the time your path first crossed the aforementioned causal information chain is flagged as the time at the center. And these facts also generalize.

his word 'arthritis'; in other words, he does *not* understand his own word 'arthritis'. Such is the lesson of anti-individualism. But since, on the Jackson–Chalmers picture, it is impossible in the example for the patient not to understand his word 'arthritis', this picture cannot accommodate the fundamental anti-individualist nature of this and a large family of other natural-language expressions.[33]

2.5 *A More Satisfactory Framework*

Consider some truisms. The proposition that A & B is the conjunction of the proposition that A and the proposition that B. The proposition that not-A is the negation of the proposition that A. The proposition that Fx is the singular predication of the property F of x. The proposition that there exists an F results from existentially generalizing on the property F. And so on. These truisms tell us what these propositions are essentially: they are by nature conjunctions, negations, singular predications, existential generalizations, etc. These are rudimental facts that require no further explanation and for which no further explanation is possible. This was pretty much the dominant view on propositions in the history of logical theory.

By adapting techniques developed in the algebraic tradition in extensional logic, one is able to develop this nonreductionistic approach. Examples like those just given isolate fundamental logical operations—conjunction, negation, singular predication, existential generalization, etc. Intensional entities are then taken as *sui generis* entities; the aim is to analyze their behavior with respect to the fundamental logical operations.

How are we to integrate definite descriptions? On the Fregean approach, the singular term 'the F' refers to the unique item satisfying the predicate 'F' if there is one; if there is not, 'the F' has no reference, in which case the sentence 'The F Gs' lacks truth-value. To incorporate this intuitive theory, we consider a logical operation *the* (which is akin to the Frege–Church operation ι) associated

---

[33] The Jackson–Chalmers approach does not deal with a number of related challenges facing an account of linguistic understanding. (1) A characterization of overly deferential, incomplete understanding (e.g., as in Putnam's beech/elm case). (2) A solution to the circularity problem created by the fact that a speaker might fail to understand some of the *auxiliary* words or concepts involved in the characterization of relevant possible cases. (3) An account of other ways of failing to understand a word or concept besides the sort of incomplete understanding associated with deference, for example, the sort of misunderstanding created by the ubiquity of *false* information in one's web of belief. (4) An account of the phenomenon of mere local misunderstanding versus full-fledged misunderstanding. (The account in section 3 is designed to deal with these and other concerns.)

with the word 'the'. One may think of the values of *the* as 'individual concepts': *the*(F) would then be the individual concept of being the F. Consider the property of being G and the individual concept of being the F. What is the relation between them and the proposition that the F Gs? Not singular predication: when the operation of singular predication is applied to the property of being G and the concept of being the F, the value is the proposition that the concept of being the F Gs. This is a *very* different proposition! The relation of singular predication is thus not the relation holding between the property of being G, the concept of being the F, and the proposition that the F Gs. Rather, the relation holding between them is a quite distinct kind of predication, which may be called *descriptive predication*. Thus, the proposition that the F Gs is the result of descriptively predicating G of the concept that results from applying our operation *the* to F.

In this informal account, the entities playing the subject roles in descriptive predication are individual concepts (or properties). But we could instead think of them more generally as modes of access or modes of presentation (*Arten des Gegebenseins*). Besides these purely Platonic entities, certain *constructed* entities also present things to us. For example, pictures do. Certain *socially* constructed entities also function in this capacity; the most prominent are linguistic entities. Indeed, linguistic entities provide the only access most of us have to various historical figures. These linguistic entities have the important feature of being *public*, shared by whole communities. Names are one kind of linguistic entity that provide us with this kind of access to objects.[34]

This suggests that certain Frege-style puzzles may be dealt with by relying on such non-Platonic modes of presentation. (I will use double-quoted expressions to denote such names: "Hesperus", "Phosphorus", etc.) The object "Hesperus" presents = Hesperus = Phosphorus = the object "Phosphorus" presents. This is so despite the fact that these two non-Platonic modes are distinct (i.e., "Hesperus" ≠ "Phosphorus").

The key idea is that relevant logical operations should be defined for all modes of presentation, non-Platonic as well as Platonic. So, in particular, the

---

[34] In what follows, names will be understood, not as mere phonological or orthographic types, but as fine-grained entities whose existence is an empirical fact and for which it is essential that they name what they do. For example, Cicero the Illinois town and Cicero the famous orator share a name in the phonological or orthographic sense, but not in the fine-grained sense. In the latter sense, but not the former, the existence of the two names is an empirical matter: the name of the town is fairly new; the name of the orator is very old. Given that the name of the town exists, it is essential to it that it name the town; likewise, given that the name of the orator exists, it is essential to it that it name the orator. This conception meshes with Kripke's rigid-designator theory of names. See Kripke (1980: 8 n. 9), Kaplan (1989: 603 ff.), Bealer (1993*b*: 35 f) Fine (1994).

operation of descriptive predication may take as arguments, say, the property of being a physical object and the non-Platonic mode "Hesperus". The result of this descriptive predication would be a proposition. Likewise, for being a physical object and "Phosphorus". The point is that these non-Platonic modes—as opposed to descriptive properties obtained from them by means of *the*—are the arguments in these descriptive predications.

The resulting two propositions have the following salient features. First, as noted, they are distinct (since "Hesperus" and "Phosphorus" are distinct). Second, they are necessary, reflecting Kripke's doctrine that every physical object is *necessarily* a physical object. Third, they are distinct from all propositions expressible by the use of definite descriptions (with or without actuality operators); in other words, they have *no* descriptive content (except, of course, for that associated with the predicate 'physical object'). Finally, these non-Platonic modes of presentation are neither *in* nor *parts* of these propositions. These propositions are seamless; only in our logical analyses do these modes appear.

Taken together, these features are exactly the salient features of the proposition that Hesperus is a physical object and the proposition that Phosphorus is a physical object. This suggests the hypothesis that they *are* these propositions. If this is correct, the analogous thing will hold for identity propositions of the sort responsible for Frege's puzzle itself. For example, the logical analysis of the proposition that Hesperus = Phosphorus will be a descriptive predication involving both "Hesperus" and "Phosphorus", whereas the logical analysis of the proposition that Hesperus = Hesperus will only involve "Hesperus". This ensures that the former proposition is nondescriptive, necessary, and a posteriori, while the latter is nondescriptive, necessary, but a priori. We thus have a provisional solution to this instance of Frege's puzzle.

I do not say that all instances of Frege's puzzle (or even the above instance) have exactly this style of solution. What I do claim (Bealer, forthcoming) is that, by using this and certain other techniques provided by the nonreductive algebraic framework, all instances have solutions. If so, theories that deny the existence of necessary a posteriori propositions would be baseless.

3 Rationalist Modal Epistemology

With an adequate logical framework in place, we are now ready to outline a moderate rationalist account of modal epistemology. Central to this account of our modal knowledge is an analysis of what it is to understand one's concepts, which will be sketched in section 3.1. This account, in turn, leads in section 3.2 to an account of our a priori knowledge of *categories*, an account that can then be used to explain our knowledge of a posteriori necessities of the kind discussed by SE. Finally, these accounts of the source and justification of our modal knowledge will be applied in section 3.3 to the question of modal error.

3.1 *Moderate Rationalism and Understanding Our Concepts*

I argued (Bealer 1992) that intuitions are in fact evidence. And in Bealer 1987 and 1996 I argued that intuition is in fact a *basic* source of evidence, and that the only satisfactory explanation of this fact is provided by *modal reliabilism*: the doctrine that something counts as a basic source of evidence iff there is an appropriate kind of modal tie between its deliverances and the truth. Modal reliabilism implies a form of moderate rationalism and an associated autonomy of the a priori disciplines. But why should the indicated tie to the truth exist? The answer is provided by the analysis of what it is to understand one's concepts. Giving this analysis creates an exegetical dilemma—either to give a very compressed sketch or to provide a lengthy exegesis and accompanying justification. In this setting, I have opted for the former, being all too aware of its shortcomings.[35]

There are two senses in which a subject can be said to possess a concept. First, a weak nominal sense:

> A subject possesses a given concept at least nominally iff the subject has natural propositional attitudes toward propositions that have that concept as a constituent content.

Possessing a concept in this sense is compatible with what Tyler Burge (1979) calls misunderstanding and incomplete understanding of a concept ('misunderstanding' for cases where there are errors in the subject's understanding of the concept, and 'incomplete understanding' for cases where there are gaps), and it is compatible with having concepts partly in virtue of the mere attribution practices of third-party interpreters. Second, there is a robust sense of concept possession, which requires *understanding* the concept:

> A subject understands a concept iff (i) the subject at least nominally possesses the concept and (ii) the subject does not do this with misunderstanding or incomplete understanding or merely by virtue of satisfying our attribution practices or in any other such manner.

---

[35] I give a more complete discussion in Bealer 1987 and 1999, and the full presentation in my forthcoming book *Philosophical Limits of Science*.

I will use the technical term 'determinately understand a concept' for this kind of concept possession.

Examples provide the basis for our analysis. Here is an illustration (see Bealer 1987). Suppose that in her journal a sincere, wholly normal, attentive woman introduces *through use* (not stipulation) a new term 'multigon'. She applies the term to various closed plane figures having several sides (pentagons, octagons, chiliagons, etc.). Suppose her term expresses some definite concept—the concept of being a multigon—and that she determinately understands this concept. By chance, she has neither applied her term 'multigon' to triangles and rectangles nor withheld it from them; the question has just not come up. Eventually, however, she considers it. Her cognitive conditions (intelligence, etc.) are good, and she determinately understands these concepts. Suppose that the property of being a multigon is either the property of being a closed, straight-sided plane figure, or being a closed, straight-sided plane figure with five or more sides. (Each alternative is listed under 'polygon' in my desk *Webster's*.) Then, intuitively, when the woman entertains the question, she would have an intuition that it *is* possible for a triangle or a rectangle to be a multigon if and only if being a multigon = being a closed, straight-sided plane figure. Alternatively, she would have an intuition that it is *not* possible for a triangle or a rectangle to be a multigon if and only if being a multigon = being a closed, straight-sided plane figure with five or more sides. That is, the woman would have *truth-tracking* intuitions. If she did not, the right thing to say would be that either the woman does not really understand one or more of the concepts involved, or her cognitive conditions are not really good.

Our judgments about other relevant examples also fit this pattern. Naturally, these judgments are defeasible, given that all sorts of incidental factors might in misleading ways affect a person's dispositions to have such truth-tracking intuitions. Consistent with this, however, are the following ideas. The person (or an appropriate epistemic *Doppelgänger* of the person) would have *ever more reliable* intuitions if his cognitive conditions (intelligence, etc.) were to improve and his auxiliary conceptual repertory were to enlarge (given, of course, that in the process of these developments there is no shift in the way the person understands his original concepts or propositions involving them). Thus, as the person's cognitive conditions improve and his auxiliary conceptual repertory enlarges, the degree to which the person's intuitions are truth-tracking will ever more accurately reflect how well the person understands the relevant concepts. This suggests that determinate understanding can be explicated in terms of the associated metaphysical possibility of this sort of truth-tracking intuition: determinate understanding is that mode of understanding that constitutes the categorical base of this possibility.[36] I will work up to the final analysis in stages.

3.1.1 *A Priori Stability*

Suppose x understands a given proposition p in some mode m (determinately, indeterminately, etc.). (For brevity, I will say that x understands p m-ly.) Then, I will say that x settles with *a priori stability* that p is true iff, for cognitive conditions of some level *l* and for some conceptual repertory *c*, (1) x has cognitive conditions of level *l* and conceptual repertory *c*, and x attempts to elicit intuitions relevant to the question of whether p is true, and x seeks a theoretical systematization based on those intuitions, and that systematization affirms that p is true, and all the while x understands p m-ly, and (2) necessarily, for cognitive conditions of any level *l'* at least as great as *l* and for any conceptual repertory *c'*, which includes *c*, if x has cognitive conditions of level *l'* and conceptual repertory *c'*, and x attempts to elicit intuitions bearing on p and seeks a theoretical systematization based on those intuitions, and all the while x understands p m-ly, then that systematization also affirms that p is true.[37] In other words, once x achieves cognitive conditions *l* and conceptual repertory *c*, theoretical systematizations of x's intuitions always yield the same verdict on p as long as p continues to be understood m-ly throughout. That is, p thereafter always gets settled the same way.

Using this notion of a priori stability we arrive at the following candidate analysis:

> determinate understanding = the mode m of understanding such that, necessarily, for all x and property-identities p understood m-ly by x, p is true iff it is possible for x to settle with a priori stability that p is true.[38]

[36] Some people have objected that relying in this way on intuition's tie to the truth is unacceptable, for it simply amounts to invoking a 'dormative virtue'. The analogy fails, however, for in the present context the explanandum is a modal fact—i.e., intuition's qualified *necessary* tie to the truth. And necessities call for a very different sort of explanation from that called for by contingencies. In the explanation of necessities, it is wholly appropriate to articulate essences, and it is of the essence of determinate understanding of concepts that intuitions involving those concepts be correct—modulo suitably good cognitive conditions, notably intelligence. This is compatible with its being of the essence of intelligence to have the complementary property. In fact, this complementarity is paradigmatic of functionally definable sets of basic (i.e., non-Cambridge) properties.

[37] When I speak of higher-level cognitive conditions, I do not presuppose that there is always commensurability. In order for the proposal to succeed, I need only consider levels of cognitive conditions *l'* and *l* such that, with respect to *every* relevant dimension, *l'* is at least as great *l*.

[38] By property-identities p, I mean the following. Suppose a primitive predicate 'F' expresses a given concept. Then the associated property-identities p are propositions expressible with sentences of the form 'The property of being F = the property of being A', or the denials of such sentences (where A is some possible formula). The reason for the restriction to property-identities is to avoid certain potential counter-examples to the definition (and, in turn, to moderate rationalism).

The sufficiency claim in this biconditional is a *correctness* property. The necessity claim is a *completeness* property. The correctness property tells us about the potential *quality* of x's intuitions: it is metaphysically possible for x to get into a cognitive situation such that, from that point on, theoretical systematizations of x's intuitions yield only the truth regarding p, given that x understands p m-ly throughout. The completeness property tells us about the potential *quantity* of x's intuitions: it is metaphysically possible for x (or a qualitative epistemic counterpart of x) to have enough intuitions to reach a priori stability regarding the question of p's truth, given that x understands p m-ly throughout.

3.1.2 *Scientific Essentialism*

As it stands, the completeness clause clashes with scientific essentialism, which tells us that there are property-identities that are essentially a posteriori. For example, this clause wrongly requires that x be able to settle with a priori stability that the property of being water = the property of being H_2O. To solve this problem, we need to weaken the completeness clause so that it requires only *categorial mastery*. The easiest way to do this is to replace the original completeness requirement with the weaker requirement that it merely be possible for x to settle with a priori stability that there could exist some true proposition that is a twin-earth counterpart of p.[39] Thus:

determinate understanding = the mode m of understanding such that, necessarily, for all x and property-identities p understood m-ly by x,

(a) p is true *if* it is possible for x to settle with a priori stability that p is true.
(b) p is true *only if* it is possible for x to settle with a priori stability that p has a counterpart that is true.

Note that, if a test proposition p is *semantically stable*, it is entirely immune to scientific essentialism. Consequently, for semantically stable property-identities, the weakened completeness clause entails the strong completeness clause of the earlier analysis, which in turn implies a form of moderate rationalism and autonomy of the a priori disciplines.

3.1.3 *Anti-individualism*

This weakening of the completeness clause, however, creates a problem concerning the *noncategorial* content of our concepts. Suppose x has mere categorial mastery of a certain pair of concepts—say, the concept of being a beech and the

---

[39] For example, if p is the proposition that being water = being H_2O, x would need to be able to settle with a priori stability that there could be a twin-earth relative to which there is a true proposition that is the counterpart of the proposition that being water = being H_2O.

concept of being an elm. None the less, x might not be able to determine whether trees are beeches or elms, no matter how long and carefully he studies them. In this case, x certainly would not understand these concepts determinately (although the above analysis implies, wrongly, that he would). His 'web of belief' would be too sparse. What x needs is, roughly, enough information to 'begin doing the science' of beeches and elms.

We can resolve this difficulty by making use of the idea of *truth-absorption*. If x has categorial mastery of certain of his concepts but none the less does not understand them determinately, then, by absorbing ever more true beliefs, x will eventually switch out of his deficient mode of understanding and come to understand those concepts determinately. By contrast, people who already understand their concepts determinately can always absorb more true beliefs without switching out of their determinate understanding. This suggests the following:

> determinate understanding = the mode m of understanding such that, necessarily, for all x and all p understood m-ly by x,
>
> (a) p is true *if* it is possible for x to settle with a priori stability that p is true.
>
> (b.i) p is true *only if* it is possible for x to settle with a priori stability that p has a counterpart that is true.   (for property-identities p)
>
> (b.ii) p is true *only if* it is possible for x to believe m-ly that p is true.
>   (for p believable by x)[40]

The reason why this analysis is successful is that, absent intuition, one's web of belief is the default basis on which determinateness rides. Where there is the possibility of a priori intuitions, however, they are determinative.

Thus, to understand a proposition determinately is to understand it in a certain mode. What distinguishes this mode from other natural modes of understanding are three essential properties:

> (a) correctness
> (b.i) categorial completeness
> (b.ii) noncategorial completeness

(a) A mode m has the correctness property iff, necessarily, for all individuals x and all propositions p that x understands in mode m, p is true *if* it is possible for x (or someone starting out in qualitatively the same sort of epistemic situation as x) to settle with a priori stability that p is true, all the while understanding p in mode m.

---

[40] Perhaps 'believe' should be strengthened to 'rationally believe', and p restricted to propositions that x can rationally believe.

(b.i) A mode m has the categorial completeness property iff, necessarily, for all individuals x and all true (positive or negative) property-identities p which x understands in mode m, it is possible for x (or someone starting out in qualitatively the same sort of epistemic situation) to settle with a priori stability that there exists some true twin-earth-style counterpart of p, all the while understanding p in mode m.

(b.ii) A mode m has the noncategorial completeness property iff, necessarily, for all individuals x and all true propositions p that x understands in mode m and that x could believe, it is possible for x to believe p while still understanding it in mode m.

3.2 *Categories*

How does one justify the step from the empirical information that all and only samples of water are samples of H_2O (i.e., from the coextensiveness of water and H_2O) to the *modal* conclusion that, necessarily, water = H_2O? One bridges this 'modal gap' by combining the empirical information with *intuitions about hypothetical cases*—for example, twin-earth cases (see Bealer 1987).[41] What accounts for these intuitions? The analysis (just given) of what it is to understand one's concepts provides an answer. But in the case of these crucial intuitions still more light can be shed by an idealized rational reconstruction (ibid.).

The first step is to divide our concepts as follows: (1) category concepts (predication, number, identity, property, relation, proposition, quality, quantity, stuff, compositional stuff, functional stuff, etc.); (2) content concepts (phenomenal concepts and concepts of psychological attitudes); (3) naturalistic concepts. What distinguishes the concepts in the first two categories from those in the third is that they are *semantically stable*. The idea is that our mastery of these semantically stable category and content concepts is what drives the concrete-case intuitions (twin earth, etc.) that bridge the modal gap.

Consider the following categorial principle: if a sample of a given purely compositional stuff has such-and-such composition, then, necessarily, all other samples of that purely compositional stuff also have that composition. This principle is semantically stable, so the analysis of what it is to understand our concepts tells us that if we determinately understand the concepts involved in the principle, then our intuitions concerning the principle will be reliable. Accordingly, the principle can be known a priori.

---

[41] Not by the implicit descriptivist route of Jackson and Chalmers. Incidentally, a dialectically critical datum in the mind–body debate is that we simply lack crucial psychophysical analogues of these twin-earth intuitions (see Bealer 1994).

Now by simple universal instantiation on this principle, we get the following principle: if water is a purely compositional stuff, then if a sample of water has such-and-such composition, then, necessarily, all other samples of water also have that composition. But this principle in turn implies the following: if water is a purely compositional stuff, *then* if all and only samples of water here on earth have such-and-such composition, then if there were a twin-earth that is macroscopically like earth but on which the samples corresponding to the samples of water on earth had composition so-and-so ($\neq$ composition such-and-such), those samples would not be samples of water. Instantiating on 'such-and-such composition' and 'composition so-and-so', we obtain: if water is a purely compositional stuff, *then* if all and only samples of water here on earth have H_2O as their composition, then if there were a twin earth that is macroscopically like earth but on which the samples corresponding to the samples of water on earth had XYZ ($\neq H_2O$) as their composition, those samples would not be samples of water. The consequent of this principle (following '*then*') states the chief twin-earth intuition used in the defense of SE.

But what about the antecedent of this principle: namely, that water is a purely compositional stuff? This principle is itself necessary, but how is it known? A simple answer would follow if we were to make the simplifying assumption that 'water' was originally introduced by means of a Kripkean baptism, in which the baptizer picked out water by, among other things, identifying its category: namely, purely compositional stuff. On this oversimplified account, the baptizer would then be in a position to know a priori that, if it exists, water is a purely compositional stuff. This a priori knowledge would be an instance of the kind of a priori knowledge one gets when giving any stipulative definition. Now, through use, the term 'water' enters the vocabulary of other speakers, so that whoever *determinately understands* the term will then be in a position to elicit a priori intuitions supporting the thesis that water is a purely compositional stuff. By this process, the baptizer's original a priori knowledge is transmitted to other speakers. (A similar story holds for 'H_2O'.)

Of course, to come to know the *specific* SE necessity that all and only samples of water are samples of the purely compositional stuff H_2O (and therefore that, necessarily, water $= H_2O$), something more is needed. We must supplement the above a priori knowledge with the a posteriori scientific knowledge that all and only samples of water here on earth are samples of the purely compositional stuff H_2O. This blending of a priori knowledge and a posteriori knowledge is what accounts for knowledge that is both necessary and a posteriori.

Next we remove the oversimplifications in this picture. One obvious source of oversimplification is the fact that the baptism story is wholly implausible in the case of a common noun so central to practical life as 'water'. But let us

maintain this fiction a moment longer, for the main source of oversimplification lies elsewhere: namely, in the fact that 'water' was successfully put into use
long before anyone had any idea that various standard samples of water were
composed of a single purely compositional stuff. So it is implausible that any
baptizer would (on pain of vacuity) have restricted the reference of 'water' to a
purely compositional stuff: for all the baptizer knew, there was no such stuff.
But still, in fixing the reference of 'water', our (fictitious) baptizer would have
needed to invoke *some* relevant categorial concept, if only to distinguish water
from, say, the *functional stuff* drink and the water-like *macroscopic stuff* (whose
actual extension is the same as the actual extension of the purely compositional
stuff water), and so forth. The way to do this would have been by means of an
implicit categorial concept that, when analyzed, is equivalent, not to the fundamental concept of being a compositional stuff, but to an ordered conjunction of default categorial conditionals. For example, the concept of being the
stuff S such that (1) if all and only samples of S in our acquaintance are samples
of some purely compositional stuff, then S is that purely compositional stuff;
(2) if there is no such purely compositional stuff and if, instead, all and only
instances of S in our acquaintance are instances of some not too complicated
impure compositional stuff (akin to the impure compositional stuff jade), then
S is that impure compositional stuff; (3) if there is no such pure or impure compositional stuff and if, instead, all and only instances of S in our acquaintance are
instances of some not unwieldy macroscopic stuff, then S is that macroscopic
stuff; and so forth. (This illustration is merely heuristic.)

Suppose, then, that our baptizer introduced the term 'water' by means of
some such implicit categorial concept. By virtue of this, the baptizer would
know a priori that water falls under that concept. Then the baptizer would still
be in a position to have all the pro-SE twin-earth intuitions that we are trying
to explain. For our baptizer would be in a position to know a priori that water
satisfies the conjunction of default conditionals. And, much as before, the pro-
SE intuitions are immediate logical consequences of this analysis plus the relevant corresponding general categorial principles. In particular, the hypothesis
that all and only samples of water in our acquaintance are samples of a purely
compositional stuff is an instance of the antecedent of the first conditional in
the conjunction of default conditionals and, at the same time, the antecedent of
the twin-earth conditional.

Now, just as in the simpler setting, the baptizer's more refined a priori
categorial knowledge about water (i.e., the knowledge that, when analyzed,
is equivalent to the ordered conjunction of default conditionals) can be transmitted through use to other speakers—specifically, to those who have come
not just to use the word 'water', but to understand it determinately. Then these

speakers would likewise be in a position to have all the indicated pro-SE twin-earth intuitions. The rest follows *mutatis mutandis*.

Finally, let us remove the fiction that the term 'water' was introduced by a Kripkean baptizer. This is an unrealistic picture of how common nouns (in this case, naturalistic mass terms) typically function in natural language; rather, the community of speakers over time repeatedly reaffirms—and sometimes refines—the conventions governing the use of such terms. This process of reaffirmation and revision determines the implicit a priori categorial content of such terms, and having the potential (in relevantly good cognitive conditions) for a priori knowledge of that categorial content is a necessary condition of a speaker's determinate understanding of such terms (as was made clear in our analysis of determinate understanding).

The above picture may be generalized to all other terms to which SE is applicable. Moreover, the account may be used to explain further features of our intuitions—or, more accurately, our lack of intuitions—concerning natural kinds. For example, it explains why we lack intuitions that, *per impossibile*, would underwrite a priori knowledge of necessities that SE deems to be a posteriori.[42] For example, why do we lack an intuition that it is metaphysically impossible for there to be a sample of water containing no hydrogen? Our rational reconstruction provides an answer. *The general categorial principles that would underwrite such natural kind intuitions intuitively do not hold*. Specifically, the proposition in this water-without-hydrogen example is an instance of the following general categorial principle: for all purely compositional stuffs W and U, it is metaphysically impossible for there to be a sample of W that contains no U. But this general categorial principle is intuitively false. According to our rational reconstruction, to have an intuition that it is metaphysically impossible for there to be a sample of water containing no hydrogen, that intuition would need to be underwritten by this (or a kindred) general categorial principle concerning purely compositional stuffs. Since it is not, we lack such an intuition. So goes the explanation.

I will close with a question about modal error, which I will then try to answer in section 3.3. Consider the following false modal proposition: it is metaphysically possible for there to be a puddle of water containing no hydrogen. This proposition is an instance of the following general categorial principle: for all purely compositional stuffs W and U, it is metaphysically possible for there to be a sample of W containing no U. But, like its instance, this categorial principle is intuitively false. (On the contrary, the following general

---

[42] I certainly lack such intuitions. If someone reports having them, this would be an instance of the phenomenon considered in my example (4) in Bealer 1998: 28.

categorial principle is intuitively true: it is metaphysically possible for there to be compositional stuffs W and U such that, necessarily, every sample of W contains U.) Because the cited general categorial principle is intuitively false, the above explanation scheme predicts that we should *not* have an intuition that it is possible for there to be a puddle of water containing no hydrogen. The problem is that, prior to learning of twin-earth and the other pro-SE examples, a great many of us *did* have this possibility intuition and many others like it. How can our intuition have been erroneous in this way?

3.3 *Modal Error II: Categorial Misunderstanding*

Stephen Yablo (1993) presents an account of modal error—specifically, how anti-SE modal intuitions can be in error. (Yablo's discussion is stated in the idiom of 'conceivability' and 'inconceivability'; I will be reformulating it in what follows in the idiom of modal intuition, as defended in section 1.2.) Yablo is not concerned with errors resulting from conceptual illusions, limitations on intelligence, inattentiveness, and so forth. Nor is he concerned with the allegedly contradictory intuitions that exercised Kripke (e.g., the intuition that the identity of Hesperus and Phosphorus is necessary if true and the intuition that it could have turned out either way whether Hesperus = Phosphorus). We saw in section 1.4 that Kripke's worry dissolves as soon as we remember the distinction between the 'could'-of-metaphysical-possibility and the 'could'-of-qualitative-epistemic-neutrality and apply our little 'translation' test. Yablo's underlying concern is rather with full-fledged errors in intuitions about metaphysical possibility that arise in the context of scientific essentialism. Yablo holds that these errors have two potential sources, in each case mistaken *beliefs*: (a) mistaken a posteriori beliefs (e.g., someone who mistakenly believes that Hesperus ≠ Phosphorus might have the intuition that Hesperus could outlast Phosphorus) or (b) mistaken beliefs regarding the relationship between such a posteriori beliefs and associated modal truths (someone might deny that, if Hesperus = Phosphorus, then necessarily Hesperus cannot outlast Phosphorus). I am here less interested in class (a), for practiced dialecticians have the ability to proceed using exclusively 'pure' a priori intuitions: namely, those that survive even under the hypothesis that such a posteriori beliefs (both pro and con) are unjustified or mistaken.[43]

---

[43] In fact, by exercising this ability in the context of pure a priori philosophizing, one's natural kind intuitions will actually diminish, thereby all but eliminating disagreements of the sort associated with class (a).

How do people come to have erroneous modal intuitions belonging to the second class? Yablo's answer is that they are somehow produced by underlying class (b) beliefs, which, by hypothesis, are false. But it is plausible that the preponderance of such class (b) beliefs, albeit false, would at least be *justified*, and, as we know, such justification should ultimately be a matter of intuitions—presumably, intuitions about relevant concrete cases (twin-earth, etc.). But since a person's class (b) beliefs, which are justified by these concrete-case intuitions, are, by hypothesis, false, presumably a number of these justifying intuitions must themselves be false. What explains why these justifying intuitions go wrong? If the explanation is that they too are produced by false class (b) beliefs, we risk going in a circle. It seems, therefore, that we need something besides, or at least in addition to, Yablo's belief-based explanation of class (b) intuition errors.

Suppose two empirically well-informed, dialectically skilled philosophers have conflicting concrete-case SE intuitions (twin-earth, etc.). For example, suppose Putnam has the intuition that in his twin-earth example the samples of XYZ would not be water, whereas Carnap has the contrary intuition. One of them is in error. How are we to explain this error without going in a circle?

Our analysis of what it is to understand a concept determinately (and, specifically, the role of categorial mastery in that analysis) provides the missing pieces. One candidate explanation using these ideas is that either Putnam or Carnap simply does not determinately understand—indeed, misunderstands—the concept of being water. In some cases, this is no doubt the right explanation, but surely not in the case of Hilary Putnam or Rudolph Carnap. Certainly, *they* do not misunderstand the everyday concept of being water! For them, a subtler explanation is therefore needed. What has happened is that Carnap is the subject of a *local* categorial misunderstanding of the concept; that is, his categorial mastery of the concept is locally disrupted. An example will help to explain what I mean.

A student of mine, musing about prime numbers, realized that he did not know whether negative integers could be prime or, indeed, whether in the definition of prime number the domain is restricted to natural numbers or whether it includes all integers. Fortunately, he had a firm intuition that primes are divisible only by themselves and one, and he had the intuition that every negative integer, $-n$, is the product of itself and the number one and is also the product of n and -1, from which he inferred that negative integers cannot be prime. Then he had the intuition that 3 is prime but that $3 = 1 \times 3$ and $3 = -1 \times -3$, from which he concluded that only natural numbers were permitted in the definition of prime. In view of this performance, the student plainly *understood* the concept of being prime all along; specifically, he had full categorial mastery of it. What went wrong early on was that he suffered a *local* lapse in his categorial mastery. His a priori (dialectical) process, however, was able to correct this lapse, therein manifesting his categorial mastery of the concept.

Carnap is in a somewhat similar situation. Not only does he have the intuition that, on twin earth, samples of XYZ would be water, he also would (if asked) have the general categorial intuition that water is a macroscopic stuff (individuated by its macroscopic properties). But this categorial misunderstanding is (we may suppose) only local: it is correctable by the a priori (dialectical) process—specifically, by careful examination of further cases, say, *other* sorts of twin-earth cases (e.g., the diamond and cubic zirconium twin-earth case[44]), and by systematization of the results. That is, left to his own a priori devices, Carnap would in the fullness of time become a scientific essentialist.

The point is that, at least in a large family of cases, the quality of one's categorial mastery holds the key, not only to the correctness of one's intuitions, but also to their *incorrectness*; furthermore, whether or not that mastery has lapsed only locally is the key to whether or not it is correctable a priori. And this, of course, is the solution to the problem at the close of the previous section. For, presumably, if Carnap has the intuition that in the twin-earth example the samples of XYZ would be water, he would likewise have the intuition that it is possible for there to be a puddle of water containing no hydrogen. The source of the intuition error in each case is the same local categorial misunderstanding.

The larger moral of this discussion is thus that, besides Yablo's class (a) and class (b) belief-based errors, there are two other classes: (c) those resulting from local categorial misunderstanding and (d) those resulting from out-and-out categorial misunderstanding.

4 Modality and the Mind–Body Problem

In this closing section, I shall examine the bearing that the above formulation of moderate rationalism has on modal arguments in philosophy of mind.[45]

4.1 *Hill's Critique and Categorial Misunderstanding*

Christopher Hill (1997) gives a new style of criticism of the familiar modal arguments (e.g., Kripke's) against the Identity Theory. His idea is that the

---

[44] The diamond-appearing samples on twin earth are samples of cubic zirconium (the comparatively cheap material from which fake diamonds are commonly made on earth). Would Carnap really have had the intuition that those samples are diamonds?!

[45] See also the closing paragraph of sect. 1.3.

possibility intuitions used in these anti-materialist arguments belong to a large, general class of possibility intuitions that are united by a shared form of psychological explanation and that are typified by error-prone intuitions of the kind we have just been considering (e.g., that it is possible for there to be water without hydrogen, heat without molecular motion, etc.). Because of this shared pathology Hill concludes from this that the possibility intuitions upon which these anti-materialist arguments are based lose their evidential force and that, consequently, those arguments do not go through.

But in section 3.3 we saw that, even though this type of possibility intuition (water without hydrogen, etc.) can be subject to error resulting from local categorial misunderstanding (as in the Carnap example), the error is typically correctable a priori (as long as the concepts involved really are understood). Indeed, such intuitions typically just disappear when one submits them to the sort of pure a priori dialectical process mentioned early in section 3.3 (and n. 43). So, for those who have already gone through this a priori process, the threat of this kind of anti-SE modal error pretty much disappears, at least for mainstream SE concepts (water, heat, gold, etc.) and concepts closely akin to them. Because intuitions in this family are thus not subject to any in principle pathology, they are immune to Hill's attack, and for those of us with this kind of SE dialectical background, it is perfectly legitimate to rely on them evidentially. Furthermore, in connection with our overall theme of moderate rationalism, the specific kind of pathology involved in these pre-SE style errors pertains entirely to semantically unstable intuitions and is not found in semantically stable modal intuitions. (This, of course, is not to say that the latter intuitions are immune to error.)

Despite this happy outcome, however, there is still an SE worry concerning certain anti-materialist modal intuitions with which Hill is concerned.

4.2   *Yablo's Disembodiment Argument*

Stephen Yablo (1990) gives an argument for the metaphysical possibility of his own disembodiment. The argument proceeds in three steps. First, he elicits the intuition that his disembodiment is indeed possible. Second, he uses his belief-based account of modal error to argue that, dialectically, anyone wishing to undermine the evidential force of this intuition must show that it has been corrupted either by a false class (a) belief or by a false class (b) belief. Third, he argues that his materialist opponents cannot do this without violating the presumption that an intuition is correct unless an independent reason for doubting it can be given.

I will make two points. First, many people report not having any intuitions like Yablo's, and they report having the opposite intuitions. Moreover, many people who do have intuitions like Yablo's find themselves unable to shake their suspicions about them. For these reasons, one should hardly expect this disembodiment argument to produce many converts; to win converts, anti-materialists will need to provide additional argument.

Second, since 'I' is paradigmatically semantically *unstable*, so is the intuition report 'I could exist as a purely mental being'. So the usual SE question is then apt: what category of thing is 'hit' by use of the semantically unstable term 'I'? A *person*, to be sure. But consider a parallel case: although we know that 'water' hits a stuff, SE teaches us that one can (as in the Carnap case) be locally in the dark about what *subcategory* of stuff is hit (compositional, functional, macroscopic, etc.; see section 3.2). So, too, we could be locally in the dark with 'I': what prevents the subcategory from being that of *essentially embodied person* (at least for some utterances of 'I')? SE seems to open up this threat, and something needs to be done to close it.

We know that, at least initially, intuitions involving semantically unstable concepts are often prone to errors of the sort produced by local categorial misunderstandings and that, as a result, the presumption of correctness should at that point be suspended for such intuitions. Nevertheless, we also saw that this presumption should be restored for intuitions involving (concepts closely akin to) mainstream SE concepts as soon as one has gone through the relevant a priori process (twin-earth examples, etc.). Now, given that we have already gone through this process for mainstream SE concepts, is there, as a result, a presumption of correctness for our 'I' intuitions?

Consider an analogy. Unlike water's categorial profile, fire's remains puzzling (at least to me), despite our SE background. Is fire a process (akin to digestion and photosynthesis), a stuff (as the ancients seemed to think), a state (much as liquid is a state of matter), or what? The problem is not, I gather, a lack of relevant empirical information. In view of this, it is at least plausible that many (most?) of us suffer from some kind of local categorial misunderstanding or incomplete understanding of the concept of fire. This seems to provide reason for withholding (at least for now) the presumption of correctness from various modal intuitions about fire. Can there be fire without there being some physical object that is burning? Many people have the negative intuition. Others positive. (Presumably, some ancients would have been among the latter, for if fire were really an element, fire without any corresponding burning physical object ought to be possible.)

Now it is not implausible that we are in a somewhat similar situation with respect to the subcategory of 'I'. If this is right, our dialectical situation differs from that which Yablo describes. Specifically, at least for now, the presumption of correctness is rightly questioned for the pivotal semantically unstable intuition that I could exist as a purely mental being, and for this reason, Yablo's disembodiment argument at least supplemental support.[46]

4.3   *Two-Dimensional Modal Arguments against Materialism*

4.3.1   *Chalmers's Zombie Argument*

Whereas the possibility of disembodiment would undermine the thesis that physical properties are substantive necessary conditions for mental properties, the possibility of zombies would undermine the thesis that they are sufficient conditions. But only the right sort of zombies would have this effect: namely, zombies that are *perfect physical duplicates* of us—that is, zombies that have *exactly the same* physical properties as we have. Of course, the weak zombie intuition that there could be zombies that, physically, are *functional* duplicates refutes various forms of materialistic functionalism (e.g., that of Lewis, Harman, Shoemaker). But this intuition does not refute traditional materialism generally; in particular, it does not refute materialism of the traditional *matter-chauvinist* variety (espoused by certain Identity Theorists and also by brute-supervenience advocates). These 'right wing' materialists (as opposed to their more liberal-minded functionalist cousins) believe that, amongst the various arrays of physical properties which, physically, are functionally equivalent to one another, only certain arrays (perhaps even some unique array) are sufficient conditions for our actual mental properties. What makes the difference is the kind of matter involved: it must be outright identical to the kind of matter we have in the actual world.[47]

---

[46] There is another tension in Yablo's philosophy of mind. On the one hand, he defends the metaphysical possibility of his own disembodiment. On the other hand, he adopts the supervenience of the mental on the physical as a (for him intuitive) premise in his account of mental causation (1992). But if it is possible for embodied beings—say, you and I—to be disembodied, shouldn't it also be possible for us to switch bodies with no accompanying purely physical change? My intuition of the former possibility seems to have no more nor less evidential weight than my intuition of the latter. If such body switching is possible, however, supervenience would fail: for example, after the switch your original body would have various mental properties which it lacks in the actual world: e.g., being the body of a certain thinking being, namely, *me*. A related source of tension is that there are people who have anti-supervenience intuitions that are just as strong as Yablo's disembodiment intuitions. It seems that Yablo's method would direct these people to give their anti-supervenience intuitions the same evidential weight that Yablo gives his disembodiment intuitions, thereby threatening stalemate between these people and Yablo over supervenience.

[47] Neither the weak zombie intuition (the possibility of physical functional duplicates having no mental properties) nor the strong zombie intuition (the possibility of perfect physical duplicates of us having no mental properties) is anywhere close to being universal and, of course, the reliability of these intuitions is hotly challenged. (Compare these intuitions with the multiple-realizability

Even though a full refutation of materialism requires the indicated strong zombie intuition, Chalmers's anti-materialist zombie argument is built on a zombie intuition that seems distinctly weaker (even though it is not as weak as the anti-functionalist zombie intuition). Chalmers's intuition may be reported thus: the primary intension (i.e., 'primary proposition') of the sentence 'Such-and-such physical properties are instantiated even though no qualitative conscious properties are' is possibly true. Here 'such-and-such physical properties' is meant to be a specification of the physical properties instantiated in the actual world.[48] This specification would of course contain various microphysical expressions—'electron', 'charge', and the like. For simplicity, let us assume that this specification is entirely microphysical; doing so will not affect the argument substantially.

Two-dimensional semantics is designed so that, typically, the primary intension and the secondary intension of natural kind predicates differ markedly from one another. If this is so for any of the expressions just indicated, then the mere fact that the primary intension of 'Such-and-such physical properties . . .' is possible does not tell us whether the *secondary* intension is possible. In turn, it does not tell us whether it is possible for such-and-such physical properties to be instantiated even though no conscious properties are. But, as noted, materialism will be refuted only if these very physical properties (electron, etc.)—not some contingently associated properties (primary intensions)—can be instantiated absent mental properties. Ironically, the whole point of two-dimensionalism was to separate the meaning of natural kind expressions— 'water', 'heat', and, one would think, 'electron'—into two distinct kinds, primary and secondary. If two-dimensionalism does its job *uniformly*, Chalmers's intuition fails to refute materialism.

Chalmers is aware of this alleged 'wrong-intuition' problem and tries to show that 'it relies on an incorrect view of the semantics of physical terms' (1996: 135). According to Chalmers, 'Not only is reference to electrons fixed by the role that electrons play in a theory; the very concept of an electron is

intuition that there could be intelligence absent exactly our sort of complex electrochemical property.) For these reasons, most anti-materialists know that they will have few converts if their arguments depend on such intuitions—just as they know that they will have few converts if they rely on either the weak disembodiment intuition (that there could be a disembodied being) or the strong disembodiment intuition (that *we* could be disembodied).

[48] Recall that, for Chalmers, the primary intension ('primary proposition') of a sentence is possible iff it is true in some possible world iff it has the value True for some possible world. Note, also, that in Chalmers's framework, the above intuition is equivalent to the intuition that 'Such-and-such physical properties . . .' is epistemically possible. See sect. 1.5 and also the close of sect. 1.3.

defined by that role, which determines the application of the concept across all worlds' (1996: 136). If Chalmers were right about this, it would follow that in the case of 'electron' (and kindred terms), the secondary intension would be effectively the same as the primary intension. In this case, the secondary intension of the strong zombie sentence 'Such-and-such physical properties . . . ' would likewise be effectively the same as its primary intension. So, if the latter is possible, the former should be, too. In this event, Chalmers's intuition would refute materialism after all.[49]

But it is not his critic's view of the semantics of physical terms, but rather Chalmers's own view, that is unsatisfactory.[50] I mention three of its problems. First, the hypothesized deviation from normal two-dimensional semantics looks extremely *ad hoc*, and it is unexplained why there should be an about-face just at the point that it is needed to save the zombie argument. Second, since this semantics is committed to a Jackson-style implicit-theory descriptivism, it is refuted by the two dilemmas (see section 2.4.1) that plague the 'Platitudinous Conception' version of implicit descriptivism (for example, reminiscent of the people in communities c_1 and c_n, people who understand the term 'electron' can have very significant disagreements about the correct theory of electrons). The third problem may be brought out by means of an example.

Consider three worlds, w_1, w_2, w_3. In w_1 all particles have a certain property F that plays no identifiable causal role in the physical theory discoverable by

---

[49] I say 'effectively the same' because of the technicality that primary intensions are defined on centered worlds whereas secondary intensions are defined on ordinary (uncentered) worlds and, therefore, that primary and secondary intensions can never be identical. In what follows, I will for simplicity suppress the difference associated with this and related technicalities.

[50] True, Chalmers argues against the matter-chauvinists' view (that, in the case of 'electron', the primary and secondary intensions are different and, in turn, that the property of being an electron differs from the property of playing the electron role—i.e., the role electrons play in physical theory), and he does this by invoking the following claim: 'The notion of an electron that has all the extrinsic properties of actual protons does not appear to be coherent' (1996: 136). But his argument is a fallacy based on a confusion between necessary and sufficient conditions. Chalmers's matter-chauvinist opponents are free to agree with him that the indicated description of an electron is incoherent. Their point is that, even if all actual extrinsic electron properties were necessary for something's being an electron (thereby preventing electrons from having the envisaged extrinsic proton properties), these extrinsic electron properties would not be sufficient—something more is needed to be an electron. Chalmers's argument plainly does not touch this point. Given this, his argument does nothing to prevent our matter-chauvinists from going on to make the further claim that only the sum total of all these physical properties (including the 'something more') is sufficient for our conscious properties. Consequently, the matter-chauvinists' view of the body–mind relationship is also untouched by Chalmers's argument.

w_1's inhabitants. This holds, in particular, for the particles the inhabitants on w_1 call 'electrons'. Let us call these particles Felectrons. World w_2 is a kind Putnamian 'twin-earth world' of w_1: the particles in w_2 fall into the same number of kinds as those in w_1, and they interact with one another in the very same pattern as do the corresponding particles in w_1. There is a difference, however: namely, that instead of having property F, these particles have a certain property G. Like F in w_1, G plays no identifiable causal role in the physical theory discoverable by w_2's inhabitants. The particles these people call 'electrons' I will call Gelectrons. w_3 is a more or less symmetrical world. World w_3 may be thought of along the lines of Putnam's 'two-planet' twin-earth world. The particles on one half of w_3 (call it 'Rightland') are numerically the same as those in w_1: they are all F-particles (including Felectrons). The particles on the other half of w_3 (call it 'Leftland') are numerically the same as those in w_2: they are all G-particles (including Gelectrons). In interactions with one another, the F-particles behave exactly as they do in w_1; likewise, in interactions with one another, the G-particles behave exactly as they do in w_2. In interactions between F-particles and G-particles, however, something wholly novel occurs—say, mutual annihilation. In other words, the laws governing FF interactions in w_1 still govern them in w_3, and the laws governing GG interactions in w_2 still govern them in w_3. In addition to these laws, there are further laws governing FG interactions. (I believe it to be possible for all three sets of laws to hold in worlds w_1 and w_2 as well. On this scenario, the difference would be that GG-laws and FG-laws are uninstantiated in w_1, and FF-laws and FG-laws are uninstantiated in w_2. Although this is how I prefer to think of the example, this is not crucial.)

In the language of the 'Rightlanders' in w_3, would their term 'electron' apply to Gelectrons as well as Felectrons? Heavens no, Gelectrons actually destroy their paradigmatic electrons! Conversely, in the language of the 'Leftlanders', their term 'electron' would apply to Gelectrons but not Felectrons. Now, Rightlanders are numerically and epistemically the same people as they were in w_1, and the 'electron-ish things of their acquaintance' in w_1 and w_3 are numerically the same. Certainly, if the Rightlanders' term does not apply to the Gelectrons in w_3, the term 'electron' in the w_1 language would not apply to Gelectrons in w_3, either. And if it does not apply there, surely it would not apply to them in w_2. We thus have a counter-example to Chalmers's semantical picture. For in w_2 Gelectrons interact with one another and other G-particles in exactly the way FF-laws characterize the interaction of Felectrons with one another and other F-particles, but the w_1 term 'electron' does not apply to Gelectrons in w_3, contrary to what Chalmers's semantics predicts. This (perhaps supplemented with other examples) shows that fundamental particles, forces, and so on cannot be defined by Ramsifying on any semantically stable base.[51]

We may draw two further conclusions. First, there can be physical properties that are 'hidden' in one world (as F is in w_1 and G is in w_2) but that can nevertheless be extremely significant physically—and not at all 'hidden'—in other worlds (as F and G are in w_3). Indeed, the difference between F and G plays a dominant role in the 'revealed' physical theory for w_3: namely, in the FG-laws. In other words, 'hiddenness' is not an in-principle property of F and G.[52] Second, and most importantly, if, as in the example, the physical properties F and G can be revealed to have different physical consequences (F-particles annihilate G-particles but not other F-particles), what is to prevent them—or properties akin to them—from being revealed to have different mental consequences as well? For example, what prevents F-particles from necessitating consciousness even though G-particles do not? Nothing prevents it, says the matter-chauvinist, thus defeating Chalmers's zombie argument.

Chalmers has one last response to the matter-chauvinist: namely, to abandon his original dualism and to replace it with another, which he enunciates thus: 'The dualism of "physical" and "nonphysical" properties is replaced on this [new view] by a dualism of "accessible" and "hidden" physical properties, but the essential point remains' (1996: 136).[53] But this is not so. As we just saw, the matter-chauvinist's challenge does not turn on essentially hidden properties, and, consequently, it impinges with equal force on this fall-back 'dualism' of alleged accessible and hidden physical properties.

---

[51] By the way, in w_3 there are two distinct sequences of properties (the sequence consisting of F-particle followed by G-particle and the sequence consisting of G-particle followed by F-particle) that simultaneously satisfy the conjunction of all three sets of laws. Could we not break this symmetry by including semantically unstable terms in the theory? Yes, but this would result in a difference between the primary intension and the secondary intension of 'electron', again contradicting Chalmers's position.

[52] How, would the terms 'Felectron' and 'Gelectron' be introduced in w_3? It appears that there is no alternative but to turn from Lewis's picture of theoretical terms to Kripke's: since natural kinds are not in general definable by Ramsification on a semantically stable base, they are successfully named only by taking advantage of our situatedness at some stage of naming or other. At the same time, although the significance—physical or mental—of what we are naming might be locally unclear, it need not be hidden in principle.

[53] Chalmers also makes the suggestion that the sorts of physical property upon which matter-chauvinism is based are 'protophenomenal'; but such renaming is one more violation of the terminological maxim alluded to at the outset. Successful reductions of Xs to Ys are trivialized by saying that Ys were really just proto-Xs all along.

By the way, Chalmers entertains, favorably, a kind of Identity Theory according to which there are 'protophenomenal' physical properties that, either alone or in combination, are identical to

4.3.2 *Two-Dimensional Modal Arguments and the Identity Thesis*

Kripke really offered two modal arguments against the Identity Thesis. One aimed to establish that it is metaphysically possible for something to have firing C-fibers without pain (thereby refuting the sufficiency condition). The other aimed to establish that it is metaphysically possible for something to be in pain without having firing C-fibers (thereby refuting the necessity condition). When the first argument is reconstructed in the style of Chalmers's two-dimensional zombie argument, the resulting argument has the following main premises (analogous to those in Chalmers's argument): (a_1) the modal premise that the primary intension of 'Something has firing C-fibers without being in pain' is possibly true; (b_1) the semantic premise that this sentence's secondary intension is identical to its primary intension. Similarly, when Kripke's second argument is reconstructed in this way, it has two analogous premises: (a_2) the primary intension of 'Something is in pain without having firing C-fibers' is possibly true; (b_2) this sentence's secondary intension is identical to its primary intension. But each of these arguments fails because its semantic premise is false (just as the corresponding semantic premise in Chalmers's original zombie argument, in section 4.3.1, was false). The underlying reason is that there will always be alternate worlds in which, say, you★ (the qualitative epistemic counterparts of you) use 'C-fiber' for a natural kind very different from real C-fibers (e.g., in a science fiction case, you★ and me★ use 'C-fiber' for silicon fibers in the heads of the human-appearing androids who, along with you★, populate the planet). (As we saw in section 1.3, Kripke's arguments also failed because of this sort of semantic instability of 'C-fiber'.)

The above two-dimensional argument against the sufficiency condition is in principle unsalvageable (see section 4.4). It turns, out, however, that the above argument against the necessity condition can be salvaged as long as the secondary intension of 'firing C-fibers' entails (i.e., has as a necessary condition) the secondary intension of some predicate *C* for which the associated pair of premises hold: (a_3) the modal premise that the primary intension of 'Something is in pain without having *C*' is possibly true; (b_3) the semantic premise that this sentence's secondary intension is the same as this primary intension. Now, in fact, there are such predicates *C* (e.g., '74,985,263 or more functionally related nonconscious parts'—or whatever is the minimum number needed for

---

our phenomenal properties. This Identity Theory, however, is inconsistent with a possibility to which Chalmers's larger argument is committed: viz., the possibility of disembodied (and hence, nonphysical) beings whose phenomenal properties are nevertheless the same as ours.

having firing C-fibers). Furthermore, (a_3) and (b_3) trivially entail that the secondary intension of 'Something is in pain without having C' is possibly true. Therefore, since the secondary intension of 'firing C-fibers' entails the secondary intension of C, we obtain the conclusion: the secondary intension of 'Something is in pain without having firing C-fibers' is possibly true. But, for any English sentence S, if S's secondary intension is possibly true, it is metaphysically possible that S. It follows that it is metaphysically possible that something is in pain without having firing C-fibers. In other words, the Identity Thesis fails in this instance because having firing C-fibers fails to be a necessary condition for being in pain.

Ironically, this success on the part of two-dimensionalism reveals that two-dimensionalism is just a gratuitous complication, contributing nothing substantive to the refutation of the Identity Thesis. Why? Because the above two-dimensional argument can, without loss, be dropped in favor of an 'equivalent' but essentially simpler 'one-dimensional' argument.[54] The argument has two premises: (a_4) it is epistemically possible that something be in pain without having C; (b_4) the proposition that something is in pain without having C is semantically stable. Since a semantically stable proposition's epistemic possibility entails its metaphysical possibility, it follows from (a_4) and (b_4) that it is metaphysically possible that something be in pain without having C. Therefore, since the property of having firing C-fibers entails the property of having C, it follows that it is metaphysically possible that something is in pain without having firing C-fibers. The desired result.

The moral. Two-dimensional arguments against the Identity Thesis (viz., against its necessity condition) go through iff the primary and secondary intensions of 'Something is in pain without having C' are identical iff the sentence is semantically stable. (I suppress difference in individual- and community-centered meaning.) Hence, the two-dimensional argument goes through in just those cases where the primary/secondary distinction plays no role in so far as the sentence at issue is semantically stable and so able to underwrite an essentially simpler one-dimensional argument. Two-dimensionalism is just a third wheel: it succeeds only where it is not needed.

The indicated simpler pattern of argument generalizes. If we wish to show that a semantically unstable property U is not a necessary condition of a

---

[54] Equivalent in that these biconditionals hold: The primary intension of 'Something has pain without having C' is possibly true iff it is epistemically possible that something has pain without having C. Suppressing issues of private vs. public meaning (sects. 2.2.3; 2.4), the primary and secondary intensions of 'Something has pain without having C' are the same iff the sentence is semantically stable. The secondary intension of 'firing C-fibers' entails the secondary intension of C iff the property of having firing C-fibers entails the property of having C.

semantically stable property S, it suffices to find some necessary condition U' of U such that: (a) it is epistemically possible for S to be instantiated without U', and (b) U' is semantically stable. This general strategy provides a systematic routine for disarming scientific essentialism's threat to a large family of modal arguments in philosophy. And it does so without commitment to any particular semantical theory (especially one whose adequacy is already in doubt on independent grounds) but merely a commitment to the semantic stability/ instability distinction. The first goal of my early paper on mental properties (1994) was to isolate and defend this general strategy—and to apply it, in particular, against the Identity Thesis. The second goal was to demonstrate that this method's 'dual' (i.e., the corresponding method for showing unstable U not to be sufficient for stable S) is unsound, and, in particular, that it cannot refute the Identity Thesis.

4.4 A Middle Way

If Yablo's disembodiment argument were to go through, it would imply that mental properties do not have physical properties as substantive *necessary* conditions. But we saw that the argument is not likely to convince his materialist opponents, and their reservation is not without foundation, given the semantic instability of the key modal intuition. Analogously, if Chalmers's zombie argument were to go through, it would imply that mental properties do not have physical properties as *sufficient* conditions. Our notion of semantic instability allows us to see the failure of this argument in a similar way. From this point of view, the most that this style of argument could ever succeed in showing is that mental properties do not have any *semantically stable* physical properties as sufficient conditions. But this leaves untouched matter-chauvinism, which, in this idiom, amounts to the view that, even if semantically stable physical properties cannot be sufficient conditions for mental properties, certain semantically unstable physical properties can.[55]

For me the challenge has been to find a way to overcome this dialectical situation. More specifically, my goal (1994, 1997, 2000) has been to find a way to rely on only very weak, but very compelling, semantically stable intuitions (as in the previous subsection), thereby skirting entirely the issue of scientific essentialism.[56] When these epistemically safe intuitions are combined with our moderate rationalism, they yield all the same anti-materialist conclusions as the original, but inconclusive disembodiment and zombie arguments.

[55] Many matter–chauvinists believe that this is the secret of phenomenal qualities (sensing red, etc.). This phenomenon (and others) also creates problems for the Knowledge Argument.

[56] See the close of sect. 3.1 and n. 14.

REFERENCES

Bealer, George (1987), 'Philosophical Limits of Scientific Essentialism', *Philosophical Perspectives*, 1: 289–365.

—— (1992), 'The Incoherence of Empiricism', *Aristotelian Society*, supp. vol. 66: 99–138.

—— (1993*a*), 'A Solution to Frege's Puzzle', *Philosophical Perspectives*, 7: 17–61.

—— (1993*b*), 'Universals', *Journal of Philosophy*, 91: 185–208.

—— (1994), 'Mental Properties', *Journal of Philosophy*, 91: 185–208.

—— (1996), '*A Priori* Knowledge and the Scope of Philosophy', *Philosophical Studies*, 81: 121–42.

—— (1997), 'Self-Consciousness', *Philosophical Review*, 106: 69–117.

—— (1998), 'Propositions', *Mind*, 107: 1–32.

—— (1999), 'A Theory of the A Priori', *Philosophical Perspectives*, 13: 29–55.

—— (2001), 'Rationalism, Concept Identity, and the Solution to Frege's Puzzle', MS.

—— (forthcoming), *Philosophical Limits of Science* (New York: Oxford University Press).

Burge, Tyler (1979), 'Individualism and the Mental', *Midwest Studies in Philosophy*, 4: 73–122.

Chalmers, David (1995), 'Facing Up to the Problem of Consciousness', *Journal of Consciousness Studies*, 2: 200–19.

—— (1996), *The Conscious Mind: In Search of a Fundamental Theory* (New York: Oxford University Press).

Church, Alonzo (1950), 'On Carnap's Analysis of Statements of Assertion and Belief', *Analysis*, 10: 97–9.

Fine, Kit (1994), 'Essence and Modality', *Philosophical Perspectives*, 8 (Atascadero, Calif.: Ridgeview), 1–16.

Hill, Christopher (1997), 'Imaginability, Conceivability, Possibility and the Mind–Body Problem', *Philosophical Studies*, 87: 61–85.

Hirsch, Eli (1986), 'Metaphysical Necessity and Conceptual Truth', *Midwest Studies in Philosophy*, 11: 243–56.

Jackson, Frank (1993), 'Armchair Metaphysics', in Michaelis Michael and John O'Leary-Hawthorne (eds.), *Philosophy in Mind* (Dordrecht: Kluwer), 23–42.

—— (1998), *From Metaphysics to Ethics* (Oxford: Oxford University Press).

Jubien, Michael (2001), 'Propositions and the Objects of Thought', *Philosophical Studies*, 104: 47–62.

Kaplan, David (1989), 'Afterthoughts', in Joseph Almog, John Perry, and Howard Wettstein (eds.), *Themes from Kaplan* (New York: Oxford University Press), 565–614.

Kripke, Saul (1980), *Naming and Necessity* (Cambridge, Mass.: Harvard University Press).

Putnam, Hilary (1975), 'The Meaning of "Meaning" ', in *Language, Mind, and Knowledge*, Minnesota Studies in the Philosophy of Science, 8 (Minneapolis: University of Minnesota Press), 131–91.

Schiffer, Stephen (1987), *Remnants of Meaning* (Cambridge, Mass.: MIT Press).

Yablo, Stephen (1990), 'The Real Distinction between Mind and Body', *Canadian Journal of Philosophy*, supp. vol. 16: 149–201.

—— (1992), 'Mental Causation', *Philosophical Review*, 101: 245–80.

—— (1993), 'Is Conceivability a Guide to Possibility?', *Philosophy and Phenomenological Research*, 53: 1–42.

2

Berkeley's Puzzle

John Campbell

1 The Possibility of Existence Unperceived

Berkeley famously claimed to be unable to conceive of existence unperceived, from which he famously concluded that existence unperceived is impossible. Here is the famous passage, section 23 of *The Principles of Human Knowledge*:

But say you, surely there is nothing easier than to imagine trees, for instance, in a park, or books existing in a closet, and nobody by to perceive them. I answer, you may so, there is no difficulty in it: but what is all this, I beseech you, more than framing in your mind certain ideas which you call books and trees, and at the same time omitting to frame the idea of anyone that may perceive them? But do you not yourself perceive or think of them all the while? This therefore is nothing to the purpose: it only shows you have the power of imagining or forming ideas in your mind; but it doth not shew that you can conceive it possible, the objects of your thought may exist without the mind: to make out this, it is necessary that you conceive them existing unconceived or unthought of, which is a manifest repugnancy.

There is, in the literature on Berkeley, a standard objection to this argument. The objection is that Berkeley's argument depends on a confusion between conceiving and imagining. The most he is entitled to, the objection runs, is that we cannot imagine existence unperceived. There is a use of 'imagine' on which

Thanks to the editors, Tamar Szabó Gendler and John Hawthorne, for a helpful set of comments on an earlier draft. This chapter draws on the discussion of these topics in my *Reference and Consciousness* (Oxford: Oxford University Press, 2002).

it means something like 'visually imagine', or 'imagine seeing'. Perhaps it is true that you cannot imagine seeing a tree, without imagining the tree being seen. But it hardly follows that you cannot conceive of a tree that is not being seen. You can, for example, write down a perfectly coherent block of prose in which the tree figures unseen by anyone. There will be no explicit or implicit contradiction in such a story. So Berkeley's inference from unimaginability to inconceivability, and hence to the impossibility of existence unperceived, is just a mistake.

There is, indeed, a subsidiary literature, challenging Berkeley even on whether it is possible to visually imagine a tree unperceived. The challenge was launched by Bernard Williams in 'Imagination and the Self' (1973), where he argued that just as in watching a film or a play, we do not in general take ourselves to be provided with the visual experience of some character in the film or play, so too we could, in imagining, be sketching the content of a scene without thereby sketching the content of anyone's perception of it.

I want, though, to focus on the standard objection to Berkeley's argument, because it seems to me to be an extremely superficial response; and reflecting on why it is unsatisfactory brings out something of the depth of Berkeley's line of thought here. The key point I want to make is that Berkeley is trying to respect a principle about the relation between experience and concepts that is both important and difficult to keep in place. This is what I will call the *explanatory role of experience*. The principle is that concepts of individual physical objects, and concepts of the observable characteristics of such objects, are made available by our experience of the world. It is experience of the world that explains our grasp of these concepts. The puzzle that Berkeley is addressing is that it is hard to see how our concepts of mind-independent objects could have been made available by experience of them. The resolution he finds is to acknowledge that we do not have concepts of mind-independent objects.

Berkeley's puzzle was formulated in a context defined by Locke. Locke too aimed to respect the explanatory role of experience. The problem he faced was that experience seems, on the face of it, incapable of providing us with the conception of anything beyond itself. So you might acknowledge that experience matters for grasp of colour concepts, on the grounds that colour properties, properly understood, are nothing more than propensities of objects to produce colour experiences in us; and having the colour experiences might be thought to be essential to grasping concepts of colour experiences. The trouble with this is that experience of shape, for example, also seems to play a role in grasp of shape concepts. Suppose you had someone who was taught the functional characteristics of a range of shape properties: that the round things roll, that the jagged things can be used for tearing, and so on. You can suppose that such a person learns that there are various properties $P_1, P_2, P_3, \ldots$ and so on, that have all these functional characteristics. Someone could learn all there is to know about the functional characteristics of shape properties, without it occurring to them that these are properties they encounter in experience. What does such a person learn when they find out that roundness is that perceived property— when, for the first time, they see what roundness is like? On one view, the person simply learns about yet another functional characteristic of roundness. They learn just what kinds of sensation roundness produces. That is not Locke's view. Locke is taking it that experience of shapes provides you with knowledge of what the categorical shape property is. The puzzle is to see how that can be. How can experience of shape provide you with anything more than the conception of a propensity to produce a particular type of experience? It is at this point that Locke is compelled to appeal to his notion of resemblance: the idea that the experience of roundness intrinsically resembles the shape property itself. This desperate manœuvre has no hope of success, and Berkeley's stricture, that there can be no intrinsic resemblance between an idea and a physical property, is perfectly reasonable. But for the present, the important point is to see the pressure that drives Locke to this position. The pressure comes to a head over our grasp of concepts of ordinary physical objects, such as the tree in the quad. We think that various modal and temporal properties are possessed by such an object: that it could have existed even if no one had ever observed it, that it could have been in existence now even though it was currently unobserved, and that it continues to exist even at times at which it is in fact unobserved. But how could experience play a role in making available to us the conception of such an object? Without Locke's notion of resemblance, Berkeley insists, the thing cannot be done. We must either deny that experience is what makes the concepts of the external world available to us, or we must admit that the only concepts we have are concepts of mind-dependent objects.

I will argue that we do have to acknowledge the explanatory role of experience, and that Berkeley's puzzle must consequently be taken seriously: how can experience of an object explain our grasp of the possibility of existence unperceived? And I will argue that what makes it difficult to find the resolution of this puzzle is the difficulty of finding a clear view of the conception of experience that we need to understand how experience could be what explains our grasp of concepts. The two mistakes it is easy to make are, first, to suppose that experience is exhausted by its propositional content, and second, that experience is only caused by the object it is of. I will argue that we have to think of experience of an object as a cognitive relation more primitive than thought about the object, that none the less makes it possible for us to think about that thing. I call this the *relational view* of experience.

2   Locke and Putnam's Proof

Locke supposes that simple ideas of perception are signs of their regular causes, whatever they are. And he thinks that we understand the words we use by connecting them to ideas of perception. Now consider a sceptical hypothesis, such as the proposition that, for example, my experiences of redness are not caused by redness but by something else, or the proposition that my experiences of squareness are not caused by squareness but by something else, or that my experiences of water are not caused by water but by something else. Locke's answer to this is that simple ideas 'conform to their archetypes', are 'real', 'adequate', or 'true'. His point is that since the simple idea is merely a sign only of its regular cause, whatever that is, and the word given meaning by its association with that idea therefore stands only for the regular cause of that idea, whatever it is, the sceptical hypothesis amounts to the hypothesis that the regular cause of a simple idea is not what the idea signifies; but whatever the regular cause of an idea is, that just is what the idea signifies. Here is Locke putting the case:

simple Ideas, which since the Mind, as has been shewed, can by no means make to it self, must necessarily be the product of Things operating on the Mind in a natural way, and producing therein those Perceptions which by the Wisdom and Will of our Maker they are ordained and adapted to. From when it follows, that *simple* Ideas *are not fictions* of our Fancies, but the natural and regular production of Things without us, really operating upon us; and so carry with them all the conformity which is intended; or which our state requires; For they represent to us Things under those appearances which they are fitted to produce in us; whereby we are enabled to distinguish the sorts of particular Substances, to discern the states they are in, and so to take them for our Necessities, and apply them to our Uses. Thus the Idea of Whiteness, or Bitterness, as it is in the Mind, exactly answering that Power which is in any Body to produce it there, has all the real conformity it can, or ought to have, with Things without us. (*Essay*, IV. iv. 4)

I should emphasize that Locke's point here is about simple ideas generally; the last sentence of the quotation applies to all simple ideas of perception, not just to ideas of secondary qualities. If we put the upshot of this discussion in contemporary terms, and ask, How do I know that I am not a brain in a vat?, where the point of the question is that if I were a brain in a vat, the regular causes of my perceptions would be other than I take them to be, the answer is that my words just do stand for the regular causes of my perceptions, whatever they are. So it is a priori that I am not a brain in a vat. Locke's view here is, in fact, as will now be evident, a form of Putnam's argument that we can't be brains in vats.

One way in which Locke finds a role for experience here is that experiences are the vehicles of content. They are the reliable signs of their regular causes. But once we have reached this point, it is natural to wonder whether experience is really playing any essential role in the account of content. Surely, anything could serve as a reliable sign of its regular cause. Indeed, the main line of objection to the idea that there is an essential role for consciousness in our grasp of concepts comes from what I will call 'causal correlation' views of content. This embraces a vast family of different views. The idea common to all these views is that the prototype of all representation is one state of affairs being causally correlated with another, so that one can serve as a sign of the other. So the idea is that brain states can be causally correlated with external states of affairs, in that a brain state may be reliably produced by just one type of external condition, and so serve as a sign that the external condition obtains. The proposal is that this kind of causal correlation is all that is involved in all representations, whether the representations involved in cognitive processing or those involved in conceptual thought. This, of course, is a powerful idea, which can be developed in many different ways. And there may be types of representation for which it can, without much complication, provide a correct analysis. In any simple development of this view, though, there will be no immediate role for consciousness in explaining how we understand the representations we use. So it is natural to ask whether we cannot use a view like this to give an analysis of how we understand propositions about the world around us—the kinds of propositions we use in ordinary deductive inference, for example—without appealing to our experience of our surroundings. In that way you might hope simply to finesse Berkeley's problem. If our representations are caused by mind-independent objects, isn't that enough for us to have representations of mind-independent objects?

One way to see what is problematic in such a picture of content is to consider Hilary Putnam's (1981) reply to the sceptic. Putnam's reply, a reformulation of Locke's, depends very heavily on a 'causal correlation' view of content; it brings out quite dramatically what the view commits you to. Sceptical worries are often formulated as questions about the right whereby I take it that my perceptions are caused in the way I think they are. Perhaps, the sceptic says, my perceptions are caused in some quite different way: by the machinations of a malevolent demon or the operation of the vat-tending machinery. Putnam's point, in opposition to this kind of scepticism, is that the way in which my perceptions are caused will affect the contents of my thoughts. And however my perceptions are caused, the contents of my thoughts will be correlatively affected in such a way that they come out true. So I will always be right when I say, 'I am not a brain in a vat.'

This way of putting the matter misses the possibility that the sceptic might shrug aside these alternative causal hypotheses as simply dramatic devices which can be thrown away as inessential to his point. The key sceptical possibility, he may say, is that the perceptions I have may not be caused at all. They may have no external cause. Perhaps there is only a sequence of images. Perhaps all there is, constituting the entire universe, are images and the void. Another type of reservation has to do with the point that I might have lived a regular life for long enough for my words to have acquired all the usual references, but then have been envatted, without being advised of it, just five minutes ago. But let me set aside these reservations; I think they are correct, but not to my present purpose. I want instead to focus on another problem with this argument, which seems to me more instructive in bringing out the limitations of a causal correlation view of content.

The intuitive reservation is this. We ordinarily think that we know what the world is like. If the world is that way, it is not a bit like a vat. So, if you are told that were you to be in a vat, all your thought tokens would be systematically reinterpreted so that they came out true, this is not likely to seem reassuring enough. The world would still not be the way you think it is.

It is hard to formulate this puzzle competently, and I think the best way to do it is to recall Locke's position. Locke is certainly an externalist about content: on his view, simple ideas of perceptions are signs of their regular causes. They are signs of external phenomena in something like the way in which smoke is a sign of fire. The immediate problem this raises is that although my ideas are signs of their causes, I do not yet know what any of those causes are like. If all I ever get is smoke, how do I know what fire is like? Any causal correlation view will in the end face some version of this question. How can effects provide you, the subject, with any conception of what their causes are like?

This is where Locke introduces his notion of 'resemblance': some ideas, the idea of primary qualities, intrinsically resemble their causes. Those ideas do show what their causes are like. Ideas of secondary qualities, on the other hand, do not resemble their causes. They represent the world perfectly accurately, but they do not show you what the world is like. Now Locke's notion of resemblance is generally mocked. One possibility is that 'resembles' is interpreted in representational terms—the world is the way represented—in which case it does not get the intended effect; all we have is that the representations are, one way or another, being interpreted so that they come out true. Locke is trying to respect the explanatory role of experience, and merely appealing to it as a bearer of representations does not acknowledge its role in explaining how we can understand such representations. Alternatively, 'resemblance' requires that the intrinsic properties of the perceptual idea should be like the intrinsic properties of the object. That is the intuitively attractive idea at this point in the dialectic. But it is hopeless. Berkeley's rejoinder, that an idea can be like nothing but an idea, is, at this point, perfectly just.

Although Locke's solution does not work, the problem to which he was responding is perfectly real. It is, indeed, the key motivation for current disjunctivist or naïve realist views of experience, which criticize the conception of conscious experience as something that is merely an effect of external objects. As Bill Child (1994) puts it, if all you ever perceive are spots, how could that give you the conception of what it is to have measles? Or as John McDowell (1998) puts it, Locke's type of externalism leaves us with a view on which 'all is dark within'.

From this perspective, Putnam's proof is not reassuring. It simply writes large the darkness within. It merely emphasizes the conclusion that we have no conception at all of what the world is like. Wildly different scenarios, on which perceptions have massively different external causes, are all quite consistent with having a representational system within which you accept only truths. But what you would have commonsensically hoped for is some intimation that the world is the way you think it is. And you do not get that reassurance by being told that one way or another, your representational system is expressing truths. That is the intuitive reservation about Putnam's proof. When you think it through, it is actually a reservation about the causal correlation view of content, precisely because the causal correlation view of content, on any simple development of it, gives no role to consciousness in providing us with our conception of what the world is like. We can accept Putnam's proof only if we accept that we have no conception of what the world is like, only a set of representations which one way or another will be interpreted so as to come out true, whichever way the world is.

3 The Relational View of Experience

On a disjunctivist view of experience, there is no experiential factor in common between the case in which you see an object and the case in which you have a hallucination of such an object. When you see an object, the object itself is a constituent of your experience. The argument for this view is given by John McDowell in these words:

The threat that the Cartesian picture poses to our hold on the world comes out most dramatically in this: that within the Cartesian picture there is a serious question about how it can be that experience, conceived from its own point of view, is not blank or blind, but purports to be revelatory of the world we live in. (1998: 243)

This objection to the common factor view is stated crisply by Bill Child:

to think of conscious experience as a highest common factor of vision and hallucination is to think of experiences as states of a type whose intrinsic mental features are world-independent; an intrinsic, or basic characterisation of a state of awareness will make no reference to anything external to the subject. But if that is what experience is like, the disjunctivist objects, how can it yield knowledge of an objective world beyond experience, and how can it so much as put us in a position to think about such a world? (1994: 148)

Although McDowell and Child both tend to emphasize the epistemological dimension of this argument, I want to suggest that the argument that knowledge would not be possible on a 'common factor' interpretation is not the fundamental objection. The common factor theorist could as readily as anyone else define a notion of 'knowledge' that more or less matched the ordinary concept. For example, there is no evident difficulty in the idea that a 'common factor' perceptual image could be a reliable sign of an external phenomenon. If you already have the conception of that phenomenon, there is no particular difficulty about using a reliable sign of it to give you knowledge of it. The fundamental objection to the common factor approach is that, on it, experience cannot play its explanatory role: we cannot understand how experience, so conceived, could be what provides us with our concepts of the objects around us. As Child puts it, 'to conceive of experience in such terms is to make it unintelligible how our experience could put us in a position to . . . think about an objective, mind-independent world' (1994: 149).

This argument is very sketchy, but it is intriguing, and I want to work through how it should go fully enough to allow some serious assessment of it. The argument presses very hard the idea that experience of objects has an explanatory role to play. Experience of objects has to explain how it is that we can have the conception of objects as mind-independent. The objection to the common factor view is that, on it, experience of objects could not be what explained our having the conception of objects as mind-independent. There is something intuitive about this. On the common factor view, all that experience of the object provides you with is a conscious image of the object. The existence of that conscious image is in principle independent of the existence of the external object. The existence of the image, though, is dependent on the existence of the subject who has the conscious image. So if your conception of the object was provided by your experience of the object, you would presumably end by concluding that the object would not have existed had you not existed, and that the object exists only when you are experiencing it. We cannot extract the conception of a mind-independent world from a mind-dependent image; this is the traditional problem with Locke's doctrine of abstraction. It seems as though it ought to be possible, though, to extract the conception of a mind-independent world from an experience which has a mind-independent object as a constituent, which is what the disjunctive view ascribes to us.

I think that this is the intuitive argument to which the disjunctive view is appealing. I think it has some immediate force, but there are some issues that need further discussion here. It is striking how hard the explanatory role of experience is being worked. You might have thought that the immediate response of a common factor theorist to this argument is that the image provides the conception of an objective world simply by displaying the world as objective. Even if I am hallucinating, the objects I seem to see, seem to be mind-independent objects. So a common factor image can present objects as mind-independent; and surely that is all that is needed. The problem with this reply is that it takes for granted the intentionality of experience. That is, it takes it for granted that experience of the world is a way of grasping thoughts about the world. To see an object is, on this conception, to grasp a demonstrative proposition. There are many ways in which you can grasp a proposition: you can grasp it as the content of speech or as the meaning of a wink or a sigh. One way in which you can grasp a proposition is as the content of vision. The common factor theorist says that ordinary vision involves grasping demonstrative propositions as the contents of experiences. And you could grasp such propositions whether or not the external objects exist.

The disjunctive theorist might reply that this simply begs the question; the disjunctivist's view is, after all, that you cannot grasp demonstrative propositions whether or not the external objects exist. But the disjunctivist was trying to state an objection to the common factor view, so an attempt to shift the burden of proof at this point is simply to give up; the two views are equally probable. Anyhow, the disjunctivist has a better reply. The argument turns on an appeal to the explanatory role of experience. Experience is what explains our grasp of the concepts of objects. But if you think of experience as intentional, as merely one among many ways of grasping thoughts, you cannot allow it this explanatory role. Suppose someone said: 'Actually, reading newspapers is the fundamental way in which you understand the concepts of a mind-independent world. All your conceptual skills depend on your ability to read newspapers.' The natural response to this would be that reading newspapers does indeed involve the exercise of conceptual skills, but it is simply one way among many of exercising those conceptual skills. Just so, if all there is to experience of objects is the grasping of demonstrative thoughts about them, then experience of objects is just one among many ways in which you can exercise your conceptual skills. When we grasp thoughts as the contents of vision, or as the contents of newspaper reports, or as the meanings of signposts, they have different vehicles and different accompaniments, but that is all, on this view. At this point we do not have any way of explaining why there should be anything fundamental to our grasp of concepts about experience of objects.

It is when we press the explanatory role of experience like this that we can see the force of the disjunctivist's argument. We are not to take the intentional character of experience as a given; rather, experience of objects has to be what explains our ability to think about objects. This means that we cannot view experience of objects as a way of grasping thoughts about objects. Experience of objects has to be something more primitive than the ability to think about objects, in terms of which the ability to think about objects can be explained. The question now is whether the common factor picture of experience provides a view of experience on which it could be what explains our ability to think about objects. And at this point the question as to whether something essentially mind-dependent could provide for the conception of a mind-independent world really does seem forceful. Yet, once we have reached this understanding of the argument, we can see that there is also something wrong with the formulation of disjunctivism given by McDowell and Child. For they both take it for granted that the way in which to state the disjunctivist view is as the view that experience involves the grasping of demonstrative thoughts about objects, together with the claim that those demonstrative thoughts are object-dependent. But this robs experience of its explanatory role. For experience to have its explanatory role, it must be prior to, and not require, demonstrative thoughts. Disjunctivism is thus no better placed than the common factor view to acknowledge the role of experience in explaining how we have the conception of the world that we do.

Since disjunctivists do take experience of objects to be intentional, I will talk instead of the 'relational' view of experience, as being what is motivated by the above line of argument. On the relational view, experience of objects is a more primitive state than thought about objects, which none the less reaches all the way to the objects themselves. In particular, experience of an object is what explains your ability to grasp a demonstrative term referring to that object.

Philosophers who discuss the role of experience in our understanding of concepts tend to suppose that it has to do primarily with verifying simple observational propositions about demonstrated objects, and perhaps with the role in action-explanation of simple observational propositions. But the common factor theorist could acknowledge that role for experience; the image could do that work. The relational view is asking how common factor images could do further explanatory work: that is, it is asking how experience can be what provides for the conception of objects as mind-independent. That is, experience of objects has to explain our ability to grasp the modal and tensed propositions that express the mind-independence of objects: it has to explain my understanding of propositions to the effect that the object could have existed even though I had not, or that the object exists even at times at which I am not experiencing it. The common factor view cannot acknowledge this role for experience; the relational view can.

4 Criteria of Identity

Our topic is the role of experience in providing the conception of objects as mind-independent. How can experience of an object provide you with a grasp of the idea that the object can continue in existence through gaps in the observation of it? How can perceptual experience of objects be what provides you with a grasp of the possibility of existence unperceived? This is Berkeley's puzzle.

It is natural to think that part of the answer here has to be provided by the subject's grasp of a criterion of identity for the objects perceived. Grasping that the object is mind-independent is a matter of grasping that the criterion of identity for the object does not depend on its relation to mental states or a mind. But what is it to grasp the criterion of identity for an object? We can think of grasp of the criterion of identity for a particular object as a procedural matter: it has to do with how you proceed in establishing or finding the implications of propositions about the object. For example, there is the kind of reasoning you have to engage in when you want to demonstrate that this tree, seen here, now, is the same one as the tree that you saw here yesterday. The ability to engage in this kind of reasoning constitutes your grasp of the identity of the tree over time. You know how to demonstrate that the tree encountered at one time is the same as the tree encountered at a later time. Or there is the kind of argument required to show that the tree I can see through this window is the same one as the tree I can see through that window. If you know how to verify this, then you know what it takes for it to be one and the same object that is in question. Mastery of these patterns of reasoning, which is a matter of what you do with the evidence available to you, constitutes your grasp of the criterion of identity for the object.

Grasp of these patterns of inference is a procedural matter: it is a matter of which inferences you regard as valid, which patterns of reasoning you use and regard as compelling. Grasp of these patterns of inference will constitute grasp of the identity of the object across time. It will also constitute a primitive grasp of what is possible for the object. Grasp of the patterns of inference relating to when there is still an object around, greatly changed perhaps, but still identical to our original, and when there is no such object, will constitute a grasp of when the object is still in existence and when it has stopped existing, for example. This will constitute a grasp of which changes it is possible for the object to survive, and which changes involve destruction of the object. It is often pointed out that our grasp of such principles as the necessity of identity or the necessity of origin can be seen as depending on our grasp of a priori truths such as 'if a is identical to b then, necessarily, a is identical to b', or, 'if a's parents are b and c, then, necessarily, a's parents are b and c'. (No doubt this second principle needs refinement, but these refinements are not to the purpose here.) The point is rather that a capacity to establish the antecedents of these conditionals already requires a primitive grasp of what is and what is not possible for the objects in question. Your willingness to argue that a is identical to b, even though there have been interruptions between the observations on the basis of which you referred to a and the observations on the basis of which you referred to b, is enough already to display some primitive grasp of the mind-independence of the things you are talking about.

In these terms, Berkeley's puzzle is: what justifies our use of such a pattern of inference? It does not sound right to say that we can lay down whatever criteria of identity—whatever patterns of use for singular terms—we like, since the correctness of a pattern of use surely does depend on which objects there are out there. And the kinds of inference that would be used to demonstrate that 'this river' is the same as 'that river' will be different from the kinds of inference involved in demonstrating that 'this woman' is the same as 'that woman'. So what makes it right to use one rather than another pattern of inference? In discussing this question, we should focus on how we establish identity statements in which at least one of the singular terms is a perceptual demonstrative, since (a) these terms seem to be the most basic singular terms we have, and (b) it is in our use of these terms that we are most likely to find the role of experience in justifying our use of particular criteria of identity.

The basic constraints have to be supplied by our understanding of the demonstratives, knowledge of which object is being referred to. Suppose that someone says to you, 'What is that mountain over there?' To understand the question, you have to know what is being referred to, which mountain she is talking about. The ordinary way in which you have this knowledge is by seeing the mountain. You could, of course, always construct some description that would uniquely identify the mountain: something like 'the mountain she is looking at' or 'the mountain that has caught her eye'. But ordinarily, if the mountain is right there in front of you, you do not need to construct any such description. You are conscious of the mountain itself, and that experience of the mountain is what allows you to interpret the demonstrative; it is because of the experience that you know what is being referred to. So, on the face of it, your experience of the object has to provide your justification for one pattern of use rather than another. Your experience of the object provides you with knowledge of the reference of the term, and it is your knowledge of the reference of the term that explains your knowledge of how to use it.

In effect, Berkeley acknowledges all this. He thinks that we do indeed have patterns of use that seem to imply the possibility of sameness of object through a gap in our perception of it, and that we suppose our experience of objects to provide us with a justification for this pattern of use. For we think that our experiences acquaint us with mind-independent objects. But, as he writes in the concluding sentences of section 23 of *The Principles of Human Knowledge*, the section with which I began, Berkeley thinks that there is a fallacy here. We think we can rely on experience of objects to justify the pattern of use. None the less:

When we do our utmost to conceive the existence of external bodies, we are all the while only contemplating our own ideas. But the mind taking no notice of itself, is deluded to think it can and doth conceive bodies existing unthought or without the mind; though at the same time they are apprehended or exist in itself.

So what Berkeley says is: we think our experience of objects will justify the use of the ordinary patterns of inference, in which we do verify identities between objects over gaps in perception of them. We suppose that our perceptions do provide the mind-independent objects for which those patterns of inference would be correct. But that supposition is one that we make entirely because we make a mistake. The mistake is that, 'the mind taking no notice of itself', we forget that what the mind supplies is only more experiences. It cannot supply anything mind-independent. So the idea that experience of objects—whatever that is—can supply a justification for the use of these patterns of inference is just a mistake. It arises from supposing, of what is in fact an experience, that it could be a mind-independent object.

You might reply to this that what experience supplies is a range of propositions about the world around you, contents representing how things are. Since those propositions make reference to mind-independent objects, you might say, the mistake is in Berkeley's idea that experience can provide nothing more than what is mind-dependent; the content of an experience can involve reference to objects that are not mind-dependent. But as we have seen, that response simply does not acknowledge the role of experience in explaining our grasp of concepts. In particular, it would leave no room for an appeal to experience in justifying our use of patterns of inference that identify objects through gaps in our experience of them. If the propositional content of experience already involves the use of terms subject to these patterns of inference, it cannot be what justifies the use of these patterns of inference.

So long as we hold on to the picture of experience as either possessed merely of propositional content or as merely an effect of the environment acting on us, we will not be able to meet Berkeley's challenge. The challenge is to (a) respect the explanatory role of experience, and (b) describe how experience of objects can justify our use of the patterns of inference that express the mind-independence of experienced objects. The only way to do this is to acknowledge that experience is not exhausted by its propositional content—we have to do this to acknowledge that experience is what explains our grasp of propositional content—and to maintain that experience of an object is not merely an effect produced by the object. Rather, experience of the object involves the mind-independent thing itself as a constituent.

This is, I think, the common-sense picture. On the relational view, your experience of the object directly justifies your use of the pattern of inference. There is, on the one hand, the way in which you use the demonstrative in patterns of inference which establish informative identities in which the demonstrative figures. On the other hand, there is your experience of the object. And the pattern of use is justified by the experience of the object.

What we want is that your experience of the object should explain the correctness of, and causally sustain use of, the patterns of inference in which you use the demonstrative. It is often said that facts about what is or is not possible for an object—which changes it can undergo while continuing to exist, for example, and which changes would involve destruction of the object—have to be grounded in categorical facts about the way the object actually is. I think that we can see this idea as being articulated in the notion that the patterns of inference in which we use the demonstrative, which define our conception of what is and is not possible for the demonstrated object, are grounded in our experience of the thing. Similarly, it is sometimes said that an object, in contrast to an event, is 'all there at any one time'. I think that you can see this idea as being articulated in the point that the patterns of cross-temporal inference in which you use the demonstrative have an explanatory justification in your experience of the categorical object at a single time. Your experience of the object at a single time can causally sustain, and justify, your use of a particular pattern of inferences involving the term. It is when we conceive of experience on the relational view that we can see how experience, so conceived, provides us with a conception of objects on which they are, *pace* Berkeley, mind-independent.

5 Objects as Functional versus Objects as Categorical

I want finally to contrast another line of thought you might take in response to Berkeley. You could suppose that the notion of a physical object is a theoretical notion that we bring to bear on experience. You might think that we somehow grasp the notion of a physical object as a component in a theory designed to explain our experiences. This, the suggestion runs, would allow us to resist the relational conception of experience, on which the object is a constituent of the experience, and instead hold on to the picture of experience as merely an effect of the external world.

What would the theory look like? It would detail the kinds of link that hold between the earlier and the later stages of one and the same object. For example, we might here use Salmon's conception of mark transmission:

Suppose the object would, in the absence of interactions with other objects, remain uniform with regard to characteristic Q over a period of time. Then a mark—a modification of Q into Q′—is transmitted over the period if the object has Q′ at all points throughout the period without additional interventions. (Salmon 1984: 148)

Suppose we take a simple example of mark transmission. Suppose that while at school you carved your initials on a desk. When you revisit years later, there they still are. The mark has been transmitted over the period. Just to work through how this illustrates Salmon's definition: in the absence of interactions with other objects, the surface of the desk would have remained smooth over the period from my arrival at the school to the present day. After my modification of the smoothness of the surface of the desk into one bearing my initials, the desk bore my initials at all points during the period without further modifications. So, by the definition, that mark was transmitted over the period. And the desk had the potential for the transmission of any of endlessly many such marks over the period.

We could regard the idea that there are physical objects that exist through gaps in our observation of them in the following way: we could regard this idea as amounting to the hypothesis that there are objects, their existence postulated by us, that are capable of transmitting marks over periods during which they are not observed by us. There will be more to the hypothesis that there are physical objects than this, of course: they will be assumed to have further functional characteristics, to do with the ways in which they interact with one another and with us, and the kinds of physical properties they have that determine how they behave in such interactions.

Would this give a way of replying to Berkeley's puzzle? The idea here is that experience is being appealed to only as providing the data which the postulation of objects, with their functional characteristics, is designed to explain. Experience does not provide us with any more direct conception of the object than that. So, on this view, there is no need to appeal to the relational conception of experience. We can as well hold on to the conception of experience as merely an effect produced by the object, so that an intrinsically identical experience could equally well have been the product of sunstroke. But we have none the less succeeded in explaining with what right we can claim to have grasped the possibility of objects existing unperceived by us.

There are, however, a number of problems with this proposal. The first is that we seem to have no right to postulate such a theory, given the kinds of data to which it is responsible. The point the sceptic quite rightly makes is that if we set up such a hypothesis as this, it is easy immediately to generate a variety of alternative hypotheses about the causation of experience, so conceived.

Secondly, it seems unlikely that we will in fact be able to formulate the required functional characterization of physical objects in such a way as to reflect accurately the ways in which we ordinarily think about physical objects. On this approach we have to try to reflect all the distinctions we make about sameness and difference of object in terms of the functional characterization alone. So, for example, we have to say that what makes it true that this tree now is the same as the tree I observed yesterday is the possibility of this tree bearing marks transmitted by the earlier tree. However, if we are not allowed to take the identity of the object as given in determining which marks are being transmitted, then we may find that all kinds of cases count as mark transmission in which we do not have identity of object. For example, if a forger copies a painting, then the marks on the forgery are there because of the markings on the original; but that does not make the forgery into the original painting. Or again, we can imagine that some objects might lose their marks easily; when you mark them, they simply reset themselves to their initial condition. In general, we would ordinarily think of these functional considerations about the relations between earlier and later objects as providing evidence for sameness or difference of object, rather than as actually constituting sameness or difference of object. We would think that sameness or difference of object is a categorical fact. We would think that sameness of object is the reason for the correctness of various counterfactuals, such as the counterfactuals relating to mark transmission. Seeing my initials carved on the desk is evidence for thinking that it is one and the same categorical object again. But, on the functionalist approach to physical objects that we are considering, there is no way of explaining how we could have formed such a conception of the physical object as categorical; physical objects have the status merely of posits invoked to explain experience.

If experience of the object is to be what explains our grasp of the object as categorical, then we cannot think of experience of the object as consisting merely of grasp of a demonstrative thought about the object; it has to be what explains our capacity for demonstrative thought about the thing. So experience of the object should not be regarded as consisting in grasping a thought about the object, 'in the mode: vision', as we might say. Rather, consciousness of the object has to be a more primitive state than thought about the object, which makes thought about the object possible by revealing the object to you. We cannot either, though, think of experience of the object as a matter merely of grasping what kinds of experience the object tends to produce in us; that would provide you with only the conception of yet another of the effects of the object, rather than with a grasp of the categorical object itself. So at this point there seems to be no alternative to the relational view of experience. We have to regard experience of the object as reaching all the way to the object itself, and thereby providing us with the conception of the categorical object.

REFERENCES

Berkeley, George ([1710] 1975), *The Principles of Human Knowledge* (London: Everyman).
Campbell, John (2002), *Reference and Consciousness* (Oxford: Oxford University Press).
Child, T. W. (1994), *Causality, Interpretation and the Mind* (Oxford: Oxford University Press).
Locke, John (1975), *An Essay Concerning Human Understanding*, ed. P. H. Nidditch (Oxford: Oxford University Press).
McDowell, John (1998), 'Singular Thought and the Boundaries of Inner Space', in *Meaning, Knowledge and Reality* (Cambridge, Mass., and London: Harvard University Press), 228–59.
Putnam, Hilary (1981), *Reason, Truth and History* (Cambridge: Cambridge University Press).
Salmon, Wesley (1984), *Scientific Explanation and the Causal Structure of the World* (Princeton: Princeton University Press).
Williams, Bernard (1973), 'Imagination and the Self', in *Problems of the Self* (Cambridge: Cambridge University Press), 26–45.

3

Does Conceivability Entail Possibility?

DAVID J. CHALMERS

There is a long tradition in philosophy of using a priori methods to draw conclusions about what is possible and what is necessary, and often in turn to draw conclusions about matters of substantive metaphysics. Arguments like this typically have three steps: first an epistemic claim (about what can be known or conceived), from there to a modal claim (about what is possible or necessary), and from there to a metaphysical claim (about the nature of things in the world).

We find this structure in many different areas of philosophy: in arguments about whether the mental is reducible to the physical (or vice versa), about whether causation and laws are reducible to regularities in nature, about whether knowledge is identical to justified true belief, and so on. Many arguments in these domains first seek to establish an epistemic gap between two phenomena (e.g., that we can know or conceive of one without the other), argue from there to a modal gap (e.g., that it is possible that one could exist without the other), and step from there to a metaphysical gap (e.g., that one is not reducible to the other).

I have presented this material at Arizona State University, New York University, Princeton University, and the Mighty Midwestern Metaphysical Mayhem conference at Notre Dame. Thanks to many on those occasions and elsewhere for discussion of these issues. Special thanks to Chris Evans, Tamar Gendler, John Hawthorne, Bernie Kobes, and David Sosa for comments on the paper, and to Steve Yablo for very helpful discussion and correspondence.

Here, I will mostly be concerned with the second step: the bridge between the epistemic and modal domains. The most popular bridge here is the method of conceivability. One argues that some state of affairs is conceivable, and from there one concludes that this state of affairs is possible. Here, the kind of possibility at issue is *metaphysical* possibility, as opposed to physical possibility, natural possibility, and other sorts of possibility. Metaphysical conclusions turn most directly on matters of metaphysical possibility: if one domain is reducible to another, the facts about the second should metaphysically necessitate the facts about the first. So it is metaphysical possibility that is relevant in the three-step argument above. And there is at least some plausibility in the idea that conceivability can act as a guide to metaphysical possibility. By contrast, it is very implausible that conceivability entails physical or natural possibility.

For example, it seems conceivable that an object could travel faster than one billion meters per second. This hypothesis is physically and naturally impossible, because it contradicts the laws of physics and the laws of nature. The hypothesis may be metaphysically possible, however, since there might well be metaphysically possible worlds with different laws. If we invoke an intuitive conception of a metaphysically possible world as a world that God might have created: it seems that God could have created a world in which an object traveled faster than a billion meters per second. So in this case, although conceivability does not mirror natural possibility, it may well mirror metaphysical possibility.

In recent years, conceivability arguments have faced considerable opposition. Many philosophers hold that the step from conceivability to metaphysical possibility has been shown to be invalid, not least due to a number of apparent counter examples. For example, it is often suggested that complex mathematical falsehoods (such as Goldbach's conjecture or its negation) are conceivable but impossible. It is also widely believed that emprical identities provide counter-examples: on this view, it is conceivable but not possible that Hesperus is not Phosphorus, and that water is not H_2O.

To properly assess this matter, we must first clarify what is meant by 'conceivability'. This term can be understood in many different ways. In some senses of the term, an entailment from conceivability to possibility is out of the question; in other senses, things are not so clear. Here I will isolate three dimensions of difference between notions of conceivability: prima facie versus ideal conceivability, positive versus negative conceivability, and primary versus secondary conceivability. These distinctions are largely independent of each other, so there may be up to eight sorts of conceivability in the vicinity: prima facie primary positive conceivability, and so on. By making these distinctions, I think at least one plausible and defensible conceivability–possibility thesis can be formulated, free of any clear counter-examples.

As I will be using the term here, conceivability is a property of statements, and the conceivability of a statement is in many cases relative to a speaker or thinker. I think that conceivability is more deeply a property of propositions, but I will not talk that way here, since many philosophers have theoretical views about propositions that can confuse these issues. For a statement S, we will have eight or so ways of disambiguating the claim that S is conceivable for a given subject. I will first give rough characterizations of the various dimensions of difference. Then I will examine various specific notions of conceivability that result, and address the question of the extent to which these notions of conceivability support an entailment from the conceivability of S to the possibility of S. For ease of discussion, I will use sentence symbols such as 'S' loosely, allowing context to disambiguate whether the corresponding sentence is being used or mentioned.

1 Prima Facie and Ideal Conceivability

S is prima facie conceivable for a subject when S is conceivable for that subject on first appearances. That is, after some consideration, the subject finds that S passes the tests that are criterial for conceivability. The specific criteria will depend on a substantive notion of conceivability, as outlined in the discussion of the remaining dimensions of conceivability, to remove the apparent circularity. For example, one substantive notion of conceivability (a version of negative conceivability) holds that S is conceivable if no contradiction is detectable in the hypothesis expressed by S. Under this notion, S will be prima facie conceivable for a subject when that subject cannot (after consideration) detect any contradiction in the hypothesis expressed by S.

S is ideally conceivable when S is conceivable on ideal rational reflection. It sometimes happens that S is prima facie conceivable to a subject, but that this prima facie conceivability is undermined by further reflection showing that the tests that are criterial for conceivability are not in fact passed. In this case, S is not ideally conceivable. Given the substantive notion of (negative) conceivability above, for example, S will be ideally conceivable when ideal rational reflection detects no contradiction in the hypothesis expressed by S, or equivalently, when ~S is not a priori.

An example is provided by any mathematical statement M whose truth-value is currently unknown, but which will later be proved to be true. Here ~M is prima facie conceivable in the sense above (i.e., prima facie negatively conceivable) at least for current subjects. But it is not ideally conceivable, as ideal reflection will rule out ~M a priori.

The notion of ideal rational reflection remains to be clarified. One could try to define ideal conceivability in terms of the capacities of an ideal reasoner—a reasoner free from all contingent cognitive limitations. Using this notion, we could say that S is ideally conceivable if an ideal reasoner would find that it passes the relevant tests (if an ideal reasoner could not rule out the hypothesis expressed by S a priori, for example). A strategy like this is taken by Menzies (1998). One problem is that it is not obvious that an ideal reasoner is possible or coherent. For example, it may be that for every possible reasoner, there is a more sophisticated possible reasoner. Alternatively, one can dispense with the notion of an ideal reasoner and simply invoke the notion of undefeatability by better reasoning. Given this notion, we can say that S is ideally conceivable when there is a possible subject for whom S is prima facie conceivable, with justification that is undefeatable by better reasoning. The idea is that when prima facie conceivability falls short of ideal conceivability, then either the claim that the relevant tests are passed will be unjustified, or the justification will be defeatable by further reasoning. For ideal conceivability, one needs justification that cannot be rationally defeated.

I will not try to give a substantive characterization of what good reasoning consists in, or of what counts as a cognitive limitation to be idealized away from. I suspect that any such attempt would turn out to be open-ended and incomplete. In general, my approach is to take certain rational notions as primitive, and to see what sort of connection to modal notions emerges. In this case, I am simply appealing to our intuitive grasp of notions of reasoning and of when one reasoning process defeats another. I note that the notion of undefeatability invoked here is also implicit in our concept of knowledge: it is generally held that if one's justification for a belief that P is defeatable by better reasoning, then one does not know that P. So the notion of conceivability is not obviously worse off than the concept of knowledge.

There is also a fairly direct parallel between the idealization present in the notion of ideal conceivability and that present in the familiar notion of apriority. If I cannot know that P independent of experience, but another less limited being could do so, then it is a priori that P. And if I believe that P, but the justification for my belief is defeatable by better reasoning, then it is not a priori that P (unless there is another undefeatable justification). So the notion of apriority idealizes away from cognitive limitations in much the same way as the notion of ideal conceivability. This is not to say that either of these idealizations is perfectly clear, but at least the idealization is a familiar one. In practice, the idealizations are easy to apply. We will see that there are certain difficult cases at the far end of idealization where things get tricky; but dealing with such cases may allow us to further clarify the idealization.

There are a couple of things that should be clarified in advance, however. First, it is important that 'better reasoning' about conceivability not be defined, even in part, as reasoning that better tracks possibility. Such a criterion would trivialize the link between ideal conceivability and possibility. Fortunately there is no reason to expect that such a criterion will come into play, at least on most of the substantive notions of conceivability we will be considering. For examble, where conceivability is defined in terms of what is ruled out a priori, for example, we have an entirely independent grounding for the notion. Only if conceivability is directly defined in terms of possibility—perhaps as what a subject judges to be possible—will there be a danger of triviality.

Second, in most cases (with an exception to be discussed later), the reasoning in question is restricted to a priori reasoning, and the further reasoning involved in the idealization will remain within the a priori domain. Sometimes this will be an automatic consequence of a given notion of conceivability (e.g., the negative notion of conceivability above), and sometimes it can be seen as a stipulation. Either way, this restriction is important if this issue is to shed light on the issue of a priori access to modality.

2 Positive and Negative Conceivability

Negative notions of conceivability hold that S is conceivable when S is not *ruled out*. For example, a sense of 'conceivable' in common usage holds roughly that S is conceivable when it is not ruled out by what one knows, or by what one believes. I will set this popular usage aside as tangential to our main purposes here: philosophers are usually concerned with senses in which S can be conceivable even when one knows that S is not actually the case. More relevant notions of negative conceivability can be obtained by constraining the ways in which S might be ruled out.

The central sort of negative conceivability holds that S is negatively conceivable when S is not ruled out a priori, or when there is no (apparent) contradiction in S. One can disambiguate the notion by applying the distinction between prima facie and ideal conceivability. We can say that S is prima facie negatively conceivable for a subject when that subject, after consideration, cannot rule out S on a priori grounds. And we can say that S is ideally negatively conceivable when it is not a priori that ~S.

One subtlety concerns cases of indeterminacy. For some S (perhaps statements that are not truth-evaluable or some statements involving vague predicates), it may be a priori that it is indeterminate whether S. If so, it is not a priori that ~S. In such a case, is S negatively conceivable? For various reasons, it seems best to say that it is not. In these cases, the possibility that S is not truly left open. To handle such cases, one can say that S is negatively conceivable when det(S) cannot be ruled out, and that S is ideally negatively conceivable when it is not a priori that ~det(S). Here 'det S' expresses the claim that S is determinately the case, and '~det(S)' expresses the claim that S is false or indeterminate. (In other frameworks for dealing with indeterminacy, one can adopt a corresponding definition.) In the case of a priori indeterminacy above, it will be a priori that ~det(S), so S will not be ideally negatively conceivable.

Positive notions of conceivability require that one can form some sort of positive conception of a situation in which S is the case. One can place the varieties of positive conceivability under the broad rubric of *imagination*: to positively conceive of a situation is to imagine (in some sense) a specific configuration of objects and properties. It is common to imagine situations in considerable detail, and this imagination is often accompanied by interpretation and reasoning. When one imagines a situation and reasons about it, the object of one's imagination is often revealed as a situation in which S is this case, for some S. When this is so, we can say that the imagined situation *verifies* S, and that one has *imagined that* S. Overall, we can say that S is positively conceivable when one can imagine that S: that is, when one can imagine a situation that verifies S. (This definition, and the following discussion, is indebted to the discussion of conceivability by Yablo (1993).)

Different notions of conceivability correspond to different notions of imagination. One such notion is tied to *perceptual imagination*. A subject perceptually imagines that S when the subject has a perceptual mental image that represents S as being the case. This happens when the image is relevantly related to a perceptual experience that represents S as being the case (see Gendler and Hawthorne, forthcoming). For example, one can perceptually imagine that a pig flies by forming a visual image of a flying pig, where this can be understood as an image that relevantly resembles a visual experience as of a flying pig.

Perceptually imagining that P differs from supposing that P, or from entertaining the proposition that P, in that it involves an attitude not just toward P, but toward some specific situation that stands in a certain relationship to P. To perceptually imagine that pigs fly, we form a mental image that represents a specific situation (one with a certain configuration of animals), and we take this to be a situation in which pigs fly. Here, we can say that the imagined situation verifies 'Pigs fly'. More generally, one can say that when one perceptually imagines that P, one perceptually imagines a situation that verifies P. Unlike entertaining or supposing that P, the phenomenology of perceptually imagining that P has a mediated objectual character, with an attitude toward an intermediate mental object (here, an imagined situation) playing a crucial role. This objectual character (noted by Yablo (1993)) is distinctive of positive conceivability.

This objectual character is also present in cases of imagination that are not grounded in imagery. There is a sense in which we can imagine situations that do not seem to be potential contents of perceptual experiences. One can imagine situations beyond the scale of perception: for example, molecules of H_2O, or Germany winning the Second World War. One can imagine situations that are unperceivable in principle: for example, the existence of an invisible being that leaves no trace on perception. And one can imagine pairs of situations that are perceptually indistinguishable: for example, the situations postulated by two scientific hypotheses that make the same empirical predictions, or arguably the existence of a conscious being and its zombie twin (an unconscious physically identical duplicate).

In these cases, we do not form a perceptual image that represents S. Nevertheless, we do more than merely suppose that S, or entertain the hypothesis that S. Our relation to S has a mediated objectual character that is analogous to that found in the case of perceptual imaginability. In this case, we have an intuition of (or as of) a *world* in which S, or at least of (or as of) a situation in which S, where a situation is (roughly) a configuration of objects and properties within a world. We might say that in these cases, one can *modally imagine* that P. One modally imagines that P if one modally imagines a world that verifies P, or a situation that verifies P. Modal imagination goes beyond perceptual imagination, for the reasons given above, but it shares with perceptual imagination its mediated objectual character.

'Modal imagination' is used here as a label for a certain sort of familiar mental act. Like other such categories, it resists straightforward definition. But its phenomenology is familiar. One has a positive intuition of a certain configuration within a world, and takes that configuration to satisfy a certain description. When one modally imagines H_2O molecules, for example, one imagines a configuration of particles. To modally imagine Germany winning the Second World War, one might imagine a world in which certain German armies win certain battles and go on to overwhelm Allied forces within Europe. When one reflects on these imagined (parts of) worlds, they reveal themselves as (parts of) worlds in which there are H_2O molecules, or in which Germany won the Second World War.

Just as modally imagining that S goes beyond entertaining the proposition that S, modally imagining a world that verifies S goes beyond entertaining a proposition (even a highly specific proposition) that implies S. If this were all there were to modal imagination, then we could modally imagine any proposition trivially: just take the proposition itself and conjoin it with further propositions if necessary. But there are many propositions that are not easy to modally imagine: complex unknown mathematical propositions, for example. In these cases, we have no intuition of a world verifying such a proposition

M, even though we can entertain many specific propositions that imply M. So imagining a world is not merely entertaining a description. Of course, it may be that imagining a world involves standing in *some* relation to a detailed description of that world (one presumably uses one's conceptual resources to imagine a world), but if so, this relationship goes beyond mere entertaining or supposing. Rather, it is a relation that is distinctive of modal imagination.

We can say that an imagined situation verifies S when reflection on the situation reveals it as a situation in which S. Understood this way, verification is a broadly epistemic relation, tied to certain rational processes. Importantly, verification is stronger than a mere evidential relation. We have seen that one can imagine situations in which no perceptual evidence is involved, as with the cases of unperceivability and perceptual indistinguishability discussed. One can also imagine a situation in which one has strong evidence that S, such that the imagined situation is nevertheless epistemically compatible with ~S: a situation where experimental results point to a certain sort of particle behavior, for example, or where usually reliable witnesses testify that someone committed a crime. In such cases, consideration of the imagined situation alone does not reveal it as a situation in which S (as opposed to a situation in which there is strong evidence for S), so the imagined situations do not verify S. In this respect, verification of a statement by an imagined situation is broadly analogous to an entailment of one statement by another (a priori entailment, in the central cases): if it is coherent to suppose that the situation obtains without S being the case, then the situation does not verify S.

Just as imagining a unicorn does not entail the existence of the imagined unicorn, so imagining a situation does not entail the existence of the imagined situation, and imagining a world does not entail the existence of the imagined world. Nothing here entails that one should be ontologically committed to situations or worlds at all. Rather, for our purposes, these can be regarded as mere intentional objects, useful in characterizing the cognitive or phenomenological structure of modal imagination. It should also be noted that nothing here presupposes that when one imagines a situation or a world, there is a metaphysically possible situation or world that corresponds to the object of one's imagination. Again, these can simply be seen as *apparent* situations or worlds, of the sort represented in an act of imagination. For all that has been said so far, the imagination of situations and worlds may greatly outstrip the bounds of metaphysical possibility.

Indeed, it is arguable that one can modally imagine S when S involves an a priori contradiction. An example may be a case in which one imagines a geometric object with contradictory properties. In cases like this, one imagines a situation in something less than full detail. Another example may be a case where one imagines that a true mathematical claim (Goldbach's conjecture, perhaps) is false, by imagining a situation in which experts announce it to be false. In this sort of case, one might misinterpret the imagined situation as a situation in which S; here, the situation is merely one in which one has evidence for S.

To avoid cases like these, one can isolate a notion of *coherent modal imagination*, and hold that S is positively conceivable when one can coherently modally imagine a situation that verifies S. A situation is coherently imagined when it is possible to fill in arbitrary details in the imagined situation such that no contradiction reveals itself. To coherently imagine a situation that verifies S, one must be able to coherently imagine a situation such that reasoning about the imagined situation reveals it as a situation that verifies S. This notion is our core notion of positive conceivability: I will henceforth say that S is positively conceivable when it is coherently modally imaginable.

One can then introduce prima facie and ideal versions of positive conceivability. S is prima facie positively conceivable when one can modally imagine a situation that one takes to be coherent and that one takes to verify S. S is ideally positively conceivable when S is prima facie positively conceivable, and this positive conceivability cannot be undermined on idealized reflection. In effect, we can distinguish prima facie coherence from true coherence, and prima facie verification from true verification, where the 'true' notions involve idealization on rational reflection. True coherence requires that arbitrary details can be filled in with no contradiction revealing itself on idealized reflection, whereas prima facie coherence requires merely the appearance of coherence. True verification requires that the imagined situation is revealed as a situation in which S even on idealized reflection, whereas prima facie verification requires merely the appearance that the imagined situation is a situation in which S. Then (invoking the 'true' notions) one can say that S is ideally positively conceivable when one could coherently imagine a situation that verifies S.

When S is ideally positively conceivable, it must be possible in principle to flesh out any missing details of an imagined situation that verifies S, such that the details are imagined clearly and distinctly, and such that no contradiction is revealed. It must also be the case that rational reflection on the imagined situation will not undermine the interpretation of the imagined situation as one in which S is the case. These strictures are demanding, but they are not unreasonable.

These same strictures are typically applied to good thought experiments. A typical philosophical thought experiment starts with prima facie positive conceivability. A subject does not imagine a situation in fine detail: for example, microphysical details are usually left unspecified. Instead, a subject imagines a situation with certain important features specified, notes that a situation of this kind appears to verify S, and judges that the remaining details are not crucial: they can in principle be filled in to yield a full, coherent conception of a situation that verifies S. For the thought experiment to yield the intended conclusion, this prima facie judgment must be correct, so that S is ideally positively conceivable. If better reasoning would reveal that the details cannot be coherently filled in, or that the situation does not truly verify S, then the thought experiment will typically fail in its purpose. If the prima facie judgment is not defeatable in this way, however, the thought experiment succeeds, and S is ideally positively conceivable.

Clear cases of prima facie positive conceivability without ideal positive conceivability are surprisingly hard to come by. Possible examples might include the two cases above: imagining an impossible object and imagining a situation in which mathematicians announce that M (for some false M). In these cases, however, even a moment's reflection is enough to undermine the positive conceivability. In the first case, one can easily detect a contradiction (or the inability to fill in crucial detail). In the second case, reflection reveals the situation as one in which one has evidence that M, but not clearly as a situation in which M. So these cases will be prima facie positively conceivable under only the most superficial of reasoning processes.

A slightly better example of prima facie without ideal positive conceivability may be the Grim Reaper paradox (Benardete 1964; Hawthorne 2000). There are countably many grim reapers, one for every positive integer. Grim reaper 1 is disposed to kill you with a scythe at 1 p.m., if and only if you are still alive then (otherwise his scythe remains immobile throughout), taking 30 minutes to do it. Grim reaper 2 is disposed to kill you with a scythe at 12:30 p.m., if and only if you are still alive then, taking 15 minutes to do it. Grim reaper 3 is disposed to kill you with a scythe at 12:15 p.m., and so on. You are still alive just before 12 p.m., you can only die through the motion of a grim reaper's scythe, and once dead you stay dead. On the face of it, this situation seems conceivable—each reaper seems conceivable individually and intrinsically, and it seems reasonable to combine distinct individuals with distinct intrinsic properties into one situation. But a little reflection reveals that the situation as described is contradictory. I cannot survive to any moment past 12 p.m. (a grim reaper would get me first), but I cannot be killed (for grim reaper n to kill me, I must have survived grim reaper $n+1$, which is impossible). So the description D of the situation is prima facie positively conceivable but not ideally positively conceivable.

Note that the mathematical case is a case in which the subject has coherently imagined a situation, but in which the imagined situation does not verify S on reflection, while the Grim Reaper and impossible object cases are cases in which a situation has not been coherently imagined. Of course in both these cases, the problem is revealed by a little reflection. One might say that in this case (and in the mathematical case above), even if we have prima facie positive conceivability, we do not have secunda facie positive conceivability.

Cases of secunda facie positive conceivability without ideal positive conceivability seem to be extremely thin on the ground. Perhaps the best candidates involve rational but false beliefs in an a priori domain such as mathematics. In general, the details of an imagined situation will be irrelevant to the positive conceivability of a mathematical claim, since reflection suggests that the truth of the mathematical claim is independent of the imagined goings-on in the world. Rather, a mathematical claim will be positively conceivable insofar as there is rational reason to accept that claim; in that case, any imagined situation can be taken to verify the claim. One will have secunda facie positive conceivability without ideal positive conceivability when these reasons stand up to secunda facie scrutiny, but are undermined by ideal reflection. The claim that there is a set of all sets may be such a case: Frege had good a priori reasons for accepting this claim that survived considerable reflection, but ideal (or at least Russellian) reflection revealed a deep contradiction.

If S is positively conceivable, S is negatively conceivable (in both the prima facie and the ideal cases). If one can coherently imagine a situation verifying S, then one cannot rule out that S (though this interacts a little with the primary/secondary distinction below). The reverse is not the case, at least where prima facie conceivability is concerned: many statements are prima facie negatively conceivable without being prima facie positively conceivable. For example, as we saw above, many complex mathematical statements M are such that one cannot rule out M's truth, but one cannot imagine any situation (any part of a world) that would verify S. Something similar goes for statements in other a priori domains. Even in empirical domains, it may be that one cannot rule out M, but one cannot conceive of a situation in which M, due to limited powers of imagination, for example.

Clear cases of ideal negative conceivability without ideal positive conceivability are much harder to find. One might try mathematical statements that are true but not knowable a priori by any possible being. If there were such statements, they and their negations would be ideally negatively conceivable, but probably not ideally positively conceivable. But it is far from clear that there are any such statements. I will return to this matter later.

Positive conceivability, rather than negative conceivability, seems to be what most philosophers have had in mind when discussing conceivability. It is positive conceivability that corresponds to the sort of clear and distinct modal intuition invoked by Descartes, and that reflects the practice in the method of conceivability as used in contemporary philosophical thought experiments.

When Yablo (1993) dismisses the first Goldbach example as not really being an instance of conceivability, he is in effect saying that negative conceivability is not true conceivability, and there is something to this.

Still, it must be conceded that negative conceivability is at least better defined than positive conceivability. The characterization of positive conceivability that I have given here, invoking the notion of modally imagining a situation, cannot be considered a reductive definition. At best, it is something of a clarification. Nevertheless, there seems to be a reasonably clear intuitive notion in the vicinity, of which most people seem to have a grasp. It may be that the notion can be given a more rigorous definition, or it may be that it should be taken as primitive; this is one of the central open questions in the area.

The distinction between positive and negative conceivability bears at least some relation to van Cleve's (1983) distinction between strong and weak conceivability. According to van Cleve, S is strongly conceivable for a subject when the subject sees that S is possible; and S is weakly conceivable when the subject does not see that S is impossible. There is an obvious link between one reading of 'seeing that S is impossible' and the idea of ruling out the hypothesis that S. And the notion of 'seeing that S is possible' can be read as a sort of modal intuition that S of the sort that goes along with modally imagining that S.

I think that it is best not to import the notion of possibility so directly into a definition of conceivability, to avoid the threat of trivializing the link with possibility. In particular, there is a threat that the idealized version of seeing that S is possible will collapse into correctly judging that S is possible, which will be linked trivially to possibility. Still, the idea is closely related to that of coherently imagining a world (or a part of a world) that verifies S: both involve a sort of modal appearance. The main advantage of the construal I have given is that it builds in no presupposition that the imagined world is metaphysically possible, or even that it seems metaphysically possible. It builds in some broadly modal elements, in the ideas of imagining a world, of coherence, and of verification. But, importantly, the modalities here are cognitive or epistemic, and presuppose no tie to the metaphysical. To imagine a world is simply to engage in a distinctive and familiar sort of mental act; and the notions of coherence and verification are wholly grounded in rational notions. So there is no danger of trivializing the link between positive conceivability and possibility.

3 Primary and Secondary Conceivability

The distinction between primary and secondary conceivability draws its motivation from Kripke's discussion of the necessary a posteriori. In the wake of Kripke's arguments that a posteriori statements such as 'Hesperus is Phosphorus' are necessary, it has become a familiar observation that there is a sense in which 'Hesperus is not Phosphorus' is conceivable, and a sense in which it is not. The first of these senses corresponds to primary conceivability, the second to secondary conceivability.

We can say that S is *primarily conceivable* (or *epistemically conceivable*) when it is conceivable that S is *actually* the case. We can say that S is *secondarily conceivable* (or *subjunctively conceivable*) when S conceivably *might have been* the case. This corresponds to two different ways of thinking about hypothetical possibilities: epistemically, as ways the world might actually be, and subjunctively, as counterfactual ways the world might have been. I have written more on these distinctions elsewhere, but I will give a short characterization here.

It is simplest to start with the case of positive conceivability. When one imagines a situation, one can consider it *as actual* (as a way the world might actually be), or one can consider it *as counterfactual* (as a way the world might have been). It is often the case that one will describe a situation differently depending on whether one considers it as actual or as counterfactual. We can say that S is primarily positively conceivable when one can coherently imagine a situation that verifies S when considered as actual, and that S is secondarily positively conceivable when one can coherently imagine a situation that verifies S when considered as counterfactual.

Primary conceivability is grounded in the idea that, for all we know a priori, there are many ways the world might be. The oceans might contain H_2O, or they might contain XYZ; the evening star and the morning star might be the same or distinct; and so on. We can think of these ways the world might be as *epistemic possibilities*, in a broad sense according to which it is epistemically possible that S if the hypothesis that S is not ruled out a priori. When S is epistemically possible, there are usually a number of imaginable situations such that, if they actually obtain, S will be the case. These situations can be taken to verify S, when they are considered as actual.

For example, it is epistemically possible in this sense that Hesperus is not Phosphorus (it is not a priori that Hesperus is Phosphorus). In the background of this epistemic possibility are many specific epistemically possible situations in which the heavenly bodies visible in the morning and evening are distinct. Upon consideration, these epistemically possible situations are revealed as instances of the epistemic possibility that Hesperus is not Phosphorus. There is a clear sense in which these situations *verify* the claim that Hesperus is not Phosphorus: for example, if one hypothetically accepts that such a situation actually obtains, one should rationally conclude that Hesperus is not Phosphorus. This sort of relation among epistemic possibilities plays a central role in our thought.

When we consider situations as actual, we consider and evaluate them in the way that we consider and evaluate epistemic possibilities. That is, we say to ourselves: what if the actual world is really that way? One hypothetically assumes that the situation in question is actual, and considers whether, from that assumption, it follows that S is the case. If so, then the situation verifies S, when considered as actual. In the case above, for example, the situations in question (considered as actual) verify 'Hesperus is not Phosphorus'. So 'Hesperus is not Phosphorus' is primarily positively conceivable.

(Primary conceivability is related to what Yablo (1993) calls 'conceivability$_{ep}$', which requires that one can imagine believing something true with one's actual P-thought, but it is not quite the same. One difference is that primary conceivability does not require that a conceived situation contain a P-thought. So it is primarily conceivable that nothing exists, or that no one thinks—these are not ruled out a priori, and are verified by certain situations considered as actual—but they are not conceivable in Yablo's sense.)

Negative, positive, prima facie, and ideal versions of primary conceivability are easy to formulate. We can say that S is primarily negatively conceivable when it is not ruled out a priori that S is actually the case, or, more briefly, if S is not ruled out a priori. Positive primary conceivability, by contrast, requires coherently imagining a situation (considered as actual) that verifies S. Prima facie and ideal versions of these notions can be straightforwardly formulated as in the previous section. Primary positive conceivability implies primary negative conceivability for both the prima facie and the ideal versions, but the reverse is not obviously the case.

Primary conceivability is always an a priori matter. We consider specific ways the world might be, in such a way that the true character of the actual world is irrelevant. In doing so, empirical knowledge can be suspended, and only a priori reasoning is required.

Secondary conceivability works quite differently. It is grounded in the idea that we can conceive of many counterfactual ways that the world might have been but is not. When we consider imagined situations as counterfactual, we consider and evaluate them in the way that we consider and evaluate counter-factual possibilities in the subjunctive mode. That is, we acknowledge that the character of the actual world is fixed, and say to ourselves: if the situation *had* obtained, what *would have been* the case? If we judge that, had the situation obtained, S would have been the case, then we judge that the situation verifies S when considered as counterfactual.

Take an imagined situation in which the morning star is distinct from the evening star. Along with Kripke, we can say that if this situation had obtained, it would not have been the case that Hesperus was not Phosphorus. So when this situation is considered as counterfactual, it is revealed not as a situation in which Hesperus is not Phosphorus, but rather, as a situation in which at least one of the objects is distinct from both Hesperus and Phosphorus (at least if we take for granted the actual-world knowledge that Hesperus is Phosphorus, and if we accept Kripke's intuitions). The reason is that (if Kripke is right) the application of a term like 'Hesperus' to a counterfactual situation depends on whether the actual Hesperus (i.e., the planet Venus) is present within that situation, and of course the actual Hesperus and the actual Phosphorus are one and the same. So, when considered as counterfactual, this conceivable situation does not verify 'Hesperus is not Phosphorus'. More generally (if Kripke is right), there is no coherently imaginable situation, considered as counterfactual, that verifies 'Hesperus is not Phosphorus'. If so, 'Hesperus is not Phosphorus' is not secondarily positively conceivable.

Unlike primary conceivability, secondary conceivability is often a posteriori. It is not secondarily conceivable that Hesperus is not Phosphorus, but one could not know that a priori. To know this, one needs the empirical information that Hesperus is actually Phosphorus. This aposteriority is grounded in the fact that the application of our words to subjunctive counterfactual situations often depends on their reference in the actual world, and the latter cannot usually be known a priori.

There are various ways to formulate prima facie and ideal versions of secondary conceivability. One might say that a subject prima facie secondarily conceives of S when the subject imagines a situation and judges that if that situation had obtained, S would have been the case. One can say that S is ideally secondarily conceivable if S is prima facie secondarily conceivable, and if the secondary conceivability is not defeatable by idealized rational reflection and complete empirical knowledge. To avoid trivializing a link between conceivability and possibility here, it is probably best to restrict the empirical knowledge in question to nonmodal knowledge.

This characterizes positive versions of secondary conceivability. One might say that S is negatively secondarily conceivable when a priori reflection and empirical nonmodal knowledge reveal no incoherence in the hypothesis that S might have been the case. In any case, as secondary conceivability turns on a posteriori considerations, it will not be our central concern, and most of these varieties can be set aside.

4 Gaps between Conceivability and Possibility

With the distinctions above in play, it is relatively easy to classify potential gaps between conceivability and possibility.

(1) *Prima facie conceivability is an imperfect guide to possibility.*

Given that there is a gap between prima facie and ideal conceivability, it is only to be expected that there is a gap between prima facie conceivability and possibility. Prima facie conceivability judgments are sometimes undermined by continued rational reflection, isolating a contradiction or a misdescription in an apparently conceivable state of affairs. When this happens, then any grounds that the conceivability judgment provided for a claim of possibility will also be undermined.

This gap is widest in the case of prima facie negative conceivability judgments. When such a judgment is not backed by a corresponding prima facie positive conceivability judgment, it provides, at best, weak evidence for possibility. Mathematical cases, such as the prima facie negative conceivability of both Goldbach's conjecture and its negation, provide an obvious source of gaps here. So likewise does any domain in which one might expect to find deep a priori truths.

Prima facie positive conceivability is a much better guide to possibility, but it is still imperfect. The case where one conceives of mathematicians announcing a proof of Goldbach's conjecture (or its negation) is best seen as a case where a superficial prima facie positive conceivability judgment is undermined by a moment's reflection. Other cases of prima facie positive conceivability without possibility may be provided by the Grim Reaper paradox and the case of impossible objects.

Cases of secunda facie positive conceivability, where a prima facie positive conceivability judgment survives a reasonably searching process of rational reflection, are a still stronger guide to possibility. In the great majority of cases with a gap between prima facie and ideal positive conceivability, the prima facie judgment is easily undermined by a little reflection. Gaps between secunda facie positive conceivability and ideal positive conceivability seem to be very rare, although perhaps the Frege case is an example.

In any case, if we are looking for a notion of conceivability such that conceivability tracks possibility perfectly, we must focus on ideal conceivability. In this sense conceivability is not a merely psychological notion; it is a *rational* notion, in much the same way that apriority and rational entailment are rational notions. If there is to be a plausible epistemic/modal bridge, it will be a bridge between the rational and modal domains.

(2) *Positive conceivability is a better guide to possibility than negative conceivability.*

We have seen that prima facie negative conceivability is a relatively weak guide to possibility. The canonical case here is the prima facie negative conceivability judgment, except for a very superficial judgment in one case, of both Goldbach's conjecture and its negation. These cases are not backed by a corresponding prima facie positive conceivability. So at least where prima facie conceivability is concerned, positive conceivability is a much better guide to possibility than negative conceivability. This fits the usual practice in philosophy, where the conceivability judgments that are usually taken as evidence of possibility are almost always positive conceivability judgments. (For just this reason, the Goldbach case was never a very compelling counter-example to this practice.)

With ideal conceivability, things are less clear. Certainly ideal positive conceivability is at least as good a guide to possibility as ideal negative conceivability, since the former entails the latter. What is less clear is whether there are cases of the latter without the former, and if so, whether those cases correspond to possibilities.

The most obvious potential case here is an extension of the Goldbach case above. If either Goldbach's conjecture or its negation is provable (or otherwise knowable a priori), then only one will be ideally negatively conceivable. But perhaps (as noted earlier) there are some true or false mathematical statements whose truth-value cannot be settled even by ideal rational reflection. If so, we would have cases of ideal negative conceivability without ideal positive conceivability and without possibility. It is not at all clear that cases of this type exist, however. I will discuss this and other potential counter-examples to a link between ideal negative conceivability and possibility later. It seems that there are at least no clear counter-examples, so a link between ideal negative conceivabilty and possibility remains tenable.

Overall, we can say that both ideal positive conceivability and ideal negative conceivability are promising as guides to possibility, but that due to its added strength, the former is in a slightly better position to be a perfect guide than the latter.

(3) *Primary conceivability is an imperfect guide to secondary possibility.*

The other standard source of gaps between conceivability and possibility arises from Kripkean cases. It is often said that it is conceivable that Hesperus is not Phosphorus, or that water is not H_2O, or that heat is not the motion of molecules, but none of these states of affairs is in fact possible. In these cases, we have a posteriori necessities and impossibilities, out of reach of a priori methods.

There are a couple of things to be said here. Clearly, the main sense in which these states of affairs are conceivable involves primary conceivability. As discussed earlier, the states of affairs in question are not secondarily conceivable. At best, they might be prima facie secondarily conceivable for a subject lacking relevant empirical knowledge. They will not be prima facie secondarily conceivable for a subject with the relevant knowledge, and they will not be ideally secondarily conceivable as that notion is spelled out above.

One might then try to save a conceivability–possibility link by suggesting that ideal secondary conceivability entails possibility. This thesis is not implausible, but it is not helpful for our purposes here. The reason is that secondary conceivability, and especially ideal secondary conceivability, is deeply a posteriori. So, even if secondary conceivability is a guide to possibility, it will yield no a priori access to modality.

(Around this point, it seems to me that the otherwise excellent discussions of conceivability and possibility by Menzies (1998), van Cleve (1983), and Yablo (1993) all give up too soon, settling for conceivability–possibility theses that are more attenuated than necessary.)

If we are interested in modal rationalism, we should instead focus on ways in which primary conceivability might still be a guide to possibility. Even if it is conceded that, strictly speaking, it is not possible that water is H_2O, it can still be argued that the primary conceivability of 'water is not H_2O' is revealing something about metaphysical possibility. When we apparently conceive of a world in which water is not H_2O, we conceive of a situation in which some other substance (XYZ, say) is the clear liquid surrounding us in the oceans and lakes, and so on. And this situation is indeed metaphysically possible—so our act of conceiving has indeed yielded access to a possible world. It is just that in a certain sense we have misdescribed it in calling it a world where water is not H_2O, or a world in which water is XYZ. If Kripke is right, it is in fact a world in which XYZ is watery stuff, but not water, and a world in which the only water that exists is H_2O.

Further, there remains a sense in which a world with XYZ in the oceans can be seen as satisfying the statement 'water is not H_2O'. Here, I will give a very brief version of a story that I have told in more detail elsewhere (e.g., Chalmers 1996, forthcoming a; see also Evans 1977; Davies and Humberstone 1980; and Jackson 1998).

As discussed earlier, there is clearly a broad sense in which it is *epistemically* possible that water is not H_2O, in that the hypothesis is not ruled out a priori. Intuitively, there are ways our world could turn out such that, if they turn out that way, it will turn out that water is not H_2O. And if we consider the XYZ-world as an epistemic possibility—that is, we consider the hypothesis that the world with XYZ in the oceans is *our* world—then this epistemic possibility can be seen as an instance of the epistemic possibility that water is not H_2O. We can rationally say, 'If our world turns out to have XYZ in the oceans (etc.), it will turn out that water is not H_2O.' This might be put as a simple indicative conditional: 'If XYZ is in the oceans and lakes (etc.), then water is XYZ.' Compare: 'If Prince Albert Victor committed those murders, then he is Jack the Ripper.' Here, the indicative conditional 'If P, then Q' can be evaluated using the

Ramsey test: if one hypothetically accepts the belief that P, does one rationally arrive at the conclusion that Q?

All this reflects the fact that we have a systematic way of evaluating and describing epistemic possibilities that differs from our way of evaluating and describing subjunctive counterfactual possibilities. In both cases, we consider and describe worlds; but in the epistemic case, we consider them as actual, whereas in the subjunctive case, we consider them as counterfactual. These two modes of consideration of a world yield two ways in which a world might be seen to satisfy a sentence. When the XYZ-world is considered as actual, it satisfies 'water is XYZ'; when it is considered as counterfactual, it does not.

Given a statement S and a world W, the *primary intension* (or *epistemic intension*) of S returns the truth-value of S in W considered as actual. Three heuristics for evaluating the primary intension of S in W correspond to the three tests mentioned above. One can appeal to direct evaluation of epistemic possibilities: is the epistemic possibility that W is actual an instance of the epistemic possibility that S? One can appeal to indicative conditionals (evaluated by the Ramsey test): if W is the case, is S the case? Or one can appeal to the 'turns out' locution: if W turns out to be actual, will it turn out that S?

Primary intensions can be formally defined in terms of a priori entailments. In particular, we can say that the primary intension of S is true in W if the material conditional 'if W is actual, then S' is a priori: that is, if the hypothesis that W is actual and S is not the case can be ruled out a priori. S's primary intension is false in W if the conditional 'if W is actual, then ~S' is a priori; and S's primary intension is indeterminate in W if neither of these conditionals is a priori. For example, the hypothesis that the XYZ-world is actual and water is H_2O can plausibly be ruled out conclusively by rational reflection alone. If so, the material conditional 'if the XYZ-world is actual, then water is not H_2O' is a priori, and the primary intension of 'water is H_2O' is false in the XYZ-world. For more on the definition of primary intensions, see the further discussion below.

Primary intensions are grounded in the *epistemic* evaluation of statements in worlds: that is, the evaluation of statements in worlds considered as actual. One can also define the notion of a *secondary* (or *subjunctive*) intension, grounded in the subjunctive evaluation of statements in worlds: that is, the evaluation of statements in worlds considered as counterfactual. The secondary intension of a statement S is the function that maps a world W to the truth-value of S in W considered as counterfactual. These correspond to a much more familiar notion of intension in contemporary philosophy, so I will say less about them here.

To characterize secondary intensions with a heuristic, one can appeal to subjunctive conditionals: if W had obtained, would S have been the case?

Or one can appeal directly to intuitions about counterfactual possibilities: is W a counterfactual possibility in which S would have been the case? Heuristics of this sort are frequently invoked by Kripke in his evaluation of possible worlds; and his influential claims about possibility are almost always grounded in subjunctive claims about what might have been the case. So the intensional notions that arise from Kripke's work are all closely tied to secondary intensions.

A paradigmatic example involves the subjunctive evaluation of a statement such as 'water is XYZ' at the XYZ-world, a world that is similar to our own except that the watery liquid in the oceans and lakes is XYZ. If Kripke and Putnam are correct, then if the watery stuff in the oceans and lakes had been XYZ, it would nevertheless not have been the case that water was XYZ: at best, XYZ would have been watery. Correspondingly, W does not seem to represent a counterfactual possibility in which water is XYZ. So the secondary intension of 'water is XYZ' is false at the XYZ-world.

We can then say that S is *primarily possible* (or 1-possible) if its primary intension is true in some possible world (i.e., if S is true in some world considered as actual). S is *secondarily possible* (or 2-possible) if its secondary intension is true in some possible world (i.e., if S is true in some world considered as counterfactual). Primary and secondary necessity can be defined analogously.

Secondary possibility and necessity correspond to the standard conception of what it is for a statement to be metaphysically possible or necessary. For example, 'water is H_2O' is plausibly 2-necessary, and 'water is XYZ' is 2-impossible, reflecting their metaphysical necessity and impossibility (as standardly understood) respectively. On this understanding, we can say that a statement is metaphysically necessary iff it has a necessary secondary intension.

Primary possibility and necessity correspond much more closely to epistemic notions such as apriority. It is clear that when S is a priori, it will have a necessary primary intension, so it will be 1-necessary. Whether the reverse entailment (from 1-necessity to apriority) holds is one of the central issues in this paper, but for now we can note that at least the clearest cases of 1-necessary statements are all plausibly a priori: witness '2+2=4', or 'Hesperus, if it exists, is visible in the evening' (1-necessary and a priori), as opposed to 'tables exist' and 'water is H_2O' (1-contingent and a posteriori).

The existence of primary and secondary intensions suggests that expression tokens have a complex semantic value that involves both intensions. These intensions will play important roles when the expression is embedded in different contexts. In constructions such as 'it might have been the case that S' and subjunctive conditionals, S's secondary intension will be relevant. In constructions such as 'it is a priori that S' and indicative conditionals, S's primary intension will be relevant. Both intensions are part of the content of S in both contexts (S is not ambiguous): it is just that the different contexts exploit different aspects of S's content. The propositional content of S might be understood in more than one way, but if one holds that the apriority and necessity of S is a function of the proposition that S expresses, then the proposition expressed by S will be reducible to neither its primary intension nor its secondary intension. Rather, it will involve at least the structure of both.

We can now see how primary conceivability can act as a guide to possibility. When we find it conceivable that water is not H_2O, there is no possible world that satisfies 'water is not H_2O' when the world is considered as *counterfactual*, but there is a possible world that satisfies 'water is not H_2O' when the world is considered as *actual*. Put differently, the secondary intension of 'water is H_2O' is true in no world, but the primary intension is true in some (centered) worlds. The XYZ-world, and other centered worlds that we might conceive of when we conceive that water is not H_2O, all satisfy the primary intension of 'water is H_2O'.

We can put this by saying that primary conceivability is an imperfect guide to secondary possibility, but is a much better guide to primary possibility. In all the Kripkean cases in which S is primarily conceivable, S is also primarily possible (or at least, Kripke's discussion gives no reason to deny this). There is a (centered) possible world satisfying the primary intension of 'Hesperus is not Phosphorus' (e.g., a world where heavenly bodies visible from the center in the morning and the evening are distinct), of 'heat is not the motion of molecules' (e.g., a world where something else causes heat sensations), and so on. These worlds are all first-class metaphysical possibilities.

So Kripke's examples are entirely compatible with the thesis that conceivability is a guide to possibility. We just need to make sure that the relevant notions are aligned: primary conceivability is a guide to primary possibility, and secondary conceivability is a guide to secondary possibility. This is no surprise: it would be odd to expect conceivability of a situation considered as actual to be a guide to possibility of a world considered as counterfactual, or vice versa! So we are still left with significant a priori access to the space of possible worlds.

5 Sideline: On Defining Primary Intensions

Primary intensions are intensions that capture the distinctive way in which a statement is used to describe and evaluate epistemic possibilities. The primary intension of a statement could be defined in various ways, but the most useful definition is in terms of a priori entailments: the primary intension of S is true at W if the material conditional 'if W is actual, then S' is a priori. I elaborate and defend this conception of a primary intension in other work; here I will make a few observations about the definition of primary intensions and about their properties. This material can be skipped by those who are not interested in the fine details of the two-dimensional framework.

(i) For a world to be considered as actual, it must be a *centered* world: a world marked with a specified individual and time. The reason is that an epistemic possibility is not completely determined until one's 'viewpoint' is specified. For example, an objective description of the world will not allow me to settle the question of whether I am in Australia or in the USA, but a 'centered' specification will do this. The hypothesis that a centered world W is actual, for me, will include the hypothesis that I am the being marked at the center and that now is the time marked at the center. A primary intension can then be seen as a function from centered worlds to truth-values. The primary intension of 'I am a philosopher', for example, will be true at those centered worlds in which the subject at the center is a philosopher.

(ii) The evaluation of a conditional involving 'If W is actual . . .' requires a *canonical description* of W. We can say that the primary intension of S is true at W if the material conditional 'if D, then S' is a priori, where D is a canonical description of W. The notion of a canonical description can be elaborated in various ways (see chalmers forthcoming *b*). One needs to isolate a semantically neutral vocabulary in which worlds can be described, and to require a certain sort of complete description within this vocabulary. On the first point, a semantically neutral expression might be seen intuitively as one that behaves the same way in epistemic and subjunctive evaluation, so that it is not susceptible to Twin Earth thought experiments (supplemented by indexicals such as 'I' and 'now' to handle centering). On the second point, one might require a complete description to be ontologically complete, or qualitatively complete, or epistemically complete, in the terms from later in this paper. If the theses of this paper are correct, these different notions of completeness are coextensive. If the theses are incorrect, these notions may come apart, yielding different primary intensions. In that case, it is probably best to require epistemic completeness in the definition.

(iii) Primary intensions are defined here as functions over (centered) possible worlds. One can also define a closely related intension as a function over an independently characterized *epistemic space* of maximal epistemic possibilities. Epistemic space is defined not in terms of metaphysical possible worlds, but rather in terms of epistemic notions such as apriority: maximal epistemic possibilities correspond roughly to maximally specific a priori consistent hypotheses concerning the actual world. One can define an intension over this space much as one defines a primary intension. In other work (e.g., Chalmers, forthcoming *a*, *b*), I have called this an *epistemic intension*.

What is the relationship between the two notions? It turns on the relationship between epistemic space and the space of centered possible worlds, which in turn is closely tied to the relationship between ideal negative conceivability and primary possibility. If this paper's theses are correct, there is a direct correspondence between the two spaces, so that primary intensions and epistemic intensions as defined here are almost identical. If the theses are incorrect, then the definitions come apart: there will be maximal epistemic possibilities that correspond to no centered possible worlds, so the intensions will be defined over different spaces.

For many purposes, especially within the epistemic domain, the notion of an epistemic intension is more fundamental. For example, necessity of epistemic intension is constitutively tied to apriority and other epistemic notions, inde- · pendently of any views about metaphysical possibility. So epistemic intensions can be used for epistemic purposes regardless of one's further views. For present purposes, the link between the epistemic and the metaphysical domain is the central focus, so I concentrate here on primary intensions understood as functions over metaphysically possible worlds. If what I say here is correct, the two intensions may ultimately be collapsed.

(iv) The primary intension of some terms can vary between speakers. For example, Leverrier might use 'Neptune' to pick out whatever causes certain orbital perturbations within a world, whereas a friend might use it to pick out (roughly) whatever Leverrier refers to with the name, irrespective of any perturbing role. If so, their primary intensions will vary accordingly. All this reflects the fact that certain conditionals of the form 'if W is actual, then Neptune is such-and-such' are a priori for Leverrier, but not for his acquaintance. This happens not because of any difference in their rational capacities (which we are idealizing away from), but because of differences in the inferential roles associated with the term. Something similar can happen with most names and natural kind terms.

It follows that at least where names and natural kind terms are concerned, primary intensions are not candidates for linguistic meaning, the sort of meaning common to all tokens of an expression type. (See Chalmers, 2002 *a*.) To accommodate this phenomenon, primary intensions should be associated in the first instance with expression tokens (or perhaps with types as used on occasions), not with expression types. We can define primary intensions more precisely by saying that the primary intension of a statement token S (used by a speaker) is true in W if the material conditional 'if W, then S' is a priori for the speaker. Here, a sentence T will be a priori for a speaker if the belief (or the hypothesis) that the speaker expresses with T could be conclusively justified, on ideal rational reflection, with justification independent of experience. On this account, different material conditionals will be a priori for Leverrier and his friend, so their primary intensions for 'Neptune' will differ accordingly.

Note that the notion of apriority (whether speaker-relative or speaker-independent) requires the same sort of rational idealization as that present in the notion of ideal conceivability. I have defended the claim that relevant conditionals are a priori elsewhere (see also the discussion of scrutability later in this paper). If someone is skeptical about this, or skeptical about the very notion of apriority, it may nevertheless remain plausible that the material conditionals in question have *some* distinctive epistemic status that can be used to define a corresponding notion of primary intension.

(v) To evaluate the primary intension of S in W, it is not required that W contain a token of S. The heuristics and definition above give no special role for such a token, even when it is present. On another approach, one could define the *contextual intension* of S as a function defined across worlds containing a token of S at the center, returning the truth-value of that token. Contextual intensions are closely related to Stalnaker's *diagonal proposition* (1978), which is also defined in terms of the semantic values of a token in a different context. These notions differ in fundamental respects from the current notion of a primary intension, which is grounded in the epistemic domain. Contextual intensions turn on the context-dependence of a statement's extensions, while primary intensions turn on the use of a statement in evaluating epistemic possibilities.

To see some differences, note that the contextual intension of statements such as 'language exists' will plausibly be nowhere false, but the primary intension of 'language exists' will be false in many (language-free) centered worlds. This reflects the (broad) epistemic possibility of such worlds: it is not a priori that language exists. Something similar applies to 'nothing exists' (whose primary intension is true of an empty world) and many claims about thinkers and about language. The contextual intension also requires an account of what it takes for a token to count as an instance of S's type, raising problems (pointed out by Block and Stalnaker (1999)) that tend to break the link between contextual intensions and epistemic notions. If we individuate S's type orthographically, 'bachelors are unmarried' has a contingent contextual intension; if we individuate by familiar sorts of semantic content, 'water is XYZ' has a necessarily false contextual inten-sion; if we individuate by 'narrow content' or some such, then we need an inde-pendent account of that sort of content. This issue does not arise for primary intensions. The effect is that primary intensions are much more directly con-nected to the epistemic domain than are contextual intensions.

This distinction is useful in assessing the relationship between the conceiv-ability–possibility theses I am putting forward here and a related thesis put forward by Kripke (1980). Kripke suggests that when a necessary claim (such as 'heat is the motion of molecules') is 'apparently contingent', then in a qualitatively identical evidential situation, a qualitatively identical statement might have been false. Translated into the existing framework, this appears to come roughly to the thesis that when S is primarily conceivable for a subject, there is a world at which a certain sort of contextual intension of S is true. This contextual intension is defined at worlds whose center contains a subject in a evidential situation qualitatively identical to that of the original subject, uttering a qualitatively identical statement. At this world, the contextual intension returns the truth-value of the statement uttered at the center.

This thesis roughly parallels the thesis I have offered here, except with a sort of contextual intension in place of an epistemic intension. It is not entirely clear how to understand the notions of 'qualitatively identical' here, but however the notion is understood, the thesis appears to be false. The reasons are closely tied to the considerations already mentioned about 'Language exists' and the like. We can let 'Bill' be a term introduced to rigidly designate whatever color quale is in the center of my visual field now, or let 'L' be a term introduced to rigidly designate the number 1 if there are languages, and 0 if there are no languages. Then 'Bill = blue' and 'L>0' are a posteriori necessities, associated with the usual sense of apparent contingency. But they fail Kripke's test: they have a necessary contextual intension (of the relevant kind), and all qualitatively identical statements uttered in identical evidential situations will be true. The same problem applies to an adaptation of Kripke's thesis by Bealer (1996), suggesting that a posteriori necessities do not arise with expressions using 'semantically stable' terms—terms whose meaning does not vary across qualitatively identical epistemic situations—so that a priori modal intuitions using these expressions are reliable. Terms such as 'Bill' and 'L' are semantically stable by Bealer's definition, but still yield a posteriori necessities.

In contrast, the thesis I have offered handles these cases straightforwardly. 'Bill = blue' and 'L = 1' have a contingent primary intension: the first is false at a world where the subject at the center has no blue experiences, and the second is false at a world without language. So the inference from primary conceivability of these statement's negations to their primary possibility goes through straightforwardly. This suggests that epistemically defined notions are more fundamental than contextually defined notions for present purposes. (For much more on this matter, see Chalmers, forthcoming *b*.)

(vi) Yablo (Ch. 13 below) considers various ways in which the epistemic evaluation of statements in worlds might be defined. He rejects both the indicative conditional heuristic and the 'turns out' heuristic, on the grounds that they give the wrong result in certain metalinguistic cases. For example, 'tail are wings' should be false in a world (considered as actual) where 'tail' is used to refer to wings. But Yablo suggests that the indicative conditional 'if "tail" refers to wings, then tails are wings' is intuitively correct, as is 'if it turns out that "tail" refers to wings, then it will turn out that tails are wings'.

I think that these judgments of intuitive correctness are unclear, and that there is at least a reasonable reading of the locutions on which the conditionals in questions are incorrect. (Compare the reasonable conditional: 'if "tail" refers to wings, "tail" does not refer to tails'.) But even if Yablo were right about this, it would show only that the heuristics are imperfect, giving the wrong results in special cases. The problem does not arise for the definition I have given here in terms of a priori material conditionals.

To see this, note that the claim that 'tail' refers to tails is not a priori, but represents substantive a posteriori metalinguistic knowledge. It is a posteriori that the orthographic string 'tail' means anything at all, and it is a posteriori that it means what it does. So there is no a priori entailment from claims involving ' "tail" ' to corresponding claims involving 'tail'. And in particular, there is no a priori entailment from ' "tail" refers to wings' to 'tails are wings'. More generally, there are plausibly no substantive a priori connections between claims about the orthographic string 'tail' and claims about tails, since any inferential connections between these claims rest on a posteriori metalinguistic knowledge. If so, the way that 'tail' is used in such a world will be irrelevant in evaluating the primary intension of statements such as 'tails are wings' in that world. In particular, there is no danger that 'tails are wings' will be true in a world (considered as actual) in which 'tail' refers to wings.

Someone might suggest that there is a semantic concept of 'tail' that builds in semantic constraints as well as orthographic constraints, so that it is a priori that 'tail' refers to tails. But then the worlds that Yablo considers, in which the orthographic string 'tail' refers to wings, will not be worlds in which 'tail' (construed semantically) refers to wings, so there is no danger that they will be worlds (considered as actual) in which tails are wings. Either way, the usage of the orthographic string 'tail' in a world will be irrelevant in evaluating the primary intension of 'tails are wings' in that world.

Yablo himself endorses a mixed view, on which it is a priori that 'sister' refers to sisters (like the semantic view), but on which it is not a priori that 'sister' refers to female siblings (like the orthographic view), even though it is a priori that sisters are female siblings. A mixed view like this cannot be accommodated in the current framework: the framework requires that apriority is preserved under a priori entailment, but Yablo's view violates this. (For the relevant A, B, C, it is a priori that A, that B, that if A and B then C, but not that C.) But it can plausibly be argued that this violation of closure is reason enough to reject Yablo's mixed view. (The view seems to be grounded in an idiosyncratic conception of a priori knowledge, according to which a priori knowledge that S depends on metalinguistic knowledge concerning 'S'. I think that such a view should clearly be rejected.) In any case, it seems that any residual problems here arise from Yablo's somewhat idiosyncratic view of these metalinguistic cases, and not from the cases themselves.

For his own view of the epistemic evaluation of statements in worlds, Yablo endorses a 'could have turned out' heuristic: 'If it had turned out that W, would it have turned out that S?' Although I have occasionally used this heuristic myself in earlier work, I am less comfortable with it than with the 'turns out' heuristic, as the subjunctive conditional here can easily be read nonepistemically, and it is too close to the subjunctive 'If it had been that W, it would have been that S' for comfort. (I am also worried that Yablo's paper has the wrong title—most uses of 'coulda', 'woulda', and 'shoulda' go with secondary intensions, not primary intensions.) Still, it may be that there is at least a reading of this locution that gives approximately correct results in most cases.

6 Conceivability–Possibility Theses

To summarize: if any variety of a priori conceivability entails possibility, it must be a variety of ideal primary conceivability, and the variety of possibility that is entailed must be primary possibility. And positive conceivability is always at least as good a guide to possibility as negative conceivability. This leaves us with the following as the most plausible entailment between conceivability and possibility:

(1) *Ideal primary positive conceivability entails primary possibility.*

That is, if S is ideally primarily positively conceivable, then there is some metaphysically possible centered world satisfying S's primary intension (or that satisfies S when considered as actual).

We have also left open the status of the following:

(2) *Ideal primary negative conceivability entails primary possibility.*

For completeness, I note that the following two theses also remain plausible, although neither suffices for a thoroughgoing modal rationalism:

(3) *Secunda facie primary positive conceivability is an extremely good guide to primary possibility.*

(4) *Ideal secondary (positive/negative) conceivability entails secondary possibility.*

We have seen that the first thesis is compatible with the standard clear counter examples to a link between conceivability and possibility, as is the second (although there are some unclear counter examples that may threaten the second). So if there are any counter examples to these two theses, they must come from a different source, and their existence will gain no support from the standard cases.

For my part, I think that thesis (1) is almost certainly true, and that thesis (2) is very likely true. In most of the rest of the paper, I will discuss what counter examples to these theses would involve, and will give a quick sketch of reasons to think the theses true.

Note that because the conceivability and possibility of a statement are speaker-relative, the conceivability–possibility theses above must be interpreted in a speaker-relative way: if S is conceivable for a speaker, S is possible for that speaker. There are two main sources of speaker-relativity here: variation in cognitive capacity, which affects prima facie conceivability, and variation in primary and secondary intensions of terms, which affects primary conceivability/possibility and secondary conceivability/possibility respectively.

For the central theses (1) and (2), only the second sort of variation is relevant. This variation manifests itself in phenomena such as the following: 'Neptune does not perturb the orbit of Uranus' may be ideally primarily conceivable for Leverrier's friend but not for Leverrier himself; it will also be primarily possible for Leverrier's friend but not for Leverrier himself. In a similar way, 'I am not David Chalmers' may be ideally secondarily conceivable for you, but not for me; it is also secondarily possible for you, but not for me. Because the variation here affects conceivability and possibility equally, it does not threaten an inference from conceivability to possibility. It suggests at most that in cases where this variation is present, the inference must be speaker-relative.

One might worry that because the notion of ideal conceivability itself involves the notion of possibility (for example, in claims about what some possible being could conceive, or about what is defeatable), there is a danger of circularity. There are a few different issues here. First, one might worry that this rules out a reduction of possibility to conceivability. But I am not trying to give such a reduction; I am simply investigating the connection between the two notions. Second, one might worry that circularity will make the conceivability–possibility thesis trivial. But the notion of possibility enters into the definition of conceivability in such a roundabout way that the thesis clearly remains substantive. Finally, one might worry that defining conceivability in terms of possibility renders conceivability toothless as an epistemic guide to possibility, and so defeats modal rationalism. But this is not so: modal rationalism holds that modality is a priori *accessible*, and so invokes the notion of possibility in a precisely parallel manner. If ideal conceivability tracks possibility, then modal facts are rationally accessible, as required.

(If one wanted to give a reductive account of possibility in terms of conceivability, there is one strategy that would be worth trying. Instead of invoking possible beings in the definition of conceivability, one could invoke conceivable beings. There might then be a sort of bootstrapping definition. First, the notion of conceivability would be grounded in our own prima facie conceivings. Second, we can conceive of beings who are better reasoners than us, with fewer cognitive limitations. Third, those beings could presumably conceive of better reasoners still. And so on. It is not out of the question that this process might lead to some sort of limit or fixed point. If so, one might obtain a recursive (not circular) definition of possibility in terms of conceivability. I cannot pretend that this matter is entirely clear, however.)

Does this account leave room for modal error? If theses (1) and (2) are correct, then modal errors arising from conceivability judgments will stem either from the difference between prima facie and ideal conceivability or from the difference between primary and secondary conceivability (and possibility). These modal errors will fall into one or more of the following classes:

(i) Prima facie negative conceivability judgments can go wrong in cases where a 'deep' a priori contradiction is not revealed by prima facie reasoning.

(ii) Prima facie positive conceivability judgments can go wrong when (a) an imagined situation that is taken to verify S does not in fact verify S, upon rational reflection; or when (b) an imagined situation is not coherently imagined, because of the failure to notice a deep contradiction, or because of the inability to fill in crucial details.

(iii) Primary conceivability judgments can go wrong if a subject mistakenly expects them to be a guide to secondary possibility.

(iv) Prima facie secondary conceivability judgments can go wrong as a guide to secondary possibility when a subject is misinformed about relevant nonmodal empirical facts, and perhaps when an incautious subject is merely ignorant of those facts.

7 From Negative to Positive Conceivability

In the remainder of the paper, I will focus on the status of the central conceivability–possibility theses (1) and (2), discussing what is required in order for them to be true, what form counter examples must take, whether there are any plausible counter examples, and what might ground the truth of the theses. Given space limitations, this discussion will only scratch the surface, but I hope to convey at least a broad view of the terrain. In discussing these theses, we can restrict our attention mostly to ideal primary positive conceivability, ideal primary negative conceivability, and primary possibility. 'Ideal primary' should be understood throughout, in references to positive and negative conceivability, and 'possibility' should always be read as primary possibility. The speaker-relativity of the relevant claims should also be understood throughout.

I will first address the question of whether (ideal primary) negative conceivability entails (primary) possibility. Here I will factor out the question, addressed later, of whether positive conceivability entails possibility, and address the question of whether negative conceivability entails positive conceivability.

I call the (empty or nonempty) class of statements that are negatively conceivable but not positively conceivable the *twilight zone*. Potential members of the twilight zone come from two sources: inscrutabilities and open inconceivabilities.

8 Inscrutabilities

The class of inscrutabilities can be introduced by considering an attractive thesis about truth and reference:

Scrutability of Truth and Reference: Once we know how the world is qualitatively, we are in a position to know what our terms refer to and whether our statements are true.

Take the case of reference first. Often we do not know what our terms refer to, but this knowledge is usually grounded in some qualitative ignorance of the way the world is. Given enough qualitative information (typically information about physical and mental states, although more on this later), we are in a position to know what our terms refer to. This reflects common practice in the theory of reference: in thinking about reference of a term in actual and hypothetical situations (considered as actual), it suffices to give a complete enough qualitative description of relevant features of those situations. From here, reference can be determined.

There are a few difficulties with the thesis of scrutability of reference. The first is that it is not entirely obvious what it means to 'know what a term refers to'. Presumably this is to be able to give some sort of alternative description of the referent; but just which alternative descriptions qualify? The second is that there may be a degree of indeterminacy in the reference of our terms over and above what is present in the truth-values of our statements. Examples might include terms like 'number' and 'symphony', or Quine's examples of mass-nouns and count-nouns in Japanese (see Benacerraf 1965, Horgan 1986, and

Quine 1960, respectively). In these cases, it seems that there are multiple ways to assign referents to our terms, each of which captures our intuitions about the truth-values of our statements, insofar as these truth-values are determinate. In these cases, it is not at all clear that there is a fact of the matter between these assignments of reference.

For both of these reasons it is easier to focus on the scrutability of truth. On the first issue, there is no analogous problem making sense of what it is to know the truth-value of a statement. On the second issue, almost all of the indeterminacies discussed above drop out when it comes to the truth-values of statements. (The exceptions may be such statements as 'the number two is a set of sets', and the like, but now we are at least down to an isolated problem in the metaphysical domain, as opposed to a problem that arises with every use of the word 'two'.) And most of the intuitive backing behind the scrutability of reference (e.g., that, given enough qualitative information, we can know who Jack the Ripper is) is reflected in the scrutability of truth (e.g., that, given enough qualitative information, we can know whether Jack the Ripper was Prince Albert Victor).

The scrutability of truth can be formulated somewhat more precisely as follows:

Scrutability of Truth (second pass): If D is a complete qualitative description of the world, then for all T, T $\supset$ (D $\rightarrow$ T).

Here and elsewhere, 'A $\supset$ B' is a material conditional, and 'A $\rightarrow$ B' is true iff 'A $\supset$ B' is a priori. When 'A $\rightarrow$ B' is true, we can say that A *implies* B. So the scrutability thesis says, in effect, that all truths are derivable through a priori reasoning from a complete qualitative description of the world. The thesis can also be weakened somewhat to hold that all truths are derivable from a complete *enough* qualitative description, thus avoiding the need to invoke a description of the whole world for every truth; but I will use the simpler, if less practical, formulation in what follows.

This way of putting things is not only more precise than 'Once we know A, we're in a position to know B'; it also overcomes a problem posed by the paradox of knowability. Let P be a truth that I don't currently know, and let Q be 'P and I don't know that P'. Then Q is true but unknowable. (To know Q, I would have to know P; but once I know P, then Q is false.) So Q is in danger of coming out inscrutable on the first formulation—it is a truth such that having full qualitative information about the world doesn't suffice to know it. Nevertheless, it may remain the case that Q is implied by a full qualitative description of the world. The 'paradox' gives no special reason to deny that, given such a complete qualitative description D, I can know a priori that if D, then Q.

We can also put the scrutability thesis in terms of *epistemic completeness*, where an epistemically complete statement is one that, roughly speaking, epistemically settles everything that could be settled. More precisely, let us say as before that a statement D is epistemically possible (in the broad sense) when D is not ruled out a priori: that is, when it is not a priori that ~D (or that ~det(D), to cover cases of indeterminacy) or, equivalently, when D is ideally negatively conceivable. Then:

> A statement D is *epistemically complete* iff (i) D is epistemically possible, and (ii) for all F, if D ∧ F is epistemically possible, then D→F.

Then the scrutability thesis, reformulated, says that a complete qualitative description of the world is epistemically complete. The second formulation implies the first, since if D is a complete qualitative description of the world and T is the case, then D ∧ T is true, so D ∧ T is epistemically possible, so (by the second formulation) D implies T. In the other direction: if D ∧ F is epistemically possible, then D does not imply ~F, so (by the contrapositive of the first formulation) ~ ~F, so F, so (by the first formulation) D implies F. (Worries about indeterminacy are handled by the observation that if D ∧ F is epistemically possible, D does not imply ~det(F), so the indeterminacy of F is excluded.)

The residual unclarity, of course, is in the notion of a 'complete qualitative description of the world'. What counts as a complete qualitative description? One idea is that a complete enough qualitative description is one that specifies all truths; but this will not do for our purposes, since it renders the scrutability thesis trivial. Intuitively, a qualitative description of the world is a basic description from which many other truths might be derived.

A second and promising idea says that a complete qualitative description is a complete description in terms of fundamental natural properties (plus indexical information). That is, it involves a description in terms of fundamental microphysical properties (perhaps such as mass, charge, position, and spin), and perhaps also in terms of those fundamental properties (if any) that are not microphysical (on some nonmateralist views, phenomenal or protophenomenal properties). So understood, the scrutability thesis would come to the claim that the fundamental natural truth about the world, in conjunction with indexical truths, implies (a priori) all truths.

We might formalize this by understanding this sort of description of the world as an *ontologically complete* description of the world: roughly speaking, one that metaphysically necessitates all truths about the world. In order for a resulting scrutability thesis to be tenable, the relevant sort of metaphysical necessitation must be 1-necessitation (recalling that a statement is 1-necessary if its primary intension is true in all centered metaphysically possible worlds). More precisely, we can say:

A statement D is *ontologically complete* if (i) D is 1-possible, and (ii) if $D \wedge F$ is 1-possible, then $D \supset F$ is 1-necessary.

The resulting scrutability thesis is:

Strong Scrutability: If D is an ontologically complete truth, then D is epistemically complete.

The strong scrutability thesis is interesting and not obviously false, and is closely related to thesis (2) connecting ideal negative conceivability and possibility (in fact, it is a consequence of that thesis). But it does not cut things quite finely enough for our purposes here. The thesis would be denied by a materialist who holds that it is positively conceivable that there are zombies (or other worlds physically identical to ours and phenomenally distinct), but that zombies are not metaphysically possible. (I have elsewhere called this view type-B materialism, as opposed to type-A materialism on which zombies are not even conceivable.) According to such a materialist, phenomenal truths about the world are not implied by the complete fundamental truth about the world, which is microphysical, so strong scrutability is false. This sort of denial of strong scrutability raises issues somewhat distinct from those I am concerned with here. For now, I am concerned with potential gaps between negative and positive conceivability, but this denial is best assimilated to a potential gap between positive conceivability and possibility. So it is useful to factor out a weaker scrutability thesis that this denial does not contravene.

The weaker scrutability thesis requires a sense of 'complete qualitative description' such that on the type-B materialist view, a microphysical description is not a complete qualitative description. Intuitively, the microphysical description seems incomplete (in a sense) as a qualitative description precisely because it does not specify the phenomenal truths, and the phenomenal truths seem to be (in a sense) qualitative truths. And the sense in which these are qualitative truths seems to correspond to the fact that such truths will be required for a fully clear and distinct conception of what the world is qualitatively like. That is, they are required for a description of the world to the limits of positive conceivability.

A qualitatively complete description of the world, then, should be understood as a description to the limits of positive conceivability. That is, it is a description that specifies a unique positively conceivable situation. We can define this more precisely as follows:

A statement D is *qualitatively complete* if (i) D is positively conceivable, and (ii) if $D \wedge F$ is positively conceivable, then $D \rightarrow F$.

On the type-B materialist view, a complete microphysical description of the world will not be qualitatively complete. For various phenomenal truths F, D ∧ F will be positively conceivable, as will D ∧ ~F, but D will imply neither F nor ~F. On this view, a complete qualitative description of the world will require at least something akin to a full microphysical and phenomenal description.

With the notion of qualitative completeness in hand, we can now formulate our final version of the scrutability thesis.

Scrutability (final version): If D is a qualitatively complete truth, then for all S, S ⊃ (D → S).

Or, equivalently:

If D is a qualitatively complete truth, then D is epistemically complete.

We can say that S is an *inscrutable truth* if S is true and some qualitatively complete truth D does not imply S. The scrutability thesis above says that there are no inscrutable truths.

It is easy to see that if S is inscrutable, then both D ∧ S and D ∧ ~S (for a relevant D) are in the twilight zone. D ∧ S and D ∧ ~S are negatively conceivable, since their negations (D ⊃ ~S, D ⊃ S) are not a priori. But they are not positively conceivable: if they were, then D could not be qualitatively complete. So, if there are inscrutable truths, there are inhabitants of the twilight zone, and negative conceivability implies neither positive conceivability nor possibility.

Are there any inscrutable truths? To assess this, it helps to have an idea of what a qualitatively complete truth involves. Such a truth presumably must include at least full microphysical information, including microphysical laws. It may or may not require phenomenal information (a type-A materialist view will deny this), but it cannot hurt to include it (specified in the sort of 'pure phenomenal' vocabulary discussed by Chalmers (2002)). On any of the type-A materialist, type-B materialist, and property dualist views, a qualitatively complete truth implies the complete microphysical and phenomenal truth, so anything not implied by the former is not implied by the latter. Indexical information is required, since more than one conjunction of complete objective truths with indexical claims is positively conceivable. Finally, in order to rule out situations containing extra nonphysical, nonphenomenal goings-on, qualitative completeness requires a 'totality' claim, holding that the world is a minimal world that satisfies the physical, phenomenal, and indexical claims.

Elsewhere (Chalmers and Jackson 2001), this conjunction of microphysical, phenomenal, indexical, and totality claims is referred to as PQTI. It is not entirely implausible that PQTI is itself a complete qualitative description of the world: for the most part, even where there are candidates for truths not implied by PQTI, these do not seem to be associated with intuitions of distinct positively conceivable situations analogous to the intuitions in the zombie case. In any case, even if PQTI is not itself qualitatively complete, we can at least say that any inscrutable truth will be a truth not implied by PQTI.

Possible candidates might fall into a number of classes.

(i) *Ordinary macroscopic truths.* One might first question whether ordinary macroscopic truths about the natural world, such as 'grass is green' and 'there is water in my pool' can be derived by a priori reasoning from PQTI. I have argued elsewhere (Chalmers 1996; Chalmers and Jackson 2001) that they can be, and I will not repeat that case here. But the basic idea is that straightforward a priori reasoning from PQTI puts one in a position to know all about the physical composition, the phenomenal appearance, the spatial structure, and the dynamic behavior of macroscopic systems, along with facts about their relation to oneself and their distribution in space and time; and this information, in turn, puts one in a position to know all ordinary macroscopic truths S about such systems, as long as one possesses the concepts involved in S. The information will include all the information on which ordinary perceptual or theoretical knowledge that S might be based, along with sufficient information to conclusively rule out skeptical counter possibilities. If so, it is very plausible that PQTI implies S.

One worry arises with names and natural kind terms: someone might object that truths involving these terms cannot be a priori entailed by PQTI, as the relevant a priori connections are not built into the semantic content of these terms. In response, recall that we are working with a speaker-relative conception of apriority and primary intension. It may be that in cases such as 'Neptune' or even 'water', the primary intension and a priori connections of a term vary between speakers, so that if 'semantic content' must be common to all speakers, primary intensions and a priori connections are not determined by semantic content. But all that is required here is that the conditional 'PQTI ⊃ S' be a priori for any given speaker. This thesis is quite compatible with the variation in primary intension, and it can be argued for straightforwardly along the lines of the previous paragraph.

(It might be thought that Kripke's epistemological arguments tell against even speaker-relative a priori entailments, but it is easy to see that they have no power against the entailments at issue here (see Chalmers 2002a). At most, they suggest that a term's primary intension cannot be captured by a description. Special issues come up for expressions that are used with semantic deference, as when a speaker defers to other speakers in fixing a term's reference. I think that even these expressions can be accommodated on this framework, but for present purposes it is easiest to stipulate that we are concerned only with nondeferential uses.)

(ii) *Certain mathematical truths.* Someone might suggest that there are true mathematical statements that are not a priori: that is, that are not knowable even on ideal rational reflection. For example, one might suppose that certain Gödelian statements in arithmetic (the Gödel sentence of the finite human brain?) or certain statements of higher set theory (the Continuum Hypothesis or its negation?) may be determinately true without being ideally knowable. If such truths exist, they will plausibly not be implied by a qualitatively complete description of the world, so they will be inscrutable.

However, it is not at all clear that such statements exist. In any given case, one can argue that either (1) the statements in question are knowable under some idealization of rational reasoning, or (2) that the statements are not determinately true or false. In the arithmetical case, one can argue that for any statement S there is some better reasoner than us that could know S a priori. Our inability to know a given Gödel sentence plausibly results from a contingent cognitive limitation: perhaps our limitations in the ordinal counting required for repeated Gödelization (which can be shown to settle all truths of arithmetic), or even our contingent inability to evaluate a predicate of all integers simultaneously (Russell's 'mere medical impossibility'). In the case of unprovable statements of set theory, it is not at all clear that truth or falsity is determinate. Most set theorists seem to hold that the relevant cases are indeterminate (although see Lavine, forthcoming, for an argument for determinacy). Even if these statements are determinate in some cases, it is not out of the question that possible beings could know the truth of further axioms that settle the determinate statements.

There is more to say about this issue. I think that the mathematical case is the most significant challenge to scrutability, and even if it fails, it clearly raises important questions about just what sorts of idealizations are allowed in our rational notions. For now, however, it suffices to note that there is no strong positive reason to hold that cases of mathematical determinacy without apriority exist.

(iii) *Vague statements.* It is plausible that some statements involving vague predicates (e.g., 'person X is bald') cannot be known to be true or false, even given complete qualitative information. Complete qualitative information will tell us how much hair a person has, but may leave the question of baldness unsettled. On the standard view of vagueness, this will not be a case of inscrutability, since the statements themselves will be neither true nor false. On the epistemic theory of vagueness, however, such statements are determinate even if we cannot know their truth-values: there is a precise border between the bald and the nonbald, but we cannot know where it is. Some versions of the epistemic theory may hold that this is due to rational limitations on our part (so that more intelligent creatures might be able to locate the border between baldness and nonbaldness); but we can consider a version on which even this epistemic connection fails. On such a view, some statements involving vague predicates will be inscrutable truths.

For example, let us assume for simplicity that baldness supervenes on number of hairs. On this version of the epistemic theory, some truths of the form 'X is bald' will not be implied by truths of the form 'X has n hairs'. Here, 'X has n hairs and is not bald' will be ideally negatively conceivable, but impossible. Here, the two statements 'X has n hairs and is not bald' and 'X has n hairs and is bald' are negatively but not positively conceivable. When we consider any imagined situation in the vicinity—one in which X has n hairs and has further qualitative properties that are inessential here—it verifies neither 'X is bald' nor 'X is not bald'. So these statements fall into the twilight zone.

(Contrast the zombie case in the philosophy of mind, where it seems that 'physical structure P and conscious' and 'physical structure P and not conscious' are each positively conceivable, verified by two different modally imaginable situations. In the baldness case, and other cases of vagueness, there are no two such distinct modally imaginable situations: at best, there are two coherent descriptions. So in these cases, unlike the zombie case, there is no need to include information about baldness explicitly in a qualitatively complete description of the world; the existing description is already qualitatively complete, at least as far as the matters here are concerned. So the truths about baldness (on the epistemic theory) fall into the gap between negative and positive conceivability, yielding inscrutability, whereas truths about consciousness do not.)

Of course all this is contingent on the truth of the epistemic theory of vagueness, and the epistemic theory is widely regarded as very implausible. In fact, one might trace the implausibility of the epistemic theory at least in part to the way it denies inscrutability. In these cases, it seems that a subject has all the qualitative information that could possibly be relevant, and it seems almost obvious that, given that information, the subject is in a position to know all there is to know about baldness here. So it might be argued that the intuitive implausibility of the epistemic theory is grounded in an intuitive endorsement of scrutability, at least in this domain.

One might worry about the status of vague statements even when the epistemic theory is rejected. Here the answer depends on one's view of vagueness. If one accepts the law of the excluded middle ($S \vee \sim S$), then one must also accept $(PQTI \rightarrow S) \vee (PQTI \rightarrow \sim S)$. If one rejects the law of the excluded middle (the best option, on my view), then one will reject the corresponding claim about implication. If there are determinacy operators 'det' and 'indet', and cases in which indet(S), then PQTI must imply indet(S). One might also consider a weaker construal of scrutability, requiring only that det(S) entails that PQTI implies S. Overall I do not think there are any fatal problems for scrutability here, over and above the problems that arise in analyzing vagueness in general.

(iv) *Moral claims.* Many philosophers hold that the truth or falsity of moral claims, such as 'eating animals is bad', is not determined a priori by natural truths. This can be argued by a generalization of Moore's open question argument, suggesting that two people possessing full natural information might disagree on the truth of a claim like this, without either of them displaying incapacities of reasoning or failing to grasp moral concepts. This view is often combined with the view that moral claims are not strictly true or false at all; but some philosophers hold that moral claims are true or false despite being epistemically underdetermined by the natural truth in this way. On this view, moral truths are not implied by PQTI. As in the case of vagueness, there do not seem to be distinct positively conceivable situations verifying $PQTI \wedge M$ and $PQTI \wedge {\sim}M$, where M is a moral claim. If so, then moral truths are inscrutable truths.

As in the case of vagueness, this view of morality is controversial, so it certainly does not provide a clear case for inscrutable truths. Proponents of this sort of view sometimes argue for it by appealing to Kripke's distinction between the a priori and the necessary, but there are strong disanalogies: Kripke's cases are compatible with an entailment from (negative) conceivability to possibility and with the scrutability of truth, whereas this view is not. Furthermore I think that there are good arguments against the view, based on considerations related to scrutability (Horgan and Timmons (1992) give related arguments). In any case, the view helps to illustrate what an inscrutable truth might be.

(A related issue: Yablo (Ch. 13 below) worries that in the moral case, given the nonapriority of $PQTI \supset M$ and $PQTI \supset {\sim}M$ and a principle connecting nonapriority of ${\sim}S$ with primary possibility of S, one could infer the primary possibility of both $PQTI \wedge M$ and $PQTI \wedge {\sim}M$, which seems wrong. In response: if one denies the apriority of the conditionals and also rules out the position above, then the most plausible position remaining is that moral claims are not strictly true or false but are indeterminate; and it is plausible that if this view is true, it is a priori. If so, then it is a priori that ${\sim}\det(PQTI \wedge M)$ and that ${\sim}\det(PQTI \wedge {\sim}M)$. If so, then (given the official characterization of ideal negative conceivability) $PQTI \wedge M$ and $PQTI \wedge {\sim}M$ are not ideally negatively conceivable, so they will not be primarily possible.)

(v) *Metaphysical claims.* Many issues within philosophy are such that it is not obvious that they can be settled conclusively by rationally reasoning from the information in PQTI. This applies especially to questions at issue within meta-physics: Do mereological sums exist? Do all dispositions have categorical bases? Are properties universals or tropes? What is required for identity over time? Do numbers exist? Is an A-theory or a B-theory of time correct? And even, does conceivability suffice for possibility?

There is no space here to consider these issues separately. But, in general, given any one of these issues, an advocate of scrutability can take one of three strategies. (1) One can argue that sufficient rational reflection—perhaps more than has been done to date—can conclusively settle the issue (perhaps the issues about numbers and conceivability fall here). (2) One can argue that the issue is positively conceivable either way, so that PQTI needs to be supplemented by further information to yield a qualitatively complete description of the world (perhaps the issues about categorical bases and about time fall here). (3) One can argue that there is no fact of the matter about the issue, or that it can only be set-tled by terminological refinement (perhaps the issues about mereological sums and identity over time fall here). In each case, there is room for argument, but it certainly seems that there are no clear cases where all three of these strategies fail.

Overall, it seems that there is no clear counter-example to scrutability. At best, there are some unclear potential counter-examples, none of which carries enormous antecedent plausibility, although some deserve further investigation.

Stepping back for a moment, why should we accept the scrutability thesis? One way to argue for it is to suggest that any reasonable candidate for an inscrutable truth will be an unknown and unknowable truth, since what we know is limited to information gained through perception (and so present in, or implied by, PQTI), plus that derived from rational reflection (and so implied by PQTI). One can also argue that all unknown truths stem from either igno-rance of the qualitative nature of the world or from insufficient a priori reasoning, and that the only unknowable truths stem from ignorance of the qualitative nature of the world. If this is so in general, then there are no inscrutable truths.

None of this yields a knockdown argument, but it does give reason to take the scrutability thesis very seriously.

To address this, it is useful to generalize the scrutability thesis slightly, so that it applies not only to complete qualitative descriptions of the actual world and to actual truths, but to any complete qualitative descriptions and to any truths. The generalized thesis is that a complete enough qualitative description of *any* world leaves no truth about that world epistemically open. After all, it would be odd if scrutability turned out to be true in this world but not in others; the thesis seems to have a much more general source than that.

Generalized Scrutability: If D is qualitatively complete, then D is epistemically complete.

Clearly generalized scrutability implies scrutability: the earlier scrutability thesis is the special case where D is a qualitatively complete *truth*. Scrutability does not logically imply generalized scrutability, but it is natural to think that if scrutability is true, generalized scrutability is probably true. If scrutability holds, it seems unlikely that it holds accidentally in the actual world. Rather, its truth would seem to reflect something deep about concepts, truth, and reason. If this is right, then the two theses are likely to stand and fall together.

9 Sideline: Modal Rationalism and Logical Empiricism

As Yablo (Ch. 13 below) notes, the scrutability thesis has something in common with some versions of logical empiricism. A common logical empiricist thesis was that phenomenal truths analytically entail all truths. The main differences between the theses are: (1) in appealing to a qualitatively complete truth, the scrutability thesis allows much more in its entailment base than just phenomenal truths (in particular, it allows the complete microphysical truth); and (2) scrutability as I have characterized it appeals not to analyticity but to apriority (which I think is a more basic notion).

Yablo suggests that the problems of logical empiricism may infect the modal rationalism that I advocate. The problem on which Yablo focuses is the underdetermination of theory by evidence. Underdetermination of theory by *local* evidence is no problem for a sufficiently holistic logical empiricist, but underdetermination of theory by *total* evidence is a problem. It seems easily conceivable that different states of affairs might provide the same evidence, or that some truths might leave no trace on our evidence; and there are even pairs of real-life scientific theories (as in quantum mechanics) that save all appearances while making different microphysical claims. These considerations are all tied to the limitations of observation, however: they suggest that phenomenal truths or observational truths underdetermine theory. They do nothing at all to suggest that the complete qualitative truth (including microphysical truths) underdetermines theory. So the most common worries about underdetermination do nothing to threaten the scrutability thesis.

To make a stronger parallel argument, Yablo appeals to a different worry, about the role played by a posteriori considerations of 'reasonableness' and 'sensibility' in moving from evidence to theory. There seem to be a number of separate arguments here, although I am not certain that Yablo intended all of them.

First: considerations of reasonableness cannot be reduced to a set of a priori rules (as in 'the dream of an a priori inductive logic'). Response: there is no reason to suppose that a priori truths, or a priori entailments, must be reducible to some basic set of explicit formal principles. (See Chalmers and Jackson 2001 for more on this.) So this is a red herring. At best, this point might affect a thesis cast in terms of analyticity, if analyticity is defined in terms of logic plus definitions.

Second: the modal rationalist requires too much of our 'grasp of meaning', by requiring knowledge of the relevant conditionals. Response: on the rationalist view, knowledge of the relevant conditionals need not be built into grasp of meaning, and need not be possessed by every subject who possesses the relevant concepts. Where present, the knowledge is usually a product of substantive reasoning, grounded both in possession of the relevant concepts and in rational reflection.

Third: there are cases where rational reflection on qualitative information underdetermines theoretical truth, which is settled only by pragmatic factors. Response: if the pragmatic factors are rationally underdetermined, then these are cases where originally indeterminate statements become determinately true or false because of terminological evolution. (See Chalmers and Jackson 2001.) So there is no point at which there are inscrutable truths.

Fourth: the inference from PQTI to macroscopic truths may depend on 'peeking', as when one perceptually imagines the appearance of a situation. Response: this point might threaten a scrutability thesis based on PTI, which excludes information about appearances. But given the phenomenal information Q about appearances (in a pure phenomenal vocabulary), peeking comes for free. Knowledge of PQTI yields knowledge of the phenomenology of the appearances, and this puts one in as good a position to reason from those appearances to macroscopic truths as if one had experienced the appearances directly. (See also the further discussion below.)

Fifth: the general exercise of 'sensibility' is a posteriori, since it involves introspective knowledge of concept application in one's own mind. Response: no introspective knowledge is needed to know the entailment from PQTI to S. One merely needs to deploy the concepts involved in S; one does not need to observe their deployment.

There is more to say here, but it seems that at least on a first look, the scrutability thesis is unthreatened by its parallels with logical empiricism. Still, the parallels certainly exist, both with logical empiricism and other broadly phenomenalist and anti-realist views. These anti-realist views hold (in a sense) that when it comes to truth, nothing is hidden. The scrutability thesis does not suggest this, and is perfectly compatible with a realist view. But it suggests a weaker thesis: *given* complete qualitative knowledge (and ideal reflection), nothing is hidden. There is perhaps a tiny residue of anti-realism here: if a claim cannot be settled by a priori reasoning on the basic qualitative facts, then there is no fact of the matter about that claim. But one does not have to be a logical positivist to find this thesis attractive. (There are some things that it is perfectly reasonable to be anti-realist about.) Indeed, in almost all cases where a claim cannot be settled in this way, as we have seen, it is independently plausible that the claim is indeterminate. So the scrutability thesis may well embody a principle that is tacit in our reasoning.

10 Open Inconceivabilities

The second potential source of a gap between negative and positive conceivability arises from states of affairs that are *inconceivable*, but that are nevertheless not ruled out a priori.

There are quite likely many prima facie inconceivabilities: a rich source is provided by statements about phenomenal properties quite distinct from our own. For example, the claim that there are creatures with 12-dimensional phenomenal color spaces cannot be ruled out a priori, but it may be beyond our capacity to conceive of a situation verifying this claim. Such a conception might require phenomenal concepts (and ultimately phenomenal experiences to ground those concepts) that we simply lack. If so, such a claim is prima facie negatively conceivable, but not prima facie positively conceivable. This is not obviously a case of ideal inconceivability, however. We have already seen that the inconceivability here stems from a lack in our repertoire of phenomenal concepts, and this limitation is contingent. If we idealize away from this conceptual lack, then the situation in question will plausibly turn out to be conceivable after all. Presumably there are possible creatures with the relevant concepts, and such creatures would have no difficulty in conceiving of the situations in question.

Still, perhaps there are some features of the world, or of some world, that simply cannot be positively conceived at all. One example might be provided by intrinsic properties that are not phenomenal properties and are not conceptually related to them. One might argue that the only way to form a conception of an intrinsic property is by direct acquaintance, as in the phenomenal case, or perhaps by a priori reasoning from concepts of intrinsic properties that one has direct acquaintance with; think of the missing shade of phenomenal blue. (Of course, one might form an extrinsic conception of an intrinsic property, such as 'the property that is causally responsible for such-and-such', but this is not good enough here, as such a conception leaves open multiple epistemic possibilities as to the nature of the property.) And one might argue that the only intrinsic properties with which any subject can be directly acquainted are phenomenal properties. If so, then any intrinsic properties that are not phenomenal properties will be in the relevant sense inconceivable.

Of course, all the assumptions going into the case above are highly contestable, but the possibility of inconceivable features of the world does not seem easy to rule out. This can be exploited to yield perhaps the most plausible example of an open inconceivability: namely, 'There are inconceivable features of the world'. This statement is, by its nature, verified by no positively conceivable situation, but it is also not easy to rule out a priori. Unless some way can be found to rule out this statement a priori, it will be (ideally) negatively conceivable, but not positively conceivable, and hence will be in the twilight zone.

More precisely:

S is an *open inconceivability* if S is negatively conceivable, but for all qualitatively complete D, D → ~S.

(Note: to handle indeterminacies, the last clause should hold that for all D, D implies ~det(S). If S is negatively conceivable, det(S) is not ruled out a priori; if, nevertheless, for all D, D implies that S is indeterminate, then S should be an open inconceivability.)

We have seen that 'There are no inconceivable features of the world' is one potential open inconceivability. Another is 'There is no qualitatively complete description of the world'. At a more specific level, the case of nonphenomenal intrinsic properties, on the assumptions above, will provide examples of open inconceivabilities insofar as there are ways to express relevant inconceivable truths (e.g., 'There are nonphenomenal intrinsic properties', if nothing else). Still, none of these yield clear cases, so we can at least formulate a relevant thesis opposed to them:

Noinconceivability: No S is an open inconceivability.

It is not clear how best to argue for this thesis. One might argue for any property that there is some creature than can form a conception of it—perhaps any intrinsic property can be known by acquaintance, and any nonintrinsic property by description. And one might argue that this principle is itself a priori. If that is so, then it plausibly follows that there are no open inconceivabilities. But the central claim here is far from obvious.

Like inscrutabilities, open inconceivabilities (if they exist) provide a gap between negative and positive conceivability. They differ from inscrutabilities, however, in that they may not provide a gap between negative conceivability and possibility. That gap depends on whether the open inconceivabilities in question correspond to real possibilities (e.g., properties we cannot form a conception of), or whether they correspond to impossibilities that we cannot rule out a priori (perhaps all properties are conceivable, but we can't rule out the alternative a priori). If all open inconceivabilities are of the former sort, then negative conceivability might still be a guide to possibility—it is just that the possible will outstrip the positively conceivable. If some are of the latter sort, then negative conceivability will be an imperfect guide to possibility.

11 The Structure of the Twilight Zone

We have seen that potential members of the twilight zone stem from at least two classes: inscrutabilities and open inconceivabilities. In fact it is not hard to see that all members of the twilight zone stem from these two classes.

Negpos: Ideal negative conceivability entails ideal primary positive conceivability.

The negpos principle says that there are no members of the twilight zone. Then it is not hard to demonstrate the following thesis: Negpos is true iff generalized scrutability and noninconceivability are true.

Proof: Left-to-right: Given negpos, any qualitatively complete statement will be epistemically complete, so generalized scrutability will be true. Given negpos, any negatively conceivable statement will be positively conceivable, so will be entailed by some qualitatively complete D, so noninconceivability will be true. Note that the second part requires the principle that any positively conceivable statement is implied by some qualitatively complete statement. This seems reasonable, as it encapsulates the idea that a statement verified only by 'uncompletable' situations will not be ideally positively conceivable.

Right-to-left: Let S be negatively conceivable. Noninconceivability implies that there is a D such that $\sim(D \rightarrow \sim det(S))$. Generalized scrutability implies that D settles S's truth-value, so D implies S. (Note that the determinacy operator in the definition of open inconceivability is needed here, in order to exclude the possibility that D implies neither S nor $\sim$S, due to indeterminacy.)

So, in order to close a potential gap between (ideal primary) negative and positive conceivability, it is necessary and sufficient to rule out generalized inscrutabilities and open inconceivabilities.

In order to close a potential gap between negative conceivability and possibility, it is necessary to rule out generalized inscrutabilities (if S is a generalized inscrutability, then both $D \rightarrow S$ and $D \rightarrow \sim S$ will be negatively conceivable for a relevant D, but both cannot be possible). It is not necessary to rule out all open inconceivabilities, but one must rule out all *impossible* open inconceivabilities. If some open inconceivabilities are also impossibilities, then negative conceivability does not entail possibility. But if all open inconceivabilities are possibilities (which is not entirely implausible), then an entailment between negative conceivability and possibility is not threatened.

12 From Positive Conceivability to Possibility

Does (ideal primary) positive conceivability imply (primary) possibility? A counter-example to this principle must involve what I have elsewhere called a *strong necessity*: a statement that is falsified by some positively conceivable situation (considered as actual), but which is nevertheless true in all possible worlds (considered as actual). For such necessities to exist, the space of positively conceivable situations must outstrip the space of possible worlds.

There are certainly no clear examples of strong necessities, and the only candidates are highly tendentious. I have discussed this matter at some length elsewhere (Chalmers 1999), so I will say only a little about some possible candidates here.

(i) *The existence of God*. On many theist views, a god exists necessarily, so that every possible world contains a god. But a theist may hold that it is not a priori that a god exists, and that a godless world is positively conceivable, even on rational reflection. On this view, it is natural to hold that 'no god exists' is primarily positively conceivable, but not primarily possible. So if this view is correct, then 'a god exists' is a strong necessity. Of course, the theist thesis here is highly controversial, so this is not a strong counter-example, but it illustrates what a counter-example must involve.

One further worry: if a god does not exist necessarily, then 'A necessary god exists' is impossible. But it may seem that a necessary god is at least conceivable (see Yablo 1999). In response, I deny that a necessarily existing god is ideally conceivable. A god's existence may be conceivable, but to conceive of a god's necessary existence is much harder, especially given its conceivable nonexistence. In effect, one must conceive (metamodally!) that conceivability does not imply possibility. But it is not clear that this is more than prima facie negatively conceivable. On my view, it is a priori, if nonobvious, that conceivability entails possibility (see below for the sketch of an a priori argument). If so, then the denial of the entailment is not ideally conceivable, and so neither is the necessary existence of a god.

(ii) *Laws of nature.* Some philosophers hold that the laws of nature are metaphysically necessary. On some views of this sort (e.g., those discussed by Fine and Sidelle in Chapters 6 and 8), this necessity arises for broadly Kripkean reasons: the reference of terms such as 'mass' is fixed a posteriori to a certain very specific property, so that worlds with different laws do not contain mass. I think this view is implausible, but in any case it is compatible with an entailment from primary conceivability to primary possibility. If G′ is a counter-nomic statement (say, an adjusted statement of gravitational laws with a different constant), then G′ is both primarily conceivable and primarily possible. G′ is verified by a metaphysically possible world W considered as actual, although not by W considered as counterfactual. (Considered as counterfactual, W contains 'schmass', not mass.) So there are no strong necessities here.

There is a stronger view on which the laws of every world are exhausted by actual-world laws, applying to actual-world properties. On this sort of view, even 'schmass' worlds are metaphysically impossible: G′ will be primarily conceivable, but not even primarily possible. On this view, laws of nature are strong necessities. There is no reason to accept this view, however. (It is notable that Fine and Sidelle quickly dismiss such a view as too extreme to be plausible.) Proponents of necessary laws usually appeal to Kripke's necessary a posteriori for support, but the Kripkean cases support at best the weak view in the previous paragraph. Nothing here gives reason to suppose that worlds with different laws are impossible; at best, it suggests that they are misdescribed as breaking our laws. So there is no good reason here to deny the conceivability–possibility thesis.

(iii) *Response-enabled concepts.* Yablo (Chapter 13 below) considers a class of *response-enabled* concepts whose extension and whose meaning are fixed by our responses. He suggests that 'oval' is in this class: the reference of 'oval' is fixed by picking out whatever looks oval-shaped to us, irrespective of any pure geometric description of this shape. I think the example is imperfect, since 'oval' is arguably a pure geometric concept, picking out certain geometric shapes regardless of the responses they cause in us. But there may be other terms that function as Yablo suggests, so I will play along with his suggestion that 'oval' works this way.

Following Yablo, let 'cassini' be a term for a certain class of mathematically defined geometric figures, of a sort that actually cause 'oval'-responses. Then (given Yablo's view of 'oval'), it is not a priori that cassinis are ovals. So, 'cassinis are not ovals' is ideally negatively conceivable. 'Cassinis are not ovals' is also plausibly ideally positively conceivable, since it is verified by a situation in which cassinis are not the sort of object that cause 'oval'-responses. But Yablo suggests that 'cassinis are ovals' is nevertheless true in all worlds considered as actual: in all such worlds, cassinis fall under the extension of 'oval'. If this is correct, then ideal (negative or positive) primary conceivability does not entail primary possibility.

In response: As I have characterized considering-as-actual, it is clear that 'cassinis are oval' is true of some worlds considered as actual. Let W be a world in which cassinis cause 'oval'-responses. Let us grant that it is a priori that if W is actual, cassinis cause 'oval'-responses. (Yablo raises no objection to this.) We can also note that if 'oval' functions as described, then a material conditional such as 'if Hs cause oval responses, then Hs are ovals' is pretty clearly a priori. (Yablo himself allows that there may be an a priori connection here.) It follows that the material conditional 'if W is actual, cassinis are ovals' is a priori. So, as I have defined things, 'cassinis are ovals' is true in W considered as actual, and is primarily possible.

Why does Yablo resist this straightforward conclusion? It seems to me that he is operating with a different conception of how statements are evaluated in considering a world as actual, one tied to the 'if it had turned out' locution and to certain claims about 'conceptual necessity'. I am not sure that I fully grasp this conception, but for present purposes I need not deny that it is coherent or that it captures some feature of our concepts. But it is clearly distinct from the conception I am operating with, on which considering-as-actual involves a priori reasoning about epistemic possibilities. Yablo gives no reason to deny that this conception is coherent, or that it yields the results I have suggested. So the conceivability–possibility link that I have advocated is not threatened by Yablo's discussion.

Something similar applies to other claims that Yablo discusses, including 'unless we are greatly misled about the circumstances of visual perception, what looks green is green'. If this (or something like it) is a priori, then, like all a priori statements, it will automatically hold in all worlds considered as actual, at least on my conception of considering-as-actual (though perhaps not on Yablo's). And the statement 'Fs are not red', where 'F' involves a complete intrinsic characterization of something that is actually red, will be a posteriori, primarily positively conceivable, and primarily possible on my conception: it will be straightforwardly true in a world (considered as actual) where Fs do not look red.

At one point Yablo raises another worry about response-dependent concepts: physical and phenomenal truths may not imply truths about yellowness (say), since a characterization of the relevant phenomenology may not enable one to identify the 'yellow' responses a priori. I think this is not a problem. The relevant responses are phenomenal kinds, characterized by what it is like to have them. In particular, knowledge of what it is like to experience an object (in normal circumstances) enables knowledge of whether the object is yellow, with no further empirical justification required. Further, physical and phenomenal knowledge enables knowledge of what it is like to experience the relevant objects (in normal circumstances), with no further empirical justification required. It follows that the physical and phenomenal truths imply the truths about yellowness.

(iv) *Psychophysical laws*. A final example is given by some type-B materialist views, on which there is an epistemic gap between the physical and the phenomenal, but no ontological gap. On such a view, zombies (and the like) are positively conceivable, but not possible. Type-B materialists often appeal to Kripkean cases for support, but it is not hard to see that these do not help, since those cases are compatible with the primary conceivability–possibility link, and the mere primary possibility of zombies causes problems for materialism (see below). In response, some type-B materialists deny that zombies are even primarily possible. On such a view, psychophysical laws (of the form 'if P, then Q' for physical P and phenomenal Q) are strong necessities.

Again, this view is highly controversial, so it does not provide any clear counter-example. This view is usually put forward on the grounds that it is the only tenable way to preserve materialism, given the epistemic gap; but of course that falls well short of a positive argument for the view, especially when the truth of materialism is at issue. Indeed, one can suggest that the conceivability–possibility link that holds elsewhere itself provides a strong argument against this view. Given the discussion above, it seems that the strong necessities required here will be unique. (Even if one thinks that God and laws of nature provide partners in crime, it is notable that the sort of strong necessity at issue there cannot save materialism: in those cases, strong necessities connect ontologically distinct existences!) Some type-B materialists (e.g., Loar 1997, 1999, and Hill 1997) have bitten this bullet and tried to give an explanation of why strong necessities should uniquely arise in the phenomenal domain. I have argued elsewhere (Chalmers 1999) that these explanations fail.

In summary: in each case, the claim that there are strong necessities rests on very controversial assumptions. One might more plausibly argue in reverse: in each of these cases, the elsewhere unbroken link between conceivability and possibility provides an argument against the assumptions in question. In any case, there are no clear counter-examples to the conceivability–possibility thesis here.

Still, at best this makes a negative case for the conceivability–possibility thesis, by defeating potential counter-examples and explanations. It remains to make a positive case for the thesis, giving reasons why we should expect it to be true. I make a start on this case in Chalmers (1999). I hope to expand on this further elsewhere, but here I will just recapitulate the case briefly.

The argument involves locating the roots of our modal concepts in the rational domain. When one looks at the purposes to which modality is put (e.g., by Lewis (1986: ch. 1)), it is striking that many of these purposes are tied closely to the rational and the psychological: analyzing the contents of thoughts and the semantics of language, giving an account of counterfactual thought, analyzing rational inference. It can be argued that for a concept of possibility and necessity to be truly useful in analyzing these domains, it must be a *rational* modal concept, tied constitutively to consistency, rational inference, or conceivability.

It is not difficult to argue that even if not all conceivable worlds are metaphysically possible worlds, we *need* a rational modal concept tied to rational consistency or conceivability to best analyze the phenomena in question. We might call the corresponding notion of possibility *logical* possibility. For example, even if all worlds with different laws of nature are metaphysically impossible, it will still be tremendously useful to have a wider space of logically possible worlds (or world-like entities) with different laws, to help analyze and explain the hypotheses and inferences of a scientist investigating the laws of nature. Such a scientist will be considering all sorts of rationally coherent possibilities involving different laws; she will make conditional claims and engage in counterfactual thinking about these possibilities; and she may have terms and concepts that are coextensive at all worlds with our laws, but that intuitively differ in meaning because they come apart at worlds with different laws. To analyze these phenomena, the wider space of worlds is needed to play the role that possible worlds usually play.

Further, there is no bar to a space of such worlds. If one does not want simply to postulate them, one can easily construct them in an 'ersatz' way. For example, one can identify them with equivalence classes of qualitatively complete (or epistemically complete) descriptions (for such a construction, see Chalmers, forthcoming *c*). One can then introduce means of semantically evaluating expressions at these worlds, on both epistemic and subjunctive dimensions. The worlds and the semantic evaluation are perfectly well-behaved, yielding a modal space that is useful for all sorts of purposes. (If one has qualms about using the term 'world' for these entities, nothing turns on the word: one can equally call them 'scenarios', or some such, instead.)

One can then argue that this space of worlds suffices to account for all modal phenomena that we have reason to believe in. Such a space will analyze such rational and psychological matters as counterfactual thought, rational inference, and the contents of thought and language as well as any other modal space can. And with the help of two-dimensional semantic evaluation, it can accommodate such 'metaphysical' modal phenomena as the concept/property distinction, a posteriori necessities, and so on. These phenomena emerge directly from two-dimensional semantic evaluation over a single space of worlds. The two-dimensional semantics in question will be grounded in a priori conceptual analysis plus nonmodal facts about the actual world. (The first dimension is grounded straightforwardly in a priori conditionals. The second dimension is grounded in a priori conditionals, such as 'if water is H_2O, it is necessary that water is H_2O', plus empirical nonmodal facts, such as 'water is H_2O'.) So one modal space plus conceptual analysis plus nonmodal facts gives us everything, as long as this modal space is tied constitutively to the rational domain.

If this modal space is all, we have *modal monism*, with a single modal primitive. The believer in strong necessities, by contrast, must embrace a *modal dualism*, with distinct primitive modalities of logical and metaphysical possibility, neither of which is reducible to the other. There is no good reason to accept such a modal dualism, when modal monism can explain all the untendentious phenomena. There are no further modal data for a distinct metaphysical modality to explain: what needs to be explained is already explained. This is not just a simplicity argument. One can argue further that there is no distinct *concept* of metaphysical possibility for the second modality to answer to. The momentary impression of such a concept stems from a confused understanding of such ontic/epistemic distinctions as that between apriority and necessity and that between concept and property, all of which are easily subsumed under a modal monism with the help of some two-dimensional semantics.

Ultimately, there is just one circle of modal concepts, including both the rational modal concepts (validity, rational entailment, apriority, conceivability) and the metaphysical modal concepts (possibility, necessity, property). The result we are left with is *modal rationalism* in more senses than one: a priori access to modality and constitutive ties between the modal and rational domains.

Conclusions

We can sum up the lay of the land by labeling some varieties of modal rationalism:

Weak Modal Rationalism: (Ideal primary) positive conceivability entails (primary) possibility.

Strong Modal Rationalism: Negative conceivability entails possibility.

Pure Modal Rationalism: Positive conceivability $\equiv$ negative conceivability $\equiv$ possibility.

Then, pure modal rationalism is equivalent to the conjunction of weak modal rationalism with negpos. The left-to-right direction here is obvious, and the right-to-left direction follows from the observation that possibility entails negative conceivability (no primary possibility is ruled out a priori). Combining this with the previous result about the nature of the twilight zone, it follows that pure modal rationalism is equivalent to the conjunction of weak modal rationalism, generalized scrutability, and noinconceivability.

It follows that to establish pure modal rationalism, we must rule out strong necessities, generalized inscrutabilities, and open inconceivabilities. Here I am most confident about the first, reasonably confident about the second, and unsure about the third. I have outlined a case against strong necessities here, and given tentative reasons to be doubtful about inscrutabilities, while the status of open inconceivabilities is unclear. In any case, it seems to me that each of these three is a distinct and substantial philosophical project, and that the investigation of each raises deep philosophical questions and promises significant philosophical rewards.

If weak modal rationalism is the best we can establish, then we will have done enough to support conceivability arguments as traditionally used, although the overall picture of modality and of modal epistemology will remain somewhat messy. We will have distinct notions of positive and negative conceivability, and thus a mild dualism within the rational modal sphere (though it will be a dualism that is forced on us by the phenomena). If there are generalized inscrutabilities, then although conceivability will guarantee access to a possible world, it may not yield access to all truths in that world. And if there are open inconceivabilities, there will be worlds to which conceivability offers no access.

Pure modal rationalism yields a simpler picture of modal space, and a correspondingly elegant epistemology. Looking at its three components in turn: the first says that positive conceivability gives us access to only possible worlds, the third says that it gives us access to all the possible worlds, and the second says that we can know all the truths about these possible worlds. In effect, we have a telescope that gives us access to all and only the stars, and that tells us the exact composition of every star. If this thesis is true, the epistemology of modality, at least when idealized, will be simple and beautiful.

APPENDIX: THE MIND—BODY PROBLEM

With these conceivability–possibility theses in hand, it is interesting to apply them to various conceivability arguments against materialism in the philosophy of mind.

Historically, the most important such argument has been Descartes's conceivability argument. This argues from the conceivability of my existing without a body to the possibility of my existence without a body, and from there to the claim that I am not physical. The soundness of this argument is often doubted, and the standard reasons for doubt can be expressed straightforwardly in the current framework. The sense in which it is clearly conceivable that I am disembodied is primary positive conceivability, from which the 1-possibility of disembodiment follows. The sense in which physical things are essentially physical involves 2-necessity (as do all claims of *de re* necessity). But the 1-possibility of disembodiment is quite compatible with the 2-impossibility of disembodiment, so the claim that I am physical is not threatened by Descartes's argument.

More recently, the knowledge argument and the zombie argument against materialism have been widely discussed. Here, let P be the conjunction of physical truths about the world, and let Q be a phenomenal truth. The zombie argument claims that zombies, and therefore $P \wedge \sim Q$, are primarily positively conceivable. (Here, Q might be 'someone is conscious'.) The knowledge argument claims that Q cannot be derived a priori from P, so that $P \wedge \sim Q$ is primarily negatively conceivable. (Here, Q might be 'someone is having a such-and-such experience'.) From here, both step to the denial of materialism. If we use the current framework to analyze these arguments, a first pass might yield something like the following:

(1) $P \wedge \sim Q$ is ideally primarily positively (negatively) conceivable.
(2) If $P \wedge \sim Q$ is ideally primarily positively (negatively) conceivable, then $P \wedge \sim Q$ is primarily possible.
(3) If $P \wedge \sim Q$ is primarily possible, materialism is false.

———————————

(4) Materialism is false.

Here, premise (2) is a special case of the two main conceivability–possibility theses already outlined. It is notable that the zombie argument requires a weaker epistemic-modal premise here: the thesis connecting positive conceivability to possibility is weaker than the thesis connecting negative conceivability to possibility. (It requires excluding only strong necessities, not inscrutabilities.) This is offset to some extent by the fact that the knowledge argument requires a weaker epistemic premise: the claim that $P \wedge \sim Q$ is negatively conceivable is weaker than the claim that it is positively conceivable.

What of the epistemic premise (1)? This is widely, although not universally, accepted in the knowledge argument case, and to a somewhat lesser extent in the zombie case. A materialist might deny it in two ways: either by denying even the prima facie conceivability of $P \wedge \sim Q$, or by accepting prima facie conceivability but denying ideal conceivability. Some type-A materialists will deny even prima facie conceivability, but this denial is not easy to defend, since it runs counter to a very strong intuition. Others accept prima facie conceivability but deny ideal conceivability, holding that there may be a deep epistemic connection between P and Q and a deep a priori contradiction in the notion of a zombie.

The second position, exploiting the gap between prima facie and ideal conceivability, may seem particularly promising, especially in the view (which I have elsewhere called 'type-C materialism') that holds that there is a deep epistemic connection that we have not found yet, or perhaps cannot find. But there are two problems. First, this materialist will concede that zombies are not just prima facie but secunda facie positively conceivable, and we have seen that secunda facie conceivability is an extremely good guide to possibility. Second, defeating ideal conceivability will require an a priori entailment from physical to phenomenal, which requires that phenomenal concepts can support that entailment. Given the structural-dispositional nature of the physical concepts in P, this requires a structural or functional analysis of phenomenal concepts. But there is good reason to believe that any such analysis of phenomenal concepts is a misanalysis. So, while type-C strategy is an interesting strategy that deserves investigation, I think we have reason to believe that it will not succeed.

That leaves premise (3). Here, one runs up against the same problem as in the Cartesian argument. Materialism requires that the physical truths *secondarily* necessitate all truths, and so requires that $P \wedge \sim Q$ is secondarily possible. But there is no clear inference from the primary possibility of $P \wedge \sim Q$ to its secondary possibility. So the argument seems to be unsound as it stands. (An eliminativist who denies Q might deny (3) for different reasons, but I will set that position aside here.)

In this case, unlike the Cartesian case, the argument can be rescued. First, one can observe that *if* P and Q both had identical primary and secondary intensions (up to centering), then premise (3) would be straightforwardly true. Further, it is very plausible that the most important phenomenal concepts do indeed have the same primary and secondary intensions (see Chalmers 2002), so that Q at least can be accommodated here. And even if this is false, Q's primary intension can be seen as the secondary intension of some other truth Q', which stands to Q roughly as 'watery stuff' stands to 'water'. As long as P has the same primary and secondary intension, then the primary possibility of $P \wedge \sim Q$ will entail the secondary possibility of $P \wedge \sim Q'$, which will itself entail the falsity of materialism.

Here a loophole emerges: it is not clear that P has the same primary and secondary intension. It can reasonably be argued that physical concepts have their reference fixed by some dispositional role, but refer to an underlying categorical property. If so, their primary intensions pick out whatever plays a certain role in the world (irrespective of its categorical nature), while their secondary intensions pick out instances of a certain categorical property (irrespective of its role). If so, the purported 'zombie world' in which the primary intension of $P \wedge \sim Q$ holds may be a world in which the secondary intension of P is false, so we cannot infer the secondary possibility of $P \wedge \sim Q$ (or $P \wedge \sim Q'$).

However, this loophole opens up only a small space for the materialist. Consider the conceived world W, in which the primary intension of $P \wedge \sim Q$ holds. Because the primary intension of P holds, this world must be structurally-dispositionally isomorphic to the actual world, with the same patterns of microphysical causal roles being played. If P's secondary intension fails, it can only be because these microphysical causal roles have different categorical bases in W (or, just possibly, no categorical bases at all). This difference is the only microphysical difference between our world and W. If physicalism is true, it is this difference that is responsible for the presence of consciousness in our world and its absence in W.

What results is a view on which the existence of consciousness is not necessitated by the structural or dispositional aspects of the microphysics of our world, but is necessitated by the categorical aspects of microphysics (the underlying categorical basis of microphysical dispositions), perhaps in combination with structural-dispositional aspects. This is an important view: it is the view put forward by Russell (1926) and discussed in recent years by Maxwell (1978), Lockwood (1989), and others. In effect, the view holds that consciousness stems from the underlying categorical aspect of microphysics. On this view, the nature of the categorical aspect is left open by physical theory, but it turns out to involve special properties that are collectively responsible for constituting consciousness. We can call these special properties *protophenomenal*: they might not themselves be phenomenal properties, but they stand in a constitutive relation to phenomenal properties. We can call the view as a whole *panprotopsychism*.

It is not clear whether this sort of panprotopsychism qualifies as a version of physicalism. That question turns on whether the underlying protophenomenal properties are best counted as physical properties, or not. We need not settle that question here. We need only note that if it is a sort of physicalism, it is a quite unusual sort, and one that many physicalists do not accept. In many ways, it has more in common with nonmaterialist views, in virtue of its postulation of fundamental protophenomenal properties whose nature is not revealed to us by physical theory.

In any case, we are now in a position to reformulate the relevant argument:

(1) $P \wedge \sim Q$ is ideally primarily positively (negatively) conceivable.
(2) If $P \wedge \sim Q$ is ideally primarily positively (negatively) conceivable, then $P \wedge \sim Q$ is primarily possible.
(3) If $P \wedge \sim Q$ is primarily possible but not secondarily possible, then panprotopsychism is true.
(4) If $P \wedge \sim Q$ is secondarily possible, materialism is false.

———————

(5) Materialism is false or panprotopsychism is true.

The argument (in both versions) is valid, and I have given reasons for accepting all the premises. Note that one can substitute the secondary possibility of $P \wedge Q'$ for the secondary possibility of $P \wedge Q$ in the third and fourth premises, if necessary. Note also that I have said nothing about the role of indexicals and centering. One might think that these open another loophole in the argument (around premise (3)), by opening another gap between primary and secondary possibility. It is not hard to give a fuller version that takes this role into account but I omit the details here for reasons of space.

Finally, a note on Stalnaker's paper in this volume (Chapter 11), concerning the zombie argument. Stalnaker (through his character 'Anne') questions the argument, by questioning the inference from conceivability to possibility. In effect, he invokes a notion of conceivability distinct from those discussed here, which we might call *1-2-conceivability*. It is 1-2-conceivable that S if it is primarily conceivable that S is secondarily possible; or, more precisely, if 'possibly S' is 1-conceivable, where the modal operator here represents 2-possibility. Stalnaker accepts that zombies are 1-2-conceivable (property dualism is not a priori false, and if property dualism is true, then zombies are 2-possible). But he notes that the 1-2-conceivability of S does not entail the possibility of S: the epistemic possibility of property dualism is compatible with the truth of materialism and with the 2-impossibility (and 1-impossibility) of zombies.

Stalnaker is right that the conceivability of zombies, in this sense, does not directly entail the falsity of materialism. But this sort of conceivability plays no role in the arguments I have given. What is relevant is simply the *1-conceivability* of $P \wedge \sim Q$. In the knowledge argument, the argument aims to directly establish the non-apriority of $P \supset \sim Q$, and so the prima facie negative conceivability of $P \wedge \sim Q$. In the zombie argument itself, the claim is that it is conceivable that *in the actual world* P holds, but no one is conscious. (Of course, I know that I am conscious, but this is a posteriori knowledge; that issue can also be bypassed by considering only the epistemic possibility that P holds while *others* in the actual world are zombies.) That is, the claim is that $P \wedge \sim Q$ is primarily positively conceivable. Stalnaker says nothing to cast doubt on this claim (or the analogous claim about negative conceivability), and he says nothing to cast doubt on the inference from primary conceivability to primary possibility. So his discussion leaves this argument untouched.

REFERENCES

Bealer, George (1996), 'A Priori Knowledge and the Limits of Philosophy', *Philosophical Studies*, 81: 121–42.

Benacerraf, Paul (1965), 'What Numbers Could Not Be', *Philosophical Review*, 74: 47–73.

Benardete, José A. (1964), *Infinity: An Essay in Metaphysics* (Oxford: Oxford University Press).

Block, Ned, and Stalnaker, Robert (1999), 'Conceptual Analysis, Dualism, and the Explanatory Gap', *Philosophical Review*, 108: 1–46.

Chalmers, David J. (1996), *The Conscious Mind: In Search of a Fundamental Theory* (New York: Oxford University Press).

—— (1999), 'Materialism and the Metaphysics of Modality', *Philosophy and Phenomenological Research*, 59: 473–96, consc.net/papers/modality.html.

—— (2002*a*) 'On Sense and Intension', *Philosophical Perspectives*, 16, consc.net/papers/intension.html.

—— (2002*b*), 'The Content and Epistemology of Phenomenal Belief', in Quentin Smith and Aleksandev Jokic (eds.), *Consciousness: New Philosophical Essays* (Oxford: Oxford University Press), consc.net/papers/belief.html.

—— (forthcoming *a*), 'The Nature of Epistemic Space', consc.net/papers/espace.html.

—— (forthcoming *b*), 'The Foundations of Two-Dimensional Semantics', consc.net/papers/foundations.html.

—— and Jackson, Frank (2001), 'Conceptual Analysis and Reductive Explanation', *Philosophical Review*, 110: 315–61, consc.net/papers/analysis.html.

Davies, Martin, and Humberstone, I. Lloyd (1980), 'Two Notions of Necessity', *Philosophical Studies*, 38: 1–30.

Evans, Gareth (1977), 'Reference and Contingency', *Monist*, 62: 161–89.

Gendler, Tamar Szabó, and Hawthorne, John (forthcoming), 'Imagining the Impossible', MS.

Hawthorne, John (2000), 'Before-Effect and Zeno Causality', *Nous*, 34: 622–33.

Hill, Christopher (1997), 'Imaginability, Conceivability, Possibility, and the Mind–Body Problem', *Philosophical Studies*, 87: 61–85.

Horgan, Terence (1986), 'Psychologism, Semantics, and Ontology', *Nous*, 20: 21–31.

—— and Timmons, Mark (1992), 'Troubles on Moral Twin Earth: Moral Queerness Revived', *Synthese*, 92(2): 221–60.

Jackson Frank (1998), *From Metaphysics to Ethics: A Defense of Conceptual Analysis* (Oxford: Oxford University Press).

Kripke, Saul (1980), Naming and Necessity (Cambridge, Mass.: Harvard University Press).

Lavine, Shaughan (forthcoming), *Skolem was Wrong*, book manuscript.

Lewis, David (1986), *On the Plurality of Worlds* (Oxford: Blackwell).

Loar, Brian (1997), 'Phenomenal States', second version, in Ned Block, Owen Flanagan, and Güven Güzeldere (eds.), *The Nature of Consciousness: Philosophical Debates* (Cambridge, Mass.: MIT Press).

—— (1999), 'On David Chalmers' *The Conscious Mind*', *Philosophy and Phenomenological Research*, 59: 465–72.

Lockwood, Michael (1989), *Mind, Brain, and the Quantum* (Oxford: Blackwell).

Maxwell, Grover (1978), 'Rigid Designators and Mind—Brain Identity', in Wade C. Savage (ed.), *Perception and Cognition: Issues in the Foundations of Psychology*, Minnesota Studies in the Philosophy of Science, 9 (Minneapolis: University of Minnesota Press), 365–403.

Menzies, Peter (1998), 'Possibility and Conceivability: A Response-Dependent Account of their Connections', in Roberto Casati and Christine Tappolet (eds.), *Response-Dependence*, European Review of Philosophy, 3 (Stanford, Calif.: CSLI Press), 261–77.

Quine, Willard van Orman (1960), *Word and Object* (Cambridge, Mass.: MIT Press).

Russell, Bertrand (1926), *The Analysis of Matter* (London: Kegan Paul).

van Cleve, James (1983), 'Conceivability and the Cartesian Argument for Dualism', *Pacific Philosophical Quarterly*, 64: 35–45.

Yablo, Stephen (1993), 'Is Conceivability a Guide to Possibility?', *Philosophy and Phenomenological Research*, 53: 1–42.

—— (1999), 'Concepts and Consciousness', *Philosophy and Phenomenological Research*, 59(2): 455–63.

4

Desire in Imagination

GREGORY CURRIE

Moral truths, if there are any, may all be necessary truths. But that ought not to stop us imagining alternative moralities. After all, plenty of strict impossibilities in the purely factual realm are, or seem to be, perfectly imaginable, as with stories in which it turns out that Gödel misled us about the unprovability by finite means of the consistency of arithmetic.[1] None the less, imagination is peculiarly inhospitable to alternative moralities. We are not, Hume remarked, repelled by the factual errors of writers from other times and places; with 'a turn of imagination' we enter easily into all their opinions. But with stories that presuppose an alien morality, 'I cannot, nor is it proper that I should, enter into such

Versions of this paper were read at the Research School of Social Sciences, Australian National University; the Leonard Symposium on Imagination at the Meeting of the American Society for Aesthetics, Reno, October 2000; the Moral Sciences Club, Cambridge; and the Department of Philosophy, University of Sheffield. Thanks to the audiences on all these occasions for more help than I can possibly record. Special thanks go to Tamar Szabó Gendler and John Hawthorne for their careful reading of an earlier draft.

[1] Alternatives to the so-called metaphysical necessities such as water's being H_2O are not, I think, good examples here. I follow the two-dimensionalists in denying that there are two kinds of necessity, metaphysical and conceptual. The necessary proposition expressed by 'water is H_2O' is conceptually necessary. The question is, which proposition is it? That question gets answered by empirical inquiry, and the answer is that it is the proposition which is true just in case H_2O is H_2O. One can imagine that 'Water isn't H_2O' expresses a true proposition, but that is not a case of imagining an alternative to any kind of necessary truth. See, e.g., Jackson (1998: 67–86).

sentiments.'[2] While we take fiction's violations of history and even of physical law in our stride, many of us balk at stories that presuppose the rightness of slavery or the wickedness of unbelief. We also find it difficult to embrace the bad in our own acts of imaginative pretence. Speculating on the origins of representational art, Ernst Gombrich noted our resistance to defacing the portrait (even an otherwise worthless image from a newspaper) of someone we admire. Gombrich's observation was intended to strengthen the claim that art originated in magical ideas of control: 'Somewhere there remains the absurd feeling that what one does to the picture is done to the person it represents.'[3] That way, resistance is explained in terms of belief; we believe, subconsciously or at least in some way less than fully integrated with our other beliefs, that damaging the picture will harm the person. But resistance to defacement can be explained in other ways. Poking holes in the relevant bits of the photograph might be very apt to prompt us to imagine that we are poking out the eyes of the person represented.[4] Perhaps we simply don't want to imagine doing such a terrible thing—just as we don't want to engage, even in imagination, with moralities that oblige or allow us to do that which we actually think would be terribly wrong.[5]

Some people hold that we cannot *really* believe in the impossible. So, they might add, we can't really imagine impossibilities either, for belief and imagination (of the relevant kind) are so similar that the limits of belief are the limits of imagination as well. So, they might continue, it is unsurprising that imagination is resistant to the morally impossible. I agree about the similarity between belief and imagination; I explore that similarity in some detail below. But a blanket ban on imagining the impossible needs to account for Escher-imagining. You can see an Escher drawing which represents an impossible state of affairs; with a good visual memory, you ought to be able to visualize, that is, visually to imagine, that impossibility. And even if you can account for this and like phenomena, insisting on the general impossibility of imagining the

---

[2] Hume (1757: 246). For more recent work see Walton (1994), Tanner (1994), Moran (1994), Williams (1999), and especially Gendler (2000). I return to Gendler's argument in the final section. Hume does not always distinguish between imagining and believing in his discussion; at one point he suggests that embracing the poetic works of earlier authors would require us to share their *judgements* of right conduct, and that this is what we find difficult ('a very violent effort is requisite to change our judgement of manners'). To this we may respond that neither are we free to judge the earth flat or the wind the breath of gods. Hume's postulation of an asymmetry between the moral and the factual makes sense only so long as we understand him to be focusing on what we can imagine.   [3] Gombrich (1984: 20). See also Gombrich (1960: ch. 3).

[4] I take it this is Walton's view; see Walton (1990: 154–5). On games of pretence with pictures as props see ibid., ch. 8.   [5] I return to Gombrich's example in sect. 4 below.

impossible mislocates our problem. For imaginative resistance to alternative moralities is a special problem, with special features not apparent in other sorts of cases. The resistance I experience to the invitation to imagine, say, female infanticide being right is quite different from that which arises in the case of imagining the consistency of arithmetic to be provable by finite means. Indeed, in the latter case, it is not clear that I *experience* any imaginative resistance at all. At most, I might on reflection conclude that I was not really imagining what I took myself to be imagining. When it seemed to me that I was imagining the provability of consistency, it seemed also that I was imagining this without any effort or difficulty. And anyway, it would be wrong to suppose that the problem of imaginative resistance arises only for people (us, presumably) who have correct moral views. People whose morals are, by our lights, very misguided experience imaginative resistance to better views when they are exposed to them; if it were not so, moral education would be an easier business. But, by hypothesis, the opinions they are resistant to are not incoherent. There is something psychologically distinctive about imaginative resistance to values we find alien, and my aim here is to find out what.[6] Before I start, I want to show a connection between this issue and one about moral and factual learning.

Whether we are moral realists or anti-realists, we agree, I take it, that some degree of open-mindedness in moral matters is a good thing. Collectively and individually, we have embraced the bad in the guise of the good too often for us to be confident that our present position is beyond improvement. We shall, of course, disagree about what this involves, with moral realists insisting that the problem concerns the recognition of moral truth, and anti-realists wanting to put it some other way. And moral realists will disagree among themselves about whether moral error consists in taking what is merely a moral possibility for a moral truth, or whether it is more like error in mathematics, where there are no unactualized possibilities. So let us say, more neutrally, that change of moral outlook is sometimes change for the better. The problem is then to decide how to make changes in such a way that they have at least a good chance of being changes for the better. Occasionally it is suggested that imagination can play an important role here. According to David Lewis, values are those things we would desire to desire under ideal conditions of imaginative involvement.[7] And Martha Nussbaum has argued that imaginative engagement with fictions can make us better moralists. She claims that

---

[6] Gendler (2000) also points out that resistance of the kind we experience to immoral moralities also occurs where possibility is not at issue; see her fable of the mice (sect. 7).

[7] See Lewis (1989).

literature encourages us to take on the role of a judicious and impartial judge, whose sympathies are engaged via imaginative identification, tempered with 'external assessment'. Thus reading is a kind of training in moral judgement, a training that allows us to approach the position of Adam Smith's judicious spectator.[8]

But here there is a peculiar asymmetry between the factual and the moral. We find it easy, on the whole, to imagine alternative factual circumstances. But we don't think that such exercises of the imagination will make us better, more reliable believers. We see no special connection between imagining P and being a reliable believer of P, perhaps because it is just *too* easy for us to imagine factual alternatives. On the other hand, we find it difficult (as I hope I have indicated above) to engage imaginatively with alternative moralities. But it seems, to some of us at least, that this is exactly what we need to do in order to be better moralists. There is a special connection—though not one that it is easy to state—between openness in imagination to alternative moralities and developed moral character.

This is, I know, rather vague and rhetorical. But we cannot get clear about the problem until we are clearer about the nature of imaginative resistance. My aim here is to provide some of this clarity. I shall do so by focusing on the nature of the imagination itself, and on the different kinds of imaginings that there are. In particular, I want to argue that there is such a thing as imagining that is desire-like. Desire-like imagining will turn out to be fundamental to the problem of imaginative resistance.

1 Modes of Imagining

An inquiry into the structure of the imagination might well begin by noting the different kinds of imaginings we can engage in. We can imagine in a perceptual mode, as when we visualize something. Visualizing is not seeing, but it is, surely, seeing-like: our spontaneous description of it in visual terms suggests that visualizing and seeing are phenomenologically similar, and experiments show that the information content of visual imagery and of vision are presented and processed in ways that are strikingly alike.[9] I am suggesting that there are modes of imagining that are comparably similar to propositional

[8] See Nussbaum (1995).

[9] Many of these processing similarities are described in Kosslyn (1994). For criticism of the conclusions that Kosslyn draws from this concerning the underlying form of mental representation in imagery, see Abell and Currie (1999).

attitudes like beliefs and desires.[10] I shall call them 'belief-like and desire-like imaginings'. I shall say a great deal about them in sections 3–5.

I claim that belief-like imagining is just what we more often call assuming or supposing. It has been argued that supposing and imagining must be different, because they have different properties. I shall try to show that this argument is plausible only so long as we do not also recognize the category of desire-like imagining. But belief-like imaginings first.

An important feature of beliefs is their occupation of characteristic inferential roles: believing something tends to lead to believing other things, depending on what else you already believe.[11] Philosophers interested in belief dynamics assume that imagining is belief-like in this respect when they offer the Ramsey test as a means of deciding whether you should accept a conditional. According to the Ramsey test,

> given an overall state of belief G, you should accept the conditional 'If P then Q' if you should accept Q in the overall state G⋆P,

where G⋆P is the belief state that results from revising G in the light of P.[12]

How do I apply the Ramsey test? If I could add P to my beliefs and settle into a new overall state of belief, I could then just see whether Q seemed reasonable or not. But I can't add to the stock of my beliefs at will. Anyway, I do not wish to take on beliefs irrespective of their truth-values just in order to evaluate conditionals. The idea is that, instead of adding P as a belief, I can add it 'in imagination', and since imagination preserves the inferential patterns of belief, I can then see whether a new imagining, Q, emerges as reasonable in the light of this. If it does, I have reason to think that adding P to the stock of my beliefs would lead me to add Q as well, and so I can add the conditional 'If P then Q' to my beliefs.[13]

That there is a kind of imagining inferentially like belief is further supported by what we know about our imaginative engagements with fiction, backed up by some things that psychologists have recently discovered. If you imagine the novel's heroine in London one day and in Chicago the next, you will also imagine that she flew there, unless there is a strong indication in the work that

---

[10] Comparably similar, but not, as we shall see, similar in the same respects.

[11] In her account of what she has called 'replication' and now prefers to call 'co-cognition', Jane Heal (1995) places much emphasis on the capacity for imagination to preserve the inferential role of belief. But Heal makes it clear that she would oppose a functionalist theory of the individuation of mental states.   [12] See Stalnaker (1968).

[13] Note that here I am assuming that supposing is a form of imagining. The argument will come later.

she got there by another means. As readers, we let our imaginings mingle with our beliefs, and further imaginings emerge which, so far as their contents go, are identical with what would emerge from the operation of inference on belief alone. Sometimes fictions defeat our attempts to fill them out via the commingling of imagining and belief; if the story set in 1800 has the character on one side of the Atlantic one day and on the other side the next, I may decide that this is just error on the author's part. My beliefs, together with the kinds of imaginings I think the work entitles me to, don't get me to a plausible scenario. But where interpretation works at all, it works by mixing up beliefs and imaginings and seeing what results. There are occasions where we read that the character in 1800 crossed the Atlantic in hours, and are not confused about what to imagine. That's because we have come across some indication in the work that, say, magical modes of transport are available, and we have imagined that as well. The appearance that a fiction has us conclude something that we would not conclude on the basis of belief alone is due to our having left out of account some important element in what we are being asked to imagine—like magical modes of transport.

It is this capacity of imaginings to mirror the inferential patterns of belief that makes fictional story telling possible. If imaginings were not inferentially commensurate with beliefs, we could not draw on our beliefs to fill out what the story tells us, and story-tellers would have to give us all the detail explicitly. But that is more than they could ever give, and more than we could stand listening to.

Incidentally, this sheds important light on the 'problem of truth in fiction'. David Lewis (1983: 264) once remarked that inferences undertaken by consumers of fictions are peculiar. For example,

> It is fictional that Sherlock Holmes is human.
> All humans are mortal.
> So,
> It is fictional that Holmes is mortal.

This is an inference in which the conclusion is governed by the intensional operator *It is fictional that*, but where only some of the premises are so governed. What rules would justify such inferences? But it is not clear that these are in fact the inferences we undertake. Rather, the reader's inference might be something like this:

> Holmes is human (something she imagines).
> All humans are mortal (something she believes).
> So,
> Holmes is mortal (something she imagines).

Here the inference is perfectly conventional; what is notable about it is the commingling of attitudes—belief and imagination. And the only rule, apart from standard logical ones, that governs the making of such inferences is that, where the inference is from premises at least one of which is an imagining, the conclusion will be an imagining as well.

Recent work in child psychology has shown that the preservation of inference in imagination emerges very early; it is not likely that children first engage in imaginings that are not inferentially constrained and then learn somehow to constrain them. In one experiment children are shown a range of soft toy animals. There is also an empty cup which the children are encouraged to imagine is full of water. The cup is up-ended over one of the animals: the lion, say. The children will spontaneously imagine that the lion is wet, though the animal is in fact dry (since the up-ended cup was in fact empty) and no one has mentioned the idea of it being wet.[14] It looks as if the children's imagining that the animal had water poured over it mingles with their beliefs about water-pouring situations, and arrives, belief-like, at the imagining that the animal is wet.

There are other ways that imagination can be like belief. Reasoning can be practical as well as theoretical, and you can undertake a piece of practical reasoning based on what you imagine as well as on what you believe; the result will be a decision, in imagination, to do something. Imagining something can also have consequences for emotion and affect that are very like the emotional and affective consequences of believing it; when we read stories or watch films and are imaginatively involved with their events, we often experience emotions that are both powerful and apparently continuous with those we experience in response to situations in real life.[15] But fully to understand the mechanisms underlying imaginative practical reasoning and emotion-generation, we need the concept of desire-like imagining, and I shall introduce that idea only in section 3 below.

[14] Paul Harris and Robert Kavanaugh (1993) found that children from 24 months reliably showed this kind of competence. It was more difficult to elicit it from younger children, but even children around 21 months, when they responded at all, tended to show that they understood which of several animals was wet.

[15] Keith Oatley describes the results of some work on emotional responses to fiction done by his students: 'adults and adolescents reading short stories by James Joyce, Alice Munro and Carson McCullers, could readily mark the margins of texts where emotions occurred while reading a story, and could later describe these emotions, say what caused them, and rate their intensities. Emotions occurring while reading were similar to those of ordinary life. During reading they were typically experienced around the midpoint of a scale of intensity, ranging from 0 = barely noticeable to 10 = the most intense ever experienced, and sometimes towards the top of this range (1994: 54).

All this concerns ways in which belief-like imagining is like belief. But belief-like imagining must differ from belief in various ways, otherwise it is not anything different from belief. And it does differ. Beliefs are constrained in various ways that imaginings are not. It is said that beliefs have to form a rational system, in the sense that one's beliefs form an internally rational whole, are justified by the perceptual states that lead to them, and justify or rationalize the actions to which they lead. Such constraints can be overstated: few want to insist that there can never be tensions between one's beliefs, that beliefs are never held in opposition to the evidence, that actions are always rational. But the more a putative belief presses against these constraints, the less confident we should be in attributing it. And beyond some vague boundary, we seem no longer to be talking about belief at all. That is why the various kinds of delusional beliefs that people are sometimes said to possess—that thoughts are being inserted into their heads, that alien forces control their bodies, that loved ones have been replaced by strangers of similar appearance—pose real problems for anyone who takes these constraints seriously.[16] And people who are not suffering from independently identifiable psychopathologies do at least acknowledge that inconsistency in belief is a problem, though they may shelve the problem posed by a known inconsistency in what they believe because there are more urgent matters to confront or because no obvious solution presents itself. Imaginings are not similarly constrained. We are happy to attribute to someone the imagining that P, despite the fact that she never had any perceptual experience that would justify P, never engaged in any action that would be appropriate if P were true, and possessed many beliefs that contradict P. And we do not expect her to treat the inconsistency between what she imagines and what she believes as a problem she ought to face up to at some stage.

How is all this compatible with there being an inferential fit between belief and imagination? Imaginings have limited—usually very limited—duration. When we imagine P, the tendency is for any belief that contradicts P, or which stands in substantial probabilistic tension with P, to fall into the background for the duration and purposes of the imagining. The imagining then combines inferentially with other relevant beliefs that don't contradict or stand in tension with it. When we stop imagining P, our beliefs, including those that were backgrounded by the imagining, are still available for theoretical and practical reasoning. Beliefs are supposed to obey the constraints of inferential rationality long-term and globally; ideally, all our beliefs are always consistent. But the most we ask of imaginings is that they carve out a consistent subset of our beliefs with which to connect in the short term.

---

[16] See Coltheart and Davies (2000).

2 Why Belief-Like Imagining isn't a Kind of Belief

That our imaginings need not be consistent with anything other than a small subset of our beliefs explains why we can't assimilate imagining to belief. The attractions of assimilation are summed up in the following response to what I have said so far. 'You have said that belief-like imagining is like belief in some ways and unlike it in others. But you assume that there is a single conception of belief, and that is not so. One conception is the neo-behaviourist one: whether one believes that P is a matter of whether one is disposed to act in a way that is appropriate, given that P is true.[17] We can agree that imagining is not believing in that sense. But there are other accounts of belief. L. Jonathan Cohen, for example, says that the belief that P is the disposition to feel that P is true,[18] and one can have that disposition without being apt to satisfy one's desires in worlds where P is true. Perhaps these different accounts of belief are not rivals; perhaps they identify different points on a belief spectrum. In that case there is a broad concept of belief that would cover belief as neo-behaviourists understand it, as well as various less demanding conceptions.[19] And perhaps we can locate imagining somewhere along this spectrum.'

We can't, for the following reason. We can take a liberal view of what counts as a belief, including as beliefs a variety of states that do not meet any version of the neo-behaviourist condition. But belief, however weakly characterized, is normative, in that an agent who has contradictory beliefs (in any sense of belief) is in a less than ideal epistemic situation. And it is no defect in our imaginer's epistemic condition that she imagines things contrary to what she believes. An otherwise consistent and coherent believer who imagines that Desdemona is murdered is not in any way failing to meet constraints of epistemic virtue. While imagining is like belief in various ways, it is not to be classed with beliefs, however weak a sense of belief we opt for.

But don't confuse the false view that imagination lies on a continuum *of* belief states with the true view that imagination lies on a continuum—or better, within a many-dimensional space—*with* belief. The space that beliefs and imaginings both lie in is a space of states which are functional kinds. Beliefs of the kind I have been focusing on have certain characteristic relations to perception, desire, decision, action, and other states. There may be other kinds of beliefs, with different functional characteristics; perhaps, together, all these belief states form a vaguely bounded irregular solid within the space. And there might be another irregular solid which includes the states of belief-like

---

[17] See Stalnaker (1984).   [18] Cohen (1989: 368).   [19] See Morton (1980).

imagining that correspond to each of these belief states. At various places these two solids may come very close together. But they do not intersect.

Perhaps there are other reasons why imaginings are not beliefs. But the strength of the argument from normativity given above can be brought out by comparing it with an argument that doesn't work. The argument is this. Beliefs—or, at least, reasonable beliefs— are context-independent. But imaginings are highly context-dependent; what I imagine relative to one context (e.g., reading *Jane Eyre*) is quite different from what I imagine relative to another (e.g., watching *The Mummy*). This argument is lifted, with modification, from Michael Bratman, who argues that acceptance is not belief, because what one accepts varies between contexts.[20] But Bratman's argument leaves open the possibility that to accept P might be simply (i) to believe P and (ii) to have one's belief that P play a certain role in a given piece of reasoning. And a belief that plays this role in one piece of reasoning need not play that role in another. That way, acceptances could be beliefs; beliefs, *qua* beliefs, are context-independent, *qua* acceptances they are context-dependent. After all, conscious belief is context-dependent—one consciously believes something in one context and not in another—but conscious belief is still belief. Imaginings might then similarly be beliefs, but beliefs that have characteristics over and above those definitive of beliefs and that make them count as imaginings in some contexts and not in others. But the argument from normativity given above survives this objection; if imaginings were beliefs-that-occupy-imagination-defining-roles, then, in order to imagine things contrary to what one believes, one would have to have contradictory beliefs.

3 Imagination and Desire

Recall that imagination can be belief-like in respect of inferential role: imagining that P leads to new imaginings in the way that believing P would lead to new beliefs. But beliefs also prompt action, where they combine with our desires to produce decisions. And imaginative projections often involve the re-creation of motivation; we imagine ourselves in this situation and then, in imagination, we decide to do something. And we may conclude from this that that *is* what we would do in that situation. Imaginative projection should involve more than just a shift of belief; sometimes I need to shift my desires

---

[20] See Bratman (1992). But Bratman has other arguments for the distinctness of belief and acceptance; I am not here quarrelling with those other arguments.

as well, because in the imagined situation I would desire something I don't actually desire. But this can't involve *really* taking on a new desire, exactly because desires have connections to actions; if imagining led me to have desires appropriate to a merely imagined situation, I might end up acting in dangerous ways. The shift of desire must itself be a shift in imagination. There must be desire-like imaginings, as well as belief-like ones.[21]

Postulating desire-like imaginings helps explain the affective consequences of imagination. Sometimes, emotional responses are dependent on cognitive states: I feel envious because of what I believe about your success, and I would feel no envy without those beliefs or beliefs relevantly like them. And my emotional reaction to a fictional situation depends similarly on my belief-like imaginings; Desdemona's death affects me in the way it does partly because I imagine that it is the outcome of a wicked design. But where emotions depend on beliefs, they depend on desires as well; if I didn't desire your success or success relevantly like it, I would not be envious. And so it must be with emotions that depend on belief-like imaginings; to be genuinely belief-like, these imaginings ought to have emotional consequences only in conjunction with states that are desire-like. The phenomenology of spectatorship supports this. Our emotional response to the death of Desdemona is very different from our reaction to the death of Macbeth, a disparity which it seems natural to explain in terms of differences of desire: we say that we *want* Macbeth to be killed and Desdemona to be saved. Only these are not really desires, but desire-like imaginings. Why? For one thing, desires, like beliefs, face normative constraints, and these constraints on desire do not govern what we call 'wanting Desdemona to be saved'. Desires can be shown to be unreasonable, or at least unjustified, if they fail to connect in various ways with the facts; the reasonableness of my desiring punishment for someone depends on the facts about what they did.[22] But the reasonableness of my (as we say) wanting punishment for Macbeth—compared to the unreasonableness of wanting punishment for Desdemona—is not undercut by the fact that there is no such person as Macbeth, and so no such person ever did anything deserving of punishment.

[21] Shaun Nichols and Steve Stich argue against the idea of desiring in imagination, preferring an account in terms of real desires. When children play mud pies, and pretend to eat the pies, 'The motivating desire is not an imaginary desire to eat a pie, but a real desire to behave in a way that is similar to the way that the imagined person behaves' (2000: 134–5). In this chapter I do not consider whether imaginings can motivate; I argue for the existence of desire-like imaginings on other grounds. For arguments that imaginings can motivate, see Currie and Ravenscroft (2001: ch. 6). See also Velleman (2000).

[22] It will depend on other things as well, such as moral principles.

You might reply that the theatre-goer's state *is* accounted for in terms of a real desire she has; it's just that we misdescribe it when we say that she desires that Othello not kill Desdemona. We should say that she has the perfectly respectable real desire that, *in this fiction*, Desdemona not be murdered. Desiring that, in this fiction, someone not be murdered is a real desire, but it is not the desire that someone not be murdered, because *in this fiction* is a propositional operator that behaves like *believes*, or *possibly*: Desiring that S believes that P, or that possibly P is not desiring P, and neither is desiring that in the fiction, P.

This is not a very useful proposal unless it is generalized to other kinds of cases of imaginative projection, as when I shift my perspective in imagination from mine to yours, because I want to figure out what you will do, and I think that imaginative projection into your situation will help me. Perhaps a case like that can be thought of as involving a little fiction of my own construction, a fiction in which I am in your situation, and which I desire to turn out in a certain way. But since, as we shall see, the proposal won't work even for *Othello*-type cases, we shan't need to ask whether generalization really is possible.

One problem with the proposal is that it obscures the distinction between attitudes towards characters, like Desdemona, and attitudes towards fictions, like *Othello*.[23] On the proposal, everything that has the appearance of being a desire-like state concerning fictional characters turns out to be a real desire concerning the fictional narratives that describe them. But this would make it difficult to understand the ways we react emotionally to fictional situations. When I am sorry and upset about the fate of Desdemona, I am not sorry that this fiction has it that an innocent and good-hearted girl suffers a cruel fate. One might be sorry about that, deploring that there are fictions with such unhappy and unjust outcomes. But this is not what at least many of us are sorry about; we are glad that Shakespeare's fiction has it this way, and not the way that a rewritten version with a happy ending would have it. Part of the inner tension that we experience on watching this play derives from the fact that we have a desire-like imagining that Desdemona flourish, combined with a (genuine) desire that the play be one which will ensure that that desire-like imagining is unsatisfied. In that case desire-like imaginings do not seem to be dispensable, even in contexts where dispensing with them seems most likely to work: namely, where there is an independently acknowledged fiction to appeal to.

---

[23] Another is that theatre-goers often know how the play is going to end; desiring that it not end that way would then seem to involve a sense of hopelessness at odds with the very real tension one actually feels concerning the outcome.

Another proposal for doing without desire-like imaginings is this: there is one unified state of imagining, and what we are calling 'belief-like imaginings' and 'desire-like imaginings' are accounted for by saying that in the one case we imagine that we believe something, and in the other that we imagine that we desire it. That way we get by with three categories—belief, desire, and a generic imagining—instead of my four—belief, desire, belief-like imagining, and desire-like imagining. The difference between my proposal and this new one is that, on my proposal, I imaginatively project into the situation of one who believes P and desires Q when I have the belief-like imagining that P and the desire-like imagining that Q. But on the new proposal what I do is imagine (in some generic sense) that I believe P and desire Q.

This proposal makes all imagining self-imagining, imagining in which one deploys a self-concept, as well as such psychological concepts as belief and desire. For it is part of the content of what I imagine, not merely that P, but that I believe P. But imagining that there is beer in the fridge surely does not require me to deploy psychological concepts. And consider imagining that Smith will win the election even though no one believes he will. If this means imagining that I believe that Smith will win the election even though no one believes he will, I am required to imagine something contradictory.[24] Perhaps it is possible to imagine explicitly contradictory things like this. But imagining that Smith will win the election even though no one believes he will does not seem to involve imagining anything contradictory; we should be suspicious of a theory that says otherwise.[25]

Desire-like imaginings don't seem to figure much in folk-psychological thought and talk about the imagination. If I ask you to imagine so-and-so, you are unlikely to complain that my request is ambiguous as between the request for you to come up with an imagining that is belief-like and one that is desire-like. Should this make us suspicious that the latter category is just a theoretician's artefact with no psychological reality? I don't think so. When people get down to detail about their imaginings, especially in response to fictions, talk of desire-like states starts to emerge; we say that we wanted Othello to believe in Desdemona's innocence. I've argued that attempts to explain such statements as referring to genuine desires won't work; they have to be understood as referring to desire-like imaginings.

---

[24] Thanks to Martin Davies for the example.

[25] This argument is the analogue, for belief-like imagining, of a familiar argument concerning perceptual imagining; can we consistently imagine, in the visual mode, an unseen tree? [For related discussion, see John Campbell 'Berkeley's Puzzle', Ch. 2 above—eds.]

One reason why desire-like imaginings don't figure prominently in our folk theory of imagination is this. When story-tellers invite us to imagine things, they generally concentrate on shaping our belief-like imaginings, and leave desire-like imaginings to follow our natural inclinations. Thus story-tellers make it explicit, or at least easily inferable, that Desdemona is innocent, that Oliver wants more, that Peter Pan kicks Hook over the side of the ship. These are not things we could be counted on to imagine simply by following our own inclinations; story-tellers have to make it clear that these are the things they want us to imagine. But they generally don't tell us what kind of desire-like imaginings to have concerning these events; they assume that we will desire in imagination much as we do in real life. For it is harder, much harder, to get people to desire in imagination against the trend of their own real desires than it is to get people to believe in imagination against the trend of what they really believe. (The latter, we know, is easy; otherwise, fantasy and science fiction would not be popular genres.) So story-telling makes belief-like imagining very salient, and desire-like imagining not very salient. This will be important in the next section.

Why should there be this asymmetry between belief-like and desire-like imagining?[26] It will help if we consider only ideally rational agents. Such an agent is constrained in her believings, not by personal inclination, but by the evidence. For such a person, belief is externally, but not internally, constrained. But our ideally rational agent is not devoid of moral character; her tendency to desire is constrained by a complex set of dispositions that may, perhaps, be thought of as higher-order desires, but that, since they constitute her basic moral character, are not easily changed. And the effect of shifting from beliefs and desires to belief-like and desire-like imaginings is to free the subject from external constraint. And that is where the asymmetry starts to emerge. Belief-like imagining becomes free, but desire-like imagining remains responsive to the dictates of moral character.[27]

---

[26] Thanks to Tamar Szabó Gendler for pressing me on this.

[27] Edward Craig has objected that there are internal constraints on belief formation. We form new beliefs in response to incoming evidence in ways that favour the conservation of previously held beliefs. So belief formation is constrained by our own history of believing. But we have seen that belief-like imagining is not substantially constrained in this manner; as imaginings are formed, beliefs in tension with them merely fall into the background. And the same, presumably, can be said of desire and desire-in-imagination. The formation of new desires is constrained by what we already desire, but desire-like imaginings, when they do make their way into our mental economy, merely push aside conflicting desires for the duration of the project. So we can ignore this kind of internal constraint as not significant for imagination, either in its belief-like or in its desire-like form.

4 Supposition

What I have called belief-like imagining is what you may be inclined to call supposition: we make suppositions and slip them into our reasoning alongside our beliefs, getting out conclusions that are also suppositions. I agree, more or less. Roughly speaking, belief-like imagining is supposition (perhaps there is more than one kind of supposition; I'm content to say that belief-like imagining is one kind). One argument against this identification draws on the kind of imaginative resistance I mentioned at the beginning. Tamar Szabó Gendler argues that 'imagination requires a sort of participation that mere hypothetical reasoning does not. . . . What this suggests is that imagination is distinct from belief on the one hand, and from mere supposition on the other' (2000: 80–1).[28] I am resistant to believing a moral proposition if it conflicts with what I believe, and I am similarly resistant to believing a non-moral one; belief evinces no asymmetric resistance to moral propositions as opposed to non-moral ones. And I am happy to suppose both the moral proposition and the non-moral one; no asymmetry here either. But there is, according to Gendler, an asymmetry in imagining. We have no problem, she says, in imagining that female infanticide takes place; but we do, many of us, have great difficulty in imagining that female infanticide is good, and our experiencing this sort of barrier to imaginative participation in alien moralities explains some of our discomfort with certain kinds of fictions. So imagination differs from supposition in the way that imagination differs from belief. So imagining is neither believing nor supposing.

The asymmetry that Gendler describes seems to me an important one if we are trying to assess the role of imagination in the enlargement of moral possibility. And I agree that imagining is not belief; I spent part of section 2 arguing for exactly that. But I think it is wrong to say that supposition and imagination are fundamentally different kinds of things. I propose instead that supposition is a special form of imagining: a form of imagining that is more flexible than the kind of imaginative engagement that we typically experience when engrossed in a vivid and arresting story.

What, then, is the difference between merely suppositional imagining and imagining of the richer kind that displays resistance to alien morality? My answer will be that a richly imaginative projection has a desire-like component,

---

[28] Moran holds a similar view, though in his formulation it does not amount to the denial that supposition is a kind of imagining: 'Imaginatively adopting a perspective on something involves something different from the sort of imagination involved in ordinary counterfactual reasoning' (Moran 1994: 105).

while supposition is simply belief-like imagining.[29] Recall Gendler's argument: we have no problem in supposing that female infanticide is good, but we do have difficulty in imagining this. In general, I am happy to suppose both moral propositions and non-moral ones; but while I am happy to imagine non-moral propositions, I experience discomfort with, and resistance to, imagining certain kinds of moral propositions. So imagining is not supposing. But if we recognize desire-like as well as belief-like imagining, we need not accept this argument. We can say instead that there are different kinds of imaginative projects. One kind is confined to belief-like imagining, and displays no resistance to alien moralities.[30] But there is another kind, which involves both belief-like and desire-like imagining, and which does display resistance.

However, I shall not argue that imaginative resistance is confined to imaginings that are desire-like. I want to argue for something a little more complicated. I think there are cases where belief-like imagining exhibits resistance, but that is because of its connection with desire-like imagining. I'll say more about the connection below. So my claims will be these: (i) that resistance is primarily a characteristic of desire-like imagining and only secondarily, or through its relation to desire-like imagining, a characteristic of belief-like imagining; and (ii) supposing is belief-like imagining that does not stand in the kinds of relations to desire-like imagining that tend to produce resistance.

That imaginative resistance is at least not exclusively a characteristic of belief-like imagining is indicated by the fact that there are cases of imaginative resistance to fictional points of view even where the truth of an alien morality is not at issue. Take the case I cited at the beginning: defacing a picture as part of the project of imagining poking out someone's eyes. We surely are resistant to such a project, though it cannot be necessary to its undertaking that we imagine that poking people's eyes out is good. It seems much more natural to say that what we resist is desiring, in imagination, to poke out someone's eyes. Also, we are often resistant to taking on, in imagination, the point of view of a

---

[29] Moran says: 'By contrast [with hypothetical reasoning], imagination with respect to emotional attitudes may require such things as dramatic rehearsal, the right mood, the right experiences, a sympathetic nature' (Moran 1994: 105). This sounds right to me, because dramatic rehearsal and the rest sound to me like just the sorts of things that require desire in imagination. Moran goes on: 'If we understood better why imagining in such cases requires your heart to be in it, we would understand better what is being resisted when we resist' (ibid). I claim that desire in imagination, and its subservience to moral character, helps us to explain exactly this.

[30] In contrasting imagination with supposition, Gendler seems pretty clearly to have belief-like imagining in mind. She says: 'imagining involves something in between belief on the one hand, and mere supposition on the other' (2000: 56), and throughout she uses 'imagine' interchangeably with 'make-believe'.

wicked character, even when the moral world of the fiction itself is not alien, and where the wicked character does not himself believe that his project is moral; Iago would surely be contemptuous of the idea that his project was a morally good one. I suggest that our difficulty is just that we cannot easily construct for ourselves imaginative replicas of his wicked desires. Indeed, the asymmetry between belief-like and desire-like imagining here is striking. We tolerate astonishing amounts of cruelty and suffering being represented in fictions, and are very willing to imagine that innocent people like Desdemona are murdered for no good reason, as long as we are not asked to take on in imagination the desires of the characters who bring about and delight in that suffering.

But isn't it true, as Gendler says, that we are resistant to imagining alien values, when that imagining is belief-like? Aren't we resistant to imagining that female infanticide is good? I agree that this is true, but the reason is that there are internal connections between moral beliefs and desires, and similar connections between belief-like and desire-like imaginings. Quite what these connections are is hard to determine; we should not say, for example, that believing that F is good always involves desiring F; one can hold F as valuable and not desire F. We can make out a more plausible connection via the idea of an ideal spectator: someone who is sufficiently rational, well-informed about, and disinterested in the action she surveys for it to be the case that, were she to think a certain outcome to the action morally right, she would desire that outcome, and were she to think that outcome morally wrong, she would desire its non-occurrence. And, as Martha Nussbaum has argued, readers of fiction frequently approximate to the condition of being ideal observers of the fictional worlds they survey: their reason, interest, and moral sensitivities are engaged, but not in the service of their own ends.[31] So their desire-like imaginings will tend to be in harmony with their belief-like imaginings about the rights and wrongs of the action. And for such a person, resistance in desire-like imagining will translate into resistance in belief-like imagining as well; if it is difficult for her to have the desire-like imagining that female infants be killed, she can have the belief-like imagining that female infanticide is right only at the expense of the harmony between belief-like and desire-like imagining which is the natural stance of the intelligent and sensitive reader.

What, then, is supposition? I say that it is belief-like imagining that is isolated from, or at least not substantially affected by, desire-like imagining. (That's why I agree only 'more or less' that supposition is belief-like imagining; strictly, it is belief-like imagining under certain conditions.) When I am asked to suppose

---

[31] Nussbaum (1995: 77).

some (possibly alien) moral proposition, I succeed if I manage to restrict my imaginative engagement to the re-creation of belief-like states. This turns into an imaginative project which is more than merely suppositional if my desire-like imaginings are engaged as well. I might, by great effort, manage to take on in imagination the desires that conform to this alien moral proposition, desiring female infanticide to flourish, for example. In that case my supposition has become a more richly imaginative project that probably does not any longer deserve the label 'supposing' (though I am not assuming there is any sharp boundary here). I have, at this point, started 'really getting into' that value, if only in imagination. But if my imagining does start to engage my desire system at all, it is likely that I shan't be able to summon the appropriate desire-like imagining in favour of female infanticide at all, and then the imaginative project will be derailed.

Whether, and to what extent, we succeed in insulating belief-like imagining from desire-like imagining, and thus engage in an act of supposing, will depend on a number of factors, including natural capacities that vary between persons. But one important factor will be the rhetorical and descriptive features of what prompts the imagining in the first place. If I simply ask you, without embellishment, to suppose, for the sake of the argument, that female infants should be killed, you may well succeed in forming the relevant belief-like imaginings without bringing the desire system into play. But if I create, as novelists and film-makers do, a vivid and detailed world in which to situate these circumstances, this mental partitioning will be much more difficult. We cannot say, therefore, that this or that proposition is something I can suppose, while some other proposition is beyond my suppositional powers. The most we can say is that this proposition, in this context of presentation, given my natural inclinations, present thoughts, recent experiences, and so forth, is or is not something I can insulate from desire-like imagining.

Are there kinds of imaginative resistance that this proposal could not explain? Kendall Walton asks us to consider a story in which a joke is told; actually, the joke is very feeble, but in the story it is said to be extremely funny. There are grave barriers, he says, to *imagining* it as funny, just as there are barriers to imagining the rightness of female infanticide. Yet there does not seem to be any obvious explanation of resistance to imagining the joke funny in terms of the rigidity of desire.[32]

I don't think we know enough about the psychology of humour to rule out the possibility that jokes depend for their reception on our having, or being

---

[32] Walton (1994) discusses the joke case. I thank him for raising it, in conversation, as a problem for my approach.

able to summon in imagination, certain desires. But I won't base my response to Walton on the claim that they do. For what is it, exactly, that we cannot do in response to the story with the feeble joke? If you can imagine being much amused by something, you can surely imagine reacting in *that* way (that amused way) to the story's feeble joke. In my terms, you can have the belief-like imagining that the joke is funny. Perhaps you can even imagine, of your (actually) disdainful reaction, that it is a reaction of extreme amusement.[33] What you can't do is actually be amused by it. But then the case is no longer one of *imaginative* resistance; it is akin to our incapacity to believe stories with fantastical plots, and in that region, the asymmetry of response that is our focus here does not show itself.

Still, I agree that there are cases of resistant imagining which are not cases of resistant desiring in imagination. Take the case of pain. Suppose you and I play *The Spanish Inquisition*, having at our disposal some life-like bits of equipment. And suppose you pretend to tighten those very real thumbscrews on my hands. I am likely, in that situation, to have what surely deserve to be called 'pains in imagination': experiences that are not really pains, and certainly are not caused by bodily damage, but that are unpleasant and localized to the relevant bodily part. We sometimes have these experiences sympathetically, when people relate painful experiences to us. Now suppose we vary the game a bit so that in the game-world torture is inflicted not with the thumbscrews but with the comfy chair. In that case I think it unlikely that I shall experience pain-like imaginings. It may be part of the story that sitting on the comfy chair is excruciating, but my body just won't co-operate to give me the right imagined pains. And the explanation for this is surely found not in terms of resistant desiring, but in terms simply of what I am apt to find painful. I don't say that resistant desiring is the only kind of imaginative resistance there is. I say that it is the kind that explains our resistance to alien moralities.

There have been some simplifications here. I have spoken as if people are always resistant to alien desires, and to the values that, as ideal spectators, they would take on in imagination only if they took on correspondingly alien desires. Neither is strictly true. Sometimes we find evil attractive and wish to explore, in imagination, an evil outlook. Sometimes we are simply drawn into desiring morally alien things by subtle rhetoric that makes us unaware, or less than fully aware, of what we are doing. And we might be rationally persuaded that imagining the alien perspective would be a good thing; by taking on in imagination values and desires that are abhorrent, we may be better able to

---

[33] For such *de re* imaginings, see Walton (1990).

understand why people do take them on in reality, and perhaps we can thereby come up with sensible suggestions for preventing the spread of evil ambitions. Also, belief-like imagining is not infinitely biddable. Stories sometimes ask us to imagine, in a belief-like way, things we may find it difficult to imagine. In *Ivanhoe*, Walter Scott has one of his characters, a colourful fellow called Athelstan, struck dead by a blow that the narrator clearly sees as fatal; but later the character reappears, having recovered from what we are now told was a superficial wound. Readers find this difficult to integrate with the imaginative project they have been engaged in up to that point. And Scott, evidently, did not expect them to imagine it; he says in a footnote that the character was revived at the instruction of the printer, who refused to set the work until it was done. So the asymmetry between compliant belief-like imaginings and resistant desire-like imaginings is not absolute. But it does require a special effort, and we feel it needs a special justification, consciously to take on alien desires in imagination, simply because they are alien desires. And there is no comparable resistance to taking on alien beliefs of a factual kind, except for special reasons like those that move us in the *Ivanhoe* case.

REFERENCES

Abell, Catherine, and Currie, Gregory (1999), 'Internal and External Pictures', *Philosophical Psychology*, 12(4): 429–45.

Bratman, Michael (1992), 'Belief and Acceptance in a Context', *Mind*, 101: 1–14.

Cohen, L. Jonathan (1989), 'Belief and Acceptance', *Mind*, 98: 367–89.

Coltheart, Max, and Davies, Martin (2000) (eds.), *Pathologies of Belief* (Oxford: Blackwell).

Currie, Gregory, and Ravenscroft, Ian (2002), *Recreative Minds: Image and Imagination in Philosophy and Psychology* (Oxford: Oxford University Press).

Gendler, Tamar Szabó (2000), 'The Puzzle of Imaginative Resistance', *Journal of Philosophy*, 97(2): 55–81.

Gombrich, Ernst (1960), *Art and Illusion* (Princeton: Princeton University Press).

—— (1984), *The Story of Art* (Oxford: Phaidon).

Harris, Paul L., and Kavanaugh, Robert D. (1993), 'Young Children's Understanding of Pretense', *Monographs of the Society for Research in Child Development*, 58(1).

Heal, Jane (1995), 'How to Think about Thinking', in M. Davies and T. Stone (eds.), *Mental Simulation: Evaluation and Applications* (Oxford: Blackwell), 33–52.

Hume, David (1757), 'Of the Standard of Taste', in E. Miller (ed.), *Essays Moral, Political and Literary* (Indianapolis: Liberty Fund), 226–49.

Jackson, Frank (1998), *From Metaphysics to Ethics* (Oxford: Oxford University Press).

Kosslyn, Stephen (1994), *Image and Brain: The Resolution of the Imagery Debate* (Cambridge, Mass.: MIT Press, Bradford Books).

Lewis, David (1983), *Philosophical Papers* (Oxford: Oxford University Press).

——(1989), 'Dispositional Theories of Value', *Proceedings of the Aristotelian Society*, supp. vol., 63: 113–37.

Moran, Richard (1994), 'The Expression of Feeling in Imagination', *Philosophical Review*, 103: 75–106.

Morton, Adam (1980), *Frames of Mind* (Oxford: Clarendon Press).

Nichols, Shaun, and Stich, Stephen (2000), 'A Cognitive Theory of Pretense', *Cognition*, 74: 115–47.

Nussbaum, Martha (1995), *Poetic Justice* (Boston: Beacon Press).

Oatley, Keith (1994), 'A Taxonomy of the Emotions of Literary Response and a Theory of Identification in Fictional Narrative', *Poetics*, 23: 53–74.

Stalnaker, Robert (1968), 'A Theory of Conditionals', in N. Rescher (ed.), *Studies in Logical Theory* (Oxford: Oxford University Press), 98–112.

——(1984), *Inquiry* (Cambridge, Mass.: MIT Press).

Tanner, M. (1994), 'Morals in Fiction and Fictional Morality/II', *Proceedings of the Aristotelian Society*, supp. vol. 68: 51–66.

Tulloch, G. (1997), Introduction to Walter Scott, *Ivanhoe* (Oxford: Oxford University Press).

Velleman, J. David (2000), 'The Aim of Belief', in *The Possibility of Practical Reason* (Oxford: Oxford University Press), 244–81.

Walton, Kendall (1990), *Mimesis as Make-Believe: On the Foundations of the Representational Arts* (Cambridge, Mass.: Harvard University Press).

——(1994), 'Morals in Fiction and Fictional Morality/I', *Proceedings of the Aristotelian Society*, supp. vol. 68: 27–50.

Williams, Christopher (1999), 'False Delicacy', in Anne Jaap Jacobson (ed.), *Re-Reading Hume* (State College, Pa.: Pennsylvania State University Press), 239–62.

5

Essentialism versus Essentialism

MICHAEL DELLA ROCCA

> Here, then, the notion of 'counterpart' comes into its own.
>
> Kripke, 'Identity and Necessity'

A great deal seems to be at stake in the debate over whether conceivability is a guide to possibility. Depending on the connection that obtains between the two, one may be in a position to deploy certain arguments for robust and startling claims of nonidentity. Perhaps most prominently, such arguments have been advanced in the philosophy of mind in order to establish various dualist, anti-physicalist views. But such conceivability arguments abound elsewhere as well, in order to reach conclusions about the individuation of events and of material objects, and so on.

The general form of such arguments is as follows: Consider two items *a* and *b*. Let's say that it is conceivable that *a* has a certain feature and it is not conceivable that *b* has that feature. From this difference between *a* and *b* with

Thanks to friends at Yale who offered comments on an earlier version of this paper presented to a Philosophy Department discussion group, to the participants at the Metaphysical Mayhem Conference at Syracuse in August 2000, and, in connection with the latter occasion, thanks especially to Tom McKay who served as commentator. For very helpful discussions or written comments or both, I am grateful to the editors of this volume, Tamar Szabó Gendler and John Hawthorne, and Katalin Balog, Tad Brennan, Shelly Kagan, Trenton Merricks, Laurie Paul, Carol Rovane, Kevin Zaragoza, and the participants in my seminar at Yale in the fall of 1999 during which I developed the ideas presented here.

regard to conceivability, it follows that there is a modal difference between them: *a* possibly has the feature in question, and *b* does not possibly have this feature. This is the first step in conceivability arguments, and in drawing this conclusion, one would be presupposing a strong connection between conceivability and possibility. From the claim that there is this modal difference, it follows—or so the proponents of conceivability arguments say—that *a* and *b* are not identical. This is the second step in such conceivability arguments. The second step—from a modal difference to a claim of nonidentity— is usually regarded as uncontroversial by both proponents and critics of such arguments.[1] The first step—which relies on a substantive connection between conceivability and possibility—has been far more contentious. This is the place usually targeted by those who want to avoid the claims of nonidentity to which such arguments lead.

We see this in the current, long-standing debate with regard to a dualism of phenomenal and physical properties. David Chalmers, following Saul Kripke, acknowledges that, in certain cases and for certain specified reasons—which we will be examining in detail—conceivability is not a good guide to possibility and so cannot be relied on to yield the relevant claim of nonidentity. However, Chalmers, again following Kripke, goes to great lengths to argue that those reasons do not apply in the case of the relation between phenomenal and physical properties, and so one can mount a successful argument for nonidentity in this case.[2] Stephen Yablo, Brian Loar, and many others go to equally great lengths to argue that the considerations that Chalmers and Kripke see as licensing in this case the inference to possibility from conceivability are mistaken, and that no genuine modal difference, and thus no claim of nonidentity, emerges from the conceivability differences that Chalmers and Kripke appeal to.[3] This is the standard way of attempting to short-circuit conceivability arguments for claims of nonidentity, not only in the mind–body domain, but generally.

Here I will explore a road less traveled, at least nowadays. I want to challenge not the first step, but the second step in the conceivability arguments for nonidentity. Since the legitimacy of the second step is common ground between the opposing sides of the conceivability–possibility debate, by calling this commonality into question, I intend also to cast doubt on the significance of the debate over whether conceivability is a guide to possibility. For if one

---

[1] Chalmers notes this on the first page of 'Does Conceivability Entail Possibility?', Ch. 3 above.

[2] See Chalmers (1996: Ch. 4; 1999). Chalmers also makes the stronger claim that phenomenal properties do not supervene on physical properties. See Chalmers (1996: 131). Chalmers's account is, of course, much more complex than this sketch suggests.

[3] See Loar (1998, 1999), and Yablo (2000 and Ch. 13 below).

cannot infer claims of nonidentity from modal differences, then, even if there is a stronger connection between conceivability and possibility than Chalmers, Kripke, and other friends of conceivability arguments would allow, one cannot capitalize on this connection to establish, as such friends want to, any relevant claims of nonidentity.

But how do I propose to do such an extraordinary thing as call into doubt the legitimacy of the apparently trivial step from a modal difference between *a* and *b* to their nonidentity? Notice that this step presupposes the doctrine that the modal properties of a thing are independent of the way that thing is referred to or described or thought of. For if modal properties are not independent in this way, then, whether or not a given object is possibly F may depend on how it is referred to, and thus, for example, '*a* is possibly F' may be true, while '*b* is possibly F' may be false, despite the fact that *a* = *b*. If so, then one could not, of course, infer from a modal difference between *a* and *b* that *a* and *b* are not identical. Thus the second step of the conceivability arguments relies on the claim that the modal properties of a thing are independent of the way in which the thing is referred to or described or thought of. In presupposing this, such arguments are presupposing essentialism; for, as I will make clear shortly, the truth or falsity of essentialism turns largely on whether or not modal properties enjoy such independence. I intend to challenge the second stage of conceivability arguments by criticizing essentialism. In effect, I will be arguing, therefore, that even if conceivability is a guide to possibility, possibility (and modality generally) may not be reference- or description-independent, and thus essentialism may not be true.

I announce this with some trepidation because essentialism is, of course, the orthodox position in contemporary metaphysics. Indeed, I myself used to be a card-carrying essentialist; but my essentialist faith has been shaken. In this chapter, I will try to show why. Precisely by starting with the intuitions undergirding essentialism—intuitions that always seemed congenial to me and that concern the role of similarity in modal claims—I will develop a line of argument that shows, I contend, how these intuitions, in a surprising way, undermine themselves or, at least, render themselves unjustified. I intend to show, in other words, how the motivations for, and defense of, essentialism, when properly understood, lead to the downfall of those very motivations and that very defense. This self-undermining character of the intuitions behind essentialism necessarily makes anti-essentialism a more viable and attractive option than it might otherwise seem. If this challenge to the second step of conceivability arguments is successful, it will also, and thereby, constitute a challenge to the metaphysical significance of any direct connection between conceivability and possibility.

I will begin by offering, in section 1, a new characterization of the debate between essentialists and their opponents. In section 2, I will employ this characterization in order to develop my argument against essentialism. Throughout, I will be treating Kripke's views as expressed in *Naming and Necessity* as paradigmatic of essentialism. Near the end, I will briefly discuss a version of essentialism, Yablo's, that departs from Kripke's in an important respect, one relevant to the conceivability–possibility debate.

1   The Debate between Essentialism and Anti-essentialism

Essentialism comprises two claims:

(a) Individuals have some properties essentially or necessarily.[4]
(b) The modal properties of an individual (properties such as being essentially F or possibly G) are had independently of the way in which the individual is referred to.[5]

These two claims allow for two ways to be an anti-essentialist: by rejecting (a) or by rejecting (b). I am going to take for granted here that (a) is true; the only people who would disagree are those who hold the position that there is no sense in which any individual has any properties necessarily. Although such a view deserves to be taken seriously,[6] most people find it unpalatable, and most of the really important philosophical issues arising from the debate between essentialists and anti-essentialists take (a) as common ground. For simplicity, I will follow suit and assume that (a) is true. Thus the kind of anti-essentialism I am interested in is the one that denies (b). The real contention in the literature has been over precisely this point, and that is why my guiding question will be: 'Do individuals have their modal properties independently of the way they are referred to?' Kripke, of course, answers this question in the affirmative. For Kripke, and for essentialists in general, the modal properties of an individual— properties such as being possibly the winner of the 1968 election, being

---

[4] I will not here be distinguishing between the necessary and the essential properties of an individual.

[5] Or described or thought of. I intend this last disjunct to cover features of the context of an utterance that may color the ways in which the object is being thought of. For simplicity I will sometimes, in what follows, not mention all these disjuncts when speaking of this requirement of essentialism. With regard to (b), see the characterization of essentialism in Quine (1976*b*: 175–6).

[6] As does, e.g., Stalnaker (1979).

necessarily a human being, etc.—apply to the individual independently of the way in which the individual is referred to.[7]

The claim that modal properties are in this way reference-independent helps generate an argument for the necessity of identity, for the claim that if an object *a* and an object *b* are identical, then they are necessarily identical. One way to see how this depends on essentialism, on the reference-independence of modal properties, is as follows. Let us say that '*a*' is a name for a particular object: namely, *a*. *a* has the property of being necessarily self-identical. To deny this would be to hold that *a* could fail to be identical with itself, an absurd claim. Given that *a* is, of course, identical to *a*, we can say that *a* has the property of being necessarily identical to *a*. If modal properties are independent of the way in which the object is picked out, and if '*a*' and '*b*' (which picks out *b*) are different ways of picking out the very same object—that is, if $a = b$—then whatever modal properties can truly be asserted (or denied) of *a* can also be truly asserted (or denied) of *b*. Thus, since *a* is necessarily *a*, and $b = a$, it follows that *b* is necessarily *a*. The point applies generally, and thus, on this line of thought, we can conclude that whenever identity holds, it holds necessarily and not contingently.[8] Thus, for example, since Cicero = Tully, Cicero and Tully are necessarily identical.

Notice that the above inference to the claim that *b* and *a* are necessarily identical is a specifically essentialist inference. The inference from the modal properties of *a* to the modal properties of *b* goes through only on the assumption that modal properties apply to a thing in a reference-independent way. Were we to drop the assumption that modal properties are independent of the way in which the object is picked out, then the above inference would be invalid. Indeed, as far as I can see, any argument for the necessity of the identity of *a* and *b* crucially presupposes the claim that modal properties are reference-independent; that is, any such argument presupposes claim (b) of the characterization of essentialism. In this way, the necessity of identity is an inherently essentialist claim: essentialism is part of the reason for accepting the necessity of identity. And, for this reason, any anti-essentialist of the kind that denies (b) is committed to allowing that claims of identity, such as 'Hesperus is identical to Phosphorus' may be only contingently true.

Having introduced the necessity of identity, I must add an important complication, one that Kripke emphasizes. It may seem that in the above argument for the claim that *a* is necessarily *b*, I was not entitled to skate so blithely

---

[7] See Kripke (1980: 41–2). Unless otherwise noted, all references to Kripke will be to this work.

[8] The argument here goes back, at least, to Barcan (Marcus) (1947). See also Kripke (1980: 3; 1977: 89), Wiggins (1980: 110).

over the claim that *a* is necessarily *a*. After all, there are some cases in which such a claim does not seem true or does not seem clearly true. For example, take a case in which an object is not picked out by a name, such as '*a*', but by a description, such as 'the inventor of bifocals'. Is it really true to say that the inventor of bifocals is necessarily the inventor of bifocals (a claim that might seem to be of the same type as '*a* is necessarily *a*')? Can't we truly say of the inventor of bifocals (i.e., Franklin) that he is not necessarily the inventor of bifocals?[9] Surely we can imagine a situation in which someone other than Franklin, say Spinoza, had this honor. And this worry leads to a worry about the earlier argument for the claim of the necessity of identity. For that argument turned on this inference:

(i) *a* is necessarily *a*.
(ii) *a* = *b*.
Therefore,
(iii) *b* is necessarily *a*.

If the inventor claim—that is, if 'the inventor of bifocals is necessarily the inventor of bifocals'—is false, why can't we say the same of (i)? And, if so, then the inference to (iii) or the necessity of identity won't go through.

Kripke diagnoses the problem this way. He draws a distinction between two kinds of expression: rigid and nonrigid designators. A rigid designator is a term that designates the same object in all possible situations in which that object exists and does not designate any other object in other possible situations.[10] A nonrigid designator, by contrast, designates different objects in different possible situations. Thus 'the inventor of bifocals' is a nonrigid designator, as we can see by deploying modal intuitions that we have already, in effect, introduced: since someone other than the inventor of bifocals might have invented bifocals (e.g., Spinoza might have), it follows that 'the inventor of bifocals' is not a rigid designator. By contrast, Kripke wants to say, Cicero is, intuitively, necessarily Cicero; that is, no one other than Cicero might have been Cicero; no one other than Franklin might have been Franklin, and nothing other than *a* might have been *a*. Thus, for Kripke, the terms 'Cicero', 'Franklin', and '*a*' are all rigid designators.[11]

Kripke holds that the argument for a claim of necessary identity goes through only in cases where the terms flanking the identity sign are both rigid

---

[9] Cf. Kripke (1980: 48): 'someone other than the U.S. President in 1970 might have been the U.S. President in 1970.'

[10] Stanley (1997: 556). Cf. Kripke's intuitive test for rigid designation (1980: 48–9).

[11] Stanley (1997: 566) brings this out well. Bealer (1987: 313–17) has a good discussion of the reliance on intuition in Kripke's claims about rigid designation.

designators (as in the Cicero/Tully case or the *a/b* case above). If one or both of the terms is nonrigid, then one cannot make the relevant claim of necessary identity. Thus, despite the identity of Franklin and the inventor of bifocals, it is not true that Franklin is necessarily the inventor of bifocals, and it is not true precisely because the latter of the two terms is not rigid. So, for Kripke, the falsity of 'the inventor of bifocals is necessarily the inventor of bifocals' need not cast doubt on the claim that *a* is necessarily *a*, and need not render problematic the inference from (i) and (ii) to (iii).

One of Kripke's central themes—again, argued for on the basis of modal intuitions—is that proper names in general, such as 'Cicero' and 'Humphrey', are rigid designators. These terms refer to the same object in all possible situations, as Kripke argues based on his modal intuitions that no one other than Humphrey might have been Humphrey, no one other than Cicero might have been Cicero, and so on. But it is important to notice again that such intuitions, if accepted, lead to the claim that Cicero and Tully are necessarily identical only because essentialism is true and, in particular, only because modal properties apply to a thing independently of the terms used to pick it out. For if Cicero is necessarily Cicero, and if Cicero=Tully, it follows that Tully is necessarily Cicero only on the assumption that the modal properties of individuals apply to those individuals no matter how the individuals are picked out. That is, if we accept what Kripke takes to be intuitively obvious claims such as 'Cicero is necessarily Cicero', then we must see essentialism as entailing the necessity of identity. And, relatedly, an anti-essentialist of the kind that denies (b) does not think that one can move directly from 'Cicero is necessarily Cicero' and 'Cicero=Tully' to 'Cicero is necessarily Tully'.

So we've seen that essentialism has a plausible way to make sense of modal claims such as 'Humphrey might have won the election' and that, given certain modal intuitions such as 'Humphrey is necessarily Humphrey' or 'Hesperus is necessarily Hesperus', essentialism straightforwardly entails the necessity of identity.

Of course, not everyone is convinced. I want to lay out briefly two historically important criticisms of essentialism. I emphasize these reasons because, despite the fact that they have come under much attack, they can help us get at Kripke's underlying motivations for essentialism, and also because I want to rehabilitate versions of these criticisms later.

The first criticism I call the worry about arbitrariness. According to almost every version of essentialism, objects have some properties essentially or necessarily, and other properties only contingently. (The exception would be super-essentialism—a view according to which all properties of individuals are necessary.) Thus Humphrey is the loser, but is so only contingently, and so

Humphrey is possibly the winner. However, equally intuitively it seems, Humphrey is not possibly a light switch. That is, Humphrey is necessarily not a light switch. What is the principle behind this distinction between properties that an object has necessarily and those that apply only contingently to an object? What is it in virtue of which it is true that an object is necessarily F and only contingently G? Absent such a basis, it might seem as if any distinction between necessary and contingent properties of an object can at best be arbitrary. The first charge against essentialism is that the essentialist can provide no legitimate ground for such a distinction. Why should being a non-light switch be a necessary feature of Humphrey, and being a loser merely a contingent feature? According to this line of criticism, there is no good answer that an essentialist can give, and the distinctions to which the essentialist appeals are thus 'invidious', and essentialist metaphysics can seem hopelessly ill-grounded.[12]

A related worry is what I call 'the epistemic worry'. According to this objection, one cannot legitimately claim knowledge of the modal properties of an object if the modal properties are, as the essentialist conceives them, properties of the object itself and not dependent on our way of referring to the object. According to the epistemic worry, if essentialism is correct, we would have no way of telling which modal properties an object has and which ones it lacks. Part of the reason for this epistemic worry may be the very arbitrariness of the distinction between necessary and contingent properties. If the distinction were, instead, well-grounded—if there were something about the object that accounted for its modal properties—then the basis for the distinction, whatever it is, might be able to serve also as a means for deciding or coming to know which properties of an object are essential and which are not, and more generally for coming to know what the modal properties of the object are. But, if there is nothing about the object that accounts for its modal properties, it might also seem as if there can be nothing that enables us to know what the object's modal properties are.[13]

Notice that anti-essentialism of the kind we are discussing readily avoids these worries.[14] If the modal properties of an object are not fully 'out there',

---

[12] A version of this worry and the famous use of the term 'invidious' can be found in Quine (1976a: 184).

[13] A classic statement of the epistemic worry is presented, but (of course) not endorsed by Kripke (1980: 42–3). For other versions of the epistemic worry, the arbitrariness worry, or both, see Lewis (1973: 39–41; 1986: ch. 4, sect. 4); Sidelle (1989: ch. 4).

[14] Actually, anti-essentialism of the other kind (the kind that denies (a)) avoids them too, but in a different way. Anti-essentialism of this other kind denies that objects have any properties essentially and holds that all properties are contingent. On this view, then, there is no line to draw between the essential and nonessential properties of objects. Thus there is no need to ground such a distinction, and no need to explain how we can know how to draw such a distinction.

but instead are in part a function of our way of conceiving of, or referring to, the object, then we can readily see what makes it true that certain modal properties apply to an object, and we can readily account for our knowledge of such truths. For an anti-essentialist, the modal properties of things are grounded not in the things themselves, but in our way of thinking about, or referring to, the things. A single object, x, may be essentially F, relative to one way of thinking about that object, and not essentially F, relative to another way of thinking about the object.[15] Thus x might be essentially not a light switch when thought of as 'the senator from Minnesota with an alliterative name', but not essentially not a light switch when thought of as 'the object five feet to the left of the doorway to the Senate chamber'. According to the anti-essentialist, there is something that grounds the modal distinctions we want to make, so they are not arbitrary. However, this something lies not in the object itself, but in our different ways of thinking about the object.

The skeptical worry is handled in a similar way: for the anti-essentialist, we can know the modal properties of the object because, as we have just seen, modal properties are a function of our ways of thinking about the object, and, in principle, we can know the ways in which we are thinking about the object. There is no insuperable obstacle to modal knowledge for the anti-essentialist.

A well worked-out version of anti-essentialism that clearly meets both the arbitrariness and the skeptical worries is Lewis's counterpart theory.[16] On Lewis's view, each individual, x, has many different counterparts. An object's counterparts are those objects (typically) in other possible situations that are similar to the object in certain relevant respects. If one of an object's counterparts is F (even if the object is actually not F), then that is what it is for it to be true that x is possibly F. Roughly, if all of x's counterparts are F, then x is necessarily F.

However, this statement of Lewis's views must be modified to allow for variation in which respects of similarity are seen as relevant. Thus, consider Humphrey, an actual human being who is five feet from the door of the Senate chamber and who runs for President in 1968. Consider also a possible situation which contains an object, y, which is a light switch five feet from the door of the Senate chamber but which, of course, does not run for President. Is y a counterpart of Humphrey? Well, y is similar to Humphrey in some respects and dissimilar in others; y shares with the actual Humphrey the property of

---

[15] Thus (b) is rejected.

[16] It is, of course, important to distinguish the idea behind Lewis's counterpart theory from his modal realism: one can accept one without the other. Thus I see my qualified defense of something like counterpart theory later in this chapter as providing no aid or comfort to modal realism. Other versions of counterpart theory can be found in Stalnaker (1986), Sider (1996, 1999), and Forbes (1985: chs. 3 and 7).

being five feet from the door of the Senate chamber, and differs from Humphrey with regard to the property of being a human being and the property of running for President, and so on. Whether y counts as a counterpart of Humphrey depends on which respect of similarity we are emphasizing. If, for some reason, the property of being five feet from the door of the Senate chamber is particularly salient in our thinking about Humphrey, then any object in another possible situation that is similarly located counts as a counterpart of Humphrey. Thus y would count as a counterpart of Humphrey. And, if we are thinking in this vein, y would make it true that Humphrey might have been a light switch. This is true because, on this way of thinking of Humphrey, Humphrey has a counterpart that is a light switch. However, if, as is more natural, we are thinking about Humphrey more saliently as a politician from Minnesota who runs for President, then y no longer counts as a counterpart of Humphrey, but instead z does. z is a person in another possible situation who is a Minnesota politician who runs for President and wins in 1968. z is similar enough to Humphrey to count, on this way of thinking about him, as a counterpart of Humphrey, and z would make it true that Humphrey might have won. He might have won precisely because there is, in another possible situation, someone (relevantly) similar to Humphrey who wins.

Thus, for Lewis, modal predication is inherently relative to the manner in which an object is specified or thought about and is thus, as he puts it, 'inconstant'. This is an anti-essentialist view.[17]

Notice that the key notion in Lewis's account of the modal properties of an object is *similarity*. An object, x, has certain modal properties in virtue of the fact that, in some situations, objects similar to x have certain features. Modality turns on similarity for Lewis. And I think that this feature of Lewis's version of anti-essentialism is true of many anti-essentialist views.[18]

---

[17] Lewis (1971; 1986: ch. 4). See also Noonan (1991). Gibbard (1975) holds a similar view, but with important differences from Lewis's view, as Lewis notes (1986: 256 n. 40). Forbes (1986: sect. 5), raises some, admittedly inconclusive, doubts about the kind of relativity to manner of conception that Lewis espouses. Also, it is important to note that when Lewis first introduced counterpart theory in 1968—the year, incidentally, in which Humphrey ran and lost—he did not then hold that modal predication and the counterpart relation vary with different ways of thinking about the object. Thus his earliest view was actually a version of essentialism and not anti-essentialism, and he explicitly said this at the time (1968: 119–20). Lewis gives good reasons for abandoning this version of counterpart theory in Lewis (1971). Notice that since there can be an essentialist version of counterpart theory, it would not be correct to characterize essentialism as the view of modality which rejects counterpart theory. It is better to characterize it in terms of theses (a) and (b), as I did at the outset.

[18] Though not, perhaps, all. For example, Quine, an anti-essentialist, does not explicitly rely on similarity in the way Lewis and others do.

This important point about Lewis and at least some other anti-essentialists leads to a crucial point about Kripke. In his defense of essentialism against the two worries—concerning arbitrariness and modal skepticism—Kripke famously rejects any kind of similarity account of modal claims. Consider the epistemic worry. Kripke says that in order to know the modal properties of Humphrey, we don't need, as Lewis contends, first to consider the relevantly similar objects in other possible situations and *then* consider whether any of these similar objects, say, wins the 1968 election. No, Kripke plausibly says, one can just *stipulate* that there is a situation in which Humphrey wins. Similarity is simply irrelevant: there is no need to make a detour through considerations about similar objects or through any considerations beyond the modal fact that Humphrey might have won. There is, of course, a limit, Kripke says, to what we can legitimately stipulate. We can stipulate a situation in which Humphrey wins, but we cannot stipulate a situation in which he is a light switch. What accounts for this difference? Kripke says, again plausibly, that we should let modal intuitions be our guide here. We have the intuition, Kripke says, that Humphrey might have won, and we have the intuition that Humphrey is necessarily a human being and not a light switch. These intuitions allow us to stipulate a situation in which Humphrey wins and prevent us from stipulating a situation in which Humphrey is a light switch.[19] Thus these intuitions provide us with direct knowledge of modal facts—direct in the sense that they are not derived from considerations about objects similar to Humphrey. Given such intuition-based stipulative knowledge, the skeptical worry is no longer a worry.[20]

Further, since, according to Kripke, modal facts about an object can be stipulated regardless of considerations concerning similar objects in other possible situations (and, indeed, regardless of anything beyond the modal facts themselves), he denies that modal facts need to be grounded in, for example, similarity, as Lewis and other anti-essentialists hold. Kripke rejects the demand for any kind of grounding of modal properties, and so he would reject the arbitrariness worry—which arises from a felt need for some such grounding—as seriously misguided.

Thus Kripke's key claim in response to the two worries is that, contra Lewis and other anti-essentialists,

(1) Modal claims, such as 'Humphrey might have won', are not to be accounted for in terms of similarity.

---

[19] Kripke is explicit about his reliance on intuitions in his challenge to the anti-essentialist. See Kripke (1980: 42).

[20] For a good account of the importance of such stipulation, see Salmon (1996). Salmon offers more general critiques of counterpart theory in (1981: esp. appendix 1); and (1986: esp. sect. VI).

In other words, Kripke denies that the truth of 'Humphrey might have won' depends on the fact that there is a possible situation in which someone relevantly similar to Humphrey wins. Perhaps the best expression of this point of view occurs in this passage:

> if we have such an intuition about the possibility of *that* (*this man's* electoral loss), then it is about the possibility of *that*. It need not be identified with the possibility of a man looking like such and such, or holding such and such political views, or otherwise qualitatively described, having lost. We can point to the *man*, and ask what might have happened to *him*, had events been different. (1980: 46, emphasis in original)

Kripke's invocation of (1) is, I believe, necessary for defending essentialism against the kind of similarity account of modal claims that Lewis and other anti-essentialists offer. This role of (1) in the argument for essentialism is what I now want to focus on. I will attempt to show that Kripke, in his defense of (1), may undermine his whole case for essentialism.

2 Steps toward Adjudicating the Debate

I now want to develop reasons against Kripke's crucial claim, (1), and thus against his defense of essentialism: reasons that are continuous with, though quite distinct from, the standard worries about essentialism that I have already presented. The arguments I shall offer are, specifically, not so much reasons against (1) itself, but rather reasons for thinking that, in the context of his overall argument for essentialism, Kripke is not justified in asserting (1), and so not justified in accepting essentialism itself. This charge of lack of justification *may* be able to be parlayed into the charge that essentialism is actually false. I'll investigate this matter briefly near the end of the chapter.

To begin the argument against Kripke, recall that Kripke's crucial point is that the claim that Humphrey is possibly the winner is not to be understood in terms of similarity: that is, the truth of this claim does not depend on the fact that in some other possible situation someone (relevantly) similar to the actual Humphrey wins the election. I grant that Kripke's point is intuitively appealing. But its appeal may begin to fade when we focus not on the claim 'Humphrey is possibly the winner', but rather on different modal claims that also seem intuitively correct, but which, unlike 'Humphrey is possibly the winner', Kripke says must be accounted for in terms of similarity.

To see an example of this other kind of modal claim, let us turn to another endlessly fascinating case, that of Hesperus and Phosphorus. 'Hesperus' is a name for a certain heavenly body, and 'Phosphorus' is another name for the very same heavenly body: namely, Venus. That is, Hesperus=Phosphorus. Kripke contends that this identity claim is not only true but necessarily true. This is because 'Hesperus' and 'Phosphorus', as proper names, are rigid designators, as Kripke has already argued on the basis of certain modal intuitions. And, as we have seen, Kripke holds (because of his essentialism) that identity claims involving rigid designators are necessary if true. Thus 'Hesperus=Phosphorus' is necessarily true.

Although Kripke admits that this claim is intuitively well-grounded, he also admits to having the nagging feeling that there is *some* contingency involved here. We have, Kripke says, in addition to the intuition of rigidity that leads to the claim of the necessity of the identity of Hesperus and Phosphorus, the intuition that things might have turned out otherwise, that Hesperus might not have been identical to Phosphorus. Kripke confesses to having this intuition:

Look, Hesperus might not have been Phosphorus. Here a certain planet was seen in the morning, and it was seen in the evening; and it just turned out later on as a matter of empirical fact that they were one and the same planet. If things had turned out otherwise, they would have been two different planets, or two different heavenly bodies, so how can you say that such a statement is necessary? (1977: 90)[21]

So we have the intuition that Hesperus might not have been Phosphorus. Given that 'Hesperus' and 'Phosphorus' are rigid designators, this intuition conflicts with the necessity of identity, and so any good essentialist must reject it. But, of course, Kripke must tread carefully here: in rejecting this modal intuition, he must not impugn our faculty of modal intuition generally. As we have seen, his entire essentialist system and the argument for it require taking certain modal intuitions as reliable—for example, 'Humphrey might have won' and 'Hesperus is necessarily Hesperus'. So, in rejecting certain intuitions, Kripke must be careful not to call into doubt the reliability of modal intuitions generally. His way of carrying this out is as follows.

Kripke says that Hesperus *is* necessarily Phosphorus. But, he goes on to say, when we intuit 'Hesperus might not have been Phosphorus', what we're really intuiting is a genuine possibility of nonidentity, but *not* a genuine possibility of the nonidentity of Hesperus and Phosphorus, a nonidentity which, for Kripke, is not possible. Rather, Kripke says, we are intuiting a genuine possibility involving the nonidentity of Phosphorus and an object similar to Hesperus. Alternatively, we are intuiting a genuine possibility involving the nonidentity of an object similar to Phosphorus and an object similar to Hesperus. In

---

[21] See also (Kripke 1980: 103).

particular, for Kripke, the modal intuition of contingency is not appropriately expressed as

(A) Hesperus might not have been Phosphorus,

but as

(B) There is a possible situation in which the object that appears in the evening sky is not identical to the object that appears in the morning sky.

Kripke contends that when we expressed our intuition of contingency as (A), we were subtly confusing (A) with (B), a claim that is actually quite different from (A). Notice that (B) involves no rigid designators, and (A) two. Thus, given the identity of Hesperus and Phosphorus, (A) cannot be true, though (B) may be. (A) cannot be true because its truth would be tantamount to the contingent truth of an identity claim involving two rigid designators. But, for Kripke, there can be contingent identity claims only where at least one of the terms flanking the identity sign is not a rigid designator. And this is why (B) may be true, but (A) may not.[22]

Why, according to Kripke, is this confusion of (A) with (B) so easy for us to fall into? Kripke answers: the proper names 'Hesperus' and 'Phosphorus' have definite descriptions associated with them, which enable us to fix the reference of the name. Thus, I might go into my backyard one evening and say 'the object that appears in the evening sky I name "Hesperus" '; the name 'Phosphorus' analogously acquires a reference via the description, 'the object that appears in the morning sky'. Kripke holds that, given the close connection between names and identifying descriptions, it is, perhaps, understandable that we would be guilty of the subtle confusion involved in expressing a claim such as (B) in terms of (A).

This reconstrual of (A) as (B) allows Kripke to say that our faculty of modal intuition is trustworthy in the sense that it was indeed getting at some truths— as we have seen, it is crucial for Kripke to preserve the reliability of our faculty of modal intuition, since his entire essentialist system presupposes this reliability.[23] But it also allows Kripke to avoid a conflict with the necessity of identity, a claim that is crucial to his essentialist system.

Of course, Kripke applies his method of reconstrual more broadly. He applies it, in effect, wherever intuitions of contingency, such as 'Hesperus is possibly not

---

[22] Instead of (B), with no rigid designators, the intuition of contingency could be expressed with one rigid designator and one nonrigid designator, as in 'there is a possible situation in which the object that appears in the evening sky is not identical to Phosphorus'. This reconstrual of (A) would serve Kripke's purposes too, because it, like (B), would remove any apparent threat to the necessity of identity.

[23] Later we will consider a way in which Yablo, an essentialist, tries to preserve this reliability without having to say that in this case there is some modal truth which our faculty does get at.

Phosphorus', 'Cicero might not have been Tully', 'Water might not have been H$_2$O', and the like, threaten the necessity of identity.[24] I would like to point out two important features of this method. First, in all these cases, Kripke is motivated to reconstrue an intuition precisely because of his essentialism. We can see this as follows. The Hesperus intuition, for example, is in conflict with Kripke's claim of the necessity of the identity of Hesperus and Phosphorus. So Kripke's acceptance of the reconstrual is motivated by his acceptance of the necessity of identity.[25] But, as we saw, the acceptance of the necessity of identity is motivated by the acceptance of the claim that the modal properties of a thing are reference- or description-independent. (Recall the way in which the proof of the necessity of identity presupposes something like claim (b) of the characterization of essentialism.) Thus Kripke's essentialism motivates his acceptance of the reconstrual of the Hesperus intuition. Without essentialism, Kripke would not accept the necessity of identity, and so there would be no need to reconstrue the Hesperus intuition in order to preserve the necessity of identity. The whole enterprise of Kripkean reconstrual thus has a point only against the background of Kripke's essentialist commitments. This point will be crucial shortly.

The second point I want to emphasize is that Kripke's reconstrual of (A) is a reconstrual in terms of similarity. (B) is not, in the first instance, about Hesperus itself in other possible situations, but rather about objects similar to Hesperus in other possible situations. To see this, it is important to note that, for Kripke, a reference-fixing description need not involve a property that (necessarily) suffices for being that object; that is, the reference-fixing description need not be a rigid designator. Thus something other than Hesperus (that is, something other than Venus) might have appeared in the evening instead of, or in addition to, Hesperus; for example, Jupiter might have appeared in the evening. Since the identifying property is not sufficient for being Hesperus, when we talk, as in (B), about a possible situation involving the object that appears in the evening, we are not talking directly about Hesperus itself, Kripke says. We are, he insists, merely talking about objects in other possible situations that are similar to Hesperus in a certain respect—namely, with regard to the property of appearing in the evening. The similarity in question here is what might be called 'epistemic similarity'. The relevant point for Kripke is that, in reconstruing the Hesperus intuition, we consider a situation *epistemically* the same as the actual situation—that is, a situation which would appear to us just as the actual situation does. However, the situation is one in which things need not be

---

[24] Kripke (1980: 142–4) gives a general formula for reconstrual. See the general discussion of the methodology in Chalmers (1996: ch. 4) and Yablo (2000).

[25] Such a motivation for reconstrual is especially evident in (1977: 100. n. 18).

metaphysically the same as they are in the actual situation. That is, the possibility we are considering need not be a situation involving the very same objects as are involved in the actual situation. In this way, one might say that the kind of possibility at work in the intuition that Hesperus might not have been Phosphorus is epistemic, as opposed to metaphysical, possibility.[26]

Kripke explicitly calls attention to the point that he accounts for certain intuitions of contingency in terms of such epistemic possibility. In the following
passage, he is speaking not of (A), but of the intuition that this table, which is in fact made of wood, might have been made of ice. Given Kripke's acceptance of the essentiality of origin (which we need not go into here), such an intuition of contingency violates his essentialism as much as (A) does.[27] Kripke suggests a reconstrual of this intuition in terms of possible situations involving similar tables. Thus:

What, then, does the intuition that the table might have turned out to have been made of ice or of anything else, that it might even have turned out not to be made of molecules, amount to? I think that it means simply that there might have been *a table* looking and feeling just like this one and placed in this very position in the room, which was in fact made of ice. In other words, I (or some conscious being) could have been *qualitatively in the same epistemic situation* that in fact obtains, I could have the same sensory evidence that I in fact have, about *a table* which was made of ice. The situation is thus akin to the one which inspired the counterpart theorists . . . *This* table could not have had an origin different from the one it in fact had, but in a situation qualitatively identical to this one with respect to all the evidence I had in advance, the room could have contained *a table made of ice* in place of this one. Something like counterpart theory is thus applicable to this situation, but it applies only because we are *not* interested in what might have been true of *this particular* table, but in what might or might not be true of *a table* given certain evidence. It is precisely because it is *not* true that this table might have been made of ice from the Thames that we must turn here to qualitative descriptions and counterparts. To apply these notions to genuine *de re* modalities is, from the present standpoint, perverse. (1980: 142, italics in original)[28]

---

[26] For an elaborate account of epistemic possibility (or, to use Yablo's preferred term, 'conceptual possibility'), see Ch. 13 below. In Chalmers's terminology in Ch. 3 above, that Hesperus is not Phosphorus is primarily conceivable, but not secondarily conceivable.

[27] See especially Kripke (1980: 114–15 nn. 56, 57). See also Salmon (1981: Ch. 7).

[28] In addition to the reconstruals of intuitions of contingency, one can also construct Kripkean reconstruals of intuitions of necessity in terms of similarity. Thus (on the assumption that Humphrey is picked out via the description 'the most famous senator from Minnesota'), 'Humphrey is necessarily not a plastic pencil holder' would be reconstrued as 'In all possible situations, the most famous senator from Minnesota is not a plastic pencil holder'. Similarly, 'Hesperus is necessarily Hesperus' would be reconstrued as 'In all possible situations, the Evening Star is the Evening Star'. I stress, however, that although these reconstruals are available, Kripke wouldn't endorse them or find them plausible *qua* reconstruals.

From my point of view, what is most interesting about this passage is the fact that Kripke admits that he is making a limited use of the method of counterparts.[29] He believes that he can employ a similarity account of modal claims—an account that is something like a counterpart theoretic account—in a few limited cases within the context of an overall essentialist and non-counterpart-theoretic account of modal claims. I want to argue now that this belief—that he can have just a little bit of the method of counterparts—is false. A little counterpart theory goes a long way, and much further than Kripke can tolerate.

Although Kripke holds that

(A) Hesperus might not have been Phosphorus

is to be accounted for in terms of similarity (as we have just seen), he also holds—and this is precisely what (1) asserts—that modal claims in general, such as 'Humphrey might have won', are *not* to be accounted for in terms of epistemic similarity in this way. This raises a fundamental question: why should the Hesperus intuition and the Humphrey intuition (as I will often refer to them hereafter) be treated so differently? Why, for Kripke, does the Hesperus intuition require treatment in terms of epistemic similarity, whereas the Humphrey intuition (and many other modal intuitions) does not require such treatment? Or, to put the point yet another way, why should the Hesperus intuition be interpreted in terms of epistemic possibility and the Humphrey intuition in terms of metaphysical possibility? So far, all Kripke has done is to give an explanation, in terms of epistemic similarity, of why we might have been led to express our intuition of contingency in the Hesperus case in a way that was, strictly, false, but was also some kind of expression of a genuine modal fact. But, in light of the treatment that the Hesperus intuition has received, we are naturally led to wonder: perhaps the Humphrey intuition, the intuition that Humphrey might have won, also involves a similar understandable mistake. Perhaps it is the case that this intuition, too, is really about a person similar to Humphrey, and thus not particularly about Humphrey himself. Perhaps 'Humphrey might have won' is to be understood in terms of epistemic, and not metaphysical, possibility.[30]

If Kripke does not have a response to such doubts, then his reconstrual of the Hesperus intuition and of other intuitions would threaten his entire essentialist system. As we have seen, it is ultimately because of his essentialism that he

---

[29] Consider also this chapter's epigraph: 'Here, then, the notion of "counterpart" comes into its own', a claim made in the context of Kripke's discussion of his method of reconstrual (1977:93 n. 15).

[30] In Chalmers's terminology, the point would be that perhaps 'Humphrey wins the election' is primarily, but not secondarily, conceivable.

puts forth the reconstruals. But now it seems that the reconstruals that Kripke adopts succeed only in raising a doubt about his view that the Humphrey intuition and modal intuitions generally are not to be accounted for in terms of similarity. That is, Kripke has, in effect, raised a doubt about

> (1) Modal claims, such as 'Humphrey might have won', are not to be accounted for in terms of similarity.

Since, as we have seen, (1) is a crucial premise in the Kripkean argument for accepting essentialism, as opposed to a version of anti-essentialism that relies on similarity, the doubt about (1) that Kripke's reconstrual of the Hesperus intuition raises is, ultimately, a doubt about essentialism itself.[31]

To allay this doubt, Kripke now needs to find a relevant difference between the Hesperus intuition and the Humphrey intuition, a difference that would explain why, although the Hesperus intuition is to be accounted for in terms of similarity and is to be treated as a mere expression of epistemic possibility, the Humphrey intuition is not to be accounted for in terms of similarity, but is instead to be regarded as an expression of a genuinely metaphysical possibility. This difference would then be part of the defense of Kripke's (1), and thus part of the case for essentialism.

What might such a difference be? The answer is not immediately obvious. The two intuitions are intuitions of contingency. Obviously, the Hesperus intuition is an intuition of contingent *identity*, and the Humphrey intuition is not. But it is not clear why this difference should be relevant. In any event, Kripke insists on reconstruals of intuitions of contingency that are not intuitions of contingent identity (e.g., the intuitions that this table might have been made of ice, that water might not have been a compound, etc.). And, just like the reconstrual of the Hesperus intuition, these other reconstruals are motivated by Kripke's essentialism.

The *only* plausible candidate for a relevant difference that I can find, though, is related to concerns about contingent identity and emerges from the very motivations that Kripke has for reconstruing the Hesperus intuition. Recall that Kripke was prompted to reconstrue the Hesperus intuition because of his essentialism, and, in particular, because the intuition, if accepted as is, would

---

[31] It is also a doubt about the legitimacy of rigid designation. If modal claims involving the term 'Humphrey' are to be accounted for in terms of similarity, then, when we make such claims, we are speaking, in the first instance, about objects similar to Humphrey in other possible situations, and not directly about Humphrey himself. Thus it would no longer be clear that we would be using the term 'Humphrey' to pick out the very same object in all possible situations, and thus it would no longer be clear that 'Humphrey' is a rigid designator. Similar doubts could be raised about other purported rigid designators.

conflict with the necessity of identity. But there is no such reason to reconstrue the Humphrey intuition. Accepted as is, and not reconstrued in terms of similarity, the claim 'Humphrey might have won' is perfectly compatible with the necessity of identity, so essentialism provides no motivation for the reconstrual. So here, then, is a difference between the two intuitions: the Hesperus intuition is such that a reconstrual of it is motivated by essentialism; by contrast, the Humphrey intuition is not such that a reconstrual of it is motivated by essentialism, and thus it can be left unmodified. And this difference might seem to be well-placed to explain why the Hesperus intuition must be treated so differently from the Humphrey intuition.[32]

There's a certain plausibility to this line of thought, but, unfortunately, Kripke is not entitled to it. Let me explain. I have raised a doubt about Kripke's claim

(1) Modal claims, such as 'Humphrey might have won', are not to be accounted for in terms of similarity.

by noting that Kripke does account for other modal claims, such as the Hesperus intuition, precisely in term of similarity. To allay this doubt, I suggested appealing to the following claim:

(2) The Hesperus intuition is to be reconstrued in terms of similarity, and the Humphrey intuition is not, because reconstruing the Hesperus intuition in terms of similarity is motivated by essentialism, but reconstruing the Humphrey intuition is not so motivated.

But why should we rely on (2)? It's clear that Kripke accepts something like (2), only because he accepts essentialism. Kripke is an essentialist, and so he is motivated to do things (such as reconstruing some modal intuitions) that are motivated by essentialism. Anyone who accepts (2) and, for this reason, decides whether or not to reconstrue a modal intuition does so out of a prior commitment to essentialism. Thus the doubt about (1) is allayed by acceptance of (2), and so by a prior acceptance of essentialism itself.

But now here is the problem for Kripke: not only does essentialism seem to be part of Kripke's defense of (1), and thus part of his reason for accepting (1), but, as we saw earlier, (1) is a crucial part of Kripke's reason for essentialism. Kripke uses the rejection of a similarity account of the Humphrey intuition (and of modal intuitions generally) as a reason for accepting essentialism, and, on the suggestion I am now developing, he uses essentialism to support a

---

[32] Such a line of thought is suggested by Kripke's claim (1980: 142), quoted earlier, that it is 'perverse' to apply the method of reconstrual to 'genuine *de re* modalities'—i.e., presumably, to cases such as 'Humphrey might have won'.

rejection of a similarity account of the Humphrey intuition (and of modal intuitions generally). And so we have a circle.

Another way to put this point is as follows: Kripke's reasons for accepting essentialism are called into doubt unless he can appeal to a distinction between certain modal intuitions, but this distinction can be drawn only by first appealing to essentialism itself. So the doubt about essentialism, for Kripke, is to be allayed by appealing to essentialism itself. Rather than allaying doubts about essentialism, such a circular line of thought exacerbates them.[33]

In his discussion of the Hesperus intuition, Kripke begins with the best of intentions. He seeks to reconcile a conflict between the Hesperus intuition and the necessity of identity—a thesis Kripke holds because of his essentialism—by *explaining away* the Hesperus intuition. This was potentially a good strategy. The problem is that Kripke's very way of explaining away the Hesperus intuition serves only to cast doubt on his basis for essentialism itself. Further, Kripke does not have, it seems, the resources within his system legitimately and non-question-beggingly to answer the newly raised doubt concerning essentialism itself. Essentialism thus seems inevitably incapable of being justified.

I want to consider now two important objections to my argument against Kripke.

(i) My objection was premised on the need to find a reason for treating the Humphrey intuition differently from the Hesperus intuition. I argued that this demand for a reason cannot be met, and so Kripke has no good reason for accepting essentialism and for avoiding anti-essentialism. It might be granted that once the demand for a reason for treating the cases differently is accepted, once one accepts that there must be something about the two intuitions that justifies us in treating them differently, then Kripke is in trouble. However, the first objection to my argument would go, it is wrong to think that we can treat the two cases differently only if we can point to some difference between the two cases that justifies us in treating them differently. According to this challenge, there need be no such difference, for we can just intuit that the Humphrey intuition is not to be accounted for in terms of similarity, and we can also intuit that the Hesperus intuition is to be accounted for in terms of similarity. In other words, we can just see with the help of a moment's reflection that the Hesperus intuition must be handled in terms of epistemic possibility and the Humphrey intuition in terms of metaphysical possibility. We have, in effect, second-order intuitions about the way the Hesperus and

---

[33] Cf. Bealer (1987: 336–7).

Humphrey intuitions are to be handled. Such second-order intuitions obviate the need for any deeper explanations for why the two intuitions are to be treated differently, in much the same way that one's first-order modal intuitions, according to Kripke, obviate the need for any deeper explanation of why certain modal properties do, and others do not, apply to Humphrey. In particular, such second-order intuitions would obviate the need to rely on essentialism in order to explain why the Hesperus intuition needs to be explained in terms of similarity.

In response to this challenge, I claim that any such second-order intuition presupposes essentialism—that is, it rests on a prior acceptance of essentialism—and so cannot be used to defend essentialism from the objection I have raised. To see this, consider the essentialist's reconstrual of the Hesperus intuition. A crucial point about this reconstrual, I have argued, is that it is adopted for a reason: namely, that the intuition 'Hesperus might not have been Phosphorus', if left unmodified, would conflict with the necessity of identity—a thesis at the heart of essentialism itself. Reflection on essentialism and, in particular, on the necessity of identity and on the view that the modal properties of things apply to those things no matter how they are described is behind the acceptance of the reconstrual in the Hesperus case. Certainly, without some prior commitment to the necessity of identity and essentialism, one would not see anything wrong with the Hesperus intuition as initially expressed. Yes, the essentialist finds the reconstrual appealing in this case; but, I stress, he does so only because of his previous commitment to essentialism. The second-order intuition that the Hesperus intuition is to be construed in terms of similarity is thus a theory-laden intuition, and the theory it is laden with is essentialism.

Now return to the intuition, 'Humphrey might have won'. I have been asking: what reason is there not to reconstrue in this case as well? Given that the Hesperus intuition was reconstrued because of essentialism, if the essentialist is not to reconstrue the Humphrey intuition, that must be, in part, because essentialism does not provide any reason for such a move. My point here is that the essentialist's clear reason for reconstruing the Hesperus intuition makes it the case that any legitimate case of nonreconstrual must also be for a related reason. Had the essentialist reconstrued for no reason in the Hesperus case, then he could, perhaps, legitimately and without reason fail to reconstrue in the Humphrey case. But, given that he reconstrued for a certain reason in one case, any failure to reconstrue in other cases must be in part because of the absence of that very reason for reconstruing. So I am not demanding here that there must be a reason for any difference whatsoever in ways of handling modal intuitions; rather, I am demanding that if some reconstruals occur for a reason, then cases of nonreconstrual can legitimately occur only (in part at least) for the reason that that very reason is absent.

Here's another way to make this point. Let us say that we run into a Kripkean, and, as inquiring minds who want to know, we ask: 'Why don't you reconstrue the modal intuition about Humphrey?' The Kripkean's answer, perhaps, would be: 'Well, it just seems right not to reconstrue in this case, and I'm at peace with that. It just seems right to treat the Humphrey claim in terms of metaphysical possibility without reconstruing it in terms of epistemic possibility.' I would say in response: 'Don't you need to be sure that the reason you yourself had for reconstruing in other cases (such as the Hesperus case) doesn't apply here, before you go ahead and reject any reconstrual in the Humphrey case?' The point is that the whole challenge stemming from the Hesperus example was that, perhaps, the Humphrey intuition, too, should be understood as a mere claim of epistemic, as opposed to metaphysical, possibility. In response to this challenge, it will do no good to assert, as the second-order intuitions do, that 'Humphrey might have won' is to be understood as involving metaphysical, and not epistemic, possibility, because that point is precisely what is in question.

I should say that the reconstrual of the Humphrey intuition in terms of similarity is not one that I find plausible independently of my argument here. That is, prior to this argument, I did *not* say, 'The Humphrey intuition is obviously to be understood in terms of similarity,' and I *was* inclined to find a Kripkean no-similarity account of that intuition itself intuitively plausible. But once I consider the claims I have made about the need for reasons for handling certain intuitions in certain ways, I accept that the Kripkean essentialist can give me no reason to understand the Humphrey intuition as he understands it, and so he can give me no reason for accepting essentialism itself. In short, I am led not to trust my initial intuition in favor of the Kripkean understanding of the Humphrey intuition. And I believe that the fact that this lack of trust has arisen is really the essentialist's own fault.

(ii) My argument against Kripke and essentialism starts from the fact that Kripke acknowledges that he, at least initially, has the intuition that Hesperus might not have been Phosphorus. When Kripke backtracks and tries to reconstrue this intuition, he gets into trouble, as I have argued. A defender of essentialism might interject here: 'Well, Kripke should never have admitted to having the Hesperus intuition. I don't feel, and have never felt, any pull toward the claim that Hesperus might not have been Phosphorus. On the contrary, it has always seemed to me intuitively obvious that "Hesperus might have been Phosphorus" is false.'

In response, I say that Kripke is getting at a real intuition with the Hesperus claim, and that it is just not plausible to assert that one has *never* had the intuition. Certainly, before one comes to know that Hesperus is Phosphorus, the intuition that Hesperus and Phosphorus are possibly distinct would need to be taken seriously.

However, a more subtle version of this objection may now be advanced: instead of picking on the fact that my argument against Kripke presupposes that one initially has the Hesperus intuition, this version of the objection focuses on the fact that my argument emerges from Kripke's offering of a reconstrual of the intuition. My whole approach so far turns on Kripke's claim that the Hesperus intuition must give us access to some modal fact, and that we must provide an alternative way of expressing the intuition—an alternative in terms of similarity—when we discover that the Hesperus intuition must be false as it stands. It is this reliance on a similarity substitute that gets Kripke into trouble, I have argued. But why couldn't Kripke just ditch the Hesperus intuition outright and leave nothing in its place? Granted, Kripke needs to give up the Hesperus intuition as stated, why does he have to go on to give a way of expressing the intuition that substitutes for the original false expression? Perhaps, Kripke's mistake is to think that he needed to engage in the method of reconstrual, instead of the simpler method of just giving up the intuition. According to this objection, one grants that one *did* feel the intuitive pull of 'Hesperus might not have been Phosphorus', but one holds that *now*, when one has become apprised of certain facts, even without invoking a reconstrual, one no longer feels any pull toward that claim.

Yablo elegantly defends such a view,[34] and this defense is central to his argument for a weaker connection between conceivability and possibility than philosophers such as Kripke and Chalmers insist on. I do not here want to enter into the relative merits of the method of reconstrual versus the method of just giving up the intuition. This is because my aim is, as I have said, to undercut a presupposition (viz., essentialism) common to both sides of the debate over the connection between conceivability and possibility. Thus, instead of turning to an evaluation of Yablo's method of giving up, versus Kripke's method of reconstrual, I will try to establish the more important point that the method of giving up faces the same kind of problem that, I have just argued, the method of reconstrual does.

---

[34] Yablo (2000) and Ch. 13 below. (For a similar strategy, see Loar 1998, 1999.) Although Yablo claims that we do (or should) just give up the intuition that Hesperus could (or might) have been distinct from Phosphorus without reconstruing that intuition in terms of objects relevantly similar to Hesperus and Phosphorus, he does hold, in Ch. 13 below that, even after we reject that intuition, we do continue to hang on to 'It could have *turned out* that Hesperus was not Phosphorus'. I'm not sure I agree with Yablo that there is a sharp distinction between 'could have been' and 'could have turned out', but even if this distinction is correct, the fact that Yablo rejects 'Hesperus could have been distinct from Phosphorus' leads to problems for his position, as I will now argue in the text.

Despite the fact that Yablo sees no need to offer a reconstrual of the Hesperus intuition, he does recognize the need to deny it as stated, and he denies it for precisely the same kinds of reason that Kripke reconstrues it. That is, he recognizes that the truth of 'Hesperus might not have been Phosphorus' would conflict with the empirically established identity of Hesperus and Phosphorus and with what Yablo sees as the necessity of this identity claim.[35] Without one or the other of these points, Yablo would not be prompted to reject the Hesperus intuition.

That claim is all I need to get my argument going. First we ask of Yablo: if you reject the Hesperus intuition, why don't you reject the Humphrey intuition? Yablo's answer, presumably, would be, in part, that there is no empirical result that shows that the Humphrey intuition comes into conflict with the necessity of identity. That is, the reason for rejection that applies in the Hesperus case does not apply in the Humphrey case.

Let us give Yablo this point for the time being. However, a problem still lurks. I want to focus now on a different intuition associated with the Hesperus case: namely, the intuition that Hesperus is necessarily Hesperus. I will call this the rigidity intuition because, as I explained early in the chapter, it is an intuition employed to establish that 'Hesperus' is a rigid designator. Now, as we have seen, Yablo simply rejects the intuition that Hesperus might not have been Phosphorus. In light of this, we are prompted to ask: why isn't the rigidity intuition to be rejected as well? We have good reason to ask this question. Given Yablo's history of rejecting certain modal intuitions, the demand for an explanation of the difference between the two intuitions seems apposite. We are naturally led to wonder whether the kind of reason that Yablo himself appeals to in rejecting the intuition that Hesperus might not have been Phosphorus also applies to the rigidity intuition.

It might seem that Yablo can meet this demand, for he can simply appeal to the fact that the reason for rejecting the intuition that Hesperus might not have been Phosphorus—namely, the need to preserve the necessity of identity—is not in place in the case of the rigidity intuition, the intuition that Hesperus is necessarily Hesperus. The rigidity intuition does not come into conflict with the necessity of identity (on the contrary, it helps to establish the necessity of identity), and so there is not the same reason to reject the rigidity intuition as there was to reject the intuition of contingency. Thus part of Yablo's reason for

---

[35] Yablo (2000: 119). More generally, Yablo's point is that rejection of an intuition that E is contingent requires the existence of a defeater, D, such that (a′) D is true, and (b′) if D is true, then E is impossible. Yablo gives this illustration: 'Hammurabi was able to conceive it as possible for Hesperus to exist without Phosphorus only because he didn't realize that the two were identical, and (maybe also) that identicals necessarily coexist' (2000: 119).

not rejecting the rigidity intuition has to be that such a rejection is not demanded by the necessity of identity.

But if *this* is Yablo's response to my demand, then it seems that his justification for not rejecting the rigidity intuition presupposes the necessity of identity. Yablo here lets the decision about whether or not to reject an intuition be guided by the desire to preserve the necessity of identity, and so his reason for not rejecting the rigidity intuition presupposes the necessity of identity. However, the intuition that Hesperus is necessarily Hesperus is used by Kripke, Yablo, and other essentialists to *establish* the necessity of identity or, at least, the necessity of the identity of Hesperus and Phosphorus. As we have seen, rigidity intuitions are used to establish the necessity of identity. In this light, it would be circular to use the necessity of identity to shore up a rigidity intuition or to defuse a doubt about it. Thus the doubt cannot be allayed in this way, nor can I think of any other way to allay it. Had Yablo not rejected the intuition of contingency, there would have been no opportunity for a doubt about the rigidity intuition to arise. But once Yablo rejects the intuition that Hesperus might not have been Phosphorus, and rejects it for the reasons I have discussed, he opens the door to doubting the rigidity intuition and seems to leave himself no way legitimately to remove the doubt. In a similar way, other rigidity intuitions—such as 'Humphrey is necessarily Humphrey'—would also be called into doubt.[36]

If Yablo is thus not entitled to hold that 'Humphrey' is a rigid designator, then he is also not entitled to the view that our intuition that Humphrey might have won is not to be accounted for in terms of similarity. Here is why: If 'Humphrey' is not a rigid designator, then 'Humphrey' designates different objects in different possible situations. Why would just these objects be picked out by 'Humphrey'? The answer, I believe, would have to be that 'Humphrey' has associated with it a certain description or a certain property, and that all these objects come to be picked out by this term precisely because they satisfy the description or share this property. But, if this is the account of the nonrigid reference of 'Humphrey', then we see that the referents of the nonrigid designator 'Humphrey' are selected by virtue of some similarity that they all bear to one another; and thus sentences containing this term, sentences such as 'Humphrey might have won', are made true in part in virtue of such similarity

---

[36] I would also argue, though I will not develop the point here, that the considerations that I adduced to show that Kripke has no reason not to reconstrue 'Humphrey might have won' in terms of similarity also show that he has no reason not to reconstrue rigidity intuitions in terms of similarity. Thus, I contend, rigidity intuitions are no more immune to Kripkean reconstrual than modal intuitions generally, in the same way that rigidity intuitions are no more immune to Yablo-style rejection than other modal intuitions. (See n. 28 on reconstruals of intuitions of necessity, such as 'Hesperus is necessarily Hesperus'.)

relations. Thus, as soon as Yablo loses justification for treating 'Humphrey' and other proper names as rigid designators, he loses justification for (1), the statement that modal claims such as 'Humphrey might have won' are not to be accounted for in terms of similarity.[37] But we have seen that Yablo loses justification for treating 'Humphrey' as a rigid designator as soon as he rejects (without reconstruing) the intuition that 'Hesperus might not have been Phosphorus'. So it seems that Yablo's method of just rejecting the intuition leads to a doubt about (1). But (1) is, as I have emphasized, crucial to the essentialist's defense of essentialism; therefore, Yablo's method of just rejecting the intuition leads to a doubt that renders essentialism itself unjustified, just as Kripke's method of reconstrual does. Thus, whether or not Yablo's method is superior to Kripke's on other grounds (and it may well be), it falls prey, I believe, to the kind of reasoning I have deployed against Kripke.

The general point in criticism of Yablo and Kripke is this: in rejecting or reconstruing certain intuitions because of a commitment to a certain thesis (viz., essentialism), one should not thereby generate ineliminable doubts about the reasons for accepting that thesis in the first place, for then one's commitment to the thesis serves only to render it unjustified.

What are the implications of this problem that I have raised for essentialism? If I am right, essentialism can be justified only circularly, and, more particularly, essentialism raises doubts about itself that cannot be answered non-question-beggingly. For this reason, even if essentialism is true, we cannot know that it is true, and, in particular, we have no reason to believe that modal claims— such as 'Humphrey might have won'—are true in the way that the essentialist understands them. That is, we have no reason to believe that Humphrey, independently of the way he is described, might have won. And thus, given my argument, if essentialism is true, and if it is a fact that Humphrey, independently of the way he is described, might have won, then we are cut off from know-ledge of this and similar modal facts. Thus the truth of essentialism would involve a kind of skepticism about modal reality.

Such self-generated skepticism does seem unpalatable and does provide some reason to reject essentialism and to treat anti-essentialism as a live option. Of course, I have not shown here that anti-essentialism does not also raise ineliminable doubts about itself or lead to a kind of modal skepticism. But here, it seems, the prospects are brighter. Anti-essentialism regards modal facts as determined by our ways of thinking about objects, and, as I have said, there seems to be no in-principle obstacle to acquiring knowledge of such ways, and

---

[37] Cf. the connection between rigidity and similarity in n. 31.

thus acquiring knowledge of modal facts, as the anti-essentialist conceives them. Further, and importantly, nothing about anti-essentialism itself, as far as I can see, generates doubts about that very thesis. By contrast, I have argued, there does seem to be an in-principle obstacle to acquiring knowledge of modal facts as the essentialist conceives them—an obstacle that is, in effect, raised by the essentialist's own methodology. These epistemological consider-ations provide, I believe, a substantial reason for preferring anti-essentialism to essentialism. Regardless of any advantages that may be claimed for essentialism, the skepticism about itself and about modal facts generally that essentialism engenders, seems too high a price to pay.

3 Conclusion

In a way, the criticism I have leveled against essentialism is a souped-up version of the standard objections (concerning arbitrariness and modal skepticism) that I considered in the first half of the chapter. Thus I have argued that the essen-tialist must treat two different modal intuitions differently for no principled rea-son. This is analogous, at least, to the earlier charge that the essentialist must draw modal distinctions arbitrarily. Further, I have argued that essentialism leads to a form of modal skepticism. Again, this parallels the earlier epistemic objection.

Despite these parallels to the standard objections, I believe that my objections cut deeper. Consider again the key claim in Kripke's defense of essentialism:

(1) Modal claims, such as 'Humphrey might have won', are not to be accounted for in terms of similarity.

Rather than attacking this premise directly, I challenge it by showing that, by the essentialist's own lights, he cannot legitimately use (1), and so cannot argue for essentialism.

This turning of the tables on the essentialist is more effective than a direct approach that simply denies any intuitive appeal for (1). It is more effective because many philosophers (including Kripke and me for most of my adult life so far) just do find (1) intuitively appealing. So a simple denial of this intuitive appeal will tend to bring the debate to a standstill, instead of furthering it. Also, the standard arguments directly against (1)—the standard arguments from modal skepticism and from arbitrariness—are, I have claimed, inconclusive or, at least, are objections to which Kripke has a plausible response. My objection to Kripke avoids such impasses. I begin as a friend of essentialism and grant that the essentialist can resist the direct attacks on (1) found in the literature. I also grant that (1) is intuitively appealing. In general, I am willing to accord the essentialist maximal leeway in developing his system free from the onus of having to convince those who don't share the essentialist's guiding intuition, (1). All I ask of the essentialist (and, believe me, I don't ask for much!) is that he not develop his system in a way that undercuts the intuitive justification for accepting essentialism—that is, in a way that raises doubts about essentialism's guiding intuition. This simple demand is manifestly fair to the essentialist (unlike, perhaps, the demand that an essentialist provide some kind of grounding of modal properties that can serve also as a basis for modal knowledge). If the essentialist cannot meet this basic demand, then he fails to meet a demand that any friend of essentialism, and indeed the essentialist himself, would reasonably impose on essentialism. I have argued that, in fact, the essentialist cannot meet this demand. Thus, ultimately, essentialism is pulled up short by the essentialist himself, rather than by one who was hostile to essentialism all along and never shared its guiding intuition. This undercutting of the motivation for essentialism by the essentialist's own hands shows, if I am right, that there is something more deeply wrong with essentialism than the standard arguments against it would—even if successful—lead us to suspect. These doubts about essentialism also afford us a new perspective on the conceivability–possibility debate; for if, as I have suggested, essentialism is false, then no matter what strength of connection there is between conceivability and possibility, conceivability arguments will not by themselves enable us to establish claims of nonidentity.[38]

---

[38] It might be helpful to readers of my earlier paper (Della Rocca 1996) if I were to say a few words about the relation between that paper and this one. This chapter rejects a crucial aspect of the earlier paper, but otherwise extends key insights in the earlier paper. In that paper, I argued that close attention to Kripke's method of reconstrual shows that essentialists cannot legitimately employ modal intuitions to argue for claims of nonidentity, arguments that essentialists, such as Kripke, had seen as some of the most important implications of essentialism. In the earlier paper, I held that the method of reconstrual is not at all in tension with essentialism; I simply wanted to purge essentialism of a method of arguing for nonidentity that was, I held, incompatible with the method of reconstrual that was crucial to Kripke's essentialism. This chapter also focuses on the method of reconstrual, but, by considering how that method is bound up with the role that similarity plays in the essentialist's argument for essentialism itself, I argue that not only must essentialists regard certain arguments for nonidentity as unjustified, but that they must also regard their own argument for essentialism itself as unjustified. *This* conclusion undermines essentialism itself or, at least, its justification, in a way that the former paper did not aspire to. Thus I reject the earlier paper's claim that the method of reconstrual is not in tension with essentialism itself. I now claim that it is, but I do so in part because of the kind of examination I gave to the method of reconstrual in that earlier paper.

REFERENCES

Barcan (Marcus), Ruth (1947), 'The Identity of Individuals in a Strict Functional Calculus of Second Order', *Journal of Symbolic Logic*, 12: 12–15.

Bealer, George (1987), 'The Limits of Scientific Essentialism', *Philosophical Perspectives*, 1: 289–365.

Chalmers, David (1996), *The Conscious Mind: In Search of a Fundamental Theory* (New York: Oxford University Press).

—— (1999), 'Materialism and the Metaphysics of Modality', *Philosophy and Phenomenological Research*, 59: 473–96.

Della Rocca, Michael (1996), 'Essentialists and Essentialism', *Journal of Philosophy*, 93: 186–202.

Forbes, Graeme (1985), *The Metaphysics of Modality* (Oxford: Clarendon Press).

—— (1986), 'In Defense of Absolute Essentialism', in French *et al.* (1986), 3–31.

French, Peter A., Uehling, Theodore E. Jr., and Wettstein, Howard K. (1979) (eds.), *Midwest Studies in Philosophy*, iv: *Studies in Metaphysics* (Minneapolis: University of Minnesota Press).

—— —— —— (1986) (eds.), *Midwest Studies in Philosophy*, xi: *Studies in Essentialism* (Minneapolis: University of Minnesota Press).

Gibbard, Allan (1975), 'Contingent Identity', *Journal of Philosophical Logic*, 4: 187–222.

Hale, Bob, and Wright, Crispin (1997) (eds.), *A Companion to the Philosophy of Language* (Oxford: Blackwell).

Kripke, Saul (1977), 'Identity and Necessity', in Stephen P. Schwartz (ed.), *Naming, Necessity and Natural Kinds* (Ithaca, NY: Cornell University Press), 66–101.

—— (1980), *Naming and Necessity* (Cambridge, Mass.: Harvard University Press).

Lewis, David (1968), 'Counterpart Theory and Quantified Modal Logic', *Journal of Philosophy*, 65: 113–26.

—— (1971), 'Counterparts of Persons and their Bodies', *Journal of Philosophy*, 68: 203–11.

—— (1973), *Counterfactuals* (Cambridge, Mass.: Harvard University Press).

—— (1986), *On the Plurality of Worlds* (Oxford: Basil Blackwell).

Loar, Brian (1998), 'Phenomenal Properties', in Ned Block, Owen Flanagan, and Guven Guzeldere (eds.), *The Nature of Consciousness* (Cambridge, Mass.: MIT Press), 597–616.

—— (1999), 'David Chalmers's *The Conscious Mind*', *Philosophy and Phenomenological Research*, 59(2): 465–72.

Noonan, Harold (1991), 'Indeterminate Identity, Contingent Identity and Abelardian Predicates', *The Philosophical Quarterly*, 41: 183–93.

Quine, W. V. (1976a), 'Reply to Professor Marcus', in Quine (1976c), 177–84.

—— (1976b), 'Three Grades of Modal Involvement', in Quine (1976c), 158–76.

—— (1976c), *Ways of Paradox*, rev. enlarged edn (Cambridge, Mass.: Harvard University Press).

Salmon, Nathan (1981), *Reference and Essence* (Princeton: Princeton University Press).

Salmon, Nathan (1986), 'Modal Paradox: Parts and Counterparts, Points and Counterpoints', in French *et al.*(1986), 75–120.

—— (1996), 'Trans-World Identification and Stipulation', *Philosophical Studies*, 84: 203–23.

Sidelle, Alan (1989), *Necessity, Essence, and Individuation* (Ithaca, NY: Cornell University Press).

Sider, Theodore (1996), 'All the World's a Stage', *Australasian Journal of Philosophy*, 74: 433–53.

—— (1999), Review of Michael Jubien, *Ontology, Modality and the Fallacy of Reference*, *Nous*, 33: 284–94.

Stalnaker, Robert (1979), 'Anti-Essentialism', in French *et al.* (1979), 343–55.

—— (1986), 'Counterparts and Identity', in French *et al.* (1986), 121–40.

Stanley, Jason (1997), 'Names and Rigid Designators', in Hale and Wright (1997), 555–85.

Wiggins, David (1980), *Sameness and Substance* (Cambridge, Mass.: Harvard University Press).

Yablo, Stephen (2000), 'Textbook Kripkeanism and the Open Texture of Concepts', *Pacific Philosophical Quarterly*, 81: 98–122.

6

The Varieties of Necessity

KIT FINE

Necessity abounds. There are the necessary truths of logic, mathematics, and metaphysics, the necessary connections among events in the natural world, the necessary or unconditional principles of ethics, and many other forms of necessary truth or connection. But how much diversity is there to this abundance? Are all necessary truths and connections reducible to a single common form of necessity? And if not, then what are the different ways in which a truth might be necessary or a necessary connection might hold?

It is the aim of this paper to show that diversity prevails. I shall argue that there are three main forms of necessity—the metaphysical, the natural, and the normative—and that none of them is reducible to the others or to any other form of necessity. Thus, what it is for a necessity or possibility of any of these forms to obtain does not consist in the obtaining of some other form or forms of necessity or possibility.

Although the focus here falls squarely within the philosophy of modality, some of my arguments may be of broader interest. For certain currently fashionable views on scientific essentialism and ethical naturalism entail the collapse of forms of necessity that I would wish to keep distinct. Thus I have found it crucial to indicate what it is in these views that I take to be in error; and this has required consideration of questions from within the metaphysics of natural kinds and the epistemology of ethical belief.

I should like to thank Roberta Ballerin, Ruth Chang, Tamar Gendler, John Hawthorne, Chris Peacocke, Stephen Schiffer, Bartosz Wieckowski, Nick Zangwill, the members of a seminar at Princeton, and the audience at a talk at UCLA for much helpful comment and discussion.

1   Necessities

A proposition is necessary if it *must* be true and possible if it *might* be true. On the face of it, there are different ways in which a proposition might be necessary or possible. Suppose I ask, 'Is it possible to get from London to New York in under an hour?' Then I might answer 'No', meaning that it is impossible given the currently available means of transport; or I might answer 'Yes', meaning that it is scientifically possible. Or again, suppose I ask, 'Is it possible to get from the earth to the sun in under 2 hours?' Then I might answer 'No', meaning that it is scientifically impossible; or I might answer 'Yes', meaning that it is logically possible.

Given that there are these different ways in which a proposition might be necessary, then how are they related? Is it possible to define, or otherwise explain, some in terms of others? And if it is, then which are the most basic?[1]

I suspect that many philosophers, in response to these questions, might be attracted to some version of modal monism. They would maintain that there was a single underlying modal notion in terms of which all others could be defined or understood. However, philosophers of this persuasion might well be tempted to adopt different views of what that underlying notion was. Many philosophers of the 'old school' would take it to be that of logical necessity in the narrow sense. This is the sense in which it is necessary that anything red is red, though not necessary that nothing red is green or that I am a person. The philosophers of the 'new school', on the other hand, would take the single underlying notion to be that of logical necessity in the broad sense, or what is sometimes called 'metaphysical' necessity. This is the sense of necessity that obtains in virtue of the identity of things (broadly conceived). Thus, in this sense it is necessary not only that anything red is red or that nothing is both red and green, but also that I am person or that 2 is a number.

Depending upon which notion of necessity one starts with, there are two main strategies for defining the other notions of necessity.[2] Suppose one starts with the narrow notion of logical necessity (or with some other suitably narrow notion). The main problem will then be to define the broader notions of necessity; and the obvious way to do this is by relativization. Consider the case of conceptual necessity—the necessity that holds in virtue of the identity of concepts. It will be necessary in this sense that nothing is both red and green, though not necessary that I am a person. Now let it be granted that there are

---

[1]   I take necessity to be a feature of propositions, though nothing of any importance for my purposes will turn on this assumption.

[2]   I do not wish to suggest that these two strategies represent the only possible ways of defining one notion of necessity in terms of others.

some basic conceptual truths—perhaps given by the *definitions* of the various concepts—and that the class of such truths can be defined without appeal to any modal notions (besides logical necessity). We might then define a proposition Q to be a conceptual necessity if it follows from the definitions: that is, if the conditional, 'if P then Q', is logically necessary for some conjunction P of basic conceptual truths. 'The conceptually necessary truths, in other words, may be taken to be those that are logically necessary *relative to*, or *conditional upon*, the basic conceptual truths.

Suppose, on the other hand, that one starts with the broad metaphysical notion of necessity (or with some other suitably broad notion). The main problem will then be to define the narrower notions of necessity; and the obvious way to do this is by restriction. Consider the case of mathematical necessity, the form of necessity that pertains to the truths of mathematics. We may then define a proposition to be mathematically necessary if it is necessary in the metaphysical sense and if, in addition, it is a mathematical truth—where this latter notion is presumably one that can be defined in non-modal terms. In this case, the new form of necessity is defined by means of a restriction that can be stated in non-modal terms (or, at least, without appeal to further modal notions).

I am inclined to think that the second of the two strategies *can* successfully be pursued. Given the notion of metaphysical necessity, the various narrower notions of necessity—be it logical, mathematical, conceptual, or the like—can each be defined by restriction.[3] Each of them can be regarded as a *species* of metaphysical necessity.

The feasibility of the first strategy, however, is open to serious doubt. It is, in the first place, not at all clear that metaphysical necessity can be defined in terms of logical necessity; for it is not clear that one can provide a non-modal characterization of some basic metaphysically necessary truths from which all other metaphysically necessary truths will be a logical consequence. But even if one sets this problem aside and allows the use of both logical and metaphysical necessity, there would appear to be concepts of necessity that are broader still, yet equally resistant to definition.

The two main concepts of this sort are the concepts of natural and normative necessity;[4] and it is my aim in the rest of the chapter to show how these

---

[3] Some of my reasons for thinking this are outlined in Fine (1994: 9–10), though much more needs to be said on the question.

[4] Another possible candidate is the concept of historical necessity, that form of necessity for which the past is 'closed' yet the future may be 'open'. The interesting question of whether the concept of natural necessity is merely a special case of this other concept is not one that I shall consider. Nor do I consider the epistemic, deontic, or tense-logical modalities, since I do not view them as constituting genuine forms of necessity.

concepts raise serious problems for the doctrine of modal monism. There are two main ways, in either case, in which the doctrine might be defended. It might be denied that either of the other concepts of necessity is genuinely broader than the metaphysical concept; natural and normative necessity should be regarded as *restricted* forms of metaphysical necessity. Or it might be maintained that the other concept is indeed broader, yet definable as a *relative* from of metaphysical (or logical) necessity. I have attempted to show, in each case, that neither line of defence can be made to work.

It is important to bear in mind some limitations in my approach. First, I have not directly addressed the question of whether there might be some other concepts of necessity that cannot be understood in terms of the three upon which I have focused. One should think of the discussion as representing an 'end-game' in which the other candidate concepts of necessity have been removed from the board. Second, I have not considered all possible ways in which one of the remaining concepts of necessity might be defined or understood in terms of others. But if there are others, then I do not know what they might be. Finally, my concern throughout has been to arrive at the most basic modal concepts: that is, those that are not to be defined or understood in terms of other modal concepts. I have not directly considered the question of whether it might be possible to break out of the sphere of the modal and understand it in altogether different terms. Thus my conclusions have no direct bearing on the issue of modal realism—that is, on whether the modal facts are themselves most real—for I may merely have tracked modality down to its penultimate source, within the sphere of the modal, rather than to a possibly more ultimate source.[5]

2 Natural Necessity: Subsumption

Natural necessity is the form of necessity that pertains to natural phenomena.[6] Suppose that one billiard-ball hits another. We are then inclined to think that it is no mere accident that the second billiard-ball moves. Given certain antecedent conditions and given the movement of the first ball, the second ball *must* move. And the 'must' here is the *must* of natural necessity.

---

[5] All the same, my conclusions may provide some succour for the realist concerning modality. For realism about possible worlds will not be plausible given that there are different primitive notions of necessity; and a reductive form of anti-realism will not be plausible given that the modal does not supervene on the nonmodal.

[6] [For an extended discussion of issues related to those raised in this section, see Alan Sidelle, Ch. 8 below—eds.]

The above elucidation of natural necessity does not presuppose that the notion has primary application, or even *any* application, to natural law. However, it is very plausible to suppose that if there are particular necessary connections of the above sort, then there are also general necessary connections of this sort. Thus, not only will it be necessary that this billiard-ball move in these particular circumstances, it is also necessary that any billiard-ball will move in relevantly similar circumstances.

What is the relationship between metaphysical and natural necessity? Is every natural necessity a metaphysical necessity? And is it therefore possible to regard the one form of necessity as a restricted form of the other?

The answer to these questions would appear to be a straightforward 'No'. For surely it is conceivable, and hence metaphysically possible, that the one ball should strike the other in the given circumstances without the other moving. And surely it is conceivable, and hence metaphysically possible, that many of the natural laws that govern our universe should fail to hold, that bodies should attract one another according to an inverse cube law, for example, rather than the inverse square law.[7]

However, ever since Kripke (1980), we have learnt to be suspicious of such considerations. For can we be sure that the hypothetical situation in which an inverse cube law is envisaged to hold is one in which the bodies genuinely have mass? Perhaps they have some other property somewhat like mass, call it schmass, which conforms to an inverse cube law. And can we be sure that the hypothetical situation in which the second billiard-ball is envisaged not to move is one which genuinely contains the given billiard-balls rather than some schmassy counterparts?

In either of these cases, the proposed counter-example would fail; and if the same is true for any other counter-example that might be proposed, then the way would be clear towards maintaining that every natural necessity was a metaphysical necessity. Indeed, several philosophers have recently been attracted towards such a view[8] and it might also be thought to be especially congenial to my own way of thinking. For I take metaphysical necessities to be those that are rooted in the identity of 'things' (Fine 1994: 9); so natural necessities might then be taken to constitute the special case in which the things in question are the natural properties or kinds. Natural necessities would simply be the special case of those essentialist truths that arise from the identity of natural kinds.

---

[7] For expository purposes, I take an oversimplified view of what the scientific laws are.

[8] They include Shoemaker (1980: 244; 1998), Swoyer (1982), and Ellis (1999). Kripke raises the issue (1980: 99, 164) but without taking a stand.

However, it seems to me that the scope of these counter-considerations is severely limited, and that the restrictionist view remains highly problematic.[9] It may be conceded that we should exercise caution in judging a natural necessity to be metaphysically contingent—for what is taken in a given hypothetical situation to be a property or kind that figures in the natural necessity may be no such thing. But this, I believe, should merely lead us to adopt a more discriminating view as to which natural necessities are metaphysically contingent, rather than to give up the idea that there are any such necessities.

To see why this might be so, let us return to the putative counter-example to the metaphysical necessity of the inverse square law; and let us concede that the envisaged hypothetical situation involves schmass, rather than mass, and that the counter-example therefore fails. Still, that very same hypothetical situation may be used to provide a counter-example to the metaphysical necessity of a *different* natural necessity. For consider the proposition that there is no schmass (i.e., that there are no instances of schmass). Then this proposition should be taken to be a natural necessity. For our original judgement was that the inverse square law was a natural necessity, though not a metaphysical necessity. Now that we see that the metaphysically possible worlds in which it was taken to fail are ones with schmass rather than mass (and given that our universe is taken to be completely governed by the Newtonian Laws), we should take it to be a natural necessity that there is no schmass. In either case, the 'fabric of the universe' is envisaged as excluding a certain sort of behaviour—whether this be the deviant behaviour of mass or the normal behaviour of schmass. Moreover, my opponent should concede it to be a metaphysical possibility that there is schmass, since it was through postulating schmass—or the like—that the original putative counter-example to the metaphysical necessity of the inverse square law was reinterpreted. So he should grant that the absence of schmass is a natural, though not a metaphysical, necessity.

Indeed, there is no reason in general why the sophisticated post-Kripkean should not agree with the naïve pre-Kripkean as to which of the metaphysically possible worlds are naturally impossible. For whereas the pre-Kripkean will take such a world to be a natural impossibility because of the straightforward failure of a law, the post-Kripkean will take it to be a natural impossibility because of the instantiation of an alien property or kind. Thus even though sensitivity to the cross-world identity of natural properties or kinds may lead one to re-describe the hypothetical situations in which a natural law is taken to fail, it should not lead one to reject the natural impossibility of those situations.

---

[9] Further criticisms of the subsumptionist view are made by Alan Sidelle in Ch. 8 below.

It might be objected that there is not even a *putative* counter-example to the metaphysical necessity of the inverse square law. But such a view is too outlandish to deserve consideration;[10] and once we have the putative counter-example, then we have the basis, if I am right, for deriving an actual counter-example. It might also be objected that the proposition that there is no schmass remains true in the hypothetical situation in which the inverse square law is thought to fail, since it means that there is no *body* with schmass and, in the hypothetical situation, there are only schbodies, not bodies. Thus 'body' goes the way of 'mass'. But, if that is the objection, then let us formulate the proposition that there is no schmass with an absolutely unrestricted quantifier: there is nothing whatever with schmass. Or, alternatively, we might use the proposition that there are no schbodies (again with an unrestricted quantifier).

A more serious objection concerns the existence of the relevant properties or kinds. It might be thought that the properties or kinds that figure in natural law are *immanent* in the sense of only existing if instantiated. The kind *schmass* will therefore not exist. It might also be thought that a proposition exists only if the items it directly concerns exist. So, since the kind *schmass* does not exist, nor does the proposition that there is no schmass; and so we have no counter-example to the subsumption of natural under metaphysical necessity.

Whether this is so depends upon exactly what the subsumption thesis is taken to be. If it is the thesis:

> every (actual) proposition is such that it is natural necessity only if it is metaphysical necessity,

then no counter-example has been given under the stated assumptions. But if it is the thesis:

> necessarily$_M$ every proposition is such that necessarily$_M$ it is a natural necessity only if it is a metaphysical necessity,

or even the weaker thesis:

> necessarily$_M$ every proposition is such that actually it is a natural necessity only if it is a metaphysical necessity,[11]

then there is a counter-example. For the proposition that there is no schmass exists in the hypothetical situation in which there is schmass, and this very

---

[10] Perhaps even for someone like Shoemaker (1998:n. 11), who believes that nothing but H_2O could behave the way water ordinarily behaves, since what is at issue here is whether something other than water might behave in some other way.

[11] I use the subscripts 'M' (and 'N'), here and elsewhere, to indicate the kind of necessity in question.

proposition is a natural necessity in the actual world, though not a metaphysical necessity. Moreover, in standard formulations of modal logic, it is the stronger theses that are required if natural necessity is to be eliminable in favour of metaphysical necessity.

In any case, there are counter-examples that require no appeal to uninstantiated properties or kinds. Let P, Q, ... be an exhaustive list of all the kinds (or all the fundamental kinds) that there actually are. Then presumably it will be a natural necessity that every object (or every fundamental object) is of one of the kinds P, Q, ..., but it will not be a metaphysical necessity. Or again, suppose that determinism is true and holds of natural necessity: it is a natural necessity that every event has a cause. (Or, if we wish to avoid appeal to the notion of cause, we can say: it is a natural necessity that for any event e there is a preceding event c such that it is a natural necessity that e occurs only if c occurs.) But surely it is a metaphysical possibility that determinism is false. It would be absurd for my opponent to maintain that the hypothetical situation in which determinism appears to fail is one that does not really involve events or time. Thus, given that it is a metaphysical possibility that determinism should hold, we have the metaphysical possibility of a natural necessity not being a metaphysical necessity.

We can even construct a counter-example on the basis of standard laws. Consider the inverse square law as an example. Now my opponent will maintain that this law is still true in the hypothetical situation in which there is schmass rather than mass, though vacuously. But surely he will concede that, even though the law is true in this hypothetical situation, it is not a *law*—or, at least, not a law that *prevails*—in that situation.[12] Indeed, if it were, then, by parity of reasoning, the inverse cube law for schmass would have to be a law that prevails in our world; and surely it is not. But now, whatever it takes to be a prevailing law, it seems clear that it is a natural necessity that the inverse square law is such a law. Not only is there no natural possibility of its failing to hold, there is no natural possibility of its failing to be a law that governs the universe. But then the proposition that the inverse square law is such a law is another actual counter-example to the thesis that every natural necessity is a metaphysical necessity.

The lesson to be learnt from these counter-examples is not that we should go back to our pre-Kripkean intuitions of metaphysical contingency, but that we should attempt to be more discriminating about which laws of nature are to be regarded as metaphysically contingent and which is not. There is an intuitive

---

[12] Cf. Shoemaker (1980: 248): 'Nothing I have said precludes the possibility of there being worlds in which the causal laws are different from those that prevail in this world.'

distinction to be drawn here. That electrons have negative charge, for example, strikes one as metaphysically necessary; it is partly definitive of what it is to be an electron that it should have negative charge. But that light has a maximum velocity or that energy is conserved strikes one as being at most naturally necessary. It is hard to see how it could be partly definitive of what it is to be light that it should have a given maximum velocity, or partly definitive of energy that it should be conserved.[13] It is equally a defect of the old view that saw all laws of nature as metaphysically contingent and of the new view that sees them all as metaphysically necessary that they fail to heed this distinction; rather than take a blanket view of the modal status of these laws, we should attempt to refine and systematize the intuitive discriminations that we are naturally inclined to make among them.[14]

Although I have emphasized the way in which natural necessities may outrun the metaphysical necessities, it seems to me that there is one respect in which this may not be true. For I am inclined to think that there are no distinctive *de re* natural necessities. Let us suppose that x and y are two particles, and that it is a natural necessity that they attract one another (assuming, of course, that they exist!). Then it is plausible to suppose that this should follow from (a) its being a metaphysical necessity that each of the particles is of the kind that it is and (b) its being a natural necessity that particles of this kind attract one another. Thus the *de re* natural necessity will reduce to a *de re* metaphysical necessity and a *de dicto* natural necessity; and it might be thought that something similar should be true of any *de re* natural necessity or, indeed, of any form of *de re* necessity whatever. All forms of *de re* necessity (and of essence) will be fundamentally metaphysical, even though some forms of *de dicto* necessity may not be.

3 Natural Necessity: Definition

Even if post-Kripkean sensitivity to the cross-world identity of natural kinds does not enable one to *subsume* natural necessity under metaphysical necessity,

---

[13] Lowe (2000) has also stressed the metaphysical contingency of the values born by the fundamental physical constants, and Chalmers (1999: 13–14) has stressed the metaphysical contingency of the conservation laws.

[14] Thus I do not share Shoemaker's scepticism on this point (1980: 249–51). It is not that we need a general criterion for saying when we have one kind of necessity as opposed to another but a clearer conception of what, in particular cases, might plausibly be taken to be relevant to the identity of a given natural property. Where he sees a problem, I see an interesting project. The present distinction is somewhat akin to the Kantian distinction between the 'pure' and 'empirical' parts of science, which was later taken up by some of the logical positivists (see Friedman (1994) for a general discussion).

it might still appear to hold out the hope of defining it as a *relative* form of metaphysical necessity. For suppose we uphold the doctrine of immanent universals. We may then let the existence of natural properties or kinds be our guide to the natural possibilities for a given world, a possible world being a natural possibility relative to a given world if it contains only (or perhaps all and only) those natural kinds that exist in the world.[15] A world of schmass, for example, will not be a natural possibility, since the kind *schmass* does not actually exist; and, in general, any objects that behaved in a nomically irregular way within a given world would have to be of kinds that do not actually exist, and hence would belong to a world that was not a natural possibility. (And, of course, once given the naturally possible worlds, we can define the natural necessities as those that hold in every such world.)

Instead of presupposing the doctrine of immanent universals in formulating the definition, as is often done, we may appeal instead to what is taken to be required for a kind to exist. Thus we may say that a world is a natural possibility if it instantiates only those kinds that are actually instantiated, and thereby side-step the issue of the conditions under which a universal exists. Nor is there any need to place such emphasis on instantiation as the condition for the existence of universals. Perhaps we can allow kinds to exist in the manner of Hume's missing shade through being suitably related to other kinds that exist, even though they are not themselves instantiated. If we free up the account in both these respects, then we are left with the general idea that the natural possibilities for a given world will turn upon the status and distribution of its natural properties and relations.

But accounts of this sort, it seems to me, are subject to a familiar form of objection. It is sometimes pointed out that two possible worlds might *merely* differ as to what is a natural necessity and that regularity-type views must therefore be mistaken, since they would be unable to distinguish between the two worlds. This objection will not work against the present view, since it might be argued that any difference in the natural laws would make a difference to the natural properties that exist in the two worlds. But a variant of the objection *can* be made to work.[16]

Consider, for example, a metaphysically possible world w_N that is Newtonian. Then bodies in this world will have mass, be subject to force, and so on (or have

---

[15] Clearly, the natural kinds should also be taken to include the various fundamental physical relations.

[16] Carroll (1994: sect. 3.1) advances a similar line of objection, though without attempting to take care of the rejoinder that the two worlds might differ in their natural properties. Similar objections to Humean accounts of objective chance have also been considered in the literature.

something similar to mass and be subject to something similar to force, since actual mass is not itself strictly Newtonian). By the same token, there will be a metaphysically possible world w_M which is Schmewtonian. The bodies in this world behave like bodies in w_N but are subject to the inverse cube law or some other variant of the Newtonian Laws. The bodies in this world will not have mass, according to our opponent, but they will have something similar to mass, say schmass; and likewise for force and the rest. Now surely it is a natural possibility in both w_N and w_M that there be no bodies; after all, there is nothing in the natural laws of either world that requires that there be anything to which they apply. So there is going to be an empty world v_N that is a natural possibility for w_N, and an empty world v_M that is a natural possibility for w_M. Since v_N is a natural possibility for w_N, it will verify all of the natural necessities of w_N; so, since it is a natural necessity in w_N that there is no schmass, it will be a natural necessity in v_N that there is no schmass.[17] Moreover, since the world w_M contains schmass, we may safely assume that it is a natural possibility in the empty world v_M that there be schmass; for it would be bizarre in the extreme to suppose that the non-existence of any bodies somehow precluded the possibility of there being schmass.[18] So the empty worlds v_M and v_N differ as to what is a natural possibility. But it is hard to see how there can be any difference in the status of their natural properties; for the natural properties that exist in the two worlds and their pattern of instantiation are just the same.[19]

A similar counter-example (though not subject to worries over empty space-time) runs as follows. Consider a metaphysically possible world w_D for which mind–body dualism is true. The world w_D may not consist of mental and physical events as we conceive them, but it will then consist of related kinds of events—the mental$_D$ and the physical$_D$, say. Let us suppose that epiphenomenalism is also true in w_D, so that the mental$_D$ and the physical$_D$ events of w_D are each subject to their own laws, but with no nomological interaction between them. By the same token, there should be a metaphysically possible epiphenomenal world w_E in which the physicalistic events are subject to essentially the same laws as in w_D, but the mentalistic events to somewhat different

[17] I have assumed that natural necessity is subject to the S4 axiom, $\Box A \rightarrow \Box \Box A$. But even without the benefit of this assumption, it would be odd to suppose that, in w_N, the non-existence of bodies somehow required the possibility of there being schmass.

[18] Alternatively, we could appeal to the assumption that natural necessity was subject to the S5 axiom, $A \rightarrow \Box \Diamond A$, though nothing so strong is required in this particular case.

[19] One might maintain that the kind mass exists in v_N but not in v_M, but that is presumably only because the instantiation of mass is a natural possibility in the one but not the other, and so the concept of natural possibility is already presupposed.

laws. It is reasonable to assume, or at least to allow, that the physicalistic events of w_D and w_E are of the same kind, even though the mentalistic events are not.

Now surely it is a natural possibility in both w_D and w_E that, under given physical conditions, there be nothing mentalistic in the world. Thus there will be a mind-free world v_D that is a natural possibility for w_D, and a physically similar mind-free world v_E that is a natural possibility for w_E. But then by the same line of reasoning as before, w_D and w_E will differ on what is a natural possibility (for the mentalistic part of the world), even though there is no difference in the 'status' or distribution of their natural properties.

Of course, if these counter-examples are correct, then they tell not only against the property-based definitions, but also against any other account that would make the natural possibilities supervene, as a matter of metaphysical necessity, upon the non-nomic facts.

There is, however, another, more radical objection to be made. So far I have argued that any definition of natural in terms of metaphysical necessity will be extensionally incorrect—there will be a difference, or at least a possible difference, in the propositions that fall under the definiendum and those that fall under the definiens. But it might be argued that even if we had an extensionally correct and non-circular account of natural necessity, it still would not be likely to provide an adequate definition.

We may illustrate the nature of the difficulty with the doctrine of logical fatalism. Suppose one holds, for whatever reason, that every truth is necessary. Then:

($\star$) for every proposition p, p is necessary iff it is true;

and since this proposition is itself true, it follows:

($\star\star$) necessarily, for every proposition p, p is necessary iff it is true.[20]

But even the logical fatalist will not accept ($\star\star$) as a correct *definition* of necessity, despite the presence of necessary coincidence and the absence of circularity, since it will be important for him to maintain that the necessity of a proposition does not *consist* in its being true. It so happens, if I may put it this way, that every true proposition is necessary; but the proposition's being true is not that in which its necessity consists.

Another, though somewhat more problematic, case is provided by the standard definition of logical necessity (narrowly conceived) in terms of invariance. For let it be granted, if only for the sake of argument, that:

necessarily$_M$, a proposition is logically necessary iff its truth is preserved under any substitution for its non-logical constituents.

---

[20] I here ignore the difficulties over including merely possible propositions within the scope of the definition.

Still, it might be maintained that such invariance is not what it is for a proposition to be logically necessary. After all, the proposition that B.C. is not an angel remains true under any substitution for the constituent B.C. but is not, on that account, a necessary truth. So why should it be any different in the logical case? What we have *at best*, on this view, is a definition of logical *truth*, rather than of logical *necessity*.

One might even argue against my proposed definition of metaphysical necessity in terms of essentialist truth along similar lines (Fine 1994: 9). I wish to claim:

necessarily$_M$, a proposition is metaphysically necessary iff it is true in virtue of the identity of some (possible) objects.

But it might be argued that what we have on the right hand side is merely an account of the source of the proposition's truth and not of its modal status. Essentialist truth is no more capable than logical truth of conveying modal import.[21]

A similar problem, I suspect, is bound to arise for any proposed definition of natural necessity in terms of metaphysical necessity. For it will usually be possible to see such a definition as a case of relativization. Certain propositions will be picked out by means of a suitable description, call it 'being a law'; and a proposition is then taken to be a natural necessity iff it is entailed by the propositions that satisfy the description—that is, by the laws.[22] But such an account is subject to the obvious objection that it does not provide an adequate account of the natural necessity of the 'laws' themselves. For where the proposition P is a law, its being a natural necessity, according to the definition, will consist in: (a) its being entailed by the various 'laws', including P itself; and (b) its being a law. But (a), which is merely a matter of self-entailment, can hardly contribute to the given proposition's being a natural necessity; and it will be hard to see, in any given case of (b), how the defining feature of a 'law' might constitute an adequate account of the *necessity* of the given proposition. Consider the definition proposed above by way of illustration. This may be put in the form: a proposition is a natural necessity iff it is entailed by the proposition that K_1, $K_2, \ldots$ are the only kinds that there are, where $K_1, K_2, \ldots$ is an inventory of all

---

[21] Another illustration of the distinction is provided by Quine's arguments against analyticity, which have as their principal target a certain kind of truth, rather than a peculiarly modal status. Almog (1991) draws a similar distinction between a 'primal', or constitutive, truth and its modal import.

[22] I have supposed that the laws are picked out by a description that is external to the entailment, but one might also provide an analysis of the form L $\rightarrow$ P, as long as one is prepared to resort to double indexing, as in van Fraassen (1977).

the kinds that there are. The 'law' here is the proposition that $K_1, K_2, \ldots$ are the only kinds that there are, and its being a 'law' essentially consists in its being true. But we are inclined to think that, in so far as it is a natural necessity that there are no other kinds, it is because there is something in the nature of the world that prevents there being other kinds; and the mere fact that there *are* no other kinds can hardly be taken to constitute an adequate account of what this force, or form of necessity, might be.

The general problem is that a definition of natural necessity as a form of relative necessity will tend to make the necessity of the propositions with respect to which the necessity is relative a trivial or insubstantial matter; yet we are inclined to think that the necessity attaching to the laws and the like is not of this trivial sort. Any true proposition whatever can be seen as necessary under the adoption of a suitable definition of relative necessity. Any proposition that I truly believe, for example, will be necessary relative to the conjunction of my true beliefs, and any proposition concerning the future will be necessary relative to the conjunction of all future truths. The problem therefore is to explain why the necessity that issues from the definition of natural necessity is not of this cheap and trivial sort; and I doubt, in the case of any otherwise reasonable definition that might be proposed, that this can be done.

One might wish to press the objection further and claim that no definition stated entirely in terms of metaphysical necessity could capture the peculiarly modal force of truths that are naturally necessary yet metaphysically contingent. Just as it has been supposed that there is a conceptual barrier between normative and non-normative concepts, so one might think that there is a conceptual barrier, not merely between modal and non-modal concepts, but also between different 'grades' of modality. But even though I would wish to endorse this more general claim, there is no need to appeal to it in arguing against the plausibility of particular accounts of what this peculiar 'modal force' might be.

I conclude that there appears to be no reasonable way of understanding natural necessity as a restricted or relative form of metaphysical necessity.[23]

4 Normative Necessity: Naturalism

There is a familiar distinction between accidental and non-accidental generalizations within the natural sphere, but what is not so often appreciated is that

---

[23] Among recent theorists, Armstrong (1983: 92–3) and Fales (1993: 140) have been attracted by the view that some form of natural necessity or necessary connection might be primitive.

a similar distinction can be drawn within the moral sphere. This may be illustrated by the claim that every war is wrong. For this might be meant in the sense that every war, in the circumstances that actually prevail, is wrong; or it might be meant in the sense that every war, in whatever circumstances might prevail, is wrong. In the latter case, the claim is taken to be necessary—to hold unconditionally, or in all possible circumstances; while in the former, the claim is not taken to be necessary, but merely to hold conditionally upon the circumstances that actually obtain.

The distinction between accidental and necessary generalizations in nature is often drawn in terms of the ability to sustain counterfactuals. A necessary generalization that all F's are G's will sustain the counterfactual 'if this were to be an F it would be a G', while the corresponding accidental generalization will not. The distinction may be drawn on a similar basis in the moral case. For the *de facto* pacifist need not commit himself to the view that if there were a war of such-and-such a hypothetical sort, then it would be wrong, though the more radical pacifist will be so committed. Indeed, it is perhaps only in so far as moral judgements bear this counterfactual force that they can be of any real help as a guide to action; for even if we do not do something, we still wish to know whether it would have been better if we *had*.

The sense of necessity in which the radical pacifist wishes to maintain that it is necessary that any war is wrong I propose to call *normative*. I am inclined to think, as the term 'normative' suggests, that the same kind of necessity has application to other normative domains; but I shall bracket this question in what follows and simply focus on the moral case.

It is in this sense of necessity that the moral supervenes on the natural, and, indeed, such cases provide the least contentious examples of normative necessity. Suppose that D is a complete description of the world in naturalistic terms. Then we will be inclined to make certain moral judgements about the world so described—that such-and-such a consequence was unfortunate or such-and-such an action wrong. But in so far as we are prepared to make such judgements, we will also be prepared to say that it was no accident that they are true. In those particular circumstances, the consequences *had* to be unfortunate, the action *had* to be wrong.

It is perhaps only because moral truths may hold with this kind of necessity that it is appropriate to talk of ourselves as being subject to moral *law*. For just as we are inclined to think that if one billiard-ball hits another in given circumstances, then the other *must* move, so we are inclined to think that if I make a promise to someone in given circumstances, then I *must* keep the promise. And here the 'must' is not merely the 'must' of obligation. I am obliged to keep the promise, but that I am so obliged is something that is *required* by my having made the promise in the first place. The obligation is itself something that falls under the rubric of necessity.

How should normative necessity be understood? Is it a species of natural or metaphysical necessity? Or somehow definable in terms of these other forms of necessity?

It seems bizarre to suppose that normative necessity is a species of natural necessity. Indeed, it is commonly held that there are no natural necessities that essentially involve normative concepts. But from this we would hardly wish to conclude that there are no non-trivial normative necessities.

Whether normative necessity is a species of metaphysical necessity is more contentious. One reason for thinking that it is derived from the traditional doctrine of naturalism, according to which any moral property will be coextensive, as a matter of conceptual necessity, with some natural property.[24] In order to see how the argument from the one to the other might go, let us suppose that a given proposition P, say that lying is wrong, is a normative necessity. This may be symbolized as follows:

(1) $\boxed{\text{n}}\, P\,(\text{W})$,

with the predicate 'W' for 'wrong' made explicit. Given naturalism, it is a conceptual necessity that wrongness is coextensive with a certain natural property N:

(2) $\boxed{\text{c}}\, (x)\, (\text{W}x \leftrightarrow \text{N}x)$.

Let us use the notion of normative necessity in an inclusive sense so as to include all of the conceptual necessities. Or, to put the matter differently, we shall not allow something to be a normative possibility unless it is also a conceptual possibility. It then follows from (2) that wrongness and the natural property N are coextensive as a matter of normative necessity:

(3) $\boxed{\text{n}}\, (x)\, (\text{W}x \leftrightarrow \text{N}x)$.

Since this is so, one may be substituted for the other in (1), and we obtain that it is a normative necessity that lying has the naturalistic property N:

(4) $\boxed{\text{n}}\, P(N)$.

But that lying has the property N is a purely naturalistic proposition, and so, given that it is a normative necessity, it must also be a conceptual necessity; for normative necessity merely serves to restrict the *connection* between the

---

[24] The traditional form of naturalism is to be distinguished from the more contemporary form, in which all that is required is that the moral 'supervene' on the non-moral. Under certain assumptions, which need not be subject to doubt in the present context, the two will be equivalent.

naturalistic and the normative possibilities, it does not serve to restrict the naturalistic possibilities themselves. So:

(5) $\boxed{c}\,P(N)$.

But again, given, by (2), that W and N are coextensive as a matter of conceptual necessity, one may be substituted for the other in (5); and we obtain that it is a conceptual necessity that lying is wrong:

(6) $\boxed{c}\,P(W)$.

In this way, any normative necessity can be shown to be a conceptual necessity (and hence also to be a metaphysical necessity under the traditional view).

The argument rests on two general assumptions. The first, which we may call *Inclusion*, is that every conceptual necessity is a normative necessity. Or, in schematic form:

Inc $\boxed{c}\,A \to \boxed{n}A$.

The second, which we may call *Conservativity*, is that every naturalistic normative necessity is a conceptual necessity:

Cons $\boxed{n}\,A \to \boxed{c}\,A$, for A naturalistic.

If these assumptions are themselves taken to hold of conceptual necessity, then it may be shown to be a conceptual necessity that any given normative necessity is a conceptual necessity.

Ever since Moore, however, most moral philosophers have taken naturalism in its traditional form to be an instance of the 'naturalistic fallacy'; and if, as I think, they are right, then the present route to subsuming the normative notion of necessity under the conceptual notion will be blocked. This is not the place to attempt a vindication of this objection to naturalism, but let me make a few comments on how I think it might best be understood. Moore thought that if there were an analysis of an ethical property in terms of a naturalistic property, then it would no longer be an open question whether things with the naturalistic property had the ethical property. But, as has often been pointed out, it may not be obvious that a correct analysis is indeed correct, so such an analysis could still leave open the question of the connection between analysandum and analysans.

Perhaps a more satisfactory way to formulate the objection is as follows.[25] If there is a correct analysis of *good*, say, as what promotes pleasure over pain,

---

[25] A rather different way to obtain a version of the open question argument is to 'reverse' the argument given above. For suppose we reject the conclusion of the argument: i.e., take it to be a conceptual possibility that something holds of normative necessity though not of conceptual necessity. Then, granted the conceptual necessity of the assumptions (Inc) and (Cons), it follows that (2), the doctrine of naturalism, will be false. This also strikes me as being a powerful objection to naturalism.

then something's being good must consist *in nothing more* than its promoting pleasure over pain.[26] But we have a strong intuition that it *does* consist in something more. Here we are not relying on the purported *epistemic* status of a correct analysis, as is Moore, but on its *metaphysical* consequences.

This argument, moreover, can be strengthened. For suppose one merely takes it to be a conceptual necessity that something is good if it promotes pleasure over pain. Now, if this is true, then presumably it must also be true that something is good in virtue of promoting pleasure over pain. Indeed, it is only because something is good in virtue of promoting pleasure over pain that there is the conceptual connection between the one and the other. But now what is this in-virtue-of relationship that accounts for the conceptual connection? The only possible answer, it seems, is that it is the relationship of one thing *consisting in no more than* some other; for this would appear to be the only in-virtue-of relationship capable of sustaining a conceptual connection. But if this is right, then the argument can also be taken to apply to statements of conceptual implication, and not merely to analyses.

5 Normative Necessity: Neo-naturalism

Many philosophers have recently been willing to grant that normative necessity is not a form of conceptual necessity, but have been tempted, all the same, by the view that it is a form of metaphysical necessity.[27] This alternative view does not appear to have been based upon any serious consideration of the matter. It is observed that there is a necessary connection between the naturalistic and the normative features of a given situation, and it is simply assumed, given that the connection is not conceptual, that it must be metaphysical. These philosophers sometimes appeal to the fact that the connection holds in all possible worlds, but it is only if these worlds are themselves taken to be metaphysically possible that the metaphysical necessity of the connection would thereby be established. No insight into the status of the necessary connection is to be gained in this, or any other, case by an appeal to possible worlds.

If metaphysical necessity is taken to be that form of necessity that derives from the nature of things, then it is prima-facie highly implausible that the necessary connection between the naturalistic and normative features of a

[26] The notion of *consists in*, which I appeal to at various places in the chapter, is discussed at greater length in Fine (2001).

[27] Their number includes Dreier (1992: 15), Klagge (1984: 378), McFetridge (1985: 251–2), Shoemaker (1985: 441), and Zangwill (1995).

given situation should be taken to be metaphysical. For there would appear to be nothing in the identity of the naturalistic or normative features that demands that they be connected in the way they are. It is no part of what it is to be pain that it should be bad, and no part of what it is to be bad that it should include pain. There is a striking, intuitive difference between the connection between being water and being composed of H_2O, on the one hand, and the connection between being a pain and bad, on the other. For the identities of the respective features require that the connection holds in the one case, though not the other. I might also note that my previous argument against normative necessity as a form of conceptual necessity would appear to work equally well against its being a form of metaphysical necessity, since it is hard to see how a metaphysically necessary connection between the naturalistic and the normative could hold without the latter simply consisting in the former.

There is, however, a way in which this line of reasoning might be resisted. For it might be maintained that the normative features may have a 'hidden' nature, and that, once it becomes clear what this is, it will be apparent how these features may be connected, as a matter of metaphysical necessity, with appropriate naturalistic features. The elaboration of such a view is to be found in the new 'metaphysical' version of naturalism. This differs from the old 'conceptual' version of naturalism in two main respects. First, the naturalistic property in terms of which 'good', or what have you, is analysed is a high-level 'functional' property, rather than a low-level 'criterial' property. Second, the extension of the term 'good' is taken to be 'fixed' by means of such a property. Thus an analysis of 'good' (one that is meant to reveal our understanding of the term) may be put in the following general form:

(*) for any x, x is good iff x has the property that actually fits the good-making role.

We might suppose, for example, that for a property to fit the good-making role is for it to be what is valued under ideal conditions of valuation, and that the property that actually fits this role is the property of promoting a balance of pleasure over pain. It would then be a metaphysical necessity that:

(**) for any x, x is good iff x promotes a balance of pleasure over pain.

However, in contrast to traditional versions of naturalism, (**) would be a posteriori, since it would be an a posteriori matter that the property of promoting a balance of pleasure over pain is what is valued under ideal conditions of valuation.[28]

---

[28] Wiggins (1987: 206), Lewis (1989: 132), Smith (1994: 190–2), and Jackson (1998: 143) are among those who have been tempted by a view of this sort.

An immediate consequence of this view is that it enables one to see normative necessity as a straightforward case of metaphysical necessity. For the normative necessities are merely those metaphysical necessities that arise from looking at the naturalistic content of the ethical predicates, without regard to how that content might have been fixed. Thus (**) above, the paradigm normative necessity from which all others follow, will also be a metaphysical necessity. The view is also able to preserve the distinction between the substantive criteria for goodness and what it is to be good; and it is not subject to our previous argument for the collapse of normative and conceptual necessity, for it is readily shown that the Inclusion assumption should be given up. Indeed, if it were to hold—that is, if each conceptual necessity were taken to be a normative necessity—then the Conservativity assumption would fail.[29]

However, I believe that the view is still open to serious objection.[30] Even though it may be capable of yielding a better account of the metaphysics of mortality than the traditional naturalist account, it is still not capable of yielding a satisfactory account of its epistemology. For it is unable properly to respect the non-empirical character of ethical belief.

In explaining what this is, there are two main problems that need to be addressed. The first is that of which ethical judgements should be taken to be non-empirical. The second is: in what should their non-empirical character be taken to consist. It clearly will not do to say that *all* ethical judgements are non-empirical; for that Joey did something wrong yesterday is clearly an empirical judgement, since its truth rests upon the empirical naturalistic fact that he did one thing rather than another. We might attempt to pre-empt the relevance of empirical judgements in this way by making the ethical judgements in question conditional upon a complete description of the facts. Thus an ethical judgement will now take the form: if this is how things are naturalistically (there follows a complete naturalistic description of how things might be), then this is how things are morally (there follows a partial account of how things should be). However, such a judgement might be true, not because the consequent is true, but because the antecedent is false, and in this case there would be no reason to expect it to be non-empirical. In order to get round this problem, I propose that we consider instead the normative necessity of the above judgement. Thus the judgement is now of the form: it is (normatively)

---

[29] Indeed, necessity will collapse to truth. For suppose that S is the case. Then it is a conceptual necessity that the actual truth-value of S is the truth-value of S, and a metaphysical necessity that the actual truth-value of S is True. So if the two necessities could be combined, it would be necessary that the truth-value of S is True, and hence necessary that S.

[30] As will become clear, the objection is also likely to apply to versions of naturalism that insist on functionality without also insisting on rigidity.

necessary that if this is how things are, then this would be good (say); or, to put it in counterfactual terms, if this is how things *were*, then this *would* be good.[31] Call such judgements *world-bound normative conditionals*. Then one formulation of the claim that ethics is non-empirical is that every world-bound normative conditional should be non-empirical.

We must now say in what the non-empirical character of an ethical judgement is to consist. One could adopt here a traditional characterization of the non-empirical, or a priori, as what can be known independently of experience. But this makes the claim that world-bound judgements are non-empirical highly problematic, both because it is not altogether clear that we can arrive at *knowledge* of such judgements, and also because it is not clear what epistemic role should be assigned to moral imagination and the like. I myself would not shrink from ascribing a strong form of aprioricity to ethical judgements. But in order not to prejudge the issue, I shall take the non-empirical character of ethics to consist in its conformity to what one might call *the criterion of perceptual independence*.

Let us use the term 'inner experience' to refer to experience that the subject does not take to be a case of veridical perception (we might also add the condition that the experience actually not be a case of veridical perception); and let us use the term 'outer experience' for any other kind of experience. The *criterion* for a judgement to be non-empirical is then:

> the reasons one can have for making the judgement (or its negation) on the basis of inner experience are as good as any reasons one can have;

and the corresponding *principle of perceptual independence* for ethics is that:

> the reasons one can have for judging a world-bound normative conditional to be true (or false) on the basis of inner experience are as good as any reasons one can have.[32]

---

[31] It may not be necessary to give a complete description of a world, but merely one that is qualitatively complete. And, in this case, what we may have is not strictly speaking a conditional, but a universal claim of the form $\forall x\ (Fx \supset Gx)$, where F is naturalistic and G normative. I shall not concern myself with such niceties in the text.

[32] It might be argued that if every world-bound normative conditional is non-empirical, then so is any normative necessity whatever. For let $D_1, D_2, \ldots$ be an exhaustive list of all world descriptions, and suppose A is a normative necessity. Then:

(i) $\boxed{n}\,(D_1 \lor D_2 \lor \ldots)$;

and

(ii) $\boxed{n}\,(D_i \supset A)$ for each world description D_i.

Now $\boxed{n}$ A logically follows from (i) and (ii), and so, given that (i) and (ii) are non-empirical, it is plausible to suppose that $\boxed{n}$ A is also non-empirical.

The principle does not commit one to having some special kind of a priori access to ethical truth, since it is perfectly compatible with inner experience providing us with an empirical basis for our ethical beliefs. Thus it allows one to steer a middle course between embracing a strong form of empiricism for ethical inquiry, on the one hand, and a strong form of apriorism on the other. Nor does the principle require one to deny that outer experience could be helpful in coming to the conditional judgements. It merely requires that, in such cases, the experience be dispensable—that whatever probative value it might have could always in principle be matched by the probative value of some inner experience. Thus someone who took himself to be a brain in a vat (and perhaps is a brain in a vat) will be in as good an epistemic position to arrive at the judgements in question as a creature firmly ensconced in the real world.

Before applying the principle, it will help to clarify it further. In the first place, it should be clear that the principle is intended to apply to an ideal cognizer who is capable of grasping a complete description of a world. This idealization is merely a device to factor out irrelevant empirical considerations and, in actual applications of the principle, could probably be weakened. For all that we require is that the antecedent of the conditional should incorporate anything that might be empirically relevant to the truth of consequent. We might be in a position, for example, to say that there is something bad about a situation involving intense suffering, whatever other circumstances might prevail.

Second, even to grasp the concepts involved in the conditional judgement might require us to have certain outer experience.[33] Thus it should be taken for granted that the cognizer has had whatever outer experience is required in order to grasp the judgements in question. This means that our reformulation of the principle in terms of a brain in a vat may not be altogether accurate, since we must assume that the brain in the vat (perhaps in a previous 'embodied' existence) has had whatever outer experiences are required in order to grasp the relevant concepts.

Third, there are some reasons that are parasitic upon other reasons, in the sense that their cogency rests wholly upon the cogency of those other reasons.

However, the assumption that (i) is non-empirical is not entirely unproblematic. I am inclined to think it holds, since I take normative necessity to coincide with conceptual necessity in its application to naturalistic statements. But, on a view in which it is taken to coincide with metaphysical necessity, the assumption might be subject to doubt.

[33] I merely make this concession for the sake of argument. My own view is that the most basic ethical principles can be formulated in terms of concepts whose possession does not require any contact with the external world. Instead of talking of *human beings*, for example, which appears to require such contact, we can talk of *moral agents* or *conscious beings*, which does not.

Testimony is a clear case of what I have in mind; since the cogency of testimonial evidence rests upon the cogency of the reasons available to the person from whom the testimony is drawn. Now it is possible in cases of this sort that the parasitic reasons may have greater probative value than the reasons upon which they depend. I may have good reason to believe some testimony, for example, even though the person providing the testimony has no good reason for saying what he does. Let us call a reason of this sort *unsustainable*. The principle should then be restricted to sustainable reasons, since it may not be possible to match an unsustainable reason, obtained on the basis of outer experience, with a reason obtained on the basis of inner experience.[34]

With these clarifications in place, I hope it is clear that the principle is indeed plausible. For how might outer experience provide reasons for forming an ethical judgement? One way is for it to inform me of the circumstances in which the moral concepts are to be applied. But this is irrelevant in the present case, since the relevant circumstances are already completely specified in the antecedent of the conditional. Another way is for it to make vivid to me *how* the concepts are to be applied in any given circumstance. It may be through seeing one person torture another, for example, that I learn to appreciate how awful torture is. But in so far as outer experience teaches me this lesson (without also informing me of the relevant circumstances), then it would appear to be irrelevant that the experience is, or is taken to be, veridical. Suppose, after what I take to be an experience of seeing one person torture another, I learn that the experience was not veridical. Does this make the moral lesson I take away from the experience any less worthy of consideration? Surely not. Surely what I learn from the experience is something that I could have learnt from a virtual form of the experience or even from a highly developed moral imagination.[35] Finally, a trusted moral authority might inform me that such-and-such an ethical judgement was correct. But in that case, given that my reason for trusting the authority is sustainable, I can simply take myself to have whatever reason the authority might have. If it is constituted by inner experience, all well and good; if it is not, then it can ('by induction') be replaced by whatever inner experience might serve in its place. It seems to me that these are essentially the only kinds of case that can arise; so, granted the adequacy of my responses, the principle is secure.

---

[34] It was an objection of Tony Martin's that made clear to me the need for a qualification of this sort.

[35] It is partly for this reason that fiction can function so effectively as a substitute for experience in the development of moral sensibility.

Let us return to the neo-naturalist. There will be for him world-bound normative conditional truths that are a posteriori. For whether a property *P* fits the good-making role is presumably a contingent (and a posteriori) matter. Indeed, if it were not, then the use of 'actually' in the formulation (★) of the position would be unnecessary, and the view would collapse into a version of the traditional form of naturalism. Consider now a world-bound normative conditional, such as: necessarily, if this is how things are, then this is good. Then, in general, to determine whether this is true will require determining what property actually satisfies the good-making role.

But the neo-naturalist now faces an intolerable dilemma. For consider his account of the good-making role. There are two possibilities: (i) it is egocentric in the sense of being indexed to the speaker; (ii) it is not egocentric—that is, it is either indexed, though not simply to the speaker, or not indexed at all. The first case is illustrated by 'the property *I* would value (under ideal circumstances)', and the second two cases by 'the property *we* would value' and by 'the property *everyone* would value'. Now in any plausible version of the first option, there will be no genuine possibility of moral disagreement; for each of us, in talking about what is good, will essentially be talking about ourselves. We might attempt to secure the possibility of moral disagreement by adopting the other option. But the non-empirical character of ethical judgement will then be lost. For whether a world-bound conditional holds will in general depend upon what in fact fits the good-making role; and this, in turn, will depend upon how things are 'outside' myself. But, in that case, it is hard to see why having a window on the world (or taking myself to have such a window) would not put me in a better position to determine whether the conditional holds. Thus it appears that our neo-naturalist must either deny that there are genuine moral disagreements or must give up on the non-empirical character of ethical belief.

One might attempt to finesse this difficulty by taking the good-making role to be a question of our ideal valuational dispositions and yet taking it to be an a priori matter that we all have the same ideal dispositions. Thus it will be sufficient to ascertain my own dispositions (on the basis of inner experience) in order to ascertain them all. But the problem with this intermediate position is in seeing how it might be contingent that I have the ideal dispositions that I do and yet a priori that you have the same dispositions as me. How can my other possible self be so different from you?

There is another version of neo-naturalism that appears to avoid these difficulties. It holds, in common with the previous version, that it is an a posteriori metaphysical necessity that goodness is (or coincides with) such-and-such a naturalistic property, but it denies that any specific good-making role is part of our understanding of the term 'good'. The reference of the term, on this view, is taken to be determined 'empirically' rather than 'conceptually'. It is given by causal or other such links between our use of the term and the real world—in much the same way, so it has been supposed, as the reference of natural kind terms, such as 'electron' or 'water'.[36]

This approach avoids the previous dilemma, since it no longer provides us with any descriptive content for the good-making role by which the dilemma might be stated. But it is still subject to a serious epistemological problem. For what is this mechanism for fixing reference, that both allows for genuine disagreement on matters of morality and yet respects the non-empirical character of moral belief, meant to be? How can the reference of the terms hook up to the real world, yet our justification for believing a substantive body of ethical truths not require any access (or any substantive access) to that world?

On this point, the much-vaunted analogy with natural kinds is of little help, and actually stands in the way of seeing what the mechanism might be. For our beliefs concerning natural kinds are not in general independent of perceptual experience. If we were to learn that most of our perceptual experience was non-veridical, then little would be left of our knowledge of natural kinds. The brain-in-the-vat is at a severe epistemic disadvantage in coming to any form of scientific knowledge; and if there really were an analogy between our understanding of scientific and of ethical terms, then one would expect him to be at an equal disadvantage in the effort to acquire moral wisdom. It is for this reason that the continuity in moral and scientific inquiry so much stressed by writers such as Boyd (1988: 123–4) and Railton (1986: 138) appears entirely misplaced. A much better analogy is with our understanding of mathematical terms, for which the idea of a hook-up with the real world is far less plausible.

I conclude that naturalism, in either its traditional or contemporary versions, is unable to rescue the doctrine that normative necessity is a species of conceptual or metaphysical necessity. There remains the possibility, of course, that normative necessity might somehow be definable in terms of another form of necessity; and two proposals along these lines may briefly be considered. One is that a normative necessity should be taken to be a normative (or moral) proposition that is true in all possible circumstances, where the circumstances are given in entirely naturalistic terms, so that there is no danger that the form of possibility by which they are qualified is moral. The error in this suggestion is that if the circumstances are taken to be naturalistic, then the idea of a moral proposition's being true *in* such a circumstance—that is, of there being a necessary connection between the circumstance and the truth of the proposition—presupposes the very notion of necessity in question.

---

[36] Sturgeon (1984), Boyd (1988), Brink (1989), and Railton (1986) adopt a view of this sort.

The second proposal is that normative necessity be taken to be a form of relative necessity. We specify the moral laws without appeal to the notion of normative necessity, and then define a normative necessity to be whatever is entailed by the moral laws. But it is not altogether clear how we might define the moral laws without appeal to the notion of normative necessity, and the view is subject, in any case, to the difficulty that it trivializes the form of necessity possessed by the moral laws themselves.

The notion of normative necessity would therefore appear to constitute yet another basic form of necessity.[37]

6 Modal Pluralism

There remains another possibility for defining the notions of metaphysical, natural, and normative necessity. For perhaps one or other of these notions can be defined as the restriction of a more comprehensive notion of necessity. Indeed, if each could be defined as the restriction of the most comprehensive notion of necessity, then modal monism could be saved.

Perhaps the most plausible suggestion of this sort is that metaphysical necessity be defined as a restriction of the (inclusive) notion of natural necessity. In this case, there is arguably no difficulty in stating the relevant restriction in non-modal terms. For the metaphysical necessities can be taken to be those natural necessities that are essential truths. This definition is reminiscent of the earlier proposal that metaphysical necessity be defined as essentialist truth, but it does not suffer from the same difficulty over modal force, since modal force is now included in the requirement that the essentialist truth should be a natural necessity.

There is, however, a related difficulty. For we do not thereby appear to capture the *relevant* modal force. There appears to be an intuitive difference to the kind of necessity attaching to metaphysical and natural necessities (granted that some natural necessities are not metaphysical). The former is somehow 'harder' or 'stricter' than the latter.[38] If we were to suppose that a God were capable of breaking necessary connections, then it would take more of a God to break a connection that was metaphysically necessary than one that was naturally necessary. It would be harder, for example, to break the connection

---

[37] As far as I know, Moore (1922: 275) was the first to suggest that there might be a distinctive form of normative necessity, in his marvellous paper 'The Conception of Intrinsic Value'.

[38] It seems to be something like this that Kripke (1980: 99) has in mind when he talks of necessity 'in the highest degree'.

between the truth of P & Q and the truth of P than the connection between cause and effect. It is also because of this difference in strictness that it is so much more plausible to think of the natural necessities as already including the metaphysical necessities than it is to think of the metaphysical necessities as already including the natural necessities.

It is difficult to say in more precise terms what this difference comes to. But one way to bring it out is in terms of the consequences of a proposition failing to be necessary. A proposition may fail to be metaphysically necessary even though it is naturally necessary. Perhaps it is a natural necessity that *e* causes *f*, though not a metaphysical necessity. Now we are inclined to think in such a case that there exists a genuine possibility of the proposition's being false. On the other hand, if a proposition were a metaphysical necessity, though not a natural necessity (in the narrow sense), then there would be no genuine possibility of its being false, since the 'hardness' of the metaphysical necessity would stand in the way.

I am inclined to think that the objections become more compelling when we consider the possibility that natural and normative or metaphysical and normative necessities might both be restrictions of a more comprehensive notion of necessity. For the character of the necessities seems even more strikingly different in these cases, and, in addition, there are difficulties in seeing how the relevant kind of restriction might be defined. It will not do to say, for example, that a normative necessity is a comprehensive necessity that essentially involves moral (or other normative) components. For under certain strange theological views, it may be a natural necessity, and hence a comprehensive necessity, that what in fact is the actual world is the best of all possible worlds. This is a comprehensive necessity that essentially involves a normative component, yet it is not naturally taken to be a normative necessity, for normative necessity is biased not towards things going well, morally speaking, but merely towards things going in the appropriate moral manner, good or bad, given how things are.

I conclude that there are three distinct sources of necessity—the identity of things, the natural order, and the normative order—and that each gives rise to its own peculiar form of necessity. Neither form of necessity can be subsumed, defined, or otherwise understood by reference to any other forms of necessity; and any other form of necessity, if my survey is complete, can be understood by reference to them. I have no a priori commitment to there being these three forms; but I must admit to finding some satisfaction in the thought that the three main areas of human inquiry—metaphysics, science, and ethics—should each give rise to their own form of necessity.

There has been a tendency in recent discussions of modality to focus on the notion of metaphysical necessity, just as earlier there had been a tendency to focus on the narrow notion of logical necessity. But it needs to be remembered that there are other forms of necessity, not intelligible in terms of these, that are equally important for philosophy, and equally worthy of study. Philosophers like to think of themselves as having found the key to the universe. But where there are many locks, it should be recognized that we may have need of many keys.

REFERENCES

Almog, Joseph (1991), 'The What and the How', *Journal of Philosophy*, 88(5): 225–44.

Armstrong, David (1983), *What is a Law of Nature?* (Cambridge: Cambridge University Press).

Bacon, John, Campbell, Keith, and Reinhardt, Lloyd (1993) (eds.), *Ontology, Causality and Mind: Essays in Honor of D. M. Armstrong* (Cambridge: Cambridge University Press).

Boyd, Richard (1988), 'How to be a Moral Realist', in Geoffrey Sayre-McCord (ed.), *Essays on Moral Realism* (Ithaca, NY: Cornell University Press), 181–228; repr. in Darwall *et al.* (1997), 105–36.

Brink, David (1989), *Moral Realism and the Foundations of Ethics* (Cambridge: Cambridge University Press).

Carroll, John W. (1994), *Laws of Nature* (Cambridge: Cambridge University Press).

Chalmers, Alan (1999), 'Making Sense of Physical Laws', in Sankey (1999), 3–15.

Darwall, Stephen, Gibbard, Alan, and Railton, Peter (1997) (eds.), *Moral Discourse and Practice: Some Philosophical Approaches* (Oxford: Oxford University Press).

Dreier, James (1992), 'The Supervenience Argument against Moral Realism', *Southern Journal of Philosophy*, 30(3): 13–38.

Ellis, Brian (1999), 'Causal Powers and Laws of Nature', in Sankey (1999), 21–42.

Fales, Evan (1993), 'Are Causal Laws Contingent?', in Bacon *et al.* (1993), 121–44.

Fine, Kit (1994), 'Essence and Modality', in James Tomberlin (ed.), *Philosophical Perspectives*, 8: 1–16; repr. in Grim *et al.* (1994), 151–66.

—— (2001), 'The Question of Realism', *Imprint*, 1(1): 1–30.

Friedman, Michael (1994), 'Geometry, Convention and the Relativized A Priori: Reichenbach, Schlick, and Carnap', in W. Salmon and G. Wolters (eds.), *Logic, Language, and the Structure of Scientific Theories* (Pittsburgh/Konstanz: University of Pittsburgh Press), 21–34; repr. in Grim *et al.*(1994), 167–80.

Grim, P., Mar, G., and Williams, P. (1994), *The Philosopher's Annual*, xvii-94 (Atascadero, Calif.: Ridgeview).

Jackson, Frank (1998), *From Metaphysics to Ethics: A Defence of Conceptual Analysis* (Oxford: Oxford University Press).

Klagge, James (1984), 'An Alleged Difficulty Concerning Moral Properties', *Mind*, 93: 370–80.

Kripke, Saul (1980), *Naming and Necessity* (Oxford: Blackwell).

Lewis, David (1989), 'Dispositional Theories of Value – II', *Proceedings of the Aristotelian Society*, supp. vol. 63: 113–37.

Lowe, E. J. (2001), 'Kinds, Essence, and Natural Necessity', forthcoming.

McFetridge, Ian (1985), 'Supervenience, Realism, Necessity', *Philosophical Quarterly*, 35: 245–58.

Moore, G. E. (1922), *Philosophical Studies* (London: Routledge & Kegan).

Railton, Peter (1986), 'Moral Realism', *Philosophical Review*, 163–207; repr. in Darwall *et al.* (1997), 137–66.

Sankey, Howard (1999) (ed.), *Causation and Laws of Nature* (Dordrecht: D. Reidel).

Shoemaker, Sydney (1980), 'Causality and Properties', in Peter van Inwagen (ed.), *Time and Cause* (Dordrecht: D. Reidel), 109–35; repr. in *Identity, Cause and Mind: Philosophical Essays* (Cambridge: Cambridge University Press, 1984), 234–60.

—— (1985), 'Review of S. Blackburn's "Spreading the Word"', *Nous*, 19: 438–42.

—— (1998), 'Causal and Metaphysical Necessity', *Pacific Philosophical Quarterly*, 79: 59–77.

Smith, Michael (1994), *The Moral Problem* (Oxford: Blackwell).

Sturgeon, Nicholas L. (1984), 'Moral Explanations', in D. Copp and D. Zimmerman (eds.), *Morality, Reason and Truth: New Essays in the Foundations of Ethics* (Totowa, NJ: Rowman & Allenhead), 49–78.

Swoyer, Chris (1982), 'The Nature of Natural Laws', *Australasian Journal of Philosophy*, 60: 203–23.

Van Fraassen, Bas (1977), 'The Only Necessity is Verbal Necessity', *Journal of Philosophy*, 74(2): 71–85.

Wiggins, David (1987), *A Sensible Subjectivism?*, Aristotelian Society Series, 6 (Oxford: Blackwell).

Zangwill, Nick (1995), 'Moral Supervenience', *Midwest Studies in Philosophy*, 20: 240–62.

7

A Study in Modal Deviance

GIDEON ROSEN

*Despite the indulgence of the editors, I have been unable to complete my own contribu-
tion to the present volume in time for publication. In its place I offer the following 'meditation' (for lack of a better word). The author is a distant cousin of mine from the old
country—a professor of arithmetical philosophy at the University of——, and (to judge
from a mimeographed Festschrift presented to him by his students) a notoriously unreliable melancholic. The document arrived in a box with the rest of my cousin's literary
remains. Internal evidence suggests that it was drafted during the period of his final ill-
ness—a 'fever in the brain', according to the lamentably terse cover note. I have been
unable to verify the anthropological citations. (G.R.)*

These notes are prompted by a report in a recent number of the *Journal
of Metaphysical Anthropology* (von Feld *et al.*, 'Modal Deviance among the
Q', *J. Met. Ant.* (Brest Litovsk), 17: 1253). The observation concerns a small
population concentrated in the gloomy forests of our northern district. The Q,
as they are called, are remarkably sophisticated in many ways. They cultivate
fluency in the major European languages, and the library at the small technical
university in their principal village receives scientific materials from around the
world—though often late, as the mail can take years to reach them, and always

I would like to thank Tamar Szabó Gendler and John Hawthorne for their patience and for their
very helpful comments on this paper.

with certain passages excised by the censor. Their doctrines are for the most part unexceptionable. (Their curious rituals are another matter.) In mathematics, in particular, they are admirably orthodox. As children, they master basic arithmetic, geometry, and some algebra. As advanced students, they are introduced to the higher reaches of the subject, and their scholars are responsible for charming contributions in several areas. Their peculiar deviance is not mathematical, but metaphysical.

The Q have followed recent trends in modal metaphysics with some avidity. The dog-eared copy of *Naming and Necessity* in the university library has been checked out by nearly everyone in the village at one time or another. Indeed, it is not uncommon among the Q for houses to be decorated with framed extracts from this and other beloved texts, carefully copied on to yak skin and illustrated with colorful diagrams. Von Feld and his colleagues were able to interview several informants on modal matters, and for the most part their modal opinions are quite conventional and quite correct. The Q regard the truths of logic—for them, classical second-order logic—as metaphysically necessary (though they are aware of distant controversy on this point), and they take a similar view of 'analytic' or 'conceptual' truths. Their intuitions concerning the essences of ordinary individuals, kinds, and stuffs are coincident with our own. They believe that Napoleon is essentially (at least initially) human, that his origin is essential to him, that the water in their wells could not possibly have been an element, and so on. There is lively controversy on certain questions which our scholars also have not resolved. (There are two synagogues in the village: one for strict adherents of S5, one for those who advocate more liberal systems.) But in most respects the Q-villagers would not be out of place in a seminar on modal metaphysics in my own university—their frankly idiotic local costumes notwithstanding.

Their perversity is for the most part confined to a single topic. The Q believe that the truths of pure mathematics—and in particular, the truths of arithmetic—might have been false. They understand that this is a deviant view, and that with the exception of the reliably perverse John Stuart Mill, no philosopher in the canon from which they draw their instruction has ever held it.[1] They find this puzzling. They note it, but they cannot explain it. For their part they find it perfectly obvious that certain facts of number theory might have been otherwise: that, unlike the facts of logic and like the facts of human history, they are metaphysically contingent: true in some genuinely possible worlds, false in others.

---

[1] Robinson (1979: 69 ff.). A related view is defended by Hartry Field (1993). Field's discussion is restricted to the 'conceptual' modalities. He rejects the notion of metaphysical necessity in terms of which the Q (and we) frame the issue.

Von Feld was able to elicit extensive testimony upon this topic. His affable informants were pleased to encounter emissaries from what is for them a baffling orthodoxy. For some time there has been a current of speculation among the Q that a powerful argument for the absolute necessity of mathematics must be known to the tradition despite its absence from their sources. The Q were eager to explain their views in the hope that the investigators might disclose to them the details of this vanished argument.

I have in my possession a facsimile of von Feld's shorthand field notes from his interviews with the Q. These notes are meticulous: I can almost hear the voices of these distant farmers. And much as I would like to dismiss their perversity as yet another ethnological curiosity, I am beginning to suspect that the encounter has affected my nerves. I am losing sleep. My head has begun to itch—on the inside! Sometimes my own firm conviction begins to waver. I shall copy out the crucial passages below.

Von Feld: You accept standard number theory. So you believe that as a matter of fact $2+3=5$, there are infinitely many prime numbers, and so on. And yet you regard these truths as contingent. Perhaps you think that in another possible universe $2+3=6$?

Vozmozhinski (a small professor at the technical university): Not at all. We reject the possibility of a 'queer' arithmetic in which the arithmetical relations among the natural numbers are somehow altered. The very idea involves a contradiction. Nothing deserves to be called a bachelor unless it is unmarried; and likewise, no collection of things deserves be called '2', '3', '5', and '+' unless they satisfy the condition '$2+3=5$'. Of course this particular constraint is not basic. The basic constraints in the area include a version of what is sometimes called 'Hume's Principle':

> *A* deserves to be called 'the number of *F*s' iff for all *G*, *A* is the number of *G*s iff there are just as many *F*s as *G*s.

They also include definitions of the individual numerals and the arithmetical operations:

> *A* deserves to be called '0' iff for some *F*, *A* is the number of *F*s and there are no *F*s.
>
> *A* deserves to be called 'the successor of *B*' iff for some *F* and *G*,
>
> > *A* is the number of *F*s and *B* is the number of *G*s and there is exactly one thing that is *F* but not *G*.
>
> *A* deserves to be called '1' iff it is the successor of 0; '2' iff it is the successor of 1, etc. *C* deserves to be called 'the sum of *A* and *B*' iff for some *F* and *G*:
>
> > *A* is the number *F*s and *B* is the number of *G*s and no *F* is a *G* and *C* is the number of (*F* or *G*)s.

And so on. These metalinguistic constraints correspond to statements in the language of arithmetic, all of which strike us as manifestly 'analytic'. To deny any one of them is to come as close as one can come to outright contradiction short of asserting 'Fred is a yak and not a yak'. But these facts rule out the possibility of a substantive nonstandard arithmetic. So as far as we are concerned, a universe in which $2+3=6$ is like a world of married bachelors: an absolute impossibility.

But of course there might have been no bachelors—that's clearly possible—and if there had been no bachelors, then the bachelor-theoretic facts would have been different. And likewise we think: there could have been no numbers—that's clearly possible—and if there had been no numbers, the number-theoretic facts would have been different. '$2+3=5$' entails 'There is such a thing as the number 5'. And like every existential theorem of arithmetic, this claim might have been false. Of course the universal theorems of number theory would have been vacuously true even if there had been no numbers. So we don't see how *they* could possibly have been false. But the existential truths of number theory? True in this world, false in others.

Von Feld: So you believe that in some other possible world there are exactly two yaks in the field—$\exists x \, \exists y$ (x is a yak in the field, and y is another yak in the field, and nothing else is a yak in the field)—but the number of yaks in the field is not 2? Is that not also a contradiction in terms?

Vozmozhinski: Not that I can see. It would be a contradiction if it were given that numbers exist in this world. A conditional version of the principle connecting numerically definite quantification with explicit attributions of number is indeed analytic:

> *If there is such a thing as the number of Fs*, then the number of Fs$=n$ iff there are exactly *n* Fs.

But since it's contingent whether numbers exist, the consequent of this conditional is also contingent.

Von Feld: But it is customary to suppose that the numbers exist necessarily. Even Kripke says, somewhere . . . as if it were obvious . . . Hand me that book, please. Yes, here it is:

> the peculiar character of mathematical propositions (like Goldbach's conjecture) is that one knows (*a priori*) that they cannot be contingently true; a mathematical statement, if true, is necessary.[2]

Vozmozhinski: We know he says that. We just can't see why—and that's what puzzles us. Most of the modal metaphysics that comes to us from abroad

---

[2] Kripke (1980: 159).

seems so sensible. When some learned author claims that this or that modal judgment is 'intuitive' or 'obvious', we agree. But when it comes to the necessary existence of numbers, we just don't get it. It strikes us as perfectly obvious that there might have been no snakes. And it strikes us as just as obvious that there might have been no numbers.

Von Feld: Can you tell me *why* you believe that the existence of numbers is a contingent matter? I am not asking for the causes of your opinion. I am curious about your reasons.

Vozmozhinski: Well it's just obvious, isn't it? Do we need more of a reason than that?

Von Feld: When the experts are unanimous in rejecting your position, perhaps you do need something more. But in any case, we can sometimes offer reasons for what we find obvious, as when we prove from first principles that $2+3=5$. What would you say if one of your children asked you to justify your position? Can you do no better than to say, 'Well it's just obvious, isn't it?'

Vozmozhinski: Well, the children do sometimes wonder about this. (They also wonder about the existence of the external world!) And when they do, we have answers for them. I'd be happy to review them for you, if you promise later on to tell me why *you* believe that numbers exist necessarily.

Von Feld: Very well. [Does the great von Feld's hand begin to tremble here? Yes, I believe it does.]

Vozmozhinski: We have three arguments for the contingency of numbers. We don't pretend that they're conclusive. Each one appeals to a defeasible form of inference or to a controversial modal principle. They tend to work on our children, but perhaps that's not saying much. In any case, we're hoping you'll tell us where exactly they go wrong.

The argument from vivid conceivability

I might have had eleven fingers. How do I know? I don't derive this modal claim from some more general modal principle. Rather, I can *vividly conceive* a world in which I have eleven fingers. I can represent such a world—in this case, I can imagine it; but I could also draw you a picture—and when I do, the world I represent strikes me as a possibility: it seems possible to me. This modal seeming is analogous in certain respects to visual seeming. How do I know that my tunic is blue? Well it looks blue to me, and I have no special reason to doubt my senses. Such visual seeming—the tunic's looking blue to me—is not itself a judgment. When I see an oar in the water, it looks broken in the relevant sense, even when I know (and hence judge) that it is intact. Visual seeming is a pre-doxastic intentional state that often causes a corresponding belief. It is phenomenologically vivid: it is typically conscious and introspectible. And it is a resource for justification. It is a general principle of epistemology that if it visually seems to you that x is F, then you are justified in believing that x is F unless you have some special reason for discounting the appearances. Likewise in the modal case: if you can vividly conceive a world at which you have eleven fingers—if such a world strikes you as clearly possible—then you are justified in believing that you might have had eleven fingers, unless you have some special reason to resist the inference from vivid conceivability to possibility in this case.

The analogy is not perfect. In the visual case we possess a reasonably developed account of the underlying mechanism, and we know quite a bit about the conditions under which its reports are reliable. In the modal case we have no analogous account. But even in the visual case the transition from 'seems' to 'is' does not *require* such a theory. (The Neanderthal were justified in treating visual appearance as a guide to reality.) So if you can vividly conceive a world in which there are no numbers, then you have a reason to believe that numbers might not have existed, unless you have special grounds for doubting your faculties.

But of course you *can* conceive a world in which there are no numbers. Start by conceiving a world where standard arithmetic is true. The actual world will do; but it will not be enough simply to open up your eyes and look around. It will be important to bring the relevant mathematical aspects of actuality into relief. And this is not straightforward. The numbers are invisible, after all. So it will not do simply to call up an image and to say to yourself, 'Let's consider a world that looks like *that*'. But this is not to say that images and pictures are irrelevant. When a physicist thinks about the standard model of particle physics, the content of his thought is not exhausted by the images he entertains. But it would be surprising if images did not figure centrally in his thinking, and rightly so. Images play a legitimate (if undertheorized) role in metaphysical thinking as well. (Of course they can mislead us. But what form of thinking can't?) So the first order of business is to call up an image of the actual world—a diagram or a cartoon, if you like—that highlights the mathematical aspects of reality that interest us.

Now a world in which arithmetic is true is a world in which numbers exist. (If you doubt this—if you think that it might be true that there are ten prime numbers less than 30 even though there are no numbers—then we really don't know what to say. You are perhaps already too far gone.) Moreover, a world in which numbers exist must contain infinitely many distinct objects. A 'model' for standard arithmetic requires nothing more. A world with infinitely many Roman emperors or space-time regions supplies a model in this sense. And yet it seems reasonably clear that our conception

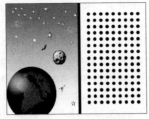

Fig. 1. A world containing infinitely many pure abstract objects.

of the numbers requires something more. As Frege says, we know a priori that Julius Caesar is not a number,[3] and the same goes for the volume of space-time Caesar occupies. A world that featured only Julius Caesar and his ilk would therefore be a world without numbers, no matter how extensive its inventory. The point is usually made by saying that numbers are abstract entities, and that's fine so long as nothing very definite is intended. It is clearly some sort of a mistake to suppose that the number 11 might exist in Lenin's tomb, or for one brief shining moment in 1917. That numbers are abstract in this sense does not follow from the standard axioms for arithmetic. But that just means that axiomatic arithmetic provides a partial account of what it takes to be a number.[4]

A world in which standard arithmetic is true is thus a world containing infinitely many pure abstract objects. And it is easy enough to picture—or better, diagram—a world of this sort.

The picture is crude, needless to say. But you may object that it is also misleading in one crucial respect. We have just finished saying that the numbers are in some good sense nonspatial. And yet the picture (you may say) represents them as located at some *distance* from the natural world. And yet surely, you may say, a picture that gets so much wrong at the start is worse than useless as an aid for modal thinking. (See Figure 1.)

But this is to misconstrue the diagram. The images that represent the numbers are certainly located in space, and there is a spatial gap between these number-images and the image of the concrete world. But the number-images are also small, black, and round. And yet you were not even tempted to suppose that *according to the picture, the numbers are small black dots*. The spatial gap in

---

[3] Frege (1980: sect. 66).

[4] Crispin Wright and Bob Hale have proposed to derive the abstractness of numbers from their preferred axiomatization (by means of Hume's Principle) together with the claim that axiomatization suffices to explain the concept of number. But even if the requisite derivation is unavailable, it might still be built into our concept of number that numbers are nonspatial, nonphysical, and the rest.

the picture is not an icon. It is not meant to resemble the state of affairs it depicts. It is rather a diagrammatic representation of a fact that is otherwise hard to picture: the fact that numbers and ordinary concrete things are *mereologically distinct* from one another. Not only is Caesar not a number. He is not made of numbers, and numbers are not made of him; nor do they have any ingredients in common. Numbers are neither parts nor aspects nor constituents of concrete things; and vice versa, numbers are neither made of, nor constituted by, nor constructed from, concrete individuals.

This may be part of what is meant by saying that numbers are *pure* abstract objects. The set containing Pushkin and Chekov is apparently constituted from these two great authors: if they had not existed, it would not have existed. Pushkin's masterpiece, *Evgenii Onegin*, is also somehow entangled with the concrete world. It is not itself an aggregate or set of material things. But if Pushkin had not written or spoken certain (concrete) words, there would be no such poem. The poet's literary activity somehow grounds (and indeed, plausibly suffices for) its existence, even if the poem itself does not contain Pushkin's inscriptions as literal parts or constituents.

In the case of numbers, however, there would appear to be no such entanglement. There are many ways in which one thing can be made up out of, or constituted by, or grounded in, other things. But the numbers are not made out of emperors in any sense. That is what the spatial gap in the picture is meant to signify. And once we've said this explicitly, the picture should not mislead us. It may still be crude in any number of respects. But for all we have seen, it does not embody an outright falsehood.

If you understand the sort of world the picture is meant to illustrate, and if such a world strikes you as clearly possible (perhaps because actual), then you can conceive a world in which infinitely many pure abstract objects exist. This may be equivalent to conceiving a world in which the numbers exist. But even if it is not—even if the existence of the numbers requires more— clearly any world at which numbers exist must be a world of this sort. And that being so, there's an easy recipe for conceiving a world without numbers.

Start with the actual world as pictured in the diagram: then erase the right-hand side. You are now conceiving a world just like the actual world in concrete respects, but altogether bereft of pure mathematical objects. If you can't perform the exercise, then I don't know what to say. We find it perfectly straightforward. Of course you won't get anywhere if you try to picture a contrast between how things would *look* to similarly situated agents in the two worlds. The worlds will look just the same from the inside—or from the outside, for that matter. The numbers are invisible, after all. If you insist on the etymological connection between 'image' and 'imagine', then we concede that the contrast is strictly speaking unimaginable. Even so, this is not to say that a world without numbers cannot be imagined; it is only to say that there is no difference between imagining a numberless world and imagining an otherwise similar world replete with numbers. (In the same sense there is no difference between imagining a man grimacing in genuine pain and imagining a man pretending to grimace in pain. But no one would suggest that we cannot imagine a man who is grimacing in genuine pain.) And in any case, 'imagination' is not the crucial concept for our purpose. Even if you cannot 'imagine' a world without numbers, you can conceive one by means of images. If you can conceive a world that corresponds to the original picture, you can conceive a world that corresponds to the reduced version in which the right-hand side has been erased. And in conceiving the latter world you are conceiving a different world—one in which standard arithmetic is false because there are no numbers.[5]

A 'Humean' argument

This pictorial argument is an application of a familiar modal principle: the Humean stricture against necessary connections between distinct existences. And for those who are wary of the appeal to pictures in metaphysics, we sometimes offer an explicitly 'principle-driven' version of the case.

The most straightforward statement of the Humean stricture has it that if A and B are distinct—if they share no common part or ingredient or constituent—then it is possible for the one to exist without the other. But this is clearly too strong. Some individuals have relational essences. Sometimes it is essential to A that A bear R to B, even though A and B are distinct, and in cases of this sort the straightforward principle does not hold. I am distinct from my paternal grandfather in the relevant sense. But there is no possible world in which I exist but he does not.

A more plausible version of the principle is due to David Lewis:[6]

(HS) If A and B are distinct, then it is possible for a perfect intrinsic duplicate of the one to exist without the other.

HS is not liable to the counter-example. It is possible for a perfect duplicate of me to exist in the absence of any duplicate of my grandfather. Indeed, it is possible for a perfect duplicate of me to exist in the absence anything distinct

---

[5] [*Vivid conceivability* corresponds roughly to what David Chalmers calls '(ideal) positive conceivability'. See his Ch. 3 above.—G. R.]   [6] Lewis (1986: sect. 1.8).

from it. And indeed, this would seem to be a general principle (somewhat stronger than (HS)):

(HS$\star$) For any individual A, it is possible for there to be a perfect intrinsic duplicate of A and nothing distinct from it.[7]

Now when it comes to the natural numbers, it is unclear what 'perfect intrinsic duplication' would amount to. Mathematics itself has nothing to say about the qualitative nature of the numbers. The negative theology that is embodied in our ordinary understanding tells us very little: the numbers are *not* in space-time (whatever that means), and so they do not possess qualities that can only be instantiated by spatial things: shape, color, mass, and the like. For all we know, the objects of pure mathematics are like featureless abstract points. But equally, for all we know, they possess an abundance of intrinsic properties whose natures we cannot begin to fathom.

For present purposes, however, it does not matter whether we can make sense of the idea of a 'duplicate' of the number 17. The spatiotemporal world—the world on the left-hand side of our cartoon—is a large concrete particular with a complex intrinsic nature. If HS$\star$ is true, then there exists a possible world that contains a duplicate of the concrete world as it is *and nothing else*. But since the numbers would have to be something else if they existed, this would have to be a world in which the numbers do not exist.

An argument from 'strong coherence'

Finally, for those who reject the appeal to pictures and who find this particular application of Hume's stricture unconvincing, we offer the following (rather more speculative) argument from what we call 'strong coherence'.

Some philosophers believe that numbers do not exist, and that arithmetic is therefore false in the actual world. Since you accept standard arithmetic, you believe that these nominalists are mistaken. But even so, you know perfectly well what they think. You understand their position. You can reason about its consequences; you can pretend to believe it—try it on for size, as it were—and even if you still don't believe it, you know exactly what you're doing.

By itself, this does not entail that nominalism might have been true. After all, you know perfectly well what Frege meant when he endorsed the naïve principle of class abstraction. But we do not regard Frege's theory as a genuine possibility.

---

[7] If a thing is distinct from the space it occupies, then an exception for this space must be supplied. For present purposes this is an irrelevant complication.

There is, however, an important difference between the cases. Frege's system entails a contradiction—a manifest impossibility—and when we see this, it no longer strikes us as possible.[8] When we work our way through the nominalist's system, on the other hand, we encounter neither contradiction nor manifest absurdity. We can flesh out the nominalist's premise in any number of ways, making explicit what is implicit in the available formulations, stipulating detailed answers to questions the view leaves open, and so on. The limit of this process—a complete account of a single nominalistic world in all its specificity—is unattainable. But as we consider more and more detailed, more and more determinate, specifications of the nominalist's conceit, it becomes increasingly plausible that there is nothing incoherent in the position. The view may still strike us as wildly *implausible*, of course. It may strike us as on a par with Russell's hypothesis that the world was created five minutes ago with all the traces of an extensive past in place. But implausibility is one thing, incoherence another. And for all its craziness, nominalism would appear to be coherent.

Now of course, this appearance itself may be mistaken. The view may be self-undermining or absurd in ways that have yet to come to light. But those of us who have given the matter some thought are inclined to think otherwise. The compelling objections to modern nominalism are methodological rather than metaphysical.[9] The view is revisionary and (as we tend to think) under-motivated. It involves a gratuitous departure from the natural attitude towards mathematics. (In this respect it is analogous to more familiar forms of skeptical doubt, which involve a gratuitous departure from the natural attitude towards common sense or settled science.) The fictionalist stance that Field endorses may be rationally permissible.[10] But the arguments for the view purport to undermine the alternatives, and these destructive arguments are unconvincing.[11] But that is just to say that the positive case for Field's position is unpersuasive. It is not to say that the view is intrinsically incoherent. It may be misguided, but it is not absurd.

Now, coherence in this sense does not entail possibility. The ancients believed that pure water was a simple substance. That view is not absurd. You can think your way through it until the yaks come home with landing yourself in absurdity. But for all that, there is no possible world in which it is true.

---

[8] This has been denied. cf. Priest (1987).
[9] I have in mind the nominalism defended by Hartry Field (1980, 1989).
[10] For a defense of this claim, see Rosen (2001).
[11] For discussion, see Burgess and Rosen (1997).

But once again, there is an important difference between the cases. The hydrology of the ancients is *a priori coherent*. It does not entail, *a priori*, any manifest absurdity. But it is not, as we shall say, *strongly coherent*.[12] Let ϕ be a catalog of the categorical, nonmodal facts about the actual world. To say that *P* is strongly coherent is then to say that the conjunction, 'ϕ & $\Diamond P$' is a priori coherent. If *P* is strongly coherent, then there is no lurking contradiction or absurdity in the supposition that the actual world is, in all categorical respects, just as it actually is, while *P* holds in some other possible world. Somewhat less accurately, if more vividly, *P* is strongly coherent if a logically omniscient agent with full information about the nonmodal character of the actual world would see no incoherence in the supposition that *P* is possible. If you are ignorant or mistaken about the composition of water, you may see no incoherence in the supposition that it might have been an element. But if you know that water is a compound of hydrogen and oxygen—and if you know, moreover, that that is *what it is to be* water[13]—then you should find it incoherent to suppose that in some other possible world *that very substance* is an element. It is incoherent to suppose that what is by nature composite might have been simple. Ancient hydrology thus fails to be strongly coherent.

Now we hold (with certain qualifications that have no bearing on the present case) that *strong coherence is sufficient for genuine possibility*.[14] If the supposition that *P* holds in some possible world is neither intrinsically incoherent nor incoherent given the way the world is, then *P* might have been the case. Moreover, it is plausible that the nominalism is strongly coherent. We have already said that, so far as we can tell, the view is coherent in itself. So if it is strongly incoherent, there must be some nonmodal fact given which it is palpably absurd to suppose that there might have been no numbers. But not only are we unable to point to such a fact. We cannot imagine what it could possibly be. It is a fact, for example, that numbers exist in actuality. But even when we bear this in mind, it does not strike us as absurd or self-contradictory to suppose that there are genuine alternatives to actuality in which numbers do not exist.

Just to say it one more time, we could be wrong about this. Just as there might be some intrinsic absurdity in the nominalist's view, there might be some actual fact with which the supposition of its possibility is incoherent.

---

[12] [*Strong coherence* corresponds roughly to what David Chalmers calls 'ideal negative conceivability'. See his Ch. 3 above—G. R.]

[13] Facts about the real natures of individuals, stuffs, and properties—facts about what it is to be an F—are nonmodal in the relevant sense (if they exist at all). See Fine (1994).

[14] [For a discussion of these qualifications, see my, 'The Limits of Contingency', forthcoming in a volume edited by Fraser MacBride—G. R.]

But there comes a point at which failure to turn up a plausible example of such a fact counts as powerful grounds for thinking that none exists. There would appear to be no *obstacle* to the possibility of nominalism. There is no intrinsic absurdity in the view. It would appear to be coherent upon reflection informed by the facts. And given this we ask: Why couldn't it have been the case? If the plan makes sense, why couldn't God have followed it? We know why God could not have made a world in which water is a simple substance. Given that he didn't, the supposition that he could have is absurd. But why couldn't God have made a world without numbers?

That's it for the arguments. As we say, we don't pretend they're conclusive. The argument from vivid conceivability would be undermined if we could be persuaded that our (seeming) capacity vividly to conceive a *P*-world did not provide a prima-facie reason for thinking that *P* is possible, or if that reason could be overridden in this instance. The argument from Hume's stricture would be undermined if it could be shown that the stricture fails to apply in this (admittedly peculiar) case. The argument from strong conceivability would be undermined if strong conceivability turned out to be compatible with impossibility. And all of the arguments would come to nothing if it turned out that the supposition of a world without numbers involves a contradiction. Still, from where we sit, it now simply strikes us—thanks to these arguments and perhaps also thanks to some more immediate modal intuition—that numbers need not have existed. As Yablo has stressed,[15] when it strikes you that *P* is possible, the only dialectically effective antidote takes the following form: There must be an independently plausible case for some proposition *A*, and for the proposition that if *A* is true, then *P* is impossible. And that's our question for you. What is this proposition *A*? What is the *obstacle* to the possibility of a world without numbers? We've been more than forthcoming. Now it's your turn.

Here von Feld's notes leave off, but I am confident that he did not reply. Von Feld is an anthropologist—a towering figure—but he is not an evangelist. His job is to understand the Q, not to change them. But suppose he had been inclined to 'convert' the Q by answering. What could he have said? What can I say—I who believe as I have always believed: that the truths of pure arithmetic could not have been otherwise?

These yak farmers are not insane. To the contrary, they seem the very voice of sobriety. And upon reflection I must admit: their general precepts for modal argument ring true to my ears. I believe that our capacity vividly to conceive a

[15] Yablo (1993).

P-world gives us reason to believe that *P* is possible. I accept Hume's stricture against necessary connections between distinct existences. And (while the idea has never occurred to me before) it seems right that *P* is possible if the assumption of a *P*-world involves no absurdity given the actual facts. I do not believe that nominalism is incoherent in this sense. If challenged to cite an obstacle to the possibility of a nominalistic world, I am at a loss. Could it be that I—I who have devoted my long, miserable life to the single-minded cultivation of modal lucidity—could it be that I have nothing to say to the Q?

The game is lost if we concede that the world of numbers is a separate world of abstract things. This 'simple platonism' is at odds with the necessitarian orthodoxy that I so cherish. It is incoherent to suppose that there exists a domain of inexplicably robust abstract particulars, altogether distinct from the natural world and ungrounded in anything else, each of which exists as a matter of absolute necessity. Let it be that in our world a zoo of pure abstracta exists. We can imagine a world in which there are no such things. No incoherence results from the supposition of their absence. It is simply incredible to suppose that such things might nonetheless exist of necessity. You might as well say that the great cathedral just now visible from my attic window is a necessary being, despite my capacity vividly to conceive its absence.

No, what is needed is a reduction. We must make plausible some claim of the form:

To say that numbers exist is just to say that *A*,

or,

For it to be the case that numbers exist just is for it to be the case that *A*,

where *A* is an indisputably necessary truth—a truth even the Q would regard as necessary.

When I run through my library, I find no shortage of suitable proposals—developed doctrines in the foundations of mathematics that entail that 'Numbers exist' is in one way or another strongly equivalent to one or another necessary truth:

Numbers exist ⇔ If the Peano axioms are true, then numbers exist.
Numbers exist ⇔ The Peano axioms entail that numbers exist.
Numbers exist ⇔ It is consistent to suppose that numbers exist.
Numbers exist ⇔ Numbers might have existed.
Numbers exist ⇔ An ω-sequence might have existed.
Numbers exist ⇔ Countably many objects might have existed.
Numbers exist ⇔ For some concept/plurality *F*, there are just as many *F*s as there are *F*s.

In each case the right-hand side is a necessary truth. I am confident that even the Q would not deny this. But I am equally certain that they would reject the claim of strong equivalence (whether understood in semantic or in metaphysical terms)—not from pig-headedness, but in all honesty. I can just imagine their puzzled voices:

As far as we can tell, we speak the language well enough. But as we understand it, the sentence 'Numbers exist'—or, more minimally, 'There exist infinitely many pure abstract objects'—is not synonymous with any of the indisputably necessary truths you have enumerated. It does not feel like a contradiction to say that there might have been numbers (or numerals, or infinitely many objects, or what have you), but as a matter of fact numbers do not exist. If the equivalences are nonetheless analytic in the language we speak, then they must be among the unobvious analyticities, on a par with 'Second cousins share great grandparents' and the ε-δ analysis of continuity. But unobvious analytic principles can normally be made obvious, either by reflecting on their consequences or by deriving them from more basic analyticities. How are the derivations supposed to go in these cases? We are of course aware of some of the proposals. Your neo-logicists purport to derive all of arithmetic from what is meant to be some sort of necessary truth:

The number of Fs$=$the number of Gs iff there are just as many Fs as Gs.[16]

We do not deny that the axioms of Peano arithmetic follow analytically from this principle, given standard definitions of 'number', 'successor', and the rest. But the biconditional does not strike *us* as a conceptual truth—as true in virtue of meaning, as indisputable on pain of linguistic incompetence. It strikes as a substantive hypothesis—true, but contingent—to the effect that whenever there are just as many yak as there are reindeer, there exists an immaterial object—a number—to which the yak and the reindeer are both related. The nominalist may believe that there are just as many yak as reindeer; but as he sees it, this commitment does not entail the existence of anything as un-yak-like as a number. The nominalist may be wrong about the mathematical facts; but we do not believe that his rejection of this and similar principles signals imperfect mastery of the language. If you think that two sentences can be 'conceptually equivalent' even though an utterly competent speaker (a) accepts the one but rejects the other and (b) cannot be led to recognize his mistake by reflection and the exercise of his linguistic abilities, then we just don't know what you mean by 'conceptual equivalence'. Given the meanings we find ourselves in a position to attach to this phrase, the neo-logicist biconditional and the other proposed equivalences are not analytic in the language as we understand it. So if they are necessary, then they are necessary for some other reason.

But perhaps you will concede this point. Perhaps you will say, 'It is not a matter of meaning, but nevertheless: the *fact* that the number of Fs$=$the number of Gs simply

---

[16] See Wright (1983); Hale (1988).

consists in the fact that there are just as many *F*s as *G*s. Perhaps you will even say that they are one and the same fact.

And perhaps you would be right. There may be pre-modal truths about how the nonbasic facts are 'constituted'. The fact that Fred is a yak may consist in the fact that Fred is descended from the ur-yak; the fact that a yak is grazing on the moor may consist in the fact that the quarks and leptons are arranged thus-and-so. If the existence of numbers consists in one or another indisputably necessary fact in some such sense, then the nonexistence of numbers is not strongly conceivable after all. There is a fact—a nonmodal fact about the actual world—given which it is inconceivable that there should be a world without numbers. Our seeming capacity to conceive a numberless world depends upon our ignorance of just this fact. If it were known to us, the evidential force of these conceivings would be defeated. We would have an answer to our question, 'What prevents God from making a numberless world?' The answer would be: 'For numbers to exist just is for it to be the case that *A*, and clearly—even you will admit it—God could not have made a world at which *A* fails to be the case.'

But of course it is not enough to *assert* that some such pre-modal connection is in place. You must give us some reason to believe that it is in place. We are willing to believe that part of what it is to be a yak is to be an animal. But we are willing to believe this (in part) because, having learned that yaks *are* animals—and not, for example, robots controlled from the moon—we can no longer conceive a world in which yaks (*that very sort of thing*) exist but are not animals. If we thought that we could conceive a world in which yaks were machines, then we would reject this claim about what it is to be a yak until we were given some good reason to accept it. You could tell me that part of what it is for this samovar to exist is for there to be no fewer than 1,000,000 chickens in Novaya Zembla—and hence that the existence of this samovar entails the existence of a million chickens. But since I can picture the samovar in a chickenless world, I would not believe you unless you had much more to say. So you can't just assert that the existence of infinitely many pure abstract objects consists in some indisputably necessary state of affairs. If it still *seems* to me that the latter might obtain without the former, then I will not be in a position to believe what you say.

And I am afraid that the Q would be right about all this. The appeal to preexisting synonymy or to facts of pre-modal 'constitution' is dialectically weak, even if it is ultimately correct. If the Q have good reason to believe that there are worlds in which numbers do not exist of the sort rehearsed above, then it will reasonably strike them as implausible that 'Numbers exist' should be necessarily equivalent to a necessary truth. They will need to be shown that this is so. But how?

The latest number of the journal has just arrived, and it contains a curious report that gives me some small hope (H. Geofroi *et al.*, 'State-Sanctioned

Modal Structuralism among the Z', *J. Met. Ant.* 18: 1311). Geofroi and colleagues report an encounter with a highland tribe on St. Hilaire which in many ways echoes von Feld's encounter with the Q. The Z, as they are called, are similarly dedicated to philosophy and mathematics. However, unlike the Q, they regard the truths of pure mathematics as straightforwardly necessary. The Z are distinctive in possessing an argument for this necessitarian thesis—an argument that adverts to their peculiar system of mathematical education.

The Z do not learn arithmetic as we do (and as the Q do), by immersion in a practice of counting and calculation followed by self-conscious theory building and axiomatization. Rather, they are introduced to the subject as young adults by explicit instruction. After having mastered the metaphysical modal idiom in the usual way—that is, by immersion, followed by axiomatization and semantic reflection—the Z are introduced to the language of arithmetic as an *uninterpreted formalism*. They are told that the language contains a one-place predicate, N, a unary function symbol, s, and a constant symbol o, and that the well-formed formulae are defined in the standard way. But they are not told anything about what these novel sentences are supposed to mean. They are then invited to consider the conjunction of the second-order Dedekind–Peano axioms (PA) as an uninterpreted sentence in this new language. They are encouraged to practice operating with this sentence— to construct 'proofs' of novel sentences according to the standard rules of inference, to evaluate claims of entailment and consistency by constructing models, and so forth. But at this point this is little more than an exercise in formal logic.

The interpretation of the new language is then given by stipulation. Geofroi and colleagues quote at length from their *First Course in Arithmetic*.

Each sentence A in the language of arithmetic has a *modal structural counterpart*, $A^\star$, which may be constructed in stages. Begin with the material conditional:

(0) PA $[N, s, o] \supset A [N, s, o]$.

Now replace the nonlogical terms with new variables of the appropriate type and bind those variables with existential quantifiers:

(1) $\exists F \, \exists f \, \exists x \, (\text{PA} \, [F, f, x] \supset A \, [F, f, x])$.

Since any system of object satisfying the matrix PA $[F, f, x]$ must be infinite, this nonmodal conditional is vacuously true if the domain is finite. But consider its necessitation:

(2) $\Box \, \exists F \, \exists f \, \exists x \, (\text{PA} \, [F, f, x] \supset A \, [F, f, x])$.

This says that, as a matter of metaphysical necessity, if there exists a system of objects satisfying PA $[F,f,x]$—that is, an ω-system—then that system satisfies a certain structural condition derived from A. And claims of this form can be nontrivial, even if the domain of actual individuals happens to be finite. (You may verify this by taking A to be '$0 \neq 0$'.) For certain purposes it suffices to treat (2) as the modal structural counterpart of A. Strictly speaking, however, one further modification is required. Begin by noting that for pairs of 'contradictory' claims A and $\sim A$ in the language of arithmetic, the corresponding instances of (2)

$\Box \; \exists F \, \exists f \, \exists x \; (\text{PA} \; [F,f,x] \supset A \; [F,f,x])$
$\Box \; \exists F \, \exists f \, \exists x \; (\text{PA} \; [F,f,x] \supset \sim A \; [F,f,x])$

are not logically incompatible, since both will be true at all worlds in any frame where the individual domain is finite. It is desirable, however, that the mapping from claims in the arithmetic to claims in the modal language preserve the logical relations suggested by the surface syntax of the language of arithmetic. For this reason, the modal structural counterpart of A is given by the conjunction:

$(A\star) \; \Diamond \; (\exists F \, \exists f \, \exists x \; (\text{PA} \; [F,f,x] \; \& \; \Box \; \exists F \, \exists f \, \exists x \; (\text{PA} \; [F,f,x] \supset A \; [F,f,x]).$

In words: there might have been an ω-sequence of objects, and as a matter of necessity, if there had been an ω-sequence, then a structural condition derived from A would have been true of it.[17]

Instances of $A\star$ are sentences in the language of pure second-order modal logic, a language you already understand. The language of arithmetic itself is so far uninterpreted. However, the Academy of Meaning has stipulated that its sentences are to be interpreted according to the following semantic rule.

(RULE) For each sentence A in the language of arithmetic, A is to mean the same as $A\star$.

It is easily verified that PA itself is true on this interpretation, and that the classical rules of inference preserve truth when applied to sentences in the language of arithmetic. You are thereby authorized to operate with these sentences according to these familiar rules, as if they had the logical syntax they appear to have. Not only are you authorized to assert the axiom PA itself: you are authorized to assert any sentence that can be derived from this axiom by the standard rules. The semantics guarantees that this procedure will never lead you into error.

This is the account of pure arithmetic. The introduction of the cardinality operator #, without which there can be no application of arithmetic, is more complex.[18] But even in this case we have the following result: in all operational respects, the language of arithmetic functions among the Z just as it does among us. They will agree with us (and with the Q) about which arithmetical

---

[17] [For a related account, see Hellman (1989)—G. R.]
[18] For pertinent details, see Burgess and Rosen (1997: ch. B).

claims are true, and about how such claims may be warranted by proof within formal arithmetic. There are, however, two crucial differences.

First, when called upon to *justify* their acceptance of pure arithmetic—with its apparent commitment to infinitely many numbers—the Z have a straightforward answer. (We may have our answers, but they will not be straightforward.) The Z will simply say: 'Look, PA may look like some bold speculation about the invisible denizens of another world. But we know exactly what it means. It means that there might have been an ω-sequence, and necessarily, if there had been an ω-sequence, then there would have been an ω-sequence. Now, the first conjunct may not be *absolutely* trivial. (The second clearly is.) But we have never heard a good reason for denying it, not even from the finitists who suspect that the actual world may well be finite. But in any case, given the official interpretation of the language, the challenge to justify PA reduces to the challenge to justify this altogether uncontroversial modal claim.'

Second, and for my purposes much more importantly, if pressed to justify their commitment to the *necessity* of pure arithmetic, the Z once again have a straightforward answer: 'According to the official interpretation, the truths of arithmetic are modal truths—that is, truth-functional compounds of sentences whose main connectives are modal operators. We happen to accept as a general rule that for modal statements A, if A is true, then A is necessary. But one need not accept this principle in full generality in order to find its application to pure arithmetic convincing. How could it be a contingent matter whether ω-sequences are possible? How could it be a contingent matter whether, if there had been an ω-sequence, it would have satisfied a certain purely logical condition? Once you have convinced yourself that a claim of the form $A^\star$ is true, you will find it *perfectly evident* that it expresses a necessary truth. (Even the Q, with their deviant modal doctrines, do not deny this.) But of course, if $A^\star$ is a necessary truth, then so must A be. There is thus no doubt that the true sentences of pure arithmetic express necessary truths. We know this *a priori* with as much confidence as we know anything about modality.'

The existence of the Z raises many questions—questions that would still arise if they were merely fictional. There is no doubt a sense in which the Z have arithmetic. Not only do they accept a collection of sentences that look and sound just like the arithmetic we accept. The uses to which those sentences are put (and the manipulations to which they are held to be subject) are by and large just the uses to which we put our arithmetic. On the other hand, the sentences that comprise their arithmetic are *by stipulation* nothing more than code for a range of claims expressible in the language of pure modal logic, and this is not so for us. The contrast with the Q in this respect is perhaps more striking. The Q understand the modal language, and they concede that the modal-structural counterparts of the truths of arithmetic are uniformly necessary. But since they regard the (existential) truths of arithmetic as themselves contingent, they take this observation to block any claim of equivalence.

Evidently, then, the Z and the Q mean different things by their arithmetical claims, despite the fact that the difference comes to nothing 'in practice'. It should not be surprising that this is possible. One of the striking things about mathematical discourse, after all, is that it admits of so many determinate construals, all of which leave the first-order practice of counting and calculating and theorem proving in place. The pressing question for me is whether the Z have a response to the questions which von Feld declined to answer. With what right do *we* take the truths of pure arithmetic, as we understand them, to be necessary? Should the existence of the Z lead the Q to reconsider their anti-necessitarianism?

I can imagine a line of thought that runs as follows. The Q were quite sensibly vague about what it takes for the claims of standard arithmetic to be true in a possible world. They were willing to entertain the thought that the truth of standard arithmetic requires nothing more than an infinity of (abstract) objects. Their case for the contingency of arithmetic turned on an argument for the contingency of this proposition. But don't the Z have an argument, a priori, for the necessary existence of infinitely many objects? The Z clearly do have an argument for the claim that a certain sentence, PA, expresses a necessary truth in their language. Moreover, they claim to have an argument for the soundness of the standard canons of inference as applied to arithmetical claims taken at face value. Now PA entails, in this sense, the non-arithmetical statement

(3) $\exists F \, \exists f \, \exists x \, \text{PA}[F, f, x]$,

and (3) is true only in infinite domains. But if (3) follows logically from a necessary truth, then it must itself be necessary. And if this is so, then it must be incoherent to suppose that the existence of an ω-sequence is a contingent matter.

But here we must be careful. Let us bracket the question whether the existence of an ω-sequence—any ω-sequence—would suffice for the truth of arithmetic. Suppose that this is so. It would be remarkable enough in any case if the Z were in a position to demonstrate a priori that, as a matter of necessity, the domain of individuals must be infinite. But is there such an argument?

The intuitive line of thought depends on the claim that the ordinary canons of inference are sound (on the Z-semantics) when applied to the claims of arithmetic taken at face value. But whether this is so depends on what is meant by a 'claim of arithmetic'. (3) is a purely logical sentence. It does not contain any special arithmetical vocabulary. It is the sort of claim that the Z–initiate is supposed to understand prior to his introduction to the language of arithmetic. And for this reason it is natural to suppose that it does not fall within the scope of the RULE. But if this is right, then the claim of 'soundness' is incorrect. After all, on the Z–semantics, PA is an abbreviation for the modal sentence:

(4) $\Diamond \, (\exists F \, \exists f \, \exists x \, (\text{PA} \, [F, f, x]) \, \& \, \Box \, \exists F \, \exists f \, \exists x \, (\text{PA} \, [F, f, x] \supset \text{PA} \, [F, f, x]))$.

But (4) does not entail (3) as a matter of logic.

Given the official interpretation of the Z–sentence PA, then, the inference from PA to '$\exists F \, \exists f \, \exists x \, (\text{PA} \, [F, f, x])$' is invalid. The argument for the necessary existence of an ω–sequence is therefore blocked. As the Z understand it, PA could be true even if there were only finitely many objects in the actual world.

Here is another way to make the same point. It is easy to confirm that the following sentences express necessary truths in the language of arithmetic as the Z understand it:

(5) $\exists x \, x = 0, \exists x \, x = s(0), 0 \neq s(0)$.

One might therefore think that the Z have an a priori argument for the impossibility of monism. But notice that, as the Z understand it, there is no license for the inference from (5) to (6)

(6) $\exists x \, \exists y \, x \neq y$.

The latter is an ordinary sentence in the language of pure logic that receives no special interpretation from the stipulations. But the official translations of sentences in (5) do not entail (6) as a matter of logic.

The general claim of soundness is thus incorrect. The 'singular terms' and 'quantifiers' in the language of arithmetic as it is understood among the Z do not have the inferential roles or ordinary singular terms and quantifiers. It is therefore a mistake to interpret Z–arithmetic as entailing the necessary *existence* of infinitely many objects, despite the fact that it guarantees the necessary truth of the sentence PA.

Of course it is possible to read the RULE as covering sentences in the language of pure logic as degenerate cases of sentences in the language of arithmetic. The *First Course* might have said explicitly,

When one is engaged in arithmetical reasoning, a sentence *S* in the language of pure logic is to be understood to mean *S*★.

(*S*★) $\Diamond \, (\exists F \, \exists f \, \exists x \, (\text{PA} \, [F, f, x]) \, \& \, \Box \, \exists F \, \exists f \, \exists x \, (\text{PA} \, [F, f, x] \supset S)$.

On this interpretation, the inference from PA to '$\exists F \exists f \exists x$ (PA $[F, f, x]$)' will be valid, as will the inference from (5) to (6).

The effect of this procedure, however, is to introduce an ambiguity into the language. Sometimes '$\exists x \exists y \; x \neq y$' will mean that there are at least two objects. Sometimes it will mean that there might have been an ω-sequence, and necessarily, if there had been, then there would have been at least two objects. And it may be thought that, given our interests, this defeats the purpose of the construction. The intuitive argument sought to demonstrate, from materials implicit in the story of the Z, that, as a matter of necessity, infinitely many objects *exist*. What we have now is a demonstration that, on one interpretation, the sentence '$\exists F \exists f \exists x$ (PA $[F, f, x]$)' expresses a necessary truth. The trouble is that on this interpretation the sentence does not say that an ω-sequence *exists*. It says (more or less) that if there had been an ω-sequence, then there would have been an ω-sequence. And that is not to say that an ω-sequence in fact exists.

But perhaps this is tendentious. It is sometimes said that we have more than one 'notion' of existence, and in particular, that the existential idiom means one thing in mathematics and something else in other contexts. This suggestion is usually put forward on dubious verificationist grounds. (The evidence for an existence claim in number theory is rather different from the corresponding evidence in Roman history. But *this* does not show that 'exists' means different things in different contexts.) The idea itself, however, is by no means preposterous. It is an important datum in the philosophy of mathematics that our own mathematicians will often balk at questions like, 'Do numbers (really) exist?'[19] In response, some will say, 'Look, either this is a trivial mathematical question—of course numbers exist *in mathematics* or *in the mathematical sense*—or it is a metaphysical question that I don't begin to know how to answer.' And of course that is just what the mathematicians among the Z are likely to say.

We are not the Z. We do not learn the mathematical use of 'there exists' by explicit semantic stipulation. Nonetheless, the fact that at least some of us are inclined to balk at some of the questions that arise when one insists on treating 'there exists' as univocal across discourses provides some ground for thinking that we are like the Z in some respects. And if that is so, then the fact may have some bearing on our problem.

---

[19] The datum, needless to say, does not interpret itself. The man on the street will balk at being asked whether his hands exist. But that does not show that the sentence 'My hands exist' is ambiguous, or indeed that it is anything but obviously true.

The Q will presumably be unmoved by the story of the Z. They will say: 'We do not have this nonstandard notion of existence, and it cannot possibly clarify matters to introduce yet another ambiguity into the language. What the Z really ought to do, if they want to be completely above board, is to apply their holophrastic stipulations to a brand new language—a language that includes not only some novel nonlogical vocabulary, but also novel 'quantifiers', 'variables', and other particles. They already have a symbol, ∃, which means simply 'there exists'. So let them introduce a new symbol, ∃* (pronounced 'there shmexists'), and apply the modified RULE that includes S↔S* to sentences containing it. It will then be a trivial truth—and a necessary one—that there shmexists an ω-sequence of objects. But let's not confuse this claim with the equally true but utterly contingent claim that an ω-sequence exists.'

This is surely correct, as far as it goes. And yet it might be maintained that ∃*, though distinct from ∃, nonetheless expresses a genuine *notion* of existence: that to schmexist is to exist *in a sense*. Perhaps the close formal (inferential) analogy between ∃ and ∃* suffices to range them both under a single genus. And if that is right, it may then be said in response: 'You may not have the concept of schmexistence yet, but we can easily explain it to you by exploiting the existential idiom you already understand along with your understanding of the modal operators. And when we do, you will have no choice but to concede that, while it is obscure whether it is necessary that numbers exist *in the basic sense*, it is straightforwardly necessary that they exist *in this secondary sense*.'

Now it is hard to imagine a softer question than 'Does ∃* express a genuine notion of existence?' If the everyday mathematical uses of 'there exists' clearly meant 'there schmexists', then I suppose the answer would be 'Yes'. But this claim of semantic equivalence is not *clearly* correct. And given this, it seems to me that the answer to the question must itself be unclear.

But to say that 'there exists' in mathematics is not *clearly* equivalent to 'there schmexists' is not to say that the two notions are clearly (or determinately) distinct. We should perhaps be alive to the following possibility: 'There exists' in mathematics is indeterminate in sense. Our practice with the idiom is for the most part consistent with its meaning just what it means elsewhere in the language—though the fact that we count mathematical existence claims as straightforwardly necessary tells against this. But it is also consistent with its meaning 'there schmexists' (or something of the sort). If this is so, then there is a sense in which ∃* expresses *a* notion of existence, since the notion it expresses is a candidate meaning (though not the only one) for certain serious uses of 'there exists' in ordinary language.

Suppose this is correct, and let us return to our encounter with the Q. Our question concerned the modal status of the existential claims of arithmetic. And the answer to it depends on what these claims are supposed to mean. If they are *ordinary* existence claims—if 'there exists' in arithmetic means just what it means in Roman history—then the principles and procedures for modal argument invoked by the Q are compelling. It is compelling that if *A* and *B* are distinct, then it is possible for (a duplicate of) the one to *exist* without the other. It is compelling that there is no incoherence in the thought that numbers do not *exist*, and so on. But if 'there exists' in arithmetic means 'there schmexists'—or if it sometimes means *something like* 'there schmexists', or if it is unsettled whether it sometimes means something like 'there schmexists'—then these principles are problematic. From the fact that the natural world and the numbers are distinct, it does not follow that there is a possible world in which the natural world is as it is, but the numbers do not schmexist. It is (quite plausibly) incoherent to suppose that possibly, the numbers fail to schmexist. And so on.

Enough already. Tomorrow I shall begin a note to the Academy on these reflections. My conclusion will be as follows: On one straightforward interpretation of the language—the interpretation favored by the Q—the existential quantifier is univocal across discourses, and the existential claims of arithmetic are at best contingent. On another interpretation—the interpretation supplied by the Z—'there exists' means one thing in arithmetic, and something else in Roman history; and on the former interpretation, the existential truths of arithmetic are noncontingent truths. If the latter interpretation[20] is determinately excluded as an interpretation of *our* use of the existential idiom, we should concede that the Q are correct about the modal status of arithmetic. In the absence of some compelling reduction or grounding of the arithmetical facts in noncontingent facts of some more basic sort, it is sheer dogmatism to insist that the facts of arithmetic are noncontingent. On the other hand, if the devious interpretation favored by the Z is not determinately incorrect as an account of the existential idiom in arithmetic, then a more subtle verdict is in order. If it is not clearly false that we mean something like what the Z mean, then it is not clearly false that the facts of arithmetic are noncontingent.

---

[20] And its ilk. There are many ways to associate arithmetical truths (falsehoods) with indisputably necessary truths (falsehoods) in one or another pre-mathematical idiom in such a way as to secure the validity of the ordinary rules of inference in arithmetic. Nearly every reductive program in the philosophy of mathematics supplies such a mapping. The anti-necessitarian conclusion follows only if each such interpretation is determinately excluded as an interpretation of the ordinary language of arithmetic.

REFERENCES

Burgess, John, and Rosen, Gideon (1997), *A Subject with no Object* (Oxford: Clarendon Press).

Field, Hartry (1980), *Science without Numbers* (Princeton: Princeton University Press).

—— (1989), *Realism, Mathematics and Modality* (Oxford: Blackwell).

—— (1993), 'The Conceptual Contingency of Abstract Objects', *Mind*, 102(406): 285–99.

Fine, Kit (1994), 'Essence and Modality', in J. E. Tomberlin (ed.), *Philosophical Perspectives*, viii: *Logic and Language* (Atascadero, Calif.: Ridge view), 1–15.

Frege, G. (1980), *Foundations of Arithmetic*, trans. J. L. Austin (Oxford: Blackwell).

Hale, Bob (1988), *Abstract Objects* (Oxford: Blackwell).

Hellman, G. (1989), *Mathematics without Numbers* (Oxford: Clarendon. Press).

Kripke, Saul (1980), *Naming and Necessity*, 2nd edn. (Cambridge, Mass.: Harvard University Press).

Lewis, David (1986), *On the Plurality of Worlds* (Oxford: Blackwell).

Priest, Graham (1987), *In Contradiction* (Dordrecht: Martinus Nijhoff).

Robinson, J. M. (1979) (ed.), *Collected Works of John Stuart Mill*, ix: *An Examination of Sir W. Hamilton's Philosophy* (London: Routledge and Kegan Paul).

Rosen, Gideon (2001), 'Nominalism, Naturalism and Epistemic Relativism', in J. E. Tomberlin (ed.), *Philosophical Perspectives, xv: Metaphysics* (Atascadero, Calif: Ridgeview), 69–91.

Wright, Crispin (1983), *Frege's Conception of Numbers as Objects* (Aberdeen: Aberdeen University Press).

Yablo, Steve (1993), 'Is Conceivability a Guide to Possibility?', *Philosophy and Phenomenological Research*, 53(1): 1–42.

8

On the Metaphysical Contingency of Laws of Nature

ALAN SIDELLE

In the old days—good or bad, depending on your views—it would have been very hard to propose that the laws of nature are necessary 'in the strongest sense' and be taken seriously.[1] After all, what the laws of nature are is a matter for empirical investigation, and however they turn out, we can imagine them having been otherwise. When scientists look for laws, there are various hypotheses as to what the laws might be, and so long as there is no hidden contradiction, any of these is conceivable, and so represents what the laws *are* in some (set of) possible world(s). Certainly, the laws of nature may represent, or underlie, weaker sorts of necessity—physical, biological, psychological, or economic necessity—but such necessity would be understood as being compatible with contingency in a wider sense. Maybe, as things are, this unsupported cup has to fall—but surely the laws could have differed so that under the very same conditions, it would *not* fall. We can surely *imagine* it, and in the old days, this would have been enough.

I would like to thank Thomas Blackson, Berent Enc, Ted Everett, Marie-Louise Mares, Elliott Sober, and Tamar Szabó Gendler and John Hawthorne for helpful thoughts and support.

[1] For an exception, see Kneale (1949).

Saul Kripke changed all that, with help from Hilary Putnam.[2] They convinced most philosophers that there are necessary truths which are not analytic or a priori, and before long, all kinds of things which seemed clearly contingent, on grounds of being empirical and the imaginability of their negations, were being claimed to be necessary. More specifically, the idea that one could establish a possibility by conceiving or imagining it (or refute a proposed necessity by imagining its negation) has come in for harsh treatment, and it is far from uncommon to see such conceivability arguments, or considerations, simply brushed aside like so many tea-leaves.

Thus it no longer seems so clear to many that the laws of nature are metaphysically contingent, and a number of philosophers actively propose that they are, in fact, necessary in the strongest sense,[3] and many more philosophers are willing to take the idea seriously, despite the seemingly clear contrary testimony of the traditional tests for necessity and possibility.

I think the old days were the 'good' old days, and while I agree that there are necessary a posteriori truths, I don't think they are in any interesting sense 'metaphysical', or that they warrant a general suspicion of appeals to imagination as the basic method of modal inquiry.[4] Correspondingly, I think the laws of nature are either contingent, or, if they are necessary, that this is much less interesting than it may appear at first glance. I shall try to show why in this chapter. While the laws of nature are my explicit topic, I intend this as an illustration of the more general misuse, or misinterpretation, of the possibility of a posteriori necessities, and of the importance of traditional imagining, conceiving, and thought experiment to modal inquiry.

1 Imagining Our Laws of Nature Not to Obtain

In this section, I will describe a number of ways in which we can conceive our actual laws of nature to fail to obtain. If these conceived situations are genuine possibilities, then the laws do not obtain with full, or metaphysical, or 'the widest kind' of necessity. Some may find the number of examples a bit much— the conceivability is obvious from the start, so why not just posit it and move on? And some will find it wholly irrelevant (a partially overlapping group),

---

[2] Kripke (1971, 1980); Putnam (1975).

[3] Among the more visible are Shoemaker (1984, 1998); Swoyer (1982); Harré and Madden (1975); Fales (1993); Tweedale (1984).

[4] I argue this in Sidelle (1989), henceforward *NEI*. See also sect. 2 below.

since the necessity of laws of nature is presumably metaphysical, not conceptual, so we are in the realm where 'conceivability is no proof of possibility'.[5]

The latter charge I will address in sections 2 and 3. For now, notice that even the arguments of Kripke and Putnam, showing that we can, on occasion, conceive the impossible (or conceive something other than we think), rely on such thought experiments. In fact, they rely on thought experiments of *just the form* we are using: take for granted that some fact *actually* obtains, and then consider whether it might nonetheless fail in some other possible situation.[6] So, while I grant that such imaginings are defeasible—we can be argued out of them—those who have been convinced by Kripke and Putnam have no basis for denying, and are in no *position* to deny, that these sorts of imaginings constitute at least a prima-facie case for the possibility of their contents.

As for the charge of overkill, my hope is that seeing the nature and variety of ways in which the laws of nature seem to be contingent will help us better see both the difficulty of plausibly maintaining that they are necessary (at least, in a metaphysically interesting way) and the inability of the purported necessity to do the jobs for which it has been postulated. So—on to the examples, most or all of which have probably been presented in various contexts by other philosophers.[7]

1.1 *'Obvious' Imaginability—Non-Incoherence*

The simplest way to see that the laws of nature can be imagined otherwise is just by noting that they are not analytic or a priori, and so there is no incoherence in postulating their falsity in some other situation. We can always construct models involving the same properties, magnitudes, and/or forces, models that involve no explicit contradictions. One can just keep it at this level, or give

---

[5] Putnam (1975: 233).

[6] Thus, for instance, suppose water is actually composed of H_2O; could this fail to obtain in another possible situation? This contrasts with the more traditional, more simple 'Can you imagine water not composed of H_2O?' While Kripke's and Putnam's arguments, if accepted, show that the simpler imaginings can mislead us about possibility, the same does not apply to the 'premised on actual fact' sort—indeed, as I say, the arguments *rely* on such attempted conceivings, although admittedly there are arguments adduced to influence our judgments about the proper way to describe these imagined situations.

[7] I should say in advance that some of the cases may not be fundamentally different; if so, I apologize, but nothing hinges on the total number. For some other, and often related, examples, see Kit Fine's 'The Varieties of Necessity', Ch. 6, sect. 2 above. The presentations differ, in part, because our purposes criss-cross. Fine's main aim there is to show that not every natural necessity is metaphysically necessary, whereas I want to show that *none* is 'deeply' metaphysically necessary—which is compatible with *all* being 'metaphysically' necessary.

simple examples. Hume gives us some—imagine one ball striking another at such-and-such a speed and angle, so that, given the actual laws, the second ball must move in such a direction with such a speed: now simply imagine the contact, while the second ball stays in place, or goes off in another direction, or at a different speed, or turns into a tiger-shaped object and eats the first ball.[8] One's first instinct may be to insist that other forces must be in play for one of these things to happen—but why? It's my imagination, and I'm telling you that the balls are just as they in fact are, with *no* other forces.[9]

One may note that I've assumed that the laws (in these conditions) do entail that the second ball would move in a certain way. But what if the laws are probabilistic? Of course, the probabilities would have to be nonzero for *all* the alternatives we can imagine for this to even seem a useful reply, but let us suppose that it is so. Still, we are left with the question of whether in our imagined world, the probabilistic laws that actually obtain, obtain there as well, and while a single imagined instance doesn't show that they don't, we can multiply them to the point where there is scarcely any credibility to the claim that the probabilities there are just what they are here, especially if we imagine the universe to extend infinitely in time, with actual frequencies coming nowhere near the postulated probabilities. Of course, any (nonzero) probability assignments may be logically compatible with any strings of unlikely instances. But it is hard to see what meaning to attach to the claim that in those cases, the probabilities would nonetheless be the same, especially insofar as to respond to *all* the cases we can imagine, one would need to say that no matter *what* the actual frequencies, the probabilities—which, again, are not supposed to be determined simply by logic or meaning—would be exactly the same.[10] This is especially

---

[8] Replies that these situations are not really possible due to the real natures or essences of the properties involved will be addressed in sections 2 and 3; here, I consider only objections that the cases don't even pass minimal, *a priori* conditions: e.g., that they are not internally coherent, or do not constitute even apparent possibilities of the falsity of the law. (This is another contrast with Fine's presentation, which jumps right into considering such replies.)

[9] There is no problem here insofar as any 'new forces' are the products of the interaction of our objects and properties, and if, in some of the examples, one wants to insist that laws and causal claims by *definition* require forces, then fine, we either have such new forces, or the old forces themselves work somewhat differently. Either way, since the interactions don't produce the actual forces according to the actual laws, we are imagining situations where our laws don't obtain. Throughout the chapter, 'no extra forces' is to be understood this way.

[10] Sense can sometimes be attached in terms of inner features of the properties or magnitudes involved—e.g., a coin that is perfectly evenly weighted may meaningfully be said to have a 50 percent probability of landing tails, even in worlds where it always lands heads. But insofar as probabilities are supposed to be in this way dependent, we can ask whether the probability assignments based on the 'determining' feature are a priori or empirical. If the former, we again don't have

clear when the probabilities are fundamental. (I return briefly to probabilistic laws in (1.5), below.)[11]

Another source of alternative laws focuses on the fact that most (all?) laws express mathematical relationships; they take the form of mathematical formulas. Now, if these are laws of nature, the formulas are not themselves mathematical (plus definitional) truths. So, to conceive the laws of nature being different, we simply need to imagine the specific values in the equations being different; so long as there are no inconsistencies, we will then have a model of a possible situation. One range of alternatives comes from the physical constants. Take, for example, the universal gravitational constant—roughly, $6.67 \times 10^{-11}(\text{N} \star \text{m}^2/\text{kg}^2)$. Surely that could have been different in countless ways. No doubt, change it, and lots of other things change too (supposing no other changes of law, beyond those already entailed)—but we don't need to describe a whole world to know that one differing in this way has mathematically consistent models. Another range of similar cases focuses instead on the relationships, rather than the constants—for example, the gravitational force between two bodies is inversely proportional to the square of the distance between them.[12] Why not to the cube, or some other power or function, of their distance? Or why must the force be directly proportional to the *product* of the masses of the objects? Why not some more complex mathematical relation? In some cases of this sort, there may be some threat that the theoretical terms involved are in fact defined by the relations expressed in the law—maybe 'mass of n grams' is *defined* in terms of the force an object exerts—and there, some purported imaginings will fail. But if the law itself is not simply a truth of definition and mathematics, not all of the terms will be so defined in any such law, so it will just be a matter of figuring out which term should be understood as independent, and conceiving the alternative law accordingly. Additionally, laws that are derived will not be possibly different without a change in the laws from which they are derived (supposing the derivation is in fact deductively valid)—so a consistent model would have to alter any more basic laws.

---

genuine laws of nature, and if the latter, we can ask what is the basis for determining the connection between that feature and the probabilities. Whatever it is, our imagined world will be one in which that basis differs so as to alter the probability distribution. If there *is* no basis, then it is presumably a brute fact, and consequently, we can just stipulate the equally brute possibility of an alternative probability assignment.

[11] Of course, we could *stipulate* that actual world probabilities be assigned in all these other worlds—but that is right away to dismiss the metaphysical force of the necessity of the law's obtaining.

[12] For simplicity, I'm sticking with Newton here. I hope it is clear that nothing depends on Newton's being right.

But again, (a) we can just start off at the fundamental level, altering the mathematical relationships therein, and (b) given that the laws are empirical, there will always be a way of making any more basic laws so consistent, to provide a coherent model.

Finally, there are other 'physical necessities' that seem in a broader way contingent—why must the total quantity of mass-energy remain the same? Why can't anything travel faster than the speed of light? There doesn't seem to be much trick to imagining these otherwise.

1.2 *Theory Competition*

Many of the above cases seem so easy to imagine because we know that the determination of the laws was a product of defeasible empirical inquiry. The gravitational constant was determined long after the acceptance of Newton's Laws, and the nature of the relationships was fought out among various possible theories. Now of course, we don't want to confuse the possibility of having *found out* otherwise with the possibility of things having *been* otherwise—as Putnam and Kripke have argued. Nonetheless, that is clearly not in place in many of these cases. Is there any inclination to say that since the constant *is* G, in worlds where objects produce a force between them, directly proportional to their masses and inversely proportional to the square of the distance between them, but of a somewhat different coefficient, the force would not be gravity? This seems unlikely.[13] So in many, though quite likely not all, cases of competing theories, those that have turned out false provide us with ways the laws could have been different—metaphysically, not just epistemically.

1.3 *Can the Laws of Nature Change?*

In discussing the problem of induction, one may hear the proposal that even if there have been natural laws in place up until now, how do we know they won't change? This suggests another argument for the contingency of our laws of nature. First, consider a world like ours up to some time—now, or 1968—but in which things then change, in one of the various ways we earlier described: perhaps the constants change, or the relations between properties and magnitudes

---

[13] It might be claimed that 'gravity' is nonrigid, so that even though the force would be gravity, this doesn't show that the *gravitational force* itself might have been different. This, however, doesn't seem to affect the claim that while the law is that objects gravitationally attract each other with a force of $[(6.67 \times 10^{-11} \text{N} \star \text{m}^2/\text{kg}^2) \text{ mm}']/\text{r}^2$, that might have been false.

change. At any rate, aspirins cease to relieve headaches, instead causing rashes; straight contact causes angular motion; shadows don't have the shapes of their objects—and none of this is due to different forces. Things just happen differently—though with as much claim to law-likeness as before. We may suppose that, for a while, scientists try to hold onto the old laws and explain these changes by extra parameters, but they ultimately decide—correctly (why mightn't they be right? Let our world be one where they are)—that they would do better just to look for what new equations could account for events since the change. And indeed, they are there to be found.

Now, how are we to describe such a world? There seem to be the following options: (a) A natural description is the one with which we started: the laws changed at t. If this is right, we immediately have the contingency of our laws—if the necessity of a law is supposed to imply its *always* holding (as opposed simply to its holding in every possible world, at least at some time)— or we can get there by imagining a world just like this world, except only *after* t, so that our laws are *never* in force. (b) One may insist that laws are incapable of change. If so, one may try the claim that there are laws, but they are more complex than our laws—perhaps they make reference to a particular time: for example, instead of '$F = Gmm'/r^2$',[14] we have 'at $t < 1968$, $F = Gmm'/r^2$, at $t > 1968, F = G\star mm'/r^2$', or whatever. On the other hand, one may deny that this could really be the form of a law, saying instead that there would be no laws in such a world.[15] Either way, our laws clearly do not obtain here, so we again have conceived the possibility of their failing to obtain. (c) A final possibility here is to maintain that the laws in this world do not change, but that the properties, magnitudes, and forces that appear in the world before t, and that *seem* to still be around after t, really cease to be instantiated after t; instead, there are 'look-alike' properties, and so forth. Consequently, the same laws hold throughout, but before t, half have no application, since the properties they govern have no instances, and after t, the other half (ours) are in that position. This view will presumably be attractive only to those already invested in the claim that the laws of nature hold necessarily, so my reply will wait until section 3. For now, we may simply note that it sure *looks* like we have the same properties— hitting an object at an angle of 42 degrees, moving at 5 feet per second, accelerating at 32 feet per second^2—so this at least looks like a situation, however described in accord with either (a) or (b), in which our laws fail to obtain.

---

[14] This is the law of gravity. F is gravitational force, G is the universal gravitational constant, m and m' are the masses of the attracting objects, and r is the distance between them.

[15] See David Armstrong for both of these options (1983: 100–1; 1993: 147–8).

1.4 *Mini-Worlds*

We can imagine the world being very short, or very small—one object for one second, one object changeless throughout, a time-slice of the actual world, preceded and followed by nothing, to name a few. Need we suppose that in all of these our actual laws obtain? Of course, setting aside probabilistic laws (see above, and notes 10 and 11), if actual properties and forces, and so on are instantiated, with nothing extra, then these worlds constitute examples of the sort considered under (1.1) above—if there is a ball made of concrete, and the next moment nothing, or if the ball is moving at 3 miles an hour and then just stops, and neither of these is due to extra forces, then our laws can't obtain there. The briefness of the worlds' histories just helps make this vivid.

But there is another point here, which will lead to our last argument. Doesn't it seem gratuitous to suppose that in such worlds there are *any* laws, or at any rate, any laws rather than any others which are equally compatible with the few events in our world?[16] Or, put a bit differently, if we *can* understand the claim that there are laws in such worlds—for example, that there is a factual (and not trivial or definitional) answer to what would have happened had the world continued—can't we make equally good sense for *any* candidate law, that there are mini-worlds just like ours in its history, but in which this other law is in place? If so, once again, we have worlds in which our laws fail to obtain, either because there are no laws,[17] or because there are alternative, incompatible laws.

Now, this last question raises the more general question of whether the laws of nature in a world supervene upon its history. Classic regularity theories imply that they do, while more recent views, most notably the view that laws

[16] As Tamar Gendler has pointed out to me, and as Fine notes in his chapter, our laws may imply that at least some of these worlds are actually physically possible. In such cases, clearly, it is not gratuitous to say of these worlds that they obey our laws. But (1) not every such world will be so physically possible, and (2) we have to be careful about what is or is not gratuitous here. When we say 'the world could have had this history,' we may be making a claim of either nomological or metaphysical possibility. When making the former, of course, we are accessing a world—if there is one—that shares our laws, and so it is not at all gratuitous to say of that mini-world that it does so. But if we are—as I was—making a claim of metaphysical possibility and just describing the world with no implicit legal baggage, the question is whether the description as so given requires our laws to obtain. And that is why I call the supposition of a particular set of laws here gratuitous: given that we aren't constrained by 'physical accessibility', we want to know what *in the history and contents of the world itself*—for this is all that has been specified—gets us one set of laws rather than another. But this anticipates (and leads to) the argument of the next section.

[17] Those who prefer 'no laws' might propose that it can't hurt to assign our laws to such worlds, insofar as what happens there doesn't contradict them. But while we can agree to say this, it hardly makes it *metaphysically* so—indeed, the claim *is* that *really*, there are no laws.

of nature are relations between universals,[18] would suggest that they do not. For the most part, I have tried to make my examples acceptable, whatever account of laws one accepts. But at least the most recent argument is not so neutral—if worlds cannot differ in their laws without differing in what happens at the worlds, then I cannot argue that for each mini-world there are actually a plethora of possible worlds differing in their laws. On the other hand, if the laws *are* supervenient, we return to the somewhat doubtful content of ascribing any laws—but more specifically our own—in the mini-worlds. However that may be, we may use the issue of supervenience to pose one final argument.

1.5 *Do the Laws of Nature Supervene on the History of a World?*

Laws of nature either exhibit what has been called 'Humean supervenience' or they do not. As characterized by David Lewis, Humean supervenience 'is the doctrine that all there is to the world is a vast mosaic of local matters of particular fact . . . there is no difference without difference in the arrangement of qualities. All else supervenes on that.'[19] According to this, laws of nature would so supervene, so that pairs of worlds differing in no local matter of fact could not, then, differ in their laws. This view has come under regular recent attack, but is still fairly commonly held; I will argue that, either way, we have a clear case for contingency.[20]

If laws of nature don't supervene, it is quite easy to imagine them otherwise and, especially, in a way fully compatible with the magnitudes, properties, and the like, that are actually governed by those laws nonetheless being instantiated. On the most standard non-Humean view, laws of nature are relations among universals (see note 18). But without supervenience, these relations are not determined by the actual distribution of instantiations of the governed properties—indeed, the relation, if anything, is supposed to be explained in the other direction. But, as is well known, any number of imaginable laws—conceivable relations among universals—could, if actual (combined with the actual initial conditions, if any), produce just the actual history of the world. Indeed, this is generally noted as a possible problem in theory selection, and for some Humeans, as a problem in giving real content to the claim that one rather than another of these sets of laws is the actual one. So, there is nothing to imagining a world where the laws of nature are different—imagine a world *just*

---

[18] This view is sometimes called 'the Dretske–Tooley–Armstrong view', after its early proponents. The classic citations are Dretske (1977); Tooley (1977, 1987); and Armstrong (1983).

[19] Lewis (1986: pp. ix–x).

[20] See, e.g., Carroll (1990, 1994), as well as the writings cited in n. 18.

like ours, so far as its particular history goes, but differing in the relations among universals, or, more neutrally, differing in the laws in virtue of which this history comes to pass. Notice that this is equally vivid, if not more so, for probabilistic laws.

So, what if the laws *do* supervene? Actually, for the most part, those who think that the laws *do* supervene are the least likely to think them metaphysically necessary, since the laws, in a way, do not so much *explain* the history, as sum it up or organize it. Be that as it may, we have an independent, and equally straightforward, reason to think that the laws could have been different within this view—just imagine the history different. Now of course, it isn't *so* simple— not every alternative history is incompatible with the actual laws. But it is easy enough to select one that is, and we've seen various samples above. What is useful, I think, in viewing those examples from the current perspective is the idea that in imagining them, we *thereby* imagine the laws to be different, in a way that is perhaps more direct than if we think that when considering these cases, we imagine the laws to be different only by implication.

So, the laws supervene or they don't, and either way leads pretty directly to plenty of conceivable ways in which our actual laws could have failed to obtain.

By now, you have no doubt had enough. Yes, we can imagine that our laws of nature do not hold. So what, then, of those who think the laws are nonetheless necessary? Surely, they have not overlooked the fact that we can imagine their failing to hold! Rather, we can expect them to maintain that here is a case where conceivability and possibility come apart: we should discard this evidence, and embrace the laws as a posteriori necessities.

2 Necessity A Posteriori

As we noted earlier, most philosophers now believe that there are necessary truths that can be known only a posteriori. The standard examples are empirical identity statements (where both terms are rigid designators), like 'Hesperus is Phosphorus' (ordinary identifications like 'That's Joe!' are less-discussed examples, but more indicative of the pervasiveness of such truths) and scientifically discovered property identifications (and their logical consequences), like 'Water is H_2O' (and 'water contains hydrogen'); also commonly offered are truths of kind membership—'Lassie is a dog' (this is not a priori—we could discover she was a very weird looking pony) and 'Cats are mammals'—and more controversial statements of material origin, like 'Queen Elizabeth originated in sperm s and egg e'. In each case, there are arguments that these truths are necessary, despite their not being knowable a priori. But, in not being so knowable, they are all, like our laws of nature, subject to conceivable falsity: we can—or can seem to—imagine that Lassie was a pony, and that Superman was not Clark Kent. Since these conceivings are compatible with the truths' nonetheless being necessary, perhaps the laws of nature are in the same boat.

Unfortunately for the necessitarian, this is not, I believe, a metaphysically interesting boat. I have argued elsewhere (see note 4), that each necessary a posteriori truth should be seen as derived from a combination of an analytic principle of individuation that has empty spaces to be filled in by empirical findings and a particular empirical finding that of itself carries no modal weight. For example, in the case of water's being necessarily H_2O, the analytic principle might be 'Nothing counts as water in any situation unless it has the same deep explanatory features (if any) as the stuff we call "water"', and the empirical fact, which makes the result a posteriori, is that the deep explanatory feature of the stuff we call 'water' is being composed of H_2O.[21] It is clear that each argument for some necessary a posteriori truth, if successful, establishes some such more general principle, and in each case, the argument looks a priori—we establish a priori what (sort of) empirical fact will generate a necessary truth, and empirically discover the particular fact. The modal force, then, of necessary a posteriori truths comes from the principles, which we have compelling reasons, I think, to treat as analytic and as representing linguistic conventions, rather than as revealing metaphysically deep features of reality.[22]

My arguments for this last conclusion were epistemological, metaphysical, and semantic.[23] Epistemologically, short of postulating a mysterious faculty of intuition, the only way to understand how our a priori methods—principally, thought experiments of the sort described above—could give us knowledge of these principles is to suppose that they reflect the meanings we have attached to the relevant terms, like 'water', 'natural kind', and singular terms.[24] Metaphysically, it is hard to see what real necessity could *be*—*especially* when we consider that for each necessary a posteriori truth, there is a genuine possibility which is *just what* the negation of that truth would be like, except that it requires a different description. For example, while there is supposedly no world in which water fails to be H_2O, there are worlds in which stuff other than H_2O does basically what water does, and occupies the roles that water does here. But one might have thought that if water's being necessarily H_2O was a

---

[21] For fuller discussion, see Sidelle (1989: Ch. 3). Similar accounts have been offered by Frank Jackson (1998) and David Chalmers (1996).

[22] [For related discussion of these issues, see Chalmers, Ch. 3 above, and Yablo, Ch. 13 below—eds.] [23] See Sidelle (1989: Ch. 4, as well as 1992*a* and 1995).

[24] On this last, see Sidelle (1992*b*).

real metaphysical necessity, it would at least have to rule out situations like that. If not, what erstwhile possibilities *does* it rule out? It only rules out that this stuff can be water—but we might wonder if that can really amount to anything more than that, given the rules of English, we cannot *call* it 'water'. And this leads to the semantic argument: given these other genuine possibilities, it is easy to imagine that people just like us, given all the same information, introduce proper names, 'water', and the rest in just the situations we introduce them, with no other conscious thoughts than we have—but who offer different judgments and descriptions of the possible worlds that we use as our main arguments for the necessity of some a posteriori truth, and who are not moved by whatever further considerations we offer.[25] For example, they say XYZ *is* water, and Jimmy Olson's pop *would* be Superman[26]—and they continue to do so in the face of whatever we may say which we have found convincing in favor of our alternative descriptions.

Argument one: Isn't it much more plausible to say that they are employing the relevant terms differently than we are, than to say that they are simply wrong? They have associated different criteria of individuation with 'water'. But then, what makes 'water is H_2O' necessarily true in *our* case is the fact that *we* have associated particular criteria with 'water'—and that is to say that the general principle is analytic. Argument two: In order for 'water is H_2O' to express a necessary truth (and so, for dissenters to be wrong), 'water' must refer to H_2O rather than, say, 'functional kind W', or, as some call it, 'Thwater'. How can it do so? Since every actual instance of water is an instance of thwater, it can't be just because the stuff we call water *is* necessarily H_2O—for these samples also instantiate something that *isn't* necessarily H_2O. There must be something in our intentions in using the terms—exhibited in our judgments of what counts as water in various counterfactual situations—that determines one rather than another as the referent. But then it is not the fact that 'this stuff' is necessarily H_2O that makes our counterfactual judgments true but, rather, our counterfactual judgments that determine that we are talking about a sort individuated by deep structure rather than (say) functional features. So again, it has to be built into the meaning of the term that this is how to apply it counterfactually—and again, the general principle is analytic, and the necessary truth reveals our linguistic conventions, not any metaphysically deep essential feature.

---

[25] We don't need to imagine such people—they are actual.

[26] There are two interpretations of this latter: one is that 'Superman' is not being used as a rigid designator; the other is that it is being used rigidly, but the associated criterion of identity is not that for persons: Superman is constituted by different people in different worlds.

Of course, one may argue that, for all this, it is nonetheless true that there *is* a real kind whose deep metaphysical essence is 'being composed of H_2O', and that all my argument shows is that we cannot refer to this kind without certain referential intentions, and that if we had different intentions, we would have referred to something else. But this is gratuitous: once it is granted that the general principle is analytic, we have an explanation of the necessity of 'water is H_2O', and of all the evidence in support of this, which doesn't posit any such metaphysical essence—beyond, perhaps, the logical necessity of H_2O being H_2O—and this is all to the good, given the further epistemological and metaphysical puzzles.

This, then, is my general take on necessary a posteriori truths. If I am right, much of the rhetoric that has gone with, and followed upon, the acceptance of such truths involves misinterpretation. Metaphysically, it is misleading to speak of essences and natures, as if they were more than semantically determined; by the same token, it is at best misleading to say—as many philosophers often do— 'well, of course you can imagine that a is F, or some F is G—but perhaps *the very nature* of a, or F, makes this really impossible'. This is especially important, because this sort of 'real natures' talk is often what underwrites the sense that considerations of what we can imagine should not be expected to shed any light on what is genuinely possible. If 'real natures' are properly understood according to my account, no such suspicion of the epistemic force of imagination is warranted—it is just that we sometimes need to try to imagine something on an assumption (i.e., that it is in fact false), because only so will it reveal the nature of our conventions. And of course, we have independent reason here to think that any such conclusions, suspicious of imaginative appeals, start by underappreciating the role of these very appeals for necessary a posteriori truths themselves—all the modal work, epistemically, is done by traditional a priori methods, not science.[27] And so, as I said earlier, not only is a general suspicion of imaginative appeals *unwarranted* by, but it is actually *inconsistent* with, taking these very necessary truths to have been successfully argued for.

If the laws of nature are necessary in *this* way, their necessity, too, would not be of the sort its advocates seem to have in mind. And insofar as most of the above arguments apply to necessary a posteriori truths *by their nature as a posteriori*, and not simply because of details of the actual cases (though that helps make things even more vivid), I think they must apply to any such truth, and so to laws of nature, if, indeed, they are necessary at all. But rather than just stand

---

[27] For more along these lines, see Bealer (1987).

on this, let's look at the actual arguments, and see whether they can establish a necessity for the laws of nature beyond the convention-based sort we've been discussing.

3 The Purported Necessity of the Laws of Nature

There have been two major sorts of argument advanced in support of the necessity of laws of nature. The first, and more common, uses the fact that laws of nature carry modal weight, both directly and in the fact that they support counterfactuals, and argues that the only way to understand this is in terms of the broadest metaphysical necessity of the laws.[28] The second argument looks not directly at laws of nature, but at the properties governed by the laws.[29] Properties—or, at any rate, *these* properties—must be individuated by their causal powers, and these are precisely what are specified by their governing laws. Thus, these properties cannot fail to be governed by these laws, so our laws at least obtain in every world where these properties are instantiated[30]—a strong enough conclusion—and one might think that it at least doesn't hurt to say that the laws obtain even where the properties are not instantiated: after all, given the nature of the properties, all the counterfactuals entailed by these laws obtain—for example, if this object *did* have positive electric charge, it would do such-and-so (this counterfactual has to be true if positive charge is, as the position maintains, individuated by all its causal powers). I will look at each of these arguments in turn, and try to show how either the position, or the argument for it, founders when considered in combination with the conceivings presented in section 1.

First, the argument from counterfactuals. Even if we grant that laws of nature support counterfactuals and claims about what 'must', in some sense, happen, it seems, at first glance, hardly to provide a basis for the broad necessitarian claim we are considering. After all, many opponents of the position are happy to grant a sort of natural necessity to laws of nature or, at least, to the events they govern—why do we need anything stronger? And true counterfactuals always seem to coexist with *some* worlds where the antecedent is true and the consequent false—that's why counterfactuals are typically interpreted

[28] See all the writers mentioned in n. 3, other than Shoemaker.

[29] This argument is most famously associated with Shoemaker, but a version of it is also offered by Swoyer.

[30] As Elliott Sober pointed out to me, this argument does not apply to noncausal laws.

in terms of what is true in worlds *close to ours*, when the antecedent is true, instead of requiring truth in *all* such worlds.

However, it is maintained that we cannot understand the law-supported counterfactuals—with the force they have—short of supposing that their consequents are true in *every* world where the antecedents (and, of course, other causally relevant facts) hold. Similarly, if there *are* worlds where, say, I let go of the ball in just these conditions and it doesn't drop, then there is no acceptable way to accommodate the claim that it really *has* to drop.

The argument goes something like this: if there are worlds where the ball drops, and worlds where it doesn't, how is its dropping necessary *at all*? How does it differ from any other fact that obtains in some, but not all, possible worlds? Perhaps, one might try, it is an instance of something that always obtains in the actual world—but now we have the problem, which the modal force of laws was supposed to address, of distinguishing between laws and accidental generalizations. The latter also always obtain, and do so in some but not all other worlds. And if one interprets the necessity as truth in all worlds where the laws of nature obtain, there is still no difference from accidental generalizations, since it is true in every world where all the coins in my pocket are nickels that, if I have a coin in my pocket, it is a nickel. If the sort of necessity in question is just, in effect, truth in all worlds where some (actually) true generalization obtains, *every* true generalization supports such necessities. Since instances of laws have some more *robust* sort of necessity, their necessity cannot be understood in a relative, partial way.

The very same considerations apply to the counterfactuals that laws support. It is natural to say that what is strictly true is that, if I were to drop it, the ball would fall *in all worlds with the same laws as our world has*, and when we count the counterfactual true *without* the qualification, it is because we are holding the laws of nature fixed, or, if one likes, treating similarity in laws as required for a possible world to be sufficiently close for evaluating the counterfactual. However, here again, *any* fact—in particular, accidental generalizations—will support counterfactuals if they are held so fixed; if, to be acceptably close, a world has to be one where all the coins in my pocket are nickels, then it is *true* that, had there been another coin in my pocket, it would have been a nickel. If the way in which laws support counterfactuals is not of this trivial sort—which it must not be if laws support counterfactuals and true accidental generalizations don't—it can only be because there *is* no restriction: the consequents are true in *every* world where the antecedents are true.[31]

---

[31] Here is Fales's presentation: 'So it is with law-supported counterfactuals. Conventions have a role here, too. They tell us, roughly, to hold fixed all causally relevant aspects of a situation

There are a number of replies to this interesting argument. The first is that it is simply not clear that the modal and counterfactual-supporting force of laws of nature is as objective as proponents of this line suggest. It isn't clear that we really *can* suppose that counterfactuals have determinate truth-values short of an at least implicit complete specification of the antecedent which entails the consequent—so the necessity would just be logical and hypothetical. It is also hardly mysterious that, in general, our counterfactuals would hold the laws of nature fixed; while it is a convention, it is a deep convention.[32] The laws of nature are among the most general, pervasive features of the world, and provide the basic terms in which we couch our explanations. Given our general purposes in asserting and asking counterfactuals, one would expect the assumption of common laws. Of course, this reply needs a way of distinguishing laws from accidental generalizations *other* than by their independent support, or lack thereof, of counterfactuals. But it isn't wholly clear that our confidence in particular counterfactuals *is* independent of our views about what the laws are, so this does not seem a hopeless project. But I won't pursue it here.

A second point is that, whatever the force of the claim that laws support counterfactuals and have modal force, we have already presented at least prima-facie grounds for thinking that they are not necessary in the widest sense, that there are possible worlds where the antecedents are true and the consequents false, and where the events that 'must' happen *don't* happen. Thus, the postulation of metaphysical necessity for laws seems to prove too much—it may offer an explanation of what we want explained, but it has other entailments that seem false. This, of course, is the basis for the traditional idea of nomological necessity as a weaker sort of necessity. But, according to the argument at hand, we can't really understand such a middle modal status: anything weaker than real, full-blooded necessity will leave the laws in the same position as accidental generalizations that don't have modal force or support counterfactuals.

Why should this be? Most of those who take the necessity of laws seriously are anti-Humeans who advocate causation as some sort of natural necessity.[33]

---

except those to be counterfactually varied. But they could not instruct us to "hold fixed" the supporting law itself. Were they to do that, the truth of the counterfactual would become a mere artifact of convention (as, for example, it would be if we were to claim that accidental generalizations support counterfactuals in virtue of some newly laid-down convention that fixes the accidental generalizations themselves). To objectively ground a counterfactual, a law must itself be necessary. Only thus will what happens in worlds whose antecedent conditions differ from ours be a matter of objective and determinate fact' (Fales 1993: 128).

[32] See Armstrong (1993: 146).

[33] Other Humean opponents would be friends of real, probabilistic causation, but they, of course, would hardly be giving this argument.

Now, isn't the apparent fact that such connections are *not* necessary in some broader sense *of itself* sufficient grounds for thinking that there is some such notion to be made sense of? The attempts made, by Fales and others, to consider how something short of metaphysical necessity could be adequate are all of a distinctly Humean stripe—they don't postulate some weaker sort of necessity, but instead try to explain the apparent necessity in terms of *logical* relations given certain assumptions. But why suggest something so deflationary? If one thinks this necessity is something real, let's get it out there! Why can't the 'force' of causal necessitation determine an accessibility relation, in virtue of which the relevant counterfactuals hold? We don't need to think of all the possible worlds as self-contained little units only possibly related by similarity—the laws of nature give us (physical, or whatever) access to some, but not all, metaphysically possible futures, and so to some, but not all, worlds. Why isn't this a basic sort of relation among worlds that binds some together in a way that not just *any* similarity does? This, at any rate, *seems* to be what postulating genuine natural necessity amounts to; and, if so, it gives us both a restricted sense of necessity that is not trivial and objective support for counterfactuals that isn't afforded by just any true generalization. I don't mean to advocate this view— I tend to the first reply—but *insofar as* one rejects Humeanism, and is willing to postulate natural necessity, why can't it be some such weaker postulation? And if it can, isn't it preferable to the stronger claim—not merely because it is weaker, yet sufficient, but because it is consistent with the rest of our modal evidence?

This brings me to my third, and most important, reply. It seems to me that postulating metaphysical necessity here cannot really serve the purpose of explaining the truth of counterfactuals *in the way* its proponents maintain they need to be explained to have adequate objectivity. To make this point, we need to first recall our imagined worlds of section 1, and consider what the friend of the necessity of laws of nature can say about them.

The standard line, following Kripke in *Naming and Necessity*, maintains that in our conceivings we have established *some* possibility; but when what we imagine, or seem to imagine, is genuinely impossible, we have misdescribed the actual possibility. So, for instance, our purported imagining of Hesperus not being Phosphorus gets at a genuine possibility: namely, that the first celestial body visible in the morning—which, in the situation, we call 'Phosphorus'— might not be the same as the first celestial body visible in the evening—there called 'Hesperus'. In one such situation, we would actually be naming Hesperus 'Hesperus', and in another, Phosphorus 'Phosphorus'—but we can't, in either, be giving *both* names to their actual world referents. Similarly, in apparently imagining non-H_2O water, we are cottoning on to the real possibility of differently constituted stuff behaving just as water does and occurring in just the same situations—but that stuff is not, in fact, water (assuming we agree that water must be H_2O).[34] Call this the 're-description' approach.

How would that be applied here? The proper description of these worlds must be such that our laws actually do obtain there. Since the laws and events we have described are at least not in *accord* with our laws, it could only be because the properties, magnitudes, and so on instantiated in these situations are not *our* properties, magnitudes, and the rest—so our actual laws can still obtain, although in most of our cases, vacuously. (This is the approach we put off considering in section 1.3(c).) Unfortunately, this will often be of dubious plausibility. Is the angle at which this light hits this object not 42 degrees? Is this ball not moving with a velocity that, according to our actual laws, must lead to the other ball's moving off in a way other than it does in our imagined case? If objects attract each other with a force not governed by Gmm'/d^2, is this force not gravity? Or must we have mistakenly assigned masses to the two objects? Or mistakenly identified the distance? I think that 'mass is wrong' is the only move with a prayer here, but even it looks implausible if we imagine the quantity to still be governed by other actual laws, such as $F = ma$. Perhaps some other imaginings can be more plausibly re-described, especially when the concepts in the laws are sufficiently theoretical—maybe when we think we imagine nonradioactive radium, there is good reason to say we haven't really imagined radium, because it must have this atomic composition, and that is ultimately what radioactivity *is*. But it seems implausible as a general rule.[35] Consequently, at least some of our examples cannot be plausibly re-described, and those laws, then, still seem contingent.

But suppose we try to gain strength from our argument. It is a law that objects attract each other with force Gmm'/d^2, and so we have true counter-factuals of the form 'if the mass of the Earth swelled to M, then it would attract

[34] I have adopted Kripke's description of these situations as only seeming imaginings of impossible situations, and in fact genuine imaginings of possible situations, which are wrongly described (Kripke 1980: 102–5, 113–14, 124–5, 128–55). If one prefers Putnam's claim that we can conceive of the impossible, one can delete my use of 'seeming' or 'apparent' as applied to these conceivings; it remains that for each impossible situation we can imagine, there is a (or a set of) corresponding *possible* situation(s)—so that even if it is possible to imagine the impossible, there is always *some* possibility genuinely established by the imagining.

[35] As will become clear, nothing in the main argument *depends* on this—the natural necessities that are 'fully' necessary are, by my account, conventionally, not 'metaphysically', so, even if *all* natural necessities are absolutely necessary. It just seems to me that in a fair number of these cases, our handle on the contents of our imaginings is pretty unproblematic—which is why the 'concession' about radium doesn't seem to license a general claim that we may always be wrong.

Venus with force F'—and whatever other dire consequences. The claim is that we can only understand this as objectively true if in every world where Earth has mass M (and all other actual causal factors are the same), the attraction is F. So, in worlds, like some of those we imagined, where the attraction is *not* F, we *have* to reckon that either the mass of Earth is *not* M, or else that the attractive force is not really gravity.

Now, in effect, I have already responded to this. But there is a deeper point I want to make. Suppose, in order to maintain the counterfactual-support argument, we allow these re-descriptions of our imagined worlds. Still, *even the re-described worlds undermine the counterfactuals, if they are supposed to hold with objective, absolute necessity.* Remember, one of the key ideas is that laws are supposed to support counterfactuals in an objective, nonconventional way. It is the internal nature of the workings of the world, not what we tacitly build into our descriptions, that is supposed to make these true. And so much as a single possible world where the antecedent obtained without the consequent would, on this view, undermine the necessary objectivity. But look at the world we have now been forced to re-describe, or any such world that seems to violate the counterfactuals supported by our laws. Do the re-descriptions undercut the fact that things could be, in all relevant respects other than the supposed identity of these particular properties, exactly the same, while events took a different course? It is *this* that, it seems to me, has to be impossible according to the counterfactual-based argument—but it is not. The 'impossibility' in question seems just a matter of linguistic decision—failure to satisfy this counterfactual, and that *alone*, will suffice for this to be a different property (or, to not satisfy this predicate)—and this undermines the supposed objective, metaphysical force which the postulation of metaphysical necessity was supposed to vouchsafe for the counterfactual. We may re-describe all the properties and quantities we want—if the re-described possibility is genuinely possible, then, while the counterfactual may be exceptionlessly preserved in letter, is has not been saved in spirit.

Put this another way. Suppose we ask, 'Why doesn't Earth, when not attracting Venus with F, have mass M?'—or, more generally, 'Why doesn't a have property p/magnitude m (but only p⋆)?' The only available answer is: 'Because then it would obey these laws, which it doesn't.' Then it is the fact that the counterfactuals fail—and *simply* that fact—that determines the magnitude, rather than the other way around. If anything *else* about m determined these counterfactuals to be true, they would have to be true for our 'alternate' quantities as well. But we see that they are not, and describing our imagined properties or quantities as other than our actual properties or quantities cannot change this fact. It is *simply the failure to satisfy the counterfactuals* that drives the re-description, and this undermines the pretext that it is the 'nature' of the properties themselves, given the laws that actually govern them, that rule out *any* possibility of the holding of the antecedent without the consequent. (This is perhaps clearest if one considers the examples of the laws changing over time (section 1.4).)

Thus, since the re-description of our imagined cases undermines the supposedly needed force of the counterfactuals, I conclude that our cases show that counterfactuals just *don't* have that force, and thus that this argument cannot show that laws of nature are necessary a posteriori. Notice the similarity between this argument and the metaphysical (and semantic) arguments for my rejection of a 'realist' reading of the more familiar necessary a posteriori truths—in both cases, there are acknowledged genuine possibilities that undermine the supposed force of the purported necessity. The difference is that in those other cases the re-descriptions are independently plausible, while they are not, in general, so here. Thus, the case for re-description here requires argument, and the current argument requires—what is *not* needed for the more familiar necessary a posteriori truths—that the postulated necessity be real, rather than conventional. Since this it cannot be, I conclude that, rather than a case for (what would be a) conventional necessity, we have no case for necessity—beyond perhaps natural necessity—at all.

Things are a bit different when we turn to the other argument, the argument from the causal individuation of properties. Here, I think, we *do* find some reason to think that at least *some* laws are necessary. But, I will claim, we have as much reason to reckon these necessities as convention-based as we do the more familiar necessities a posteriori.

Why should we think that properties governed by laws must have the causal powers ascribed to them by these laws? Here is one fast argument: if we have already accepted truths like 'water is H_2O' as necessary, it is presumably because we are individuating substances by their deepest explanatory features. Well, don't laws, in general, tell us things' deepest explanatory features? And what are the 'explanatory features' of a property, or magnitude, other than its causal powers—or anyway, that in virtue of which it has its causal powers?[36]

The force of this argument will vary greatly with how one has interpreted the necessity of water's being H_2O. If one has given it a realist reading, it

---

[36] Some properties, like being a bachelor, or being grue, would seem not to actually be individuated by their 'deepest explanatory features'—but Shoemaker would maintain that this is because they aren't law-governed at all (as such), and so, by his lights, are not genuine properties (I'm not entirely sure whether he would accept this for bachelorhood) (1984: 207–9, 219).

may look quite compelling. But, on the interpretation I have given, it has limited force. First, and most obviously, since it is just an extension of the earlier arguments, it would at best establish the sort of convention-based necessity for laws of nature that we have found applies to the earlier necessities; all of the earlier arguments would apply with equal force, with the semantic and metaphysical arguments applying because of the cases we discussed in section 1. Those worlds would fail to be worlds where our laws didn't obtain *simply* because our conventions require that we describe them so—that we say the properties, magnitudes, and so on are not our properties, but look-alikes— 'schmass, schlight, scharge'. But second, insofar as the necessities *are* dependent on our conventions, we cannot just assume that all our scientific terms are governed by the same sorts of conventions. Maybe some explanatory features count for more, in identifying this or that property in another situation, than another, for any number of reasons.[37] We need, basically, to conduct the relevant thought experiments. Insofar as most of the terms in laws are theoretical (though see some exceptions below), and (I think) we as laymen defer to the experts in their use,[38] then we would need to have practicing scientists perform the relevant thought experiments before we could determine which causal powers (and so, laws) are, and which are not, necessary a posteriori. However, there is no doubt good reason to think they *would* re-describe quite a few of our sort of cases, and so, by implication, judge many causal powers, and so laws, to be so necessary. And so, we have here, I suspect, good reason to think at least some laws *are* necessary a posteriori. But again, the results would just show us how scientists use the terms, and the necessity would be based in analyticity.

There is one more argument here that doesn't seem to be just an extension of the traditional arguments, and hence is a candidate for showing us that

---

[37] This addresses an argument Shoemaker gives (1984: 228–30). Of course, Shoemaker *is* there assuming that the causal necessities are metaphysical, and so reasonably asks how some, but not all, causal powers can be necessary. But, having already addressed his charge that conventions cannot make for *de re* necessities (Sidelle 1989: ch. 3), we have the wherewithal to see how there could be discrimination here.

[38] That is to say, if we are asked the relevant counterfactuals, and it is built into these that scientists would judge the cases other than we might have been inclined to, we will go along with the scientists. Insofar as we do, that is part of our referential intention in the use of the term, which goes into the necessity-determining analytic truth. It may be urged that in these cases, our imaginings are no guide to possibility—but this would be a mistake for two reasons. First, it is our imaginings which indicate the modal significance of the scientists' judgments, and second, they still establish *some* possibilities, which possibilities form the basis for our arguments against the *metaphysical* significance of the necessities that we will accept from the scientists' judgments.

laws of nature are broadly necessary in a really metaphysical, not conventional, way. This is Shoemaker's argument, which he calls 'broadly speaking, epistemological',[39] though it has a metaphysical side. Suppose, Shoemaker asks, that properties could differ in their causal powers.[40] Then, two properties ought to be able to 'switch' their causal powers, either across worlds or across time.[41] But this, Shoemaker contends, is incompatible with the fact that we often know what properties things have, and that some object has continued to have some property over time. Both these results stem from the basic, and obvious, fact that we know what properties objects have in virtue of the causal powers these properties confer—either causal powers to affect us, as in being green or round, or to affect other things, getting to us more indirectly, as in having a mass of 2 micrograms or containing two free electrons. The time argument is easy—if we know that a is F due (directly or indirectly) to the causal powers of a, conferred upon it by F, but property G could come to confer those powers while F loses that ability, then the apparent absence of change in a, with respect to F, could be due to a's coming to be G, while F and G have switched roles. So how can we ever know, for any a and F, that a is still F? In the case of properties differing across worlds, the argument is this: we believe that a is F because of some sort of causal interactions between a and whatever. But if being G could produce those same results, how can we tell that a is F, rather than G? Of course, when the overlap is only partial, we can conduct other tests to discriminate. But when being F or being G will produce just the same results in *any* circumstances, no test *could* distinguish. And lest one say that this is only a problem in worlds where F and G *do* confer the same causal powers, we can note that we seem devoid of resources for telling that we are not in such a world; that is, while there are some properties that we know don't confer the same powers as other properties, there could always be two, or lots of, properties with the causal powers in virtue of which we believe that a is F. On the more metaphysical side, the very possibility is supposed to be disconcerting; surely we have *some* way of identifying properties across worlds, and if there could be such complete switches of causal powers, how is this possible?[42]

    As interesting as this argument is, it is in another way quite perplexing. One would *think* that taking it seriously might start us worrying whether we really *do* know that objects have retained their properties, or that a *is* F (where F is not

---

[39] Shoemaker (1984: 214).

[40] A causal power of a property is to be understood as a power conferred upon objects with that property to bring about P in conditions C, where C includes the instantiation of other properties.   [41] For further discussion of these matters, see Hawthorne, forthcoming.

[42] For something like this metaphysical argument, see Swoyer (1982: sect. II).

itself trivially identified causally: for example, 'has the power to make me feel pain'). Is our confidence that we know these things greater than our confidence that pairs of properties couldn't—or don't—switch their causal powers? If we came to learn that there in fact is—or is even a suspicion of—a property G just like F except in the causal powers it confers in cases quite unlike those that any of us encounter—it would hardly be to the point to insist that we often know that some a is F, so there really can't be any such G. To dismiss this purported G, we would need independent grounds, and if we were to uphold our knowledge of F without such a denial, it would have to be on some sort of *epistemic* grounds. While Shoemaker might insist that the cases differ because we could at least in principle distinguish this F and G, this doesn't seem relevant to the apparent need for either an independent argument or an epistemological solution. In short, it isn't clear why Shoemaker hasn't identified an epistemo-logical *puzzle*, by identifying an underlying, but unnoticed and problematic, *assumption* of many of our ordinary beliefs, rather than an argument for a strong metaphysical position.

A similar point can be made by noting the similarity of Shoemaker's position with a response that might be offered to an argument associated with Locke and Kant, about personal identity. Locke and Kant point out that, assuming immaterial souls to be the seat of thought, we cannot tell, by introspection (or presumably, any other methods), that from day to day—or minute to minute—we have the same souls, *assuming that souls can 'switch' contents*. Since, it is claimed, we *do* know that *we* are around from day to day—even if these switch-ings are taking place—we cannot be our souls. Now, suppose that one con-cluded from this scenario *not* that we can't be our souls, but that our souls *cannot* switch their contents, as Shoemaker concludes that properties cannot switch their causal powers. I think we would have to say either (a) that we can clearly see that they *can*, or (b) that insisting on this just in effect *defines* 'souls' in terms of contents, and so the pretext that we know that our souls are the same from day to day simply redounds to the fact that we know that certain *contents*, or relations between contents (or whatever), are the same day to day, and insofar as one had been thinking of souls as 'that in which thoughts reside', it remains perfectly true that we don't know that *they* are the same from day to day, and sameness of person cannot be the same as sameness of that 'container'. In other words, the reply accomplishes nothing as far as preserving our previously accepted knowledge that we always have the same souls—*unless* it was just already true that we used 'soul' in the more metaphysically innocuous way, in which case the *force* of the claim that souls cannot change their contents becomes trivial—not metaphysical. Just so, I wish to say about applying Shoemaker's metaphysical solution to his epistemological quandary. Either we *mean* by many of our predicates something like 'that which is responsible for producing E in circumstances C (and E′ in C′, etc.)'[43]—so we save our knowledge, but there is no *metaphysical* necessity to these causal powers—or we are really thinking of properties as something distinct from the clusters of causal powers, in which case we need an *epistemological* solution, for the metaphysical solution does nothing to undermine the fact that if there are these extra things beyond the causal powers, we *can't* distinguish them, and they might be distinct.

In addition, it seems clear that for many properties that figure in laws, and that Shoemaker discusses, there *are* ways of identifying them—and so, of being sure of at least some of our knowledge—quite short of *all* their causal powers. Here are some: the angles of incidence, reflection, and refraction of a ray of light hitting some surface. These all figure in laws, and so have causal powers (here I include powers to *be* caused in certain ways)—but if we identify these by their causal powers, it is only by a small subset of them: if we imagine that an angle of incidence of 45 degrees could reflect at 60 degrees, do we have to suppose that we never know that light in fact *does* hit a mirror or prism at 45 degrees? It seems just obvious that the essence—or, to be obvious, definition—of 'contact at 45 degrees', as applied to rays of light, is independent of the actual legal relations between angles of incidence, reflection, and refraction, and that 'incidence', 'reflection', and 'refraction' are also independently defined, and independently identifiable. Velocity and acceleration are another couple of central law-governed properties which seem easily knowable and identifiable aside from many of their actual causal powers.

Of course, the *way* in which these cases handle Shoemaker's epistemological problem is by being properties that *cannot* trade *all* of their causal powers with other properties, because they have features—in many cases, causal features—which suffice for being that property. But this returns us to our earliest reply, which is that these are trivial—either analytic (as in all these cases) or by being the actual values of more general analytic principles of individuation. If we can be sure of our knowledge, independent of epistemological principles, it is because we know that these features, or these causal features, suffice for something to have F—and this is because of how we use the term 'F'. Again, our examples from section 1 help make this vivid. Perhaps our use of 'mass' or 'electricity' or 'quark' makes it such that some of those worlds are best described not as worlds violating our laws, but as worlds instead instantiating 'schmass' and 'schmarks'—but that does not make these worlds go away, and the only way to

---

[43] By 'mean', here, I don't require that the actual causal powers be specified—we could instead, and presumably often do, have the more general 'place-holding' sorts of definitions, as that earlier suggested for 'water'.

understand how 'schmass' is not mass obeying different laws is by taking ourselves to be governing 'mass' by the laws, and causal powers, actually governing mass. There is no call for a more metaphysical interpretation; nor is our understanding of anything enhanced thereby.

Before concluding, it must be admitted that my arguments here—especially my assimilation of the case of laws of nature and causal powers to that of other purported a posteriori necessities—have depended on my assumption that what we can conceive is *somehow* possible; that in the case of a posteriori necessities, we have imagined, but misdescribed, some genuinely possible situation. It has largely been in terms of such situations, and their genuine possibility, that I have disparaged the purported value of postulating the broadest sorts of necessity in order to handle the way in which laws support counterfactuals and the knowledge Shoemaker cites us as having. This is, as I say, an assumption that is standardly accepted by the advocates of necessary a posteriori truths; it is implicit in the standard re-description strategy. However, there is one other strategy for approaching the seeming conceivability of the negations of these necessities, and Shoemaker himself seems to advocate it, so let me briefly comment on it in closing. Rather than allow that we have misdescribed a genuine possibility, we may give a more cavalier dismissal of the supposed imagining: So what? This doesn't admit *any* sort of possibility, beyond the merely epistemic 'This is logically compatible with what else I believe'.[44] Call this 'the dismissal'.

I think that what gives the dismissal whatever attraction it has is the idea, already discussed, that at least some possibilities and necessities stem from the real natures of things, and that there is no reason to think that our imaginations give us any special insight into this. I have already argued that we have no real conception of 'real natures', and certainly no reason to suppose there are any or that we have any knowledge of them. But even if we allowed all this, it would provide us with *no* reason to doubt the possibility of our imagined look-alike worlds. Even if we first thought them up, confusedly, as potential counter-examples to some purportedly necessary truth, we can just as well think of them directly, and insofar as we are not even *purporting* to imagine, say, non-H_2O water, or a gravity-defying 10-pound object, no lack of insight into the 'real natures' of water and mass can be grounds for suspicion. But once the possibilities are so acknowledged, they undermine the pretense of real, as opposed to conventional, necessity, via the metaphysical and semantic arguments, and in some cases—like the two we have considered—they will

---

[44] See Shoemaker (1998: 70–4 and n. 11). Of course, I don't mean to suggest that Shoemaker advocates this for *every* purported imagining, even when the content is the negation of some necessary a posteriori truth.

undermine the argument or rationale for thinking of the proposition as necessary in the first place.[45]

Shoemaker suggests that we imagine either in phenomenal terms—in which case, we only establish the possibility of the world *looking* a certain way, or even the possibility of our undergoing a certain sequence of qualitative states—or else we do it in objective terms. 'But the more theoretical the concepts involved in such a description, the less confident we can be that there is not a contradiction or incoherence that escapes our notice' (1998: 74). I hope it is clear that many of our cases do *not* fall into the first category, and I think it is obvious that many fail to fall into the second as well. At any rate, we have already explained how it can *appear* that our imaginations are irrelevant in theoretical cases—namely, we may intend to let the experts' use of these terms guide our use. After all, they are the ones fundamentally using these terms. But even so, (1) our imaginings are still relevant to showing that it *is* scientific use which determines the proper description of the possibilities, and (2) we have no reason whatsoever to doubt that scientists equally well see the prima-facie imaginability of the scenarios in section 1—even those they are willing or inclined to re-describe—and this can hardly be attributed to their failure to understand the terms. Thus, we have all the same reasons for thinking that the scientists' use has to be understood as determining analytic rules for the use of these terms, and that their counterfactual judgments reflect these intentions, rather than real metaphysical necessities.

My main responses to both these approaches to make out the laws of nature as metaphysically necessary have focused on the fact that the existence of genuine possibilities, established by imagination, undermine any explanatory force (beyond explaining our linguistic behavior, in terms of conventions) or metaphysical punch that these supposed necessities are supposed to have. I considered other replies as well, but they are just gravy. I hope the discussion has made it apparent that this sort of reply will be available for any attempt to establish an a posteriori truth as necessary—in being empirical, there will be at least apparently imaginable cases where the truth fails to obtain, and if these cases do not undermine the claim to necessity, they will at least undermine any metaphysical pretense thereof, and show the necessity to be grounded in convention. It is seeing this that I had in mind in the introduction, in saying that I intended this investigation as a case study in the necessary a posteriori,

---

[45] While I have allowed that some laws are necessary, it has not been on the basis of the arguments we have considered; instead, they are established via the neo-traditional 'ask competent speakers what they would say, given the actual facts'.

and the general significance of imagination and conceivability on both the epistemology and our very understanding of possibility and necessity.

REFERENCES

Armstrong, David (1983), *What is a Law of Nature?* (Cambridge: Cambridge University Press).

—— (1993), 'Reply to Fales', in John Bacon, Keith Campbell, and Lloyd Reinhardt (eds.), *Ontology, Causality and Mind* (Cambridge: Cambridge University Press), 144–51.

Bealer, George (1987), 'The Limits of Scientific Essentialism', in James Tomberlin (ed.), *Philosophical Perspectives, 1: Metaphysics* (Atascadero, Calif.: Ridgeview), 289–365.

Carroll, John (1990), 'The Humean Tradition', *Philosophical Review*, 99: 185–220.

—— (1994), *Laws of Nature* (Cambridge: Cambridge University Press).

Chalmers, David (1996), *The Conscious Mind* (Oxford: Oxford University Press).

Dretske, Fred (1977), 'Laws of Nature', *Philosophy of Science*, 44: 248–68.

Fales, Evan (1993), 'Are Causal Laws Contingent?', in John Bacon, Keith Campbell, and Lloyd Reinhardt (eds.), *Ontology, Causality and Mind* (Cambridge: Cambridge University Press), 121–44.

Harré, Rom, and Madden, E. H. (1975), *Causal Powers* (Totowa, NJ: Rowman & Littlefield).

Hawthorne, John (forthcoming), 'Causal Structuralism', in James Tomberlin (ed.), *Philosophical Perspectives* (Atascadero, Calif.: Ridgeview).

Jackson, Frank (1998), *From Metaphysics to Ethics: A Defence of Conceptual Analysis* (Oxford: Oxford University Press).

Kneale, William (1949), *Probability and Induction* (Oxford: Clarendon Press).

Kripke, Saul (1971), 'Identity and Necessity', in Milton K. Munitz (ed.), *Identity and Individuation* (New York: New York University Press), 135–64.

—— (1980), *Naming and Necessity* (Cambridge, Mass.: Harvard University Press).

Lewis, David (1986), *Philosophical Papers*, ii (New York: Oxford University Press).

Putnam, Hilary (1975), 'The Meaning of "Meaning"', in *Mind, Language and Reality* (Cambridge: Cambridge University Press), 215–71.

Shoemaker, Sydney (1984), 'Causality and Properties', in *Identity, Cause and Mind* (Cambridge: Cambridge University Press), 234–60.

—— (1998), 'Causal and Metaphysical Necessity', *Pacific Philosophical Quarterly*, 79: 59–77.

Sidelle, Alan (1989), *Necessity, Essence and Individuation* (Ithaca, NY: Cornell University Press).

—— (1992a), 'Identity and the Identity-Like', *Philosophical Topics*, 20: 269–92.

Sidelle, Alan (1992*b*), 'Rigidity, Ontology and Semantic Structure', *Journal of Philosophy*, 98(8): 410–30.

—— (1995), 'A Semantic Account of Rigidity', *Philosophical Studies*, 80: 69–105.

Swoyer, Chris (1982), 'The Nature of Natural Laws', *Australasian Journal of Philosophy*, 60: 203–23.

Tooley, Michael (1977), 'The Nature of Laws', *Canadian Journal of Philosophy*, 7: 667–98.

—— (1987), *Causation: A Realist Approach* (Oxford: Clarendon Press).

Tweedale, Martin (1984), 'Determinable and Substantival Universals', in Radu J. Bogdan (ed.), *D. M. Armstrong, Profiles*, iv (Dordrecht: Reidel).

9

The Art of the Impossible

ROY SORENSEN

Prize: One hundred dollars to the first person who identifies a picture of a logical impossibility. I may be willing to pay more for the painting itself. This finder's fee is simply for pointing out the picture. Let me explain more precisely what I seek.

1 Illegal Pictures

There is a genre of children's picture puzzles that is marked by the question 'What is wrong with this picture?' Well, that goat does not belong in the library. That clock is mirror-reversed. Ostriches do not fly. . . . The job of the viewer is to spot the incongruities.

An impossible picture features a nomic incongruity—a violation of a law. There are many pictures that depict scientifically impossible situations. René Magritte's *Collective Invention* features a reverse mermaid: woman from foot to waist, fish from waist to gills.

An impossible situation need not involve an impossible *object*. Many of Magritte's paintings feature ordinary objects in impossible *relationships*. *Zeno's Arrow* simply shows a huge rock that fails to be gravitationally related to the earth. Actually, all 'impossible objects' involve impossible relationships. For

An ancestor of this chapter was presented at the University of Saskatchewan. I thank Karl Pfeifer, Walter Sinnott-Armstrong, and the editors of this volume, Tamar Gendler and John Hawthorne, for comments and imaginative suggestions. I thank Milton Katz for permission to reprint one of his figures, and István Orosz for permission to reprint his drawings.

instance, the impossibility of Magritte's reverse mermaid involves an imposs-ible relation among body parts.

Empirical background is needed to infer that Magritte's reverse mermaid cannot be actual. Maybe empirical knowledge sometimes suffices for the identi-fication of a *necessary* falsehood. Perhaps reverse mermaids are 'metaphysically impossible'. The essentialist, Saul Kripke (1980), has argued that 'unicorn' is a necessarily empty term. He thinks that species terms work like names. Under Kripke's causal theory, only objects that bear the appropriate historical relation with a name can be denoted by that name. So Kripke must deny that a picture of a unicorn depicts an animal that could exist. He would not be claiming that the impossibility of unicorns could be inferred from the picture alone. Knowledge that unicorns do not exist is a posteriori, the result of scientific investigation.

I am interested in pictures that depict a priori impossibilities. Analyticity is a traditional source of apriority. A statement is *semantically* analytic if its truth-value is determined by the meanings of its words. W. V. Quine (1951) excited controversy about these statements that persists today. Although I am personally content with the analytic/synthetic distinction, I confine the search to a picture that avoids this controversy. Quine does not object to *syntactically* analytic state-ments. These statements owe their truth-value just to their logical words.

Any logical truth is syntactically analytic. A logical truth is a theorem of a cor-rect theory of what entails what. Standard logic (first-order predicate logic with identity) forms the core of this theory. Thus the class of logical truths includes any theorem found in logic textbooks. The negation of a logical truth is a logi-cal falsehood. So a perceptual depiction of a logical falsehood suffices for the prize.

Although 'logical falsehood' is clear enough, 'perceptually depicts a logical falsehood' is obscure. There are no plausible, precise theories of depiction. Prize-seekers need not be discouraged. People make discoveries without being able to define what they have discovered.

In a way, I am being strict. For I am not issuing the reward for a picture of a mere conceptual impossibility. One reason, aside from the desire for a clear goal, is that I am satisfied that a number of artists have composed scenes that violate geometrical truths. For instance, the relative proximity relations of the columns in István Orosz's *Cavalier* (Fig. 1) are inconsistent. I think most philosophers should be receptive to the general possibility of depicting the impossible. For most philosophers agree that it is possible to believe the impossible. And if it is possible to *believe* the impossible, then what would stand in the way of graph-ically representing the impossible?

Consider purely pictorial instructions. When frustrated by Ikea's pamphlets for assembling furniture (which are designed to rely on no knowledge of a

Fig. 1. *Cavalier*, by István Orosz. Reproduced by courtesy of the artist.

language), I have doubted the possibility of executing the instructions. I have always been wrong. But have I been *necessarily* mistaken?

There are prominent philosophers who do not believe that one can believe the impossible. Robert Stalnaker (1984) maintains that the object of belief must be a nonempty set of *possible* worlds. Ruth Marcus (1981) claims that belief relates to possibility as knowledge to truth. That is, belief has an external defeasibility condition. When we learn that p is impossible, we retract our attribution of belief. Or so she argues. Others insist that we can believe only what we can understand, and that anyone who understands a contradiction realizes that it is not true—and so does not believe it. Causal theorists say that the object of belief is the state of affairs that would cause that belief under optimal conditions. There are no such conditions for impossibilities. Some devotees of the principle of charity (which instructs us to interpret agents as rational) claim that belief in impossibilities is unintelligible. Others say that the appearance of contradiction should always trigger the postulation of an ambiguity.

All of these anti-contradiction strategies sound good in theory, but fall flat in practice. I long believed that 'The American Thanksgiving Holiday is on the last Thursday of November which is the fourth Thursday in November'. Only in November 2000, which contains five Thursdays, did I realize that these two definite descriptions only partially overlap. Of course, I long knew that November has more than twenty-eight days and that there are only seven days in a week and that the first day of the month cycles forward each year. But I did not pull together all these analytical truths.

If you do not think that the believability of contradictions can be established by the Method of Humiliating Confession, I also offer a Cartesian argument. The essential idea is that belief that someone believes at least one contradiction is infallible (Sorensen 1996). After all, if I mistakenly believe that it is impossible to believe the impossible, then that very mistake would itself be a belief in an impossibility.

In my opinion, the only theory that permits belief in the impossible is the linguistic account of the object of belief. To believe is to believe something that resembles a sentence—if not a sentence of a natural language, then a sentence in the 'language of thought'.

Are pictures sentences? John M. Kennedy (1974: 110) speaks of a 'language of lines', and supplies a vocabulary of concave corners, convex corners, occluding edges, and occluding bounds. His discussion of surface layouts can be understood as an articulation of the syntax for constructing outline pictures. The mere fact that there are computer programs for constructing illustrations shows that important kinds of pictures are combinatoric. However, many nonlinguistic phenomena are combinatoric: chemistry, checkers, building-block toys. It is one thing to convey information in a modular fashion. It is another to be the object of a propositional attitude.

2 Pseudo-Pictures

Those who regard pictures as sentences are often unclear about whether *impossible* pictures actually qualify as sentences. Linguists say that a language is a set of sentences defined by a vocabulary and a grammar specifying how the words can be combined into sentences. Therefore, ungrammatical sentences are not part of the language. Thus, if one characterizes impossible pictures as ungrammatical sentences of the picture language (Huffman 1971), then one should not count them as pictures. This seems harsh. Kennedy attempts a compromise:

Combining incompatible words makes an 'impossible' sentence, a sentence that can have no direct referent in reality. An example is 'Colorless green ideas sleep furiously.'

The sentence is grammatical—it is not nonsense like 'furiously sleep ideas green colorless.' A drawing, too, can show impossible things, things that cannot have a direct equivalent in reality. (Kennedy 1974: 146)

If 'Colorless green ideas sleep furiously' expressed an impossibility, then it would have a negation that expresses a necessary truth. But Chomsky regards 'It is not the case that colorless green ideas sleep furiously' as equally meaningless. He takes his most famous utterance 'Colorless green ideas sleep furiously' to illustrate the fact that a meaningless sentence can conform to the grammar of a language. He thinks that the sentence violates semantic rules. By contrast, Chomsky (correctly) thinks that contradictory statements fully conform to all rules of the language. They merely express propositions that are necessarily false. A grammar that fails to generate contradictory English sentences is an inadequate grammar. Grammaticality cannot be a necessary or sufficient condition for possibility.

Many of those who reject the idea that pictures are sentences will still be inclined to regard meaningless pictures as failed attempts at picturing. Happily, prize-seekers need not take sides. Contradictions are meaningful. If there were literally a language of outlines, contradictory pictures would be sentences within that language.

3 Pictures have a Role within Propositions

I agree with most philosophers in denying that pictures are discursive. I also conform to my colleagues' view that pictures cannot be believed on their own. Photographs do not lie. Nor do they tell the truth. They can be evidence of the truth by virtue of the optical information they carry. But bare photographs can no more be believed than bare fingerprints.

I can believe that a picture of a flying saucer is undoctored. I can believe that a town square in Holland remains as a sixteenth-century artist drew it. But I cannot believe the picture itself. Nevertheless, pictorial representations (drawings, maps, photographs) figure in what I believe. As David Kaplan (1996: 364) observes: 'Many of our beliefs are of the form "The color of her hair is——," or "The song he was singing went——," where the blanks are filled with images, sensory impressions, or what have you, but certainly not words.' Although raw images lack truth-values and so cannot figure as premises or conclusions, they can be part of premises that do have truth-values:

(1) The color of her hair is——.
(2) The color of her sister's hair is also——.
(3) At least two women have hair that is——.

The argument is sound, because I am thinking of two women who make the premises true and because the argument is valid. Some of our beliefs are demonstrative. Demonstratives cannot be reduced to qualitative descriptions. Hence, pictures can play an essential role in forming the objects of belief.

Nevertheless, I am not interested in the contradiction 'The color of her hair is——and is not——'. Although the image plays a role in constituting this demonstrative contradiction, the image is not doing any logical work.

I am not trying to raise the standard of representation to an impossible height. If I thought a picture of a logical impossibility were impossible, then I would feel safe in posting a large prize. In fact, I expect to pay the $100 finder's fee. I may even wind up paying someone who does not actually believe that it is possible to picture a logical impossibility. For all he needs to do is to persuade me. This conditional proof can exploit my concession that conceptually impossible pictures are possible. The prize could be won simply by demonstrating the following hypothetical: If there are pictures of conceptual impossibilities, then *this* is a picture of a logical impossibility.

The issue for me is the step from conceptual impossibility to logical impossibility. Prize-seekers will find it useful to see what standard of evidence I have applied to the acceptance of conceptual impossibilities.

4 Historical Background

On the basis of introspection, the British empiricists believed that ideas have pictorial properties. A speaker uses sentences to describe his mental images. The pictorial mode of representation is epistemically prior to the discursive mode. Nevertheless, the empiricists imposed an important, famous limit on the expressive scope of pictures. David Hume writes:

Tis an establish'd maxim in metaphysics, *That whatever the mind clearly conceives includes the idea of possible existence, or in other words, that nothing we imagine is absolutely impossible.* We can form the idea of a golden mountain, and from thence conclude that such a mountain may actually exist. We can form no idea of a mountain without a valley, and therefore regard it as impossible. (1739–40: 32)

A picture of a conceptual impossibility would generate counter-examples to Hume's principle that anything which is conceivable is possible. People would look at the picture and thereby conceive an impossible scene. The artist would have proved a philosophical proposition just as Clyde Tombaugh proved the astronomical proposition that there is a ninth planet by photographing Pluto in 1930.

Photographs can only be of actual objects. But drawings can prove the possibility of uninstantiated objects. A mathematician can convince an engineer that a larger cube can pass through a smaller cube by drawing a smaller cube with a diagonal tunnel. (A cube with a 1-meter face has a diagonal equal to the square root of 2 meters.) The proof works even if no one bothers to build the perforated cube.

If drawing X demonstrates the possibility of X, then we appear to have a quick proof that it is impossible to draw an impossible object. Drawing an impossible object would show that it is possible for an impossible thing to exist. Contradiction. Therefore, it is impossible to draw an impossible object.

This proof is sound. But only when read *de re* (as referring to a thing and then reporting a feature of it). For instance, the *de re* report 'The discoverer of the largest prime number is being drawn as a winner of the Fields Medal' entails that the discoverer of the largest prime number exists. But some depiction is *de dicto* (as concerning a representation). For instance, the *de dicto* report 'In the picture, the discoverer of the largest prime number is receiving the Fields Medal' does not entail that there is a discoverer of the largest prime number. Nor does it entail that it is possible for someone to discover the largest prime number. Any person who earns the $100 finder's fee will be giving me a *de dicto* report. He will not be claiming to have discovered an impossibility that has secured the attention of a faithful portraitist.

5 Requirements

Philosophical tradition and common sense converge on what counts as an acceptable depiction of the logically impossible. None of the requirements below are intended to indulge personal idiosyncrasies.

5.1 *Openness to Inspection*

A description of an impossible situation should be detailed enough to convey the nature of the impossibility. Ditto for depiction. Paul Tidman's (1994) joke picture of a square circle (Fig. 2) violates this requirement. Since Hume is not

Fig. 2. Square circle, side view.

present to balk Tidman's evasiveness, I balk on Hume's behalf. If evasive perspectives are permitted, anyone can 'draw' anything (see Fig. 3). A genuine

●

Fig. 3. Any object as seen in the distance.

depiction must place no limit on potential detail. I do not insist on limitless
actual detail. I merely require that the specimen be open to view.

Well, let's not be chauvinistic about vision. Any sense modality will do. A
depiction via smell or a less-known sense would be equally acceptable.

Roger Shepherd (1964) devised a tone that seems to rise endlessly.
Jean-Claude Risset (1997) has developed aesthetic possibilities of this and other
acoustic illusions (such as ever-accelerating beats) in his computer music. For
example, in *Little Big Boy*, there is a sound which goes down the scale but ends
up higher in pitch. The endless 'nontransitive descent' represents the dropping
of the atomic bomb on Hiroshima. Visual illusions are better known than
auditory illusions because artists have long been able to draw trick figures with
just a pencil. Auditory illusions generally require careful control by computer
synthesis. However, musicologists have discovered notated pitch circularity
dating back as far as 1550 (Braus 1995: 324).

The inconsistencies of paradoxical music are at the level of the medium of
representation, rather than at the level of the thing represented. It is like the
inconsistency inspired by the light–dark spectrum from nonblack to black. We
perceive the spectrum as devoid of transition points, but the spectrum as a
whole as embodying a complete transformation.

There is a strand of the empiricist tradition that favors touch over sight. The
young George Berkeley would have actually preferred a *sculpture* of a round
square—something he could put his hands on. In his *New Theory of Vision*,
Berkeley argued that touch is the primary sense modality; vision tells us about
reality only after we learn how to correlate what we see with what we feel.

5.2 *No Equivocation*

In Taxicab geometry all squares are round squares (Krause 1975). In this form
of non-Euclidean geometry, distance is measured by how a taxi travels on a

coordinate plane. A circle is a figure whose perimeter is everywhere equidistant from its center. Consequently, all circles are squares, and all squares are circles. Thus a round square in Taxicab geometry is a tautologous figure rather than a contradictory one. But this contrast is achieved by adopting a different meaning for 'distance'. When people say that round squares are impossible, they should be read as making a claim in the framework of Euclidean geometry. Similarly, I give no quarter (much less $100) to any candidate who fiddles with the meaning of 'there is', 'and', 'etc.', etc.

Drawings made in axonomic perspective or anamorphic perspective have the superficial appearance of impossibility. But unfamiliarity should not be confused with incongruity. Alternative systems of representation differ without necessarily disagreeing. I want to see a genuine clash with logic.

Stick to the standard logical concept of 'contradiction'. Soviet artists represented 'historical contradictions' in all relevant detail. Their usage echoes Georg Hegel and Karl Marx. These philosophers used 'contradiction' broadly. (Daniel Goldstick (1995) points out that Hegel and Marx also used it in the narrower sense more familiar to contemporary logicians.) Hegel and Marx included phenomena analogous to gainsaying in a dialogue. Adorno elaborated this into a dialectical metaphysics in which contradiction plays a central role. This is the famous process which begins with a thesis. The thesis stimulates an anti-thesis. The anti-thesis stimulates synthesis. The resulting synthesis between thesis and anti-thesis is itself a more comprehensive thesis. Accordingly, this higher thesis stimulates a higher anti-thesis and another round of synthesizing. Each contradiction is the effect of a limited vantage point. By building on the remains of past positions, dialectical descendants command higher ground and a more sweeping vista. Contradictions precipitate and sustain their own transcendence. Soviet artists were instructed on how the history of thought, and indeed, just plain history, is built on the backs of dead contradictions. These artists brought new meaning to the theory of perspective.

Communism encourages an itchy trigger finger. Contradictions abound—worldwide. Graham Priest (1987), uses 'contradiction' in a way that is intended to encompass ordinary scenes such as Vladimir being in a doorway (because Vladimir is both in and out of the room).

In addition to being broader than the logical sense of 'contradiction', the dialectical conception of contradiction is also narrower: the dialectical conception implies that all contradictions are divisible into self-consistent conjuncts that have the stereotypical P & ~P form. Many important logical contradictions are not divisible in this way. Consider Hegel's belief that the law of identity is false. This logical falsehood, $\sim(x)$ $(x = x)$, is not divisible into self-consistent conjuncts. Nor can we divide Bertrand Russell's early belief that there is a set for every property. Nor Ludwig Wittgenstein's Tractarian belief that there is a decision procedure for all logical truths (Fogelin 1976: ch. 4). Each philosopher contradicted himself. But none were 'of two minds'.

Those who believe that anything can be depicted also believe an indivisible contradiction. To see why, first note that some pictures depict other pictures. For instance, Watteau's *L'Enseigne de Gersaint* features an art merchant selling his merchandise. Here is a logical truth: there is no picture that depicts all and only those pictures that do not depict themselves. If this picture depicts itself, then it does not depict itself. But if it does not depict itself, then it must be amongst the pictures it depicts. Contradiction. James F. Thomson (1962: 104) discusses a whole family of contradictions that have this logical form.

This logic exercise proves decisively that there are logically impossible depictions. Artists are imaginative people. But imagination is not a resource for evading logical limits. My $100 fee can still be earned, because I want only a picture that depicts a logical impossibility, not a picture that is itself logically impossible.

For the sake of administrative ease, I will pay a $10 bonus for an indivisible contradiction. The assumption that all impossible figures are divisible into self-consistent components is commonly made by philosophers—for instance, Max Cresswell (1983). The assumption is made uniformly by psychologists.

In impossibles, each part is ecological, but the combination of the parts violates nature. They could not exist, so they are imaginary, but the fact that they are imaginary does not make them impossible. To make an imaginary object, parts are combined in possible ways. The combination can be possible but be a combination that does not exist. For example, there is nothing about surfaces and air spaces that rules out a horse with a horn, like a unicorn. Nature has not seen fit to evolve unicorns, but it could do so without contravening its own ways with surfaces and air. The parts of a unicorn are ecological. The combination of parts breaks no laws of solidity. In language, one may claim 'I saw a unicorn, a horse with a horn.' In language, as in pictures, to be imaginative is to combine familiar parts in possible but novel ways, whereas to be impossible is to combine the parts in novel ways that violate rules of nature. (Kennedy 1974: 149–50)

All mathematical analyses of impossible figures have conformed to the idea that impossible figures are built from possible parts. For instance, Diego Uribe has analyzed an infinite class of impossible figures as jig-saw puzzles of just thirty-two equilateral triangles consisting of special bar elements (Ernst 1986b: 58). This is the basis for software (available free over the Web) that enables you to mechanically construct impossible objects by manipulating these triangles. But if we take the analogy with language seriously, we should doubt that these analyses exhaust the stock of impossible figures. All natural languages can express infinitely many indivisible contradictions. If it is possible to pictorially represent a contradiction, then it should be possible to pictorially represent an indivisible contradiction.

An indivisibly inconsistent picture would side-step the problem of distinguishing inconsistency from doubt. Consider 'continuity' errors in movies. For instance, in the last ten minutes of *Mission: Impossible 2*, secret agent Ethan Hunt is riding a motorcycle in a chase scene. The last two digits of his license plate shift from 69 to 89. This production error does not make the movie inconsistent about the license plate number. Instead, the conflicting depictions merely create doubt whether the license plate ends with 69 or 89. Whenever the contradiction is divisible, there is the opportunity to interpret the scene in this uninteresting way. Depiction of an indivisible contradiction would avoid this hitch.

5.3   *The Depiction must be Perceptual*

On a purely stipulational conception of 'depict', merely intending x to be an F makes x an F. Thus, if a child scribbles on a page and says that the scribble is his mother, then the scribble is a depiction of his mother. Thinking so makes it so.

Actually, I think that this subjectivist construal of stipulation is misconceived. Stipulation is more complicated and defeasible (Horowitz 1983). Couples who simply declare themselves to be married do not thereby become married. It might be pleasant to think of them as married. But they can only marry with the help of the right sort of official conducting the proper sort of ceremony. Artistic stipulation has a similar but fainter institutional infrastructure. Like the preacher, the artist is participating in a practice that requires knowledge of procedures and institutional backing. Nearly all of us are artists in the capacious sense that we draw simple pictures. Outline drawings are understood by toddlers without training (Hochberg and Brooks 1962). Consequently, outline drawings are understood in all cultures (Kennedy 1974: ch. 5). True, unfamiliar objects are misconstrued as more familiar objects. But that kind of error only underscores a firm grasp of how drawings represent objects. Prehistoric cave paintings show that this ability has been around for a very long time. Special training and the infrastructure of an art community considerably amplify our stipulative capacity. The same applies to other stipulative activities, such as the construction of thought experiments (Sorensen 1992). Every healthy adult constructs experiments that edify by virtue of reflections on their design rather than by execution. But only those who are inducted into special fields of science and philosophy magnify this power.

In any case, if subjectivist 'depiction' sufficed, then my oldest son Maxwell would deserve the $100 reward. At age three, he loved the color green. In fact, he loved it to the exclusion of all other colors. Maxwell became a green maximizer. He drew a picture of a 'green all over rainbow' with a single green crayon. Since a rainbow must be multicolored, no scene could match my son's description.

The problem with Maxwell's picture is that it does not reveal what it would be like to see a uniformly green rainbow. In artistic contexts, 'depict' is used in a way that allows failure. When students take art classes, they want to learn how to render objects *perceptually*. Techniques such as drawing in perspective capitalize on the running start we all have from folk optics. The students already know how to depict objects discursively via pure stipulation (or stipulation plus an ancillary stick figure). Suppose the art instructor says, 'Drawing is not as hard as it looks. All you need to do is to decide what your marks on the canvas are intended to represent. Then, presto, you are done.' The art students will rightly demand a tuition refund.

One of René Magritte's most famous pictures, *The Treason of the Pictures (This is not a pipe)* consists of a picture of a pipe along with the caption 'This is not a pipe'. Peter Strawson might be tempted to say that this is not a depiction of anything. According to Strawson (1952: 2–3), a statement of the form P & not-P says nothing because the 'not-P' merely cancels out the P. Others interpret the picture as making the point that the *picture* of the pipe is not itself a pipe. This illustrates a standard alternative to viewing a picture as depicting an impossibility: one attributes an ambiguity. To forestall this attribution of an ambiguity, suppose the caption had instead been 'This is not a picture of a pipe'. Would Magritte then have pictured a contradiction?

Well, maybe. But it would not be the kind of picture I seek. I want the contradiction to be within the picture, not between the picture and its caption. I am not forbidding the kind of illocutionary variety that Wittgenstein alludes to when he notes that a picture of a boxer can be used to report or instruct or inquire. But I do forbid examples in which the content of the picture plays no role. For instance, the picture plays no role in the pictorial conundrum (inspired by Peter Geach (1948)) shown in Figure 4. Here is the enigma: Some pictures are well-titled, in that they accurately describe the picture. Other pictures are ill-titled, because they are descriptively inaccurate. But now consider *Ill-titled*. If *Ill-titled* is ill-titled, then its title accurately describes the picture, and so *Ill-titled* is well-titled. But if *Ill-titled* is well-titled, then the picture's title fails

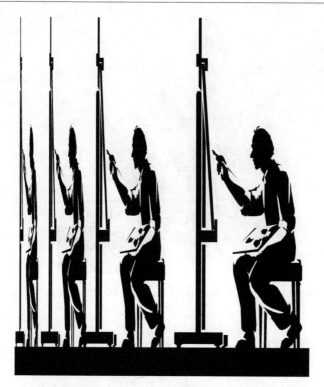

Fig. 4. Ill-titled, inspired by Peter Geach.

to describe itself, and so is ill-titled. Contradiction. Notice that the dilemma is independent of anything hanging above the caption.

I also ban pragmatic paradoxes such as *Fall of the Undepictable Domino* (Fig. 5). The very act of depicting the domino undermines its status as undepictable.

And let there be no crucial reliance on labels. Suppose there are two figures in a picture, one labeled 'Albanian tomato' and the other labeled 'Something that cannot coexist with an Albanian tomato'. This picture is inconsistent, but only discursively so. There are subtler ways to smuggle in discursive elements. There are no words in *Thought Clouds* (Fig. 6). Thought clouds are the cartoonist's iconographic symbols for thoughts. Embedding thought clouds within thought clouds suggests a kind of cognitive impossibility. This appearance of impossibility is embraced by some logicians. They try to solve the liar paradox by insisting that all thoughts be 'grounded' (Burge 1984). It is not clear that there is anything really impossible about an infinite regress of embedded thoughts. The feeling that ungrounded thoughts are impossible bears a suspicious resemblance to the feeling that an infinite past is impossible. But my main reservation about *Thought Clouds* is its employment of those

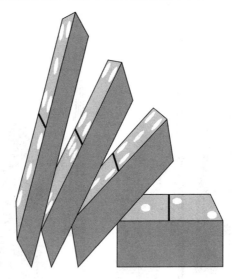

Fig. 5. Fall of the Undepictable Domino.

Fig. 6. Thought Clouds.

discursive-looking icons. I want an impossible picture, not an impossible pictogram.

Fallacious geometrical proofs often rely on mislabeled diagrams. The same applies to figures in rule books. The official rule book for Little League Baseball mandates that home plate be an irregular pentagon (Fig. 7). This figure is impossible because it requires the existence of a (12, 12, 17) right triangle

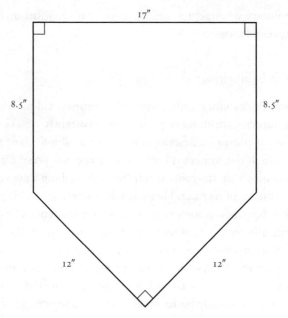

Fig. 7. Home plate.

(Bradley 1996). According to the Pythagorean theorem, the squares of the sides of a right triangle must add up to the square of the hypotenuse: $a^2 + b^2 = c^2$. But $12^2 + 12^2 = 288 \neq 289 = 17^2$. This example illustrates Wittgenstein's contention that many contradictions are inconveniences rather than disasters. 'Home plate' is used in definitions of 'strike zone', 'out', 'run', and so on. Yet thousands of valid Little League baseball games have been played with home plates that only approximate a regulation home plate.

Belief in a contradiction sometimes leads to a disaster. For instance, scheduling inconsistencies have put trains on collision courses. But a priori errors are no more likely to lead to disaster than a posteriori errors. We are more apt to regret an a priori error because we had everything needed to detect the mistake. But we only police our calendars and calculations with the same vigilance as we check our empirical assumptions. This is good evidence that the consequences of a priori error are only about as serious as the consequences of a posteriori error.

These points about quality control generalize to the visual system. A priori perceptual errors are bad, but may be acceptable given the right trade-off for speed, generality, and ruggedness. Just as a busy street portraitist may resign himself to some errors of perspective, the visual system may stray from

Euclidean geometry when representing a scene. These violations of the law do not constitute dissidence.

5.4 *Adverbial Inconsistency is not Enough*

There is a process/product ambiguity in 'inconsistent description'. When under police interrogation, most people inconsistently describe their past activities. These inconsistent descriptions are not descriptions of an inconsistent world in which the suspect is both present and not present at work on 3 January 2001 at 9:05 a.m. Instead, the testifier is describing a consistent state of affairs in an inconsistent manner. He makes *de re* reference to his past and then inadvertently assigns inconsistent properties to this sequence of events.

Most stories inherit a consistency constraint from the author's belief that inconsistencies are inaccuracies. The story purports to be accurate testimony. Inconsistencies in this kind of fictional testimony must therefore be treated in the way inconsistencies of factual narratives are treated. Standardly, the story-teller is embarrassed by his inconsistencies and regards them as mistakes. We should not interpret screen writers for *Mission: Impossible 1* as describing an impossible world in which secret agent Ethan Hunt descends head first to within one inch of a vault floor, yet then has room enough to prevent a bead of sweat from hitting the floor by catching it with his outstretched hand.

A world is not the sort of thing that can be inconsistent. The only bearers of inconsistency are representations. Consistency is just the absence of inconsistency. Nonrepresentations are trivially consistent because they do not even have an opportunity to be inconsistent.

Just as story-telling is parasitic on factual testimony, so depictions are parasitic on factual drawing. The artist purports to be presenting an accurate visual record. Consider art students learning how to draw in perspective. They are embarrassed by their inconsistent renderings of size and proximity relationships. William Hogarth (1697–1764) lampooned these errors in his widely reprinted drawing *False Perspective*.

Some errors in perspective are forced by competing aesthetic desiderata. Artists deliberately sacrifice coherence for the sake of other aesthetic advantages. For example, a fifteenth-century painting of the Archangel Gabriel telling Mary about her future son recesses a middle pillar for the sake of an uninterrupted foreground. (The picture is reproduced in Ernst (1986*a*: 76).) The artist was probably aware of the inconsistency. But this does not mean he was depicting a miraculous violation of geometry.

The opposite of forced inconsistency is gratuitous inconsistency. In Gary Trudeau's comic strip *Doonesbury*, there are often conflicting depictions of background material. A cup will appear in one frame, disappear in the next, and then reappear in a third frame. Trudeau introduces these inconsistencies in a playful manner. He is not depicting strange appearances and reappearances of household bric-à-brac. He is flippantly depicting ordinary scenes.

Good for him! When you need to say something vividly, say it with a contradiction. Caricatures are easier to recognize than pictures with strict adherence to geometrical fidelity (Ryan and Schwartz 1956; Dwyer 1967). James Shellow, the defense attorney for Sandy Murphy, contended that her husband (the Las Vegas millionaire Ted Binion) died in 1998 from the synergistic effect of heroin, alcohol, and the prescription sedative Xanax. The attorney explained that in this case $1 + 1 + 1 = 6$. (Admittedly, the jury felt it did not add up: Murphy was convicted along with her lover.)

5.5   *An Inconsistent Infrastructure is Not Enough*

The art of inconsistency must be distinguished from art that merely rests on inconsistent perceptual processes. Consider traditional engraving. The engraver creates shades of gray by scratching sharp black lines into a white surface. Take a good look at George Washington's engraved picture on a one-dollar bill. Washington's face looks gray even after you notice that the picture is composed solely of fine black lines. All engraved portraits exploit the 'spreading effect': at a sufficiently fine scale, black and white are optically fused into gray. Varying the density of the lines renders shadows and shades of gray. Many report that the optical fusion does not wipe out the perception of black and white. The same surface is seen simultaneously as gray all over and as black and white all over. Unlike the Necker cube, there is no alternation between consistent interpretations. There is a single inconsistent interpretation. Yet the portrait of George Washington is perfectly pedestrian. Inconsistent processes can yield a consistent product.

The spreading effect can be explained in terms of competing homunculi (Hurvich 1981). One feature detector analyzes the fine lines as just fine lines. A rival feature detector averages the black lines with the white spaces to obtain feature *gray*. These homunculi are not supervised, so neither is silenced or muted. Consequently, the observer sees the same surface both ways.

A parallel explanation can be offered for the waterfall illusion. If you stare at a waterfall and then look at neighboring rocks, the rocks appear to move while remaining stationary. Staring at the waterfall adapts some position detectors, but not others. When your eyes turn to the rocks, these adapted detectors indicate that a movement in the opposite direction of the waterfall is taking place. However, your unadapted detectors declare that the rocks are not moving. Absent the intervention of a censor, we see the rocks both ways at once. Some psychologists have interpreted this as an example of seeing the logically impossible:

although the after-effect gives a very clear illusion of movement, the apparently moving features nevertheless seem to stay still! That is, we are still aware of features remaining in their 'proper' locations even though they are seen as moving. What we see is logically impossible! (Frisby 1979: 101)

Tim Crane (1988) thinks this shows that concepts cannot be part of perception. One of the standard tests for ambiguity is the contradiction test. If a competent speaker believes that x is F and x is not G, then F and G must have distinct meanings that is, express different concepts. However, in the waterfall illusion, the speaker is inclined to believe that the rock is moving and not moving. The only way to retain the contradiction test and deny ambiguity is to abandon the assumption that concepts are involved in the speaker's visual judgment.

D. H. Mellor boggles at how a judgment can be inconsistent if it does not involve concepts. Just what could be the contradiction? A contradiction is a proposition, so necessarily involves concepts. He goes on to deny that there is any tendency to believe a contradiction. The waterfall illusion simply involves two inclinations that cancel out:

We could, however, be inclined to believe that Fa, while also being inclined to believe that ~Fa. And that, I submit, is what happens in the Waterfall Illusion. There isn't simply, as Crane claims, 'a contradiction in the <u>one</u> content of one attitude'. Rather we are conscious of seeing that a moves while also seeing that it doesn't. One of these two perceptual experiences gives us the corresponding belief, say that a doesn't move, which then suppresses the rival inclination to believe that it does. (1988: 149)

Mellor is proposing a divide-and-conquer solution. There is merely disagreement between two self-consistent perceptual experiences.

I disagree with Crane and Mellor. The rocks are perceived inconsistently, but it does not follow that the observer perceives a contradiction. The observer sees ordinary rocks via an inconsistent homuncular process. Such inconsistent processes are common. What is uncommon is our awareness of the inconsistency. Only in atypically simple situations do we notice incoherences that are systemic to experience.

5.6 *Ambiguity is Not Enough*

The famous psychological reaction to ambiguous figures is ambivalent alternation between equally plausible, consistent interpretations. This instability is exploited in István Orosz's balcony scene. One cannot tell which corner of the

Fig. 8. *Balcony*, by István Orosz.
Reproduced by courtesy of the artist.

balcony is closer. The eye just vacillates between both interpretations. But visual ambiguity can stimulate reactions other than ambivalence. Consider what happens when the Necker cube (Fig. 9) is stretched. At the stage of greatest elongation, the dominant interpretation is inconsistent. As Barbara Gillam notes, 'Most observers report that for much of the time it appears to be an impossible object with both ends pointing towards them at the same time' (1979: 230). They realize that this is possible only if the figure is bent. But the figure is perceived as straight rather than bent.

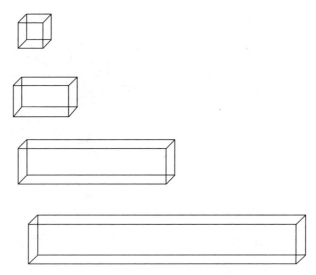

Fig. 9. Necker sequence.

Our visual system's ambivalent reaction to the Necker cube is often said to illustrate the system's insistence on consistency. However, the elongation sequence suggests that consistency is negotiable. Moving top to bottom, the inconsistent interpretation begins as a weak alternative to the consistent alternatives. But as the elongation increases, the inconsistent interpretation becomes the dominant interpretation. Thus the inconsistent interpretation prevails even though the observer is being primed on consistent interpretations.

A consistent interpretation is always logically available. Any 'impossible figure' can be interpreted as a consistent drawing by treating the drawing as a two-dimensional assembly of lines or as a conglomerate of distinct pictures. With opposite deviousness, one can also interpret any possible figure as an impossible figure. It is just a matter of connecting consistent dots in an inconsistent way (see Fig. 10).

Logical availability does not imply psychological availability. Our visual system is cognitively impenetrable. It cannot be modified to accommodate the discovery of new possibilities. For instance, topologists have acquired an excellent algebraic understanding of four-dimensional objects. They can even calculate an impossible object that would be perceived by beings who can perceive four-dimensional objects (Kim 1978). But they cannot visualize the objects and so cannot grasp the depiction at first hand.

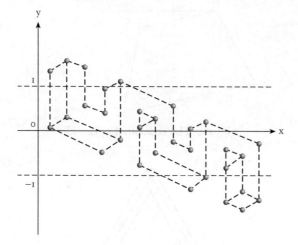

Fig. 10. The quantum sine wave.

Psychological research on inconsistency in spatial representation suggests that we routinely represent consistent states of affairs inconsistently. People memorize local geography by employing heuristics (Moar and Bower 1983): Turns are at right angles. Alternative paths are aligned perpendicularly. The greater the number of turns, the longer the distance. Stylized subway maps are pitched to these simplifications. We regularly fall into inconsistency when we apply these heuristics to the street layout of our home towns. Compare this inconsistency to the sort that mechanical calculators evince when they give conflicting answers to $1/3 \times 3 = ?$ and $3 \times 1/3 = ?$ To save memory, the calculator rounds off, and so treats 1 divided by 3 as a number slightly less than a third. Rounding errors are common, but generally can be ignored. Similarly, people make navigation manageable by rounding off geographical irregularities.

Given the strong analogy between space and time, we may conjecture that parallel heuristics lead to inconsistent mental diaries. Since we represent objects and events in a system of space and time, I further conjecture that ordinary experience is normally inconsistent. Most of the inconsistency goes unnoticed. For instance, the truncated pyramid (Fig. 11) is experienced without dissonance. Are other animals more sensitive? The prey of such an animal would have an opportunity to conceal itself as a nonexistent entity (see Fig. 12). The hyperlogical predator notes the inconsistent vertices. He moves on, leaving the starfish unmolested. No organism implements this camouflage technique. This suggests that all animals tolerate inconsistency.

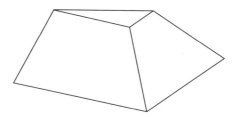

Fig. 11. The truncated pyramid.

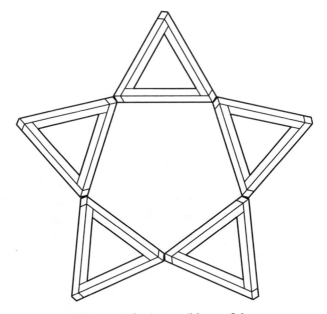

Fig. 12. The impossible starfish.

6 Why I am Optimistic

My picture of the impossible starfish is composed of five Penrose triangles. Unlike the truncated pyramid, the Penrose triangle stimulates dissonance. Unlike the elongated Necker cube, the dissonance tracks genuine incoherence. There really is something awry in the picture. The vertices are each possible, but not co-possible. One sees this without relying on labels or captions. The inconsistency is within the picture itself.

Is inconsistency too abstract a relation to be 'in the picture itself'? The worry becomes less pressing when one dwells on the range of properties to which perceivers are sensitive. When the objects in view are fewer than four, we are able to appreciate their exact number immediately. This enumerative process is called 'subitizing'. It is immediate, scale-insensitive, and virtually infallible. Counting, the process used for objects that exceed three, is slow, scale-sensitive, and error-prone. When one, two, or three objects are involved, we just see the number of objects. Even if arithmetic is not reducible to logic, statements such as $1 = 2$ have close logical counterparts. Illusions about the number of items in a picture might be harnessed to form a picture of logical impossibility. That is, if numerical properties are perceivable, then it seems likely that logical properties are also perceivable.

Or consider the difference between an asymmetrical picture and its mirror image. The two pictures have the same constituents. The internal relations between the parts are the same. Yet they clearly differ perceptually.

7 Inconsistency does not Reduce to Ambiguity

Ambiguous figures such as the Jastrow duck-rabbit show that the numerically same picture elements can be organized differently. When I see the figure as a duck, the marks on the page are organized duck-wise. When I see the figure as a rabbit, the marks are organized rabbit-wise. The difference between these two perceptions is therefore not reducible to the marks on the page. Nor is it reducible to the marks plus the low-level topographical relations that hold between the marks. The relational difference is at a higher level: being a bill rather than a pair of ears. I cannot convey the exact difference between the two perceptions by drawing a duck and drawing a rabbit. The best I can do is to distort the original picture to bias one interpretation over the other. The additional contours and shadows will prime people to see the doctored figure as a duck rather than a rabbit. But they see something topologically distinct from the original. After all, the original picture and its doctored descendant are not even identical with respect to the marks composing the picture.

'Seeing as' is compatible with there being a uniquely correct interpretation. An astronomer may undergo Gestalt switches while viewing a lunar crater. His visual system cannot settle on whether the feature is concave (a crater) or convex (a mountain). Yet there is a fact of the matter. Or consider an ambiguous photograph of a staircase (Fig. 13). There is no way to tell whether the picture is taken from the bottom of the staircase or the top. You can see the steps as going up into the darkness or have a Gestalt switch in which they are going down into the darkness. But there is an objectively correct answer. The origin of the photograph settles the matter. (Confession: Actually both answers are wrong. I took the photograph from <u>beneath</u> a stairwell. To duplicate the

Fig. 13. Photograph of a staircase, by the author.

original orientation, hold the photograph above your head with the light side closest to you.)

The artist's intention can also ensure a fact of matter. But what if the artist wants us to interpret his depicted staircase as going *both* up and down? Even if we accept the artist's authority on the matter, I would object that this is the wrong kind of impossible picture. Just as the ambiguity of the Jastrow duck-rabbit is internal, the inconsistency of a prize-winning picture must be internal.

The Penroses themselves seem unconcerned about the distinction between a picture that looks as if it depicts an impossibility and a picture that really depicts an impossibility. Lionel Penrose delighted in the construction of little staircases and ramps that look impossible when photographed (or viewed with one eye) from the appropriate angle. I like impossible construction projects too—see 'The impossible plumber's son' (Fig. 14). The top pipe segments are actually about a foot apart. The impossible boy darting through my carefully staged scene is actually my two-year-old, Zachary Sorensen.

Fig. 14. 'The Impossible Plumber's Son',
photograph by the author.

Lionel Penrose's son, Roger Penrose, analyzes the Penrose triangle as an ambiguous figure. Mathematically, there can be no genuinely impossible figures, so the analysans of Penrose's topological investigations are consistent figures that are perceived inconsistently. This is the main approach of mathematical psychologists. Accordingly, they regard 'impossible object' as a misnomer. Some prefer to call the figures 'improbable objects'.

Roger Penrose's (1991) ambiguity analysis cannot handle figures that are ambiguous between interpretations that are themselves impossible figures (see Fig. 15). If all inconsistent interpretations are actually ambiguous, then Katz's figure would involve second-order ambiguity. But all higher-order ambiguity collapses into first-order ambiguity (Sorensen 1998). Ambiguity is discretion over meaning. If there is ambiguity about whether a term is ambiguous, then the speaker has discretion over whether he has discretion about the term's meaning. But then he does have discretion about the term's meaning. For he can decide to exercise his discretion in favor of having discretion over whether the term is ambiguous. Katz's figure is not ambiguously ambiguous. Since it is ambiguous between genuinely inconsistent interpretations, it is a counter-example to the claim that all visual inconsistency is disguised ambiguity.

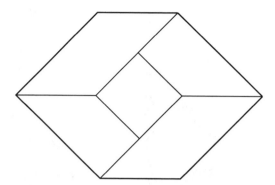

Fig. 15. Katz's figure, from Katz 1984: 221.
Reproduced by courtesy of Milton Katz.

The linguistic analogue of Katz's figure is 'Some bats are not bats'. The sentence has a reading that is a contradiction about a certain kind of winged mammal and a reading that is a contradiction about a certain piece of baseball equipment. Although the sentence is contradictory under all disambiguations, the sentence is not itself a contradiction. Similarly, Katz's figure is not itself inconsistent. It is merely inconsistent under each of its disambiguations.

A Penrose triangle could be composed of smaller Penrose triangles. Thus an impossible figure can be composed of other impossible figures. The linguistic analogue of these figures is a conjunction such as 'Some electrons are not electrons and it is not the case that some electrons are not electrons'. This statement is contradictory at two levels. At the base level it is contradictory by virtue of having a contradictory conjunct. But it is also contradictory in virtue of its overarching 'P & ~P' form.

The hierarchy could be continued upwards indefinitely. Could it extend endlessly downward? A negative answer is implied by those who think that all impossible figures can be ultimately decomposed into possible figures. But perhaps there could be impossible 'gunk'. Gunk is infinitely divisible matter. A Penrose triangle might be composed of smaller and smaller Penrose triangles, *ad infinitum*.

8 Pictorial Consistency is an Extrinsic Property

In M. C. Escher's lithograph *Ascending and Descending*, the Penrose triangle is used to construct a finite staircase that seems to rise endlessly. Escher also uses the Penrose triangle to form a perpetual motion machine in *Waterfall* and an incoherent alignment of pillars in *Belvedere*.

Shegeo Fukuda has pieced together physical models of Escher's *Waterfall* and *Belvedere*. Photographs of them (taken from exactly the right angle) look like the corresponding Escher lithographs. (The photographs are reproduced on pages 92–3 of Ernst (1986*b*).) However, these are not photographs of impossible objects. They are photographs of miniature buildings that are bent and broken to appear impossible. So if Escher depicts an impossible object, then it cannot be simply in virtue of the graphical properties of the picture. Nor can they be depicted simply in virtue of inconsistency within the perceptual processes. Shegeo Fukuda's photographs are perceptually equivalent to Escher's lithographs. Moral: the perceptual equivalent of a depiction of an impossible object need not itself be a depiction of an impossible object. This undermines attempts to define impossible depictions as those that stimulate inconsistent perceptions.

Fukuda's photograph of the Belvedere model also defeats attempts to define impossible depictions as depictions which dispose people to form necessarily false beliefs. If Graham Priest (1999: 439) mistakenly believes that Fukuda's picture is of an impossible state of affairs, then his belief is necessarily false. For if a state of affairs is possible, then it is necessarily possible. Thus there are pictures of consistent states of affairs that promote beliefs in inconsistencies.

Shegeo Fukuda's photograph further demonstrates that 'depicts an impossible object' involves an extrinsic property. The 'narrow psychology' of the artist and his audience is not enough to ensure that a picture depicts an impossibility. We must consider the origin of the picture.

The same point applies to a factual drawing of Fukuda's *Belvedere* model. Suppose a scientific draftsman draws the *Belvedere* model as seen through a pinhole from the appropriate angle. The drawing will be perceptually equivalent to Escher's drawing, but will not be a depiction of an impossible object. For a factual drawing represents in the same way as a photograph. A photograph represents an object just in case there is an appropriate causal connection between the object and the image. The beliefs of the photographer are irrelevant. That is why a photographer can be surprised by the content of his photograph.

9 Nonepistemic Conceiving

Fred Dretske (1969) focused much attention on the distinction between epistemic seeing ('seeing that'), which entails belief, and nonepistemic seeing, which is neutral with respect to belief. I can nonepistemically see a three-legged frog even though I believe it is a hallucination. I nonepistemically see object O just in case there is an appropriate causal connection between object O and myself.

The kind of representation involved in photography and factual drawing has the objectivity of nonepistemic seeing.

Fictional depiction is much more subjective. The author's beliefs about what he is depicting heavily influence what he is depicting. Nevertheless, there is still room for surprises. The imagined scenarios of thought experiments often have unanticipated properties. Bertrand Russell (1948: 112) conceived of someone having justified true belief without having knowledge. His example featured a man who reads the time from a broken clock that is coincidentally correct. However, Russell did not believe that it was possible for someone to have justified true belief without knowledge. For Russell's example was merely intended to illustrate why true belief did not suffice for knowledge. Edmund Gettier (1963) was the first to *epistemically* conceive a counter-example to the justified true belief analysis of knowledge.

Some of the debate over whether conceiving p entails the possibility of p is due to an ambiguity. Epistemically conceiving p does not entail the possibility that p. But nonepistemically conceiving p *does* entail that p is possible.

Epistemically conceiving p implies belief that p is possible, and hence raises questions about circularity. The thought experimenter seems to be in a situation reminiscent of the one in which Harold finds himself in the children's story *Harold and the Purple Crayon* (by Crockett Johnson). Harold is a polite but imaginative boy whose drawings become real. If he wants a boat, he just draws it and then sails away. Harold's command over reality leads to many confusing adventures. Eventually Harold becomes lost. So he draws a policeman to direct him home. The stick-figure officer points. Harold thanks him and proceeds in the indicated direction. But only because that is the way that Harold was independently inclined to go.

Epistemic conceiving seems circular, because it is theory-laden. The thought experimenter is pictured as merely erecting props for antecedently held convictions.

Nonepistemic conceiving also invites a charge of circularity. In the nonepistemic sense, 'conceive' is a success term. So some complain that this sense of 'conceive' is useless, because one must first establish the possibility of p to tell whether one is conceiving p. However, the precedent for nonepistemic seeing (which is also a success term) should make us doubt this charge of redundancy. We have independent tests to check whether a witness really saw a crime. There are similar tests for conceiving. Suppose a student tells you that he has conceived a counter-example to John Locke's principle that distinct things of the same kind must exist in different places. You will test him by asking him to describe the counter-example. The description must have a certain level of detail. It must disconfirm Locke's principle without circularity. The student must be able to put the counter-example in his own words. In practice, we have a rich network of tests for conceiving.

10 Depicting Inconsistencies

Stories can be told in a way that guarantees consistency. But they need not be. Graham Priest's memorial tribute to the para-consistent logician Richard Sylvan, 'Sylvan's Box', is designed to be a story in which a contradiction plays an essential role. The centerpiece of the tale is an empty box that contains something. In accompanying commentary, Priest explicitly rejects the suggestion that the characters are mistaken about the box or that the box is empty in one sense but not another. That would be a poor tribute indeed! The aptness and poignancy of the tale evaporate if we render his story consistent through the usual devices.

Fiction works like belief. If someone sincerely says that he believes that p, then that is strong evidence he believes that p. If the author sincerely says that p is part of his story, then that is strong evidence that p is part of his story. Both principles are defeasible, because we are also guided by indirect principles of belief attribution that may trump the speaker's authority.

The story-teller pretends to be reporting his beliefs. So anything that can be believed can be part of a story. Priest does not believe that Sylvan had an empty box that contained something. But he could believe it. A contradiction can be true in a story in the same way that a contradiction can be true in a belief system—that is, the contradiction is affirmed in the system. Just as the consequences of p cannot be inferred from 'Peewee believes that p', so they cannot be inferred from 'In Peewee's story, p'.

I am not sure whether Priest could convey the belief in a purely pictorial fashion. However, I am impressed with his resources. If, as I believe, experience is systematically inconsistent, and if, as I believe, there is no obstacle to inconsistent fiction, then visual depiction of a logical inconsistency seems feasible. Escher successfully pretends to be faithfully recording geometrically impossible scenes. Geometry and logic seem comparably abstract. So there does not seem to be any artistically relevant difference between the two. But when I personally try to arrive at the depiction of a logical impossibility, I draw a blank.

11 A Parting Ban on Vacuous Depiction

I have flirted with the idea that drawing a blank might be a solution. Drawing inspiration from the minimalists, my Spartan 'The empty universe' consists of a blank canvas. (Perhaps you have seen reproductions at your local art-supply store.) As suggested by its title, the work depicts a universe in which nothing exists. Logic forbids the empty universe. For the universal quantifier has existential import: 'Everything is F' entails 'Something is F'. And 'Something is F' means 'There exists something which is F'. Thus the law of identity, 'Everything is identical to itself' entails 'Something exists which is identical to itself'. My picture vacuously depicts the empty universe in all relevant detail. True, it relies heavily on its title for interpretation, but it is otherwise independent of discursive elements.

One reservation about awarding the prize to myself is the controversy that surrounds the claim that 'Nothing exists' is *logically* false. Most people believe that they can imagine an empty universe (either straight off or by subtracting until nothing remains). They take conceivability to be powerful evidence for it being genuinely possible. They are also influenced by a methodological claim: logic should only supply the structure for what exists and ought not to commit us to the content. Existence is a contingent property. So it is contingent whether anything at all exists.

This opposition to counting 'Nothing exists' as a logical falsehood does not persuade me. But I am not going to fight it. I present 'The empty universe' only to exempt it as a prize-winner. I want a *substantive* depiction of a logical impossibility. No tricks! Limiting cases will be returned to the sender.

REFERENCES

Bradley, M. J. (1996), 'Building Home Plate: Field of Dreams or Reality', *Mathematics Magazine*, 69: 44–5.

Braus, Ira (1995), 'Retracing One's Steps: An Overview of Pitch Circularity and Shepherd Tones in European Music, 1550–1990', *Music Perception*, 12(3): 323–51.

Burge, Tyler (1984), 'Epistemic Paradox', *Journal of Philosophy*, 81(1): 5–29.

Crane, Tim (1988), 'The Waterfall Illusion', *Analysis*, 48: 142–7.

Cresswell, M. J. (1983), 'A Highly Impossible Scene', in R. Baurele, C. Schwarze, and A. von Stechow (eds.), *Meaning, Use and Interpretation of Language* (Berlin: De Gruyter), 62–77.

Dretske, Fred (1969), *Seeing and Knowing* (Chicago: University of Chicago Press).

Dwyer, F. M. (1967), 'Adapting Visual Illustrations for Effective Learning', *Harvard Educational Review*, 37: 250–63.

Ernst, Bruno (1986a), *Adventures with Impossible Figures* (Norfolk: Tarquin Publications).

—— (1986b), *Optical Illusions* (New York: Taschen; trans. Karen Williams, 1989).

Fogelin, Robert (1976), *Wittgenstein* (London: Routledge and Kegan Paul).

Frisby, J. P. (1979), *Seeing* (New York: Oxford University Press).

Geach, Peter (1948), 'Mr Ill-Named', *Analysis*, 9: 14–16.

Gettier, Edmund (1963), 'Is Justified True Belief Knowledge?', *Analysis*, 23: 121–3.

Gillam, B. (1979), 'Even a Possible Figure can look Impossible!', *Perception*, 7: 229–32.

Goldstick, Daniel (1995), 'Marxism on Dialectical and Logical Contradiction', *Australasian Journal of Philosophy*, 73(1): 102–13.

Hochberg, J. E., and Brooks, V. (1962), 'Pictorial Recognition as an Unlearned Ability', *American Journal of Psychology*, 75: 624–8.

Horowitz, Tamara (1983), 'Stipulation and Epistemological Privilege', *Philosophical Studies*, 44: 305–18.

Huffman, D. A. (1971), 'Impossible Objects as Nonsense Sentences', in *Machine Intelligence*, vi (Edinburgh: Edinburgh University Press), 295–323.

Hume, David (1739–40), *A Treatise of Human Nature* (London), ed. L. A. Selby-Bigge (Oxford: Clarendon Press, 1888; 2nd edn. rev. P. H. Nidditch (Oxford: Clarendon Press, 1978).

Hurvich, Leo M. (1981), *Color Vision* (Sunderland, Mass.: Sinauer Associates, Inc.).

Kaplan, David (1996), 'Quantifying In', *Synthese* 19 (1964), 178–24; repr. in A. P. Martinich (ed.), *The Philosophy of Language* (New York: Oxford University Press), 347–68.

Katz, Milton (1984), 'A New Reversible and Impossible Object', *Perception*, 13: 221–2.

Kennedy, John M. (1974), *A Psychology of Picture Perception* (San Francisco: Jossey-Bass).

Kim, Scott E. (1978), 'An Impossible Four-Dimensional Illusion', in David W. Brisson (ed.), *Hypergraphics* (Boulder, Colo.: Westview Press), 187–239.

Krause, Eugene F. (1987), *Taxicab Geometry: An Adventure in Non-Euclidean Geometry* (New York: Dover).

Kripke, Saul (1980), *Naming and Necessity* (Cambridge, Mass.: Harvard University Press).

Marcus, Ruth Barcan (1981), 'A Proposed Solution to a Puzzle about Belief', *Midwest Studies in Philosophy*, 6: 501–10.

Mellor, D. H. (1988), 'Crane's Waterfall Illusion', *Analysis*, 48: 147–50.

Moar, I., and Bower, G. H. (1983), 'Inconsistency in Spatial Knowledge', *Memory and Cognition*, 11: 107–13.

Penrose, Roger (1991), 'On the Cohomology of Impossible Figures', *Structural Topology*, 17: 11–16.

Priest, Graham (1987), *In Contradiction* (Dordrecht: Martinus Nijhoff).

—— (1997), 'Sylvan's Box: A Short Story and Ten Morals', *Notre Dame Journal of Formal Logic*, 38(4): 573–82.

—— (1999), 'Perceiving Contradictions', *Australasian Journal of Philosophy*, 77(4): 439–46.

Quine, W. V. (1951), 'Two Dogmas of Empiricism', *Philosophical Review*, 60: 20–43.

Risset, Jean-Claude (1997), 'Rhythmic Paradoxes and Illusions: A Musical Illustration', *Proceedings of the International Computer Music Conference* (Thessaloniki) (San Francisco: ICMA), 7–10.

Russell, Bertrand (1948), *Human Knowledge: Its Scope and Limits* (New York: Simon and Schuster).

Ryan, T. A., and Schwartz, C. (1956), 'Speed of Perception as a Function of Mode of Representation', *American Journal of Psychology*, 69: 60–9.

Shepherd, Roger (1964), 'Circularity in Judgments of Relative Pitch', *Journal of the Acoustical Society of America*, 36: 2346–53.

Sorensen, Roy (1992), *Thought Experiments* (New York: Oxford University Press).

—— (1996), 'Modal Bloopers: Why Believable Impossibilities are Necessary', *American Philosophical Quarterly*, 33(1) (July): 247–61; repr. in Patrick Grim, Kenneth Baynes, and Gary Mar (eds.), *The Philosopher's Annual 1996* (Atascadero, Calif.: Ridgeview, 1998), vol. xix.

—— (1998), 'Ambiguity, Discretion, and the Sorites', *Monist*, 81(2): 217–35.

Stalnaker, Robert (1984), *Inquiry* (Cambridge, Mass.: MIT Press).

Strawson, Peter F. (1952), *Introduction to Logical Theory* (New York: John Wiley & Sons).

Thomson, James F. (1962), 'On Some Paradoxes', in R. J. Butler (ed.), *Analytical Philosophy* (New York: Barnes & Noble), 104–19.

Tidman, Paul (1994), 'Conceivability as a Test for Possibility', *American Philosophical Quarterly*, 31(4): 297–309.

10

Reliability and the A Priori

ERNEST SOSA

Numbers, properties, and propositions are said by Platonists to constitute a realm of abstracta beyond space-time. How, then, could denizens of space-time ever discern the lay of that land?

According to Hartry Field, 'we should view with suspicion any claim to know facts about a certain domain if we believe it impossible to explain the reliability of our beliefs about that domain' (1989: 232–3). But how, even in principle, could the Platonist explain why the following schema is often enough true?

(⋆) If mathematicians accept 'p' then p. (Field 1989: 230)

Explaining this regularity is a serious problem for the Platonist, or so it is argued by Field:

[There] seems prima facie to be a difficulty in principle in explaining the regularity. The problem arises in part from the fact that mathematical entities, as the platonist conceives them, do not causally interact with mathematicians, or indeed with anything else. This means we cannot explain the mathematicians' beliefs and utterances on the basis of the mathematical facts being causally involved in the production of those beliefs and utterances; or on the basis of the beliefs or utterances causally producing the mathematical facts; or on the basis of some common cause producing

This paper benefited from incisive comments by Tamar Szabó Gendler, John Hawthorne, and David Sosa.

both. Perhaps then some sort of non-causal explanation of the correlation is possible? Perhaps; but it is very hard to see what this supposed non-causal explanation could be. Recall that on the usual platonist picture, mathematical objects are supposed to be mind- and language-independent; they are supposed to bear no spatiotemporal relations to anything, etc. The problem is that the claims that the platonist makes about mathematical objects appear to rule out any reasonable strategy for explaining the systematic correlation in question. (1989: 230–1)

From this passage one might draw the following dilemma for the Platonist:

(i) Platonism is committed to the acausality and mind-independence of mathematical objects.

(ii) Any causal explanation of our mathematical reliability is incompatible with the acausality of mathematical objects.

(iii) Any noncausal explanation of our mathematical reliability is incompatible with the mind-independence of mathematical objects.

Therefore,

(iv) There is no explanation of our mathematical reliability that is compatible with Platonism.[1]

Rejection of (iii) may enable us to explain the reliability of mathematicians' beliefs, while leaving it open that the objects of mathematics be abstract, non-spatiotemporal, and mind-independent. Although truths about such objects would be *determined* by judgments in accord with best mathematical practice, the objects themselves might still exist outside space-time independently of anyone's judgments. Of course, the reliability of best judgments concerning the relevant domain would be guaranteed, since it is such judgments that *determine* what is true in that domain.

The contrast between determination and tracking is akin to the Euthyphro contrast between the good being good because it is God-loved (determination by God-love) and the good being God-loved because it is good (tracking of the good by God-love). Applied to mathematical truth, the contrast would be between 5 being prime because best opinion would think it prime (determination by best opinion) and 5 being thought prime by best opinion because it is prime (tracking by best opinion).

---

[1] John Divers and Alexander Miller (a) draw the dilemma, and (b) despite Gödel's rejection of premise (i), target (iii) as the weak link: '*Our central two-fold claim is that mathematical belief is reliable because mathematical truth is judgement-dependent, and that the judgement-dependence of mathematical truth brings no commitment to the mind-dependence of mathematical objects*' (1999: 280, italics in original). Their defense of this position, which I will now consider, draws heavily on the growing literature on response dependence, especially the work of Crispin Wright.

Constructivism views facts in a certain domain as constructed from facts in another domain, as deriving necessarily from those other facts. Most often the source facts are thought less problematic in one or another metaphysical or epistemological respect. Thus one might view supposed facts of morality as derivative from facts about moral codes, or facts about fictional entities as derivative from facts about authors and readers. Would the present 'construction' offer such advantages were it successful? Well, what is the nature of a fact as to what one should think, what it would be best to think, on a certain subject matter? This is a normative or evaluative fact, which would seem no easier to know, and no more causally accessible, than facts of mathematics. Fortunately, the approach under review goes further.

The proposal is that the conditions C enabling best opinion can be specified so as to make it a priori knowable that opinion meeting *those* conditions would hold 5 to be prime (for example). And what best explains this is said to be the fact that 5 *is* prime *because* opinion meeting those conditions would think it prime.

According to the judgment-dependence proposal, something explains or determines mathematical facts. Five is said to be prime *because* opinion that satisfied conditions C would think it so. Here is an argument, to the contrary, that nothing contingent can (fully) explain anything necessary.

Argument A

A1. If P explains why Q is true, then it cannot be that Q would be true regardless of whether P were true or not (putting aside overdetermination); in particular, it cannot be that even if P were false, as it might be, Q would still be true.

A2. But if Q is *necessarily* true, while P is contingent, then even if P were false, as it might be, Q would still be true.

A3. So, if P is contingent, and Q necessary, then P cannot explain why Q is true.

This argument may perhaps be rejected, however, for some allowable sort of explanation (for some relevant 'because', 'for the reason that', 'in virtue of', 'as a result of', etc.). Its first premise may be rejected for at least some such. Here are two potential counter-examples:

(a) Tom, Dick, and Harry are in the room, so there is someone in the room in virtue of Tom's being there (and also in virtue of Dick's being there, etc.). There are various ways in which it could have come about that there was someone in the room. There are various eventualities from which it might have *resulted* that there was someone in the room. One is Mary's being there, but she is not there, she was delayed, so that's not how it *comes about* or how it is *made to be the case* that there is someone in the room, that is not what the presence of someone in the room *results* from. One way in which it *does* come about, etc., is through the presence of Tom, which itself came about in some complex way involving perhaps plans and decisions, etc. But there would have been someone in the room even if Tom had not been there; the presence of someone in the room would still have resulted from something else: for example, from the presence of Dick in the room, even if Tom had not been there.

(b) At the washbasin, you first open the hot water faucet, so that there is then water in the basin because the hot water faucet is open. However, there would be water in the basin then regardless of whether the hot water faucet was open, since if you had not opened the hot water faucet when you did, you would then have opened the cold water faucet, so that there would still have been water in the basis at the relevant time.

In addition, there is the worry that, according to A1, it would be impossible ever to explain any necessary fact. No necessary fact would ever fail to be the case if such-and-such, no matter the such-and-such.

One might of course dig in one's heels, alleging, for example, that the cases cited are importantly different from the cases of purported explanation of the necessary by appeal to contingent judgment-dependence. However that may turn out, next I would like to consider how argument A might be supplemented through some alternative account of ontological determination, one that may be worth considering in any case.

First, we assume a distinction between positive and negative (possible) facts, facts that might or might not obtain, which prepares the way for the following sketched proposal.

A family of facts F1 is determined by a family of facts F2 iff (i) necessarily, each obtaining positive fact in F1 obtains in virtue of (obtaining) facts in F2, and (ii) there could be *no* positive facts in F1 unless there were some in F2.[2]

Our sketched account fits examples like the following: the determination (a) of facts about the shapes and spatial relations of medium-sized dry goods by facts about bits of matter and their properties and relations; (b) of etiquette facts

---

[2] We focus on nonmolecular facts, and we might think of these as those expressed in a quantificational modal language devoid of individual constants by sentences that start with either a modal operator or (in prenex normal form) an existential quantifier. Also, not just any arbitrary set of facts constitutes a 'family'. It must be a set unified in the way in which the facts of arithmetic are a unified set, or in the looser way of the facts about human conventions.

by facts about the intentions and rules adopted in the relevant group; (c) of appearance facts about photographs by facts about the coloring of small enough portions of their surfaces; and (d) of facts about fictional characters and their antics by facts about works of literature and what they say.

According to our sketched account, no family of necessary facts could possibly be determined by a family of facts that might have lacked any positive members. If so, then the facts of arithmetic could *not* be ontologically determined by facts about the judgments that people would make. There might have been no people at all, for one thing. Could there then still have been any positive facts as to how people *would* have judged *if* there had been any people to do so? Perhaps. Nevertheless, if *these* positive facts were themselves contingent, then there might be none of *these* either.

In order to safeguard the ontological derivation of positive arithmetic facts from facts as to how people would judge, accordingly, it would seem that these latter facts must themselves be necessary. If this further argument is sound, then the judgment-dependence explanation for any necessary truth of mathematics must itself be necessary.[3] Consider next an instance of the schema J crucial to that account for some recondite prime N:

L (i.e.: N is prime) ↔ R (i.e.: If C, then S judges that N is prime)

Since L, the left-hand side, is necessary, then R, the right-hand side, can explain L only if it is itself necessary, or so our argument would have it. Only if R is *necessarily* true can it be so that N is prime *because* R is true. But how plausible can it be that there are conditions, not just empty conditions of the 'whatever it takes' form, or just normative conditions of ideality, but *substantive* conditions C (of attentiveness, intelligence, etc.) such that *necessarily* anyone in those conditions will judge that N is prime. This seems particularly challenging if the conditions C are supposed to figure in a general truth J′ that will work for all primes, and even more challenging if they are to figure in a general truth J″ good for *all* of mathematics.

Could the judgment-dependence approach instead take truths one at a time? Perhaps the conditions C5 that work for the primeness of 5 are different from the conditions C7 that work for the primeness of 7, and so on, indefinitely. On this tack, however, it seems mere speculation that there would always be conditions C of the required sort for every mathematical truth. What is more, it is not clear how the view could escape this tenuous status, given that conditions C are not likely to be surveyable, enabling us to generalize.

---

[3] Hence explanation of necessary truths could not be causal, and must be formal or of some other sort.

What substantive conditions could possibly assure us that anyone meeting those conditions would get it right no matter what fact of mathematics might be targeted? Would there be some general substantive conditions applicable for all mathematical truths? Or would we need to go field by field, some conditions applying in plane geometry, some in arithmetic, and so on? Can we even be sure of finding conditions that would apply generally in arithmetic? They would have to be conditions under which all who considered the question would agree. Can we plausibly expect that we will find such conditions about which we could know a priori that anyone meeting them would deliver the right verdict? 'Intuitionists' may hope that there would be such conditions for every mathematical truth whose knowability we wished to protect, and indeed, whose very truth we would wish to protect. But they are notoriously led to abandon too much of mathematics.

Consider, finally, the response-dependence strategy of granting the mind-dependence of mathematical truth while upholding, as good Platonists, the mind-independence of mathematical objects such as the number 5. This collides with its being a mathematical fact that there are numbers, that there is, for example, such a number as the number 5. If, as Platonists, we insist that there is the number 5, this would seem to be a mathematical fact. But, according to the response-dependence strategy, it will then itself become judgment-dependent in the way of the fact that 5 is a prime. How, then, could the number 5 itself be mind-independent, while its existence is mind-dependent?

A theory about the perceptual instruments used in a certain field—the microscopes, telescopes, and even eyeglasses—can help us understand how we know facts in that field. The same goes for direct observations aided by our most basic instruments, our sensory organs. But none of this illuminates how we can know by introspection facts of our own mental life, or how we can know such contingencies as the fact that one now thinks, or even the fact that one now exists. In these cases the explanation of reliability stays largely within the realm of the a priori in the manner of Descartes (in a broad sense of the a priori as that open to epistemically justified belief independent of perceptual observation). It is because we see how such beliefs are, and must be, infallible that we understand how perfectly reliable they are. No doubt derives here from ignorance of causal mechanisms.

Moreover, such explanation of reliability is extensible far beyond *cogito* propositions. For example, we may similarly explain how we are so reliable regarding propositions expressed by 'This exists' affirmed of whatever one picks out thus in thought, and how we are so reliable regarding propositions expressed by 'This is thus' where the thought latches onto an image, say, and attributes to it a color or a shape intrinsic to that image, *as one that then characterizes the image*.[4] So, perhaps here again we might appreciate a priori how reliable such thoughts must be, as reliable as the *cogito* thoughts distinguished by Descartes.

Some traditional paradigms of reliability are comprehensible, then, through reflection on the content-determining conditions of our thought. Might we possibly extend such reflection so as to help explain how reliable we are in other realms, including that of logic, propositional or quantificational? Results in proof theory, or in metatheory more generally, might thus explain why it is that our thoughts in the relevant fields are likely to be right, or even *bound* to be right, if we follow certain methods. What rules out the possibility of such general understanding of our own reliability on the a priori, precisely by means of properly directed a priori theorizing?

Compare our potential explanation of how perceptual observation is reliable as a source of true perceptual beliefs, and how scientific theorizing is reliable as a source of scientific beliefs. How could *these* explanations fail to derive precisely from perceptual observation and scientific theorizing?

True, if we move beyond theorems known by proof to items known directly, absent proof, then the circle tightens threateningly. Our reliable intuitive knowledge of modality, and of other a priori cognoscibilia, seems subject to limits not knowable except through such intuition. But this gives sufficient reason neither to reject such intuition nor to judge its ontological status, not without first comparing our knowledge of the *cogito*, a knowledge defensible independently of any specific ontological commitments. Our *cogito* knowledge is defensible via appeal to its infallible reliability, in the manner of Descartes, without this requiring any such commitments. And the same goes for our introspective knowledge more generally. Unless one's critical attack is to extend beyond philosophy and beyond Platonism in mathematics, therefore, one will need to show what distinctive features of modal and mathematical intuition entail that it must be shown reliable—perhaps through a causal or judgment-dependence account—in some way that would require specific ontological commitments. Why should this be so if our knowledge of the *cogito* and of our own headaches requires no such commitments?

---

[4] I assume here that the conditions of contextual reference through the use of 'thus' enable its use, aided by some mechanism of attention, to pick out a color or a shape as present in that very image. Of course, the requirement of such a mechanism of attention would seem to import a need for some presupposed *nondemonstrative* concepts to give content to the attention, which means that such demonstrative reference could not be conceptually fundamental.

Your belief at a given moment as to whether you exist at that very moment can enter into no causal relationship with the fact believed so as to explain the reliability of that belief. There is here no more possibility of a causal relation between our beliefs and the relevant facts than there is between mathematical beliefs and the mathematical facts believed. Nor is it plausible that your existence at that moment is determined by what you believe or might best believe on the matter. It is plainly false that you exist simply *because* your best opinion as to whether you exist would be affirmative. For the *cogito* the explanation of infallible reliability proceeds therefore in some way that skirts both causal tracking and construction or judgment-dependence.

Could we reasonably expect to acquire the required epistemic perspective on the reliability of our mathematical beliefs through a priori reflection of the sort featured in Descartes's philosophy of the *cogito*? On a superficial view, even Descartes seems to complete only half the job. He seems able to explain our infallible reliability in *cogito* thoughts, but not thereby to explain how we so effectively avoid any contrary thoughts. It is only when we see the *cogito* as not just infallible, but also indubitable (upon consideration) that we grasp the fuller Cartesian account. Once we see that we cannot concurrently assent to a proposition and also to its very negation,[5] it becomes clear how, for Descartes, we are really reliable about *whether* the *cogito* is true, and not just reliable in thinking *that* it is true. And that stronger reliability is captured more fully by the fact that at any given time we *would* believe it upon consideration, infallibly so, *and never its negation*. Why is this so? The thought that one thinks and exists is safe even from the evil demon, but that is not quite enough; we need to explain also why we opt always for the positive, and never for the negative, on *whether* we think and exist. And what could possibly explain this if not the fact that we would not so much as understand the question if we opted for the negative. After all, you lack so much as the ability to pose the question whether you now think and exist unless you always answer yes, never no.

Analogously, we need to account not only for the reliability of our correct arithmetical beliefs, but also for how we so reliably avoid incompatible and, of course, false arithmetical beliefs. A theory of understanding again seems an attractive recourse, one that might explain how the very understanding of certain concepts—that of existence, say, and that of thinking, and our simple

---

[5] If someone assures us that they believe something of the form 'p & not-p', or even that they believe both 'p' and 'not-p' separately, would we have to take their word for it at face value? I would rather think that we no more need to do so here than we do about their beliefs that emerge at best under analysis. At a minimum, we would and should explore other ways to make coherent sense of their speaking as they do.

numerical concepts—requires some minimal complement and preponderance of correct beliefs involving them. This might potentially help explain *both* our tendency to be right in *cogito* thoughts and arithmetical beliefs *and also* our avoiding error on these subjects.

Whether that project can succeed or not, this fact remains: its success would give us an a priori component for our desired epistemic perspective, a component that, in the respect of being substantially a priori, would match the Cartesian epistemic reflections traditionally accorded the highest explanatory efficacy in epistemology. And again, these components of our epistemic perspective would require no specific ontological commitments, or any a posteriori causal story of the sort pertinent to perceptual knowledge.[6]

Accounts of a priori justification often postulate some basic *sui generis* source of such justification. It might be called intuition, or insight, or apparent insight. However labeled, such a source is proposed as fundamental, although further inferences can then be drawn from its immediate deliverances, as in some proofs of theorems from given axioms. And it is often argued that such intuition or insight works by means of a distinctive intellectual appearance that helps ground the a priori just as sensory appearance grounds the a posteriori. Must such appearances be infallible? Recent opinion preponderantly answers in the negative. Intuition is said to serve as fundamental source of a priori justification *despite* its fallibility—an answer supported by familiar paradoxes.

Simple arithmetical beliefs plausibly require no first-level evidence or inference or calculation (unlike the solution of a complex arithmetical problem). Such simple beliefs seem justified by an intellectual appearance of truth derived from the bare understanding of the proposition believed. In simple arithmetic this understanding derives in good measure from certain drills. The rote learning of arithmetical tables must be viewed not on the model of testimony, however, but rather as a way to acquire not just belief but also understanding. For many simple propositions, the tables coordinately provide both belief and understanding. Phenomenologically, such beliefs would seem to derive simply from one's understanding of their contents. Admittedly, the drills that foster understanding of arithmetic concepts might be flawed in particular cases, limiting the value of the resulting appearances as sources of justification. Already the paradoxes suggest that an appearance can be false and no less robust, powerful, and entrenched for all that, and still apparently a source of justification. Here again we see intellectual appearance that is robust, powerful, and

---

[6] Further discussion of how empirical considerations might bear on a priori knowledge may be found in Casullo (1999).

entrenched, but now perhaps only a limited and imperfect source of justification. Simple arithmetical beliefs are the case in point, but only if the drills can be reliable enough to instill understanding without being reliable enough to yield the degree of epistemic justification requisite for knowledge. For example, perhaps the manual used has enough nearby errors to make it doubtful that the subject is epistemically justified in believing that $9 \times 8 = 72$, even while remaining, overall, a good enough manual to give understanding of arithmetic in general and of that proposition in particular.

Nevertheless, the conditions that attach contents to the relevant thoughts and sayings come with a guarantee that the contents attached will be true at least preponderantly, and this seems sufficient for some at least minimal degree of epistemic justification. Moreover, the degree of justification would seem to depend on how crucial it is to believe the particular proposition involved (or how crucial it is to believe a large enough preponderance of the members of some limited family to which that proposition belongs) if one is to grasp the relevant properties and concepts. It is this element in particular that is shared with *cogito* thoughts. In both sets of cases, the conditions determinative of content determine also that the contents must be true, in every case or at least in most cases. It is this understanding-based appearance that is characteristic of a priori intuition or insight, and secures reliability, for both the *cogito* and arithmetic. Neither for the *cogito* nor for arithmetic does our explanation imply any conclusion about the allowable pertinent ontology (other than the thinnest of conclusions—namely, that one does exist; what is left open is the ontological nature of this self). The reliability of the *cogito* is compatible with almost any ontology of the self. And the like may then be true of arithmetic.

How, it may be asked, could the tables impose a reference to Platonic items outside space and time? Would not a Platonic world of numbers lie beyond our intentional reach? Well, how does one secure reference to oneself through the *cogito* despite the absence of any relevant relation, whether causal or constructive (or of judgment-dependence), between one's existence and one's thought that at that very moment one does exist? Here the connection is secured through a fact known a priori: namely, that when someone has a thought of *that sort*, the thought refers to the thinker. Might the Platonist say, similarly, that when we have thoughts of the arithmetical tables sort, we can know a priori that *such* thoughts are bound to be right? This would still leave wide open the ontology of arithmetic, just as the Cartesian explanation of the *cogito*'s reliability leaves open the ontology of the self. All we need for now is our ability to see a priori that thoughts and sayings of certain sorts are bound to be right (at least preponderantly).

It might be objected that, in order for us to grasp arithmetical concepts, we must have arithmetical abilities of discrimination, whether directly and perceptually or by way of counting or calculation, abilities that make us reliably sensitive to the cardinality of contingently existing and perceptually identified collections. Just as with colors and shapes, therefore, we need here again some theory of perception that will explain such sensitivity. This does seem right, but also unproblematic for the Platonist. The Benacerraf–Field problem presumably does not concern our knowledge by perception of the facts about the colors and shapes of environing objects. Moreover, the problem still does not arise even if these colors and shapes are abstract properties. For such properties *can*, after all, act causally on our sensory organs *by way of their exemplifications*.[7] But this now yields a curious result.

Presumably perception and inductive reason can in tandem enable knowledge of correlations expressed by means of universal claims like: $(\forall x)$ $(Fx \supset Gx)$. But the truth of such a claim is tantamount to the following fact: Every instance of F-ness is an instance of G-ness. And now we seem to know *about* abstract items, reference to which is enabled at least in part by our causal intercourse with their instances. With regard to the contingent correlation, moreover, it is not only the grasp of the abstracta that is gained via our actual or potential perception of their instances. Our required rationale for believing the general claim itself *also* derives essentially from perceptually acquired information about the instances. And here one might well wonder, with Hume, how we could possibly know something so far beyond the causal reach of our perceptual scanning as the fact that absolutely nothing anywhere anytime combines the properties of being F and being non-G, and, even more, how we could possibly know something even further beyond that scope: namely, that nothing anywhere anytime *would* combine those two properties. Would this concern give good reason to *reject* objective generality pertaining to the future, or to the past, or to anything beyond our present consciousness, and especially to reject any supposed objective generality with subjunctive force?

Suppose you grasp the properties of sphericity and cubicity, which may require your being appropriately related causally to actual or potential instances of these properties. Then consider a question you might pose once in possession of such concepts: Can anything cubical (as a whole) be (as a whole) spherical? The disposition to answer this question straight off in the negative would seem required for proper possession of the concepts of cubicity and sphericity. One can no more properly latch onto these properties, absent a negative response, than one can latch onto oneself in thought by means of a conceptual

---

[7] Which puts in doubt premise (i) of our Platonist's dilemma.

mechanism of self-reference, if one is unable to answer correctly the question of whether one then exists. Indeed, the very understanding of the question whether one then exists entails a correct affirmative response. And the very understanding of the question whether anything cubical is spherical correspondingly yields a correct negative response.[8]

Critics of Platonism may still object that we remain in the dark as to how you gain access to the arithmetical facts believing which is constitutive of both your knowledge *and* your understanding of those facts. Why should the Platonist be silenced by this, however, if he can appeal to the drills of rote learning yielding mastery of the arithmetic tables? Why not view these as rather like the maturation and training that yield one's concepts of the various colors and shapes? The symbols, or anyhow concepts that enable counting and simple arithmetic, would then serve to put us in touch with the cardinal properties that give content to our arithmetical knowledge. When we are suitably related to a collection, we can detect the presence or absence of cardinal properties of that collection through those symbols and concepts and through the practices in which they figure. Those symbols and concepts may thus play a role rather like that of rulers, which aid our access to specific lengths beyond our unaided perceptual discrimination. True, some propositions come built into the package. Thus we know that $4 > 3$, and need no counting or any other procedure in order to figure that out. But neither do we need to figure out that black is distinct from white, nor that sphericity is distinct from cubicity, nor the multitude of other such propositions built into the respective packages for understanding of the colors and the shapes.

Compare, finally, the following:

Level 1   Necessarily, nothing cubical is spherical.
Level 2   Cubicity and sphericity are necessarily disjoint.

The level 2 claim purports to *refer to, not just to express*, certain properties and to attribute a relation to them. Here it is not so hard to explain how we know. Presumably, what we know is just a correlate of the level 1 claim, and this fact should unfurrow our brow. So long as we understand generality, modality, and the substantive concepts of cubicity and sphericity, what blocks our access to the question answered by that level 1 claim?[9] So much for our access to the

---

[8] Or, in order to guard against results here analogous to those concerning simultaneity, or even to those suggested by deep logical paradoxes, one might then want to retreat to the view that we must have a strong inclination to answer our questions about sphericity and cubicity, a prima-facie inclination analogous to the perceptual ones that survive our Müller–Lyer discoveries, etc.

[9] In any case, cubicity and sphericity do have a causal presence in space-time, even if they could exist apart from space-time. They are causally present via their instances, which is also a way in

question, perhaps. But still: How can we know the answer? How can we be sure that we are adequately reliable in answering as we do? By analogy to Descartes's way of explaining our knowledge of the *cogito*, our explanation here might appeal neither to causal relations joining our knowledge-constituting beliefs to the facts believed nor to any sort of construction of those facts by those beliefs, nor to any judgment-dependence. True, our answer would derive from our exercise of the very a priori faculties whose reliability wants explaining. But, in this respect, it is not distinctively questionable by comparison with Descartes's explanation of our *cogito* reliability, or by comparison with any explanation attainable by naturalized epistemology for the reliability of our faculties of perception and reasoning.

A causal requirement is imposed by Benacerraf in his early work, but the causal theory of knowledge on which it rests has long since been refuted. By contrast, what Field requires is not that our beliefs—even our beliefs about particulars and their properties—derive causally from facts constituted by those particulars and properties, but rather that it be possible to see at least in principle how the reliability of our beliefs might be explained somehow. The explanation need not be causal, but we need at least some glimpse of how in principle an explanation might go, whether causal or not. What is supposed problematic about Platonism is not just that the realm of abstracta is causally untrackable, but that it is *neither* trackable *nor* constructible through our responses, judgments, practices, and so forth. For, according to Platonism, abstracta lie hermetically beyond space-time, while also independent of our minds. So, neither tracking nor constructing will help explain how we can be so reliable about that realm.

Field's requirement seems to me harder to reject, whether one is an externalist or an internalist in epistemology; and in fact, along with Descartes, I am both. I am an externalist about animal knowledge, as was Descartes about *cognitio*. And I am an internalist about reflective knowledge, as was Descartes about *scientia*. If Field is right about the Platonist's predicament, then Platonism would preclude our ever attaining reflective *scientia* about mathematics. Suppose Field is right that Platonists are powerless to give us so much as a glimpse of how we could possibly be reliable about numbers. Even so, *externalist* Platonists might still be able to hold onto knowledge of arithmetic. For they might contend that *we are as a matter of fact reliable* about arithmetic, even if we have no clue as to *how* we manage that, and can never have a clue.

which cardinal properties make themselves felt and known. However, we need no observational contact with their instances in observable space-time, which distinguishes cardinality from color and shape. For cardinality, like existence in the *cogito*, is exemplified also in our own consciousness, and wherever there is a plurality of items, so even in the world of abstracta itself.

I am with Field, however, in fighting shy of the corner wherein one would have to claim a reliability that avowedly one could never explain. A reliabilist might perhaps be willing to claim reliable knowledge of arithmetic, while granting that we can never have a clue as to how we manage it. Even so, it would be sad to be forever denied reflective knowledge about arithmetic. How much more coherently satisfying would be an overall metaphysics and episte-mology through which one could make sense of one's own reliability about arithmetic, and about any other realm concerning which one claims to have knowledge. Surely we would do better not to reject but to *meet* the Benacerraf–Field challenge. *This* much should seem acceptable to all, even to those unwilling to condition one's attainment of knowledge, or of a higher level of knowledge, on one's achieving any such explanation.

Field's desideratum is, again, to explain in effect the following:

(F1) Generally: [(P is a mathematical proposition and mathematicians believe P) ⊃ P is true].

But this does not seem quite the right desideratum. Compare the following:

(F2) Generally: [(P is a proposition of empirical science and empirical scientists believe P) ⊃ P is true].

Should we be suspicious of empirical science simply because we are unable to pro-vide a single explanation for F2 in one fell swoop? Surely we must be allowed to divide and conquer, offering the following as a more circumspect explanandum.

(⋆) Generally: [(P is a proposition of *arithmetic* and mathematicians believe P) ⊃ P is true].

But *this* seems explicable by noting that the propositions of arithmetic that mathematicians believe all follow from the Peano axioms. Does this give us what we need, at least for the area of arithmetic? Can we now say that what explains why (⋆) is true is simply that generally mathematicians will believe an arithmetical proposition only if it follows from the Peano axioms, and that all such propositions are true?

No, clearly this would not do. What we need is some *sort* of mathematical propositions such that, if a proposition is of *that* sort, then if you believed it, your belief would be true, and mathematicians tend to believe such propositions *because* they are of *that* sort. To properly explain the reliability of mathemati-cians in their arithmetical beliefs, then, we need to advert not just to the fact that such beliefs of theirs are generally restricted to what follows from the Peano axioms. This is true enough, but it is not explanatory in the desired way.

Compare again the *cogito*. Do you believe you exist now simply *because* that is a self-attribution of existence and you understand it thus? This would fit the model according to which truth and justification derive just from understanding, so it counts as a priori. If we use the Peano axioms analogously in explaining why mathematicians' arithmetical beliefs are generally true, then the mathematicians would be said to believe their arithmetical beliefs *because* they follow from the Peano axioms. But this is problematic in more ways than one.

In the first place, it would *not* explain why you believe the Peano axioms themselves. You do not believe them just because they follow from themselves. Secondly, most people, mathematicians included, believe particular arithmetical propositions based not on the Peano axioms but on proper calculation using the arithmetical tables. And this does explain the reliability of their belief formation, since such calculation is bound to get it right. But still, a similar question remains, as with the Peano axioms. Why do people believe the tables themselves?

Learning the tables by rote derives from drills that give you *both* understanding and belief in a single package. Through the numerals and the tables we gain access to the numbers and the cardinality properties and basic truths of elementary arithmetic. But how can we bear even so much as this relation of understanding-plus-belief to a set of facts so far removed from us? This question does remain, but is it *distinctively* a problem for Platonism?

Take any scientific theory with its general laws. These laws will be either unrestrictedly universal or at least will have a scope that goes well beyond our powers of perceptual scanning. So how are we able to tell what is or is not thus true beyond our combined powers of perception, introspection, and memory? Presumably we are able to tell because we have powers of reason, and, in particular, of inductive reason. So when we have evidence of sort $E1, \ldots, En$ in circumstances C, we accept on that basis some theory T. This manifests a *commitment* (let's call it that) on our part to reason from *such* evidence in *such* circumstances to *such* a theory. If we had *no* such commitments, there would be no theorizing. Now some such commitment, at some logical depth, is presumably unrestricted. So it has a scope that surpasses our powers of perception, memory, and introspection. It is a fact, therefore, that lies beyond our powers of scanning and retention. How, then, can we explain our reliability in accepting it? Does our inductive reason automatically come under suspicion because there is bound to be some such commitment, at some level, whose reliability is so hard to explain? It might be replied that there is an evolutionary explanation as to why our inductive reason is as successful as it is. But if this tack is successful for inductive reason, why could it not be equally successful for mathematical and deductive reasoning? In any case, and even if we had to appeal to the mathematical beliefs acquired by a priori reasoning in explaining the reliability of such reasoning (as, by the way, did Descartes), the circularity here would seem no more vicious than the parallel circularity in appealing to evolution in order to explain the reliability of our empirical faculties and modes of reasoning.

REFERENCES

Casullo, Albert (1999), 'A Priori Knowledge Appraised', in Albert Casullo (ed.), *A Priori Knowledge* (Aldershot: Dartmouth Publishing Company), pp. xiii–xxxviii.
Divers, John, and Miller, Alexander (1999), 'Arithmetical Platonism: Reliability and Judgement-Dependence', *Philosophical Studies*, 95: 277–310.
Field, Hartry (1989), *Realism, Mathematics and Modality* (Oxford: Blackwell).

II

What is it Like to be a Zombie?

ROBERT STALNAKER

Zombies are creatures that are physically exactly like ordinary people, but that have no phenomenal consciousness. A zombie world is a world physically exactly like our world, but with no phenomenal consciousness at all. The sun shines in such worlds, but the lights are out in the minds of the unfortunate creatures who live in them. These beings behave just as we do, and their internal physical and functional properties are exactly the same as ours. They make judgments, and perhaps have beliefs (or at least functional analogues of beliefs: states that represent the world), but their states have no qualitative character, no 'inside'. There is nothing it is like to be a zombie.

To really be clear about what a zombie world would be, a lot more should be said about what it means for a possible world to be physically exactly like our world. Suppose for a moment that some form of mind–body dualism is true, and that physical interactions *cause* emergent nonphysical phenomenal experience. Isn't it part of the *physical* character of this world that physical interactions have these effects, and wouldn't a world without them be *physically* different? If so, then the possibility of zombie worlds will be ruled out from the start by

I am grateful to Kati Balog, Daniel Dennett, Sydney Shoemaker, and the editors, Tamar Szabó Gendler and John Hawthorne, for very helpful comments on a prior draft of this chapter. Thanks also to audiences at Johns Hopkins University, the University of Wisconsin at Madison, the University of Illinois at Chicago, Cornell University, Stanford University, and the University of Oxford for stimulating discussion.

dualists and materialists alike. But I will assume that to say that two possible worlds are physically alike is only to say that all physical phenomena and physical powers to produce physical phenomena are the same. There will still be room for considerable debate about just what phenomena and properties count as physical, but even if we don't look too carefully at the extent of the domain of the physical, contenting ourselves with a rough intuitive distinction, it will still be controversial whether zombies, and zombie worlds, are possible, and the controversy has metaphysical consequences. There is a simple argument against materialism, and for a kind of dualism, that has as its central premise the hypothesis that it is conceivable, or conceptually possible, that there be zombies. From this it is inferred that zombies (and zombie worlds) are *metaphysically* possible. But if there are possible worlds exactly like ours with respect to all physical facts in which there is no consciousness, then the facts about consciousness in our world (assuming there are such facts) are not determined by (or supervenient on) the physical facts. So materialism—the thesis that everything is supervenient on the physical—is false.

Some have questioned the move from the premise that zombies are conceivable, or *conceptually* possible, to the conclusion that they are *metaphysically* possible, and I will consider below whether there might be a gap between conceptual and metaphysical possibility, but for the moment I will assume that metaphysical possibility is possibility in the widest sense. My aim is to try to get clearer about the nature of the disagreement between those who think zombies are possible and those who think they are not. What kind of dispute is this, and what kinds of arguments are relevant to resolving it? I am interested in getting clear about this issue mainly for the light it might throw on general questions about the nature of modal claims and about the relation between metaphysical, semantic, and empirical questions.

I will begin by describing the views of three fictional philosophers who give unequivocal answers to the question, 'Are zombies possible?' These characters may seem to resemble real philosophers with the same names, and I will not claim that the resemblances are coincidental, but I want to be able to oversimplify without getting into trouble, so I won't identify my characters, whom I will call 'Dave', 'Patricia', and 'Sydney', with any real philosophers. (It is not that the views of my characters are any less complex than those of the real philosophers on which they are based; it is just that my fictional characters can't complain when I oversimplify their views.) Dave and Patricia believe that zombies are possible, while Sydney denies this. Although Dave and Patricia agree about the possibilities, they disagree about the facts: Patricia thinks that the world we live in is a zombie world, while Dave agrees with Sydney that the world we live in is not a zombie world.

I said that Dave and Patricia disagree with Sydney about whether zombies are possible, but what sort of disagreement is this? Specifically, is it an ontological disagreement about what sorts of metaphysically possible worlds there are? Or is it a semantic disagreement—a disagreement about the meanings of the words we use to describe the possible worlds? Consider the dispute between O'Leary, who insists that it is impossible for there to be a veterinarian who never served in the military, and Daniels, who thinks that not only is this possible, there actually are such people. On closer inspection, we learn that this is not really a disagreement about what possible worlds there are: O'Leary agrees with Daniels that there are animal doctors who are lifelong civilians—he just has a misconception about some words that are used to describe these people. Is our dispute between Dave and Patricia, on the one side, and Sydney, on the other, like this? (Those who have taken the lessons taught by Quine to heart may be skeptical about the distinction I am trying to make, but let's ignore them for the moment.)

In the case of Daniels and O'Leary, a paraphrase helped to bring out that the issue was semantic rather than metaphysical. Daniels could describe the kind of world he claimed was possible without using the disputed word 'veterinarian', and when he did, O'Leary agreed that this was indeed a metaphysically possible world. The only issue that remained is whether a certain expression was correctly applied to describe such a possible world. One might, at that point, get out the dictionary, but O'Leary, like Humpty Dumpty, doesn't care how other people use words. He insists that 'veterinarian', as he uses the term, applies only to former members of the military. Once this became clear, there was nothing left to argue about. Daniels, and we, may find O'Leary's idiosyncratic speech perverse, but we don't disagree with him either about the facts or about the possibilities.

If Dave and Patricia can paraphrase their description of the world they are claiming to be possible in a way that avoids the crucial expression 'phenomenal consciousness', and related expressions, then we may be able to see whether their disagreement with Sydney is semantic or metaphysical. One can't expect this procedure to work in general. It is rarely easy to find paraphrases for controversial philosophical expressions that are not equally controversial. But in this case it turns out to be surprisingly easy. Let us define a *z-world* as a possible world exactly like the actual world in all *physical* respects, and that contains nothing except what supervenes on the physical. To use the popular metaphor, a z-world is a world in which God made and arranged the physical stuff, *and then stopped*. He did not go on and add anything else. We have not mentioned the absence of consciousness in our characterization of this world, but both Dave and Patricia should agree that our definition gives a determinate description of the world they are claiming to be possible. At least, it is as complete as their original description of the zombie world. Clearly a zombie world (if there is one) fits this description, and there cannot be two discernible possible worlds fitting the description, since we have specified all of its physical features, and added that there are no others. So one need not say more to say what kind of possible world we are talking about.

According to David Lewis, the thesis of *materialism* is true in our world if and only if the following condition is met:

Among worlds where no natural properties alien to our world are instantiated, no two differ without differing physically; any two such worlds that are exactly alike physically are duplicates.[1] (Lewis 1983: 364)

This says what it is for materialism to be true in our world. One could say more generally what it is for materialism to be true in an arbitrary possible world x by replacing 'our world' in Lewis's definition by 'world x'. Materialism is the proposition that is true in those possible worlds x that satisfy Lewis's condition. If we accept this definition of the thesis of materialism, then a z-world is just a world meeting the following two conditions: first, it is physically exactly like the actual world; second, materialism is true in it. So anyone who believes that materialism is true will believe that the actual world is a z-world.

Now Sydney is a materialist, so he believes, in agreement with Patricia, that the actual world is a z-world, and so of course that z-worlds are possible. So it seems that Sydney and Patricia agree both about the possibilities and about the facts. Their disagreement about whether zombie worlds are possible is, like the disagreement between Daniels and O'Leary, a semantic one. 'I am a materialist, but not an *eliminative* materialist,' says Sydney. 'As I use the expressions "phenomenal consciousness", "feeling", "qualia", etc., they all apply in the actual world, and so in the world that both Patricia and I agree is the z-world.' So it seems that all three of our characters agree that there are possible worlds of the kind that Dave and Patricia *call* zombie worlds. The disagreement is about whether they are properly so-called.

---

[1] Might there be possible worlds with laws that permit the emergence of nonphysical phenomena, but only in circumstances that, because of the accidents of chance or initial conditions, never in fact arise? And if there are such possible worlds, shouldn't we say that materialism is false in them? Lewis's Humean metaphysics, according to which laws are supervenient on arrangements of particular matters of fact, excludes such possible worlds, but those who want to allow for them might want to tinker with this definition (perhaps referring not to *instantiated* fundamental properties, but to properties that play a role in the fundamental laws of the world). But I don't think this issue will matter for our purposes here.

Both Sydney and Patricia are what David Chalmers has called type-A materialists: those 'who hold that consciousness, insofar as it exists, supervenes logically on the physical, for broadly functionalist or eliminative reasons'. Chalmers would distinguish both of them from type-B materialists, who 'accept that consciousness is not logically supervenient, holding that there is no *a priori* implication from the physical to the phenomenal, but maintain materialism all the same' (1996: 165–6). We will introduce a new character who is a type-B materialist later, but we should note now that all materialists, whatever their views about the epistemological status of materialism, will agree that the actual world is a z-world—that follows from the definition of materialism, and of the z-world. So any materialist who believes that we are conscious beings (any noneliminative materialist) will deny that the z-world is a zombie world. For type-B as well as type-A materialists, the ground for claiming that the zombie world is metaphysically impossible is that the candidate possible world (the z-world) is not a zombie world. If this is right, then there is no room for a defense of materialism against the zombie argument that tries to open a gap between conceivability and possibility by claiming that there are possible *worlds* that are conceivable but not metaphysically possible.[2] Any materialist will agree with Dave, Sydney, and Patricia that the z-world is not only conceivable, but metaphysically possible, and there is no other world, whatever its status, that is a candidate to be a zombie world. The question is not whether a certain conceivable situation is metaphysically possible; it is whether a certain situation that is agreed to be metaphysically possible is correctly described in a certain way.

We said above that Sydney and Dave agreed with each other (disagreeing with Patricia) about whether the actual world is a zombie world. It now seems that this was a case of only apparent agreement. It is like the apparent agreement between Daniels and O'Leary that Jones is a veterinarian. Daniels knows that Jones is an animal doctor who never served in the military, while O'Leary believes, falsely, that he served in the military, but is not an animal doctor. They disagree about the facts about Jones, but since they use the word 'veterinarian' in different ways, they agree that Jones is correctly described as a veterinarian. Their agreement in assenting to the statement 'Jones is a veterinarian' results from two disagreements—one semantic and one factual—that cancel each other out. The same seems to be true of the superficial agreement between Dave and Sydney about the truth of the statement 'The actual world is not a zombie world'. It is a result of disagreement about whether we live in a z-world, and about whether certain words are correctly applied to z-worlds.

---

[2] See Chalmers (1996: 136 ff.).

The first disagreement is the only substantial one. On the second question, Dave and Sydney may find each other's choices about how to talk perverse, but when each is clear about what the other means, there is nothing to argue about.

Or is there? The argument against materialism that motivated our inquiry depended crucially on the assumption that the z-world is a zombie world. The soundness of this argument cannot depend on an innocent choice about how to talk. Perhaps it is not so easy to separate the semantic question about how to describe the z-world and its alternatives from the substantive questions about what kind of world we live in. Let's look more closely at the way the z-world and its alternatives are specified.

The first thing to note is that we have defined the z-world in terms of the actual world, and since our characters are not omniscient, they may disagree about what the actual world is like physically (and so about what the z-world is like). So, while it is right that in defining the z-world we have specified a unique possible world (assuming we have specified a possible world at all), there will remain empirical questions about what the world we have specified is like.

Here is one way that future science might go: as cognitive psychology and neuroscience develop, they, along with commonsense psychology, converge. Both ordinary concepts for describing thought, emotion, and sensation and functional concepts developed by psychologists tend to fit together smoothly with neurophysiological concepts and categories. Introspective reports about phenomenal experience, as well as cognitive categories motivated by behavioral experiments, are found to correlate well with brain states and events revealed by new brain-imaging techniques. Call this the optimistic scenario.

Alternatively, it might happen that as neuroscience learns more about the brain and develops sophisticated methods for explaining and predicting behavior, commonsense mentalistic concepts and functional psychological theory seem increasingly irrelevant and outmoded. As we learn more about the brain, it becomes harder to reconcile what we are inclined to say about our thoughts, feelings, and sensations with what science tells us to be true about what is going on in our bodies and brains. Commonsense and cognitive concepts seem increasingly unnatural. Folk psychology comes to look increasingly like a theory with false presuppositions deeply embedded in it. Call this the pessimistic scenario.

Now Patricia is inclined to believe that the pessimistic scenario is closer to the truth, while Sydney is disposed to expect something more like the optimistic scenario to be realized, and this empirical disagreement is part of what explains their disagreement about whether the z-world is a zombie world. But it is clear that this is not the whole of the disagreement. For one thing, Dave agrees with Sydney that the optimistic scenario is more likely, but agrees with Patricia about whether the z-world is a zombie world. In addition, it is clear that Patricia and Sydney would continue to disagree about whether the z-world is a zombie world even on the hypothesis that the pessimistic scenario is correct. Sydney will grant that the pessimistic scenario is an (unlikely) empirical possibility, but he thinks that zombie worlds are not only impossible, but inconceivable. According to him, we know on conceptual grounds that phenomenal consciousness is a functional property, although just what functional property is open to further discussion, informed by consideration of both thought experiments and empirical evidence. We might well discover that, according to some particular conceptual analysis of phenomenal consciousness, there was no such thing, but that would be a compelling reason to reject the analysis as incorrect. It is not (according to Sydney) an a priori truth that we are conscious beings, but the belief that we are conscious is a datum that should play an important role in evaluating any proposed conceptual analysis.

We can characterize the semantic difference between the usage of Sydney, on the one hand, and Dave and Patricia, on the other, in a general way. The issue concerns how theoretically loaded the idea of phenomenal consciousness is. Some words carry with them a lot of theoretical baggage; the word can be correctly applied only if the theoretical presuppositions implicit in its semantics are correct. Other words are more innocent. If we discovered that we were mistaken about the fundamental nature of Fs, in the one kind of case we say that we learned that there are no Fs, while in the other kind of case we say that Fs turned out to be fundamentally different from what we thought.

Consider water: it was once believed to be a fundamental element (perhaps the one out of which all matter is made, but at least one of four fundamental elements). Imagine a more skeptical ancient scientist who expects that future science will reveal that what we call 'water' is not a fundamental kind at all, but just a heterogeneous category held together by a cluster of superficial properties. Separate from this empirical issue is a semantic question about what we should say if the second hypothesis turned out to be true. One view is that 'water' is a theoretical word—it is built into its meaning that anything correctly called 'water' is a fundamental element. On this semantic hypothesis, if the skeptical ancient scientist turned out to be right, then the right thing to say would be that there is no water. A contrasting semantic hypothesis is that 'water' is theoretically innocent. Water is the stuff we call 'water', whatever it turns out to be. If the facts were as the skeptic thought, then 'water' would turn out to be vaguer than expected, but it would still be said that the stuff we regarded as paradigms of 'water' is water. Of course, water turned out not to be one of the fundamental elements, but it is nevertheless regarded as a natural kind of stuff. The situation was different with the other fundamental elements, but we are still not inclined to say that there is no such thing as earth, air, and fire, in contrast with what we are inclined to say about phlogiston, or what we would say about oxygen or neutrinos if the theories of which they are a part turned out to be fundamentally mistaken.

It is not only that it seems descriptively right to say that 'water' is a term with little theoretical baggage built into its semantics—it is also clear that such terms are necessary to facilitate discussion when there is disagreement about the nature of the stuff we find in the world. Suppose we are having a discussion with Thales, who is defending the view that water is the fundamental element out of which everything in the world is made. 'Water', says Thales, 'is, by definition, a fundamental element. According to you crazy H_2O theorists, there is no such thing as water. You may try to paper over the paradoxical character of your theory by changing meanings, calling the stuff you think fills the rivers and lakes by the name "water", but what you really are committed to is the incredible claim that the world is *bone dry*. Isn't it just obvious that that is false?'

Now the H_2O theorist may be tempted to reply in kind: 'It is *you*, Thales, who are claiming that we live in a waterless world. The world as you think it is, is a version of Putnam's counterfactual twin earth—a world superficially like ours, but with no water (we might call your fundamental element "XYZ"). But obviously we don't live on counterfactual twin earth.' It might be more helpful to respond instead in this way: 'You may talk as you like, Thales, though we might argue about whose usage is eccentric. Your decision about what to mean by the word "water" is clear enough, and we agree that if we use the word as you are using it, our account is committed to the claim, "there is no water in the world". And we agree that this sounds like a crazy claim, but if you use words in eccentric ways, the simple truth may sound like a crazy claim. (To quote Berkeley's character Philonous: "Suppose a traveller should tell you, that in a certain country men might pass unhurt through the fire; and, upon explaining himself, you found he meant by the word *fire* that which others call *water*; or if he should assert there are trees which walk upon two legs, meaning men by the term *trees*. Would you think this reasonable?" ' (Berkeley 1979: 51).)

We don't want to quibble about words, but we do think (quite independently of our theory about the nature of the stuff in question) that it is useful to have a word that is less theoretically loaded than your word 'water', or our expression 'H_2O'—a name for the stuff whose composition is under discussion. If we have such a word, we can more easily frame our disagreement, which is primarily empirical, and not semantic. Granted, we can't completely separate questions about what is in the extension of a term from questions about the nature of the stuff, but at least in a specific context of disagreement, we can choose our words so as to describe clearly the issues that are in dispute. 'Water' seems a word that is well suited for this purpose, but whatever we call the stuff whose nature we are arguing about, it is pretty clear that we agree, in large part, about when we have a paradigm example of the stuff, and about what many of its superficial properties are.

The point might be put with the help of a distinction, and some terminology for it, introduced by Martin Davies and Lloyd Humberstone (1982). If we consider the twin-earth world as a counterfactual world (presupposing what we H$_2$O theorists know to be true—that water is H$_2$O), we describe it as a world without water, and this is a correct description of that possible world. But if we describe that counterfactual world *as actual*—imagine ourselves in it, describing it from within—then we adopt the semantics that we (or our counterparts) use in that possible world. We grant that if Thales were right about the nature of the stuff, then he would be right that the word 'water' applies to the stuff with that nature. We believe that there is no water on counterfactual twin earth, but we beg the question if we assume this in a discussion with someone who thinks that we actually are in such a world.

In using the two-dimensional apparatus to formulate this point, I do not mean to endorse the view that Stephen Yablo has called 'textbook Kripkeanism',[3] according to which a word like 'water' has two kinds of meaning or intension, one of which is a reference-fixing definition in terms of the manifest properties that we use to pick out water. Our capacity to identify water and the fact that we agree, in many cases, about where it is to be found make it possible for us to talk about it without talking past each other, but this does not imply that the facts about water that we agree about are implicit in the meaning of the word 'water', in any sense, or that we know a priori that water has the properties we use to pick it out.[4]

The contrast between more theoretically innocent and more theoretically loaded words is not meant to be a sharp or deep distinction of kind. There will be intermediate cases, and it may in some cases be an accident of lexicographic history whether one says, when a theory is overturned, 'we discovered that there were no such things as Fs' or 'we discovered that Fs are very different from what we thought'. The important thing is not to equivocate between the two.

To return to consciousness, it seems clear that Dave and Patricia are building some theoretical content into the concept of phenomenal consciousness and

---

[3] See Yablo (1999) and Ch. 13 below. Yablo (correctly, I think) refrains from attributing this line of thought to Kripke.

[4] I discuss alternative interpretations of the two-dimensional modal apparatus in Stalnaker (2001).

the cluster of related words; that is, they are treating 'consciousness' more like 'oxygen' and 'phlogiston' than like 'water', 'earth', or 'fire'. Patricia will probably agree with us about this; for her, the idea of phenomenal consciousness is inseparable from an outdated, false theory of the mind. But Dave may insist that, as he uses the expression, 'phenomenal consciousness' has a demonstrative meaning. 'Zombies are possible,' he might say, 'because there might be creatures physically just like us who do not have *this* going on in them' (inwardly demonstrating the property we all experience ourselves as having). But Dave does assume that there are some theoretical constraints on the kind of thing that we can be demonstrating. Specifically, he seems to assume that it follows from what we mean when we talk about consciousness that consciousness is non-physical. For consider what happens when Dave's zombie twin judges that he himself is conscious. According to Dave, the word 'conscious' as used by the zombie, does not refer to some property that is salient to the zombie, as one might expect with a demonstrative. (I assume that properties can be salient to zombies: they can, for example, presumably use words like 'she' to refer to a most salient female in the relevant context.) Rather, the word, as used by both Dave and his zombie twin, is constrained to refer only to a property of a certain kind. 'There is no doubt', Dave says, that his zombie twin, in judging that he himself is conscious, 'is judging that he has *some* property over and above his structural and functional properties—a property that he calls "consciousness".'[5] Even the zombie (at least the zombie who is Dave's zombie twin) is judging that he has some nonphysical property.

Sydney uses the word 'consciousness' in a contrasting way, but a way that may also be theoretically loaded. He is an analytical functionalist, so, while Dave is insisting that it is part of the meaning of the word that consciousness is *not* a functional property, Sydney is insisting that it is built into the meaning of the word that it *is* a functional property. This semantic mismatch is not conducive to a perspicuous debate about whether we in fact live in a z-world or in one of its alternatives. So let me introduce a new character—a materialist who tries to use words in a more theoretically neutral way. I will call her Anne. (Don't look for a real-world analogue of this character—at least, not one with this name.) Anne thinks that 'phenomenal consciousness' and related expressions are names for, or ways of talking about, properties that we find ourselves with, but she thinks that there is no theoretical account of the nature of these properties built into the semantics of the expressions. Perhaps they are functional properties, or physical properties. Perhaps they are irreducible nonphysical properties. Empirical inquiry will be relevant to answering the question of what kind of

---

[5] Chalmers (1996: 180).

properties they are, though the questions are obviously highly theoretical. Thought experiments, as well as empirical experiments and observations, will be relevant to deciding what kind of properties they are. Some arguments about the nature of the properties may look like something that might be called 'conceptual analysis'. But Anne—a good Quinean—thinks that the line between theoretically informed conceptual analysis and empirical discovery is difficult to draw in a nonarbitrary way. Anne is the promised type-B materialist.

Since Anne is a materialist, she agrees with Sydney and Patricia that we live in a z-world, and since she is not an eliminative materialist, she agrees with Sydney that a z-world is not a zombie world. The contrast between Sydney's and Anne's views about the semantics of the contested expressions is a subtle one. To bring it out, we need to be more explicit about the alternative to the z-world—the world that Dave thinks is actual. I argued above that it was easy to specify a unique z-world without using contested words, but this is not possible with the alternative to the z-world. And while it is common ground that there are z-worlds, it is less clear whether our characters will agree that there are possible worlds of the alternative kind. We can say this much, before running into disagreement, about what such an alternative world would have to be like: an a-world is a world that is physically just like the actual world, and so just like the z-world; in addition it has some properties not instantiated in the z-world: *alien* properties, in Lewis's sense—that is, properties that are alien relative to the z-world. (The 'a' in 'a-world' is for 'alternative' or 'alien', but if you are on Dave's side in this dispute, you can think of it as short for 'actual'.) All of our characters agree that an a-world meets these conditions, and that worlds meeting these conditions are possible. But of course, this is far from enough to specify the kind of possible world that Dave has in mind. We have to add that the extra properties in the a-world (call them the a-properties) are properties of conscious beings, and that they are the properties we are referring to when we talk about consciousness, experience, qualia, and so forth.

It is here that Sydney will balk. 'I will grant that there are possible worlds like ours, but with extra non-physical properties or substances. I will even grant that the mental/functional properties such as phenomenal consciousness that are physically realized in our world might, in some other world, be realized by alien nonphysical properties. But it has been stipulated that a-worlds and z-worlds are physically alike, so the functional properties that are physically realized in the z-world will be realized in exactly the same way in a corresponding a-world. Since I think that expressions like "phenomenal consciousness" refer, in virtue of their meaning, to such functional properties, I hold that they will refer to them, and not to the a-properties, in (or with respect to) the a-worlds. Now if we set aside the purely semantic assumption that our expression "phenomenal consciousness" and others like it refer (with respect to the a-world) to a-properties,[6] then I will grant that a-worlds are possible, and I will agree with Dave that we, or our counterparts in the a-world, are conscious there (since I think we are conscious in the physically and functionally equivalent z-world). But I deny that the a-properties he postulates have anything to do with our consciousness in such worlds. That is, I claim that phenomenal consciousness in the a-world is independent of the a-properties, which is to say that the following counterfactual is true there: *Even if none of the a-properties were instantiated, people would still be conscious, have qualitative experience; there would still be something it is like to be them.* You can hypothesize all the alien properties you like, but if they don't affect our brains or our behavior, then they won't have anything to do with our minds—and they won't be anything we could know about.'

Dave and Sydney have reached an impasse much like that of Thales and the H_2O theorist. At this point, Anne enters the discussion: 'We disagree about the nature of consciousness, but just as with water, we agree, for the most part, about when and where it is to be found. Talk of qualitative experience—of "what it is like", and so on—is somewhat elusive, but people with very different theoretical views seem to be able to understand each other when they talk about experience, at least outside an abstract theoretical debate. (Just as Thales and we can agree about whether there is water or vodka in the glass, so Dave and we can agree about exactly when a patient regained consciousness after an operation.) And just as it seems natural to describe the disagreement between Thales and the H_2O theorist as a dispute about the nature of water, so it seems natural to describe the disagreement between Sydney and Dave as a dispute about the nature of consciousness. Let's call the phenomenon whose nature is at issue "phenomenal consciousness", without prejudging its nature. We have no a priori assurance that we can identify the subject matter of our dispute in a theory-neutral way, but let's assume provisionally that there is a property that Dave thinks is an irreducible nonphysical property and that Sydney thinks is a functional property—a property that we all agree we find ourselves with. The property may be *essentially* nonphysical, or *essentially* physical, or neither, but since that is part of what is in dispute, we'll try to leave it open. I should

---

[6] Instead of stipulating that the a-properties are the ones we refer to when we talk about conscious experience, we might (Sydney suggests) more cautiously say only that the a-properties *coincide* with mental properties, leaving open whether they are identical to them. (My character wants to acknowledge help from comments by the real Sydney Shoemaker in formulating his views—he was careless in an earlier draft. But he insists that he remains fictional; neither he nor Sydney Shoemaker should be held responsible for views expressed by the other.)

say that I am not convinced that an a-world in which the inhabitants succeed in talking about properties that are epiphenomenal is really coherent, but I am setting these worries aside.[7] What we will try to do is to consider both the z-world and the a-world *as actual*: as possible worlds that are compatible with the context in which our debate is framed. What is presupposed in the context of any discussion is only what is presumed to be the common knowledge of the participants in that discussion. In the debate between materialists and dualists, some think that we are in a z-world, and some that we are in an a-world, so both kinds of world must be included in the context. But it is common ground (since Patricia has gone home) that we are conscious. So, if you are going to take our materialism seriously, you must consider the world that we think we are in *as actual*, which means entertaining the possibility that our thesis is actually true. Now of course you might argue that our position is *incoherent*—that there is no possible world of the kind we think we are in. But you grant that the z-world is possible. You think it is a zombie world, but suppose you discovered that the z-world was not only possible but actual? (God reveals to you that all there is, is supervenient on the physical.) Would you then conclude that you are a zombie—that your consciousness is an illusion? Of course not.'

Dave responds to Anne this way: 'I'm sorry, but I can't take your materialism seriously *as possibly actual*, since I know, simply by being conscious, that I am not in a zombie world, and I think that the world you materialists are claiming we live in is is a zombie world. Let's go back to the original intuition—the one with which our argument against materialism began: that it is conceivable that there are zombies (and zombie worlds). Don't even you materialists have to admit that there is at least a prima-facie plausibility to the claim that we can form a coherent conception of a world just like ours, but with the inner light of consciousness extinguished? I grant that this is in part a semantic intuition—an intuition about what we mean by "consciousness"—but isn't it a compelling intuition nonetheless? We have to take our semantic intuitions seriously, as Berkeley's Philonous reminded us earlier in the discussion.'

Anne responds: 'I agree that we have to take semantic intuitions seriously, but my worry is that, in rejecting the coherence of our noneliminative materialism, you are appealing to incompatible semantic intuitions. On the one hand, you want to insist that "consciousness" bears a theoretical load—that it is part of the meaning of the term that it refers to a nonphysical property; on the other hand, you want to insist that consciousness is a property we can know we have,

---

[7] See Chalmers's discussion of the paradox of phenomenal judgment (1996: 172–209), and Shoemaker (1999).

simply by having it. This seems to me suspicious in a way that is reminiscent of Thales' move when he noted first that it is obvious that there is water—who but a radical skeptic could deny that there is water in the lake?—and then claimed that the H_2O theorist was committed to denying this obvious fact, since "water" by definition refers to a fundamental element. I agree that "consciousness" is something we simply find ourselves with, and I can't imagine being convinced by any kind of theoretical consideration that I am not conscious—that I am a zombie. Since I can imagine being convinced, on theoretical grounds, of the truth of materialism (this takes little imagination, since I *am* convinced of it), I conclude that the existence of consciousness is compatible with materialism.'

Anne continues: 'I will, however, concede that the intuition that zombies are conceivable has considerable intuitive force, and I think that, with the help of the two-dimensional apparatus that you are so fond of, we can accommodate it. Let's look one more time at the analogy with water: We agree that in a sense it is conceivable that water be something other than H_2O, even though it is necessary that water be H_2O (and so that there is no possible world in which water is something other than H_2O). What is conceivable (and metaphysically possible) is that the XYZ theorist is right, and if he were right, then we would be referring to something other than H_2O with the term "water". The situation is symmetrical. The XYZ theorist believes that "water" refers to XYZ in all possible worlds, but grants that, as he puts it, "if the H_2O theorist were right, we would all be referring to H_2O with the term 'water', rather than to water". If the XYZ theory were true, then what he would be saying would be true (and it is conceivable that his theory is true). So much is familiar. But now consider whether it is conceivable that there should be no water in the world at all, *even though H_2O fills the lakes and streams, and falls from the sky on rainy days, just as it does in the world as we believe it to be?* That is, try to envision a possible world physically and chemically exactly like ours, but with no water. This, we say, is surely impossible, but the XYZ theorist disagrees. He thinks that the world we think is actual is a world that is correctly described in this way—as a world with H_2O, but no water, in the lakes and streams. (Just as we describe the XYZ-world as a possible world with XYZ in the lakes and streams, but no water.) Of course the XYZ theorist is wrong, but since it is conceivable that he might be right, it is conceivable that what he says is true.

'It may seem a rather artificial and oversubtle exercise to use the two-dimensional modal apparatus to describe the actual world (considered as counterfactual) from the perspective of a counterfactual world (considered as actual), but if it is really an open question—a real live disagreement—which world is actual, this may be less artificial.'

'Now we materialists don't believe that Dave's dualist theory is right, but we beg the question if we presuppose that he is wrong. So suppose he's right—suppose that we really are in an a-world—and that consciousness—this property we find ourselves with—is an irreducible nonphysical property. (I'm not convinced that this is really possible, but we're granting it for the moment.) Now consider the counterfactual "if we didn't have this property—or any of the a-properties—we wouldn't be conscious". More specifically, consider, "if we didn't have any of the a-properties, but the world were physically just as it is, then we wouldn't be conscious—we would be in a zombie world". I will grant (though Sydney would not) that if we were actually in an a-world, then this counterfactual would be true. If it is conceivable and possible that we are in an a-world, then it is conceivable, in this convoluted sense, that there be zombies.'

If zombies are conceivable in just this sense, does that mean that zombies are metaphysically possible—that there is a zombie world? If we are in fact in an a-world, as Dave believes, then there are (counterfactual) zombie worlds. But if the materialists are right, and we live in a z-world, then there are no possible worlds correctly describable as zombie worlds. Whether or not Dave's dualism is true, if we can coherently suppose that it is true, then we can coherently suppose that zombies are possible, and so can form a coherent conception of zombies. But if this is the only sense in which zombies are conceivable, their conceivability will provide no argument against materialism, since we must assume that materialism is false to be justified in inferring that zombies are possible from the fact that they are conceivable.[8]

So what is it like to be a zombie? According to Anne, it is something like being H_2O without being water.

REFERENCES

Berkeley, George (1979), *Three Dialogues between Hylas and Philonous* (Indianapolis: Hackett Publishing Company; originally published 1713).

Chalmers, David (1996), *The Conscious Mind: In Search of a Fundamental Theory* (New York: Oxford University Press).

Hawthorne, John (forthcoming), 'Advice for Physicalists', *Philosophical Studies*.

Lewis, David (1983), 'New Work for a Theory of Universals', *Australasian Journal of Philosophy*, 61: 343–77.

---

[8] Anne's attempt to accommodate the zombie intuition is similar to a line of argument that is developed (independently) in more detail by Hawthorne (forthcoming).

Shoemaker, Sydney (1999), 'On David Chalmers' *The Conscious Mind'*, *Philosophy and Phenomenological Research*, 59(2): 439–44.

Stalnaker, Robert (2001), 'On Considering a Possible World as Actual', *Proceedings of the Aristotelian Society*, supp. vol. 65: 141–56.

Yablo, Steve (1999), 'Concepts and Consciousness', *Philosophy and Phenomenological Research*, 59(2): 455–63.

The Conceivability
of Naturalism

CRISPIN WRIGHT

A central dilemma in contemporary metaphysics is to find a place for certain anthropocentric subject-matters—for instance, the semantic, moral, and psychological—in a world as conceived by modern naturalism: a stance which inflates the concepts and categories deployed by (finished) physical science into a metaphysics of the kind of thing the real world essentially and exhaustively is. On one horn, if we embrace this naturalism, it seems we are committed either to reductionism: that is, to a construal of the reference of, for example, semantic, moral, and psychological vocabulary as somehow being within the physical domain—or to disputing that the discourses in question involve reference to what is real at all. On the other horn, if we reject this naturalism, then we accept that there is more to the world than can be embraced within a physicalist ontology—and so take on a commitment, it can seem, to a kind of eerie supernaturalism. John McDowell (1994) has proposed a distinctive, intendedly

Ancestors of this material were presented at colloquia in St. Andrews and Glasgow in 1996, at the Logic and Language conference held at the University of London in April 1998, at the Language and Mind seminar at New York University in that same month, when Ned Block was commentator, and at two seminars given at Ohio State University in April 1999. My thanks to the discussants on those occasions for many helpful criticisms and questions, and in particular to Paul Boghossian, Jim Edwards, Bob Hale, Robert Kraut, Neil Tennant, and Ned Block. I am also greatly indebted to the critical feedback of the editors of the present volume, Tamar Szabó Gendler and John Hawthorne.

'non-eerie' accommodation, involving our habituation into a more 'relaxed' conception of what should rank as natural, a conception of Nature which would be hospitable to meanings, to ethical and other norms, and to psychological properties. But the position he proposes—I am speaking just of my own reaction—can too easily seem more like a triumphant reaffirmation of the common-sense categories at issue than a real response to the metaphysical dilemma they pose.

This problem provides the background to the present chapter, rather than its topic. Its topic is the famous argument, outlined in the third lecture of Saul Kripke's *Naming and Necessity*, that pain—and sensations generally—cannot be anything physical. What gives this argument its interest in the context of the concerns of the present volume is the manner in which it draws on considerations of (apparent) conceivability to substantiate a metaphysical conclusion. In the first part of what follows, I shall outline the background to the argument, develop its detail somewhat, and sustain it against what are, according to my understanding, the two most influential received objections to it. Then I shall make a case that, if good at all, it should generalize to cover not just sensations, but all items falling within the extensions of (in a sense to be explained) *transparent* concepts, with colour concepts (an example we shall stalk throughout) and secondary-quality concepts generally the obvious next port of call. At that point, the dialectical situation will be that, to the extent that the distinctive concepts of semantic, moral, and psychological discourse also approximate the relevant model of transparency, the Kripkean argument presents an outstanding challenge to any form of reductionist reaction to the metaphysical dilemma. But I do not think that dialectical situation is stable. My concluding suggestion will be that there is still an outstanding objection to the overall strategy of the argument: the assumption that drives it, that counter-conceivability is a defeater of claims of metaphysical necessity of all kinds, both a priori and a posteriori, stands in need of a (to the best of my knowledge) unremarked form of qualification. If this is right, the argument is balked even for the basic case of sensations, and the fascinating prospect of a wide-reaching exclusion of physicalism on purely conceptual grounds evaporates.

1 Kripke's Argument

1.1 *Natural Kinds and Natural Kind Concepts*

Are colours natural kinds?[1] The philosophical question, of course, is not—in the first instance, anyway—about the actual constitution of coloured things,

---

[1] One philosopher who has argued so, in a much travelled talk some years ago, is again Kripke. An account of his arguments may be found in Johnston (1992).

but about the *concept* of colour. According to the usual template, a concept is a natural kind concept if, roughly, its extension is standardly explained by reference to indicators whose status as such is viewed as contingent, and if we conceive of the real determinant of the extension as a natural property, presumed to be explanatorily associated with the indicators, of whose character we may have—and anyway need—no clear idea in ordinary commerce with the concept. The concept of water, for instance, is characteristically explained by reference to the indicator properties: tasteless, colourless liquid, occurring naturally in lakes and rivers, satisfying thirst, essential to life, solvent for many substances, and so on and so forth. But if, as is usually supposed, **water**[2] is a natural kind concept, then these marks serve not to define it but merely as pointers to an underlying natural essence—to the best of our present knowledge, that of having the chemical constitution H_2O—whose instantiation is what canonically determines whether or not a sample is water. If **water** is a natural kind concept, the indicators serve merely as *reference-fixers*: the concept of water may be glossed as, roughly, that kind of stuff whose being the kind of stuff it is explains its characteristic satisfaction of the indicators in question. A natural kind concept thus incorporates an assumption: that there is an underlying natural essence which discharges—near enough, often enough—that explanatory role. This assumption may be wrong. In that case, the concept will suffer from reference failure.[3] Colours themselves are natural kinds if colour concepts are natural kind concepts *and* they are not so afflicted.

All this is familiar. The idea that many of our general, pre-scientific concepts are concepts of this kind came into prominence with Putnam and Kripke,[4] and contrasts with an older model, associated (on no clear evidence, actually) with the later Wittgenstein, according to which the indicator properties do not bear a *contingent* relation to an underlying determinant of the extension of the concept, but determine that extension intrinsically, after the fashion of a cluster of *criteria*—in the specialized sense of the term that arose in the first generation of commentary on the *Philosophical Investigations*. Clearly there could be concepts—let's call them *criterially governed* concepts—for which this model was correct. Even if our actual concept of water is indeed a natural kind concept, we might have employed instead a concept—**schwater**—for which the water indicators did play a criterial rather than merely a reference-fixing role. To be schwater would just be to satisfy (enough of) the (more important) indicator properties.

---

[2] Except where no ambiguity arises, I shall use boldface type to indicate reference to a concept.

[3] I am going past issues to do with whether such a concept could *survive* reference failure.

[4] The *loci classici* are Putnam (1975: chs. 8 and 10–12), and Kripke (1980: lecture III).

How is it manifest which is our actual concept? Well, if 'water' expressed a natural kind concept, then should it turn out that there is no interesting, explanatorily unifying property underlying the presence of the water indicators in enough cases, we ought to regard the case as one of reference failure: water, like phlogiston, would be a fiction, exploded by science. But if the concept expressed by 'water' were criterially governed—if it were **schwater**—no such conclusion would be warranted; the use of the concept would be indefeasible by any such empirical scientific development. That's only one type of case, though. What about the other, when a criterially governed concept is such that science *does* nevertheless disclose a natural property underlying the characteristic co-manifestations of the relevant criteria, so that a corresponding natural kind concept, had we employed it, would have been successful? That would presumably be the actual situation if the concept expressed by 'water' were **schwater**: schwater would turn out to be H_2O. What in *that* case would show that the concept was nevertheless criterially governed?

It might be thought that the difference would emerge in our attitude to certain counterfactual conditionals, for instance:

Had it turned out that there was no underlying explanatorily unifying property, we would have regarded 'water' as failing of reference.

We will affirm that counterfactual, the natural thought would be, if, but only if, our concept of water is a natural kind concept. But this isn't good enough. For the counterfactual could be wrong even if the concept expressed by 'water' *is* a natural kind concept—provided that, were nature to have let us down in this way, we would then have *changed* the concept expressed by 'water' in the light of that discovery—falling back on the criterially governed analogue, as it were. And of course the question, whether, in continuing to regard the term as referential, we would have assigned to it a concept of a different status, can be answered only in the light of some *independent* determination of how possession of one or the other status would show. So the counterfactual account is no help—it needs back-up by the very thing it purported to provide.

Kripke's discussion offered a different answer, in terms of modal intuition. If water is a natural kind—say, H_2O—then it is *essentially* that kind: something which manifested all the indicators but was not so constituted would not be water but some other kind of stuff. By contrast, if **water** is actually criterially governed, then such a substance would fall under that concept, so would be water, whatever its constitution, and we ought to allow that, while water is normally made up of H_2O, it could be composed of something else. So if **water** is a natural kind concept, and it is true that water is H_2O, it is *necessarily* true that water is H_2O. But if **water** is a criterially governed concept, it is *contingent* what constitution water has—or indeed, whether it has any uniform or typical constitution at all. To determine the status of our concept of water, then, we may check our intuitions about claims such as:

Water is H_2O, but it might not have been.

Or:

Water might have had no typical physical constitution.

If **water** is indeed a natural kind concept, these should impress as conceptual solecisms. For natural kind concepts distinctively sustain certain forms of necessary (a posteriori) claim of which these are violations.

In what follows, I am going to assume that this proposal is broadly adequate: that the difference between natural kind concepts and others can be found in the kind of modal distinctions which Kripke highlighted.

1.2 *Primary and Derivative Natural Kind Concepts*

A further qualification is wanted, however. Intuitions about the necessity of identity statements have to draw on assumptions about the status of *both* the configured terms—for instance, in the particular example, it is taken for granted that 'H_2O' is itself an expression rigidly denoting a natural kind. In general, it is obvious that the class of natural kind concepts that fit the Putnam–Kripke template—concepts that purportedly denote an essential underlying property targeted by surface reference-fixers—is a secondary class, adverting by its very characterization to a contrasting background class of elite concepts—usually assumed,[5] tacitly or otherwise, to be those of developed physical science—by means of which such underlying essences may be identified canonically. For modern naturalists, indeed, the natural coincides with the physical as (best) physics understands it. Call these elite background concepts, whether or not exclusively physical, the *primary* natural kind concepts: concepts of which it is independently given that they demarcate—if anything— what are properly regarded as natural divisions and substances, properties and stuffs.[6] A *derivative* natural kind concept will then show itself by sustaining[7] an a posteriori, but necessarily true, identity statement whose other term expresses a primary natural kind concept.

---

[5] Though not, I think, by Kripke.

[6] Naturally, the identification of these concepts will be hostage to the fate of contemporary scientific theory. We take it that 'H_2O' expresses a compound such concept; but the notion that hydrogen and oxygen are primary kinds is of course empirically defeasible.

[7] —or at least: requiring that there be, if it is instantiated—

A proponent of the thesis that colour concepts are natural kind concepts thus in principle has the option of maintaining that they are primary natural kind concepts. I take that to be the view of the so-called Simple Theory of colour.[8] But I shall not return to that idea in the present discussion. The more usual way of taking the thesis is that, like **water**, colour concepts are derivative natural kind concepts: that our understanding of the concept **red**, for instance, tacitly calls for an identification:

Redness is the property thus-and-such,

whose modal and epistemic status will be exactly comparable to that of:

Water is H_2O.

1.3 *What is the Importance of Natural Kind Concepts?*

If many of the concepts for which the criterial model might initially seem attractive are in fact natural kind concepts, that is something which it is as well to know. And the adjustment will call in turn for some re-configuration of our ideas about what is involved in thinking thoughts in which such concepts are constituents—a re-configuration closely analogous to that involved in dropping the description theory of proper names, even in its most sophisticated forms, and accepting that such expressions typically facilitate the thinking of thoughts *de re*, thoughts directly targeted upon specific objects, rather than mediated via complex descriptive conditions. In short, issues are at stake here—as Kripke saw—about the character of the relation between a thought and the objects and properties it concerns.

But those issues are not our present business. Our agenda is set, rather, by a line of thought that begins with a certain simple picture of the nature and limits of natural science. The picture has it that natural science just *is* the empirical theory of natural kinds and their functional relationships: the project of natural science is to taxonomize what kinds of thing naturally occur and to describe how they are causally and explanatorily related, to detail the laws to which they are subject. If this is right, then—here is the line of thought—the spectre is raised that a concept that is not a natural kind concept—but that is nevertheless, intuitively, a concept of a *kind* of thing, state, or event—may go on to prove, in a certain sense, *scientifically recalcitrant*, and any truths that it is needed to express may consequently lie outside the domain that natural science can illuminate. In short, at least if the simple picture is accepted, the demarcation of important groups of kind concepts that are demonstrably not natural kind

---

[8] See Campbell (1993).

concepts may be just what is needed, for those philosophers inclined to want to do so, to challenge the physical naturalism that for so many has come to seem like common sense.

Any such challenge, however, will need to surmount the simple distinction touched on above. That a criterially governed concept should be intractable for physical science is certainly possible in one kind of case: namely, where it actually has a *physically heterogeneous* extension. In that case, since there will be nothing uniform at the level at which physical science operates, in which the instantiation of the concept consists, there may be no physical laws connecting its instantiation with the instantiation of other physical properties.[9] What, though, if a criterially governed concept does have a physically unified extension, nevertheless, as **schwater** actually has? In that situation we could still affirm the identity, that schwater *is* H_2O, since the term 'schwater' has a complex descriptive content—to be cashed out in terms of the indicator properties—of such a kind as to allow the identity to be true as a matter of *contingency*. The force of the identity would be that

the satisfier of (a certain descriptive condition somehow factoring in the water indicators) = H_2O,

and this could be a contingent truth because of the non-rigidity of the term on the left-hand-side. So schwater—the actual stuff—would still *be* a natural kind— namely, H_2O—even though the *concept* of schwater was not that of a natural kind; and mention of schwater, so use of the concept, could correspondingly occur in (low-level) scientific generalizations and explanations.

This is a reminder, then, that there is—of course—no *direct* way of drawing conclusions about the limitations of science from the status of particular concepts. It will be one thing—if indeed, it can be done—to make a case that colour concepts, say, are not natural kind concepts; but no immediate conclusion is to be expected about the physical-scientific role of colour. The interesting question this raises is: what sort of additional philosophical argument could encompass the stronger conclusion?

1.4 *The Counter-Conceivability Principle*

In *Naming and Necessity*, Kripke deployed his new apparatus of rigid designation, a posteriori necessities, and the rest to outline a new argument—though

---

[9] This is only a possibility, of course. The heterogeneous instances of a concept may still divide up into a manageable variety of physical types, each associated in parallel law-like ways with other kinds of physical states and events.

he did not himself endorse it—against all possibility of the physical reduction of sensation, focusing on the case of pain.

Recall that any statement identifying the essence of a natural kind will be, if true at all, necessarily so. If **water** is a natural kind concept, and it is true that water is H_2O, then it is necessarily true. It follows that evidence against the necessity of such an identification is evidence against its truth. But what should count as evidence against its necessity in the first place? Kripke's discussion turns on a major assumption on which we should pause: that *all* purportedly metaphysically necessary statements, even those—of constitution, identity, or origin, for instance—whose justification is a posteriori, are hostage to what we can, to borrow Descartes's happy phrase, clearly and distinctly conceive, for— short of its actuality—a clear and distinct conception of a situation is the best possible evidence of its possibility. This principle—the Counter-Conceivability Principle—invites us, of course, to provide an account of when a conception should rank as relevantly clear and distinct. But without taking that issue on, we can cash the principle's operational content as being that, if one has what at least *appears to be* a lucid conception of how it might be that not-P, then that should count as a good, albeit defeasible, ground for its not being necessary that P.[10] By the Counter-Conceivability Principle, all putative metaphysical necessities, even a posteriori ones, thus have to face the tribunal of what we can, as we think, clearly and distinctly conceive; and their defeat may consequently be a priori, even if their sole possible form of justification is not.[11]

Is the Counter-Conceivability Principle correct? Naturally, it is uncontroversial for conceptual necessities: any claim that a certain truth is *conceptually* necessary has to be answerable to what we can coherently and lucidly *conceive*. But to suppose that *all* absolute necessities, a posteriori ones included, are subject to constraints of conceivability may seem to be at best a substantial

---

[10] The Counter-Conceivability Principle is something that might really have *deserved* the title of 'Hume's Principle', now of course purloined by the neo-Fregean programme for the foundations of arithmetic. Recall *Treatise*, I. ii. 2: '*whatever the mind clearly conceives, includes the idea of possible existence*, or in other words, *that nothing we imagine is absolutely impossible.*'

[11] Kripke does not explicitly articulate the Counter-Conceivability Principle, but it is striking how naturally it seems to have come to him implicitly to assume it. It did not occur to him to respond to the hypothetical objector who thinks she can conceive of Hesperus turning out to be other than Phosphorus, or of heat being something other than molecular motion, by saying: 'So what? What has conceivability to do with it? I didn't claim these things were *conceptually* necessary.' Rather, the validity of the objector's prima-facie conceptions, and their prima-facie relevance, are straightaway conceded. The defence is rather that they are not what they appear to be—that what is actually conceived in these cases goes no further than *qualitative* similarity to what was intended. But I anticipate.

epistemological claim, in need of a correspondingly substantial defence. Indeed, at worst it would appear the merest blunder: the retention of an intuitively conceptualist epistemology of modality for a range of cases where modal status originates not in the character of concepts at all, but in underlying essences that may go quite unreflected in our concepts of the items whose essences they are.

That is one concern. But in addition, if accepted, the Counter-Conceivability Principle may seem to enforce an objection to the necessity of certain kinds of statement that, if they configured natural kind concepts fitting Kripke's idea of them and were true, would have to be necessary. For instance, it may seem readily conceivable that water might have turned out to have a very different chemical constitution to the one it actually has. So it cannot be necessary that water is H_2O, even if it is true that it is. And indeed, since the point will generalize, it may look as if no such identity statement—no identity statement linking a derivative natural kind concept with a specification of the purported essence of its instances—will pass the test. So the Counter-Conceivability Principle, dubious in any case, might also seem to be inconsistent with Kripke's own view of the modal status of such statements.

Kripke's argument about pain is set up by a lemma constituted by his response to this objection. What is wrong with the objection is its premiss. It is no doubt conceivable that scientific investigations with the *same physiognomy* as those that disclosed that water is H_2O might have had a different upshot— that an investigated substance, displaying all the surface indications of water, might have turned out to be XYZ instead. But then, Kripke rejoins, it would not be *water* that would have turned out to be XYZ. The problem for the objector is how to characterize the stuff of the imaginary scientific investigations. The characterization can hardly proceed except in terms of satisfaction of the characteristic indicator properties of water. But how exactly? If as the *actual* satisfier of those indicator properties, then that is a rigid designator, which will therefore produce a necessary identity when linked with 'H_2O'. And the suggestion that it is nevertheless prima-facie conceivable that the stuff which actually has those properties, namely H_2O, might not have been H_2O is counter-intuitive indeed. What *is* conceivable is that *something* that satisfies the indicator properties, or the most widespread satisfier of the indicator properties, might have turned out not to be H_2O—but that is perfectly consistent with the necessity of *water's* being H_2O.

Essentially the same point addresses the first, more general concern. Any a posteriori necessity, N, will be associated with a seemingly intelligible imaginative scenario in which the a posteriori investigations that confirm it turn out to disconfirm it instead. So much is a consequence of those investigations being a posteriori. But it does not follow that N will be prima-facie counter-conceivable unless it is granted that the imaginative scenario involves an appropriate play with the very concepts configured in N. And that is not granted. If **water** is a natural kind concept, then which concept it is depends on what is the essence of water. The impression that the Counter-Conceivability Principle is all at sea as soon as necessities originating *in rebus* are countenanced turns on the tacit assumption of a separation between concept and essence: that, as it was expressed above, 'underlying essences . . . may go quite unreflected in our concepts of the items whose essences they are'. That assumption simply misunderstands what is being proposed about the character of the relevant concepts that feature in necessities of identity, origin, and constitution.

The Counter-Conceivability Principle is thus under no immediate threat. But the manner of its defence may raise a concern about its utility. Will not the principle be impotent if a presumed necessity that is apparently open to counter-conception can always be excused by charging that an objector's scenario fails genuinely to involve the relevant concepts? Indeed, it will, unless such excuses are required to be backed up by a properly principled explanation of what the alleged shortfall consists in. If **water** is the concept of a physical natural kind, such an explanation will be available when the scenario fails to distinguish between instantiation of that kind, whatever it is, and presentation of the indicators. The crux of Kripke's argument about **pain** is that no correspondingly principled excuse is possible: that a counter-conceivability challenge against the necessity of any particular physicalistic identification of pain actually *succeeds*—or at least, stands undefeated.

1.5 *The Argument about Pain*

Suppose C-fibres are a kind of nervous pathway actually occurring in human beings. And let the proposal be that pain is C-fibre stimulation. Still, it seems readily conceivable that physiological investigation might have found no C-fibre activity in subjects suffering pain, or even that, without change in the range of our sensory afflictions, we might have lacked C-fibres altogether. So it cannot be necessary that pain is C-fibre stimulation. Ergo, since it would be necessary if true, it cannot be true. But this would go for any purported physical identification of pain. So **pain** isn't the concept of a physical natural kind.

Why is this argument any better than that about water? Because in this case the premiss really does seem to be conceivable. Suppose we try to block the argument as before. So we put the question: how is the putative scenario to justify characterizing the imagined scientific experiment as one in which it turns out that no C-fibre stimulation takes place in a *pain-afflicted* subject? Well, what are the relevant indicators? Just one, presumably: namely, a distinctive form of discomfort. But then the difference is that to conceive of something that satisfies the indicator is, in contrast with the case of water, already enough to conceive of *pain*. There is a potential difference, provided by the concept, between a substance's giving the indications of water and its being water; but there is no more to a sensation's being pain than its giving the indications of pain—that is, hurting. So while there is an epistemic gap between conceiving of something that satisfies the indicators of water and conceiving of water, there is no such gap in the case of our basic concepts of sensation. The claim to have counter-conceived the identity of pain with C-fibre stimulation thus stands undefeated.

1.6 *A Naturalist Response*

But has a physicalist any cause to object to the argument so far? After all, the conclusion, properly understood, is only that **pain** isn't a physical natural kind *concept*. Even if that is good as far as it goes, isn't the striking conclusion that Kripke himself proposed, that pain is no physical kind of thing, out of reach? As we noted, it is consistent with its being perfectly proper to conclude that **pain** is not a physical natural kind concept to reserve the thought that pain might yet be a physical natural kind. The position would be exactly analogous to the case for water, the stuff, and **schwater**, the criterially governed concept. The extension of such a concept may always be a natural kind—as indeed it presumably is in that case. So it might be with pain, **pain** and 'pain'. If **pain** were a criterially governed concept, then anything that satisfied the indicators of **pain**—that is, felt uncomfortable in the distinctive way—might indeed count as pain, and 'pain' would be thereby apt to feature in true *contingent* identities in which it was linked with physical terms.

Why do I say that the conclusion of the argument, properly understood, is only that **pain** isn't a physical natural kind *concept*? After all, if the identity statement

Pain is C-fibre stimulation

is, if true, necessarily true, then a standing objection to its necessity has to be reckoned a standing objection to its truth; and since 'C-fibre stimulation' is, in effect, just a place-holder for any physicalist reduction, that is therefore a standing objection to any such reduction. The conclusion of the argument properly concerns pain, and not just **pain**.

But this is to forget that the argument is driven by a more complex conditional than the objector implicitly allows. What we have is not

If pain is C-fibre stimulation, then it is necessary that it is, but

> If **pain** is a natural kind concept, then if pain is C-fibre stimulation, then it is necessary that it is.

So, if the major antecedent is discharged, pain's actually being C-fibre stimulation (or whatever else) will be consistent with its being so as a matter of contingency. Sure, in that case 'pain' would not be a rigid designator, just as 'water' would not be if it expressed **schwater**. And Kripke's argument against physicalism assumes that 'pain' *is* a rigid designator. But where did that premiss come from? If it is put up for *reductio* that **pain** is a physical natural kind concept, then that, to be sure, enjoins that its expression, 'pain', is rigid. But once the argument is allowed to proceed to the point where the first assumption is discharged, then—unless some independent argument on the point is supplied—it is open to the physicalist to fall back on the view that **pain** is, rather, a (very simply) criterially governed concept, that 'pain' is consequently flexible with respect to its reference among physical kinds, and that the identity of pain with any particular neural state is consequently a possibility. And this is just the classical—as we may call it, 'Australian Rules'—physicalism about the mental, originally proposed by writers such as Jack Smart, which the Kripkean framework has been standardly regarded as squeezing out.

1.7 *Rebuttal*

This line of naturalist resistance arguably fails, however, and the manner of its failure is instructive. Let's for a moment go along with the idea that 'water' expresses a criterially governed concept—that is, **schwater**. 'Water' accordingly has as its sense a complex descriptive condition, fashioned out of the relevant criteria, its possibly constitutionally variable referents so qualifying by dint of their satisfaction of that condition. Nevertheless, water itself is a *stuff* rather than a state, so there has to be a contrast between the sense of the term, 'water', standing for that stuff, and that of the description, 'the state of satisfying the criteria for being water', standing for the state that the stuff distinctively occupies. Is the description rigid or flexible? Presumably, since the criteria for a criterially governed concept are *essential* to it and thus invariant, the state of satisfying them will likewise be invariant. So the latter description— 'the state of satisfying the criteria for being water'—should be rigid in any case: that is, should denote the same state in talking of any possible world, even if 'water', whose reference in the present scenario is to whatever is in that state, is not.

What follows is that, in order for there to be any chance of assimilating the function of 'pain' to that of 'water' as currently conceived, so that it can serve as a correspondingly flexible designator, there has to be a corresponding distinction between the use of 'pain' and that of the description, 'the state of satisfying the criteria for being in pain'. For the latter, by an analogue of the argument just given, will be rigid. But here's the point: *there is no such distinction*. 'Pain', unlike 'water', *does* denote a state; moreover, and crucially, if the (single) criterion for being in pain is that mooted above—namely, feeling 'uncomfortable in the relevant distinctive way'—then our ordinary concept brooks no distinction between the state of being in pain and the state of satisfying the criteria for being in pain. So if, on the grounds reviewed, the descriptive phrase—'the state of satisfying the criteria for being in pain'—is rigid, then 'pain', too, must be rigid; for only a rigid term can sustain a necessary identity with another rigid term.

So, hey presto! Kripke's considerations, unless otherwise faulted, can indeed be extended not merely to argue that **pain** is not a physical natural kind concept but to distinguish the reference of 'pain' from any physical kind of state.

Notice that it has not been suggested that no type of physical state is *associated* with pain, and thus to that extent characteristic of it. How could philosophy establish that? The (none the less remarkable) conclusion is only that no such type of state *is* pain—that our very concept of pain contains the ingredients to prohibit any such identification.

1.8 *The Boyd Objection*

Let's review the essential moves of the argument. Its essence is that whatever physical identification of the state of pain is proposed, it will be prima-facie conceivable that it might be empirically confounded. But the identification must hold, if at all, then of necessity (if only for the rather complex reasons just reviewed). Any claim of necessity may be defeated by conceiving—albeit *genuinely* conceiving—of scenarios in which what it affirms to be necessary does not obtain. So, absent some reason to think that the relevant scenarios about pain somehow fail to portray what they purport to portray, we should (defeasibly) conclude that no identification of pain with a physical state is necessary, or therefore true. Such a reason is available in the case of the apparently conceivable scenarios in which water turns out not to be H_2O, since it has to be ensured that the stuff of the conceived scenario really is water, rather than something that merely possesses water's surface symptoms. But no such difficulty afflicts the case of pain and, say, C-fibre stimulation, since any 'surface-symptomatic' counterpart of pain is pain.

The crux, then—the point that is supposed to make all the difference—is that to conceive of a symptomatic counterpart of pain is to conceive a pain, whereas to conceive of a symptomatic counterpart of water is not, *per se*, to conceive of water. But on reflection, how can this be enough to make the difference? In order to conceive of an identity statement's failing to hold, it suffices to conceive of one term in being while the other is not. Kripke thinks that we can conceive of a pain's occurring without any C-fibre stimulation taking place, and vice versa. And sure, it seems prima-facie completely straightforward. Just imagine a situation in which you suffer pain, yet even the most sophisticated apparatus detects no C-fibre stimulation within you; or a situation in which, conversely, the C-fibre activity detectors go off the dial, while you lie relaxed in utter comfort. But the fact is that, before we can be entitled to take any prima-facie conception of the falsity of an identity statement at face value, it has to be that *both* its terms are resistant to the difficulty that Kripke makes for the attempt to conceive of water's turning out not to be H_2O. *Both* the identified items must be such that we are entitled to regard the thought experiment as really engaging *them*, rather than mere symptomatic counterparts. Yet Kripke only considers pain. The other half of the imagined scenario—that there is, or is not, C-fibre stimulation involved—is not considered at all.

Now, situations in which C-fibres are stimulated would presumably form a natural kind. So, as in the case of water, the objection continues, there ought to be a distinction between instantiation of the kind and mere symptomatic imitation. That would be enough to create a problem for the suggestion that the necessity of 'Pain is C-fibre stimulation' might be defeated by conceiving of a situation in which C-fibres were stimulated yet no pain was felt. For while, presumably, the absence of pain, too, is a state that has only to seem to be in order to be, there ought, if there is a gap with water, to be a corresponding gap between conceiving of a genuine case of C-fibre stimulation and conceiving of a symptomatic counterpart. So that form of attempt to rebut the necessity of 'Pain is C-fibre stimulation' would be blocked by Kripke's own move. Conversely, while the concept, **situation in which C-fibres are not stimulated**, is not a natural kind concept at all—since not a concept of a type of state of affairs with a unified underlying nature—essentially the same point may still seem good against the other relevant kind of counter-scenario: pain without C-fibre stimulation. Maybe I cannot fail to conceive of a pain when there is no C-fibre stimulation by dint of failing to conceive a genuine pain. But surely I may so fail by dint of failing to conceive of a *genuine lack of C-fibre stimulation*. For just as one does not conceive of a lack of water by conceiving of an absence of satisfaction of the indicator properties of water—the concept leaves provision for non-standard instances—so, it may be suggested, one will not have conceived of an absence of C-fibre stimulation merely by conceiving of a lack of satisfaction of the indicators of C-fibre stimulation, whatever they are. It will not be enough merely to conceive of an absence, as assessed by whatever operational tests are appropriate, of the *appearances* of C-fibre stimulation.

The analogy is therefore apparently restored, and now a dilemma arises. If Kripke was successful in defeating the conceivability objection to the necessity of 'Water is H_2O', then his argument against physicalism collapses for want of a relevant disanalogy between 'Pain is C-fibre stimulation' and 'Water is H_2O'. But if he wasn't successful, then the whole apparatus of a posteriori necessities on which the argument against physicalism depends is put in jeopardy in any case.

Call this the *Boyd objection*.[12] It is apt to seem a very damaging objection. But I do not think that it is persuasive at all. Let me try to explain why.

The failure of the attempted thought experiment in which water supposedly turns out not to be H_2O hinges on the claim that—when it seems that conception is possible—what turns out not to be H_2O is not distinguished from a mere water imitator, as it were. It is crucial to understand the source of this claim. In particular, it is *not* an instance of a general thesis about the limits of conceivability—there is no suggestion, for instance, that the conceiving faculty cannot encompass water *per se* at all, but only the appearances of it. The challenge to the author of the thought experiment is to specify how its subject is identified. He is not allowed just to reply, 'As water'. Matters cannot be left there, or claims of counter-conceivability will become unnegotiable, since a proponent will have no explanatory obligations. An account is owing, accordingly, of what *makes* it water that is the subject of the imagined scenario—of why what is imagined should be regarded as water—and the (plausible) suggestion is that the thinker will prove to be relying on imagined satisfaction of the surface indicators. So it is perfectly fair to reply that, according to the view that is being opposed, that is insufficient to ensure the relevance of the thought experiment. But notice, to stress, that there is no claim here that mere conceiving can make nothing of the difference between genuine water and a symptomatic imitation—that the differences between them are, so to say, opaque to the conceiving faculty—so that *any* attempt to conceive of water would be bound to be no more than a conception of a display of indicators; on the contrary, to conceive of water, as opposed to conceiving of a symptomatic imitation, is to conceive of a purported natural kind—a substance with a certain underlying essence from which those symptoms characteristically flow. And still less is there a general claim to the effect that conceiving can make nothing of the difference between an appearance and reality—that its movement

[12] See Boyd (1992).

is confined among imagined *appearances*. That would be a hopeless claim, for a reason to be noted in a minute.

Nevertheless, the Boyd objection would seem to be feeding on some such idea. To see this, reflect that in order for it to work, there has to be *as* good a reason to suppose that any apparently lucid conception of a situation in which there is, for example, pain but no C-fibre stimulation fails to represent a genuine lack of C-fibre stimulation *as* there is reason to think that the water/H_2O thought experiment succeeds in engaging no more than a symptomatic counterpart of water. Consider, then, what sort of thing might happen when someone—let her be an expert physiologist—who knows about C-fibres and their characteristic forms of activity tries to conceive a scenario in which they are inactive. Well, she'll no doubt imagine certain tests and micro-physiological investigations turning out in a certain kind of way. And one conceptual gap that there will be is that between the appearance—the *seeming* that the tests and investigations turn out that way—and the reality—their actually doing so. So it would certainly serve the purpose of the Boyd objection if it were right that the conceiving faculty cannot cross this gap: that any thought experiment can engage no more than appearances. However, that's a radical error (and no part of Kripke's original point). The price of that contention would be that any apparent contingency whatever could be claimed with impunity to be a posteriori necessary—since any apparently perfectly lucidly conceived scenario in which it failed would be properly describable merely as one in which it *appeared* to fail. The link between conceivability and possibility may be subtle and qualified, but it is genuine—and to confine conceivability to appearances would be to sever it altogether. Thus, failing some independent reason for thinking her conception comes short, it should be granted that the physiologist really can conceive not just of an appearance but of the *reality* of the relevant tests' militating against the hypothesis of C-fibre stimulation.

A proponent of the Boyd objection may try to regroup. Probably there will still be a gap—the tests may not be conclusive, or they may be liable to operational error. A situation that, by the most refined and painstaking tests that we have, must be classified as one in which no C-fibres are stimulated may still be *mis*classified as such. Agreed; but *this* gap will not suffice to drive the objection. Someone challenged to explain what makes it *water* that turns out not to be H_2O in his thought experiment doesn't—from the point of view of one who accepts that water is a natural kind—have a good answer; for the answer involves mere satisfaction of the indicators. But if our physiologist is challenged to explain what makes it a *lack of C-fibre stimulation* that figures in her thought experiment, she has available the best possible answer: namely, its seeming and continuing to seem by the most refined tests that no C-fibre stimulation is taking place. That is to be compared not to mere satisfaction of the indicators of *water*, but to the most refined evidence of the presence of H_2O. If someone thinks it is not a good enough answer, then forget about pain for a minute and ask: what could conceiving of a situation in which it turned out merely that *there was no C-fibre stimulation* consist in? But the conceivability of *that*—on its own—wasn't supposed to be in doubt.

To confirm that one who presses this objection is tacitly shifting the goal-posts—is making a move quite different from Kripke's—it ought to suffice to reflect that it would presumably be conceded on all sides that, were **water** to be supplanted by **schwater**, there should be no difficulty concerning the conceivability of a variety of substances turning out to be schwater. It is granted on all sides, in particular, that we can conceive of a symptomatic counterpart of water turning out not be to H_2O. But the attempt to disqualify the physiologist's thought experiment along the lines just reviewed demands rules of conceivability that would also disqualify that seemingly straightforward conception. For how is it given that the conceived substance is not H_2O? Wouldn't it be merely that it turned out not to be such by the most refined extant chemical tests, and wouldn't they bear a merely defeasible relation to the fact?

In summary, what I have been saying boils down to the point that the Boyd objection misses the distinction between primary and derivative natural kind concepts, and the attendant different constraints involved in conceiving of instances of them. H_2O and **C-fibre stimulation**, we may suppose, are primary natural kind concepts. Accordingly, their reference is fixed not by adverting to indicator properties, but directly, in the light of the explicit content of the concepts themselves. These concepts are thus associated with no analogues of the distinction between water and symptomatic counterparts of water, and thought experiments in which they feature cannot be faulted for insensitivity to such distinctions.[13] A primary natural kind concept does provide, to be sure, for two other types of distinction: between something's appearing to be P and its genuinely being so, and between something's passing the most refined extant tests for being P and its genuinely being so. But to insist that the Kripkean thought experiments about pain and C-fibre stimulation are flawed by insensitivity to the second of these distinctions is implicitly to disable a whole range of perfectly valid conceivings, while to fault them for insensitivity to the first is implicitly to confine conceiving to the realm of appearances, and thereby to forfeit the connection between conceivability and modality altogether.

---

[13] At least in so far as they relate to those two concepts, though there may of course be such faults in connection with the involvement of other, derivative, natural kind concepts.

1.9 *The McGinn Objection*

A second very widely received objection to Kripke's argument was first advanced by Colin McGinn (1977). Actually, McGinn's objection presents itself as more of an accommodation; it does not abrade at all against the argument as I have so far presented it. Distinguish three claims: that **pain** is the concept of a physical natural kind, that pains form a physical natural kind, and that *pains are physical*. It is the third that is the essential thesis of physicalism. But it is at most a rejection of the first two that is supported by the considerations that we have reviewed. Even if pains are not a physical kind, each and every individual pain may nevertheless be a physical state. Pains may be *token*-identical with physical states, even if not *type*-identical.

That was McGinn's point. Grant that any particular (neuro)physical type of event may coherently be conceived as dissociated from the occurrence of pains, and that this consideration can indeed be worked into a demonstration that pains are not a physical type. Still, the consideration seems powerless to engage the thought that *the particular pain* I am feeling now is token-identical with some aspect of *the particular physical state* I am in. Suppose the aspect in question is actually one of physical type F. So the supposition is that the pain I am now feeling is my being in the particular F-state that I am presently in. Plausibly, 'The pain I am now feeling' and 'The F-state that I am currently in' are both rigid designators. So the identity statement linking them, if true, holds of necessity. In the presence of the Counter-Conceivability Principle, it would therefore make trouble for the purported identity if I *could* coherently conceive of that statement's failing to hold. But while I am granted a conception of how it could be that I was in pain without being in an F-state at all, that is not to conceive of my having *this* pain without being in an F-state, *a fortiori* without being in *this* F-state. For, it is very plausible, nothing in such a thought experiment engages the *numerical* identity of my present pain. No doubt I could conceive of having a *qualitatively indistinguishable* pain, under the very same circumstances, on the very same occasion. But if token–token physicalism is true, such conceiving may be regarded as portraying the pain I actually feel only if it involves nothing inconsistent with the actual physical identity of that pain. This is not to say, note, that conceiving is necessarily insensitive to the distinction between numerical identity and quantitative identity among token pains. It is to say, rather, that the content which may permissibly be assigned to a conceived scenario has to be sensitive to the essential characteristics of the items it involves.

If this is right, then the Kripkean argument may after all be consistent with physicalism. The strongest conclusion that it will be permissible to draw will be, not that mental states—or at least, all mental states which are akin to pain in having a purely phenomenal essence—are not physical in nature, but that their physical identity is not that of a physical type.

1.10 *The Explanatory Potential of Token-by-Token Physicalism*

McGinn's point seemingly provides a way of reconciling Kripke's argument with the ontology of physicalism. But is the resulting form of physicalism worth having? In particular, to what extent can it preserve physicalism's traditional advantages? Paramount among those was the prospect of the complete intelligibility of the world via the categories of physical science. That may now seem to be in jeopardy if the identity of, say, sensations with physical states goes merely token by token.

The line of concern, more fully, is as follows. To make scientific sense of the role of any state, property, or event in a world conceived as purely physical, it will be necessary to bring the item under concepts that render physical scientific laws applicable to it. The very generality that is of the essence of physical law, however, ensures that such laws will concern physical *types*. So if—while sensations, say, may all be physical, token by token—there are no physical properties with whose possession being in particular sensational states may generally—type by type—be *identified*, then in order to make sense of the role of such states in the physical world by the application to them of physical laws, it will be necessary to bring them under concepts that are at best, as it were, fortuitously coextensive with the concepts they fall under *qua* sensations. Suppose, for instance, that—as it happens—everyone in pain *is* in a state of C-fibre stimulation, and vice versa. Still, by the Kripkean argument, the state of being in pain is not the state of C-fibre stimulation. The concepts, **pain** and **C-fibre stimulation**, must still be reckoned to present different properties. Since the former property is not to be identified with any physical property, it follows that physical science can make no sense of—can give no scientific insight into—the coextensiveness that happens to obtain. And if it cannot do that, then it can never explain, for example, why aspirin eases a headache, no matter how convincing an account it has to offer of the effects of aspirin on C-fibre stimulation. By contrast, if the identity of pain and C-fibre stimulation goes type to type, then the scientific tractability of the latter just is that of the former. If headaches *are* a kind of C-fibre stimulation, then explaining the effects of aspirin on (that kind of) C-fibre stimulation *is* explaining its effects on headache.

In brief, if being in pain is the same thing as being in a state of C-fibre stimulation—if the identity goes type to type—then explaining aspirin's effects on C-fibre stimulation is explaining its effects on headache. Headaches become potentially scientifically tractable. But for token-by-token physicalism, it seems that the best that can be said of the types is that they are coextensive. Since this coextensiveness is then left explanatorily surd, we do not get explanations of the patterns of instantiation in one of the types merely by explaining the corresponding patterns in the instantiation of the other.

The concern is prima-facie compelling. But it makes an unsupported and crucial assumption. It assumes that if we may not identify pain with a physical type, then we are barred from identifying tokens of pain with tokens of a single physical type. This seems unwarranted. Consistently with rejecting the identity of pain, as a type of state, with the state of C-fibre stimulation, we might retain all explanatory advantages of that identification—if the empirical circumstances allow—by identifying each subject's *individual pain* with *a particular episode of C-fibre stimulation*. Then, if best science were to find that, and to explain why, whenever a subject is in a state of C-fibre stimulation, its mitigation is indeed a normal effect of taking aspirin, the fact that C-fibre stimulation could not legitimately be *identified* with pain *per se* would be no obstacle to adapting this finding to the explanation of aspirin's effect upon head*aches*. True, there would now be no way of converting the explanation of why aspirin mitigates C-fibre stimulation into an explanation of why aspirin relieves head*ache*—but if each, or enough, individual headaches are token-identical with individual episodes of C-fibre stimulation, we still get an explanation of why aspirin relieves *them*. And isn't that good enough?

If this is right, it points up something important: namely, how merely token-by-token identifications with the physical can always tap into the explanatory advantages that would have been secured by corresponding type–type identifications. Thus token-by-token theories need not, *per se*, involve any consequences regarding *anomalousness*. Sure, physical laws are essentially general, so are naturally formulated in terms of types of property, event, and state. Thus, in order to harness such laws to the explanation of what we presume to be the causes and effects of sensations, it might seem that we must find types of physical state for the sensations to be. And then, if such identifications are proscribed, it may seem as though some form of anomalousness, or scientific opacity, of sensation must be the upshot. But not so fast: the simple countervailing thought is that if a law connects one type of state with another, it thereby connects their tokens. So to treat of sensation in a fully intelligible but physical-scientific way, we do not need type–type identifications: it is enough that token sensations be token physical states of (some manageable range of) types that are tractable at the level of physical law.

1.11 *A Discomfort about Supervenience*

Nevertheless, I do not think that token-by-token physicalism offers a satisfactory accommodation with the Kripkean argument. One general difficulty with the proposal concerns supervenience. Most of us believe in some form of supervenience of the psychological upon the physical. Of course, supervenience relations come in many varieties. But I am referring just to the general idea that psychological differences demand physical ones, that had the psychological history of the world been different in any respect at all, then its physical history would have had to have differed too.[14] Is this a rational belief? It is hard to be certain what exactly is its provenance. It is not empirical. Experience might suggest that many psychological differences tend to go with physical ones. But it could not suggest that they *must* so do. And if we seemed to alight upon psychological changes that went unreflected in any physical differences, we would insist that there must be physical differences all the same, though perhaps of a kind—arcane variations in brain state, maybe—of which we have no present conception.

This supervenience is certainly a rejectable thesis. It would, for instance, be rejected by Cartesian dualism. The supervenience requires that, as a matter of necessity, any change in a subject's psychological condition must be attended by a change in her physical condition. This would be utterly incomprehensible if dualism were true: how could change in one ontological realm necessitate change in another? Dualism has it that the psychological and the physical are distinct existences. There is therefore no room for them to be linked as a matter of necessity. To that extent, the entrenchment of psychological-on-physical supervenience in our ordinary beliefs is indicative that our fundamental conception of the psychological is not Cartesian. But Wittgenstein—no Cartesian—also effectively rejected the supervenience (not there so termed, of course) in *Zettel* 608–10. And it is not clear that his stance is anything which we can readily confound by direct argument, either empirical or a priori.

If we have any justification for believing in psychological-on-physical supervenience, it would seem it must have less to do with what we can support by direct argument than with a sense of commitment to it flowing from our basic metaphysics of the psychological. But what metaphysics of the psychological would account for it? How could it be *necessary* that change in one range of states of affairs might necessitate change in another? The only possible answer,

---

[14] This very general form of supervenience need not involve, of course, that the psychological supervenes upon the *internal* physiological states of the bearers of psychological properties. It is uncompromised by views that see certain psychological and semantic characteristics as *broad*.

it seems, is if they are not fundamentally of different categories but are, at bottom, states of one and the same sort, though presented in very different conceptual vocabularies. In short, if we do not believe that psychological states and processes fundamentally *are* physical ones, the claimed supervenience, far from being basic to our conception of the psychological, would be unintelligible, and the belief in it totally unmotivated.

Only some form of physicalism, it seems, can make sense of the supervenience. Thus it may appear that not only is a token-by-token physicalism *consistent* with the Kripkean argument, but that—if type-to-type physicalism is now ruled out—the supervenience of the psychological upon the physical actually *demands* it. However—and this is the advertised discomfort—it is not clear on reflection how token-by-token physicalism can actually accommodate the supervenience any better than can dualism. To be sure, if my present headache actually *is* some token physical condition of my central nervous system, then, had I not had the headache, I would have been in a different physical condition. But psychological-on-physical supervenience, in the form that is usually accepted, requires that a change in which psychological predicates may be truly applied to me requires change in a complete description of my physical state, where the latter description is precisely conceived as a compendium of the *types* of physical state I am in. Token-by-token physicalism simply cannot explain the validity of *that* principle. It requires, to be sure, that if I had not had the headache, I would have been in a different physical state; but it is open as to whether that different state could not still have been of the same type as that I am actually in. So it allows that the physical state I was in then could have been in every way *type-indistinguishable* from my actual physical state. Psychological-on-physical supervenience, as ordinarily understood, proscribes exactly that.

Note that this is not an objection to token-by-token physicalism's ability to accommodate the Kripkean argument. The point is, rather, that the accommodation is available only if we either jettison the belief in supervenience altogether or are prepared to retain it in a setting in which we have neither direct argument for it nor any broader metaphysical justification.

1.12 *Token-by-Token Physicalism and Rigidity*

The most fundamental weakness in the token-by-token response to the Kripkean argument, however, is that, far from providing an accommodation with the conclusion, it proves on reflection to be committed to arguing with the premises. To the extent, then, that someone finds those premises to be well-motivated, she is precluded from responding in the way McGinn proposed.

Recall the dialectical situation at the crucial point. We noted earlier that the Kripkean argument was only able to advance beyond the stage of a claim about **pain** (that it is not a physical natural kind concept) to a claim about *pain* (that states of pain are not a physical natural kind) courtesy of the assumption that 'pain' is a *rigid designator*—that 'is in pain' ascribes the same state on all occasions of competent use. We canvassed argument for the assumption, which is indeed independently plausible in any case.[15] But how can it be consistent with mere token-by-token physicalism about pain? For the distinctive thesis of the latter is precisely that while all pains are physical states, no single kind of physical state need be shared by subjects in pain.

More fully, the Kripkean argument appealed to the conceivability of a situation in which no specific type of (presumably) neural state is correlated with the occurrence of, say, migraine. Suppose that situation actually obtains. Still, for token-by-token physicalism, each and every migraine headache is identical to some specific token neural condition. Consider two such token headaches, say of sufferers S_1 and S_2, and the two token neural states, as it happens of utterly different physical types, say F_1 and F_2, with which those headaches are respectively token-identical. What physical states are the respective referents of the two uses of 'headache' in the two true claims 'S_1 has a headache' and 'S_2 has a headache'? Since, for the physicalist, S_1's headache just consists in her being in state F_1 and S_2's headache consists in her being in state F_2, there seems no option but to allow that the two uses of 'headache' effect reference to these two different physical states. But then, for the token-by-token physicalist, 'headache' must be an expression referring *flexibly* among those type physical states whose instantiation, on particular occasions, may constitute a subject's having a headache—it cannot be a rigid designator of any particular such state. So in a physical world—where the only real types of state are physical—it cannot be a rigid designator at all.

Now McGinn's intervention was pointless unless the Kripkean argument succeeds against the identification of pain with a physical type. It so succeeds only if 'pain' is rigid—otherwise the argument can be seen off by Australian Rules physicalism. But if 'pain' is rigid, what—physical—state can the token-by-token physicalist regard it as ascribing? The whole essence and being of her view is that no single type of physical state need constitute being in pain, that pains may be constituted by quite different types of physical state. Rather than providing a solution, then, token-by-token physicalism would seem to have no way of construing the data of the problem that McGinn introduced it to address.

---

[15] In fact, all the same intuitions kick in as those Kripke appeals to for 'Aristotle': Could pain not have been pain? Could a different state have been the state of being in pain?

The point seems decisive. But a skirmish is possible. The objection could be finessed if we could take it for granted that there are, for instance, *disjunctive* states, or *existentially general* states. Equipped with such a repertoire, the physicalist might straightforwardly allow that the reference of 'headache', on every occasion of use, is indeed rigid—it is always to the disjunctive state of having F_1 or F_2 or F_3 or . . . , where every type of physical state that can constitute a headache features as one disjunct. Or better, let the reference of 'headache' be to the state of being in *some* physical state which . . . —and here the theorist plugs in her preferred account of the *functional role* of a headache (or of whatever the unifier is conceived as being). In contrast to type-to-type physicalism, individual pains could then be states of various physical types, united by their featuring in the relevant disjunction, or discharging the relevant functional role. But 'pain' could still be a rigid designator, denoting the same logically compound—disjunctive, or existential—state in every use.

But can physicalism regard such 'logically compound states' as in good standing? To begin with, one might wonder whether there is any satisfactory, principled specification of what might serve to *unify* the disjuncts of the putative disjunctive state, or to complete the specification of the putative existential one. And there is also a serious question whether such construals of the reference of 'pain' can make anything of another datum of the problem: the transparency of pains to their subjects. But, at least in the context of a physicalist ontology, the whole idea seems off target in a more basic way—specifically, by its illicitly imposing distinctions on to the domain of reference that make genuine sense only at the level of *modes of presentation*, concepts. When we disjoin or existentially generalize on names, the results—for instance, 'Tom or John was to blame', 'Someone was to blame'—had better not be conceived as forms of expression involving reference to disjunctive or existentially general objects. There are no such objects. Why should it be different with states? Why should 'occupancy of some state with functional role R' be regarded as denoting a state at all? I do not deny the deflated sense of 'state' in which the nominalization of any significant predicative expression denotes a potential state. But physicalism is a serious ontological thesis, and one of its consequences is that the only genuine states there are, are physical. Suppose that amongst these are some with the functional role R. Clearly, 'occupancy of some state with functional role R' denotes none in particular of these, since it suffices to instantiate it that an object be in any of them. Equally, though, since these are the only states that have the functional role R, 'occupancy of some state with functional role R' does not denote some state outside that group. It follows that it does not denote a physical state at all, rigidly or otherwise. Since 'is in pain' and 'is in some state with functional role R' would be conceptually equivalent on the present physicalist proposal, it would seem that the latter must repudiate the thesis that 'pain' is a designator at all, let alone a rigid one. But that again is to deny a datum of the problem.

2 Generalizations

2.1 *Colour and Euthyphronic Concepts*

Now to the case of colour. I choose it because there is a plausible case, so it seems to me, that colour concepts exhibit a germane kind of epistemic transparency. But whatever the facts about colour, it will emerge, if I am right, that any concept that is transparent in this way will lend itself to an argument of the Kripkean kind.

To fix ideas, let me rapidly rehearse the idea of *judgement-dependent* concepts which I have discussed elsewhere.[16] Let a *provisional equation* be an instance of the following schema:

$$C\,(S, x) \rightarrow (F(x) \leftrightarrow \text{it seems to S that } F(x))$$

That is, if conditions C are met by a subject S and an item x, then x is F if and only if it seems to S that it is. A concept, F, is *Euthyphronic* if such a provisional equation can be written for it meeting each of the following four conditions:

(i) The provisional equation is true a priori, as a matter of conceptual necessity.

(ii) The conditions, C, are specified in specific, substantial terms.

(iii) The satisfaction of the C-conditions is a matter that is independent of the details of F's actual extension.

(iv) The provisional equation is *primitively* a priori—it admits of no proof from ulterior principles concerning F of such a kind as to vindicate the idea that the C-conditions merely enable a subject to *keep infallible track* of an independently determined extension.

These clauses were proposed as one way of explicating the intuitive idea of a concept whose extension is *constitutively sensitive* to those of our verdicts that are delivered under what we conceive as the very best possible circumstances, rather than merely *reflected* by such verdicts. Whether that idea can indeed be so captured, whether all four conditions are necessary to capture it, and how

---

[16] See the appendix to ch. 3 of Wright (1992).

exactly they might need to be modified or elaborated in order to succeed, are matters beyond the scope of this chapter. However, notice that **pain** plausibly sustains a very simple provisional equation meeting at least three of the specified conditions,[17] namely:

S understands what pain is and is cognitively lucid → (S is in pain ↔ it seems to S that she is in pain).

Moreover—at the price, perhaps, of a surprising degree of complication—a case can be made for thinking that the same is true at least of central colour concepts, like **red**.

The case requires a much more detailed discussion than I can digress to offer here.[18] However, to sample its flavour, consider whether you think you have any clear concept of how the redness of a red surface could escape your judgement, or how its seeming red could be deceptive, if (i) the surface is in full view, and (ii) in normal daylight, (iii) relatively stationary (i.e., stationary or slow-moving relative to you the observer), and (iv) quite close by; and (v) if you know which object is in question, (vi) observe it attentively, (vii) are possessed of actually typical visual equipment, and (viii) are free of spots before the eyes, after-images, and so on, and (ix) are otherwise cognitively lucid, and (x) are competent with the concept **red**. You can add, if you like, that (xi) the surface be presented against a matt black background,[19] and (xii) that you—the judging subject—be free of doubt about the satisfaction of any of these conditions. Anyway, the thought of one who conjectures that **red** is Euthyphronic is that it is possible in this way to construct a list of substantial conditions whose satisfaction ensures a priori that a presented item is red only if it seems so to an observer, and that the result will be a *primitive* truth about **red**: that the extension of the concept is, in such a fashion, constrained of necessity to be sensitive to our judgements under the elaborated ideal conditions.

Someone might wonder how so relatively complex a claim, which in the nature of the case lies beyond any rigorous proof, can possibly rank as a priori. But that shouldn't be a sticking point. As a rough parallel, consider *Church's thesis*, that every effectively calculable function is generally recursive, and vice versa. Effective calculability is an intuitive notion; general recursiveness is a

---

[17] The fourth, anti-tracking condition is interestingly controversial in this case. John McDowell's (1994) view, that sensations are essentially conceptualized modes of experience, is in effect the view that it is satisfied—that there is no brute phenomenal happening, pure pain, whose occurrence is indifferent to the conceptual resources of a sufferer and of which possession of **pain** merely enables him to keep track. But the fourth condition is in any case strictly inessential to the considerations to follow.   [18] For further discussion, see Wright (1989).

[19] Or maybe viewed through an apparatus—a tube, say—that occludes any background.

mathematically precise one. The thesis is precisely an attempt to give a mathematically exact characterization of something pre-formal. In the nature of the
case, it therefore admits of no conclusive formal proof. Yet, if it is true, it is
true purely as a reflection of the character of the concepts involved, and to the
extent that it can be supported by conceptual reflection—for instance, by
the striking convergences of other attempted formal characterizations of
effective calculability, and a failure to find counter-examples—to that extent, it
is supported a priori. It is similar with the provisional equation for **red**. Our
concept of the variety of ways in which the redness of an object might in principle be masked by how it seems, or in which how it seems might be deceptive,
ought to allow of correct circumscription, just as the concept of effective
calculability ought. If we alight upon such a circumscription, it will certainly
be too complicated to enable its truth to be recognizable immediately, just by
the light cast by the analytic understanding, as it were; and there is no basis on
which its truth might be recognized inferentially. As with Church's thesis, its a
priori correctness, if it is correct, will ultimately be supportable only defeasibly,
by the failure of hard reflection to find it wanting.

There is a lot more to say. But our concern here is not with the justification
of claims of judgement-dependence, but with the implications if certain concepts are judgement-dependent in accordance with the template described.
Now the key point in the Kripkean argument was the claimed counter-
conceivability of any physicalistic identification of pain. And the key assumption for that claim was that there is no coherent distinction to be drawn
between a state's seeming to its subject, S, to be one of pain and its actually being
so. But that equation is not of course unconditional: it is, again, the impressions
of a *cognitively lucid* subject, who *fully understands* **pain**, that there is no distinguishing from the fact of pain. And it is the standing prima-facie conceivability of a separation between such impressions and any specific type of physical
(neural) state that constitutes the crucial point in the argument: what is claimed
to be counter-conceivable, in other words, is precisely what results from the
provisional equation above when the left-hand side of its biconditional
consequent is replaced by a clause ascribing to S any particular physical state
taken to be identical with pain:

> S understands what pain is and is cognitively lucid $\rightarrow$ (S is in physical state
> O $\leftrightarrow$ it seems to S that she is in pain).

The crux in the Kripkean argument is thus, in effect, the contention that any
provisional equation instantiating that schema on 'O' is counter-conceivable;
but that one such would have to hold of necessity if pain were indeed a (type
of) physical state.

The possibility of generalization to **red** is accordingly evident. Assume that we can indeed formulate a (conceptually) necessarily true provisional equation for **red** meeting the outlined conditions:

(1) C (S, x) → (x is red ↔ it seems to S that x is red).

Assume also, for *reductio*, that **red** is a derivative physical natural kind concept. Since there actually are red things, there will therefore be some presumably microphysical property, O, such that

(2) Redness is O

is likewise necessary. We may take it[20] that the necessity issuing a priori from concepts and that issuing a posteriori from essences are the very same, absolute metaphysical necessity, differing in the grounds for ascribing them to particular claims, but not in what is ascribed. That being so, since (2) entails that everything red is O, and vice versa, we may infer that

(3) C (S, x) → (x is O ↔ it seems to S that x is red)

is likewise necessary. But, for reasons exactly analogous to those which applied to **pain**, (3) ought not, it appears, to be regarded as necessary. For no matter what the detail of the physical kind, O, it seems that it will be readily conceivable that the C-conditions are met—we are standing out of doors and out of shadow at noon on a typical cloudy summer's day, staring at a stationary object quite close by; we are blessed with statistically normal visual equipment, we are attentive, and so on—and that we judge that the relevant object, which looks manifestly tomato-red, is red, and yet microphysical investigation discloses that it is *not* O. (Of course, there is at this point a debate to be had about the status of our apparently conceiving that conditions are indeed C and that x is indeed not O; but this will merely recapitulate considerations which we went through in connection with the Boyd objection.) In general, the best case for supposing that, no matter what O might be, (3) is counter-conceivable promises to be exactly parallel to that for the counter-conceivability of 'Pain is C-fibre stimulation'. The only difference is the relative complexity of the C-conditions.

In the first instance, this will be a conclusion not about redness but about the concept, **red**, and, as previously, a prima-facie accommodation with the argument will be available if the physicalist about colour is willing to maintain that (2), although true, is indeed not necessary, because 'redness' is a flexible

---

[20] As of course, implicitly, did Kripke. For it is presumably a *conceptual* necessity that there is no distinction between being in pain and being in a state epistemically indistinguishable from pain.

designator among physical natural kinds, equivalent in sense, perhaps, to the (unrigidified) description, 'the physical state indicated by the property of *looking red under C-conditions*'. Now recall that when we considered the corresponding response in the dialectic concerning pain and 'pain', we confronted the physicalist with the designator 'the state of satisfying the criteria for being in pain', which is plausibly both rigid and necessarily co-referential with 'pain'. Since only a rigid designator can be necessarily co-referential with a rigid designator, it followed that 'pain' is rigid too, and that the physicalist's flexible ersatz is false to the ordinary understanding of the term. Matters can now proceed in an analogous fashion with 'redness'. We form, for instance, the description, 'that state that, necessarily, anything is in that looks red under C-conditions' (or—for an arbitrary judgement-dependent concept, F—'that state that, necessarily, anything is in that seems F under C-conditions'). Then, provided the provisional equation is necessary, the intuition is strong that 'redness' and 'that state which, necessarily, anything is in that looks red under C-conditions' are necessarily coextensive; and the latter must, of course, be rigid if it refers at all, since otherwise there is no state such that *necessarily* anything is in it that looks red under C-conditions. It follows that 'redness' is rigid, that the property it denotes is consequently identical with no physical type—and that all this is called for by our concept **red**: our concept of the kind of property redness is, if **red** is Euthyphronic. As before, the question may be raised as to whether some form of token-by-token physicalism can save the day—and specifically whether it can accommodate the rigidity of the terms in question (for if that rigidity is denied, then the Australian Rules version already has all the resources the physicalist needs to see the argument off). And, for reasons analogous to those recently canvassed, we may well feel that it cannot.

2.2 *Summary of the Recipe*

Let us take stock. The suggestion is that Kripke's argument is apt to generalize to any concept, F, of which it holds a priori, as a matter of conceptual necessity, that under certain substantially specifiable, conceivable conditions, it will seem to a thinker that the concept is instantiated just in case it is. For **pain**—as, presumably, for sensation concepts generally—the conditions in question are very simple: they are merely that the thinker grasps the concept in question and is appropriately cognitively lucid. Other cases will not be so simple: if **red** indeed comes in this category, its C-conditions will be complex. Still, the thesis is a going concern that our concepts of colour, and of Lockean secondary qualities generally, do have the requisite kind of transparency: that even if it is harder than philosophers once supposed[21] to say under what circumstances it is equivalent to an object's being red that it look red, it remains that, with care, one can produce a list of conditions such that nothing counts as an explanation of how, under *those* conditions, an illusion of colour could occur; and that the same holds for sounds, tastes, and secondary qualities generally. To have constructed such a list for a given concept F—a list for which no one can produce any prima-facie acceptable account of how under the specified conditions it could seem to thinkers that F was instantiated although it was not—will be to have an a priori, albeit defeasible, case for regarding the relevant provisional equation as holding as a matter of conceptual necessity. That, as illustrated, will then suffice to set a form of the Kripkean argument in train.

It will do so by supplying each of two needed premisses. The first premiss, the necessitated provisional equation

Necessarily: for any S and x under C-conditions, x is F iff x seems F to S

is supplied directly. The second premiss, the necessity of any true identity of the form

F is K,

where 'K' rigidly denotes a physical kind, requires that 'F' too is a rigid designator. But, as we saw, the provisional equation's holding of necessity arguably ensures that as well. It does so provided we may abstract from it to infer that being F is being in that state P such that, necessarily, any object is in P that seems F to a thinker operating under C-conditions. For again, if 'F' were flexible, there would be no single state of which it would be *necessary* that any object—in whatever world—seeming F to a C-conditioned thinker would occupy it; rather, being F might be being in P_1 in w_1, and being in P_2 in w_2, and so on, and of no P_k would it be true that in all worlds and for any thinker operating under C-conditions, x's seeming F would be necessary and sufficient for its being in P_k.

The two premisses collectively entail that 'F' may be substituted by 'K' in the first to generate a further necessary truth: that for any S and x in the appropriate C-conditions, x is K iff x seems F to S. But the necessity of this consequence is likely to be in difficulty with the Counter-Conceivability Principle, provided conditions C are ones that we can conceive to obtain—which, at least if the kind of list sketched for **red** is any guide, there seems every reason to

---

[21] Recall Wilfrid Sellars: 'But what, then, are we to make of the necessary truth—and it is, of course, a necessary truth—that x *is* red + x would *look* red to standard observers in standard conditions?'—from 'Empiricism and the Philosophy of Mind' reprinted in Sellars (1963: 142). cf. Colin McGinn: 'It is a conceptual truth that red things *typically* look red' (1983: 11).

anticipate. Moreover, since the list is likely to proceed in quite general terms of idealization—explaining wherein consist good observation conditions, competent observers, and so on—without any reference to how *in particular* things seem to a judging subject or how they actually physically are in other respects, there seems no reason why there should ever be any tension in adjoining to an imaginary scenario in which the C-conditions hold the further detail that the thinkers involved have the impression that x is F; or to that second scenario in turn the additional detail of x's turning out under examination not to be K.

In general, the Kripkean argument will thus extend to all concepts for which an appropriate conceptually necessary provisional biconditional can be constructed, the obtaining of whose C-conditions is prima-facie conceivable, and where such a scenario may prima-facie coherently be augmented by its seeming to a thinker under the C-conditions in question that a given item instantiates (or fails to instantiate) the concept in question, while that item simultaneously lacks (or has) any particular candidate to be the physical property presented by the concept F. To be sure, in view of the prima-facie (defeasible) status of the relevant conceivings, the argument is best viewed as a *challenge* to physicalism, rather than a purported refutation. An undefeated impression that one can simultaneously conceive of a thinker's meeting the C-conditions and, say, judging that x is F while x lacks candidate physical property, O, is, by the Counter-Conceivability Principle and assuming the rigidity of the relevant terms, an undefeated challenge to the physicalist identification. But views that confront undefeated challenges ought not, *ceteris paribus*, to be believed.

Kripke's argument poses such a challenge on behalf of concepts of sensation. The challenge extends, I have suggested, to concepts of colour and, one would expect, to secondary-quality concepts generally. However, we should also note that, in moving directly to the case of secondary-quality concepts, we have passed over the possibly more straightforward, intermediate case of concepts of *public subjective appearance*—**looks red, feels hot, seems pepperminty**—on which we tend to fall back in cases where there is a potential for a mistake or an illusion about a secondary quality for reasons other than the idiosyncrasies of individuals, and which one would expect to be associated with a much simpler set of C-conditions than those for secondary-quality concepts proper. The point is also salient that even if our actual secondary-quality concepts prove recalcitrant, on closer inspection, to the construction of the relevant kind of provisional equations, that would seem to be the merest *good luck* as far as physicalism is concerned. For if the primary function of secondary-quality concepts is to provide means whereby we can record aspects of the world of common subjective appearance, it is not clear that that role would be compromised in any essential way had they been so fashioned as to sustain the requirements of the argument after all. Even if **red** is not transparent in the necessary way, there *could* be a concept, **shred**, of which it was an a priori essential characteristic that the C-conditions I listed earlier were exactly right. How would the intelligibility and utility of ordinary discourse about colours be damaged if **shred** supplanted **red**, and our other colour concepts differed in parallel?

2.3   *Other Cases*

The large metaphysical dilemma with which we started mentioned semantics, psychology, and value. One might now investigate the prospects for detailed provisional equations for those discourses' characteristic concepts which satisfy the first three conditions of Euthyphronism and thereby provide the basics for the Kripkean argument. But a less demanding form of epistemic transparency may suffice. It is arguably part of our concept of ordinary intentional psychological states that they are standardly manifest to their subjects, who are in turn standardly authoritative about them. It is no mere empirical truth, that is to say, that normally a subject will know what she believes, hopes, wants, intends, and so on, and that her opinions on such matters will be right. At least in cases where one would expect self-knowledge to be non-inferential (involving no conscious self-interpretation), it belongs, plausibly, to the very concept of a subject's being an intentional subject at all that her impressions of her intentional states are generally reliable, and that those states do not generally escape her. We can, to be sure, break the conditional in either direction: sometimes it's fruitful to think of subjects as self-deceived or as self-unaware. But these don't count as good options unless an interpreter is able to back them up with independently attested details about the subject's frame of mind and an explanation of why the circumstances might have been conducive to the mismatch in question. Absent such an account, the rule is that intentional facts should be reckoned to march in step with the subject's impression of them.

This point, if granted, is enough for a variant form of the Kripkean challenge, concentrating on what we might term scenarios of *multiple exception*. Provided it is accepted that expressions denoting types of intentional state do so rigidly, there will be a standing obstacle to any proposed identification of such states with physical types posed by the apparently lucid conceivability of a world in which it is the *normal case* that subjects who have the impression that they are in particular such states fail to instantiate the appropriate physical types, while no considerations are to hand—or indeed, emerge—that would allow an interpreter to regard them as self-deceived or self-unaware.

With semantics, the trick is to revert more closely to the Euthyphronic template, but to multiply the judges. It may be arguable whether communally pervasive *ignorance* of meanings is possible: whether our concept of the meaning of an expression allows for the possibility that sentences which are, for instance, too complex or convoluted to be reliably parsed by ordinary speakers might nevertheless have determinate meanings. But it seems that we can a priori exclude any possibility of communally pervasive *error*: any possibility that all or a large majority of, by normal criteria, competent speakers should mistake the meaning of an expression—that they should take it, and recognize each other as taking it, as meaning one thing when in fact it means another. Rather, if normal speakers are mutually recognized as attaching a particular meaning to an expression, then that is what it means, *punkt*. So again, assuming that expressions of the form 'means that P' are rigid—that they ascribe the same property in speaking of expressions in any world—there will be a standing challenge to the necessity, and hence the truth, of any proposed identification of such semantic properties with (presumably relational) physical types: the challenge will be posed by the apparently lucid conceivability of a scenario in which the members of a seemingly smooth-running speech community exceptionlessly understand themselves and each other as meaning that P by an expression that lacks whatever natural properties may have been proposed as being those in which meaning that P consists.

The case of moral concepts, finally, is more qualified. There are many, usually theistic, conceptions of morality that view human moral thinking as essentially imperfect; and there are others—for instance, some forms of utilitarianism—that view it as almost always limited by ignorance of relevant, non-moral facts. But one would expect a form of the generalized Kripkean challenge to apply on many humanistic or 'ideal-observer' accounts of the moral, according to which there is no gap between moral quality and the assessment of it offered by the most rational, fortunately situated judge. For again, it looks as though there should be no barrier to conceiving of a situation in which, in the context of any particular proposed naturalistic account of some moral quality, M, a thinker rates a situation as, for example, possessing M, where the relevant naturalistic features are missing, and where there is nothing to impugn the moral credentials of the thinker in question. Assuming the rigidity of moral predicates—that expressions for moral qualities always ascribe the same qualities when used in speaking of hypothetical scenarios—there will then be the same standing difficulty, at least on such transparent conceptions of morality, to the location of moral qualities in the world of modern naturalism.

3 Denouément

3.1 *The Counter-Conceivability Principle Again*

We have now reviewed a range of variations upon the theme of epistemic transparency, seen why epistemically transparent concepts as a species may offer a Kripkean challenge to naturalist reductions, and noted that the distinctive concepts of many of the subject-matters with which modern naturalism abrades seem to be in the frame. Of course, the challenge is potentially reversible. Let it have been shown that naturalism is indeed in difficulties when it tries to accommodate the concepts in question by tending to construe them, after the fashion of **water** outlined at the start, as concepts of underlying physical kinds. That may be taken as bad news for naturalism. But it could be construed instead as bad news for the belief that the concepts in question are of things to be met with in the real—natural—world. Of course, that belief will prove pretty resilient when the concepts in question are concepts of one's own sensations! But the dialectical point remains, that there is the option of error theory: it is naturalism as a *descriptive*, rather than as a *revisionary*, metaphysics which is put under pressure by the Kripkean argument.

But is it really put under pressure at all? An appreciation of the potential generality of the Kripkean argument, far from deepening one's sense of a crisis for naturalism, is more likely to reinforce the impression that the conclusion is much too easily reached. My final point will be to corroborate that impression.

The Counter-Conceivability Principle says that a posteriori necessities, no less than a priori ones, are defeasible by lucid counter-conception: that if one can construct what appears to be a genuinely coherent scenario in which a putative necessity fails to hold, then, unless or until some shortcoming is disclosed in that conception, the claim of necessity should be regarded as defeated. Now, Kripke recognized straightaway that with a posteriori necessities in general, a prima-facie counter-conception will always be available—since one has only, apparently lucidly, to conceive of the relevant kind of a posteriori inquiry as turning out differently. Thus one may apparently lucidly conceive of an investigation into the chemistry of water that finds that it is XYZ; or apparently lucidly conceive of an astronomical investigation that discloses that the evening star is actually Jupiter; or apparently lucidly conceive of an investigation into the composition of the Macintosh computer before me whereby it turns out to be made entirely of materials of vegetable origin. It cannot plausibly be denied that some sort of coherent scenario is involved in such cases. But, assuming that the examples do involve genuine necessities of constitution and identity, the scenarios in question are not, by one who—like Kripke—accepts the Counter-Conceivability Principle, allowed to count as genuine counter-conceptions. Rather, their claim to concern the items they are supposed to concern is found wanting. It is not water but something that presents itself as water—a mere symptomatic counterpart—that one can lucidly conceive turning out not to be H_2O; it is not the evening star, but a different, though similar-looking, body, imagined as occupying the same place in the evening sky, that one can conceive turning out to be Jupiter; it is not this computer, but one just like it, that one can lucidly conceive as turning out to be of vegetable materials.

What stopped this way of protecting the Counter-Conceivability Principle being totally devoid of interest—what stopped it being simple 'monster-barring'—was that, precisely because the move is unavailable in the case of epistemically transparent concepts, the principle is allowed to retain some teeth. We do not have *carte blanche*. The claim to have conceived a scenario running counter to a putative necessity involving an epistemically transparent concept cannot be dismissed on the ground that the scenario fails to reflect the difference between a genuine instance of that concept and a mere symptomatic counterpart—for there is no such difference to reflect.

This was the ur-thought in the Kripkean argument. But it is sufficient for the purpose only if, where a posteriori necessities are concerned, there is no *other* way in which a lucid putative counter-conception may fall short than by failing to engage the distinction between an item and surface counterparts of it. For suppose there was another way. Then the apparently lucid conception of a scenario in which pain occurred without C-fibre stimulation, while it could not be dismissed as involving nothing distinguished from a mere surface counterpart of pain, might yet come up short in this other way. However, it is clear on reflection that we *must* make room for other possible kinds of short-coming in purported counter-conceptions, however vivid and lucid-seeming they may be.

Here is an example. Suppose—Kripke would agree—that I am essentially a human being, and that it is an essential characteristic of human beings to have their actual biological origins. So it is an essential characteristic of mine to be the child of my actual parents. Still, I can, it seems, lucidly conceive of my not having had those parents but others, or even—like Superman—of my having originated in a different world, of a different race, and having been visited on earth from afar and brought up as their own by the people whom I take to be my biological father and mother. I can, it seems, lucidly imagine my finding all this out tomorrow. And it is, prima facie, every bit as coherent a scenario as those involved in the water, evening star, and computer cases. But it cannot be dismissed, in the way that they were, on the ground that it fails to be sensitive to the distinction between myself and a mere epistemic counterpart, a mere 'fool's self', as it were, sharing the surface features by which I identify myself but differing in essence. It cannot be so dismissed because I don't, in the relevant fashion, identify myself by features, surface or otherwise, at all. The point is of a piece with Hume's observation that, in awareness of a psychological state as one's own, one is not presented as an object to oneself. When I conceive some simple counterfactual contingency—say, my being right at this moment in the Grand Canyon—I do not imagine someone's being there who presents them-self, on the surface, as being me. Rather, I simply imagine *my* having relevant kinds of experience—imagine, that is to say, the relevant kinds of experience from my first-personal point of view. No mode of presentation of the self need feature in the exercise before it can count as presenting a scenario in which *I* am in the Grand Canyon; *a fortiori*, no *superficial* mode of presentation, open to instantiation by someone other than myself.

The apparently lucid conceivability of the Superman scenario turning out to be the truth is a like case. Since it need involve no play with a mode of presentation of the self, it need not be open to any charge of insensitivity to the distinction between the self and a surface counterpart (whatever that would be). And of course, it would not help to try applying this complaint to other items in the conceived scenario—for instance, to the people, looking and behaving very much like my actual parents, who are now conceived as having fostered me instead. For even if the scenario is taken to be insensitive to the dis-tinction between those who actually reared me and mere surface counterparts of them, it remains part of it that I was not born to the human race at all. Nevertheless, if I was indeed born to those I take to be my actual parents and the Counter-Conceivability Principle is correct, I cannot genuinely conceive of the Superman scenario. So how am I to describe the content of the scenario which I do seem to be able to entertain, in as great a degree of fanciful detail, moreover, as may be wished?

Next consider a different kind of example altogether. We can rest assured, I suppose, that Andrew Wiles really has proved Fermat's Last Theorem, which therefore holds good as a matter of conceptual necessity. But we can imagine a sceptic about the result who flatters himself that he can still conceive of finding counter-examples to the theorem, and of finding mistakes in Wiles's proof. Of course, there will be limits on the detail of these 'conceivings', or the sceptic would be thought-experimentally finding *real* counter-examples and mistakes. Still, we should not deny that he could be conceiving *something*, and doing so moreover—subject only to the preceding point—in as vivid and detailed a way as could be wished. The last diagnosis we should propose, however, is that his conceivings are insensitive to the distinction between finding counter-examples to Fermat's theorem and finding counter-examples to an *epistemic counterpart* of it!—or to the distinction between finding a mistake in Wiles's reasoning and finding a mistake in an epistemic counterpart of that. What could that mean? Of course, we can imagine someone with only a hazy idea of the theorem or the proof. But our sceptic may be perfectly clear about both—an able (but curmudgeonly) mathematician.

If we are to retain the Counter-Conceivability Principle, then we must provide house-room for these cases. There has to be a category of conceivings that fall short of being genuine counter-conceptions to a given proposition, not because their detail fails to be sensitive to the distinction between items that the proposition is about and 'fool's' equivalents of them, but because it is insensitive to another distinction: that between genuinely conceiving of a scenario in which P fails to obtain and conceiving, rather, of what it would be like if, *per impossibile*, P were (found to be) false. The latter is what the curmudgeonly mathematician does. It is what I do when I conceive, in as much detail as you like, of my originating of a different race, elsewhere in the galaxy (or perhaps, following Descartes, of surviving my bodily death.) If time travel is metaphysically impossible, it's what anyone does who imagines himself as a Time Lord, wandering in the fourth dimension. For a large class of impossibilities, there are still determinate ways things would seem if they obtained.[22] If, *per impossibile*, Wiles's proof is flawed, and there are counter-examples to Fermat's theorem, we know how things would seem if those circumstances came to light.

3.2 *The Failure of the Kripkean Argument*

To admit such a category of conceivings is not, let me stress, to make a concession inconsistent with the Counter-Conceivability Principle. It can remain that a prima-facie lucid conception of a scenario in which not-P holds is a standing, though defeasible, objection to any claim of the necessity of P. But if even a vivid and detailed scenario is to motivate such an objection, then it needs to be able to defend against not one, but two, charges of potential insufficiency. The first is the original Kripkean charge that nothing in its detail distinguishes its objects from surface counterparts—'fool's' equivalents—of the items that it is supposed to concern; and the second is the charge that it allows of description as a scenario, merely, of how some things would or might be—for instance, what kinds of things would be experienced—if the proposition in question were false. If the scenario can be done full justice by a description of the latter

---

[22] This is one reason why semantical treatments of subjunctive conditionals that hold all with impossible antecedents to be true are unfortunate.

kind, then it will not be done less than justice if the description is modified by the insertion of the words, '*per impossibile*', and in that case it fails to constitute a genuine counter-conception at all.

Both kinds of insufficiency afflict the scenario in which water purportedly turns out to be something other than H_2O. But the price we pay for retaining the Counter-Conceivability Principle is that the second kind of insufficiency—*per impossibile* insufficiency, as it were—must be reckoned to afflict any seemingly lucidly conceived scenario that appears to jar with a necessity, whether a posteriori or not. So if P is a proposition that is known to be necessary if true (and, correspondingly, impossible if false), then in order to determine whether we have constructed a genuine counter-conception to P, as opposed merely to a lucid scenario of how in certain respects things would be if, *per impossibile*, P did not obtain, we need first to know whether P is true. If P is true, then no matter how intricate and coherent, the scenario can embody no more than a *per impossibile* counter-conception; if P is false, then there need be no barrier to its description as a valid counter-conception. But either way, the distinction turns, in the end, on matters beyond the phenomenology of conceiving.

The effect is that, although we save the letter of the Counter-Conceivability Principle, and although—for all I have said—it can continue as a defeasible operational constraint on the ascription of necessity in cases where *contingency is an epistemic possibility*, it provides no practical controls at all on the ascription of necessity in cases where necessity would follow from truth—as is the situation of all potential necessities a posteriori. The consequence is that the apparent counter-conceivability of physicalistic identifications of the instances of epistemically transparent concepts is of no modal significance whatever. Rather, the truth-values and hence—on the assumptions of the argument—the modal status of the identities of the relevant kind must be settled independently, before we can know how properly to describe the scenarios in question.

So, after all, the metaphysical prospects for naturalism cannot be dashed purely by creative exercises of the conceiving faculty, in the extraordinary fashion that the Kripkean argument seemed to promise. But I don't think that we (most of us) ever really believed they could.

REFERENCES

Boyd, Richard (1992), 'Materialism without Reductionism: What Physicalism Does Not Entail', in Ned Block (ed.), *Readings in the Philosophy of Psychology*, i (Cambridge, Mass.: Harvard University Press), 67–106.

Campbell, John (1993), 'A Simple View of Colour', in John Haldane and Crispin Wright (eds.), *Reality, Representation, and Projection* (New York: Oxford University Press), 257–68.

Johnston, Mark (1992), 'How to Speak of the Colors', *Philosophical Studies*, 68(3): 221–63.

Kripke, Saul (1980), *Naming and Necessity* (Cambridge, Mass.: Harvard University Press).

McDowell, John (1994), *Mind and World* (Cambridge, Mass.: Harvard University Press).

McGinn, Colin (1977), 'Anomalous Monism and Kripke's Cartesian Intuitions', *Analysis*, 37: 78–80.

—— (1983), *The Subjective View* (Oxford: Clarendon Press).

Putnam, Hilary (1975), *Philosophical Papers*, ii: *Mind, Language and Reality* (Cambridge: Cambridge University Press).

Sellars, W. F. (1963), *Science, Perception and Reality* (New York: Humanities Press).

Wittgenstein, Ludwig (1967), *Zettel* (Oxford: Blackwell).

Wright, Crispin (1989), 'Wittgenstein's Rule-Following Considerations and the Central Project of Theoretical Linguistics', in Alexander George (ed.), *Reflections on Chomsky* (Oxford: Blackwell), 233–64.

—— (1992), *Truth and Objectivity* (Cambridge, Mass.: Harvard University Press).

Coulda, Woulda, Shoulda

Stephen Yablo

1 Terminology

A main theme of Saul Kripke's *Naming and Necessity* (1980) is that metaphysical necessity is one thing; apriority, analyticity, and epistemic/semantic/conceptual necessity are another. Or rather, they are others, for although the relations among these latter notions are not fully analyzed, it does emerge that they are not the *same* notion.

'Apriority' and 'analyticity' are for Kripke nontechnical terms. They stand in the usual rough way for knowability without appeal to experience, and truth in virtue of meaning. Examples of apriority are given that it is hoped the reader will find plausible. And a schematic element is noted in the notion of knowability without experience; how far beyond our own actual cognitive powers are we allowed to idealize? Beyond that, not a whole lot is said.

Analyticity, though, does come in for further explanation. The phrase 'true in virtue of meaning' is open to different interpretations, Kripke says, depending on whether we are talking about 'meaning in the strict sense' or meaning in the

This paper owes a lot to discussions over the years with Ned Block, Alex Byrne, Tamar Szabó Gendler, Sally Haslanger, John Hawthorne, Frank Jackson, Joe Levine, Brian Loar, Jim Pryor, Gideon Rosen, Sydney Shoemaker, and Robert Stalnaker. A larger debt is to David Chalmers; if I still haven't got two-dimensionalism right, Lord knows the fault is not his. I thank him for years of patient explanation and good-natured debate. May heaven smile on Tamar and John for their extraordinary work on this volume, and in particular for the excellent Introduction. I am grateful, finally, to Saul Kripke for *Naming and Necessity*, three lectures so inconceivably great as to hardly seem possible.

looser sense given by a term's associated reference-fixing description. A sentence like 'Hesperus is visible in the evening' comes out loosely analytic but not strictly so, since the meaning proper of 'Hesperus' is exhausted by its standing for Venus.

Kripke stipulates that 'analytic' as he uses the term expresses *strict* analyticity, and he takes this to have the consequence that analytic truths in his sense are metaphysically necessary truths ('an analytic truth is one which depends on *meanings* in the strict sense and therefore is necessary' (1980: 122 n. 63)). He notes, however, that one might equally let the word express loose analyticity, and that on that definition 'some analytic truths are contingent' (ibid.).

Given the care Kripke takes in distinguishing the kind of analyticity that entails metaphysical necessity from the kind that doesn't, one might have expected him to draw a similar distinction on the side of apriority: there would be an apriority-entailing kind of analyticity and a kind that can be had by non-a priori statements. 'Hesperus is Phosphorus' is not a priori, but since its meaning is a proposition of the form $x = x$, and any proposition of that form is true, it could be considered true in virtue of meaning. I am not endorsing this particular example, just pointing out a move that could have been made.

Kripke seems, however, to take it for granted that analytic truths will be a priori knowable. In his characterization of loose analyticity he speaks, not of statements whose truth is guaranteed by reference-fixing descriptions, but ones whose '*a priori* truth is *known* via the fixing of a reference' (1980: 122 n. 63, italics added). A non-Kripkean line on the apriority of analytic statements will be elaborated below.

I said that apriority and analyticity were for Kripke (relatively) 'ordinary' notions. There are intimations in *Naming and Necessity* of a corresponding technical notion: a notion that explicates apriority/analyticity as metaphysical necessity explicates our idea of that which could not be otherwise. This technical notion—potentially a partner in full standing to metaphysical necessity—needs a name of its own. What should the name be?

'Epistemic necessity' is best avoided because, as Kripke says, to call S epistemically possible sounds like a way of saying that it is true (or possible) for all one currently knows.[1] A notion explicating apriority/analyticity should not be so sensitive to the extent of current knowledge. One doesn't know how to prove Goldbach's conjecture today, but one might tomorrow; it would then turn out to have been necessary (in the partner sense) all along.

---

[1] DeRose (1991) argues that this familiar condition is not enough. If contrary information is there for the taking, and/or possessed by relevant others, then S is not epistemically possible, even if it could be true for all I myself know.

'Semantic necessity' too is liable to mislead, since for some people, Kripke included, 'Hesperus' and 'Phosphorus' are semantically just alike, yet it is possible in the partner sense that Hesperus ≠ Phosphorus. As Kripke says, one is inclined to think that it could have turned out either way.

If a name is to be given, then, to the *non*metaphysical modality that features in *Naming and Necessity*, 'conceptual' is probably the least bad. It is true that Kripke doesn't use the word 'conceptual' and doesn't talk much about concepts. But his nonmetaphysical necessities do have their truth guaranteed by the way we have represented things to ourselves; and we can think of 'concept' as just evoking the relevant level of representation. Conceptual necessity will then be the technical or semi-technical notion that Kripke runs alongside, and to some extent pits against, metaphysical necessity.

2 Conceptual Necessity

An enormous amount has been done with the metaphysical/conceptual distinction. Yet, and I think this is agreed by everyone, the distinction remains not terribly well understood. One reason it is not well understood is that the conceptual side of the distinction didn't receive at Kripke's hands the same sort of development as the metaphysical side.

This might have been intentional on Kripke's part. He might have thought the conceptual notion to be irremediably obscure, but important to mention lest it obscure our view of metaphysical necessity. Certainly this is the attitude that many take about the conceptual notion today. It could be argued that much of the contemporary skepticism about narrow content is at the same time skepticism about conceptual possibility. Narrow content, if it existed, would give sense to conceptual possibility: holding its narrow content fixed, S could have expressed a truth. If one rejects narrow content, one needs a different explanation, and none comes to mind. Going in the other direction, one might try to define S's narrow content as the set of worlds *w* whose obtaining conceptually necessitates that S. Lewis remarks somewhere that whoever claims not to understand something will take care not to understand anything else whereby it might be explained. If you don't understand narrow content, you will take care not to understand conceptual possibility either.

But, although many people have doubts about conceptual possibility, a number of *other* people are entirely gung ho about it. Some even treat it (and narrow content) as more, or anyway no less, fundamental than metaphysical possibility (and broad content). An example is David Chalmers. He calls S's narrow content its 'primary intension', and its broad content its 'secondary intension'.

One suspects that the order here is not accidental. And even if the suspicion is wrong, the primary intension is certainly a partner in full standing.

In this paper I try not to take sides between the skeptics and the believers. My topic is how conceptual possibility should be handled *supposing it is going to be handled at all*. If I do slip occasionally into the language of the believers, that is because I am trying to explore their system from the inside, in order to see what it is capable of, and whether it can be made to deliver the advertised kinds of results. (I should say that my own leanings are to the skeptical side, though I think the issue is far from settled.)

3 Initial Comparisons

Kripke's theory (or picture) of metaphysical modality is familiar enough. He says that it holds necessarily that S iff S is true in all possible worlds. The word 'in' is, however, misleading. It suggests that S (or an utterance thereof) is to be seen as *inhabiting* the world(s) w with respect to which it is evaluated. That is certainly not Kripke's intent. His view is better captured by saying that S (that well-known denizen of *our* world), to be necessary, should be true *of* all possible worlds. Every world should be such that S gives a correct description of it. Every world should be such that the way S describes things as being is a way that it in fact is.

Conceptual possibility too is explained with worlds. To be conceptually possible is to be in some appropriate sense true with respect to—or, for short, true *at*—w for at least one world w. But what is the appropriate sense? Everyone knows the examples that are supposed to bring out how conceptual modality is different. It is conceptually possible, but metaphysically impossible, for Hesperus to be distinct from Phosphorus. This is because 'Hesperus $\neq$ Phosphorus' is true at a world that it fails to be true of. The metaphysical/conceptual contrast thus hangs on the contrast between true-of-w as just discussed and the notion of true-at-w that we must now attempt to develop.

Here is the obvious first stab: S is true at w iff S as uttered in w is true of w. 'Hesperus $\neq$ Phosphorus' uttered here in the actual world means that Venus isn't Venus; uttered in w, it might mean that Venus isn't Mars. If, in w, Venus indeed *isn't* Mars, then 'Hesperus $\neq$ Phosphorus' is true at w. And so w testifies to the conceptual possibility of Hesperus not being Phosphorus.

Compare now an S that strikes us as *not* conceptually possible: for instance, 'Phosphorus $\neq$ Phosphorus'. Uttered in w, this means that Mars $\neq$ Mars. Since that is false of Mars, in w or anywhere else, w does not testify to the conceptual possibility of Phosphorus not being Phosphorus. Unless there are worlds where uttering 'Phosphorus ≠ Phosphorus' is speaking the truth, that Phosphorus ≠ Phosphorus is not conceptually possible.

But, and here is where the trouble starts, there *are* worlds like that. For there are worlds in which 'Phosphorus ≠ Phosphorus' means something other than what it actually means (say, that Phosphorus is *identical* to Phosphorus) and in which the other thing is true. So it looks like we reach the wrong result. It should not make 'Phosphorus ≠ Phosphorus' conceptually possible that there are worlds in which '≠' expresses identity!

One remembers this sort of problem from Kripke's discussion, not of conceptual possibility, but metaphysical possibility. Let it be, he says, that *w* contains speakers (maybe our counterfactual selves) who understand S eccentrically from our point of view. That has no bearing on the issue of whether S is true of *w*:

> when we speak of a counterfactual situation, we speak of it in English, even if it is part of the description of that counterfactual situation that we were all speaking [another language] . . . We say, . . . 'suppose we had been using English in a nonstandard way'. Then we are describing a possible world or counterfactual situation in which people, including ourselves, did speak in a certain way different from the way we speak. But still, in describing that world, we use *English* with *our* meanings and *our* references. (1980: 77)

By 'tail', for example, the inhabitants of *w* might mean *wing*. If so, then assuming *w*'s horses resemble ours, they speak falsely when they say 'horses have tails'. That is irrelevant, Kripke says, to the metaphysical necessity issue. 'Horses have tails' is as true of *w* as of the actual world. This is crucial if statements are to come out with the right modal status. 'One doesn't say that "two plus two equals four" is contingent because people might have spoken a language in which "two plus two equals four" meant that seven is even' (1980: 77).

How much of this still applies on the conceptual side? Worlds where 'Hesperus ≠ Phosphorus' means that Venus ≠ Mars *can* (as we saw) bear witness to the conceptual possibility of Hesperus not being Phosphorus. So in judging conceptual contingency, we *do* want to look at *w*-speakers who, in a broad sense, mean something different by S than we mean by it here.

But there are limits; we are not interested in *w*-speakers who by 'Hesperus ≠ Phosphorus' mean that Hesperus is identical to Phosphorus, or that it's snowing in Brooklyn. It thus becomes important to know in what ways the meaning of S in the mouths of *w*-speakers can differ from the meaning of S in our mouths, for the truth of S as uttered in *w* to be relevant to the conceptual possibility of S here. Something has got to be held fixed, but what?

4 Holding Fixed

First try: S has got to mean the *very same* in *w* as it means here.

This holds too much fixed. 'Hesperus' and 'Phosphorus' as they are used here both mean Venus, and '≠' expresses nonidentity. A counterfactual utterance of 'Hesperus ≠ Phosphorus' that respected these facts would have to mean that Venus ≠ Venus; and so the utterance would not be true. But then it will not come out conceptually possible that Hesperus ≠ Phosphorus, as it should.

Second try: Corresponding expressions should mean the same, *or* have their references fixed by the same or synonymous descriptions.

This is all right as far as it goes, but there is a problem of coverage. If a reference-fixing description is one that picks out the referent no matter what, then reference-fixing descriptions are hardly ever available. One doesn't know of any description guaranteed in advance to pick out the referent of 'Homer' or 'water'. So the second proposal reduces in most cases to the first, which we've seen to be inadequate.

A third approach puts conditions not on S in particular, but on *w* as whole: *w* bears on S's conceptual possibility if and only if it is an 'epistemic counterpart' of our world, in the sense of confronting the speaker with the same evidential situation as he confronts here. If *w* is an epistemic counterpart of actuality, then S's meaning can change only in ways that leave the evidential situation as is; that is what it takes for S's truth in *w* to bear witness to its conceptual possibility here.

A seeming advantage of the proposal is that it no longer attempts to specify the relevant aspects of meaning (the ones that are supposed to be held fixed) explicitly. The thought is that those aspects, whatever they are, are fixed *inter alia* by fixing the entire evidential situation. This is also the proposal's problem, though. Mixed in with the semantical material we want to hold fixed will be nonsemantic circumstances that should be allowed to vary. One doesn't want to hold fixed that there seems to be a lectern present, or there seeming to be a lectern present will be classified as conceptually necessary. That is clearly the wrong result. Appearances are conceptually contingent if anything is.

5 Subjunctives

The kind of necessity we are calling conceptual is left by Kripke in a precarious state. Judging conceptual necessity is judging whether S *as uttered in w* is true of *w*. This collapses into triviality unless certain aspects of S's meaning are held fixed. And it is unclear which aspects are intended.

Why do the same problems not arise for metaphysical necessity? The usual answer is that with metaphysical necessity, one needn't bring in a counterfactual utterance at all. One considers whether *our* utterance, saying (or meaning) just what it actually says (means), gives a true description of *w*. But this doesn't give us much guidance in some cases.

Suppose we are trying to evaluate 'horses have tails' with respect to *w*. You maintain, reasonably enough, that what 'horses have tails' actually says is that tails are had by Northern Dancer, Secretariat, . . . (fill in here the list of all actual horses). You conclude that 'horses have tails' is true of *w* iff Northern Dancer, Secretariat, . . . (or perhaps just those of them that exist in *w*) have tails in *w*.

Someone else maintains, just as reasonably, that 'horses have tails' says that if anything is a horse, then it has a tail. She concludes that 'horses have tails' is true of *w* iff the things that are horses in *w* have tails in *w*. The two of you disagree, then, about how to evaluate 'horses have tails' at a world that contains all our horses (complete with tails) plus some *additional* horses that lack tails.

Who is right? What is really said by an utterance of 'horses have tails' and how do we tell whether it is true of a counterfactual world? These questions have no clear answers. One might, I suppose, look for answers in the theory of what is expressed, or what is said, by sentences in contexts. But it would be with a heavy heart (and not only because the notion of what is said is so slippery and vague). Almost every question in semantics can be framed as a question about what some S expresses in some context. It would be nice if we didn't have to do the full semantics of English before the truth-conditions of 'necessarily S' could be given.

If there were no way around this problem, I doubt that Kripke's approach would have found such widespread acceptance. One imagines, then, that the Kripkean has a response. Here is how I imagine it going: 'You are taking the "saying what it actually says" phraseology too seriously in some way. If any real weight were going to be laid on that way of putting it, then yes, a story would be needed about how it is determined what is said. But "saying what it actually says" is just a heuristic. It reminds us that it doesn't matter, in considering whether S is true of *w*, what the citizens of *w* mean by S. How in that case *is* true-of to be understood, you ask? One option is to treat it as primitive. But this option is problematic. It gives the skeptic about metaphysical possibility too big an opening: she can claim to find the primitive incomprehensible. It would be better if we could *explain* truth-of in terms that the skeptic, as a speaker of English, already understands. This can be done using the subjunctive conditional. To say that S is true of a world *w* is to say that *had w obtained, it would have been that S*.'[2]

---

[2] See in this connection Chalmers (2000).

Consider in this light the 'controversy' about horses and their tails. When we evaluate 'horses have tails' with respect to w, is it only the actual horses that matter, or do horses found only in w have to be taken into account as well? Suppose that although actual horses have tails, w's additional horses include some that are tail-less. Is 'horses have tails' true of w?

The subjunctive account makes short work of this conundrum. Had w obtained, it would *not* have been that horses had tails; there would have been some horses with tails and some without. So 'horses have tails' is false of w.

Return now to the case of a w where 'tail' means *wing*. Does the fact that w-people speak falsely when they say 'horses have tails' show that 'horses have tails' is false of w? It doesn't, and we can now explain why in a theoretically uncontroversial way. The question is whether horses would still have had tails, if people had used 'tail' to mean wing. They clearly would have; how people talk doesn't affect the anatomy of horses. Had 'tail' meant wing, 'horses have tails' would not have been true, but horses would still have had tails.

6 Disparity

All this is to emphasize the *disparity*, in the immediate aftermath of *Naming and Necessity*, between metaphysical and conceptual necessity. The first was in good shape—because it went with 'S is true of w', which could be understood as 'it would have been that S, had it been that w'. The second was in bad shape—because it went with 'S is true when uttered in w', which had to be understood as 'it would have been that S was true, had it been that w, *and had S retained certain aspects of its actual meaning*'.

Then a brainstorm was had that seemed to restore parity.[3]

Recall what we do to judge metaphysical necessity. We ask of various worlds w whether S (*our* S, natch) is true *of w*. The Kripkean tells us that to judge conceptual necessity, we need to ask, not whether S is true *of w*, but whether it is true (as spoken) *at w*. But maybe it wasn't really necessary to move S over to w.

---

[3] At least three ideas were involved. (1) Instead of moving S over to w, bring w back to S. To do that, (2) evaluate S on the hypothesis that w actually obtains. To do that, (3) evaluate the indicative conditional 'if w actually obtains, then S'. (1) and (2) are present to some degree in Evans (1979) and Davies and Humberstone (1980), and are explicit in Chalmers (1994). I am not aware of any discussion of (3) before Chalmers (1996, 2000). See also Segerberg (1972), White (1982), and Stalnaker (1972, 1990, 1991).

A different option is to move w over to actuality: to the place where the token of S that we want evaluated in fact occurs.[4]

All right, but how do we do that? It looks at first very simple. Just as, when judging metaphysical necessity, we consider w as counterfactual, so, when judging conceptual necessity, we consider it as *counteractual*. We consider it as a hypothesis about what *this* world is like. Of course, we do not in general *believe* the hypothesis. But that should not deter us; we are masters at working out how matters stand on hypotheses we reject. Evaluating S with respect to counteractual w is asking whether S holds on the hypothesis that w is (contrary to what we perhaps think) this very world.

For example, it is conceptually possible that Hesperus $\neq$ Phosphorus because, if we suppose for a moment that this world is one in which Hesperus-appearances are due to Mars and Phosphorus-appearances to Venus, then clearly (on that supposition) we are *wrong* to think that Hesperus = Phosphorus. It is not that counterfactual people are wrong about *their* world. It is we who are wrong about *our* world, on a certain hypothesis about what our world is like.

This sounds like progress, but we should not celebrate too soon, because the disparity with metaphysical modality is not entirely gone.

I said that everyone would (should!) have been unhappy if they had been asked to treat 'true of counterfactual w' as a semantic primitive. We are willing to rest so much on true of because of the *explanation* we have been given of that notion: S is true of w iff, had w obtained, it would have been that S. It is this biconditional, with 'true of' on the left and a counterfactual on the right, that convinces us that there's a there there.

Apart, though, from some suggestive talk about what to say 'on the supposition' that w obtains, we have no comparable explanation of what is involved in S's being true with respect to counteractual w. If we use 'true if w' for truth with respect to a world conceived as actual, the problem is that 'true of' has been translated into English and 'true if' has not.

---

[4] A third option is to leave S and w where they are, and treat 'true if' as a trans-world primitive. This is one possible reading of Chalmers's remark (1994) that 'we can retain the thought from the *real* actual world and simultaneously ask its truth-value in other actual-world candidates without any loss of coherence'. He adds in a footnote that 'Doing things this way . . . avoids a problem . . . raised by Block (1991) and Stalnaker (1991). The problem is that of what must be "held constant" between contexts . . . On my account, nothing needs to be held constant, as we always appeal to the concept from the real world in evaluating the referent at [an actual-world candidate]' (1994: 42). This is certainly one way to go. But it has its costs. If taking 'true of' as primitive is obscurantist, primitivism about 'true if' borders on mysticism (our pre-theoretical grip on the second is that much weaker).

7 Indicatives

One proposal about this suggests itself immediately. Since 'true of' goes with a *counterfactual* conditional, 'true if' perhaps goes with the corresponding *indicative* conditional. 'S is true if *w*' says that *if w in fact obtains (evidence to the contrary notwithstanding), then S.*[5]

The proposal is intriguing because it offers to link two deep distinctions: metaphysical versus conceptual necessity, on the one hand, and subjunctive versus indicative conditionality, on the other. The reason it is only metaphysically necessary that Hesperus = Phosphorus is that there are worlds *w* such that, although Hesperus would have been Phosphorus *had w* obtained, it is not Phosphorus if *w does* obtain.

Do the two conditionals really 'predict' the two types of necessity? Before attempting to decide this, we need to remember how we got here. It was important for metaphysical necessity to keep what–is–said fixed as we evaluate S at *w*. Subjunctives are valued because they in effect do this, without dragging us into controversies about what is in fact said. It is *not* important to conceptual necessity to keep what–is–said fixed; indeed, we are willing and eager that it should change in certain respects under the impact of this or that counteractual hypothesis. (For example, we are eager for 'Hesperus = Phosphorus' to take on a content having to do with Venus and Mars.) Crucially, though, we do *not* want S's meaning to be changeable in *all* respects. (We don't want 'Hesperus = Phosphorus' to acquire a content having to do with nonidentity.) Indicatives are attractive because they seem to deliver an appropriate measure of meaning–fixation, just as subjunctives did on the metaphysical side.

Indicatives *appear* to deliver an appropriate measure of meaning–fixation. But when you look a little closer, the appearance fades. Indicatives don't in fact deliver *anything* in the way of meaning–fixation. The meaning of S as it occurs in the consequent of an indicative conditional can be changed all you want by putting the right kind of misinformation into the antecedent. Example: If 'tail' had meant wing, horses would still have had tails. But suppose that 'tail' *does* mean wing; it has meant wing all along, not only in others' mouths but also our own; a brain glitch (or demon) leads us systematically astray when we reflect on the meaning of that particular word. Then, it seems clear, horses do not have tails. If 'tail' as a matter of fact means wing, then to say that horses have tails is to say that they have wings. Horses do not have wings. So if 'tail' means wing, then horses do not have tails.[6]

---

[5] Chalmers (2000).

[6] Indicative conditionals are conditionals with antecedent and consequent in the indicative mood. Philosophers have proposed various theories of these conditionals. One, defended by

You may say: why should it be a problem if there are counteractual worlds at which horses lack tails? That is not the problem. The problem is that there are worlds where horses lack tails *not for anatomical reasons but on account of 'tail' not meaning tail*. If horses can lose their tails that easily, then take any S you like, it is true in some counteractual worlds and false in others. It is true in worlds where S means that X, and X is the case, and false in worlds where S means Y, and Y is not the case. This spells disaster for the indicative approach to conceptual possibility. It should not make 'Hesperus ≠ Hesperus' conceptually possible that there are worlds where people use '≠' to express identity.

8 Narrow Content

The indicative is not the conditional we want. But it is close. We want a conditional A → C that is *like* the indicative except in one crucial respect: C is protected from a certain sort of meaning shift brought on by A.

An example of the 'good' or 'permitted' sort of meaning shift is the kind exhibited by 'Hesperus ≠ Phosphorus' on the supposition that Phosphorus-appearances are caused by Mars. An example of the 'bad' sort of meaning shift is that exhibited by 'Phosphorus ≠ Phosphorus' on the supposition that '≠' expresses identity.

It may seem that the answer is staring us in the face. The 'bad' kind of meaning shift is the kind that mucks with *S's narrow content*. Our conditional should be such that S's narrow content is the same when we condition on *w* as when we don't. (The indicative is wrong because the narrow content of 'horses have tails' is one thing if 'tail' means wing, another thing if it doesn't.) Calling the actual narrow content NC, attention is to be restricted to worlds such that *w* obtains → S (still) means NC.

But, although helpful as an intuitive constraint, this doesn't solve our problem. This is partly because one doesn't know what the narrow content in fact is; NC has been pulled out of a hat. Second, though, to appeal to narrow content in this context gets things the wrong way around. The reason for being interested in 'S is true if *w*' was to get a better handle on conceptual necessity.

Grice (1989), is that they are 'material', or truth-table, conditionals. Another, defended by Adams (1975), is that they are probability conditionals. Chalmers in recent work declares a preference for the material conditional, regardless of its relation, if any, to the indicative. (He requires the material conditional to hold a priori.) The objection in the text applies regardless. However the indicative is interpreted, A's a priori entailing C suffices for the apriority of 'if A then C'. The conditional 'if horses are wingless and "tail" means wing, then horses do not have tails' has A a priori entailing C, so the conditional is a priori.

But, as noted above, conceptual necessity and narrow content are two sides of the same coin. The idea is to explain narrow content using →, not → using narrow content.

9 Turning Out

Our problem now is similar to one faced earlier in connection with metaphysical necessity. It seemed that an account of true of would have to appeal to the notion of what is said. That would be unfortunate, because it would reverse the intended order of explanation. The what-is-said of an utterance (its broad content, nearly enough) is given by the worlds of which it is true. The special case in which S's broad content takes in *all* worlds is what is otherwise known as metaphysical necessity. That is why we don't want to use broad content to explain true of. Our current worry is the same, except that it concerns true if rather than true of, and narrow content rather than broad.

How did we deal with that earlier problem? By calling in the subjunctive. We said that S is true of *w* iff it would have been that S, had *w* obtained. The claim was that this construction *automatically* targets the agreement or lack thereof between *w* and S's broad content. Can a construction be found that automatically targets the agreement or lack thereof between *w* and S's *narrow* content, as the subjunctive does for broad content?

One that comes pretty close occurs in *Naming and Necessity* itself. Kripke notes that we're at first inclined to think that Hesperus and Phosphorus (although in fact identical) could have been distinct. Then we learn about metaphysical versus other types of necessity, and we lose the inclination; Hesperus and Phosphorus could not have been distinct. Even now, though, apprised of the metaphysical facts, we are still inclined to think that it *could have turned out* that Hesperus was distinct from Phosphorus.

It is this phrase 'could have turned out' that I want to focus on. Kripke is right to represent us as still inclined to think that it could have turned out that Hesperus was distinct from Phosphorus, even after we have taken on board that it could not have *been* that Hesperus was distinct from Phosphorus. The inclination persists even among practicing modal metaphysicians (who ought to know better, if there is better to know). This suggests that 'could have turned out' is special in ways we should try to understand.

It suggests it to me, anyway. Kripke apparently does not agree. He maintains that the second inclination is just as mistaken as the first. Not only could it not have been, it could not even have turned out that Hesperus was distinct from Phosphorus. This is only to be expected if 'it could have turned out that S' means, as Kripke hints it does mean, 'it could have been that: S and we believed that S and with justification'. This interpretation, however, leaves it a mystery why the second inclination outlasts the first—why we persist in thinking that it could have turned out that Hesperus wasn't Phosphorus even after giving up on the idea that Hesperus could have been other than Phosphorus.

I propose that the persisting thought is correct. Kripke to the contrary, it could indeed have turned out that Hesperus wasn't Phosphorus. That is what *would* have turned out had it turned out that Phosphorus-appearances were appearances of Mars. It could *not*, however, have turned out that Phosphorus ≠ Phosphorus, even granting that '≠' could have turned out to express identity. That is a way for it to turn out that that 'Phosphorus ≠ Phosphorus' is true, not a way for it to turn out that Phosphorus ≠ Phosphorus.[7]

10 Conceptual Possibility

It would have turned out that C, had it turned out that A shares features with both the indicative conditional and the subjunctive. It resembles the indicative in making play not with counterfactual worlds, but with suppositions about *our* world. It resembles the subjunctive in that the consequent C is protected from a certain kind of semantic influence on the part of A. The way C (narrowly) represents things as being is left untouched by 'had it turned out that A'. The role that the antecedent plays is all on the side of whether things are, on the hypothesis that A, the way that C (in actual fact, given that the hypothesis is false) narrowly represents them as being.

If 'tail' means wing, we said, then horses lack tails. → is supposed to be different in this respect. It should not be that *w (in which 'tail' means wing) obtains* → *horses lack tails*. That is the result we get if → is a 'would have turned out' conditional. For it is *not* the case that horses would have turned out to lack tails, had it turned out that 'tail' meant wing. It is not for linguistic reasons that horses have tails; so they are not deprived of their tails by the linguistic facts turning out differently.

---

[7] Chalmers employs similar wording when he introduces primary intensions: 'there are two quite distinct patterns of dependence of the referent of a content on the state of the world. First, there is the dependence by which reference is fixed in the actual world, depending on *how the world turns out: if it turns out* one way, a concept will pick out one thing, but *if it turns out* another way, the concept will pick out something else' (1996: 57, italics added). I applaud the use of 'turns out', but I think the mood should be subjunctive—if it had turned out—rather than indicative— if it does turn out. If it turns out that 'tail' means wing, then horses lack tails. But that 'tail' means something different in *w* should be irrelevant to the question of whether *w*'s horses have tails. Otherwise conceptual necessity is trivialized. See also Jackson (1994, 1998).

One can come at → from the other direction. If Phosphorus-appearances had been due to Mars, Phosphorus would still have been Hesperus. → is supposed to be different in this respect too. We want there to be worlds w such that w obtains → Hesperus ≠ Phosphorus. That cannot happen unless the broad content of 'Hesperus ≠ Phosphorus' can be changed by conditioning it on the hypothesis that w obtains. Here too, 'would have turned out' delivers the goods. Had it turned out that Phosphorus-appearances were due to Mars and Hesperus-appearances (still) to Venus, it would have turned out that Hesperus ≠ Phosphorus.

What these examples suggest is that 'would have turned out' conditionals exhibit just the right combination of (i) openness to shifts in broad content, (ii) intolerance of shifts in narrow content. I therefore propose *it would have turned out that C, had it turned out that A* as the proper interpretation of A → C. And I make a hypothesis:

(M) It is metaphysically possible that S iff some world w is such that it would have been that S, had w obtained.

(C) It is conceptually possible that S iff some world w is such that it would have turned out that S, had w turned out to be actual.

More simply, S is *metaphysically* possible iff it could have *been* that S, and *conceptually* possible iff it could have *turned out* that S.

11 Analyticity and Apriority

A priori truths are truths that can be known not on the basis of empirical evidence. How well that accords with the Kripkean notion of apriority depends on one's theory of justification. There is a danger, though, of its according very badly.

One theory says that all spontaneously arising beliefs start out justified. They can lose that status only if evidence arises against them. Suppose that this view is correct, and suppose that, on pulling the curtains open, I spontaneously come to think that the sun is shining. (I don't infer that it is shining from premises about how things perceptually appear to me.) Then I know that the sun is shining, and not on the basis of empirical evidence. And yet it certainly isn't a priori, as Kripke uses the term, that the sun is shining.

Another theory has it that our most 'basic' beliefs lack empirical justification, because they are epistemically prior to anything that might be said in their support. So, the belief that nature is uniform lacks empirical backing. If we know that nature is uniform, and let's assume we do, the knowledge is not empirical. But it isn't a priori in Kripke's sense that nature is uniform.

Apriority, then, is not *any* old kind of not-empirically-based knowability, as judged by any old theory of justification. That would let far too much in. A (very familiar) objection from the other side helps us to clarify matters. If experience cannot be appealed to at all, then shouldn't it be enough to stop S from being a priori if it is through experience that we *understand* S? The answer to this is that our interest is in how S is *justified*, our understanding taken for granted.

If that is the one and only concession made, then we wind up with a roughly Kripkean notion of apriority. S is a priori iff it is *knowable just on the basis of one's understanding of S*. Or, better, it's a priori *for me* iff *I* can know it just on the basis of my understanding of S. This is why the originator of a name is apt to know more a priori than someone picking the name up in conversation. The mental state by which Leverrier understands 'Neptune' tells him that Neptune, if there is such a thing, accounts for the perturbations in the orbit of Uranus. The mental state by which others understand 'Neptune' is liable to be much less informative about Neptune's astronomical properties.

Apriority is knowability on the basis of understanding. Understanding is, one assumes, knowing the meaning. But what meaning?

Perhaps understanding is knowing meaning 'in the strict sense': the sense that ignores reference-fixing descriptions. But Kripke calls it a priori that Hesperus = Hesperus, and a posteriori that Hesperus = Phosphorus, though the strict meanings are the same. More likely, then, it is knowledge of meaning in the *loose* sense that makes for understanding. The closest thing to loose meaning in our framework is narrow content. So it does not do *too* much violence to Kripke's intentions to say that S is a priori iff one can know that it is true just on the basis of one's grasp of its narrow content.

Kripke calls S analytic iff 'it's true in virtue of meanings in the strict sense'. This definition has to be treated with some care, since the strict meaning of 'Hesperus = Phosphorus' is a singular proposition of the form $x = x$, and Kripke does not want 'Hesperus = Phosphorus' to come out analytic. (It is not a priori, and Kripke thinks that analytic truths are a priori.) Then what is his intent in speaking of 'meanings in the strict sense'? He cannot have been trying to *include* statements ('Hesperus = Phosphorus') that are true in virtue of strict meaning as opposed to loose. He must have been trying to *exclude* statements ('Hesperus is visible at night') that are true in virtue of loose meaning as opposed to strict. This is, in effect, to limit analyticity to 'Fregean' sentences: sentences to which the loose/strict distinction does not apply. S is analytic iff it is true in virtue of its Fregean meaning, that being the only meaning it has.

Now, though, one wants to know: why should it stop S from being analytic if *in addition* to its truth-guaranteeing Fregean meaning, it has a (possibly not truth-guaranteeing) Kripkean meaning? Or, to put it in narrow/broad terms, if S has a truth-guaranteeing narrow content, why isn't that enough to make it analytic, quite regardless of whether it has a broad content in addition?

True-blue Kripkeans will reply that narrow content is not (except *per accidens*, when it agrees with broad) part of *meaning*. Narrow content is *metasemantical*, not semantical.

But this, one may feel, is just terminological fussiness.[8] Even Kripke considers it a *kind* of meaning—meaning in the loose sense—and he says explicitly that some might want to define analyticity as truth in virtue of *that*. So, it does not do *too* much violence to Kripke's intentions to let analyticity be truth in virtue of narrow content. (This fits with our account of Kripkean apriority as knowability in virtue of grasp of narrow content.)

Now, finally, we can ask the question that matters: Is conceptual necessity a kind of apriority, or a kind of analyticity, or both?

I do not think there can be much doubt that it is a kind of analyticity. A conceptually necessary sentence is one true in all counteractual worlds. These worlds comprise what Chalmers calls the sentence's *primary intension*, and primary intension is his candidate for the role of narrow content. So, a conceptually necessary sentence is one whose narrow content is such that, no matter which world is actual, it comes out true. Truth guaranteed by narrow content is analytic truth.

Is conceptual necessity *also* perhaps a kind of apriority? As just discussed, the narrow content of a conceptually necessary sentence is such as to guarantee its truth. Does it follow that someone *grasping* the content is thereby in a position to *see* that S is true?

That depends on what is involved in grasping a content (let 'narrow' be understood). S's content is, roughly, a bunch of conditionals of the form: it would (or wouldn't) have turned out that S, had w turned out to be actual. Someone who grasps the content is in a position to know the conditionals. So if S is conceptually necessary, then she is in a position to see, for each w, that had w turned out to be actual, it would have turned out that S. Doesn't this show that she can determine a priori that S?

No; in fact, we are still miles from that conclusion. Let it be that the speaker knows for each w that w obtains $\rightarrow$ S. It is wide open so far whether this knowledge is a priori. Someone who grasps S's meaning is in a position to come to know the conditionals *somehow or other*. A priori or a posteriori is an open question.

---

[8] I myself feel it is more than that, but this is the charge made by the narrow content enthusiast whose part I am playing.

You might think that the knowledge *has* to be a priori. If grasping S's content gives me knowledge of the conditionals, then I know the conditionals based on my grasp of S's content. Knowledge based on grasp of content is a priori knowledge.

This is entirely unconvincing. Grasping S's content 'gives me' knowledge of the conditionals only in the sense of putting me in a position to come to know them; my advantage over non-graspers is that I have 'what it takes' to know. That is roughly to say that understanding S is *necessary* if one wants to know whether S if *w*, or the most important necessary condition, or the only necessary condition one has to worry about. Apriority requires that understanding be *sufficient*. I have granted that understanding suffices for being in a position to *work out* whether S if *w*. If the working out involves experience, though, then the knowledge will not be a priori.

12 Peeking

I said that our understanding of S might not be enough to go on, when it comes to working out whether S holds in a world *w*. The 'official story' about evaluation at counteractual worlds strongly denies this. But the possibility has a way of sneaking in uninvited. Here is Chalmers:

[A]s an in-principle point, there are various ways to see that someone (a superbeing?) armed only with the microphysical facts and the concepts involved could infer the high-level facts. The simplest way is to note that in principle one could build a big mental simulation of the world and watch it in one's mind's eye, so to speak. (1996: 76)

Say that this is right; I am able to build a mental model of *w*, and judge whether S is true in *w* by viewing the model with my mind's eye. The question is whether viewing a model of *w* and asking myself 'how it looks' S-wise is a way of coming to know S's truth-value in *w* a priori.

Here is a reason to think not. Asking yourself how something strikes you is using yourself as a measuring device. Information acquired by use of an external measuring device is a posteriori on anybody's account. Information acquired by use of an internal one seems no different. What matters is that an experiment is done, the outcome of which decides your response.

It might be argued that mental experimentation *is* different. Knowledge gained from it is acquired within the privacy of one's own mind. You determine that S without appealing at any point to information about the outside world. Shouldn't that be enough to make the knowledge a priori?

No, for you determine that you have a headache the same way. Knowledge of headaches is certainly not a priori. The modal rationalist in particular should agree, for my headache, if a priori, would be a counter-example to the proposed equation between apriority and truth in all counteractual worlds. 'I have a headache' fails in some counteractual worlds. A priori truths are supposed to hold everywhere.

Some internally acquired knowledge presumably is a priori. If you think up a counter-example to argument form F in your head, then you know a priori that F is invalid. What distinguishes this sort of case, where you do know a priori, from the case of looking at a mental model with the mind's eye?

Two things. First, when you conjure up an image of w, you are *simulating* the activity of really looking at it. Simulated looking is not a distinct process, but the usual process run 'off-line'. Knowledge gained by internal looking is not a priori because it is acquired through the exercise of a perceptual faculty rather than a cognitive one.

Second, some imagined reactions are a better guide to real reactions than others.[9] Imagined shape reactions are a good guide, you say, and you are probably right. But it is hard to see how the knowledge that they are a good guide could be a priori. If the mind's eye sees one sort of property roughly as real eyes do, while its take on another sort of property tends to be off the mark, that is an empirical fact known on the basis of empirical evidence. I know not to trust my imagined reactions to arrangements of furniture, because they have often been wrong; now that I see the wardrobe in the room, I realize it is far too big. It is only because they have generally been right that I am entitled to trust my imagined judgments of shape.

The temptation to think of simulation as a source of a priori knowledge is due in part to there not being much that we are able to simulate. There might be beings who, given only the microphysical blueprint of, say, an exotic fruit, are able to imagine its color in much the way that we are able to imagine its shape. They come to know that rambutans are red, without ever laying eyes on one. I take it that no one would consider the knowledge to be a priori. These beings did not deduce the color from microphysics. Information was also needed about how that microphysics appears to human eyes. They obtained

---

[9] Stepping into the lake, you say, 'It's colder than I thought.' The earlier thought might have been a real judgment based on partial information (it's August, lots of people are swimming), but it might also have been a simulated judgment based on full information about the water's kinetic properties. You imagine yourself stepping into water with those properties, and it seems to feel warmer than water like that really does feel. (Most of us do something like this with temperature properties; 80 degree water is surprisingly cold.)

this information experimentally, by simulating an encounter with a rambutan, and using it to predict the outcome of a real encounter.

Suppose that we had been able to simulate reactions in other modalities. Suppose we could determine the taste and smell of a microphysically given item with the mind's tongue and nose. Would that make it an a priori matter how rambutans [insert chemical description here] tasted? No. How a thing tastes is an empirical question. One does not feel that it escapes being a priori only because of a contingent incompleteness in our nature. It would still have been an empirical matter how rambutans tasted, even if God had been more generous in the mind's sense-organ department.

These claims might be accepted but shrugged off as irrelevant. It doesn't matter if self-experimental knowledge is a posteriori, for any suggestion of self-experimentation was inadvertent. 'I looked at *w* and saw it to contain so-and-so's' is only a colorful description of something far more innocent: intellectually contemplating a world *description* and *thinking* my way to a conclusion about whether there are so-and-so's in *w*.

That is fair enough, on one condition. Self-experimentation had better not be *needed* to work out whether S holds in *w*. It had better be that one can reason from a microphysical description of *w* to a conclusion about whether or not S. *No peeking*. I assume that Chalmers would agree; for, if peeking is allowed, the inference from 'S holds in all candidates for actuality' to 'it is a priori that S' clearly does not go through. This inference is crucial to the view that Chalmers calls 'modal rationalism'.

Given how much hangs on our ability to evaluate S without peeking, one might have expected a show of vigilance on this score. If we are playing 'pin the tail on the donkey', you watch me like a hawk. You know how hard I find it to ignore information right in front of my nose. The same should apply when the game is 'decide the truth value of S'. If it is difficult to infer S ($\neg$S) from microphysics, I will be tempted to switch to sensory imagining. Knowing this, you will take pains that my mind's eye is completely shut, or completely covered by my mind's blindfold.

The need for vigilance is never mentioned, as far as I know, in the modal rationalist literature. Here is how the passage quoted above continues:

Say that a man is carrying an umbrella. From the associated microphysical facts, one could straightforwardly infer facts about the distribution and chemical composition of mass in the man's vicinity, giving a high-level structural description of the area. One could determine the existence of a male fleshy biped straightforwardly enough. . . . It would be clear that he was carrying some device that was preventing drops of water, otherwise prevalent in the neighborhood, from hitting him. Doubts that this device is really an umbrella could be assuaged by noting from its physical structure that it can fold and unfold; from its history that it was hanging on a stand that morning, and was originally made in a factory with others of a similar kind. (Chalmers 1996: 76)

When I try to 'determine' these higher-level facts, I find myself relying on visual imagining at every turn. 'Keep your mind's eye scrunched tight,' I am told. I can try, but then the higher-level facts go all mysterious. The feeling intensifies when I read how 'doubts that the device is an umbrella can be assuaged'. Never mind how they are assuaged; I do not see how the umbrella idea came up in the first place.

I realize how it's supposed to go. I start with objective, geometrical informa-tion. A chain of a priori inferences leads to 'it's shaped like an umbrella'. That conclusion combines with a host of others to establish its umbrella-hood beyond any doubt. Visualization is barred, so I have no idea of how the object looks. (Eventually it may strike me that since the object is an umbrella, it probably looks like one.)

Is this possible? It helps to look at a simpler case. I am to infer a plate's shape (it's in fact round) from premises about the arrangement of its microphysical parts. The premises might take various forms, but assume for definiteness that the arrangement is specified in analytic geometry terms. I am told that the object's teeny-tiny parts occupy the points (x, y) such that $x^2 + y^2 < 63$. (The plate is two-dimensional, no pun intended.) If I am to reason from this to the object's shape, I must know, implicitly at least, conditionals like the following:

if R is circumscribed by the points (x, y) such that $x^2 + y^2 = 63$, then R is round;
if R is circumscribed by the points (x, y) such that $x^4 + y^4 = 63$, then R is not round.

I should know many, many conditionals of this nature, one per lower-level implementation of roundness, and, I suppose, one per implementation of non-roundness. And, most important of all, I should know the conditionals a priori, just through my grasp of the relevant English words.

But, it isn't clear that I *do* know many conditionals like these. (I am tempted to say that it's clear that I don't.) And the few that I do know, I don't seem to know a priori. It wasn't learning the meaning of 'round' that taught me the formula for circles. I worked it out empirically by graphing the formula, *looking* at the figure I had just drawn, and then *reflecting* on how I was inclined to describe the figure. (I take it that no one has their first encounter with roundness in a geometry class.)

I do not say that the above shows that you *have* to peek. There may be other ways of proceeding that haven't occurred to me. All I mean to be claiming for now is that 'one can find the umbrellas in *w* without peeking, just by virtue of one's competence with the word' is a *substantive and surprising thesis*. Theses like this need to be argued for, and no argument has been given. A priori entailment has been presented as what you would expect, unless a skeptical philosopher had got to you first.

13 Recognitional Predicates

Now let me move on to urging in a positive way that there is only so much we can judge with the mind's eye averted. I think that one *can't* always tell, just by drawing inferences from a world description, whether the world is one where it turns out that S. If that is right, then the method that Chalmers didn't really mean to be advocating, and that figures only inadvertently in his narrative, is in some cases the only possible method. This will be argued for *observational* predicates (starting with the subtype *recognitional*), then *evaluative* predicates, then, finally, *theoretical* predicates.

What marks a predicate P as observational? The usual answer is that understanding P involves an ability to work out its extension in *perceptually* (as opposed to intellectually) presented scenarios. To determine P's extension in a world, I have to cast my gaze over that world—at candidate Ps in particular—and see how it strikes me.

Nothing has been said about the kind of appearance that marks a thing as P. Sometimes *x* is judged P because our experience of *x* has a quality Q notionally independent of P. So, *x* is tantalizing if, roughly, the experience of it makes one want to get closer and know more. Other times the experience that marks *x* as P is the experience of it as being precisely P. One judges *x* to be P because P is how it looks or feels or sounds . . . . This is what I am calling a *recognitional* predicate.

Examples are bound to be controversial, so let me just follow Kripke. Kripke says that 'the reference of "yellowness" is fixed by the description "that (manifest) property of objects which causes them, under normal circumstances, to be seen as yellow" ' (1980: 140 n. 71). We understand by yellowness whatever property it is that makes objects look yellow, or gives rise to the sensation of yellow. The predicate 'yellow' is recognitional on this view, since the yellow objects are picked out by their property of looking yellow.

Suppose Kripke is right about our understanding of 'yellow'. What are the implications for the way yellow things are identified in a candidate *w* for actuality? It's clear that *x* has to look yellow to be counted into the predicate's extension. But to whom? Perhaps it needs to look yellow to the *w*-folks, including one's counteractual self. If it is counteractual Steve's reactions that matter, then I don't need to experience x myself to determine if x is (in w) yellow. I can infer x's color a priori from what the relevant world description says about the experiences Steve has when experiencing x.

But what *does* the world description say about counteractual Steve's experiences? Suppose, first, that it describes them in intrinsic phenomenological terms; banana-caused visual experiences are said to have intrinsic phenomenological property K. This doesn't yet tell me whether bananas are yellow, for I don't know that K is the phenomenology appropriate to experiences of *yellow*. I can't determine that without giving myself a K-type experience and checking its content: do I feel myself to be having an experience of yellow or of green?

Suppose, on the other hand, that counteractual Steve's experiences are described intentionally, as 'experiences of yellow', 'yellow' being the predicate whose corresponding property we are trying to identify. Then we would seem to be caught in a circle. The referent of a compound expression depends on the referents of its parts. So any intelligence we might have about what it is to be an 'experience of yellow' must come from prior information about (among other things) what it is to be 'yellow'. But then the referent of each of these two phrases depends on that of the other. [10]

Kripke must have been aware of this problem. He notes that '[s]ome philosophers have argued that such terms as "sensation of yellow", "sensation of heat", . . . and the like, could not be in the language unless they were identifiable in terms of external observable phenomena, such as heat, yellowness'. And he says that 'this question is independent of any view argued in the text' (1980: 140 n. 71). Kripke doesn't mind, in other words, if one can't identify sensations of yellowness until one has identified the property they are sensations of. How, if that is so, can we hope to identify yellowness by way of sensations of yellow?

Here is what I think Kripke would say. Yellowness is identified not by a *condition* on experience ('such as to give rise to sensations of yellow'), but by the experience itself. The objects I call yellow are the ones that *look* yellow. If the yellow things were identified by an experiential *condition*, then we would face the problem of working out which experiences were of the indicated type. But that is not our situation. Far from being something in need of discovery, the experience of yellow is *part of the discovery process*. [11] I don't have to *identify* my

---

[10] One option is to say that yellowness and the sensation of it are identified together by means of a gigantic Ramsey-type theoretical definition. This is filed under the heading 'just a pipe dream until somebody supplies details'.

[11] The issue here is much like the one raised by Putnam's 'descriptivist' interpretation of the causal theory of reference. Putnam suggests that words have their reference fixed by a causal

yellow-experiences in order to learn by their exercise, any more than I have to identify my eyes in order to learn by use of them.[12]

There is a second reason why Kripke would (should) not take 'yellow' to have its reference fixed by an experience-implicating description. What will the description say about proper viewing conditions?

This is a problem that he himself raises for a related view: the view that 'yellow' is *defined* as 'tends to produce such and such visual impressions'. Tends to produce them under what circumstances, Kripke asks? Any answer will be unsatisfactory: 'the specification of the circumstances C either circularly involves yellowness or . . . makes the alleged definition into a scientific discovery rather than a synonymy' (1980: 140 n. 71). If C-type circumstances are circumstances where we are not deceived as to yellowness, then (while it may be analytic that *x* is yellow iff it looks yellow in C-type circumstances) the definition uses 'yellow', so cannot explain its meaning. If C-type circumstances are ones where (say) the light is of such-and-such a composition, no one is suffering from jaundice, the object is not a Benham's disk rotating at such-and-such a rate, etc., then, while it may be true that *x* is yellow iff it looks yellow in C-type circumstances, it is not definitionally true, but empirically so.

If this is a good objection to the idea that 'tends to . . . in circumstances C' defines 'yellow', it would seem to be equally hard on Kripke's own claim that 'yellow' has its reference fixed by that description. Either C-type circumstances are ones where we are not deceived as to yellowness, or they are ones where the light has such-and-such a composition, etc. If the first, then, while it may be a priori that *x* is yellow iff it looks yellow in C-type circumstances, the reference-fixer presupposes yellowness, and so cannot be used to identify it. If the second, then, while it may be true that *x* is yellow iff it looks yellow in C-type circumstances, it is not a priori true, as it would be if the description fixed 'yellow' 's reference.

---

condition. One finds the referent by looking for whatever stands in the right causal relation to speech. This makes for circularity problems, since one needs to know which relation causation is to work out what 'causation' denotes. From here it is a short step to radical indeterminacy of reference. The almost universal response was that reference is fixed *causally*, not *descriptively* by a condition alluding *inter alia* to causal relations. Kripke as I am reading him says something similar: reference is fixed experientally, not descriptively by a condition alluding *inter alia* to a certain sort of experience.

[12] I like what Colin McGinn says about perceptual concepts. Some think that 'When a concept is applied to a presented object that is always a further operation of the mind, superadded to the mere appearance of the object in perceptual consciousness. On my way of looking at it, concepts figure as *substitutes* for perceptual appearance—. . . they are needed for intentionality only when the object is not being perceived' (1999: 324).

One can reply in the same way as before. What marks a thing *x* as yellow isn't the *condition* 'tends to produce . . . under circumstances C'. What marks *x* as yellow is that that is how it looks. Someone can of course ask, how do you know the perceptual circumstances (including the condition of the perceiver) are right? But we do not say to this person, 'the present circumstances are of type C, and C defines rightness'. That would open us up to all the problems raised above. Our answer is, 'Why shouldn't they be right? What is it that leads you to suspect trouble?' It may not be a priori that what looks yellow under conditions C is yellow, but it does seem to be a priori that what looks yellow is yellow assuming nothing funny is happening. And that is an assumption we are always entitled to, unless and until we run into specific objections.

I hope this makes clear how our grasp of a predicate can be *recognitional* rather than intellectual. I do not reason my way to the conclusion that something is yellow from premises about what looks yellow under which conditions. The belief arises spontaneously in me when I look at a thing. That *has* to be how it works, for I have in general no a priori reliable information about which viewing conditions are appropriate. The most that is a priori is that *these* conditions are appropriate, unless there is reason to think otherwise.

If P is a recognitional predicate, then I have an a priori entitlement to '*These* conditions are (funny business aside) such that what seems P is P'. This is an entitlement that, by its nature, does not travel well. It lapses when we move from the world that really is actual to worlds only treated as actual for semantic evaluation purposes. For in lots of those worlds, we find (what from our actual–actual perspective is) funny business.

A few special cases aside, what looks yellow, is yellow. But things could have turned out so that whipped cream looked yellow—say, because a jaundice-like staining was characteristic of healthy eyes rather than diseased ones. This would not bother the people we turned out to be (they think *our* eyes are problematic), but it does bother us as we are. Whipped cream is white, and so whoever sees it as yellow is to that extent getting it wrong.

This has two semi-surprising consequences, which for now I'll just state without argument.

(1) Something known a priori need not hold in all counteractual worlds. It is a priori that funny business aside, what looks yellow, is yellow. But had our eyes turned out as described, objects would have turned out to look yellow that were in fact white. There is no mistake here, nor is anyone misled. Whipped cream is indeed what *they* mean by the word. It is just not what we mean by it, that is, it is not yellow.

(2) Something holding in all counteractual worlds might be knowable only a posteriori. Let F be a complete intrinsic characterization of some white chalk.[13] Could an F have turned out to be other than white? The chalk could have turned out yellow-*looking*, as already discussed. To have turned out *yellow*, however, it would have needed different (non-F-ish) intrinsic properties. So although it is a posteriori what color Fs in fact are, their color is conceptually necessary in the sense that it could not have turned out any different.

14 Observational Predicates

Everyone knows what it is for a figure to be *oval*. It is not hard to distinguish ovals from polygons, figure-eights, and so on. It is not even all that hard to distinguish ovals from otherwise ovular figures that are too skinny or too fat to count. To a first approximation, a figure is oval if it has the proportions of an egg, or a two-dimensional projection of an egg. I take it that few of us know in an intellectual way what those proportions are. What marks a figure as oval is not its satisfaction of some objective geometric condition, but the fact that when you look at it, it looks egg-shaped.[14]

Because our grasp of *oval* is constituted in part by how its instances look, one might be tempted to group it with 'response-dependent' concepts like *ticklish* or *tantalizing*. That would be a mistake. There are several respects in which *oval* is quite *un*like *ticklish*, which, once pointed out, make the label 'response-enabled' seem much more appropriate. Another term I shall use is 'grokking concept'. (I apply these labels to concepts, but, depending on one's other commitments, they could speak more to how the concept is grasped.)

Constitution: Why are ticklish things ticklish? That might mean 'what is the evidence that they are ticklish?' If so, the answer is that we respond to them in a certain way; they tickle us. If it means 'what qualifies them to be so regarded?', the answer has again to do with our responses. So far there is no contrast with *oval*. But suppose we now ask, 'in what does their ticklishness consist?' Eliciting or tending to elicit a certain reaction in us is 'what it is' to be ticklish. To be oval, though, is simply to have a certain shape.

---

[13] More may have to be packed into F, such as prevailing natural laws.

[14] I say *looks egg-shaped* and not *looks oval* because I want 'oval' to be an example of an observational predicate that is not recognitional.

Tracking: Our responses do not track the extension of 'ticklish'; they dictate it. It makes no sense to suggest that our tendency to be tickled by various things might not have been, or might have turned out not to be, a good guide to what is really ticklish. It is different with 'oval'. Our responses give us *access* to the extension of 'oval', but they do not dictate the extension.

Motivation: Why are the ticklish things picked out experientially? There is an in-principle reason for this: we want to classify as ticklish whatever is experienced in a certain way. Why are the oval things picked out experientially? There is no in-principle reason, but only a practical one: we have no other way of roping in the intended shapes.

Evaluation: Externalities are the same in *w* as here, but our responses are different. Suppose that our world had turned out to be *w*. What would have turned out to be ticklish? That which turned out to elicit the tickle response. What would have turned out to be oval? That which *does* elicit the oval response; that which *does* look egg-shaped. For dimes to have turned out oval, they would have had to turn out a different shape.

The 'evaluation' contrast is the one that matters, so let me dwell on it a little. Imagine someone who thinks that 'oval' applies to whatever strikes the locals as egg-shaped, in any *w* you like, considered as counteractual or counterfactual. This person has misunderstood the concept. If he were right about counterfactual worlds, then

> dimes would have been oval, had they (although still round) looked egg-shaped.

If he were right about counteractual worlds, then

> dimes would have turned out to be oval, had they (although still round) turned out to look egg-shaped.

This is false, too. The way to a thing's ovality is through its shape; you can't change the one except by changing the other. You can't make something oval by tinkering only with our responses.

What can we say to our confused friend to straighten him out? 'Oval' stands for things like *that*, the kind that we *do* see as shaped like eggs. The concept uses our responses as a tool—a tool that, like most tools, stops working if it's banged too far out of shape. The concept presupposes that our responses are what they are, and then leans on that presupposition in marking out the class of intended shapes. This is why its turning out that we saw dimes as egg-shaped would be a way for it to turn out (not that they were oval, but) that we were taking non-ovals for ovals.

A better analogy for our concept of oval is the concept expressed by 'that shape' when we say, pointing at a sculpture, that 'that shape is eerily familiar'—or the one expressed by '*this* big' in 'a room has to be at least *this* big [gesturing at the surrounding walls] to hold all my furniture'.[15] The role of '*this* big' is not to pick out whatever old size one might turn out to be perceiving: *tiny* if one turned out to have been in a tiny room suffering an optical illusion. It is, rather, that one takes oneself to be perceiving a room of a certain size, and one has no way of knowing the size other than via its perceptual appearance.

15 Analyticity without Apriority

First there are the response-*dependent* concepts: ticklish, aggravating, tantalizing, painful-to-behold. Then there are the response-*enabled* concepts: oval, aquiline, jagged, crunchy, smiley-faced. Response-enabled concepts have their own distinctive pattern of evaluation at counteractual worlds. If *oval* were response-dependent, then one could determine its extension in *w* by asking what the people there saw as egg-shaped.[16] If it is response-*enabled*, then those counteractual responses are irrelevant. Ovality is to be judged not by *as-if* actual observers, but by *actual* actual observers. A thing in *w* is oval if it is of a shape that would strike *me* as egg-shaped were I (with my sensibilities undisturbed) given a chance to look at it.

This has consequences for what comes out analytic, or conceptually necessary. Consider a world *w* about which all I'm going to tell you is that it contains Figure 1. Is 'oval' true of this figure in *w* considered as actual? The answer is clear. All we need do to determine that it is oval is look at the figure, and note that it looks *like that*—the way that ovals are supposed to look.

Once again, I have not said anything about how observers in *w* see Figure 1. Maybe there are no observers in *w*, or maybe there are, but they do not think Figure 1 has the right sort of look. It doesn't matter, for we evaluate the figure with respect to our word 'oval', understood as we understand it. Our dispositions figure crucially in that understanding, so they are part of what we (imaginatively) bring to bear on the figure in *w*.

Now let's bring in our conditional →, the conditional used to define conceptual necessity. Is it or is it not the case that *w obtains* → *Figure 1 is oval*? Would Figure 1 have turned out still to be oval, had it turned out to be shaped as shown? You bet it would. Whether an as-if actual figure is oval is completely

---

[15] Peacocke (1989).

[16] So-called rigidified response dependency is for our purposes a minor variant of the unrigidified kind.

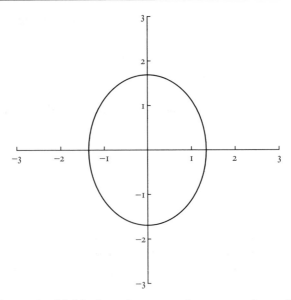

Fig. 1. Could this shape have turned out not to be oval?

determined by its shape. Things could have turned out so that Figure 1 did not look egg-shaped: we could have wound up with greater powers of visual discrimination, and as a result been 'bothered' by departures from an egg's precise shape that, as we are, we find it easy to ignore.[17] But Figure 1 would not in that case have turned out not to be oval. One wants to say, rather, that ovals would have turned out not to look the way they do look; ovals would have turned out to lack the feature by which things are recognized as ovals.[18]

Suppose we do some measurements and determine that Figure 1 is defined (up to congruence) by the equation $(x^2 + y^2)^2 - (x^2 - y^2) = 5$. Figures like that can be called *cassini*-shaped, or, for short, *cassinis*. (Giovanni Cassini (1625–1712) studied a class of figures of which this is one.[19]) 'Cassini-shaped' is an objective, third-personal predicate applying to all and only figures with

[17] Suppose for argument's sake that phenomenological similarity goes with the number of jnd's—just noticeable differences—separating one figure from another.

[18] I assume that the label 'oval' continues in the imagined case to be applied on the basis of egg-looking-ness. Does the fact that different things turn out to look that way make us (in that case) bad judges of ovality? Yes and no. Our counteractual responses are an excellent guide to what 'oval' would have turned out to mean. They are a bad guide, however, to what 'oval' does mean; they are a bad guide to what is in fact oval.

[19] The class of 'Cassinian ovals', although not all are really oval; indeed, not all are topologically connected.

the geometrical properties (that we all correctly take to be) exemplified by Figure 1.

Could things have turned out so that cassinis were not oval? If ovality in a world is purely a function of shape, then the answer is no. 'Cassinis are oval' is true in all worlds-taken-as-actual, which makes it (given our definition above) conceptually necessary.

But, of course, it is very far from a priori that cassinis are oval. To determine whether they are oval, you have to cast your eyes over (some of) them, and see how they look to you. There is no other way to do it. 'Cassinis are oval' is an analytic (conceptually necessary) truth that we are in no position to know a priori.

16 Other Intensions

If every world w is such that its cassinis are (to us) eggish-looking, then 'cassinis are oval' is analytic. Its meaning as encoded in our reactive dispositions guarantees its truth. But this is a kind of analyticity that we would not expect to make for apriority, because the route from understanding to extension and hence truth-value is inescapably observational.

To put it the other way around, one can't conclude from the fact that 'cassinis are oval' fails to be a priori that there is a counteractual world some of whose cassinis aren't oval. The premise you need for that is that 'cassinis are oval' is not *analytic*. But it *is* analytic. Given what the sentence means, it has got to be true.

Once again, the inference from (i) failure of apriority to (ii) a world that 'witnesses' the failure is crucial to modal rationalism. One might almost be forgiven for thinking that the main thing people *value* in the doctrine is its ability to deliver a counter-world. I assume, then, that modal rationalists would like, if possible, to *plug* the gap that seems to have opened up between analyticity (conceptual necessity) and apriority.

One approach harks back to the indicative account of truth in a counteractual world. For S to hold in counteractual w is, on that account, for it to be the case that if w obtains, then S. We rejected this account on the ground that it makes every sentence conceptually contingent. (If 'sibling' means parent, then sisters are *not* always siblings.) But, you may say, there is an obvious fix. It should be not merely true but a priori that if w obtains, then S. It is not a priori that if 'sibling' means parent, then sisters aren't always siblings. So a world where 'sibling' means parent is not on the new definition a world where the problematic sentence (some sisters are not siblings) holds.

Suppose we let S's *epistemic* intension be the set of worlds such that it's a priori that if *w* obtains, then S. And suppose that conceptual necessity is understood as necessity of the epistemic intension so defined. What happens to the argument above that conceptual necessity is a kind of analyticity but not a kind of apriority?

It might seem to fall apart. 'Cassinis are oval' may have a necessary primary intension, but its epistemic intension is contingent. (It is not generally a priori that if *w* obtains, then cassinis are oval; perhaps it is never a priori.) But then, if conceptual necessity goes with the epistemic intension, 'cassinis are oval' is not conceptually necessary. And so it no longer serves as a counter-example to the idea that whatever is conceptually necessary is a priori.

This assumes, however, that intensions built on a priori indicatives avoid the problems that were raised for intensions built on ordinary indicatives. Do they? What does seem clear is that the old examples no longer work. But this is for a correctable reason: namely, that sisters might, for all we know a priori, be one and all parents. It *is* a priori (let's assume) that sisters (if there are any) are not numbers. And so it is a priori too that if 'sibling' means number, then sisters (if there are any) are not siblings.

I have said that if 'sibling' means number, then sisters aren't siblings. Suppose that claim was based on empirical evidence. What would the evidence be? The only empirical fact in the neighborhood would seem to be this: 'sibling' does not in fact mean number. Call that the actual-meaning fact. Does it form part of my justification for believing that if 'sibling' means number, then sisters aren't siblings?

If it does form part of my justification, then should I *forget* 'sibling''s meaning, or come to hold an erroneous view of it, my justification would be compromised. Say I fall under the impression that 'sibling' does mean number. Have I now lost my grounds for thinking that *if* it means number, then sisters aren't siblings? Surely not. My reasons for thinking that *if 'sibling' means number, sisters are not siblings*, are just the same whether I believe the antecedent or not. How could forgetting what 'sibling' *does* mean compromise my ability to make inferences from a certain *hypothesis* about its meaning?[20]

---

[20] This is intuitive on its face, but it can also be argued for in the following way. It's agreed that I know that *if 'sibling' means number, then sisters aren't siblings*. The question is whether my justification is a posteriori, because based on the actual-meaning fact. If it is, then I lack the knowledge we've just agreed I have. Here is why. You are not said to know that *if A, then B* unless you know something from which B can be inferred, should it be discovered that A. Your justification for the conditional should therefore be 'robust' with respect to A: it should be such as to *stay in place* should one come to believe that A. (See Jackson 1979.) Your justification would not be robust if the conditional were based on ¬A. Conclusion: you don't know that *if A, then B* if your belief is

Where does this leave us? If my belief in the conditional is a priori, then there is a world that is not in the epistemic intension of 'sisters have siblings.' The same argument shows that *no* statement S, however a priori in appearance, has a necessary epistemic intension. I conclude that the a priori indicative strategy is no great advance over the plain indicative strategy. Both have the same basic problem: they make all intensions contingent, and so drain the class of conceptual necessities of all its members.

It might be held that the problem is not with the aprioritizing as such, but with the type of conditional aprioritized. A second option is to call S true in *w*-considered-as-actual iff it holds a priori that (*w* obtains → S)—it holds a priori that it would have turned out that S, had *w* turned out to be actual. The intensions that result can be called *priory* intensions. If conceptual necessity is necessity of the priory intension, maybe the inference to a counter-world can be saved. Certainly it isn't refuted by the cassini example; for although 'cassinis are oval' has a necessary primary intension, its priory intension is *not* necessary. (You need experience to establish that, had it turned out that *w*, it would have turned out that cassinis are oval.)

The priory intension is more than unnecessary, however. One can *never* tell a priori whether cassinis would have turned out to be oval, had it turned out that *w*. (I ignore the case where there are no cassinis.) 'Cassinis are oval' has, therefore, *nothing* in its priory intension. The same goes for 'cassinis are not oval'. It goes in fact for most sentences whose predicates express response-enabled concepts. If one can't determine a priori whether a counteractual object is P, then that object can't be put into P's priory intension, or ¬P's either. If the priory intensions of P and its negation are empty, then so in all likelihood are the priory intensions of sentences built on P.

Concepts like *oval* are not well-represented by their priory intensions. Still, you might say, why should that matter? The point of priory intensions is to predict epistemic status: if S fails to be a priori, there should be a world that is not in its priory intension. Why should the modal rationalist want any more?

One can see why more is wanted by considering the modal rationalist's refutation of physicalism. How does that argument go, with intensions understood as priory? First premise: it is not a priori that if PHYSICS, then PAIN. Second premise: if it is not a priori that if PHYSICS, then PAIN, then there are worlds that are not in that conditional's priory intension. Third premise: worlds not in

---

based on the premise that ¬A. Since I do know that *if 'sibling' means number, then sisters are not siblings*, my belief is not based on the premise that 'sibling' does not mean number. But that is just to say that my belief is not based on the actual-meaning fact. If it is not based on that, then it is not based on any empirical evidence.

that priory intension are zombie worlds—worlds physically like ours in which no one feels pain. Conclusion: there are zombie worlds.

The argument needs priory intensions to be like primary intensions in a certain respect. If PIs are primary intensions, then worlds that are not in a sentence's PI are worlds in which S is false. Does the same hold for priory intensions? It doesn't. If PIs are priory intensions, all we can say is that there is a *w* such that it *fails to be a priori that* it would have turned out that S, had it turned out that *w*. It might still be *true* that it would have turned out that S! There might be no way for it to turn out that PHYSICS without its also turning out that PAIN.

I present this as a problem for priory intensions, but epistemic intensions are every bit as vulnerable to it. That there are worlds lying outside S's epistemic intension does not show that there are worlds in which S is false, but only that you can't always get to S a priori. (The response will come that that is enough, since any S which cannot be verified by a priori means can be falsified by a priori means. But we have examples to the contrary, such as 'this equation describes an oval'.) I don't think that anything is gained, then, by switching to an aprioritized notion of truth at a world. The balloon just bulges in a different place. Yes, there is a world outside the intension, but there is no reason to think that it falsifies S, as opposed to just failing to a priori verify it. Better to stick with primary intensions as defined above. S is conceptually necessary iff it holds however things turn out.

17 Grasping Meaning

Why expect an analytic (conceptually necessary) sentence to be knowable a priori? Why expect a sentence whose meaning guarantees that it is true to have the further property that we can *see* that the sentence is true just from our grasp of its meaning? There might be ways of grasping meaning that do not tell us outright whether S is true if *w*, but only how to *work out* whether S is true if *w*. If S's meaning is grasped like that, then its not being a priori that S does not establish the existence of a falsifying world. The sentence might be (like 'this equation describes an oval') a posteriori but true in every world considered as actual.

The only way out is to maintain that the indicated kind of grasp is not possible. One will have to maintain that grasp of meaning always takes a certain form, a form that discloses to the grasper whether the meaning is truth-guaranteeing. If all I can do is *work out* whether $w \rightarrow S$, then I don't understand S. To understand, I have to *know* that $w \rightarrow S$.

Say that my understanding of S is *rationalistic* if it consists in whole or part of my *knowing* the conditionals. The road from analyticity to apriority would be a lot smoother if all understanding was rationalistic.

On what basis, though, can other forms of understanding be ruled out? What is the problem with grasping a word's meaning other than rational-istically? The closest thing I've found to an explicit discussion is Chalmers's reply to Loar in *The Conscious Mind* (1996).

Summarizing greatly, Loar (1990) thinks that *pain* is a recognitional concept[21] and that *C-fiber firings* is a theoretical concept, and that that is enough to make them cognitively distinct. Their distinctness notwithstanding, 'it is reasonable to expect a recognitional concept R to "introduce" the same property as a theoretical [concept] P.' So we cannot conclude from the non-apriority of 'C-fiber firings are pains' that C-fiber firings aren't pains. The failure of apriority might be because *pain* is recognitional and *C-fiber firings* isn't. If their a priori inequivalence is explained thus, then there is nothing to stop them from co-referring. These are fine things to claim, Chalmers says, but it is not clear that they can all be reconciled.

[Loar] gives the example of someone who is able to recognize certain cacti in the California desert without having theoretical knowledge about them. But this seems wrong: if the subject cannot know that R is P a priori, then reference to R and P is fixed in different ways and the reference-fixing intensions can come apart in certain conceivable situations. (Chalmers 1996: 373)

This might seem to be based on a misunderstanding. Observational con-cepts (of which recognitional concepts are a subtype) do not have their refer-ence fixed in *any* epistemically available way; hence they do not have it fixed in a different way than holds for theoretical concepts.

What can Chalmers be thinking, then? He knows that Loar *says* that 'recognitional concepts refer "directly"' . . . without the aid of reference-fixing properties' (1996: 373). He just thinks Loar is wrong about this. 'The very fact that a concept *could* refer to something else (a different set of cacti, say) shows that a substantial primary intension is involved' (1996: 373).

But, Loar can concede a substantial primary intension. The directness he is talking about is *epistemic*; one doesn't (and couldn't) *infer* that the cactus is R from its lower-level properties. A substantial primary intension is at odds only with *semantic* directness, as I now explain.

Fact: R applies to these things and not those. Why? What explains the dif-ferential treatment? If the question has an answer, as let's assume it does, it will

---

[21] This section is sloppy about recognitional versus observational, and also about Loar-recognitional versus recognitional in our sense.

be a truth of the form: R applies to x if and only if x is so-and-so. Consider this property of being so-and-so. It might be considered a reference-fixer for R; like a reference-fixer, it tells you how a thing has to be for R to refer to it. *Oval* too has a reference-fixer in this sense. Whether a figure is oval is not a brute fact about it, but depends on its shape.

A reference-fixer in the *theoretical* sense is a statement of the qualifications for being referred to by R, as these might be judged by a (smart enough) semantic theorist. A reference-fixer in the *ordinary* sense, though, is a statement of the qualifications for being referred to by R, as these might be explained by a (smart enough) user of the concept, trying to enumerate the factors she takes to make R applicable.

The claim about recognitional concepts is that they lack *ordinary* reference-fixers. Speakers do not apply *oval* on the basis of a condition that they know (even implicitly) that sums up the requisite features. Speakers do not know any conditions like that. They do not know any conditions that get the extension right no matter what. The condition that comes closest is *looks egg-shaped*. But, as we have seen, things could have turned out so that some *bona fide* oval had the wrong looks, and/or a non-oval had the right looks. I know an oval when I see one, and that seems to be enough.

Chalmers is right about one thing: it would be a mistake to deny recognitional concepts reference-fixers in the theoretical sense. That would be to deny that a thing's status as *oval* was a function of its lower-level properties. But if the claim is that recognitional concepts lack reference-fixers in the ordinary sense, then it would seem to be true. Speakers don't (and often can't) determine extensions a priori by asking what has the R-making properties.

How does all this bear on the issue that Loar and Chalmers are primarily interested in: the issue of physicalism? Chalmers, you will recall, argues as follows. It is not a priori that if PHYSICS, then PAIN; so the primary intension cannot contain every world; so there are worlds physically like this one in which pain is lacking; so physicalism is false.

The problem is (once again) with the inference from *not a priori* to *less than full primary intension*. With certain concepts the link between apriority and primary necessity breaks down. And the way it breaks down gives the physicalist an opening. She can say this: *Pain* (like *oval*) is a grokking, or observational, concept. That being so, whether an objectively described state is a case of pain cannot be determined just by rational reflection. One has to 'sample' the state by experiencing it from the right sort of first-personal perspective.

Two consequences should be noted. First, suppose there were a world w physically like ours but without pain. That world would do nothing to explain the non-apriority of 'if PHYSICS, then PAIN'; or rather, it would do nothing that couldn't be done just as well by a world *with* pain. For *w* to help, our intuition of non-apriority would have to be owing to our awareness of *w*. But the relevant fact about *w* (that it lacks pain) is not available to us as students of its microphysical description. Just as you can't tell whether *w* has ovals except by sampling its shapes, so you can't tell whether it has pain except by sampling its brain states.

Second, not only is a world like *w* of no particular help in explaining the failure of apriority, it isn't needed. Suppose that *v* is a world just like ours in every physical respect. The question of whether there is (say) pain in *v* is the question of whether there is anything there that *hurts* if sampled in the right sort of first-personal way. Whether a state hurts when sampled by someone in the state is not the kind of thing that can be decided from the armchair. If we are trying to explain why PHYSICS doesn't a priori entail PAIN, a world whose zombie-ness can't be a priori ruled out works just as well as a true zombie world would.

18 Evaluative Predicates

Our grasp of a concept is *rationalistic* if it consists in whole or in part of a certain kind of knowledge: knowledge of conditionals of the form *w* obtains → *x, y, z, . . . are the Cs*. Suppose that your conditionals put *x, y, z, . . .* into a concept's extension in *w*, while mine count *x, y, z, . . .* out. Then, by Leibniz's Law, your concept and mine are not the same. A single concept cannot have conflicting extensions in the same world.

Now, in some cases, it seems quite right that disagreements about what goes into the extension should make for differences in the identity of the concept. If you and I can't agree about whether to call a certain almost-round figure oval, and this is not because of misinformation, error, or oversight on either side, then probably we have different concepts; probably we mean slightly different things by the word. There is no question of trying to work out who is really correct, because our beliefs are not really in conflict.

Similarly, if we can't agree about whether recently widowed 98-year-old males are bachelors, and not because either of us is misinformed or confused, then probably we mean slightly different things by 'bachelor'. There is no question of trying to work out who is really right, because we aren't really disagreeing.

A phrase sometimes used for concepts of this kind is *intolerant of brute disagreement*; if we have the same concept, we should not 'brutely disagree' about what falls under it. Are all concepts like that? Imagine that we disagree about whether it was wrong of Smith to tell a lie in hopes of saving his child embarrassment. The disagreement can't be traced back to differences in factual information, or miscalculation or oversight on either side. Does this show that we mean different things by 'wrong'?

The usual view is that it doesn't. People who disagree about the extension of 'wrong' (and where the disagreement does not trace back to . . .) do not necessarily mean different things by the word. Likewise for disputes about what is beautiful or fitting or reasonable. You will get people angry if you brand these disputes 'merely verbal', just because you can't see any good way to bring the two parties into line. Some concepts, then, are *tolerant of brute disagreement*.

A lot of philosophers would claim something even stronger. So far is the meaning of 'right' from dictating a particular view of its extension that it positively *rejects* the notion that such dictation is possible. If I try to represent your side of a moral controversy as based in a misunderstanding of 'right', then I am the one who misunderstands. Questions of rightness are supposed to be *contestable* in the (rather minimal) sense that someone who brutely disagrees with you can't be charged on that basis alone with meaning something different by 'right'. Some concepts, then, seem to be *intolerant of intolerance of brute disagreement*.

How do we grasp the meaning of 'right'? If our grasp is rationalistic, then (assuming we mean the same by 'right') all of us know the same conditionals *w obtains* → *x, y, z, . . . are right and other things aren't*. Someone operating with different conditionals attaches a different meaning to the word. In that case, though, the concept is intolerant of brute disagreement. And our concept of rightness is, on the contrary, intolerant of such intolerance.

That is one argument for the conclusion that we do not grasp evaluative concepts in a purely rationalistic way. Here is another. Recall a well-known puzzle about right and wrong. On the one hand, you can't derive an ought from an is. 'If N then M', where N is descriptive and M is evaluative, cannot be known a priori. On the other hand, it does seem to be a priori that the evaluative facts are fixed by the descriptive ones. There is a tension here; we have trouble seeing how the two claims are supposed to hang together. But we do not get an outright contradiction unless it is supposed that our grasp of evaluative concepts is rationalistic.

Assume with the rationalist that if it is not a priori that S, then there's a counteractual w such that ¬S. Then, from the fact that N does not a priori entail M, we can infer the existence of a u such that *u obtains* → *(N & ¬M)*. Since it's also not a priori that if N, then ¬M, there should be a world v such that v → (N & M). But if N is descriptively complete (as we are free to suppose), then these two worlds taken together constitute a counter-example to the thesis that there can be no moral differences without underlying descriptive differences.

It could be objected that all *u* and *v* *directly* show is that things could have turned out so that N & M, and they could have turned out so that N & ¬M. To get to ◊ (N & M) and ◊ (N & ¬M), one needs to assume that M does not change in broad content between *u* and *v*. But that is a fair assumption, for the facts relevant to reference determination are descriptive facts, and these are the same in both worlds. Hence we can argue as follows:

(1) It is not a priori that if N, then M, or that if N, then ¬M.
(2) If it is not a priori that S, then there's a *w* such that *w* → ¬S.
(3) There are *u* and *v* such that *u* → *(N & ¬M)* and *v* → *(N & M)*.
(4) M does not change in broad content between *u* and *v*.
(5) ◊ (N & M) and ◊ (N & ¬M).

But (5) is an a priori falsehood. Somewhere or other a big meta-ethical mistake has been made.

I claim that the puzzle has nothing essentially to do with ethics. Consider the conditionals, 'if *x* is cassini-shaped, then it is oval', and 'if *x* is cassini-shaped, then it is not oval'. Neither is knowable a priori. Shouldn't there then be a pair of worlds *u*, *v*, exactly the same in geometrical respects but such that *u* → *cassinis are oval*, while *v* → *cassinis are not oval*? These worlds threaten to show that there can be differences in respect of ovality without underlying geometrical differences.

Where the ovality argument goes wrong is easy to see. The problem is (2). You can't get a world where cassinis are not oval out of the fact that it's not a priori that they are oval. If our grasp of ovality were purely rationalistic, then the failure of apriority *would* call for a counter-world. But it isn't, so it doesn't.

The morality puzzle can be pinned on the same mistake. You can't get a world where N and ¬M out of the fact that it's not a priori that if N, then M. It would be different if our grasp of rightness were rationalistic; then we would have a genuine paradox on our hands. I conclude that it isn't rationalistic. A similar argument can be given for other evaluative concepts. None, I claim, are grasped rationalistically. None are grasped in what modal rationalists consider to be the one way in which a concept can be grasped.

19 Theoretical Predicates

Consider, finally, theoretical predicates: acid, energy, force, mass, species, cause, mereological sum, essential nature. What can be said about our understanding of these? Do we understand 'energy' by knowing a lot of conditionals of the form 'had it turned out that *w*, such-and-such would have turned out to be the energy'?

Here are two arguments to the contrary, both harking back to the discussion of evaluative predicates. Suppose that we *do* (*qua* understanders of 'energy', etc.) know all these conditionals—that our concept of energy not only fixes, for each possible scenario, but discloses to us, for each of these scenarios, where the energy is to be found. How is it, then, that you and I continue to disagree about where the energy is to be found? (You say there is energy stored up in the curvature of space, while I deny it.) After all, there is a conditional known to both of us (as understanders of 'energy') that decides the matter. The explanation must lie in one of two places. It must be that

(i)   someone is misconstruing the lower-level facts, and so picking the wrong conditional,

or:

(ii)   someone is misconstruing their own mental states, specifically, the belief with that conditional as its content.

Whichever of these applies, our disagreement has the character of a misunderstanding. One or the other of us is laboring under a misimpression, and will (or should) change his or her tune when the mistake is pointed out. Of course, there is always the possibility that we associate *different* conditionals with 'energy'. In that case, though, we are not disagreeing at all; we mean different things by the word, so are talking past each other. None of the three scenarios allows for substantive disputes. Someone has made a mistake of type (i) or (ii), or else we are arguing over words.

This is almost as hard to accept here as it was in the evaluative case. Some disagreements *are* merely verbal, and some are based in correctable false impressions. The usual view, though, is that there's a third category: honest-to-God conflicts about what it is reasonable to believe, between people in command of the same lower-level facts. The effect of the rationalistic theory of grasp is to eliminate this third category.

The extension of 'energy' in a world is a function of what the correct scientific theory is. To find that theory, one must appeal at some point to considerations of naturalness, simplicity, nonarbitrariness, and the like—in a word, to considerations of *reasonableness*. (The positivists were the last to seriously question this.) Reasonableness is an evaluative concept and, as such, response-enabled. You can't hand responsibility over to 'rules of reasonableness'; there are no such rules, or at any rate not enough of them. You have to let yourself be led to some extent by your gut.

There are places where Chalmers sounds this theme himself. Figuring a concept's extension, he says, is not just grinding out conclusions. Judgment and discretion may be called for:

the decision about what a concept refers to in the actual world [may] involve[ ] a large amount of reflection about what is the most reasonable thing to say; as, for example, with questions about the reference of 'mass' when the actual world turned out to be one in which general relativity is true, or perhaps with questions about what qualifies as 'belief' in the actual world. Consideration of just what the primary intension picks out in various actual-world candidates may involve a corresponding amount of reflection. But this is not to say that the matter is not a priori: we have the ability to engage in this reasoning independently of how the world turns out. (1996: 58)

I suppose that we do have this ability. We can ask ourselves what is the most reasonable thing to say on various hypotheses about how the world turns out. It is not clear, though, how that argues for the matter's being a priori. We can also ask ourselves where the ovals are on various hypotheses about how the world turns out. Our conclusions in the second case aren't a priori, so why should they be a priori in the first?

If the oval example shows anything, it's that the move from 'we can tell independently of how things turn out' to 'we can tell a priori' is a *non sequitur*. For 'we can tell independently' may just mean that we can stage simulated confrontations with nature on various hypotheses about the form nature takes. It may not be obvious that searchers after the most reasonable hypothesis are doing this. But it seems to me that they are. Judgments of reasonableness and plausibility are arrived at by exercising a type of sensibility.

To be sure, the sensibility involved is not a perceptual one. And there seems less cause for worry about simulated plausibility judgments being a bad guide to real such judgments.[22] But the fact that sensibility is required should still give pause. It means that if you and I disagree about a sentence's truth-value in *w*, there may be no more we can say to each other than 'I find your position unreasonable'. The claim that everything but consciousness is a priori entailed by physics thus comes down to this: if two people disagree about a sentence's truth-value in *w*, each will find his or her own position to be the more reasonable one, unless the sentence is about consciousness, in which case each side concedes the rational defensibility of the other. Even if this were true, it is hard

---

[22] The moral case is arguably intermediate in these respects. Sensitivity to the moral aspects of things has often been likened to good vision or a keen sense of smell. And our horror at an observed case of, say, euthanasia or abortion may catch us by surprise, given our approving reaction to the imagined case. (Why else would right-to-lifers work so hard at getting us to *look* at what is being done?)

to see an argument for metaphysical dualism in it. And it is not true; the zombie hypothesis is *much less reasonable* than the hypothesis that what people seem to be feeling, they are feeling.

20 Logical Empiricism and Modal Rationalism

There were two dogmas of empiricism. One was the analytic/synthetic distinction. The other was 'semantic reductionism'—the idea that each statement is linked by fixed correspondence rules to a determinate range of confirming observations. Quine held that the two dogmas are 'at bottom the same'. For the correspondence rules are in a sense analytic. They give the sentence its meaning, so cannot fail as long as that meaning holds fixed. The dogmas are at least notionally different, though, and my focus will be on the second: the conception of correspondence rules as analytic, and therefore a priori. Although I will follow Quine in speaking mostly of analyticity, it is the apriority that is my real concern.

How is a modal rationalist like a logical empiricist? They seem initially very different. The empiricist has analytic correspondence rules connecting theory to experience. Modal rationalists aren't proposing anything like *that*. Yes, people have to be able to tell a priori whether S is true in a presented world. Gone, though, is any thought of that world being presented *in experiential terms*. There is no case, then, for a charge of *phenomenalistic* reductionism.

If one looks, though, at Carnap's writings on protocol sentences, it turns out that his sort of reductionism did not have to be terribly experiential either. Under the influence of Neurath, Carnap thinks that it is somewhat of an open question which sentences ought to be counted as protocols. Sometimes a protocol sentence is said to be any sentence 'belonging to the physicalistic system-language' which we are prepared to accept without further tests.[23] Often it is said to be a matter of *convention* which sentences will count as protocols. The important point for us is that Carnap thinks there are a priori rules connecting theoretical statements with protocols, whatever protocols turn out to be.

Another seeming difference emerges from Quine's complaint that Carnap overlooks the 'holistic nature of confirmation'. The complaint might be understood like this: One never knows whether S is really correct until all the observational evidence is in. Hence any rules portraying S as verifiable on the basis of limited courses of experience—courses of experience small enough to be enjoyable by particular observers—would be untrue to the way in which confirmation actually works.

[23] Ayer (1959: 237).

This complaint the rationalist can rightly claim to have answered. He never represents *partial* information as enough to ensure that S; the rules he contemplates take as input *complete* information:

[Quine says that] purported conceptual truths are always subject to revision in the face of sufficient empirical evidence. For instance, if evidence forces us to revise various background statements in a theory it is possible that a statement that once appeared to be conceptually true might turn out to be false.

This is so for many purported conceptual truths, but it does not apply to the supervenience conditionals that we are considering, which have the form 'If the low-level facts turn out like this, then the high-level facts will be like that.' The facts specified in the antecedent of this conditional effectively include all relevant empirical factors. . . . The very comprehensiveness of the antecedent ensures that empirical evidence is irrelevant to the conditional's truth-value. (Chalmers 1996: 55)

This is a good answer as far as it goes. But there are aspects of Quine's critique that it does not address. Quine says that

the dogma of reductionism survives in the supposition that each statement, taken in isolation from its fellows, can admit of confirmation or infirmation at all. My countersuggestion, issuing essentially from Carnap's doctrine of the physical world in the Aufbau, is that our statements about the external world face the tribunal of sense experience not individually but only as a corporate body. (1951: 41 in rpt.)

The problem here is not that S's confirmational status is underdetermined until all the empirical evidence is in. The problem is that S's confirmational status is not fully determined even by the full corpus E of empirical evidence. The degree to which E confirms S, Quine thinks, is tied up with the extent to which E or aspects of E are deducible from S. But nothing of an observational nature is deducible from S except with the help of a background theory T. Hence the degree of support that E lends to S depends on which background theory we use.

This complaint would be easily evadable if there were an analytically guaranteed fact of the matter about which theory E selects for. One could simply ask whether E supports S relative to the E-preferred theory, whatever it might be.

One has to assume, then, that this is what Quine is really concerned to deny. He denies that there are analytic connections between total corpuses E of empirical evidence and theories T of nature. Without these, there can be no analytic connections between E and particular statements S. A number of things suggest that analytic confirmation relations are indeed the target:

I am impressed, apart from prefabricated examples of black and white balls in an urn, with how baffling the problem has always been of arriving at any explicit theory of the empirical confirmation of a synthetic statement. (Quine 1951: 49 in rpt.)

This could be taken to mean just that the sought-after theory of confirmation would have to be very complicated. But Quine has something different in mind. He is aware, after all, of Carnap's attempts to work out a logic of confirmation which would tell us what to believe on the basis of given evidence. He is aware, too, that the attempt failed even for the simplest sort of examples. Carnap came up with a whole array of confirmation functions, none of them looking a priori better than the rest.

Where does this leave us? One problem with analytic confirmation relations concerns total evidence. This the rationalist has addressed. But there's a second problem: 'total science, mathematical and natural and human, is underdetermined by experience' (Quine 1951: 45 in rpt.). The version of underdetermination Quine needs is really a rather mild one. He needn't deny that there is an objectively best theory relative to a given body of evidence. He needn't even deny that there's a single most rational theory to adopt. All he need claim is that the choice between theories compatible with the evidence cannot be based just on our grasp of meaning. It 'turns on our vaguely pragmatic inclination to adjust one strand of the fabric of science rather than another. Conservatism figures in such choices, and so does the quest for simplicity'. (Quine 1951: 49 in rpt.).

This can be reconciled with the analytic view of confirmation relations only by supposing that my grasp of the language tells me how conservative I should be, and how important simplicity is, and how these sorts of desiderata trade off against one another. If two scientists judged the trade-offs differently, at most one could be considered to be speaking correctly—that is, in accordance with the meanings of her words. That, however, is not how the science game is played.

The interesting thing is that Carnap *agrees* that it's not how the science game is played. His goal, as he usually describes it, is not to uncover the true nature of meaning, but to give us tools for making our discursive practice more rational and efficient. He thinks that disputants should pick a common framework and then resolve their disagreements by reference to its assertion rules:

it is preferable to formulate the principle of empiricism not in the form of an assertion . . . but rather in the form of a proposal or requirement. As empiricists we require the language of science to be restricted in a certain way. (Carnap 1936–7: sect. 27)

Based on passages like this, one recent commentator has summarized the view as follows:

Criticisms of the meaning/belief distinction rest on the lack of a principled criterion for [semanticality]—no empirical method can be found for making it. However, for

Carnap, such a distinction is to be reached by agreement in a conflict situation. Maximize agreement on framework issues and situate disagreement on either empirically answerable problems or on questions of a pragmatic nature about the framework. (O'Grady 1999: 1026)

One can argue about whether this would really be helpful. All I am saying right now is that not even Carnap believes that it is how we really operate: that our actual practice lends itself to a distinction between semantic factors in assertion and doxastic ones.

Is there anyone who does believe that this is how we operate? The modal rationalist does, or at least, such a view is not far from the surface. We are told that grasp of S's meaning, or at least the kind of grasp you need to count as understanding S, is knowing which worlds w are such that had this turned out to be w, it would have turned out that S. This applies not just to observation-level statements, but to theoretical statements as well. It is part and parcel of knowing T's meaning to know what the world would have had to be like for it to be the case that T. And that is not obviously different from Carnap's idea of analytic confirmation rules.

I say 'not obviously different', because there may be room for maneuver on the issue of what is involved in 'knowing which worlds are S-worlds'. I have been assuming that worlds are given in 'lower-level' terms, whatever exactly that might mean. What if worlds are described more fully than that, perhaps as fully as possible? There would be no need to infer that theory T applied; it would be given that it applied in the world's initial presentation. This seems tantamount to saying that one knows the S-worlds as, well, the S-worlds, or the worlds such that if they turned out actual, it would turn out that S.

But, if a 'homophonic' grasp of the set of verifying worlds were all one needed, then there would be no reason to expect a sentence to be knowable a priori just because its primary intension contained all worlds.

This is clear from Chalmers's discussion of physicalism. Consider again the conditional 'if PHYSICS, then PAIN'. It is claimed that the only way for this to be non-a priori is for there to be worlds not in its primary intension: there have got to be zombie worlds. If our grasp of primary intensions was homophonic, the failure of apriority would present no puzzle, hence no puzzle to which zombie-worlds might be offered as a solution. The reason I don't know a priori that if PHYSICS, then PAIN is that I can't tell a priori whether the primary intension of 'if PHYSICS, then PAIN' contains all worlds. I can't tell that because I can't tell a priori whether the PHYSICS worlds are a subset of the PAIN worlds. If they are a subset, there is no puzzle as to why the understander doesn't realize it, because it is assumed from the outset that PHYSICS worlds are, for all she knows a priori, worlds without PAIN.

How, then, are worlds presented to the meaning-grasper? She must be able to pick out the S-worlds on the basis of their ground-level properties. 'If the low-level facts turn out like this, then the high-level facts will be like that' (Chalmers 1996: 55). These conditionals are thought to be analytic; indeed, they are true in virtue of the aspect of meaning to which we have a priori access. This is why I say that modal rationalists are committed to something *like* the analytic confirmation relations advocated by Carnap and rejected by Quine. The rationalist who wants to escape Quine's criticisms has got to (a) show that the criticisms don't work even against logical empiricism; (b) show that the cases are relevantly different.

To accomplish (a) would be to find a mistake in Quine's reasoning. Maybe, for example, it's just untrue that theory is underdetermined by evidence. To accomplish (b) would be to show that what the modal rationalist says is different enough from what the logical empiricist says that the Quinean critique doesn't generalize. Maybe, for example, the lower-level facts on the basis of which we can tell a priori whether S are quite unlike the 'empirical' facts on the basis of which we can't tell a priori whether S. I won't pursue the matter any further here, but I suspect that the prospects for doing either of these things are not terribly good.

21 Digression: Imaginative Resistance

Hume, in 'The Standard of Taste', points out something surprising about our reactions to imagined circumstances. Reading a story according to which S, I try to imagine myself in a situation where S really holds. The surprising thing is that we can do this quite easily if S is contrary to *descriptive* fact, but have a great deal of trouble if S is contrary to *evaluative* fact. Reading that Franco drank from the Fountain of Youth and was made young again, you don't blink twice. But reading that it was good that little Billy was starved to death since he had, after all, forgotten to feed the dog, you want to say, 'it was *not* good, I won't go along.'

Call that *imaginative resistance*.[24] Why does it happen? A number of explanations have been tried. Do we resist because what we're asked to imagine is conceptually false? No, because (i) counter-moral hypotheses are *not* conceptually false (remember essential contestability), and (ii) lots of conceptually false scenarios are *not* resisted (as readers of Calvino and Borges will attest).

---

[24] On imaginative resistance, see Gendler (2000), Moran (1989), and Walton (1994).

Do we resist because what we're asked to imagine is morally repugnant? No, because we balk at aesthetic misinformation as well. 'All eyes were on the twin Chevy 4 × 4's as they pushed purposefully through the mud. Expectations were high; last year's blood bath death match of doom had been exhilarating and profound, and this year's promised to be even better. The crowd went quiet as special musical guests ZZ Top began to lay down their sonorous rhythms. The scene was marred only by the awkwardly setting sun.' Reading this, one thinks, 'If the author wants to stage a monster truck rally at sunset, that's up to her. But the sunset's aesthetic properties are not up to her; nor are we willing to take her word for it that last year's blood bath death match of doom was a thing of beauty.'[25]

Do we resist because the scenario is repugnant along *some evaluative dimension or other*? No, because it is not only evaluative suggestions that are resisted. You open a children's book and read as follows: 'They flopped down beneath the great maple. One more item to find, and yet the game seemed lost. Hang on, Sally said. It's staring us in the face. This is a *maple* tree we're under. She grabbed a five-fingered leaf. Here was the oval they needed! They ran off to claim their prize.' Reading this one thinks, 'If the author wants it to be a maple leaf, that's her prerogative. But the leaf's physical properties having been settled, whether it is oval is not up to her. She can, perhaps, arrange for it not to have the expected mapley shape. But if it does have the expected shape, then there is not a whole lot she can do to get us to imagine it as oval.'

Imaginative resistance arises not only with evaluative predicates, but also with (certain) descriptive ones: 'oval', 'aquiline', 'jagged', 'smooth', 'lilting'. What do these predicates have in common? P makes for imaginative resistance if, and because, the concept it expresses is of the type I have called 'grokking', or response-enabled.[26]

Why should resistance and grokkingness be connected in this way? It's a feature of grokking concepts that their extension in a situation depends on how the situation does or would strike us.[27] 'Does or would strike us' *as we are*: how we are represented as reacting, or invited to react, has nothing to do with it. Resistance is the natural consequence. If we insist on judging the extension ourselves, it stands to reason that any seeming intelligence coming from elsewhere is automatically suspect. This applies in particular to being 'told' about the extension by an as-if knowledgeable narrator.

---

[25] She knows this, moreover. Why make a suggestion you know will not be accepted? There might be any number of reasons, but most likely she is just pulling our leg.

[26] [For an alternative diagnosis of this phenomenon, see Currie, Ch. 4 above—eds.]

[27] I assume that fictional situations are presented as counteractual, not counterfactual. One is to think of them as really happening.

22 (Conceptually) Contingent A Priori

I have called a lot of claims a priori. But not much has been done to explicate the notion; the focus has been more on conceptual necessity. I doubt that it is possible to explain apriority in all its guises with the materials at hand. But I'll try in the next few sections to clarify a particular type of apriority as far as I can. (Nothing argued so far depends on what is coming next.)

'Water contains hydrogen' is touted in *Naming and Necessity* as an example of an a posteriori metaphysical necessity. 'Cassinis are oval' has been touted here as an example of an a posteriori *conceptual* necessity. A posteriori conceptual necessities are the counterpart in our system of the a posteriori metaphysical necessities that Kripke emphasized.

One might wonder whether we have anything to correspond to Kripke's *other* famous category: the category of a priori but (metaphysically) contingent truths like 'Neptune is the planet if any responsible for . . .'.

I suggested above that 'unless we are greatly misled about the circumstances of perception, a figure is oval iff it looks egg-shaped' was a priori, or close enough for present purposes. But of course things *could* have turned out so that we were unable to see eggs in oval figures. Things could have turned out so that we never saw anything as egg-shaped.

Had things turned out so that nothing looked egg-shaped, would the world have turned out to be oval-free? The answer seems clear. How we see things is irrelevant to how they are shaped. It would have turned out that there were ovals which, however, did not look the way ovals are supposed to look.

I make no prediction about what we would have *said*. It may be that we would have said 'there are no ovals'. That is irrelevant unless the meaning that 'oval' would have turned out to have in that circumstance is the meaning it has actually. And it seems clear that the meanings are different. If people say 'there are no ovals' in a world geometrically just like ours, they do not mean the same thing by 'oval' as we do.

'Unless . . . , a figure is oval iff it looks egg-shaped' is an a priori but conceptually contingent truth. It could have turned out that we were not prone to see ovals as egg-shaped, perhaps because we were not prone to see anything as egg-shaped. And, approaching it from the other end, it could have turned out that almost-circular figures looked to us egg-shaped, despite not being oval.

This seems at first puzzling: how can it be a priori that 'oval iff looks egg-shaped' when it could have turned out otherwise? One has to remember that the scenario where it turns out otherwise is *also* a scenario where it turns out that 'oval' doesn't mean what we all know it does mean. A scenario in which 'oval' changes meaning can no more stop 'oval iff looks egg-shaped' from being a priori than one in which '=' means nonidentity can stop 'Phosphorus = Phosphorus' from being a priori.

23 Apriority versus Conceptual Necessity

I said that 'oval' could have turned out not to mean what we all know it does mean. What we all know it does mean is *oval*. So I could equally have said that it could have turned out that 'oval' did not mean oval. I do not shrink from this way of putting it, or even the claim that it could turn out (though it won't) that 'oval' *doesn't* mean oval.

I admit, however, that these claims sound funny. If we accept that 'oval' could have turned out not to mean oval, then it seems like we should regard as not completely insane someone (Crazy Eddie) who says that 'oval' *doesn't* mean oval. He could turn out to be right! Intuitively, though, there is no chance whatever of Crazy Eddie's turning out to be right.

What does it take for Crazy Eddie to be vindicated? It is not enough that, letting S be the sentence he uttered, it could have turned out that S. The scenario in which it turns out that S could be a scenario in which S has changed meaning. You are not vindicated unless what you said turns out to be right; it's not enough that what you turn out to have said turns out to be right. Otherwise Warrenites would be vindicated if 'Oswald acted alone' turned out to mean that Oswald had help, and he did. There is no danger of Crazy Eddie turning out to be right, because, letting M be the (actual) meaning of his words, had it turned out that M, it would have turned out that M was not what he said!

I assume that 'it could turn out that . . .' is an intensional context—that is, a context treating synonyms alike. Since 'sister' is synonymous with 'female sibling', and it could turn out (though it won't!) that 'sister' does not mean female sibling, it could turn out that 'sister' does not mean sister. The reason why it sounds funny to say it is that the statement strongly *suggests* something absurd: namely, that someone who conjectures that 'sister' doesn't mean sister could turn out to be right.

Another (not incompatible!) way to explain the funniness is this. There is a use of 'it could turn out that S' on which it means that it is not a priori that ¬S. In that (alternative) sense of the phrase, it really *couldn't* have turned out that 'sister' didn't mean sister. For we know a priori that 'sister' means sister. If it doesn't sound as bad to say that 'sister' could turn out not to mean female sibling, that might be because we don't know a priori that it does mean female sibling.

Compared to conceptual necessity, apriority is an elusive notion. One reason has already been noted. If it is a priori that 'sister' means sister, but not that it means female sibling, then 'it is a priori that . . .' is not an intensional context; it cares about the difference between synonyms. ('It could have turned out that . . .' (in the alternative epistemic sense) is therefore not intensional either.)

Stranger even than the failure of intensionality is the following. The class of a priori truths is often claimed to be closed under (obvious) logical consequence. This can't be right, if a well-known account of apriority is even roughly correct. It is a priori that S, according to the well-known account, if one can know that S is true just on the basis of one's grasp of S's meaning. Suppose I know that A and that $A \supset B$ just through my grasp of the two sentences' meanings, and then I infer B. If this is my reason for believing B, then I do not know it a priori. For my belief is based in part on my grasp of A's meaning, and A is a different sentence from B.

The failure of logical closure helps us resolve a puzzle. There are many things I know a priori. For instance, I know a priori that sisters are sisters, and that Hesperus = Hesperus. If 'S' is a sentence I understand, then I would seem to know a priori that 'S' is true iff S.[28] (More on this claim below.)

But I rarely, if ever, know a priori that a sentence 'S' is true; for truth-value depends on meaning, and my knowledge of meaning is a posteriori. I have to learn what a sentence means, even a sentence of my own idiolect. And my views on the topic are rationally defeasible under the impact of further evidence.

The question is, why can't I combine my a priori knowledge that sisters are siblings with my a priori knowledge that if they are siblings, then 'sisters are siblings' is true, to arrive at a priori knowledge that 'sisters are siblings' is true?

The problem is not that I can't *modus ponens* my way to the conclusion that 'S' is true, starting from premises known a priori. The problem is that, having done so, it is not just in virtue of understanding ' "S" is true' that I know that 'S' is true. The understanding I have of 'S' plays a role too, and that is something over and above my understanding of ' "S" is true'. (I can understand the latter while momentarily forgetting what 'S' means, or while entertaining a skeptical hypothesis to the effect that it means something other than I had thought.) Since I cannot claim to know that 'S' is true just in virtue of my understanding of that very sentence, I cannot claim to know a priori that 'S' is true.

---

[28] Notice the quotation marks. Use/mention distinctions that had been left to context are here marked explicitly.

24 Apriority

What can we say about apriority to explain these puzzling features? Since apriority is a matter of what my grasp of a sentence's meaning tells me, our account has got to bring in grasp explicitly. What aspect of grasp could function to tell me that the sentence is true? A state that tells me something is a state whereby I possess information. So our account should be in terms of the information I possess whereby I grasp meaning. Call this my *grasp-constituting information* about 'S'. The proposal is that

(AP) it is a priori (for me) that S iff for some G

(a) that 'S' is G is part of my grasp-constituting information,

and

(b) being G conceptually necessitates being true.

Let's revisit some earlier questions with (AP) in hand.

How can it be a priori that 'sister' means sister yet not a priori that it means female sibling? That 'sister' means sister is part (all?) of the information whereby I grasp 'sister'. I do of course realize 'on the side' that to be a sister is none other than to be a female sibling. But that is a collateral belief which does not figure in my grasp. Suppose the belief changed in response to some *outré* counter-example; that would be a change in what I thought sisters were, but not a change in what I meant by 'sister'.

Why are the a priori truths not closed under logical consequence? Having deduced B from A and A ⊃ B, I am in possession of information given which B has to be true. But there is no reason to expect the information to be grasp-constituting with respect to B; on the contrary, the information by which I grasp A is likely to be involved. To know B a priori, I need to know it on the basis of the information whereby I grasp B.

How can an a priori truth fail to be conceptually necessary? The information G that conceptually necessitates that 'S' is true might not be conceptually necessary information. If 'S' has a conceptually contingent property that conceptually necessitates that 'S' is true, all I can conclude about 'S' truth-wise is that it *is* true given how matters actually stand. Conceptual necessity requires more than this: 'S' must be true on *any* hypothesis about how matters stand, including the false ones.

Example: I am newly arrived in the royal court. A helpful attendant explains that 'the king' is to be understood so that 'the king is the guy giving orders, wearing the crown, and so forth' comes out true. I come as a result to know a priori that the king is the guy giving orders, and the rest. Now, as a matter of fact, it is Richard who is doing all these things; as a matter of fact, it is Richard who is the king. But things *could* have turned out so that it was an impostor Richerd who was giving orders, and so on. Would the king then have turned out to be Richerd?

I have certainly been given no reason to think so. I was told that 'the king' stood for the order-giver by someone who supposed (correctly) that the order-giver was Richard. They leaned on that supposition in defining 'the king' as the order-giver. Leaning on a supposition that they knew could turn out to be false, they were careful *not* to say that the king would still have been the order-giver however things had turned out. And indeed, he wouldn't: things could have turned out so that the king was Richard, while the order-giver was Richerd.[29] It is conceptually contingent that the king = the order-giver. Still, I know it a priori.

Why are some conceptually necessary truths not a priori? Sometimes the information that a speaker possesses about 'S' whereby she grasps its meaning is information that exhibits 'S' as true. Other times, it isn't. I am not sure what a typical understanding of 'cassinis are oval' involves, but one is not expected to realize that it is true. You should perhaps know that things looking egg-shaped are to be counted oval. But that doesn't enable you to work out that cassinis are oval until you've laid eyes on one.

If 'sisters are siblings' can turn out not to be true, yet sisters cannot turn out not to be siblings, then in some counteractual world sisters are siblings and 'sisters are siblings' is untrue. Why isn't this a world in which the T-biconditional fails? It *is* a world where the T-biconditional fails. It could have turned out that 'sisters are siblings' is untrue although sisters are siblings. This seems odd until we remember that it can happen only if 'sisters are siblings' turns out not to mean what it does mean. A world where it turns out not to mean what it does mean is a world where my grasp-making information fails. A world where that information fails is irrelevant to the issue of whether that information entails the truth of the

---

[29] A related sort of presupposition is discussed by Putnam: 'Suppose I point to a glass of water and say "this liquid is called water". . . . My "ostensive definition" of water has the following empirical presupposition: that the body of liquid I am pointing to bears a certain sameness relation to . . . most of the stuff I and other speakers in my linguistic community have on other occasions called "water." If this presupposition is false because, say, I am without knowing it pointing to a glass of gin and not a glass of water, then I do not intend my ostensive definition to be accepted. Thus the ostensive definition conveys what might be called a defeasible necessary and sufficient condition. . . . If it is not satisfied, then one of a series of, so to speak, "fallback" conditions becomes activated' (1975: 225). I would add only that the series tends to be a finite one. Some defeats you recover from; an (itself defeasible) backup condition kicks in. Eventually, though, the backups are exhausted, and the definition just fizzles.

biconditional—and so to the issue of whether it holds a priori that 'sisters are siblings' is true iff sisters are siblings.

Why does the feeling persist that if it is not a priori that S, there is a counteractual world in which ¬S? There is an argument to this effect that almost works. If there are no counteractual worlds in which ¬S, then every counteractual world is an S-world. A fact like that surely figures in the information whereby we understand 'S'.[30] The fact entails that 'S' is true, and so grasp-making information entails that 'S' is true, and so S is a priori. Contraposing, if S is not a priori, then it does not hold in all counteractual worlds. But, the sentence beginning 'a fact like that surely figures' assumes our grasp is rationalistic. The feeling persists because we forget that there are other ways to understand.

REFERENCES

Adams, E. W. (1975), *The Logic of Conditionals* (Dordrecht: D. Reidel).

Almog, Joseph, Perry, John, and Wettstein, Howard (1989) (eds.), *Themes from Kaplan* (New York: Oxford University Press).

Ayer, A. J. (1959) (ed.), *Logical Positivism* (New York: Free Press).

Carnap, Rudolf (1936–7), 'Testability and Meaning', *Philosophy of Science*, 3: 419–71; 4: 1–40.

Chalmers, David (1994), 'The Components of Content', Philosophy/Neuroscience/ Psychology Technical Report 94-04, Washington University, http://www.u. arizona.edu/~chalmers/papers/content.html.

—— (1996), *The Conscious Mind: In Search of a Fundamental Theory* (New York: Oxford University Press).

—— (2000), 'The Tyranny of the Subjunctive', http://www.u.arizona.edu/ ~chalmers/papers/tyranny.txt.

Davies, Martin, and Humberstone, Lloyd (1980), 'Two Notions of Necessity', *Philosophical Studies*, 38: 1–30.

DeRose, Keith (1991), 'Epistemic Possibilities', *Philosophical Review*, 100: 581–605.

Evans, Gareth (1979), 'Reference and Contingency', *Monist*, 62: 161–89.

Gendler, Tamar Szabó (2000), 'The Puzzle of Imaginative Resistance', *Journal of Philosophy*, 97(2): 55–81.

Grice, H. P. (1989), 'Indicative Conditionals', in *Studies in the Way of Words* (Cambridge, Mass.: Harvard University Press).

Jackson, Frank (1979), 'On Assertion and Indicative Conditionals', *Philosophical Review*, 88: 565–89; repr. in Jackson (1991), 111–35.

—— (1991), *Conditionals* (Oxford: Oxford University Press).

---

[30] This is a bit of an exaggeration, since knowing of each w that $w \to S$ is not yet knowing that $w \to S$ for all w.

Jackson, Frank (1994), 'Armchair Metaphysics', in Michaelis Michael and John O'Leary-Hawthorne (eds.), *Philosophy in Mind* (Dordrecht: Kluwer), 23–42.

—— (1998), *From Metaphysics to Ethics: A Defense of Conceptual Analysis* (Oxford: Clarendon Press).

Kripke, Saul (1980), *Naming and Necessity* (Cambridge: Harvard University Press).

Loar, Brian (1990), 'Phenomenal States', *Philosophical Perspectives*, 4: 81–108.

McGinn, Colin (1999), *Knowledge and Reality* (Oxford: Clarendon Press).

Moran, Richard (1989), 'Seeing and Believing: Metaphor, Image, and Force', *Critical Inquiry*, 16: 87–112.

O'Grady, Paul (1999), 'Carnap and Two Dogmas of Empiricism', *Philosophy and Phenomenological Research*, 49: 1015–27.

Peacocke, Christopher (1989), 'Perceptual Content', in Almog *et al.* (1989), 297–330.

Putnam, Hilary (1975), 'The Meaning of "Meaning" ', in *Mind, Language, and Reality* (Cambridge: Cambridge University Press), 215–71.

Quine, Willard van Orman (1951), 'Two Dogmas of Empiricism', *Philosophical Review*, 60: 20–43; repr. in Quine (1961), 20–46.

—— (1961), *From a Logical Point of View*, 2nd edn. (New York: Harper & Row).

Segerberg, Krister (1972), 'Two Dimensional Modal Logic', *Journal of Philosophical Logic*, 2: 77–96.

Stalnaker, Robert (1972), 'Assertion', in Peter Cole (ed.), *Syntax and Semantics*, ix (New York: Academic Press), 315–32.

—— (1990), 'Narrow Content', in C. A. Anderson and J. Owens (eds.), *Propositional Attitudes* (Stanford, Calif.: Center for the Study of Language and Information).

—— (1991), 'How to Do Semantics for the Language of Thought', in Barry Loewer and Georges Rey (eds.), *Meaning in Mind: Fodor and his Critics* (Oxford: Blackwell).

Walton, Kendall (1994), 'Morals in Fiction and Fictional Morality', *Proceedings of the Aristotelian Society*, supp. vol. 68: 27–50.

White, Stephen (1982), 'Partial Character and the Language of Thought', *Pacific Philosophical Quarterly*, 63: 347–65.

INDEX